PRESUMPTIVE MEANINGS

Language, Speech, and Communication

Statistical Language Learning, Eugene Charniak, 1994

The Development of Speech Perception, edited by Judith Goodman and Howard C. Nusbaum, 1994

Construal, Lyn Frazier and Charles Clifton, Jr., 1995

The Generative Lexicon, James Pustejovsky, 1996

The Origins of Grammar: Evidence from Early Language Comprehension, Kathy Hirsh-Pasek and Roberta Michnick Golinkoff, 1996

Language and Space, edited by Paul Bloom, Mary A. Peterson, Lynn Nadel, and Merrill F. Garrett, 1996

Corpus Processing for Lexical Acquisition, edited by Branimir Boguraev and James Pustejovsky, 1996

Methods for Assessing Children's Syntax, edited by Dana McDaniel, Cecile McKee, and Helen Smith Cairns, 1996

The Balancing Act: Combining Symbolic and Statistical Approaches to Language, edited by Judith Klavans and Philip Resnik, 1996

The Discovery of Spoken Language, Peter W. Jusczyk, 1996

Lexical Competence, Diego Marconi, 1997

Finite-State Language Processing, edited by Emmanuel Roche and Yves Schabes, 1997

Children with Specific Language Impairment, Laurence B. Leonard, 1997

Type-Logical Semantics, Bob Carpenter, 1997

Statistical Methods for Speech Recognition, Frederick Jelinek, 1997

WordNet: An Electronic Lexical Database, Christiane Fellbaum, 1998

WordNet 1.6 CD-ROM, edited by Christiane Fellbaum, 1998

Investigations in Universal Grammar: A Guide to Experiments on the Acquisition of Syntax and Semantics, Stephen Crain and Rosalind Thornton, 1998

A Prosodic Model of Sign Language Phonology, Diane Brentari, 1998

Language Form and Language Function, Frederick J. Newmeyer, 1998

Semantics and Syntax in Lexical Functional Grammar: The Resource Logic Approach, edited by Mary Dalrymple, 1998

Understanding Language Understanding: Computational Models of Reading, edited by Ashwin Ram and Kenneth Moorman, 1999

The Syntax of American Sign Language: Functional Categories and Hierarchical Structure, Carol Neidle, Judy Kegl, Dawn MacLaughlin, Benjamin Bahan, and Robert G. Lee, 2000

The Syntactic Process, Mark Steedman, 2000

Toward a Cognitive Semantics, Volume 1: Concept Structuring Systems, Leonard Talmy, 2000

Toward a Cognitive Semantics, Volume 2: Typology and Process in Concept Structuring, Leonard Talmy, 2000

PRESUMPTIVE MEANINGS

THE THEORY OF GENERALIZED CONVERSATIONAL IMPLICATURE

Stephen C. Levinson

A Bradford Book
The MIT Press
Cambridge, Massachusetts
London, England

Second printing, 2001

© 2000 Massachusetts Institute of Technology

This book was set in Times New Roman by Asco Typesetters, Hong Kong. Printed and bound in the United States of America.

Library of Congress Cataloging-in-Publication Data

Levinson, Stephen C.
  Presumptive meanings : the theory of generalized conversational implicature / Stephen C. Levinson.
    p. cm. — (Language, speech, and communication)
  "A Bradford book."
  Includes bibliographical references and index.
  ISBN 0-262-12218-9 (alk. paper) — ISBN 0-262-62130-4 (pbk. : alk. paper)
  1. Semantics. 2. Semantics (Logic) 3. Implication (Logic) 4. Pragmatics.
  5. Grammar, Comparative and general. I. Title. II. Series.
P325.L45   2000
401'.43—dc21
                                                            99-046140

For Penny
la jpasbet, kinam.

Contents

Conventions   xi

Preface   xiii

Note to Students   xvii

Acknowledgments   xxi

Introduction   1

Chapter 1
On the Notion of a Generalized Conversational Implicature   **11**

1.0   The Argument   11

1.1   Grice's Program   12

1.2   Three Layers versus Two in the Theory of Communication   21

1.3   The Argument from Design: The Maxims as Heuristics   27

1.4   A Typology of GCIs   35
1.4.1   The First (Q) Heuristic   35
1.4.2   The Second (I) Heuristic   37
1.4.3   The Third (M) Heuristic   38
1.4.4   Interactions Between Implicatures   39

1.5   Non-monotonicity and Default Reasoning   42
1.5.1   Typology of Nonmonotonic Reasoning Systems   42
1.5.2   Nonmonotonic Inference and Implicature   45
1.5.3   Investigating the Defeasibility of Scalar Implicatures   49

1.6   Against Reduction of GCIs to Nonce Speaker-Meaning   54
1.6.1   Sperber-Wilson Relevance   55
1.6.2   Implicature as Accommodation   60

1.7   Generalized Implicature and Stable Patterns of Lexicalization   64

1.8   Conclusions   71

Chapter 2
The Phenomena   73

2.1   Introduction   73

2.2   The Q Principle   75
2.2.1   Q Inferences   75
2.2.2   Entailment Scales   79
2.2.3   Q-Contrasts Based on Other Kinds of Lexical Opposition   98
2.2.4   Residual Problems: Scalar Implicature, GCIs, and PCIs   104
2.2.5   Clausal Implicatures   108

2.3   Exploring I-Inferences   112
2.3.1   Formulating the Maxim or Heuristic   112
2.3.2   Some Prominent I-Implicatures   122

2.4   M-Implicatures and Horn's Division of Labor   135
2.4.1   Horn's (1984) Division of Pragmatic Labor   137

2.5   The Joint Effect of Q-, I- and M-Implicatures   153
2.5.1   The Projection Problem   155

Chapter 3
Generalized Conversational Implicature and the Semantics/Pragmatics
Interface   165

3.1   Background   165

3.2   The Received View: Semantics as Input to Pragmatics   170
3.2.1   Grice's Circle: Implicatural Contributions to "What Is Said"   172
3.2.2   Disambiguation   174
3.2.3   Indexical Resolution   177
3.2.4   Reference Identification   180
3.2.5   Ellipsis Unpacking   183
3.2.6   Generality Narrowing   184
3.2.7   Some Interim Conclusions: Responses to Grice's Circle   186

3.3   Intrusive Constructions   198
3.3.1   Comparatives   199
3.3.2   The Conditional   205
3.3.3   Metalinguistic Negation and Other Negatives   210
3.3.4   Conclusions Regarding Intrusive Constructions   213

3.4   The Argument from Reference   217
3.4.1   How Implicatures Can Determine Definite Reference   217
3.4.2   Implicaturally Determined Reference and Donnellan's Referential/
Attributive Distinction   225
3.4.3   The Obstinate Theorist's Final Retort on Reference   230
3.4.4   Presemantic Pragmatics versus Postpragmatic Semantics   232

3.5   Some Implications   236
3.5.1   Disposing of the Existing Responses   236
3.5.2   Modularity and Control   243
3.5.3   Sag's Proposal and Possible Amplifications   245
3.5.4   Kadmon's DRT Proposal and Possible Extensions   248
3.5.5   Some Future Directions: DRT and Intrusive Constructions   251
*3.5.6   A Residual Problem: How to Get from Semantic Representations to
Propositions   256*

3.6   Conclusions   259

**Chapter 4
Grammar and Implicature: Sentential Anaphora Reexamined   261**

4.1   Grammar and Implicature   261

4.2   Implicature and Coreference   267
4.2.1   The Pragmatics of Local Anaphora   267
4.2.2   Inferring Coreference   273
4.2.3   Inferring Disjoint Reference   277

4.3   Binding Theory and Pragmatics   280
4.3.1   Introduction   280
*4.3.2   The A-First Account: Pragmatic Reduction to Binding Conditions B
and C   285*
*4.3.3   The B-First Account, with a Pragmatic Reduction of Binding Conditions A
and C   327*

4.4   The B-then-A Account: Synthesis of the A-First and B-First Accounts   345

4.5   Conclusions   359
4.5.1   Summary   359
*4.5.2   Pragmatics versus Parameters in Language Learning and Language
Change   361*
4.5.3   Pragmatics and the Generative Program   362

**Chapter 5
Epilogue   367**

5.1   Predictive Power of the Theory of GCIs   368

5.2   Presumptive Inference and General Reasoning   371

5.3   Role of GCIs in Linguistic Theory   374

Notes   379

References   425

Name Index   451

Subject Index   457

Conventions

1. TYPOGRAPHICAL

Italic is used for emphasis and mention of linguistic expressions.
Double quotes indicate utterances (i.e., uses of expressions and sentences).
Single quotes are used to gloss foreign-language expressions and pragmatic inferences.

2. SYMBOLS AND ABBREVIATIONS

&	logical conjunction
∨	logical disjunction
→	material conditional (logical "if")
~, ¬	negation
≡	logical equivalence
p, q (occasionally φ, φ, P, Q)	sentential and propositional variables
F, G	predicate variables
K (as in Kp)	epistemic modifier, to be read as 'the speaker knows p'
P (as in Pp)	epistemic modifier (the dual of K: Kp ≡ ~P~p), to be read as 'for all the speaker knows, p'
⊢	entails, as in p ⊢ q
+>	implicates, as in "p" +>'q' (uttering "*p*" implicates 'q')
++>	communicates (the sum of what is said and what is implicated)

Q+>	implicates under the Q-principle
I+>	implicates under the I-principle
M+>	implicates under the M-principle
iff	if and only if
$\langle a, b \rangle$	ordered pair
$\{a, b\}$	unordered set
$\langle S, W \rangle$	Horn scale, of linguistic expressions, such that linguistic expression S is an informationally stronger element than W.
GCI	generalized conversational implicature
PCI	particularized conversational implicature
* sentence	ungrammatical sentence
?? "sentence"	pragmatically odd or unacceptable utterance

Further symbols put to limited use are introduced in passing.

Preface

In this book I attempt to defend the notion of a *generalized conversational implicature* as a species of preferred interpretation. I do not pretend that this notion is straightforward, and I grant that it is not easy to defend. Yet I believe that the idea of a *preferred (or default) interpretation* is much too important to be ignored just because it is a difficult concept. Moreover, the existence of preferred intepretations has (for me at least) something of that brute self-evidence that Dr. Johnson invoked when he kicked a stone to dispatch Berkeley's idealism. We grope to grab and harness the beast without the slightest doubt about its existence.

I attempt in the book to justify the notion of a generalized conversational implicature, first, by trying to show that some general theoretical sense can be made of the notion of a preferred interpretation; second, by defending the notion against its detractors and exposing the deficiencies of the proffered alternatives; and third, by showing that a rather simple first approximation to a theory of such things can give us coverage of a broad range of important interpretive phenomena. This is the thrust of the first two chapters.

Then I try to show just how useful and important such a theory of preferred interpretation is for our understanding of how language works. To make the point with maximum dramatic effect, I have gone for the linguistic jugular, as it were. On the one hand, I try to show that the phenomena of preferred intepretations force us into a radical reconstruction of the entire theory of meaning. On the other, I attempt to reduce much of the alleged grammar of anaphora—central to many recent developments in syntax—to matters of preferred interpretation. I feel that these attacks are successful enough to lend powerful credence to the theory I provide.

My ambitions, in this book at least, do not extend beyond this. There are no general claims being made about the underlying mechanisms constituting a fundamental aspect of human cognition or the essence of human communication. On the contrary, I believe that a theory of preferred interpretations is just another piece in the jigsaw puzzle of the theory of meaning, that complex multifaceted landscape which the explorers of twentieth-century philosophy and linguistics have proved to be rugged terrain indeed. Thus my modest ambitions contrast strikingly with another recent attempt to recast Grice's theory of implicature, viz. Sperber and Wilson's (1986) Relevance theory, which is offered to us as a wide-ranging cognitive principle from which all pragmatic facts follow just as do facts about human attention, memory, and so on. Nevertheless, I do not believe that my narrow, technical slant is devoid of general conclusions; on the contrary, I believe that the theory of preferred interpretation that I sketch, although crude, is sufficient to show that central problems in the theory of meaning and the theory of grammar have been completely misconstrued. A scalpel cuts deep just because it is thin.

Finally, those who know other strands of my work may be puzzled that I should have written this book: the rationalist, universalist tinge may seem inconsistent with my current attempt to divert cognitive science into a proper consideration of social and cultural factors, or my previous efforts to understand some of the bases of social interaction. But I do not believe there is any inconsistency. Current perspectives on the relation between universal human nature and cultural factors often seem to me to be inverted: for example, language is held to be essentially universal, whereas language use is thought to be more open to cultural influences. But the reverse may in fact be far more plausible: there is obvious cultural codification of many aspects of language from phoneme to syntactic construction, whereas the uncodified, unnoticed, low-level background of usage principles or strategies may be fundamentally culture-independent. This is not to suggest that culture is a mere veneer that sticks just to the more rule-bound aspects of human behavior. Indeed, I think I have demonstrated that culture-specific semantic concepts can run deep in human thinking (Levinson 1996, 1997). But underlying presumptions, heuristics, and principles of usage may be more immune to cultural influence simply because they are the prerequisites for the system to work at all, preconditions even for learning language. Whether the principles explored in this book really have universal application is, given the primitive state of our knowledge in pragmatics, merely a working hypothesis, which at least seems to fit what we currently know. (Incidentally, the idea that usage principles may be much more uniform and simpler than the conventions of language is interestingly at variance with Chomsky's (1975: 25) oft-repeated pessimism about "our very limited progress in developing a scientific theory of any depth to account for the normal use of language," perhaps because "human science-forming capacities simply do not extend to this domain.")

If this picture inverting the normal presumptions is correct, then progress in this area of pragmatics, the theory of preferred interpretations, may be a prerequisite to progress in semantics, for we may eventually be able to use well-established pragmatic principles to help unravel what content is actually coded in lexemes and constructions in other languages, where we are far too prone to assume universal patterning. It may also help in the other direction, so to speak, by connecting to other, more complex, areas of pragmatics like the study of verbal interaction. Here, our patterns of preferred interpretation should provide an additional semiotic out of which the moves in social interaction must willy-nilly be constructed (see Levinson 1987a). And here, there are perhaps connections to broader strands of thinking in the social sciences, such as Bourdieu's (1977) notion of *habitus*, a structure of dispositions that generates tendencies to act and interpret in certain ways.

Note to Students

The question for students naturally is: "Do I really have to read it all?" The answer depends on your interests. Students wishing simply to get a feel for the phenomena that modern Gricean pragmaticists wrestle with may find chapter 2 all they really need. Those with theoretical interests in the theory of meaning will find chapter 3 central, and they may want to work back to check the reasoning in chapters 1 and 2. Those students whose primary interests are in the relation between form and meaning will want to concentrate on chapters 2 and 4. But the reader who attempts to shortcut the development of the book in this way will need to use the index to check back on concepts developed earlier.

This book presupposes some familiarity with the standard neo-Gricean or Radical Pragmatics approach to conversational implicature but treats only a portion of that subject. Levinson (1983, chap. 3) provides a textbook treatment that summarizes the Gricean approach and the work of Horn (1972, 1973), Gazdar (1979), Atlas and Levinson (1981), and others. Updates have been provided by Horn (1984, 1989: chap. 4 and 5 [which is also very useful bibliographically], 1992a, 1996b) and Huang (1994). The collections of Cole (1978, 1981) contain a number of relevant papers, as does the 1990 *16th Proceedings of the Berkeley Linguistics Society*. The readers edited by Davis (1991) and, more extensively, by Kasher (1998) reprint in handy form critical papers by Grice and the important early paper by Harnish (1976), with much other relevant material. Grice's (1967) William James lectures are (largely) published, together with other papers, in Grice 1989 with an epilogue, and there is useful discussion of Grice's general philosophy (together with Grice's reply) in Grandy and Warner 1986. A word of warning here: reprints of Grice's work (including his own compilation of 1989) are rarely complete—Grice 1981 for instance has substantial remarks on GCIs that are missing, without warning, from his 1989 chapter 17 (they were clearly felt to be redundant with earlier chapters of that book). This explains why I sometimes cite unpublished or earlier versions of what is apparently the same paper (quite often, for example, typographical emphasis has been removed in the reprints).[1]

Hirschberg (1985) attempts to recast many of the problems in a theory of particularized implicature but also offers useful discussion of the standard approach. Atlas (in press) presents discussion of many outstanding issues. Although Horn 1989 is a difficult, if not always unhumorous, work dedicated to negation, it contains so many important observations on generalized implicature that it is a "must" for the dedicated pragmaticist: it is a goldmine, but be prepared to use your pick and shovel (and the excellent index).

The approach developed here is sketched in Levinson 1995a, which may be a useful introduction to this book (I have drawn on parts of that paper for chap. 1). Further applications of this particular system of interacting principles have been offered by Levinson (1987b, 1991) (which I have in part drawn on for chap. 4) and especially Hawkins (1991) and Huang (1991, 1994). I have tried to lay out a wide range of data because I feel the range of application of pragmatic principles has been underappreciated—indeed the generality of the neo-Gricean account is precisely what recommends it. (Much further grist for the pragmatic mill can be found in work on linguistic typology, especially Haiman's (1985a, 1985b) pioneering studies of iconicity in language.) The danger, on the other hand, is that many of the examples will be found to be underanalyzed, but I felt it was better to point (possibly with a wobbly finger) in the direction of many future dissertations than to withhold such directions in the interest of more scholarly reticence. My inadequacies, dear student, are your opportunities!

Any intellectual program is often best understood by glancing at the rival accounts. An alternative approach with much, if not more, currency is given by Sperber and Wilson (1986), perhaps best approached though the *Behavioral and Brain Sciences* article with attendant commentary (Sperber and Wilson 1987; see also Blakemore 1992). Sperber and Wilson attempt to capture all implicatural phenomena with a single dualistic principle but are especially interested in particularized conversational implicatures. The second edition of *Relevance* (Sperber and Wilson 1995) contains a very useful bibliographical update keyed to the new "postface." On the whole, the two lines of theorizing—Relevance Theory and the neo-Gricean line exemplified by this book—are focused on quite different phenomena. However, work by Kempson (1986), Carston (1988), and others attempts to reduce generalized conversational implicatures to particularized ones using this principle of Relevance. A direct attack from this angle on my approach (of an earlier vintage) may be found in Carston 1995; my own criticisms of Relevance Theory can be found in Levinson 1989, which I have not repeated here. Another direct attack, partly from a Relevance Theory perspective, is directed at my treatment of anaphora (here enlarged in chap. 4) by Ariel (1994), although I believe she's mistaken the target. Another approach, never fully developed but still much presupposed in formal semantics, involves Lewis's concept of accommodation (see Thomason 1990). Situation semantics (Barwise and Perry 1983) at one time looked set to swallow within semantics many of the phenomena discussed here, but again, no explicit account has been published. A more recent kind of reductionist approach, based on extended versions of discourse semantics, has been proposed by van Kuppevelt (1996) and Scharten (1997). There is a fresh interest in implicature in computational and artificial intelligence circles; a good idea of what is going on can be got from glancing at the proceedings of the 1996 AAAI symposium on implicature (see also Hobbs, Stickel, Appelt, and Martin 1990).

Finally, there are a number of interesting recent dissertations on implicature to which the interested reader should refer. Those in Sperber and Wilson's framework are listed in the second edition of *Relevance* (1985, p. 296, n. 9), but especially relevant to this book are those by Hirschberg (1985), McCafferty (1987), Wainer (1991), and Welker (1994). Further bibliographical leads have been given throughout on the various topics covered.

Acknowledgments

My debts in this book reach far, far back. As an undergraduate I was trained by an ardent structuralist anthropologist, Edmund Leach, and it was at Berkeley as a graduate student that, in reaction to structuralism, I found Paul Grice's ideas about the derivative nature of conventional meaning quite revolutionary. His central idea, that "every artificial or non-iconic system is founded upon an antecedent iconic system" of representation and communication (Grice 1989: 358), is still too radical for most current thinking in linguistics and philosophy. This book explores one intriguing margin between the noniconic and the iconic systems, and it tries to establish in detail one way in which the noniconic systems trade on the iconic background. Those who share Grice's vision think that language will never be understood solely from the inside: linguistic communication is not explained by a direct form-meaning mapping but only by taking into account the intentional and inferential and indeed interactional umbrella (see, e.g., Sperber and Wilson 1986; Clark 1996).

At Berkeley in the early 1970s, Grice's ideas were being explored all around me: in sociolinguistics by John Gumperz, in grammar and meaning by George and Robin Lakoff, in philosophy by John Searle and Stephen Schiffer, and of course, there was Grice himself. Subsequently, Larry Horn, Jerrold Sadock and others in the States, and Gerald Gazdar, Ruth Kempson, and Deirdre Wilson in the U.K. rescued the crucial ideas from the collapse of Generative Semantics. Gerald Gazdar's ideas of that vintage (later published as Gazdar 1979) play a rather special role in this work, and I learned a great deal from him, reflected in my textbook of pragmatics (1983). After diversions in anthropological linguistics, a paper by Larry Horn (1984) brought the whole subject back to life for me and made me rethink the typology of implicatures, and this led to the paper (1987a, given at Viareggio, 1985) where I first explored the tripartite scheme employed here, encouraged by John Lyons, Peter Matthews, Nigel Vincent, and Yan Huang, then all at Cambridge. Meanwhile, work by Dan Sperber, Deirdre Wilson, Ruth Kempson, and associates has spurred and goaded me into some response; while at about the same time the opportunity to teach with Larry Horn at the Linguistics Institute at Stanford in 1987 greatly increased both my confidence and competence in this area, and it was there that I first adumbrated all the themes to be found in this book. That opportunity was arranged by Ivan Sag, with whom I have discussed at length on the issues in chapter 3 (we had indeed hoped to pursue some of these issues together). A year at Stanford followed, where the Linguistics Department and CSLI provided ideal conditions for discussion of many pertinent themes, and I taught a graduate course on the material in this book, where I received much helpful feedback. Herb Clark, Ray Perrault, Jerry Hobbs, and other participants in the CSLI implicature group forced me to clarify my ideas by describing their own alternative ones. Also at CSLI, conversations with Ivan Sag, Stan Peters, Craige Roberts, Nirit Kadmon, and David Perlmutter were important; and a seminar on abduction organized by Jerry Hobbs and Doug Edwards at SRI helped me understand work on the theory of inference in AI. Back in Cambridge, Yan Huang once again made me rethink my pragmatic reduction of the Binding Conditions (I had already been unsettled by discussions with Ivan Sag and K. Mohanan at Stanford, and thus recalled an earlier conversation with Ann Farmer and Robert Harnsh on the Viareggio beach). An invitation to give the Nijmegen Lectures in December 1988 gave me the opportunity to condense a meandering manuscript and gave me some valuable audience response; a workshop led by Rob van der Sandt was also most helpful. At that point, the book still lacked the survey in chapter 2, but I was given the unrefusable opportunity by the Max Planck Society to pursue a quite different line of work (see, e.g., Levinson 1996), which has proved all-consuming for many years. In the meantime, I had expected others to fill the gap. This didn't happen. The need for a book of this kind remained. Encouraged by Max Planck colleagues and fellow pragmaticists, I determined at last to recast the manuscript in line with current developments. I hope that I have succeeded in acknowledging most of the recent important contributions, but the canvas is large.

Throughout all these wanderings through the thickets of meaning, Jay Atlas has been a constant guide over 15 years; chapter 3 finds me following him in a direction I managed to resist for 10 years—somehow I had to come up with my own arguments before I could believe his conclusions. I notice a number of others making the same acknowledgment, and I look with renewed interest at all the places I still believe him to be wrong.

A number of scholars have commented on the manuscript (some, alas, in print). Most recently, I have received most helpful comments from Felix Ameka, Bob Arundale, Penny Brown, Eve Clark, Yan Huang, Eric Pederson, and David Wilkins on parts of this book, for which I am most grateful. But special mention must be made of the rich annotations I was lucky enough to receive on the whole manuscript from Jay Atlas, Kent Bach, and Larry Horn (the last two in thin disguise as referees for MIT Press). Such generous help has rescued me from numerous errors—faults and infelicities that remain are of course my own. I am also most grateful to Edith Sjoerdsma for many kinds of assistance with the preparation of the manuscript, to Elizabeth Laurençot for copyediting and Amy Brand for seeing the book through the Press.

Finally, I would like to thank the Kröller-Müller Museum, Otterlo, The Netherlands, for permission to use the reproduction of "Still life with oil lamp" by Juan Gris on the dustcover, Dover publications for use of the Rembrandt sketch in figure 0.1 (from Toney 1963), and Cambridge University Press for permission to reprint some paragraphs from two earlier articles of mine that appeared in the *Journal of Linguistics*.

Introduction

This book is about meaning, but about a rather special subpart of general utterance meaning,[1] the pragmatic penumbra closely surrounding sentence-meaning: it is about utterance-type meaning, not the utterance-token meaning that has been a major focus of recent work in pragmatics. Utterance-type meanings are matters of preferred interpretations—the presumptive meanings of the title of this book—which are carried by the structure of utterances, given the structure of the language, and not by virtue of the particular contexts of utterance. In certain ways, the ideas in this book are conservative, and the majority of them are not new (the debt to early work by Atlas, Harnish, Horn, and Gazdar will be particularly evident). But these ideas are in danger of being eclipsed and forgotten before their promise has been properly appreciated, so in the repetition of old information I remain unapologetic. Part of the motive of the book is therefore to collect these previous ideas and data together in one place, so that the systematicity of the observations can be directly judged and their implications properly appreciated. In other respects, however, the ideas presented here extend the old ideas just far enough for us to see that they are potentially quite explosive: they threaten many of the orthodoxies about meaning and form in the language sciences.

I have tried to avoid technicalities. In part, this is because half a dozen years interposed between the first and second drafts of this manuscript, and this time revealed to me the passing nature of many of the formalisms and formal theories to which the material in this book could be related.[2] The observations in this book seem to have a genuine independence from such passing clouds, and so it seems worthwhile to detach them from the technicalities. Nevertheless, I suppose it is inevitable that there will be passages that are rather hard going. I have therefore thought it worthwhile to sketch here in the introduction in a quite informal way the kind of picture of linguistic communication that will emerge from this study. I will do so partly through analogy.

Consider the Rembrandt sketch in figure 0.1 (from Toney 1963, plate 94). We interpret this sketch instantly and effortlessly as a gathering of people before a structure, probably a gateway; the people are listening to a single declaiming figure in the center. You and I may see slightly different details adumbrated: for me, the declaiming character has a beard, and the man in the foreground to the left a hat, and the sitting figures seem female, but you may have your own interpretations. Knowing something about Rembrandt's times and the subjects he was fond of, we can be fairly sure this is Christ telling parables to a crowd before a city gate. But all this is a miracle, for there is little detailed information in the lines or the shading (such as there is). Every line is a mere suggestion; some lines seem to make no sense except as flourishes of the pen, but yet we struggle to find some sense within them (see for example, the three little flourishes by Christ's right "hand," which suggest perhaps the heads of further listeners). So here's the miracle: from a merest, sketchiest squiggle of lines, you and I converge to find the adumbration of a coherent scene (that we may diverge, according to fantasy and our knowledge of art history, is of course less miraculous).

How is it possible? Although the theory of vision is considerably more advanced than the theory of the language capacity, current knowledge cannot really explain our understanding of visual information as "degraded" or physically impoverished as this (but see Changeux 1994). What we do know is that there is tremendous visual sensitivity to outlines and shading and that we can use these (although normally reinforced by multiple further sources of information like parallax, stereopsis, color, texture, and reflection) to extract three-dimensional models out of two-dimensional retinal arrays. Somehow, then, Rembrandt is exploiting the fact that we are "built" to see three-dimensional scenes in squiggles on a plane surface. He is also relying of course on cultural conventions about how to represent scenes in drawings, using the post-Renaissance preference for temporal instantaneousness and correct perspective, as opposed to, for example, the Central Australian cultural conventions in drawing a bird's-eye view from above, which represents entire episodes over time. Another important ingredient is that the sketch is presented as a representation, not, say, as scratch marks on linoleum, and as a result, there is some kind of compact between sketcher and viewer that warrants the

Figure 0.1
Rembrandt sketch

pursuit of represented detail—there is an assumption that with proper attention we should be able to recover the artist's intentions.

The problem of utterance understanding is not dissimilar to this little visual miracle. An utterance is not, as it were, a veridical model or "snapshot" of the scene it describes, although much talk of truth conditions might lead one to suppose the contrary (the work of the early Wittgenstein explored this initially attractive idea, which has never been quite washed out of our thinking since). Rather, an utterance is just as sketchy as the Rembrandt drawing. Given the way we are built and the cultural conventions that specify a particular language and its appropriate deployment, we are inexorably led, at least in most cases, to a common understanding (and, as in the Rembrandt sketch, we even have a clear sense of where we may diverge). It is the apparently deterministic nature of this process that underlines the miracle. A sentence like "It will be ready soon" is indeed sketchy like the Rembrandt drawing: *it* may refer to anything under the sun as long as it is not a human adult, *will be* specifies an infinite series of future temporal spans, and *ready* might be interpreted as 'cooked' (as when the utterance is a response to the question "When is supper?") or 'surfaced' (as in response to "When will the motorway be open?") or 'refuelled' (in response to "When does the flight leave?"). And clearly, *soon* can take on quite different values in the context of serving a meal or finishing a doctoral dissertation. But in each of these different contexts, "It will be ready soon" has its appropriate and apparently determinate interpretation effortlessly delivered to us.

How? That is the question that a theory of utterance comprehension has to answer. As with the visual processes behind the interpretation of the Rembrandt sketch, let us confess that we don't really have the faintest idea how it works. First principles even seem to suggest that the recovery of a speaker's intentions on the basis of what he has said is in principle impossible (Levinson 1995b).[3] Books like those by Sperber and Wilson (1986) or Atlas (1989) or Horn (1989), or the present effort, which attempt to spell out some of the pragmatic processes involved, are pretty much stabs in the dark. What I have tried to do in this book is detach a little part of this problem and argue that there must be powerful heuristics that give us preferred interpretations without too much calculation of such matters as speakers' intentions, encyclopedic knowledge of the domain being talked about, or calculations of others' mental processes. Such preferred interpretations may be overridden by, and are certainly supplemented with, calculations of just this complex kind. But it seems implausible that the phenomenology of instantaneous, determinate interpretation could be delivered solely by reasoning about such matters as the potentially infinite regress of what the speaker is thinking the hearer will think that the speaker is thinking, and so on, ad infinitum.[4]

Issues of cognitive processing have played an explicit role in only one pragmatic theory so far: in Sperber and Wilson's (1986) Relevance theory, the addressee infers as much as he or she can for the processing buck, following a mini-max strategy. Somehow this must have some general correlation with the speaker's communicative intention. I do not think that the Sperber and Wilson framework can offer an account of the phenomena discussed in this book, precisely because the inferences in question are relatively invariant over changes in context and background assumptions, despite being defeasible (i.e., they do not go through in the presence of contrary assumptions). It is this relative invariance that gives these inferences their *linguistic* importance, as systematic feeders to semantic processes and language change, and I think the rich observations that have been collected by Horn (1972, 1989) and others need to be preserved. Explicit processing considerations do not enter the framework offered here, but they do form part of the background, for the character of the inferences in question as default inferences can, I think, be understood best against the background of cognitive processing. The evidence, so far as it goes, from the psycholinguistic literature is that hypotheses about meaning are entertained by the hearer incrementally—as the words come in, as it were. It seems unlikely that this could be achieved without rich heuristics, because there will be early moments in utterance processing where propositional or clausal information for inferencing is simply not yet available. For this reason, the Sperber and Wilson framework is not psycholinguistically plausible, or at least it is not plausible for early moments in utterance processing. In contrast, some of the heuristics to be offered here can proceed on a word-by-word basis—for example, a scalar quantifier like *some* will, as I will show, already invoke default enrichments before the predicate is available.

Close observers of this line of thinking have noticed that it constitutes a renaissance of information-theoretic ideas:

These notions went out of fashion in theoretical linguistics—and I think this is the right way to put it—when Chomsky (1956, 1959, etc.) criticized (correctly) their association with radical, *tabula rasa*, behaviourism and finite-state models of language acquisition and of grammaticality. Their rehabilitation within the framework of more satisfactory models of the structure and use of language is very much to be welcomed. (Lyons 1995: 239–240)

Let me return now to the kernel idea behind the present work, which is disarmingly simple. The central background fact, an information-theoretic observation, is that human speech encoding is relatively very slow: the actual process of phonetic articulation is a bottleneck in a system that can otherwise run about four times faster (a point taken up in chap. 1). The pressures that this exerts on language are easy to see—for example, the pressure for frequent words to be reduced, as has been long documented (e.g., by Zipf 1949). Zipf (and, more recently, Horn 1984, 1989) saw the resulting pattern as a balance between two forces: a speaker's desire for economy and an auditor's need for sufficient information. This tension, real enough, is not the focus of the current work. Instead, I assume a kind of coincidence of interests, treating linguistic communication as a "game of pure coordination" in the game-theoretic sense of Schelling (1960), a picture I think presupposed by Grice (1957): the speaker is trying to find an economical means of invoking specific ideas in the hearer, knowing that the hearer has exactly this expectation. Now, the solution to the encoding bottleneck, I suggest, is just this: let not only the content but also the metalinguistic properties of the utterance (e.g., its form) carry the message. Or, find a way to piggyback meaning on top of the meaning.

How can this be piggybacking be achieved? Only by utilizing the form, the structure, and the pattern of choices within the utterance to signal the extra information beyond the meanings of its constituents. So, here I propose just three simple heuristics, which will serve to amplify utterance content:

1. If the utterance is constructed using simple, brief, unmarked forms, this signals business as usual, that the described situation has all the expected, stereotypical properties;
2. If, in contrast, the utterance is constructed using marked, prolix, or unusual forms, this signals that the described situation is itself unusual or unexpected or has special properties;
3. Where an utterance contains an expression drawn from a set of contrasting expressions, assume that the chosen expressions describe a world that itself contrasts with those rival worlds that would have been described by the contrasting expressions.

This description is imprecise of course. However, one can imagine formal treatments of this meaning amplification along the following lines. Let the metalinguistic information control the model in which the utterance is interpreted: let it pick out of the set of possible worlds a proper subset that has the kinds of properties signaled by the metalinguistic properties of the utterance; let it determine the domain of discourse; let it restrict the model to one in which certain extra properties obtain. In the body of the book, especially in chapter 2, many examples will be given that indicate the more precise directions in which these constraints on interpretation must be formulated. The essential point here is that no special, exotic, hermeneutic principles are being proposed: metalinguistic scrutiny by the addressee of utterance form, including the consideration of salient alternates, will be sufficient to amplify the content of utterances and ease the pressure on the encoding bottleneck; knowing which, the speaker is bound to conform to the same heuristics.

Approaches to meaning are so diverse and fractionated that it may help the reader to know where the writer stands on a wider range of issues than are directly addressed in this book. So, let me declare my cards:

1. The distinction between semantics and pragmatics is one of a number of essential distinctions in the study of meaning; it may be that in the long run the distinction will dissolve into a larger set of distinctions, but nothing is gained by lumping in our attempt to understand human communication.

2. Semantics is not to be confused with "conceptual structure" or the "language of thought"; the semantics of a language is a language-specific phenomenon, and the mapping into a "language of thought," a nontrivial relation between nonisomorphic structures (Levinson 1997).

3. Aspects of semantic content (usually only when enriched by pragmatic specifications) can be specified by the apparatus of a recursive truth definition, but this is unlikely to have a direct cognitive counterpart. Consider the analogy to vision: we can objectively specify the relation between the world that is viewed and the signals reaching the visual cortex, and compare the subjective visual experience. But this psychophysical mapping is not always truth-preserving: there are numerous conditions under which we see things that do not exist, fail to see things that do, and so on—the stock of illusions that psychophysicists take as a central part of their job to explain. Similarly, truth-conditional semantics viewed in the realist way—as a direct veridical mapping of semantic structures onto states of affairs (bypassing the head as it were)—is useful as a yardstick of human performance. Something *like* this is what the cognitive processes must do, but as in the case of visual illusions, they may fail to do so, and *how* they generally do so will be unrelated to the machinery of truth-

conditional semantics. So we can have our cake and eat it, too: we can use the insights of truth-conditional semantics without buying Realism, and without caring that it obviously fails to meet any criteria for adequacy as a cognitive model. It is a bit like buying a pair of shoes: we are glad that the salesperson can measure our feet and get the size roughly right, but in the end, it's a subjective question whether the shoes fit.

4. There is no algorithm that, given a syntactic string in a language, cranks out its unique logical form or semantic structure. The view that there *is* such an algorithm forms the basis of much linguistic theorizing, from Montague to Chomsky's most recent views. But it is patently absurd to hold such a view. First, there is the enormous range of ambiguities in natural language (requiring at least a one-to-many correspondence). Second, syntactic structures may actually be indeterminate in certain respects (Matthews 1981: 17–21). Third, pragmatic resolution is crucial before semantic interpretation or the assignment of semantic structure: nobody disputes the role of deixis here, but there are many other aspects of pragmatic resolution from the determination of anaphoric reference to the assignment of scope. The overall picture sketched by Sadock (1991) or Jackendoff (1997) is here at least correct: phonology, syntax, and semantics are areas each with their own generative capacities, and there are significant mismatches between the structural strings in each representation that, in the end, come to be associated with one another. What puts them into association with one another are correspondence rules or processes, which are not deterministic in character. Jackendoff suggests that the picture with lexical items is not in principle different: they are correspondences across phonological, syntactic, and semantic representations, but the correspondences may be partial and not one to one (compare idioms, or the mismatch between phonological and syntactic words).

5. Insofar as we can get from syntactic structures and lexical material directly to a semantic representation (which in the most part, I argue, we cannot), then such semantic representations are only partially specified; templates of partial information far too unspecified to determine truth conditions.

6. The overall role that pragmatics plays in such a picture is fundamentally different from that sketched in the textbooks (including mine of 1983). There is no scheme of the kind that syntactic structures are mapped onto semantic structures which themselves represent full-fledged propositions, these semantic structures being the input into pragmatics, which yields additional inferences or restrictions on meaning. Rather, pragmatic

processes play a crucial role in the correspondence rules mapping syntactic structures onto semantic representations, and again mapping semantic representations onto communicated thoughts or utterance meanings.

The picture of the overall theory of meaning that will emerge from this book is thus radically different from the starting point from which Gricean pragmatics began. The distinction between semantics and pragmatics was construed in the standard theory as the distinction between sentence-meaning and utterance-meaning, with the output of the semantics being the input to the pragmatics. For reasons detailed at length in chapter 3, this cannot be right. Instead, I argue, we should stop thinking of the distinction in terms of levels of representation. Instead, we should think about both semantics and pragmatics as being component processes that offer their own distinctive contributions to a single level of representation. The processes remain distinct in kind, and thus the distinction between semantics and pragmatics must be retained.

This new view of the architecture of a theory of meaning is one of the explosive consequences, mentioned at the beginning, of careful observations about the apparently minor phenomena of preferred interpretations. Another far-reaching set of consequences has to do with constraints on syntactic form, explored in chapter 4 through consideration of anaphors, where it is argued that patterns of preferred interpretation explain the distribution and typology of anaphoric expressions.

As background to all this, chapter 1 lays out the reasons to suppose that preferred interpretations do indeed exist and have a life of their own. Chapter 2 offers a catalog of these phenomena in terms of three simple neo-Gricean principles, and sketches their interaction. The reader will find many familiar facts here assembled in perhaps unfamiliar ways. A catalog may make tedious reading, but I think there is no other place where the student can find all these phenomena laid out, and it is important for the thesis of this book that the theory of preferred interpretations is seen to have perfectly general application.

This then is the structure of the book: a chapter that introduces the idea of presumptive meanings, a chapter that lays out many diverse examples and a scheme that organizes them, a chapter that explores the consequences for theories of semantics, and a fourth that explores the implications for syntax.

Chapter 1

On the Notion of a Generalized Conversational Implicature

1.0 THE ARGUMENT

In this chapter I introduce and attempt to defend the notion of a *generalized conversational implicature* (abbreviated to GCI), where what is at stake is the generalized nature of such inferences. A generalized implicature is, in effect, a default inference, one that captures our intuitions about a preferred or normal interpretation. The notion of a preferred interpretation is not one that has any special currency in the theory of language at the present time. Indeed, it is a notion that is currently either ignored or subject to virulent attack by some pragmaticists, psycholinguists, and workers in artificial intelligence. In defense of this notion, I develop a number of arguments both positive and negative.

First, looking back at Grice's program, we see that such a notion (contrary to some recent commentary) was central to his concerns; and those concerns, whatever the differences in modern implementation, seem perfectly current today. Second, I diagnose that one source of the current theoretical resistance to GCIs is a simplistic overall scheme for a theory of communication, within which there is no place for a theory of preferred interpretation. I argue that there is overwhelming evidence for the need for such a theory, evidence much broader than that for GCIs themselves, and consequently that our overall scheme must provide a niche of an appropriate sort in any case. When this is appreciated, much of the resistance to GCIs should wither away.

Next, I produce an argument from design, to the effect that a system of preferred interpretation would be much too effective a device in communication for any naturally evolved system of communication to fail to have developed such a thing. At this point, I digress to introduce the typology of GCIs that will be central to the book.

I then attempt to deal frontally with another source of resistance to the concept of a GCI—namely, the question of whether any theoretical sense can be made of the notion "default interpretation." I argue that we need to address this question in the context of the different kinds of nonmonotonic reasoning systems that have recently been developed. Although significant puzzles remain, these recent developments do offer some reassurance that formal models of default reasoning are not beyond our reach and thus that some light can be thrown from that direction on the notion of a preferred or default interpretation. (Whether these systems are essential to a proper account of default intepretations in language use is another matter, because default inferences in language may arise because of the very nature of communication.)

I turn next to some recent accounts of implicature that leave no room for a notion of a generalized implicature: Sperber and Wilson's (1986, 1995) Relevance theory, and the theories of implicature based on Lewis's (1979) notion of "accommodation" that have been developed by Hobbs (1987) and Thomason (1990). According to these theories, all implicatures are a matter of nonce (i.e., once-off) inference to the best interpretation (however that is defined), given the full richness of background presumptions. These theories, I argue, simply cannot handle the phenomena that are focal to a theory of GCIs.

As a final argument in favor of the concept of the GCI, I repeat Horn's observations that certain kinds of GCI systematically block lexicalization of certain concepts. Because these observations have an immense regularity and crosslinguistic generality, it is really quite inconceivable that anything less than a generalized, preferred species of interpretation could be responsible.

1.1 GRICE'S PROGRAM

Much of the argument in this book is developed under the assumption of what I shall call the Gricean umbrella, a general approach to the study of meaning and communication. Let us recall the essential features of these umbrella assumptions (no full explication will be made here; see, e.g., Levinson 1983: chap. 3). First, a theory of communication has as its target the full scope of Grice's (1957) *nonnatural meaning* (meaning$_{nn}$), where this constitutes communicational effects that fall under a special kind of complex reflexive intention. He suggested that a communicator S meant$_{nn}$ something by x if and only if S "intended the utterance of x to produce some effect in an audience by means of the recognition of this intention" (1957: 385). Lest such a reflexive intention, including reference to itself, prove problematic, Grice (1969, 1989: chap. 5) also phrased meaning$_{nn}$ in another more explicit way, as sketched in example (1).[1]

(1) *Grice's theory of utterer's meaning*

   S *means$_{nn}$* p by "uttering" U to A iff S intends:

   a. A to think p

   b. A to recognize that S intends (a)

   c. A's recognition of S's intending (a) to be the prime reason for A thinking p

We will call this special kind of intention an *m-intention* (for "meaning intention"); one of its interesting properties is that it is an intention that is achieved or satisfied just by being recognized. There have been many attempts at revision of this formula (see Avramides 1989 for discussion), but because nothing much will depend on this in this book we may leave the matter there. The point here is just that meaning$_{nn}$ (or something of the sort) draws an outer boundary on the communicational effects that a theory of communication is responsible for.

The second aspect of the Gricean umbrella that is important here is the claim that meaning is not homogeneous. Instead, within the circle of delimited m-intentions we may distinguish numerous different genera and species of meaning. Grice himself suggests that the semiotic pie might be cut up as in (2).

(2) *Genera and species of meaning$_{nn}$*

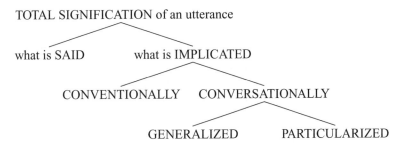

This picture is partial. Grice allows that there may be other subtypes of signification, too—for example, presupposition, nonconversational nonconventional implicatures, and so forth. None of these distinctions are straightforward (see Harnish 1976: 331ff). Additionally, the modern pragmaticist will want to add many other kinds of inference, such as those based on details of conversational organization (see, e.g., Levinson 1983: chap. 6 for review), on specific assumptions about interactional politeness, and so on (see, e.g., Brown and Levinson 1987, Leech 1983). But it is this corner of the semiotic pie that concerns us here.

Chapter 3 is quite largely concerned with the difficulties with the distinction between what is said and what is implicated, although I have little to say here about conventional implicatures. It should be noted, however, that in this scheme, what is *coded* by the linguistic system is the sum of what is *said* (roughly the truth-conditional content) and what is *conventionally implicated*. In contrast, what is *conversationally* implicated is not coded but rather inferred on the basis of some basic assumptions about the rational nature of conversational activity, as stated in the Cooperative Principle and its constituent maxims of conversations. For reference, let me briefly recapitulate Grice's maxims, with abbreviations I will use below.

The cooperative principle
"Make your contribution such as is required, at the stage at which it occurs, by the accepted purpose or direction of the talk exchange in which you are engaged." (Grice 1989: 26)

The maxims of Quality
"Try to make your contribution one that is true," specifically:
"Do not say what you believe to be false"
"Do not say that for which you lack adequate evidence" (Grice 1989: 27)

The maxim of Relation (Relevance)
"Be relevant" (Grice 1989: 27)

The maxims of Quantity
Q1: "Make your contribution as informative as is required (for the purposes of the exchange)"
Q2: "Do not make your contribution more informative than is required" (Grice 1989: 26)

The maxims of Manner
"Be perspicuous," specifically:
M1: "Avoid obscurity of expression"
M2: "Avoid ambiguity"
M3: "Be brief (avoid unnecessary prolixity)"
M4: "Be orderly" (Grice 1989: 27)

For the purposes of this book—exploring default inferences—only the maxims of Quantity and Manner are the focus of attention, and a further simplified scheme will be introduced shortly. But here, the point is that Grice argued that conversational implicatures come about on the basis of the assumption that the maxims are being preserved, at least at some fundamental level. He assumed that we can distinguish between what a speaker has said by virtue of the conventional meaning of the words or sentence (Grice 1989: 25, 87–88, 120–121) and what a speaker conversationally implicates by saying those words. Grice defines conversational implicature as follows (my abbreviation from Grice 1989: 30–31): By saying p, utterer U *conversationally implicates* q iff:

1. U is presumed to be following the maxims
2. the supposition q is required to maintain (1)
3. U thinks the recipient will realize (2)

(Grice's distinction between saying and implicating was complicated by his notion of conventional implicature. But it is also problematic for other reasons, explored in detail in chapter 3, and I defer discussion till then.)

As a result of this inferential derivation, conversational implicatures are held to display various distinctive properties:

- *Cancellability* (i.e., *defeasibility*)—the property of being an inference defeatable by the addition of premises (see section 1.5)
- *Nondetachability*—any expression with the same coded content will tend to carry the same implicatures (a principled exception has to be made for Manner implicatures)[2]
- *Calculability*—the more or less transparent derivation of the inference from premises that include the assumption of rational conversational activity
- *Nonconventionality*—the noncoded nature of the inferences and their parasitic dependence on what is coded.

To Grice's list, we may add:

- *Reinforcability*—it is often possible to add explicitly what is anyway implicated with less sense of redundancy than would be the case if one repeated the coded content (Sadock 1978, Horn 1991b)
- *Universality*—because the inferences are derived ultimately from fundamental considerations of rationality, we expect a strong tendency to universality (unlike with coded meanings, of course); conversational implicatures are motivated, not arbitrary

Apart from these reminders, I presume familiarity with all this and proceed at once to the final distinction here, that between *particularized* and *generalized* conversational implicatures. Some abbreviations are now in order: I shall often use the term *implicature* as an abbreviation for *conversational implicature* where no misunderstanding is likely to arise; and the heroes of this book, the *generalized conversational implicatures* will be dubbed GCIs, and their nongeneralized cousins, the *particularized conversational implicatures* are abbreviated as PCIs. I also use the symbol +> to signify "conversationally implicates"; more precisely, I use the convention: "S" +> 'p' to signify 'the utterance of the sentence S would (normally, or in the context sketched) conversationally implicate that the speaker knows (or believes or thinks likely) the proposition p.'

Grice (1975: 56f) provides only the following characterization of the distinction between particularized and generalized conversational implicatures (or PCIs vs. GCIs): a PCI from saying *p* would "leave no room for the idea that an implicature of this sort is NORMALLY carried by saying that *p*"; whereas in the case of a GCI "one can say that the use of a certain form of words in an utterance would normally (in the ABSENCE of special circumstances) carry such & such an implicature" (emphasis in the original).[3] Grice's intention here is clear enough although his own discussion lacks detail; the following informal formulation captures, I think, the intention:

(3) *The distinction between PCIs and GCIs*
   a. An implicature i from utterance U is *particularized* iff U implicates i only by virtue of specific contextual assumptions that would not invariably or even normally obtain
   b. An implicature i is *generalized* iff U implicates i *unless* there are unusual specific contextual assumptions that defeat it

The intuition behind the contrast between PCIs and GCIs may be highlighted by a simple example. Consider the sentence *Some of the guests are already leaving*, and consider that it might be uttered in two rather different contexts:

(4) *Context 1*
   A: "What time is it?"
   B: "Some of the guests are already leaving."
      PCI: 'It must be late.'
      GCI: 'Not all of the guests are already leaving.'

(5) *Context 2*
    A: "Where's John?"
    B: "Some of the guests are already leaving."
       PCI: 'Perhaps John has already left.'
       GCI: 'Not all of the guests are already leaving.'

Naturally enough, in the two contexts the utterance-form "Some of the guests are already leaving" carries different implicatures—it is used as a partial answer to different questions and implicates different propositions accordingly. These PCIs may be attributed to the maxim of Relevance (or Relation), construed as a principle of attending to interlocutors' goals or plans (Holdcroft 1987, Levinson 1987a, Thomason 1990).[4] But in both contexts there is also a shared inference—namely, that not all of the guests are in the process of leaving. This inference has an entirely general currency: any statement of the form "Some x are G" will, other things being equal, have the default interpretation 'Not all x are G'. One might be tempted to think about this as part of the meaning of *some*, but the semantic compatibility of *Some, but not all, x are G* seems to rule out such an explanation. It is this sort of inference that, by virtue of its prevalence and its lack of salience, has the closest connection to linguistic analysis and misanalysis and that is the focus of this book.

Grice's own treatment of the distinction between generalized and particularized implicatures is unfortunately not extended. In the immediate context of a discussion of the distinction, Grice provides only one, none too clear, example (1975: 56, 1989: 37), viz. the inference from the indefinite article to the assumption that the speaker is not in a position to be specific. Thus the assertion of (6) might normally carry the GCI inference:

(6) "I saw a woman in my office."
    GCI: 'I saw someone other than my wife/girlfriend/mother/etc.'

because "the speaker has failed to be specific in a way in which he might have been expected to be specific, with the consequence that it is likely to be assumed that he is not in a position to be specific" (Grice 1989: 38). Grice notes than an expression of the form *an X* may sometimes carry the reverse implicature in certain cases: for example, "I cut a finger" implicates 'I cut my finger' because it would require rather special assumptions to make plausible an interpretation where S cut someone else's finger but the identity of the victim was unknown or irrelevant (perhaps two manicurists might so talk!). Incidentally, I show later that the essence of

Grice's claim here can be handled in a rather different way by a systematic scalar inference.

From the brief discussion in the published versions of the William James Lectures (Grice 1989) it has sometimes been supposed that Grice attributed no great importance to the distinction between *generalized* versus *particularized* implicatures.[5] However, the lectures show just the contrary. Grice was interested in the whole phenomenon of implicature largely because it promised an account of the generally associated but defeasible inferences that rise from the use of the logical connectives.[6] And he was particularly interested in the generalized implicatures, just because they are hard to distinguish from semantical or conventional content: "noncontroversial examples are perhaps hard to find, since it is all too easy to treat a generalized conversational implicature as if it were a conventional implicature" (1989: 37). Elsewhere, he explained:

> I also distinguished ... particular conversational implicatures that depended on particular contextual features ... and ones that I thought of as relatively general which I called GENERALIZED IMPLICATURES. These are the ones that seem to me to be more controversial and at the same time more valuable for philosophical purposes, because they will be the implicatures that would be carried (other things being equal) by any utterance of a certain form, though, as with all implicatures, they are not to be represented as part of the conventional meaning of the words or forms in question. And I thought that this notion of a GENERALIZED conversational implicature might be used to deal with a variety of problems, particularly in philosophical logic, but also in other areas. In these areas there seemed to me to be quite good grounds for suspecting that some people have made the mistake of taking as part of the conventional meaning of some form of expression what was really not part of its conventional meaning, but was rather a nonconventional implication which would normally be carried, except in special circumstances. It is difficult to find noncontroversial cases just because, if this mistake has been committed, it has been committed on such a wide scale. (Grice 1981: 185, capitals in the original).

With respect to philosophical logic, he had especially the connectives in mind. Here he wished to maintain a univocal or monosemous sense, explaining frequently associated but nevertheless defeasible additional meanings as pragmatic overlays due to generalized conversational implicatures. Thus, for instance, he assumed that good arguments could be made for treating the following inferences as GCIs:

(7) a. "There is a spade either in the attic or in the basement."
+> 'The spade is not in both places and S doesn't know which.'

b. "He brushed his teeth and went to bed."
   +> 'He did so in that order.'
c. "If the President signs the treaty, then the deficit will be repaid."
   +> 'There is some non-truth-functional relation (e.g., of cause-effect) between the two events.'

Grice's own arguments are somewhat diffuse and, in the case of the conditional, convoluted, but it is worth repeating some of the ways in which he thought the inferences might arise:[7]

(8) *The disjunction*
   a. "p or q"
      +> 'S doesn't know that p, or that q.'
      Rationale: If S did know that one of the disjuncts was true, that would be more informative (and generally more relevant); therefore by the first maxim of Quantity, the fact that S hasn't said "p" or "q" implicates he's not in a position to make the stronger statement.
   b. "p or q"
      +> 'there is some non-truth-functional connection between p and q.'
      Rationale: Because the second maxim of Quality requires that S have adequate evidence for what he says, there must be some argument that concludes with 'p $\lor$ q.'

(9) *The conjunction*
   "He took off his trousers and went to bed"
   +> 'in that order.'
   Rationale: By the fourth Maxim of Manner (M4, 'be orderly'), the speaker should describe events in the order in which they occurred.

(10) *The conditional*
   a. "if p then q"
      +> 'S doesn't know that p, nor that q.'
      Rationale: No one would be interested in the truth value of the whole if they weren't interested in the truth value of the parts; therefore in saying the conditional when one knew, for example, the consequent was true, would be an infringement of the first maxim of Quantity; therefore S must be assumed to have evidence only for the less informative conditional.

b. "if p then q"
+> 'there are non-truth-functional grounds for the connection
between p and q.'
Rationale: Given the second maxim of Quality ('have adequate
evidence for what you say'), there must be an argument (almost
certainly non-truth-functional) that supports 'p → q.'

(One should note that although Grice's defense of the equation of "if"
with the material conditional no longer meets with general approval (see,
e.g., Gazdar 1979: 83ff; Strawson 1986), the pragmatic arguments are
largely unaffected. Despite that, modern accounts of the implicatures of
the conditional utilize the maxim of Quantity.)

Grice's interest in developing these arguments was to suggest that
although at first sight these inferences may appear to be part of the conventional meaning of these connectives, that may not be the case. Thus it
may be possible to maintain a relatively simple logical analysis of the
meaning of the connectives, explaining the systematic divergence in ordinary usage as due to *generalized* conversational implicatures. It is the fact
that the inferences *normally* accompany the connectives that gives rise to
the temptation to view them as part of the coded content, with all the
analytical mistakes that would follow. It is this normal, general, default
tendency of interpretation that makes it nonobvious that what we are
dealing with here is mere pragmatic inference. Thus the whole line of
argument only has force if sense can be made of the notion of a generalized conversational implicature. Grice saw this kind of analysis as having
general application to lexical meaning: he proposed (1989: 47–48) a
modified Occam's razor to the effect that "senses are not to be muliplied
beyond necessity" and suggested instead that we should always prefer an
analysis where a word has "a less restrictive rather than a more restrictive
meaning," where the more restrictive interpretations can be achieved by
"a superimposed implicature."

In modern GCI theory, the connectives are treated rather differently
(I sketch this later); in particular, the maxims of Quantity are utilized
rather than the second maxim of Quality. But the basic intellectual moves
still seem well motivated. Wherever we are faced with a linguistic expression that is apparently systematically ambiguous, we should entertain the
possibility that the correct analysis is in fact a single univocal, semantically broad sense with a defeasible set of generalized pragmatic restrictions.[8] If the restrictions were ad hoc, varying from context to context,

there would be no temptation towards a (multiple) ambiguity claim. But, if the pragmatic restrictions can constitute a preferred interpretation—that is, a systematic tendency to read an expression in one particular way—then the temptation arises and it is here that GCI theory has most to contribute to linguistic analysis.

1.2   THREE LAYERS VERSUS TWO IN THE THEORY OF COMMUNICATION

As already mentioned, in recent work there is in general both a neglect of, and an hostility to, the notion of a preferred or default interpretation.[9] The root of this resistance to the idea would seem to lie in some largely implicit, and I believe inadequate, assumptions about the nature of an overall theory of communication. In trying to understand the place of GCIs in a theory of communication, it is essential to make these issues explicit.

I believe that Grice was essentially correct in thinking of meaning as a composite notion; that is to say, he correctly considered that the full import of an utterance could only be captured by distinguishing many different kinds of content—even the coded content was divided between "the said" and "the conventionally implicated" (and later he added "the presupposed"), whereas the inferred content was divisible between particularized and generalized implicatures and perhaps other kinds of inference altogether. I believe that this recognition of the heterogeneous nature of meaning marked a fundamental advance in the theory of meaning—but others of a holistic temperament (e.g., as in so-called cognitive linguistics) consider the very variety of proposed mechanisms a sign of premature failure. We can happily concede the favoring of parsimonious explanatory principles where they seem potentially sufficient, but meaning (conceived broadly as the full scope of meaning$_{nn}$) is quite clearly not a unitary field but rather one involving cognitive principles, knowledge factors, and interactional principles, and no doubt much besides. At a time when we are happy to consider that some apparently unitary field like the heart of grammar is best treated as the outcome of distinct modules of grammatical principles, we ought surely to be willing to consider that pragmatic inference is the outcome of a set of rather different kinds of pragmatic principles.

In the composite theory of meaning, the theory of GCIs plays just a small role in a general theory of communication. In this regard, GCI theory is not in direct competition with holistic theories like Sperber and Wilson's theory of Relevance, which attempts to reduce all kinds of pragmatic inference to one mega-principle—GCI theory is simply not a general theory of human pragmatic competence. Instead it attempts to account for one relatively small area of pragmatic inference. The theoretical importance of that area derives from the generalized, stable nature of such inferences that consequently have much closer interactions with the stable body of rules of formation and construal that form a grammatical system. The point being emphasized is that a theory of GCIs has to be supplemented with a theory of PCIs that will have at least as much, and possibly considerably more, importance to a general theory of communication. It is just to *linguistic* theory that GCIs have an unparalleled import.

The overall picture of a general theory of communication that emerges is rather different from the standard picture. Although at the present time there could hardly be said to be a general theory of communication, there is nevertheless a prevailing assumption. According to the standard line (more often presupposed than justified), there are just two levels to a theory of communication: a level of sentence-meaning (to be explicated by the theory of grammar in the large sense) and a level of speaker-meaning (to be explicated by a theory of pragmatics, perhaps centrally employing Grice's notion of meaning$_{nn}$).[10] (I use the term "layer" or "level" only to indicate distinct categories of phenomena; whether these indicate distinct levels of representation or successive stages of processing is a theory-dependent matter, which as I show in chap. 3 is by no means simple.) Speaker-meaning, or utterance-token-meaning, will be a matter of the actual nonce or once-off inferences made in actual contexts by actual recipients with all of their rich particularities. This view, although parsimonious, is surely inadequate, indeed potentially pernicious, because it underestimates the regularity, recurrence, and systematicity of many kinds of pragmatic inferences.

What it omits is a third layer, what we may call the level of *statement-* or *utterance-meaning* (see Atlas 1989: 3–4), or, as I will prefer below, *utterance-type-meaning*. This third layer is a level of systematic pragmatic inference based *not* on direct computations about speaker-intentions but rather on general expectations about how language is normally used. These expectations give rise to presumptions, default inferences, about both content and force; and it is at this level (if at all) that we can sensibly talk about speech acts, presuppositions, conventional implicatures, felicity conditions, conversational presequences, preference organization, and so on and of special concern to us, generalized conversational implicatures. It is also at this level, naturally, that we can expect the systematicity of inference that might be deeply interconnected to linguistic structure and meaning, to the extent that it can become problematical to decide which phenomena should be rendered unto semantic theory and which unto pragmatics (q.v. the long-standing disputes about the semantic or pragmatic status of illocutionary force and presupposition).

The supposition of this third, intermediate layer in a theory of communication is nothing new. Austin (1962: 100ff), for example, clearly had something of this kind in mind when he proposed the three-way distinction between locutionary, illocutionary, and perlocutionary acts. The locutionary level corresponds to the level of sentence-meaning, the illocutionary to our intermediate layer formed of conventions or habits of use, and the perlocutionary (partly) to the level of speaker-meaning (i.e., the speaker's intentions to get the addressee to believe or do something as consequences of the utterance).[11] Other theorists have energetically tried to defend the notion of a *convention of use* to be distinguished from a *convention of language*; for example, such a distinction seems essential if we are to retain the idea that indirect speech acts are both partially conventional and inferentially motivated (Searle 1975; see also Bach and Harnish 1979: 192–202 on *standardization* as opposed to *conventionalization* of a nonliteral use). Without admitting the existence of such an intermediate layer, how are we to explain the use of routine formulae (like *Good luck, Bless you, See you later*) which although meaning what they literally mean simultaneously perform habitual everyday rituals (Morgan 1978)? Why is it that I can introduce myself with *My name is Steve*, but not *I was given the name Steve*; that I can express sympathy with you with *I am sorry* but not conventionally with *That saddens me*; that I express outrage with *Really!* but not with *In truth!*; that I can say *I am delighted to meet you* but not idiomatically *I am gratified to meet you*; that I can choose a pastry by saying *I'd like that one* but not *I'd admire that one*, and so on. And to every specification of proper usage there tends to be a corresponding restriction on interpretation (Levinson 1979). There is a great body of language lore here, beyond knowledge of grammar and semantics, extensively studied of course by traditional rhetoric, the ethnography of speaking, and students of translation and second language learning.

That two ways of "saying the same thing" might be unequal in their conversational import, or that one way of saying something might pre-empt another, these are surely not radical doctrines.

The theory of GCIs is not of course a theory of conventional idioms, clichés, and formulae, but it is *a generative theory of idiomaticity*—that is, a set of principles guiding the choice of the right expression to suggest a specific interpretation and, as a corollary, a theory accounting for pre-ferred interpretations. GCI theory offers a systematic account of why, for example, saying "See you on Tuesday" when tomorrow is Tuesday would suggest not seeing you tomorrow, or why saying "Some of my colleagues are competent" would suggest that not all of them are, and so on, matching a way of putting things with a favored interpretation in each case. The theory thus belongs to the intermediate level of a theory of communication, the layer of utterance(-type)-meaning.

One question that arises is whether GCIs are just the same things as other kinds of pragmatic inference that might belong to this level. First, there are perhaps more general kinds of inference that might subsume the GCIs and that also lie between the conventions of language on the one hand and the full-blown nonce inference to speaker-meaning on the other. For example, Bach has proposed the idea of a standardized inference which "shortcircuits the steps of the inferences, both as intended by the speaker and as carried through by the listener" (Bach 1975: 235, 1995).[12] Such inferences go through by default, without full calculation. But Bach's notion relies on compression by precedent (1995: 685), and GCIs, on my conception at least, are generative, driven by general heuristics and and not dependent on routinization. Second, there are more specific notions which at first blush one might want to equate with GCIs but shouldn't. One of these, the notion of short-circuited implicature (Brown and Levinson 1987 [1978]: 290, n. 35; Morgan 1978; Horn and Bayer 1984), has been developed to handle a very specific phenomenon, also arising from routinization, whereby utterances acquire morphosyntactic markers of their implicated content (examples are indirect speech acts and Neg-raising constructions; see chap. 2). Finally, various theorists have argued that not every kind of inference driven by Gricean reasoning is an implicature proper: it is variously an explicature (Sperber and Wilson 1986) or an impliciture (Bach 1994), and it may be thought that GCIs belong to one of these categories. These are essentially conceived of as a fleshing out of what was expressed (thus utterances only have one of them, but they may have many GCIs). I argue against this equation in chapter 3, but meanwhile it should be clear that my conception of a GCI is on the one hand rather catholic in the sense that it includes phenomena that others may want to consider nonimplicatures (e.g., explicatures or implicitures), and on the other hand it is orthogonal to the very general principles of short-circuiting of inference by precedence.

There are thus a number of distinct phenomena that may belong to this intermediate layer in a theory of communication. Nevertheless, that layer is constantly under attack by reductionists seeking to assimilate it either to the level of sentence-meaning or to the level of speaker-meaning; thus, for example, in the case of GCIs, Kamp, Peters, Kempson, van Kuppevelt, and others have all suggested that they should be in effect semanticized, whereas Sperber and Wilson and artificial intelligence local-pragmatics theorists have presumed that on the contrary they should be assimilated to matters of nonce inference at the level of speaker-intention. But GCIs are not going to reduce so easily in either direction, for they sit midway, systematically influencing grammar and semantics on the one hand and speaker-meaning on the other.

There is another way of course to make these distinctions, by invoking the type/token distinction.[13] On the two-leveled theory of communication we have a theory of sentence-meaning, which is a theory of the meaning of sentence-types rather than sentence-tokens,[14] on the one hand, and a theory of speaker- or utterance-meaning, which is a theory of utterance-token rather than utterance-type meaning, on the other. The theory of utterance-meaning is a theory of utterance-token meaning because theorists of this ilk conceive of speaker-meaning as a matter of nonce inference to the best interpretation taking all the particularities of the context into account. Now, from the point of view of a three-leveled theory of meaning, we need an additional distinction between utterance-token meaning and utterance-type meaning: the intermediate level is the level at which generalizations about whole classes of utterances (utterance-types) must reside. Thus GCI theory is one kind of theory about utterance-type meaning.

Reductionists, if they are willing to countenance the idea of a preferred interpretation or an utterance-type meaning at all, might propose that the phenomena can in fact be explained in terms of the structure of contexts. Faced for example with the tendency to read *John has three children* as 'John has exactly three children', an explanation might be offered in terms of nonce speaker-meaning together with a general preponderance of contexts in which absolute cardinality is relevant (Kempson (1986) perhaps holds this view). Thus we could hold onto the idea that all inferences are constructed *de novo* without reference to a default rule or a preferred interpretation, by hypothesizing that the background premises remain sufficiently constant to yield the observable bias in interpretations. It may not be easy to distinguish between this view and a theory of default interpretations, especially because such a contextual bias might itself be sufficient to engender a mental counterpart, a default rule of inference. The material difference would be that instead of having two different kinds of inference and one kind of context (as in GCI theory, where we must distinguish default GCIs from nonce PCIs), we will have one kind of inference and two kinds of context, the default context and the fully particular nonce context (amounting to a reduction of GCIs to PCIs).

My own view is that a theory of preferred interpretations is at least as plausible and much more workable; I am simply not sanguine about the possibilities of a theory of contexts able to predict the bias in interpretations in the same straightforward way. Moreover, on the theory that is advanced in this book, it is the choice of utterance-form and content, in line with perfectly general principles, that triggers the inferences in question. Such general patterns, in which, for example, marked forms suggest marked extensions, can't come out of a theory of contextual biases alone. A theory of favored contexts would have to be married to a theory of the correlation of utterance-form to kinds of contexts (some suggestions can be found in Zipf 1949). The present theory presumes such a rough correlation but goes beyond it, in that it proposes that speakers exploit such correlations for semiotic purposes.

Now it may be thought that for quite different reasons the notion of utterance-type meaning would force us into a theory of context-types. The argument would be that if an utterance is construed, as it is classically, as a sentence-context pair, the only way to abstract a type out of such a token would be to generalize over context-types.[15] But we may need to change the classical analysis of the utterance anyway. The need for such a change emerges fairly clearly from recent work in semantics; for example, in both DRT and Situation Semantics, sentence-meaning is already a matter of the relation between context and content, so we can no longer make the distinction between sentence-meaning and utterance-meaning by dragging in the context. We need to reconstruct all these concepts. One way may be to split the notion of context into different constitutive components and abstract over each of these. Thus to obtain the semantic content of "We are here" we may abstract over speakers and places, whereas to obtain the proposition expressed we must instantiate individual speakers and places of speaking; that alone will not be anything like sufficient to give us a speaker-meaning. For that, we'll need to know who are the speaker's companions and how the place including the speaker is to be effectively delimited, and so on. If we are playing hide-and-seek, then the speaker-meaning may be intentionally less specific. Another way to make the relevant distinctions might be to make speaker-meaning a three-way relation between speaker, context, and the proposition intended, whereas utterance-type meaning is just a relation between context and classes of proposition (those that the context circumscribes as possible speaker-meanings). But these are difficult issues and the precise moves we make will depend on the nature of the semantic theory we are utilizing. In any case, it is clear that we need more distinctions than the simple opposition between sentence and utterance provides, and it is likely that in talking about sentence-meaning we will already be generalizing over classes of contexts. And it is quite clear (as, e.g., demonstrated by Situation Semantics) that generalizing over classes of contexts does not amount to having a theory of default or preferred or statistically normal contexts—that should be a rather more empirical matter.

To return to the central issue, it would seem incontrovertible that any theory of utterance interpretation would have to admit the contribution of a level at which sentences are systematically paired with preferred interpretations. I will therefore presume that we need such a three-tiered theory of communication. This presumption does not presuppose that the distinctions between the middle layer of utterance-meaning and the upper and lower levels is in any way cut and dried. Indeed, there is every reason to suppose that matters of utterance-meaning will shade into speaker-meaning at the one end and sentence-meaning at the other. This is in part because there is plenty of evidence that language use is the source for grammaticalized patterns and that there is a diachronic path from speaker-meanings to utterance-meanings to sentence-meanings. Thus gray areas at the boundaries do not constitute evidence against the tripartite view, and evidence for it is the existence of preferred interpretations, default presumptions of the kind I illustrate in detail in section 1.4.

1.3   THE ARGUMENT FROM DESIGN: THE MAXIMS AS HEURISTICS

The apparently effortless speed of daily communication through language is built on much specialized and highly evolved machinery. Some of the machinery is anatomical, like the structure and positioning of pharynx and larynx; some is neurophysiological like the language specialized areas of the brain, and the special pathways for the analysis of speech signals; and some is perceptual like the precise match between the window of human auditory perception and the frequencies of human speech.[16] All this betokens a deep evolutionary history and a long honing by the processes of selection toward an optimal system of linguistic communication characterized (all things considered) by an almost miraculous speed, accuracy, and automaticity.[17]

Against this background, it is nevertheless possible to identify a significant bottleneck in the speed of human communication—a design flaw, as it were, in an otherwise optimal system. The bottleneck is constituted by the remarkably slow transmission rate of human speech (conceived of as the rate at which phonetic representations can be encoded as discriminable acoustic signals), with a limit in the range of seven syllables or 18 segments per second.[18] It is instructive (if in various ways misleading) to compare the transmission rate of human speech to the rates of information transmission that we are familiar with between relatively simple electronic devices like personal computers. As users of such devices will know, this rate is measured in bits of information transferred per second (bps), and transmission rates of 300 bps used to be the absolute and frustrating minimum at which information was transferred (the information will reflect on a screen, for example, at a much slower rate than one can read it); 2400 bps or higher is now the standard minimum and directly linked devices may communicate at 115,200 bps or higher. If we now compare human speech encoding rates we find that, making various rather optimistic assumptions, the maximal sort of data-transfer rate for normal human speech is under 100 bps.[19] That is brutally slow.

In contrast, the psycholinguistic evidence suggests that all other aspects of speech production and comprehension can run at a much higher rate. For example, prearticulation processes in speech production seem to run at a speed three to four times faster than the actual articulation rate (Wheeldon and Levelt 1995), and rates at which speech can be parsed and comprehended show the same kind of advantage over articulation rates (Calvert 1986: 178; Mehler et al. 1993).[20] It is this mismatch between articulation rates on the one hand, and the rates of mental preparation for speech production or the speed of speech comprehension on the other hand, which points to a single fundamental bottleneck in the efficiency of human communication, occasioned no doubt by absolute physiological constraints on the articulators.

Grice routinely adopted a design perspective in order to tackle fundamental problems in philosophy. He would imagine artificial life-forms, which he dubbed *pirots*, and ask how they would have to be minimally endowed in order to display the particular aspect of human behavior he was interested in.[21] Now it is quite clear that pirots, conceived of as intelligent agents with the asymmetrical abilities in thinking and speaking I have just elucidated, would find a way around the articulatory bottleneck (just as, as a matter of fact, evolution has). The essential asymmetry is: inference is cheap, articulation expensive, and thus the design requirements are for a system that maximizes inference.[22] (Hence the perspective outlined in the introduction—linguistic coding is to be thought of less like definitive content and more like interpretive clue.)

From a Gricean perspective, communication involves the inferential recovery of speakers' intentions: it is the recognition by the addressee of the speaker's intention to get the addressee to think such-and-such that essentially constitutes communication. The question has been just *how* this recognition of others' intentions is possible. Skeptics have assumed that all accounts will simply smuggle in the notion of a conventional signal (Ziff 1975; Chomsky 1975: 62–77). Griceans have put forward various accounts that trade for the most part on a notion of mutual salience. Mutual salience was shown to have quite dramatic effects on the possibility of tacit coordination, or joint action in the absence of communication, by Schelling (1960: 55), a student of strategy in economics and politics. He showed that if, for example, two subjects are told they will win a prize only if they both choose either heads or tails without communicating, nearly 90% will coordinate on heads. The trick rests on our ability to double-guess what the other party is likely to think the obvious solution, which in turn rests on what he thinks we think he will think prominent—that is, on some notion of what is mutually salient. This rather astonishing ability (utilized further below) was seized on by Griceans (Lewis 1969; Schiffer 1972), because it suggests how it may be possible to produce a communicative action that suggests the m-intention that underlies it, even in the absence of any communicative convention or signal. For example, a communicator may produce an utterance or action (say, waving an umbrella) knowing that his behavior will suggest one salient idea (say, that it may rain), and that the addressee will be looking for just such a salient suggestion. (Note that a coordination problem can involve each party doing different things, e.g., one finding the correct signal, and the other its intended interpretation; see Lewis 1969, Clark 1996.) How tacit coordination really works is admittedly a mystery, although some have suggested it is based on the fact that humans are endowed with a mental reflex to process information in particular ways (Sperber and Wilson 1986). But it is clear that any mutual expectations can serve to drastically limit the search-space for coordination solutions (see Clark 1996: chap. 3).

There is a further, related problem that has received less attention, what might be called the *logical problem* of reconstructing speaker's intentions (Levinson 1995b). Let us (following Aristotle) assume that we reason from goals to actions utilizing a logic of action, or a *practical reasoning*. Now, some theorists have assumed that intention-recognition is simply a matter of running that reasoning backwards ("turned upside down" as von Wright (1971: 96) puts it): we observe the behavior and figure out the underlying intention by the same rules that we convert intentions into the actions that will effectuate them. The logical problem is that this cannot work, for the simple reason that for all inference systems one cannot work backwards from a conclusion to the premises from which it was deduced—there is always an infinite set of premises which might yield the same conclusion (consider, e.g., the conclusion q from the sets $\{p, p \rightarrow q\}$, $\{p \,\&\, q\}$, $\{p \vee q, \sim p\}$, etc.). Given that we do indeed recognize others' intentions (not only communicative of course), there have to be further constraints that limit the search space of sets of premises. Let us call such constraints heuristics. They may be various in kind: I may take your intentions to be circumscribed because you are a shop attendant and I am a customer, or because I just asked you a question, or because I happen to know your predilections, or because we have tacitly agreed to maximize the chances of successful communication by following some specific heuristics (e.g., on this radio channel we'll only talk about air-traffic control).

Now we have two particular design requirements for our communicating pirots. First, they must find a way around the articulatory bottleneck and use inferential enrichment to bypass this physiological limitation, given that the rest of the linguistic apparatus seems to be able to outstrip the articulation rate many times over. Second, the inferential enrichment must be circumscribed in such a way that communicators can indeed zero-in or coordinate (in the Schelling sense) on the correct communicative forms and intentions. What our pirots clearly need is a set of heuristics, mutually assumed by sender and receiver, that can serve to multiply the coded information by a factor of, say, three, by licensing inferential enrichment of what is actually encoded by choice of a specific signal. These heuristics must at the same time constrain that enrichment in such a way that the overall message can still be correctly recovered, by guiding (or coordinating) the match between the chosen signal and the recoverable, augmented message.

How could such heuristics work? It may be useful to sketch a little world about which our pirots may talk to one another. But first, recollect the idea, independently developed in slightly different ways by Popper (1959) and Bar-Hillel and Carnap (1952), that the semantic information content of a message can be measured in proportion to the number of states of affairs that the message effectively rules out, given a domain of discourse. For example, in a domain consisting of Bill and Ben, and considering just the states of affairs characterized by two predicates, say 'married' and 'middle-aged', the assertion "Bill is married" will rule out just 8 out of 16 possible states of affairs (e.g., a state where Ben is married and middle-aged and where Bill is not middle-aged and not married). But the assertion "Bill is married and middle-aged" will rule out twice as many states of affairs and, by this measure, will be twice as informative. Clearly, there are limits to the utility of such a characterization of informativeness (e.g., rather a lot depends on what properties we are actually interested in).[23] But, it is useful as a first approximation—and besides, it is just about the only measure of semantic information available (for a critique, see, e.g., Cohen 1971: 135ff).

Thus, to increase the informativeness of a coded message which itself rules out some number n of states of affairs, and thus to overcome the limit on the rate of encoding, all we need are some heuristics that will serve to rule out some further possible states, yielding an incremented content $n + m$. To illustrate this graphically, imagine a simple "blocks world" of the sort made familiar by Winograd's (1972) program for understanding natural language. Let us assume that in this blocks world there are a set of cubes, cones, and pyramids of different colors. Now we can invent three simple heuristics and demonstrate their efficacy.

Heuristic 1
What isn't said, isn't

As an example, take the assertion in (11).

(11) "There's a blue pyramid on the red cube,"
    Licensed inferences: 'There is not a cone on the red cube'; 'There is not a red pyramid on the red cube'

The heuristic licences the inferences (and others of their ilk, depending on the number of objects and the number of colors in the blocks world). Because these inferences rule out a number of possible states of affairs, they multiply the informational load of what has been said by a significant factor. The heuristic is wildly underspecified, of course. It must be understood to be restricted to a set of salient contrasts—for example, the ruling out of the presence of a cone on the red cube depends on the salient opposition in the blocks world of {cones, pyramids, cubes}, whereas the ruling out of the red pyramid depends on the salient opposition {red, blue}. If the heuristic is unrestricted, then of course whatever one did *not* specify would not be the case, and that would be such a powerful heuristic it would inhibit one from saying anything (for fear of having to list everything that is the case)! Thus this heuristic depends crucially on clearly established salient contrasts. But suitably restricted, such a heuristic offers tremendous increases in communicational load.[24]

Consider now the efficacy of a different kind of heuristic, one that trades on assumptions about what is normal. Such a heuristic might be phrased, to emphasize the contrast with the previous one, as "what isn't said, is as usual." Or it might be phrased as "don't bother to say what can be taken for granted." But for reasons that will become clear, I prefer the following sort of formulation:[25]

Heuristic 2
What is simply described is stereotypically exemplified

Returning to our blocks world, consider the application of such a heuristic to:

(12) 'The blue pyramid is on the red cube."
    Licensed inferences:
    'The pyramid is a stereotypical one, on a square, rather than, e.g., a hexagonal base.'
    'The pyramid is directly supported by the cube (e.g., there is no intervening slab)';
    'The pyramid is centrally placed on, or properly supported by, the cube (it is not teetering on the edge, etc.)';
    'The pyramid is in canonical position, resting on its base, and not balanced, e.g., on its apex.'

First, we are likely to assume that the pyramid in question has a four-sided base, although the definition of *pyramid* allows any number of sides from three up. Similarly, we expect it to be a regular figure, not leaning to one side, or anything of that kind. If these conditions were not met, we'd expect to be warned by a phrase like *a pyramid with polygonal base, an irregular pyramid, a sort of pyramid,* and so on. The heuristic licenses these assumptions.

But let us concentrate on the specification of the relation between the two blocks, given by the preposition *on.* As a first approximation, we may take Miller and Johnson-Laird's (1976: 386f) gloss of the relation ON(x, y) as specifying that y supports x, and x is 'in the region of inter- action' of a surface of y's. Thus the definition of *on* will allow things to intervene between x and y (as when we say "the mug is on the table" even though there's a book underneath it) and it will certainly allow x and y to be in a momentary or precarious support relation. But the heuristic will license more restrictive assumptions, specifically for (11) that the pyramid is *directly on* the red block, and that it is not teetering on the edge of the red block, or in the process of falling off. Instead, we assume, because of the lack of warning to the contrary, that the pyramid is firmly, directly, and indeed centrally placed on the block. Similarly, the heuristic licenses the inference that the pyramid is resting on its base, the most stable way in which it could be supported.

Such a heuristic is extremely powerful—it allows an interpreter to bring all sorts of background knowledge about a domain to bear on a rich interpretation of a minimal description.[26]

This heuristic, because of its very power, carries with it the need for another complementary one that would allow the communicator to cancel the assumptions that would otherwise follow from a heuristic specifying "normal description betokens normal situation." If what is simply described can be presumed to be stereotypically exemplified, then what is described in a *marked* or unusual way should be presumed to contrast with that stereotypical or normal exemplification. I formulate the com- plementary heuristic as follows:

Heuristic 3
What's said in an abnormal way, isn't normal; or Marked message indicates marked situation

Consider the application of this heuristic to:

(13) "The blue cuboid block is supported by the red cube."
     Licensed inferences: 'The blue block is not, strictly, a cube'; 'The blue
     block is not directly or centrally or stably supported by the red cube.'

Thus, given the third heuristic, an interpreter of (13) is likely to presume that the situation described is not one in which a canonical cube is sitting directly on the middle of another. Specifically, the presumption is likely to be that there are reasons for avoiding the use of the simple expressions *cube* and *on*, the reason being that the second heuristic would license assumptions that the speaker doesn't want to encourage.

How do the suggestions come about? Note that any cube is also a cuboid (i.e., a solid with rectangular faces), but the use of the less familiar word suggests that the familiar extension is not what the speaker intends. The procedure is general: the use of the phrase the *squarish block* would also suggest 'not a cube', even though a cube is surely (at least) squarish. Similarly, opposing modes of description of the ON-relation, carry contrastive suggestions:

(14) a. The blue pyramid is *on* the red cube.
     b. The blue pyramid is *supported by* the red cube.

The use of the simple preposition in (14a) serves by the second heuristic to rule out various marked states of affairs (like indirect support), whereas the use of the circumlocution or partial paraphrase in (14b) induces the complementary interpretation by the third heuristic—the marked expression suggesting the description of a marked state of affairs. Thus the third heuristic again excludes certain interpretations, now the ones that would have risen had the stereotypical assumptions been encouraged by the use of an unmarked expression.

Here then are three simple heuristics that serve to get around the bottleneck created by the articulation rate of human speech. Each amplifies the communicative content of what is said by the measure suggested by Bar-Hillel and Carnap (1952): for each heuristic allows the recipient of a message to rule out a great many states of affairs that are in fact compatible with the content of the coded message. Taken together, the set of three heuristics serves to multiply the informational content of any message by a factor of perhaps a score, transforming the slow coding rate of human speech into something approximating the perceived speed of human communication. All that is required for such a system to work is a tacit agreement between communicators that such heuristics can be assumed to be operative unless there are indications otherwise. At the same time, because the heuristics effectively narrow the range of intended extensions of expressions, they will significantly constrain the search space for speakers' intentions and thus help to resolve the logical problem of intention-recovery.

The question that can now be raised is: could any rational and intelligent communicators, faced with a transmission bottleneck, fail to derive and utilize such a simple solution to the problem of narrow bandwidth? It seems highly unlikely. And if that is so, one of the central preoccupations of pragmatic theory should be to discover and elucidate the particular heuristics that are actually employed. And although the force of this argument does not depend on any particular proposed heuristics, the three I have sketched here seem to have both intuitive and empirical support, which I now turn to show.

1.4   A TYPOLOGY OF GCIs

There is in fact a fairly transparent relationship between the three heuristics introduced in the previous section and three of Grice's maxims of conversation. All that is necessary to see the connection is to introduce a different way of thinking about the maxims. Instead of thinking about them as rules (or rules of thumb) or behavioral norms, it is useful to think of them as primarily *inferential heuristics* which then motivate the behavioral norms. That some of the maxims and not others have a special status as inducers of GCIs more or less follows from the nature of generalized inference, as will become clear. By assimilating the new perspective to the old, we can benefit from the many observations made under more classical Gricean assumptions.

But the purpose here is to show that the three heuristics sketched in the prior section do indeed seem to be good candidates for such background inferential principles, and this can be done by taking them one by one, showing how they relate to Grice's scheme and how they collect prior observations into a tripartite typology of GCIs. At this stage, I simply wish to enlist intuitive support for the three proposed heuristics, and I shall make various rather drastic simplifications that will be modified later (see especially chap. 2).

1.4.1   The First (Q-) Heuristic

The first heuristic ("What isn't said, isn't") is more or less transparently related to Grice's first Maxim of Quantity, Q1: Make your contribution as informative as is required. Grice's Q1 maxim is the one normally held to be responsible for the classic scalar implicatures, as well as Gazdar's (1979) clausal implicatures. The essential concept behind the scalar and clausal implicatures is the notion of a contrast set, of linguistic expressions in salient contrast, which differ in informativeness (see chap. 2).[27] And, as I have just shown, the first heuristic depends crucially on a restriction to a set of salient alternates. For example, there is a scalar contrast set ⟨*all, some*⟩, such that saying (15a) implicates the rationale being that the speaker would have chosen the stronger alternate if he was in a position to do so. Similarly, for the clausal alternates ⟨*(since p, q), (if p, q)*⟩, the use of the weaker conditional stands in opposition to the use of constructions that would entail the embedded sentences (e.g., *since p, q*).

(15) a. "Some of the boys came."
      +> (scalar implicates) 'Not all of the boys came.'
   b. "If there is life on Mars, the NASA budget will be spared."
      +> (clausally implicates) 'There may or may not be life on Mars.'

Scalar implicature is thus just a special case of a whole family of implicatures based on salient alternates (mostly, but not necessarily, ranked as informationally weaker or stronger), as indicated schematically below:

Q Contrast Sets
The Q heuristic ("What you do not say is not the case") has to be restricted: for sets of alternates, use of one (especially a weaker) implicates inapplicability of another (especially an otherwise compatible stronger alternate).

   scalar: ⟨*all, some*⟩, "some" +> 'not all'
   negative scales: ⟨*none, not all*⟩, "not all" +> 'not none, i.e., some'
   clausal: ⟨*since-p-q, if-p-q*⟩, "if p then q" +> 'p is uncertain'
   nonentailment scales: ⟨*succeed, try*⟩ "try" +> 'not succeed'
   nonentailment sets: {*yellow, red, blue,...*} "yellow" +> 'not red, etc.'

Given the heuristic ("For the relevant salient alternates, what isn't said is not the case"), such sets of salient alternates then provide the basis of the following sorts of inference:

(16) a. "Some of the boys came"
      +> 'not all'
   b. "Three boys came in"
      +> 'not four'
   c. "Possibly, there's life on Mars"
      +> 'not certainly'
   d. "Not all of the boys came"
      +> 'some did'

e. "If John comes, I'll go"
   +> 'maybe he will, maybe he won't'
f. "John tried to reach the summit"
   +> 'he didn't succeed'
g. "Her dress was red"
   +> 'not red and blue'

1.4.2   The Second (I) Heuristic

The second heuristic ("What is expressed simply is stereotypically exemplified") may be related directly to Grice's second Maxim of Quantity, Q2: Do not make your contribution *more* informative than is required. The underlying idea is, of course, that one need not say what can be taken for granted.

I develop this heuristic in a particular way below, generalizing somewhat to gather in inferences to a rich interpretation that may not strictly be inferences to the stereotype. As a rough gloss, I offer "minimal specifications get maximally informative or stereotypical interpretations." Brief and simple expressions thus encourage, by this heuristic, a tendency to select the best interpretation to the most stereotypical, most explanatory exemplification. This rubric allows us to subsume under this heuristic a great number of well-known interpretive tendencies. Hence from the use of semantically general expressions we obtain the generality-narrowing in (17a–c), the strengthening of conditionals to biconditionals in (17d) (i.e., *conditional perfection*) and the strengthening of negations from contradictories to contraries in (17e), the enrichment of conjunctions by the assumption of temporal sequence and causality as in (17f) (i.e., *conjunction buttressing*), the assumption that conjoined subjects acted together as in (17g) (i.e., *together-implications*), a preference for local coreference as in (17h), and for the finding of local antecedents as in the *bridging inference* in (17i).

(17) a. "John's book is good"
        +> the one he read, wrote, borrowed, as appropriate.
     b. "bread knife"/"kitchen knife"/"steel knife"
     c. "a secretary"
        +> female one
        "a road"
        +> hard-surfaced one
     d. "If you mow the lawn, I'll give you $5."
        +> 'Iff you mow the lawn, will I give you $5.'

e. "I don't like garlic"

   +> contrary 'I dislike garlic.'

   "I don't believe p"

   +> 'I believe not-p.'

f. "John turned the switch and the motor started."

   +> p and then q, p caused q, John intended p to cause q, etc.

g. "John and Jenny bought a piano"

   +> together

   (cf.: "The Americans and the Russians launched a satellite in 1962.")

h. "John came in and he laughed"

   Preference for local coreference: John = he

i. "The picnic was awful. The beer was warm."

   Bridging: +> 'the beer is part of the picnic.'

Once again, a great deal of support can be found for the operation of some heuristic of this kind. A version of such a principle is given by Atlas and Levinson (1981), who dubbed it the *Informativeness Principle*, and following this, I call the heuristic the I-principle.

1.4.3   The Third (M) Heuristic

The third heuristic ("What's said in an abnormal way isn't normal") can be related directly to Grice's maxim of Manner ("Be perspicuous"), specifically to his first submaxim "avoid obscurity of expression" and his fourth "avoid prolixity" (Grice's M1 and M4). The underlying idea here is that there is an implicit opposition or parasitic relationship between our second and third heuristics: what is said simply, briefly, in an unmarked way picks up the stereotypical interpretation; if in contrast a marked expression is used, it is suggested that the stereotypical interpretation should be avoided. Thus we have complementary interpretations: marked expressions pick up the complement of the stereotypical extensions that would have been suggested by the use of the corresponding unmarked forms, had they been used (Horn 1984; all this developed in chap. 2 of this book).

   Again, there seems plenty of intuitive support for the existence of such a heuristic. Prototype examples are the pragmatic effects of double negatives; thus the simple positive in (18a) suggests that the plane may be late as planes often are, but the double negative in (18b) suggests that there's a rather more remote possibility.

(18) a. "It's possible the plane will be late."
          +> (by I) 'likely to stereotypical probability *n*'
      b. "It's not impossible that the plane will be late."
          +> (by M) 'rather less likely than *n*'

In the same way, use of a periphrastic alternative to a simple causative verb suggests some deviation from the expected chain of events:

(19) a. "Bill stopped the car"
          +> (by I) 'in the stereotypical manner with the foot pedal'
      b. "Bill caused the car to stop"
          +> (by M) 'indirectly, not in the normal way, e.g., by use of the emergency brake'

Similarly for more elaborate paraphrases:

(20) "The corners of Sue's lips turned slightly upward."
      M +> 'Sue didn't exactly smile'

And a particularly important instance of the opposition between unmarked and marked expressions may prove to be that between pronouns (inducing assumptions of local coreference) and full lexical NPs (resisting local coreference) as in:

(21) "John came in and the man laughed."
      +> '*the man* denotes someone other than *he* would have'

1.4.4 Interactions Between Implicatures

We now have three heuristics, each supporting a distinct family or genus of implicature. The implicatures will be generalized, that is will have the status of preferred interpretations, because the heuristics will be understood to be generally in force—it is that which gives them their communicational efficacy.

But different modes of GCI generation may yield inconsistent implicatures. This gives rise to an interesting and complex *projection problem*, which will be the subject of later attention (see chap. 2).[28] But it is important to know that although the problem is complex, it is not as intractable as it might appear. For it seems that, where inconsistent GCIs arise, they are systematically resolved by an ordered set of priorities:

Level of genus: Q > M > I (read > as 'defeats inconsistent')
Level of species: (e.g.) Q-clausal > Q-scalar

Such ordered priorities seem to account for the observable preferred interpretations where, in principle, two or more inconsistent inferences might arise (as will be described in chap. 2 in detail).

Why should the priorities be like this? There is no complete explanation at present, but here is perhaps part of the answer. First, there is a distinction between the Q- and M-inferences based primarily on linguistic alternates on the one hand, and the I-inferences based primarily on stereotypical presumptions about the world on the other. It would be essential to be able to utilize the resources of the language in order to indicate that the normal, stereotypical, rich presumptions about the world do not hold; and that is what ordering Q and M before I achieves. Both Q- and M-heuristics essentially induce a metalinguistic mode of inference, in contrast to the I-heuristic. They differ though in the kind of metalinguistic contrast that they rely on—Q relies on sets of alternates of essentially similar form with contrastive semantic content, whereas M relies on sets of alternates that contrast in form but not in inherent semantic content.

These properties provide a set of simple diagnostics for the three main genera of GCI, which I represent in a simplified way in table 1.1.[29] A few remarks on the table are in order. First, although there is some terminological confusion and some differences between lumpers and splitters, on the whole neo-Griceans are agreed about how the phenomena divide. For example, the reasons that Horn subsumes both (what are called in this book) Q and M inferences under one label should already be clear from the table—they share many properties, even though they are distinct at a finer level of granularity. In this book, I make no direct argument for the tripartite scheme here employed (for which see Levinson 1987a) but rather exemplify with how such a scheme handles the data, and so let the scheme argue for itself. Now a word on the listed properties of each type of implicature. First, by *negative inference* I have in mind that Q and M inferences are *essentially* negative, not incidentally so, because what is implicated is that the speaker is avoiding some stronger (Q) or some simpler (M) expression, and thus indicating that he or she is not in a position to use those other expressions. Making further psychological assumptions, the recipient may thus be led to believe that the speaker does not know whether the relevant sentence with those alternate expressions would be true, or even knows that those expressions if employed would express a falsehood. For this reason, both Q and M implicatures are

Table 1.1
Diagnostics for the three types of GCI

Corresponding terminologies			
Present book[1]	**Q**	**M**	**I**
Gricean maxims	Q1	M1 & M4	Q2
Horn's (1984) terms	Q	Q	R
Levinson's (1985/7) terms[2]	Q	Q/M	I
Properties of each type			
Negative inference	yes	yes	no
Metalinguistic basis	yes	yes	no
Contrast between			
semantically strong/weak	yes	no	N/A
synonymous surface forms	no	yes	N/A
Within the scope of metalinguistic negation	yes	yes	no
Inference to stereotype	no	no	yes
Overriding GCIs	none	Q	Q, M

[1] I am thus reverting effectively to the terminology in Atlas and Levinson 1981.
[2] The Q/M formulation was intended to record that in Horn's view these inferences are Quantity inferences, while in mine they are Manner ones. I am guilty of using yet another terminology in Levinson 1995a, where for purposes of perspicuous reference to Grice's maxims, I used Q1, M, and Q2 respectively.

metalinguistic in the sense that they can only be recovered by reference to what else might have been said but was not. In particular, there is metalinguistic reference to salient sets of linguistic alternates but of different kinds in the two cases: informationally ordered sets in the case of Q; sets of synonyms differing in markedness in the case of M. This last feature is what distinguishes between Q and M implicatures. Their shared metalinguistic character, however, makes it possible to deny the relevant implicature using metalinguistic negation with special stress, as in *You didn't eat SOME of the cookies, you ate ALL of them*. All these properties contrast with I implicatures, which do not have a metalinguistic basis in speaker avoidance of other expressions but are direct inferences from unmarked expressions without stronger contrastive alternates to informationally rich, often stereotypical interpretations. Finally, the three kinds of inference differ in strength, and consequently they interact in a specific way: Q inferences take priority over inconsistent inferences of other kinds, and M inferences over I inferences.

We now have in place our cast of characters, the kinds of GCI that will play an essential role in the argument throughout this book. In the next chapter, I describe them and the heuristics that give rise to them in much more detail. But now I return to the work of this chapter—the attempt to establish the very existence of a mode of inference of a kind exemplified by generalized conversational implicatures.

1.5 NONMONOTONICITY AND DEFAULT REASONING

1.5.1 Typology of Nonmonotonic Reasoning Systems

GCIs are inferences that appear to go through in the absence of information to the contrary; but additional information to the contrary may be quite sufficient to cause them to evaporate. Thus the mode of inference appears to have two important properties: it is a *default* mode of reasoning, and it is *defeasible*. Here, I try to set these properties in the context of various different kinds of nondeductive reasoning that have been explored. The underlying purpose is to show that there are a number of proposed kinds of reasoning to which the inference of GCIs might be usefully assimilated.

A reasoning system is said to be *defeasible* (or when instantiated in an argument *nonmonotonic*) if an inference or argument in that system may be defeated by the addition of further premises.[30] Deductive systems, of course, are monotonic or nondefeasible. It seems most unlikely that implicatures are derived as deductive inferences (contrary to Sperber and Wilson 1986) because implicatures are clearly defeasible:[31]

(22) a. *Assertion:* "John ate some of the cookies."
      b. *Default implicature:* 'John did not eat all of the cookies.'
      c. *Cancellation of b:* "John ate some of the cookies. In fact he ate all of them."

Indeed, it is quite possible, as Johnson-Laird (1983) has argued, that true deduction plays little part in informal human reasoning.

Our understanding of the range of alternative inference methods is still too limited to permit a proper typology. Nevertheless, a tripartite distinction between *deduction*, *induction*, and *abduction* is a useful starting place (Josephson and Josephson 1994: 27–29). A crude but effective way to approach these three modes of reasoning is through a comparison of their central syllogisms (Pople 1973):

(23) *Deduction*

$$\frac{\begin{array}{l}A(x)(P(x) \to Q(x)) \\ P(a)\end{array}}{Q(a)}D$$

(major premise)
(minor premise)
(conclusion)

(24) *Induction*

$$\frac{\begin{array}{l}P(a) \\ Q(a)\end{array}}{A(x)\ (P(x) \to Q(x))}I$$

(observed fact)
(observed fact)
(induced law)

(25) *Abduction*

$$\frac{\begin{array}{l}A(x)(P(x) \to Q(x)) \\ Q(a)\end{array}}{P(a)}A$$

(known law)
(observed fact)
(hypothesized explanation)

The idea behind this formulation is, of course, that whereas deduction gives one conclusions by instantiation in a general law, induction enables one to conclude a general law from multiple observations of singular facts, and abduction is the hypothesizing of a fact that would, in conjunction with a general law, explain an observed fact. Both induction and abduction are clearly nonmonotonic; in the former case, the discovery of a fact (e.g., 'Q(b) & ~P(b)') not in accord with the hypothesized law is sufficient to annul the law; in the case of the latter, the conclusion P(a) will be defeated if we already know that ~P(a).

To these three contrasting syllogisms we may add the following two, which characterize two further kinds of nondeductive reasoning that are currently being explored:

(26) *Practical reasoning* (Atlas and Levinson 1973 after Kenny 1966)

$$\frac{\begin{array}{l}A(x)\ (P(x) \to Q(x)) \\ Goal(Q(a))\end{array}}{Goal(P(a))}KL$$

(known law)
(desire)
(consequent desire)

(27) *Default "logics"* (see Ginsberg 1987)

$$\frac{\begin{array}{l}A(x)\ ([P(x)\ \&\ M(Q(x))] \to Q(x)) \\ P(a)\end{array}}{Q(a)}DL$$

(conditionally assume Q(x))
(known fact)
(assumed consistent fact)

Of these four kinds of defeasible reasoning, inductive reasoning has been the focus of by far the most thought; indeed there has been a lively debate since at least the time of Francis Bacon, and I make no attempt here to survey the various logical systems that have been proposed to capture notions like degree of inductive support (see, e.g., Cohen 1971; Holland, Holyok, Nisbett, and Thagard 1989).[32] However, the other kinds of system are less familiar, and I should briefly sketch the motivations behind their development.

Abduction, like practical reasoning, has a striking property illustrated in syllogism (25) above—it is an application of what in deduction would be the fallacy of affirming the consequent. This captures the essence of the informed guess, the presumption that if a fact fits with a known law, it is an instantiation of it. It may be objected here that this is a poor characterization of abduction, at least as originally conceived by Peirce—for even though he provides the simple syllogistic account in (25) above,[33] he seems to have intended that the term "abduction" should refer to the creative hypothesis of the major premise or scientific law itself and not the hypothesis of a mere fact that would make applicable a preexisting law. However, we can trivially manipulate the abductive syllogism to make the major premise the conclusion:[34]

(28) $(p \& (p \to q)) \to q$ (logical truth)

$$\frac{q}{p \& (p \to q)} A$$ (observation)

        (abduced law)

Clearly, what is fallacious in deductive reasoning (affirming the consequent) may be legitimate in hypothesis formation only under strict constraints on the antecedents one may hypothesize; otherwise any antecedent whatsoever may be posited. The strict constraints must capture, in some way, our sense of the best available explanation for the factuality of the consequent. At the same time, these constraints must suggest some heuristics that would allow the selection of reasonable hypotheses, given that, in general, there will be indefinitely many antecedents that may be hypothesized. The best explanation or hypothesis should be that one, it has been suggested (Thagard 1978), that gives us maximal predictions for minimal assumptions. In short, hypothesis formation is conservative as regards the modification of existing theory or assumptions but expansionist as regards the data that may be covered.

Theories of "inference to the best explanation" in philosophy of science may seem far afield from theories of utterance interpretation; utterance interpretation is not leisurely, ratiocinative, and globally ambitious like scientific theory. But some of the same processes may well be involved nevertheless (it would be odd if our scientific ability had no origins in everyday thinking), and transitional fields like medical diagnosis or diagnosis of mechanical failure make this plausible. AI work in diagnostic systems requires some kind of abductive inference and there has been much experimentation here.[35] But more directly pertinent is the abductive approach to implicature being developed by Hobbs and co-workers, which I review in the next section.

Practical-reasoning systems, closely allied to AI planning systems, aim to capture the reasoning from ends to means that will achieve those ends, or, if one likes, from goal to plan. They are also clearly nonmonotonic; for example, instantiating in (26), given that if one takes the 10:00 train from Cambridge one arrives in London at 11:15, and given that one wants to be in London at 11:15, then one should want to catch the 10:00 train. But suppose that one hates traveling by train; well, then, the plan is not adopted, at least if there's some alternative. Developed first in philosophical theories of action (see, e.g., Kenny 1966; von Wright 1971) and applied specifically to implicature by Atlas and Levinson (1973; see also the sketch in Brown and Levinson 1987: 64–65, 87–90), such modes of reasoning have since been explored in artificial intelligence (see, e.g., Allen 1983; Charniak and McDermott 1987: chap. 9).

Default logics aim to capture a rather different mode of reasoning—namely, the notion of a reasonable presumption, a *ceteris paribus* assumption. There are a great many different formalisms under investigation (see Ginsberg 1987), but the kind of inference that these are designed to capture can again best be indicated by instantiation in the syllogism in (28). Suppose we are told "The noise of the gun frightened off the birds." It is a natural presumption that the birds flew away; but of course the presumption is unwarranted—there are birds like penguins that do not fly at all, and others like quail that may run off along the ground or swans that may swim away. The inference from 'x is a bird' to 'x can/will fly' is an inference we seem to make *unless* there is some inconsistent assumption already made (e.g., the birds in question are penguins). So we can set up a syllogism that says, in effect, if x is a bird and x's flying is consistent with what is known, presume x flies. The inference will be defeasible given any fact that is inconsistent with it.

1.5.2   Nonmonotonic Inference and Implicature

Reviewing these forms of nonmonotonic inference, it is clear that each of them gives, by design, an account of defeasibility, the essential property for modeling inferences like implicatures. Induction alone, however, does not recommend itself as the basis for a theory of implicature just because implicatures in general, but GCIs in particular, seem to be presumed absolutely, not with such-and-such degree of inductive support; nor in general do we seem to think that a speaker meant p by U with probability n. Abduction is more attractive because it offers a circumscribed presumption—but attempts to construct an abductive system for implicature presumption require an elaborate weighting of inference rules, and even a weighting of individual facts, in order to constrain guesswork by making certain presumptions more costly than others (see Hobbs and Martin 1987, Hobbs 1987, Hobbs et al. 1993).

Practical reasoning systems, on the other hand, have a certain attraction for the modeling of implicature on first principles: if speaker-meaning is (as on the classic Gricean account) a matter of having a complex plan or intention, then understanding (and thus implicature-recovery) must be largely a matter of plan reconstruction (see, e.g., Cohen, Morgan, and Pollack 1990). A number of attempts have thus been made to model implicature in these terms (Atlas and Levinson 1973; Brown and Levinson 1978; McCafferty 1987; Thomason 1987, 1990; Welker 1994). But there is a striking problem that has never been properly addressed—namely, the fact that planning systems (like all logical systems) are asymmetrical, in the sense that plan recognition is not simply plan construction run backwards (Levinson 1995b). Just as a conclusion p might be reached from an infinite set of distinct premises (e.g., $p \,\&\, q$; or $q \,\&\, (q \rightarrow p)$; or $(p \vee q) \,\&\, \sim q$) so indefinitely many plans might converge on a single utterance. Thus even if we had an account of how a speaker plans an utterance complete with its implicatures (and see Levelt 1989 for a glimpse of the complexities), this would not directly give us an account of how the implicatures were recovered in comprehension.

Finally, only default logics clearly have the two properties that generalized implicatures (GCIs) clearly exhibit: defeasibility and default or preferred presumption. On the face of it, though, they may seem to have little to offer to a general theory of implicature because they provide a restricted set of limited inference rules, incapable of modeling the open-ended, creative, and indefinite set of inferences that come under Grice's theory. However, as an account of the inference of GCIs, just those implicatures that seem to have the default property, they may indeed have something to offer. There are a great many rather different models of default reasoning (Ginsberg 1987), but I will sketch (simplistically) how such an application might work by taking the simplest of such non-monotonic systems, the default-rule systems originating with Reiter (1980).

We can conceive of default rules, on this interpretation, as *extra-logical rules* of inference that can be used to expand the data base (the set of available premises). Such rules have the canonical form (where α and β are sentences, and M β means 'β is consistent with what is known'):

(29) $\dfrac{\alpha:\ M\beta}{\beta}$

which is read 'if α is true, and β is consistent with the data-base (what is known), then assume β'. For example, we might represent our earlier default assumption as:

(30) $\dfrac{\text{bird(a): M flies(a)}}{\text{flies(a)}}$

Thus one might assume that if *a* is a bird, then *a* flies, unless one has specific knowledge to the contrary. Turning now to GCIs, we might treat the scalar implicature from the use of the weaker existential quantifier in a precisely similar way (where α is a simplex arbitrary sentence frame):

(31) $\dfrac{\alpha\ (\text{some}):\ M\ (\alpha(\text{not all}))}{\alpha\ (\text{not all})}$

Then an utterance like "Some of them came" will implicate 'Not all of them came' wherever this further assumption is consistent with the data base. If we interpret the data base as the common ground (i.e., what is publicly taken for granted in the conversation so far), then a rule of this sort serves to augment the common ground in just the sort of way generally envisaged in pragmatic theory. Of course, the rule as stated loses all the generality that is the signal virtue of the pragmatic analysis—we want the inference to follow just from the fact that *some* is a weaker element in a Horn scale of the schematic kind ⟨STRONG, WEAK⟩. We can capture that generality, perhaps, by setting up a meta-rule of the sort in (32), which will apply to any simplex sentence frame α that contains a weak item paired with a strong item in a predetermined set of scales.

(32) $\dfrac{\alpha\ (\text{WEAK}):\ M\ (\alpha(\text{not STRONG}))}{\alpha\ (\text{not STRONG})}$

A more complex alternative is to treat the default rule as part of a modal logical system, rather than as an extralogical way of augmenting the common ground. Thus in Moore's (1985) *autoepistemic logic*, we can recast our paradigm scalar inference as a modal inference:

(33) [B(α(some)) & ∼B∼ (α(not all))] → α(not all)

which is read 'if it is believed that α (some), and it is not believed that it is not the case that α (not all), then α (not all)'. The operator here is just the strong L operator in a standard modal logic (weak S5), so the properties of such systems are well known. The intuition behind these systems is that of a rational agent inspecting his own beliefs and making the strong assumption that what he does not know is not the case (Levesque 1990). Wainer (1991) explores in detail the application of these ideas directly to the modeling of GCIs. He notes that the inference from 'John is in the attic or in the garden' to 'the speaker does not know which' (i.e., Gazdar's (1979) clausal implicatures) falls out as a consequence in such a system. But unfortunately the system also over-generates, predicting many pseudo-implicatures too.

Wainer (1991) also considers, for the purposes of modeling GCIs, another class of nonmonotonic reasoning systems based on circumscription (McCarthy 1980). Circumscription involves restricting the entities that satisfy predicates, or restricting entities in a domain to those known to exist. McCarthy (1986) notes that communication conventions rely on such circumscription, on the assumption that things are normal unless otherwise stated. This suggests that inferences due to the I heuristic (Grice's Q2) may be quite generally modeled in such systems. Wainer (1991: chap. 4) also points out that scalar GCIs might be directly generated in such systems: if one says "Two boys came," then it can be assumed that no more than two came. He notes, however, a number of problems, and in the end he outlines a model in which GCIs are generated with the semantic structure, and then such nonmonotonic reasoning systems are used to model defeasibility rather precisely under complex conditions (Wainer 1991: chap. 5).

There are a number of difficulties in the direct application of such systems to the modeling of GCIs: apart from the need to capture the generalizations inherent in GCI theory, we also need to handle many such rules that may potentially yield inconsistent inferences (although again see Wainer 1991: 175). Responding to earlier suggestions of mine, Carston (1995) draws attention to further difficulties: I implicatures, for instance, are often interpretations to stereotypical extensions and thus have a piecemeal character not easily captured by default rules (although better handled by circumscription). As well, there are patterns of defeasibility that do not seem to match this format, which I detail immediately below. Although anyone interested in formalizing GCIs should clearly investigate the potentials of this whole family of nonmonotonic logics, there are reasons to think that perhaps we should invert the argument: rather than seek understanding of implicature in theories of default inference, perhaps we should instead think of generalized implicatures as the prototype of default inferences. Meanwhile, we can look carefully at the core phenomenon itself—the defeasibility of implicatures—to discern the exact properties that such a formal theory would have to cope with.

1.5.3   Investigating the Defeasibility of Scalar Implicatures

The mechanism I call *Gazdar's bucket* gives a good first approximation to the conditions under which GCIs evaporate or are defeated. Gazdar (1979), following Hamblin (1971), Stalnaker (1972), and others, proposed that the communicative content of an utterance should be considered an ordered *n*-tuple of entailments, implicatures of various kinds, presuppositions, and so forth. The process of updating the common ground with the communicative content of a new utterance can then be treated as the ordered incrementation of that background with the entailments, implicatures, and presuppositions of the utterance.[36] Such an incremental model of dialogue has a number of virtues. For example, it allows us to capture the way in which utterances can presume background assumptions and the way in which their communicative force consists in changes to the context. Thus a permission both presumes a background prohibition and changes that background by removing the prohibition. Presupposition, illocutionary force, and anaphora all have natural accounts in this kind of model, now widely presumed. But an additional interest is how the incremental model might be used to handle the defeasibility of pragmatic inferences.

Informally and metaphorically, we can think of the common ground as a bucket, holding all the facts mutually assumed, either because they're common knowledge or because they have been asserted and accepted. Then, assuming that implicature generation is accounted for by other means, we can capture many aspects of the defeasibility of implicatures (GCIs in particular) in the following way: a new assertion will have its

content chucked in the bucket (i.e., context) strictly in the following order
and *only if each incrementation is consistent with the contents of the bucket*:

(34) Order of incremented information
  a. Entailments
  b. Q GCIs
   i. Clausal
   ii. Scalar
  c. M GCIs
  d. I GCIs

This accurately captures the following kinds of defeasibility (where $+>^*$
indicates canceled or nonarising implicature). First, there are cases where
GCIs are effectively canceled by inconsistent background assumptions:

(35) A: "A Saudi Prince has just bought Harrods."
  B: "Some Saudi princes must be pretty wealthy."
   $+>^*$ 'not all Saudi Princes are pretty wealthy.'

Thus B's assertion would by default give rise to the inference that not all
Saudi Princes are wealthy, but in a situation where the assumption is that
all Saudi Princes are wealthy, the inference will simple disappear. This
behavior is captured because one can only add implicatures to the bucket
if they are consistent with what is already assumed.

Second, there are cases where an utterance has an entailment inconsistent with an implicature, in which case the implicature is invariably
canceled:

(36) "Some Saudi Princes, and in fact all of them, are pretty wealthy."
  Entailment: 'All Saudi Princes are pretty wealthy.'
  Scalar implicature: 'Not all Saudi Princes are pretty wealthy.'

This effect is captured by ensuring that entailments are added to the
bucket before implicatures, so that when one comes to add an inconsistent
implicature the consistency requirement prevents the addition.

Third, there are cases where there are inconsistent implicatures:

(37) "Some, if not all, Saudi Princes are wealthy."
  Scalar implicature: 'Not all Saudi Princes are wealthy.'
  Clausal implicature (due to conditional): 'Possibly all Saudi Princes
  are wealthy.'

Here, an implicature of the consequent of a conditional is explicitly mentioned in the antecedent, and under such circumstances (just like pre-

suppositions, see Levinson 1983: 224), the implicature is regularly filtered or suspended. The context-increment model explains this in terms of the priority of different kinds of implicatures: a clausal GCI of epistemic uncertainty arising from conditionals has a higher priority than a scalar implicature from the consequent. Because clausal implicatures are thrown in the bucket before scalar ones, when we come to add the scalar inference, we will find the addition prevented by the consistency rule, correctly predicting the suspension of the scalar implicature only.

Thus the simple device of an ordered incrementation together with a consistency check suffices to account for many aspects of the defeasibility of implicatures. And such a consistency filter is consonant with the possibility of modeling implicature generation with default rules, as sketched in section 1.5.2. However, there are difficulties. The least of these, perhaps, is that implicatures can in fact be canceled at more or less arbitrary distance as in:

(38) "Some Saudi Princes are pretty wealthy.... Indeed, there is
       indubitable evidence that they are all billionaires."
       Implicature of first sentence: 'Not all Saudi Princes are pretty
       wealthy.'
       Entailment of second sentence: 'All Saudi Princes are wealthy
       (billionaires).'

This would require either indefinitely postponing the incrementation process, or tagging the implicatures and modifying the consistency filter so that later entailments could cancel earlier implicatures inconsistent with them.[37]

Much more interesting though are cases of implicature cancellation that are not triggered by an inconsistency at all. Here is a simple example:

(39) A: "Is there any evidence against them?"
       B: "Some of their identity documents are forgeries."
           Predicted (but nonoccurring) scalar implicature: 'Not all of their
           identity documents are forgeries.'

Assuming no special knowledge on the part of the interlocutors, there would be no inconsistency with the common ground or the entailments of B's utterance if not all of the documents are forgeries. It seems, though, that we do not let the inference through. That's because, intuitively, A is only interested in whether there is at least some evidence against the criminals; given A's question, all that is relevant is the possession of at least some evidence.

Perhaps the following example is clearer. I argue in chapter 2 that the numerals form a Horn scale in the normal way, so that saying "I have $9" will by default implicate 'I do not have $10'. Then in the following exchange (which we may imagine occurring at the entrance to a cinema), the default inference from B's utterance seems to evaporate just as in the previous example:

(40) A: "It's going to cost us ten dollars to get in and I didn't bring a cent."
       B: "Don't worry, I've got ten dollars."
       Predicted (but evaporated) scalar implicature: 'I have no more than ten dollars.'

Again, the inference would be (let us suppose) consistent with the common ground (pockets being private) and with all higher ordered inferences from the utterance itself, yet the implicature is canceled. And again, the explanation would seem to be that satisfying the very specific goal here (i.e., knowing that we can get into the cinema) can be presumed to exhaust the communicational load of the utterance.

In these cases, we can think of the situation as setting up a restricted goal: the question investigates a potential obstacle to the goal, and the reply indicates that the obstacle is not actual (see Allen 1983). I attribute this business of plan recognition and the inferences that follow from it to a maxim of Relevance, construed much as Grice intended and not at all as Sperber and Wilson (1986) reconstruct (for similar presumptions, see Holdcroft 1987, McCafferty 1987, and Thomason 1990). It seems then that Relevance implicatures, or inferences about speaker's goals, can limit the amount of further inference that is warranted. Thus even where these further inferences are entirely consistent with all that is known, they do not go through.

These sorts of examples suffice to show that consistency with an incremental common ground is not the only constraint on the addition of default implicatures to what is taken for granted. This may cast some doubt on whether default logics are the right formalism for modeling GCIs, or it might show that they simply need to be bounded by a yet to be described maxim of Relevance. But because the inferences are defeated by recognition of a goal, and because *that* kind of defeasibility is precisely what practical reasoning systems are set up to capture, perhaps these examples are indications that the plan-generation and plan-recognition types of nonmonotonic inference are what are really involved in implicature generation. Plan generation and plan recognition are, after all, what must be involved if meaning in general has the character of Grice's meaning$_{nn}$. Clearly, though, much closer work is required on *the exact nature of conditions under which inferences are abandoned*. For these are the facts that are likely to adjudicate between the different potential models of defeasible reasoning.

Two final speculations. First, one may wonder whether the intuitions that lie behind the attempts to create default logics are not in fact direct intuitions about how humans reason, but rather are primarily intuitions about communicational inferences—in fact, intuitions about the very default pragmatic inferences we are concerned with. GCIs would indeed seem to be the prototype default inferences; the root intuition is not, one may argue, that thinking of birds one assumes *ceteris paribus* that they fly. It is rather that, anyone *saying* "I scared away the birds" would have misled his audience if he did not intend to suggest (by I-inference to the stereotype) that the birds flew away. This suggestion is due of course in part to the way the world is (most kinds of birds fly); but that would only warrant a probabilistic inference. The default nature of the inference, to the surety that the birds flew away, relies on the presumption that *otherwise we would have been told*! That is, given a mutual presumption about how we use stereotypes to augment the communicational load of utterances (recollect the I-heuristic: 'what is stereotypical may be presumed'), the effect will be to convert Bayesian probabilities or hazardous assumptions into the certainties of communicational presumptions.

There is some empirical support for the rather extraordinary effect that the mutual assumption of a common heuristic can have on the probabilities of co-ordinated action. As mentioned above, Schelling (1960) showed, in some well known informal experiments, that if, for example, two people are asked to guess the same number without communicating to one another, they can do so with much greater reliability than chance—they search for a salient number that each thinks the other will also find the most salient (e.g., 1 or 100). Or, if two persons are lost in a department store they can guess where each would guess the other would go, so fixing on a single meeting place. If we think of communication as a coordination problem of the same sort (the speaker finding the signal that the recipient will interpret just as the speaker intended), a heuristic of the sort I have been describing would play the same sort of role—narrowing down the solutions to the coordination problem. Thus a mere probability that the speaker meant$_{nn}$ such and such can become converted, against tremendous odds, into a near certainty. And arguably this is just what default logics model: presumptions about interpretation based on the fact that an interpreter may assume a certain heuristic (e.g., the inference to the stereotype) and thus a particular interpretation (e.g., restricting the extension of *birds* to 'flying birds') on the basis that the speaker will have coded the message assuming the operation of the very same heuristic. Or to put it another way: when I *think* "the dog chased away the birds," I will remember the particularities of the event (whether the quail ran or flew away); it is only when I *say* it that default presumptions come into action (on the mismatch between thought and speech, see Levinson 1997).[38]

And this brings us to the second and final speculation: perhaps this account of pragmatic inference as based on stable heuristics is all we need to give an account of this species of defeasible inference. There is no need for a nonmonotonic logic to model GCIs, it might be claimed, because GCIs are simply instantiations of communicational heuristics and indeed the prototype default inferences. Just as Johnson-Laird (1983) argues that we do not need formal deduction to model deductive properties of human reasoning, relying instead on the reasoning based on instantiated mental models, so perhaps we do not need formal models of nonmonotonic argument to capture the processes of default interpretation. Some philosophers think that much of the effort expended on defeasible logics or inference systems is futile, stemming from a confusion between reasoning and rule-based inference—reasoning is always subject to revision, but deduction as least is strictly cumulative (see Harman 1986). If this category mistake has been made, it is because in the context of strong communicational assumptions—of tacit coordination and m-intentions—default inferences come to have the normative certainty that we associate with rule-based inference systems.[39]

1.6   AGAINST REDUCTION OF GCIs TO NONCE SPEAKER-MEANING

We have mentioned the current tendency to reduce utterance-meaning to speaker-meaning, or, in other words, utterance-type meaning to utterance-token meaning.[40] Thus a theory of communication is left, on these accounts, with only the level of sentence-meaning on the one hand and speaker-meaning on the other, with no provision being made for the notions of conventions of use, idiomatic use, partially conventionalized meaning, preferred interpretation, default interpretation, and so on. To theorists of this persuasion, as mentioned, the theory of GCIs is a sort of category mistake, treating pragmatic principles of inference quite inappropriately as "code-like rules" able to account for only "quite untypical examples of implicature" (Sperber and Wilson 1986: 37).[41] Instead, such theorists attempt to reduce all kinds of implicature to what we may call nonce inferences, one-off inferences to a specific speaker-meaning given the full rich body of assumptions held by the participants on that particular occasion.

The main argument against such reductionism in the case of GCIs is simply that there is no way to preserve the many simple but powerful generalizations that hold at the level of utterance-types. Thus the body of this book attempts to justify the notion of a GCI by ostension as it were in chapter 2, and then by showing how generalizations only available to a theory of utterance-types can contribute significantly to other areas of linguistic theory (chap. 3 and 4). However, here we pause to argue directly but briefly against two rival accounts that would reduce GCIs to nonce inferences.

1.6.1 Sperber-Wilson Relevance

The most prominent of the reductionist views is the theory of Relevance promoted by Sperber and Wilson (1986). This is not the place to review that theory (see Levinson 1989 for my own response and the general peer commentary in *Behavioral & Brain Sciences* 10:4, 1987), but it suffices to say that the theory holds that implicature is a side effect, as it were, of a mental automatism, a tendency to extract the maximal inferences for the minimal psychic effort.[42] There are no maxims, no heuristics, no special modes of reasoning involved in implicature derivation. Thus the fact that the GCI phenomena do not seem properly attributed to a maxim of Relevance is, on this view, beside the point; Sperber-Wilson Relevance (henceforth SW-R) is intended to replace the whole Gricean apparatus. Nor is it pertinent, apparently, that SW-R appears to be a very inadequate characterization of what pretheoretically would generally be considered the nature of relevance (as already mentioned, this seems best captured in terms of the local goals of participants at a particular locus in a conversation). SW-R is in effect a proportional measure balancing informational richness (corresponding, perhaps, approximately to my I principle or Grice's Q2) with processing effort (capturing, arguably, some aspects of my M). And the central claim is that low-cost inferences (deductive in character) will be invariably preferred.

SW-R seems to have overwhelming disadvantages as an account of implicature in general, but it faces even worse problems as an account of GCIs in particular. I raise two sample problems here.

1.6.1.1 SW-R Employs Deduction, but GCIs (and PCIs) are Non-monotonic One problem, salient in the context of the last section, is that according to SW-R all inference involved in implicature derivation is deductive, hence the inferences must be monotonic. But I have shown that they are nonmonotonic in character. Sperber and Wilson have not seriously addressed this problem, but presumably they would claim that the nonmonotonicity is illusory along the following lines:

1. where implicatures are generated, the deductive premises are part of the context;
2. where implicatures appear implicitly "canceled," the necessary premises are missing, so no inference in fact arises;
3. where implicatures are explicitly "canceled," there is an implicit adjustment of enthymematic (unexpressed) premises.

It is this last point that seems especially insuperable for such an account. Consider, for example, the following:[43]

(41) a. John has two children, if not more.
    b. John has two children and perhaps more.
    c. John has two children and in fact, now I come to think of it, maybe more.
    d. John has two children; he had two more by his first wife but they are grown up now.
    e. John has two children. Actually Sue says he has three, but I've never seen the third so I doubt he or she exists.

Intuitively, in these cases, the speaker asserts that John has two children, thereby suggesting he has no more; the additional material then suspends or cancels that suggestion. Without the suggestion, the additional material would be unmotivated—it is added precisely to suspend or cancel the suggestion. So the implicature 'at most two' must have arisen and thus on this account must have been deduced in the context (using, e.g., some premise of the sort; 'the speaker can be expected to know the exact cardinality of John's children', 'the exact cardinality is of interest to the recipient'). But if it is deduced, it can only be "canceled" by the deletion of a premise and the construction of a new deduction based on new premises (a context lacking, e.g., the premise 'the speaker can be expected to know the exact cardinality of John's children'). Thus the speaker has produced an utterance yielding inconsistent deductions—a contradiction at the level of utterance-meaning; from which every proposition under the sun will follow. Given that cancellation phrases may arise at arbitrary distance from the phrases that gave rise to the original implicature (as, e.g., in (41e)), this account would suppose that we are forced constantly to make sense of self-contradictory speakers.

Further, it won't account for the important (and long-noted)[44] asymmetry between the nonmonotonic behaviour of implicatures (allowing cancellation) and the monotonic nature of entailments (which do not allow cancellation):[45]

(42) a.   John has two children and, in fact, a total of three.

   b.   *John has two children and, in fact, a total of one.

(43) a.   John has two children. Actually, Sue says he has three, but if so I've never seen the third.

   b.   ??John has two children. Actually, Sue says he has only one, and I've never seen the second.

Although all implicatures (arguably by definition) exhibit such nonmonotonic properties, GCIs pose a special problem for any would-be deductive account because they can so plainly arise as a preferred interpretation only to be canceled or annulled later at some distance without any sense of self-contradiction by the speaker.

1.6.1.2   SW-R, if it Makes any Clear Predictions, Probably Makes the Wrong Ones   The second problem with an SW-R account of GCIs that I address is its inability to yield empirical predictions, at least of the right sort. Elsewhere (Levinson 1987c, 1989) I have suggested that SW-R is incapable of making clear predictions, partly because the theory is not clearly articulated but partly because the factor of cognitive effort, an essential ingredient in the proportional measurement of Relevance, is not empirically measurable (or at least not empirically measured). So if the theory is to be of any use, we must have some rough and ready concept of a low-cost inference such that it would be just the sort of inference favored by SW-R. Following the examples used in Sperber and Wilson (1986), I was led to think that the schema in (44) would constitute just the right kind of example.

(44) A: "If p then q"
     B: "p"
     Implicature: q

where *q* constitutes the low-cost deduction typical of an interpretation favored by SW-R. I therefore proposed (1987c) that (45) might be a counterexample to SW-R and an example that favored GCI theory.

(45) A: "If the spy had possibly more than two passports, then he may yet escape."
     B: "He had two passports."

SW-R should favor a reading of B's utterance that will make available the low-cost deduction of the consequent of A's utterance. B has said something that is consistent with the antecedent of A's utterance, and indeed on a rough gloss of the semantic content of the word *two* as 'at least two, not excluding more', B has said something almost equivalent. Thus, A's antecedent should be considered met (any minor inferences required being made), and the consequent should be deduced as:

(46) *SW-R predicted interpretation* (my guess)
     A: 'If the spy had possibly more than two passports, he may yet escape.'
     B: 'He had at least two and possibly more passports.'
     Deductive implication (alias R-implicature): 'He may yet escape.'

Now contrast the account according to GCI theory, wherein the utterance-types are sufficient to engender preferred interpretations. Two pertinent GCIs here are the I inference from the use of the conditional in A's utterance to the biconditional interpretation (i.e., conditional perfection), and of course the scalar Q inference from *two* to 'at most two' in B's utterance. This gives the following interpretations and a different deductive implication from the implicaturally-strengthened premises (in GCI theory deductive implications are just that, deductive implications, not implicatures):

(47) *GCI predicted interpretations*
     A: 'The spy may yet escape if and only if he may have had *more* than two passports.'
     B: 'He had *only* two passports.'
     Deductive implication: 'It's not the case that the spy may yet escape.'

SW-R would not favor such an interpretation, because in order to get the same yield (one deductive implication) we have had to make two gratuitous further inferences (the GCIs).

Intuitively, it seems to me that GCI theory makes the right prediction—that is, that we tend to read the exchange as suggesting that the spy will not escape. But, SW-R (on my construction of it) predicts the contrary reading, that the spy may yet escape. Thus I concluded (Levinson 1987c) that GCI theory makes the right predictions just where SW-R makes the wrong ones and, more generally, that a theory of preferred interpretations can never be superseded by a theory of nonce inference.

However, in their response, Sperber and Wilson (1987: 748) contend that their theory makes no such predictions and specifically it "does not predict that the most relevant interpretation conceivable is the right one." Rather, in this case, everything will depend on the details of the contextual assumptions and specifically on whether the interlocutors take B to be an authority on the cardinality of the spy's passports. Thus, without such further details, the authors claim that SW-R simply makes *no predictions* whatever. But this response would hardly seem to help the theory wriggle out of examples of this kind, presented here as interlocutors often experience them, without mutually assumed background assumptions of the sort SW-R calls for. There is, intuitively, a clear preference for the reading predicted by GCI theory, and it is a preference that GCI theory holds would be expected in the absence of any further specificities about the context.

Thus, either SW-R seems to make the wrong predictions about the phenomena generally considered GCIs (my claim), or it makes no general predictions about them (Sperber and Wilson's claim), and both alternatives seem equally damaging. No doubt there is plenty of room for maneuver in the application of a theory as general as SW-R to specific examples; and perhaps I continue (as alleged) to misunderstand SW-R. But certainly the two theories ought to make rather different predictions in a whole range of cases, and as far as I can see, GCI theory is bound to make the right sort and SW-R the wrong sort as far as the inferences central to GCI theory are concerned. Regardless of the success or failure of present versions of GCI theory, these rather complex examples only serve to reinforce a simple enough, indeed almost self-evident, point: expression-types do tend to have preferred interpretations (or more exactly, there are default restrictions on their extensions), interpretations that tend to go through in the absence of information to the contrary.

1.6.2   Implicature as Accommodation

There is another class of attempts to reduce implicature wholesale (including GCIs) to matters of nonce inference. These theories have in common the use of Lewis' (1979) concept of *accommodation*, which had earlier been used to account for certain properties of presupposition (Heim 1982: 370–384). Let us consider two rather different theories (Thomason 1987, Hobbs 1987) that claim that the concept of accommodation coupled with a nonmonotonic inference system may be all we need for a theory of implicature. Thomason (1987) suggests we need accommodation plus a plan-recognition inference system,[46] whereas Hobbs (1987) suggests accommodation plus his abduction system (a weighted backward-chaining, based on a constrained use of the logical fallacy of affirming the consequent). The basic idea behind accommodation is that there are reasonably well-defined felicity conditions or usage constraints on the use of particular expressions—for example, *the* X is felicitously used (it might be claimed) only where the common ground provides a uniquely salient X. Against this background of expected usage, deviant uses can then be *accommodated* by a cooperative interlocutor. Suppose I say "My car broke down. The diesel froze," in a context in which a unique mass of diesel has not been previously introduced into the discourse; well, it will take no great imagination to construct the assumption that the speaker's car runs on diesel and that the mass in question is the diesel in the fuel tank of that car.

There are thus two essential ingredients in the proposed mechanism whereby utterance U implicates proposition *p*:

1. *U* must contain a trigger *T*, some expression whose felicity conditions require that a proposition of the class *P* must be an element of the common ground if *T* is to be felicitously used;
2. if *U* is uttered and there is no proposition of the class *P* presumed in the context, then the recipient should *accommodate T* by inferring *p* such that $p \in P$, and by adding *p* to the common ground.

The essential difference between Hobbs's account and Thomason's comes down, then, as mentioned, to the mode of inference envisaged (abduction or practical reasoning).[47]

Clearly, these accounts work only where there are appropriate trigger expressions, expressions that require certain contextual assumptions that have not already been met. Thus they give reasonably good accounts of presuppositional inferences; Thomason concentrates on factive predicates (e.g., *know*) and Hobbs on the bridging inferences often required by definite referring expressions.[48] Both theorists claim that their accounts generalize to implicatures and indeed generalize right across the different kinds of implicature. But Thomason provides little reason to believe this, and Hobbs's extensions are interesting but remain within the class of presupposition-like triggers (e.g., he extends the account to noun-noun compounds like *oil alarm*, which require the inference of some unique relation between the extensions of the two nouns).

Without conceding that the account is persuasive even in these cases, we can nevertheless easily show that it offers little hope of reducing GCIs. The essential reason for this is that GCIs are not inferences that have to be made in order to maintain some particular felicity condition; the expressions that give rise to GCIs do not *require* any inference—otherwise cancellation would not be possible. Rather, GCIs are inferences that are, from the point of view of accommodation theory, essentially *gratuitous*. Another way of putting it is that accommodation theory is an account of how rule-breaking behavior is brought back into line with expectations. For example, I use a presuppositional trigger where no such presupposition is actually presumed; my interlocutor accommodates the usage by accepting the presumption. But in the case of the use of a GCI-inducing expression like scalar *some*, no rule has been broken; yet the inference to 'not all' is gratuitously made. And the very nature of GCI defeasibility— namely, cancellation in the face of inconsistent or unsupportive assumptions—makes it impossible for a GCI-inducing expression to force a presumption into the common ground.

Just to make this concrete, compare the kinds of case favorable to an accommodation account, like (48a), to the classic GCIs like scalar implicatures in (48b).

(48) a. "Sue walked into the room. The chandelier was magnificent."
        +> 'The room had a chandelier.'
     b. "Sue has two children."
        Q+> 'Sue has at most two children.'
     c. ?"Sue walked into the room. The chandelier was magnificent. It was in the cupboard."
     d. "Sue has two children. She has a third by her former husband."

Note too the ease with which the scalar implicature can be cancelled in (48d), compared to the bridging inference in (48c). The problem in (48c) is

simply that we have to find another way (other than the bridging inference) of satisfying the felicity condition of uniqueness required by the
definite article in *the chandelier*. It is the gratuitous nature of the scalar
inference, compared to the forced nature of the felicity-condition requirement, that makes cancellation so straightforward in the scalar case. Thus
the accommodation account signally fails to generalize to the class of
GCIs as a whole.

However, even in the presuppositional-type cases, an accommodation
account will not be sufficient—we still need GCI theory. The point can be
made quite well by considering further facts about definite and indefinite
reference. Compare the sentences in (49).

(49) a. "Jerry Rich came in. *He* walked over to the window."
     b. "Jerry Rich came in. *The man* walked over to the window."
        (our M +> nonlocal coreference)

Here both the expressions *he* and *the man* are definite referring expressions, with a uniqueness condition attached. In an abductive system of
inference like Hobbs's, an attempt would be made to unify the discourse
referents by linking both expressions to the antecedent *Jerry Rich*, thereby
satisfying the definiteness conditions. Indeed, both the pronoun and the
definite description would be predicted to be interpreted in the same way.
But that, of course, is contrary to intuition: the pronoun invites such
linkage to *Jerry Rich*, but the description *the man* resists it. GCI theory
gives a concise account of this: pronouns are minimal expressions that
invite maximal interpretations by the I principle discussed above, whereas
the use of a marked definite description where a pronoun could have been
used suggests by the M-principle that the speaker did not intend such
local coreference (see chap. 4).

We can press the critique further. Consider the possible analysis of the
indefinite article in accommodation theory. If the definite article requires
a previously existing discourse referent, the indefinite may be claimed to
require the setting up of a new discourse referent (Heim 1982; Kamp
1981). On this account, the sequence of sentences in (50a) would seem to
presume distinct discourse referents; this seems correct. But now examine
(50b). Here we seem happy to co-identify *the ship* and *a fine galleon*,
contrary to the theory.

(50) a. "*The man* entered. *A man* coughed."
        disjoint reference

       b. "*The ship* broke up. *A fine galleon* of the Spanish fleet had been irretrievably lost."
         +> possible conjoint reference
       c. *Scalar explanation:* ⟨DEFIN, INDEF⟩; use of indefinite Q-implicates that the use of the definite would be misleading

The best explanation of these facts seems once again to be given by GCI theory (sketched indeed originally by Grice). We should reject the analysis of the indefinite article as requiring the setting up of a new discourse referent à la Heim (1982), while accepting that definiteness does involve conditions on usage (like uniqueness).[49] We can then can set up a scalar opposition (more details in chap. 2) as in (50c), where an indefinite expression is weaker because it simply lacks the uniqueness and "givenness" conditions associated with the more specific and informative definite expression. Given a scalar opposition of this kind, a speaker using an indefinite will Q-implicate that the use of the definite would be misleading in at least one way. Thus in (50b), a speaker who said *The fine galleon of the Spanish fleet* might be thought to be communicating that there was only one fine galleon in the Spanish fleet and, wishing to avoid this inference, would use the indefinite even though it is to be coidentified with the immediately preceding discourse referent. So again, accommodation-plus-abduction gives the wrong account here, at least without rescue by GCI theory.

In sum then, whatever the success of accommodation theory in the presuppositional domain, it will not supersede GCI theory as Thomason and Hobbs have both independently suggested. On the one hand, accommodation theory simply fails to extend to the gratuitous inferences that are the focus of GCI theory, and on the other hand, without GCI theory it make the wrong predictions, over-unifying discourse referents in some cases (where M-implicatures warn otherwise) and failing to unify them in others (where, for example, a Q-inference from the use of an indefinite explains the use of the indefinite as a coreferential expression).

We may conclude this discussion of SW-R and Accommodation Theory by noting the inadequacy of such reductionist approaches in the face of the clear evidence in favor of a level of utterance-type meaning. These are not the kinds of problems that might be addressed by tinkering with the reductionist theories in limited ways. It is just because these theories are theories of speaker-meaning, or nonce inference, that they are unable in principle to capture aspects of meaning associated with the general, normal use of expressions.

1.7 GENERALIZED IMPLICATURE AND STABLE PATTERNS OF LEXICALIZATION

We may give one final positive argument in favor of a theory of generalized implicature before passing on to consider in depth and by illustration the richness of generalizations that are made possible by a theory of preferred interpretations of this sort. This argument concerns one such rich generalization which has much empirical support, and which defies explanation in any other terms. The argument is based on work by Larry Horn over 15 years, summarized in Horn 1989.

Recollect that we have described Q-implicatures as involving contrastive expression-alternatives, often arranged in scales of semantic strength, like the prototype ⟨*all, some*⟩ scale, where the use of the semantically weaker *some* will ceteris paribus Q-implicate the inapplicability of the stronger expression *all*. Recollect, too, that for each positive scale of the form ⟨S, W⟩, there will be a corresponding negative scale of the form ⟨∼W, ∼S⟩, such that asserting (in a suitable sentence frame) ∼S will Q-implicate ∼∼W (i.e., W). So, instantiating, given a positive scale ⟨*all, some*⟩, we have the negative scale ⟨*not-some (none), not all*⟩, such that asserting "Not all the boys came" will implicate 'not-none of them came', (i.e., 'some of them came').

Now, the relationship between positive and negative scales is important for a number of reasons. First, the relationship has not been understood by most commentators (despite the explanation in Atlas and Levinson 1981). Thus Gazdar (1979), Hirschberg (1985: 73), and Kadmon (1987) all claim that negation blocks implicature projection instead of seeing that negation in the case of scales simply inverts the scale, so that negative scales induce implicatures that just happen to be different from the implicatures induced by positive scales. But a second reason why the relationship between positive and negative scales is important is that it yields real insight into the nature of logical operators and in particular into the traditional *square of opposition*.

The square of opposition, that device conceived by Boethius out of Aristotle to plague monks and schoolchildren for two millennia, has the prototype instantiation shown in figure 1.1.[50]

I remind the reader of the following definitions:

p and *q* are **contraries** if *p* and *q* can't both be True,
  but they can both be False ("John is happy/sad")

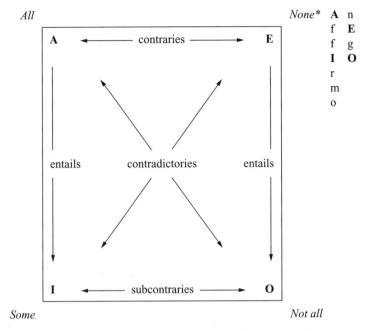

All   *None** **A** n
                                                                                         f **E**
                                                                                         f g
                                                                                         I **O**
                                                                                         r
                                                                                         m
                                                                                         o

Some   *Not all*

*Properly (traditionally) this E corner is the quantifier *no* as in *No boys came.*

Figure 1.1
The traditional square of opposition

p and *q* are **contradictories** if *p* and *q* can't both be True,
     and nor can *p* and *q* both be False—i.e., the negation of the one
     implies the other, so there's no middle ground:
     (e.g., "The number of students is odd/even")

Then we can see that the essential geometry of the square is given by
entailment relations, represented in figure 1.1 by the vertical lines (with the
entailing concepts at the top), *contrary* relations represented by the top
horizontal line, and *contradictory* relations represented by the diagonal
lines. The *subcontrary* relationship is the focus of interest here and its
proper interpretation has been controversial over the ages. Note that I
employ the traditional labeling of the vertices, A, I, E, and O, following
the mnemonics *affirmo* for the positive side of the square and *nego* for the
negative side.

Note that in essence the traditional square is nothing but a pair of
scales, here ⟨*all, some*⟩ and ⟨*none, not all*⟩ arranged vertically, so that the
strong elements *all* and *none* fall at the A and E vertices respectively, in a

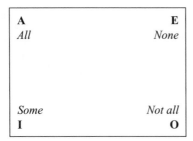

Figure 1.2
Square of quantifiers

A	E
Necessary	*Impossible*
Possible	*Possible Not*
(May$_1$)	
I	**O**

Figure 1.3
Square of logical (alethic) modals

contrary relationship to one another. It then follows by the geometry of the square that *all* and *not all* (likewise *none* and *some*) are contradictories, which the reader may verify by referring to the definition above.

Onto the geometry of the square one can map not only the quantifiers shown in figure 1.2 but also all the sets of logical operators shown in figures 1.3–1.5.

The reason that these distinct sets of logical operators map onto the same square is that there are traditional ways of paraphrasing each set in terms of the quantifiers, and the quantifiers in terms of the connectives. For example, the alethic modal *necessary that p* can be paraphrased (assuming a possible-world semantics) as 'in all worlds, p', while *possibly p* can be paraphrased as 'there is some world in which p'; while the quantificational *all Fs are G* can (assuming a finite number of entities, x_1–x_n that are F) be paraphrased as x_1 is G and x_2 is G and ... x_n is G, and so

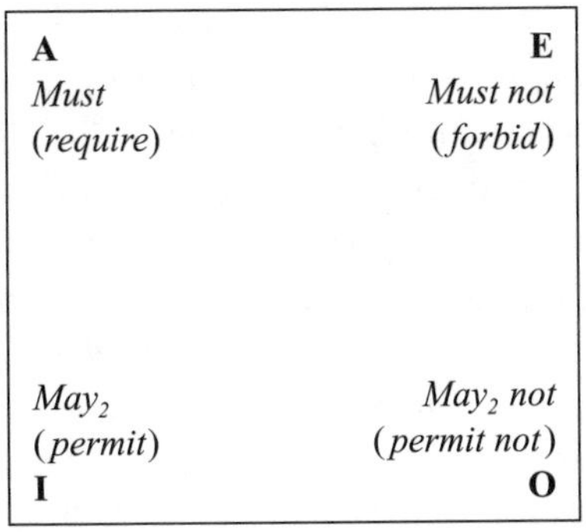

A	E
Must	*Must not*
(*require*)	(*forbid*)
May₂	*May₂ not*
(*permit*)	(*permit not*)
I	**O**

Figure 1.4
Square of deontic modals (and deontic causatives)

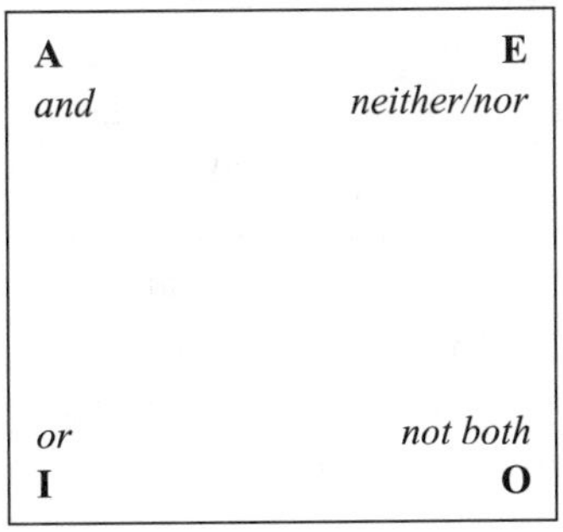

A	E
and	*neither/nor*
or	*not both*
I	**O**

Figure 1.5
Logical connectives

on, enumerating all *x*, while *some F is G* can be paraphrased as *either x_1 is G or x_2 is G or ... x_n is G*, enumerating all *x*.

And one may state the following well-known logical equivalencies directly on the relationship between the vertices of the square, thus generalizing across all the different squares (I illustrate with the quantifiers):

(51) *The duals*
$$A = \sim I \ldots \sim \quad \text{(All} \ldots = \text{Not some not} \ldots\text{)}$$
$$I = \sim A \ldots \sim \quad \text{(Some} \ldots = \text{Not all not} \ldots\text{)}$$
$$\sim A = I \sim \ldots \quad \text{(Not all} \ldots = \text{Some not} \ldots\text{)}$$
$$\sim I = A \ldots \sim \quad \text{(Not some} \ldots = \text{All not} \ldots\text{)}$$

So we come now to the pertinence of all this to GCI theory. There has in fact been two and a half millennia of confusion over the subcontrary relation, the relation between the I (e.g., *some*) and O (e.g., *not all*) vertices of the square. The question has been whether the relation should be thought of as a logical one, with the I vertex implying the O one, or whether on the contrary it should be understood as a nonlogical suggestion. Horn (1972, 1989) documents the many inconsistent positions that theorists have taken over the ages, showing how, for example, Aristotle held that in the case of the modals the I/O relation was logical but in the case of the quantifiers it was a nonlogical suggestion. Hamilton and Jespersen held the relation is logical for all the squares, De Morgan and J. S. Mill that it is nonlogical for all the squares, and so on.

The theory of GCIs helps to explain the confusion. The I (*some*) corner of the square carries a generalized scalar implicature to the effect that the O (*not all*) corner also holds. It is the generalized nature of the inference that explains the confusion even among these eminent scholars thinking deep and hard about the problem. "Some" strongly suggests 'not all', and "Not all" strongly suggests 'some', but we can say without contradiction "Some in fact all" or "Not all, indeed none," indicating that the suggestion cannot be a logical relationship. The correct answer to this perennial puzzle is given by the nature of scalar implicatures and the way in which negation reverses scales: the vertices always form scales of the form $\langle A, I \rangle$ and $\langle E, O \rangle$; so the assertion of "I" will implicate '$\sim A$', which is of course the contradictory of A, and therefore equivalent to O:

(52) a. $\langle$All, some$\rangle$; $\langle$None, not all$\rangle$
      b. "Some of the boys came" (I)
          $+>$ 'Not all of the boys came' ($\sim A = O$)
      c. "Not all of the boys came" (O)
          $+>$ 'Not-none (i.e., some) of them came' ($\sim E = I$)

Thus, given the nature of scales, it follows that there will be a regular predictable inference from the assertion of a weak item on a scale to the contradictory of the strong item on the scale, which will itself correspond to the weak item on the scale of opposite polarity. Thus there will always be a pragmatic inference from the assertion of the I (*some*) corner to the inference of the O (*not all*) corner, or from the assertion of the O (*not all*) corner to the inference of the I (*some*) corner. Despite the fact that this relation is only a defeasible pragmatic suggestion, its occurrence is so regular and predictable that theorists were misled into believing it was a semantic relation.

Here then is the first argument one can make from consideration of the I/O relation in favor of a theory of GCIs: it is evidently not easy to separate GCIs from semantic content, witness two millennia of analysts' perplexity. But if these inferences were nonce inferences, sometimes going one way, sometimes another, the pragmatic nature of the I/O relation would be self-evident. It is not self-evident precisely because there is a strong default inference, a strongly preferred interpretation that arises from the assertion of either corner to the conclusion that the other corner holds. Teasing apart preferential interpretations from semantically stipulated ones is a difficult analytical task.

A second argument for GCI theory that can be made arises from an important observation by Horn (1989: 252–267): as a matter of empirical fact, there is a strong crosslinguistic tendency for the O corner of the square to not be instantiated by a single (or at least a simple, nonderived) lexical item. In other words, the O corner of the square hardly ever lexicalizes; it is nearly always expressed by complex phrases of the form exemplified by English *not all, possibly not, not both*, and so on. This is in contrast to the strong negative apex E, where the forms routinely lexicalize, as in English *none, impossible, neither*, and so forth. In this context, the absence of **nall* (meaning 'not all'), **nalways* (meaning 'not always') or **noth* (meaning 'not both') is certainly noteworthy; and the fact that this generalization (the O corner of the square hardly ever lexicalizes) appears to hold widely across languages, indeed universally as far as we now know, is certainly remarkable.

(53) *English exemplifications of the universal lexicalization constraint on the O corner*
    not all has no lexicalization **nall* (cf. *none*)
    permit not has no form **permitn't* (cf. *forbid*)
    not always has no form **nalways* (cf. *never*)
    not . . . and . . . has no form **nand* (cf. *nor*)
    not both . . . and . . . has no form **noth* (cf. *neither*)

The patterns in English in (52) are thus typical of other languages as well. The details are telling, too: thus *Priests can not marry* is ambiguous in English between the E-reading 'are forbidden to' and the O-reading 'are permitted not to', but as soon as it is contracted and thus lexicalized (*Priests can't marry*) only the E-reading is available (Horn 1989: 259). The uncontracted form already has a preferred E-reading, and this is also a crosslinguistic, diachronic tendency, which Horn (1989: 262–263) dubs

"O to E drift." Note that *mustn't* lexicalizes 'must not', but *mayn't* (which might be expected to lexicalize the O corner 'may not') can only mean 'must not', too. The generalization is that we expect no lexicalization of a necessity modal that incorporates a negation outside its scope (e.g., 'not must'), or a lexicalization of a possibility modal with a negation inside its scope (e.g., 'may not')—both kinds of lexicalization would be at the O corner.[51]

GCI theory provides an account of this lexicalization constraint along the following lines. First, as we have just established, I and O are related by implicature: asserting I will carry a generalized Quantity scalar implicature that O. Second, it seems that what is conveyed by a GCI is generally not lexicalized; that is to say, there is a redundancy constraint on lexicalization, roughly as follows:

(54) *Redundancy constraint*
      For any lexical item W that carries a generalized Quantity implicature P, there will be no fully lexicalized counterpart W′ that lexicalizes the content of P. Because I items on a Square will always implicate O items, there will be no lexicalized O items.

Another way of putting this is: if the I item entails p and implicates q, then the corresponding O item will entail q and implicate p. Thus in an appropriate sentence frame the assertion of "some" will entail 'at least one', and implicate 'not all', whereas the assertion of "not all" will entail 'not all' and implicate 'some'. Thus the I and O items have the same overall communicational load, simply reversing the distribution of the load between what is entailed and what is implicated.[52]

We need one more ingredient in the explanation. Given that the assertion of the I (*some*) or the O (*not all*) corner will carry the same communicational load, why should I (*some*) be lexicalized but not O (*not all*)? The answer is provided by the relatively complex nature of negation (as shown by much psycholinguistic work). Given a choice between a positive term and a negative term carrying the same load, the positive term will be chosen as the basis from which to apply the redundancy constraint against lexicalization of the negative expressions. One should note that there is no general ban against lexicalization of negatives; that is shown by the tendency for the E terms to incorporate negation.[53] But given a choice between choosing the I (*some*) expressions or the O (*not all*) expressions as the basic ones and excluding the other corner from lexicalization by application of the redundancy constraint, the processing complexity of negatives favors the I (*some*) corner.

Anyone who rejects the notion of a GCI or a preferred interpretation will have to find another explanation for this lexicalization pattern. The nonce-implicature theorist cannot explain it—according to any such theory, there are no general tendencies to be found, or if there are they have the status of mere behavioral tendencies, playing no role in the systematic generation of implicatures. On such a theory, there is no more reason for *not all* to resist lexicalization than for *not some* to undergo it (*none*). Only a theory of preferred or default interpretations can explain how something as defeasible and protean as a pragmatic suggestion can impose such fundamental constraints on the lexicon.

In conclusion, then, these patterns statable across the traditional square of oppositions appear to be strong evidence in favor of a theory of generalized implicature. The nonce-implicature theorist cannot in principle, it seems, explain how there could be such a strong, reliable preference for interpretation in one direction that (a) generations of theorists themselves could be confused about whether inferences from one logical operator to another were to be explained by semantic or by pragmatic content and that (b) the language itself is adapted (by the provision of lexical gaps) to the prevailing pragmatic winds, as it were.

1.8   CONCLUSIONS

In this chapter, my prime objective has been to try and defend the notion of a generalized conversational implicature. Throughout, I have argued against the dominant current line that a theory of communication should allow only a level of speaker-meaning (or utterance-token meaning). Instead, I have argued for a third level or layer in a theory of communication, the level of utterance-type meaning interposed between the level of speaker-meaning and the level of expression-meaning. This level is to capture the suggestions that the use of an expression of a certain type generally or normally carries, by default. We may concede that the concept of a preferred, default interpretation is not an easy one to explicate and it lacks the kind of theoretical underpinning we may perhaps have for other concepts in the theory of meaning, without conceding that there is any doubt at all about the need for such a notion in a theory of communication.[54]

My arguments for the need for such a level of utterance-type meaning in general, and for the theory of GCIs in particular, have been (I recapitulate):

1. There are all sorts of other phenomena, like illocutionary force (both direct and indirect), conversational routines, presuppositions, felicity conditions, and so forth, that would themselves justify the setting up of such a level.

2. The theory of implicature as originally developed by Grice (e.g., in his application of the theory to the natural-language connectives) presupposes such a level.

3. There is an argument from design to the effect that a stable set of heuristics inducing generalized implicatures would be far too powerful and effective an instrument of communication to neglect.

4. There are a range of formal models of nonmonotonic default reasoning that offer some hope for formalization in this area. Such models, whatever their ultimate relevance to the theory of GCIs, show that it is perfectly possible to formulate relatively precise theories of preferred interpretation; thus there is nothing to inhibit the development of clearly articulated theories of utterance-type meaning.

5. I have argued that existing theories of nonce implicature when applied to the phenomena that are central to GCI theory will either make the wrong predictions or make no clear predictions at all, just where in fact there are clear predictions to be made. In contrast, GCI theory seems to make the necessary generalizations in a straightforward way.

6. Finally, I have argued that if there were no such things as GCIs or preferred default interpretations, it would be impossible to account for the strength and generality of the pragmatic inferences associated with the natural language logical operators. In particular, we would have no account at all of the reliable crosslinguistic tendency to ban lexicalization of the O corner of the traditional square of oppositions.

These arguments will be at least sufficient, I hope, for the reader to entertain the idea of a generalized conversational implicature without prejudice. We can then proceed to show how the possession of a theory of generalized implicature may contribute to the description and analysis of a great variety of linguistic facts, as detailed in the following chapters.

In making these arguments, I have introduced in a cursory way our cast of characters, the three main genera of GCI. In the next chapter, I explore this typology and its consequences in detail.

Chapter 2

The Phenomena

2.1 INTRODUCTION

In chapter 1, I argued that Grice's notion of a generalized conversational implicature (GCI) is an essential explanatory notion. It amounts to the claim that there is a special species of pragmatic mechanism that yields inferences that are both defeasible and default in character. At least some of the properties of such inferences can be captured within a number of currently available default, nonmonotonic reasoning systems. But these inferences, generated under the mutual assumption of tacit coordination through specific heuristics, have the force of strong presumptions. They belong to a broad third category or layer of meaning, midway between sentence-meaning and speaker-meaning (or utterance-token-meaning), namely utterance-type meaning, in which types of linguistic form come to have preferred, idiomatic readings. Despite many attempts to reduce this third layer away, either to aspects of sentence-meaning or aspects of speaker-meaning, it remains a robust, irreducible category of meaning, as shown by Horn's generalization of universal patterns of constraints on lexicalization that can be directly attributed to the omnipresent operation of inference patterns of this default sort.

The three main species of GCI (according to my typology) were introduced in the last chapter in a cursory way. The purpose of this chapter is to lay out the kind of phenomena that motivate the theory of GCIs. These data are the crucial observations that reductionist theories of utterance meaning have never come to terms with, and indeed cannot, as far as I can see. The phenomena are of course much more important and robust than the theory I am advocating; indeed I will not hide the fact that they are not all adequately accounted for. Nor are the observations below exhaustive; the reader should be able to find many more, similar kinds of default inference associated with specific kinds of linguistic expression. But there will be sufficient examples, I hope, to demonstrate that there is a large class of preferred interpretations, which have a systematicity both within and across languages and whose regularity makes them a frequent source of grist for the grammaticalization mill.

Although the observations have a real theory independence (having been observed as far back as Aristotle; see Horn 1973, 1989: chap. 1), I present them in terms of the tripartite classification already introduced in chapter 1—that is, in terms of Q-, I-, and M-principles or heuristics, which I feel yields more or less natural classes. So at the same time I will attempt to clarify these principles and show how the relevant examples fall under their respective predictive power. Various critiques and alternative treatments will be dealt with *en passant*, with the consequence that my assessments of them will be more cursory than some of these proposals deserve (for which I apologize in advance). Finally, at the end of the chapter, I describe the interactions between these principles, the projection problem this interaction gives rise to, and the solution that I have to offer.

Why three and just these three principles? Other estimates vary from one (Sperber and Wilson 1986) to ten or more (Leech 1983), and there is little point in arguing from first principles (but see Levinson 1987a, where I take on the lower estimates, and Atlas and Levinson 1981). As explanatory principles, we want as few as will do the job, while recognizing essential distinct genera and respecting evidence from conversation that specific principles are being oriented to (again, see Levinson 1987a). Some discussion will occur throughout this book, but a few pointers may assuage irritation at this point. Readers will note that the three principles are derived partly by elimination from Grice's original four maxims (with a total of nine submaxims). The maxim of Quality ("try to make your contribution one that is true") plays only a background role in the generation of GCIs. (There has been a tendency to assume that the Quality maxim generates implicatures of belief or commitment, despite Grice's explicit warnings against this.)[1] The maxim of Relation or Relevance (which Grice (1989: 26–27) stated simply as "Be relevant" within the overall Cooperative Principle, "Make your contribution such as is required, at the stage at which it occurs, by the accepted purpose or direction of the talk exchange in which you are engaged") has pertinence only to the immediate, ever variable, conversational goals: it generates PCIs, not GCIs. This leaves two important subprinciples of Quantity, canonized here as the Q- versus I-principles, and four subprinciples of Manner, of which two are captured in my M-principle (I suspect there is scope also for the one Grice labelled "be orderly," perhaps along the lines of Haiman's 1985a principle of iconicity). Still, it may be objected that this shows much too much reverence for Grice's ramshackle scheme, a sort of joke calqued on Kant.[2] Reverence is indeed beside the point (especially for such a delightfully irreverent intellect as H. P. Grice), but the fact is each of these three principles seem to capture a large range of phenomena (as has been noted by a number of different scholars under various rubrics). The three principles are in various ways incommensurable and even antagonistic, and therefore successful reduction looks unlikely. But for the purposes of this chapter, I ask the reader to suspend these questions and just see how the recommended scheme seems to fit the facts.

2.2   THE Q PRINCIPLE

2.1.1   Q Inferences

In chapter 1, I introduced the Q principle as a heuristic based on Grice's first maxim of Quantity, and sketched the way in which it induces inferences from the use of one expression to the assumption that the speaker did not intend a contrasting, usually informationally stronger, one. Consequently, implicatures from this principle have two essential characteristics: they are metalinguistic (and paradigmatic) in the sense that what is implicated makes essential reference to what might have been said but wasn't (i.e., to a set of linguistic alternates in paradigmatic opposition), and they are negative propositions, what is implicated being a presumption that such and such is not the case.

Now this species of inference has been more extensively explored in the literature than any other kind of implicature, and I will not repeat here the whole history of observations and commentaries (see, e.g., Levinson 1983: chap. 3). Suffice it to say that Grice (1967, 1978) employed the first maxim of Quantity to account for the implicatures from the use of the disjunction and conditional to the unknown truth value of the constituent sentences, but that it was Horn's (1972) treatment, and the subsequent formalization by Gazdar (1979), that established what we may call the standard doctrine (as reviewed in Levinson 1983: chap. 3). Since then, a number of critiques and elaborations have appeared, which I will refer to later. The version reproduced here (based on Levinson 1987b) is essentially the standard one (it is thus equivalent to "Quantity" in Atlas and Levinson 1981, to Horn's 1984 "Q-principle" minus its Manner elements, and so on). A number of problems have since been raised with this formulation, which I consider below. Additionally, I go on to assimilate a range of further inferences not normally considered to fall under its rubric.

(1) *Q-principle*[3]

Speaker's maxim: Do not provide a statement that is informationally weaker than your knowledge of the world allows, unless providing an informationally stronger statement would contravene the I-principle. Specifically, select the informationally strongest paradigmatic alternate that is consistent with the facts.

Recipient's corollary: Take it that the speaker made the strongest statement consistent with what he knows, and therefore that:

a. if the speaker asserted $A(W)$, where A is a sentence frame and W an informationally weaker expression than S, and the contrastive expressions $\langle S, W \rangle$ form a Horn scale (in the prototype case, such that $A(S)$ entails $A(W)$),[4] then one can infer that the speaker knows that the stronger statement $A(S)$ (with S substituted for W) would be false (or $K \sim (A(S))$ in Gazdar's (1979) notation, read as 'the speaker knows that it is not the case that $(A(S))$')

b. if the speaker asserted $A(W)$ and $A(W)$ fails to entail an embedded sentence Q, which a stronger statement $A(S)$ would entail, and $\{S, W\}$ form a contrast set, then one can infer that the speaker does not know whether Q obtains or not (i.e., $\sim K(Q)$ or equally, $\{P(Q), P \sim (Q)\}$ read as 'it is epistemically possible that Q and epistemically possible that not-Q')

The recipient's corollary will induce the well-known scalar and clausal Q-implicatures (Gazdar 1979; Levinson 1983: chap. 3) as illustrated here:

(2) a. *Scalar Q-implicatures*

"Some of my best friends are linguists."

$+> K \sim$ (all of my best friends are linguists)[5]

b. *Clausal Q-implicatures*

"John believes there is life on Mars."

$+> \{P(\text{there is life on Mars}), P \sim (\text{there is life on Mars})\}$

Note that the scalar implicatures are induced from ranked sets of alternates (e.g., quantifiers or scalar adjectives), whereas the clausal ones derive from contrasts between one expression that entails its embedded sentence(s) and another that does not. Further kinds of Q inferences are introduced below. I shall have relatively little to say about clausal Q-implicatures (see section 2.2.5), merely expounding Gazdar's account, whereas scalar implicatures have received considerable recent attention that will require review.

I have introduced the inferences derived from the principle with the epistemic modifications suggested by Gazdar (1979).[6] Now, these have in fact been the subject of much dispute. A first issue concerns the differential strength of implicatures from the same scale. Horn (1972: 90) originally suggested that not all scalar implicatures have the same epistemic force: in general, for scales with more than two members, for example, a scale of the form $\langle a,b,c,d \rangle$, and an arbitrary sentence frame S, assertion of "S(d)" implicates that the recipient *must* infer $K \sim S(a)$ but only that the recipient *may* infer $K \sim S(b)$, $K \sim S(c)$. Thus, for example, saying "Some came" implicates that the speaker knows that not all came, and possibly that not many or not most came (given the scale $\langle all, most, many, some \rangle$). Gazdar's formulation has equally strong epistemic commitment by the speaker for all items on the scale above the asserted one, and one may complain that this neglects Horn's correct intuition—namely, that the most salient implicature is the denial of the head of the scale. Gazdar's formulation was in fact designed to handle the projection problem; he wanted to capture the observation (see section 2.5.1) that clausal implicatures would cancel scalar ones where they were inconsistent, and he achieved this by assuring that the epistemic modification did not mask inconsistency and by stipulating that clausal implicatures take precedence. Because clausal inferences are of the form $\{Pp, P \sim p\}$, they are inconsistent with a scalar implicature of the form $K \sim p$. Atlas (1993a: 209ff) finds the clausal inference Pp implausible but will then need to reconstruct a projection solution (see section 2.5.1 and Kay 1992 for a defense of Gazdar's approach to the projection problem).

A second issue is that many authors feel that the epistemic commitments on the part of the speaker proposed by Gazdar are just much too strong (see, e.g., van der Sandt 1988: 126ff). Soames (1982, 1998: 115–120) suggests that the epistemic force of scalar implicatures is the external negation of the Hintikka operator K, so that asserting, "Some came" will carry the generalized implicature that the speaker doesn't know whether all came or $\sim K$(all came) or P(all came), which may be strengthened by the contextual assumption that the speaker would know whether or not all came, to a particularized implicature that the speaker definitively knows that not all came, or $K \sim$ (all came). He provides both telling examples and a Gricean argument to that effect. Horn (1989: 214, 233–234, 543 n. 5) essentially concurs and suggests that scalar implications are of the form $\sim Kp$ ('the speaker doesn't know that p', rather than Gazdar's $K \sim p$, 'the speaker knows that not p'), unless they are strengthened by an additional assumption that S is an expert on the subject p.[7] Soames (1998) goes on to show that if this tack is taken, scalar implicatures are not after all (at least in the classic cases) inconsistent with clausal implicatures, and Gazdar's special rule that scalars cancel clausal implicatures where they are mutually inconsistent can be dispensed with.[8]

Both more elaborate and simpler solutions are possible. Hirschberg (1985: 75ff) argues that it would be desirable to distinguish between the strong epistemic commitment associated (by the maxim of Quality) with the asserted content of utterances, and the weaker commitment, perhaps in terms of belief rather than knowledge, associated with implicatures. She therefore claims that scalars actually implicate a disjunction itself: asserting "Some came" implicates that S believes that not all came or that S doesn't know whether all came.[9] Additionally, one might wish that the relative defeasibility of different species of pragmatic implication (e.g., of scalar vs. clausal Q-implicatures) was also reflected in variable strengths of speaker commitment. On the other hand, Atlas (1993a) holds that the whole issue betrays a deep confusion (promoted by Grice's reductionist program) between utterance-meaning on the one hand and psychological states of speakers on the other: when one utters U implicating p, p is conveyed whether one believes it or not. Even if a speaker's mental states are involved in the computation that U implicated p, they are not part of the *content* of U.[10] On this account, the entire debate is beside the point: implicatures come naked, without epistemic commitments.

One central point needs to be preserved in this debate, and that is the intuitive difference between scalar implicatures, which do come with a strong presumption, arguably something close to epistemic certainty, and clausal implicatures where what is conveyed is precisely epistemic uncertainty. It is for this reason that, in what follows, I simply presume, following the Gricean tradition, that implicatures do come with some form of epistemic modification that will retain this distinction. None of the proffered solutions seem quite right,[11] and although a correct solution would be required for any formalization, I will offer none here and will remain agnostic about the directions in which such a solution may be found. Henceforth, I shall not in general mark the epistemic modification on implicatures: thus when I write "Some came" Q +> 'Not all came', this may be understood as a shorthand for 'the uttering of "Some came" will, *ceteris paribus*, implicate that the speaker judges that not all came' (where "judge" can be cashed out in various ways).[12] Where the distinction between the the scalars and the clausal implicatures needs to be highlighted, I revert to Gazdar's (1979) notation, using K and P, but with a weaker "belief" rather than "know" interpretation (where the implicated suggestion seems especially weak, I indicate this in the gloss), so that scalars will generate implicatures of the Kp form and clausal implicatures will have the form Pp, $P \sim p$, as I will explain.[13]

2.2.2   Entailment Scales

We may loosely define a Horn scale (or entailment scale, to differentiate such from non-entailment scales to be mentioned below) as an ordered *n*-tuple of expression alternates $\langle x_1, x_2, \ldots, x_n \rangle$ such that, where S is an arbitrary simplex sentence-frame and $x_i > x_j$, $S(x_i)$ unilaterally entails $S(x_j)$.[14] Classic scales of this kind come from many grammatical classes and include the quantifiers ⟨*all, most, many, some*⟩, connectives like ⟨*and, or*⟩, modals ⟨*necessarily, possibly*⟩, ⟨*must, should, may*⟩, adverbs like ⟨*always, often, sometimes*⟩, degree adjectives like ⟨*hot, warm*⟩, and even verbs like ⟨*know, believe*⟩, ⟨*love, like*⟩. They all induce Q-implicatures in the way that should already be familiar: assertion of a lower ranking (rightwards) alternate implicates that the speaker is not in a position to assert a higher ranking one—for if the speaker was in that position, he or she should, by the Q-principle, have asserted the stronger sentence. The one-way semantic entailment that orders these sets guarantees of course that leftmost items are informationally richer than rightwards ones.

Further conditions have to be put on Horn scales, lest they overgenerate (Gazdar 1979: 57f; Atlas and Levinson 1981: 44). Clearly we do not implicate the negation of every proposition that entails what we say. First, items in the same scale must be in salient opposition: of the same form class, in the same dialect or register, and lexicalized to the same degree. These considerations exclude for example a Horn scale ⟨*iff, if*⟩, for *iff* (*if and only if*) belongs to a specialized register and is not monolexemic like *if*. This lexicalization constraint holds especially for the stronger items in scales, and for good Gricean reasons: if the hearer suspects that the speaker may have avoided a stronger statement simply because it would have been clumsy and prolix (and thus contrary to Manner maxims), the hearer can clearly draw no conclusions about the speaker not being in a position to make the stronger statement (Matsumoto 1995).[15] More precisely then, the lexicalization constraint requires that stronger items on a scale be lexicalized to an equal *or greater* degree than weaker items.

Second, scalar items must be from the same semantic field, "about" the same semantic relations, and thus in conceptually salient opposition. Hence there is no scale ⟨*regret, know*⟩ because *regret* introduces semantic parameters additional to those involved in *know*.[16] Similarly, in conjunction with the requirements for sameness of word class, semantic issues rule out a scale ⟨*p because q, p and q*⟩. The same multiple constraints rule out the putative scale ⟨*necessarily-p, p*⟩, thought by Burton-Roberts (1984) to be a serious anomaly in the Gricean account (because the plain assertion of, e.g., "Two and two is four" would then imply that it is not necessarily so).

There is one apparent systematic exception to these constraints, which has to do with negative scalar items. Gazdar (1979: 56–57) blocks implicatures arising in negative contexts: otherwise, he claims, the assertion of "It is not the case that Paul ate some of the eggs" would implicate 'It is not the case that Paul ate not all of the eggs' (i.e., that Paul ate all of the eggs). The same blocking constraint is imposed by Hirschberg (1985: 73), who correctly notes, however, that Gazdar's blocking of other logical functors is unnecessary. Even Horn (1989: 234) subscribes to a blocking function that includes both overt and covert negatives (and indeed all downward-entailing operators). Now, in fact, this move arises from a misunderstanding of negative scales. The correct generalization, as pointed out by Atlas and Levinson (1981), is that negation reverses scales: for example, if ⟨*all, some*⟩ form a Horn scale, so do ⟨*none* (i.e., *not some*), *not all*⟩.[17] Hence "It is not the case that Paul ate some of the eggs" (or more simply "Paul didn't eat some of the eggs") asserts an item at the strongest end of a scale (*not some = none*), from which as always no implicature follows. The process is entirely general, and no special projection apparatus is required. However, given the generalization noted by Horn (1973, 1989) described in chapter 1, that the (*not all*) O corner of the traditional square of oppositions regularly fails to lexicalize, whereas the (*none*) E corner does, this arguably constitutes a regular exception to a constraint that items in Horn scales must be of equal lexicalized status. When the constraint is formulated, as above, so that it requires strong scalars to be lexicalized to a same or greater degree than weak items on the same scale, negative scales are in fact no longer exceptional (note, e.g., that *not some* lexicalizes to *none* on the ⟨*none, not all*⟩ scale). Still, there is a special pattern here to the nature of negative expressions, given the systematic O-corner resistance to lexicalization. This special pattern may be recognized by introducing negative scales by meta-rule: for any scale of the form $\langle x_1, x_2, \ldots, x_n \rangle$, there will be a corresponding scale of the form $\langle \sim x_n, \ldots, \sim x_2, \sim x_1 \rangle$. The psychological counterpart to this move is the claim that we process such negative scale items as *none* by reference to the equivalent expressions containing the relevant positive scalar items, like 'not some', a decompositional claim that is consistent with the known processing difficulties associated with negatives.[18]

There are some well-known diagnostics for scalar implicature. If we entertain the hypothesis that two expressions, call them S and W for "strong" and "weak," form a scale ⟨S, W⟩, then they should permit the following embeddings:

(3) a. *Canceling phrases*
       "W and even S"   (e.g., "Some and even all of them came.")
       "Not only W, S"   (e.g., "Not only some of them, all of them came.")
       "W in fact/indeed S"   (e.g., "Some, in fact all of them, came.")

     b. *Suspending phrases*
       "W or possibly/even S"   (e.g., "Some or possibly all of them came.")
       "W if not S"   (e.g., "Some, if not all of them, came.")

The rationale, of course, is that because implicatures unlike entailments are defeasible, it is possible to assert the contrary, or explicitly raise its possibility, without any sense of contradiction. The last type, the suspension of the implicature by mention in an *if*-clause, or by mention of the strong alternate in an *or*-clause, was taken as an especially important diagnostic (called "suspenders") by Horn (1972, 1989: 234–234). For non-entailment scales where we cannot order expressions on simple entailment grounds, Horn suggested we could use "suspenders" to establish that items belong to a single scale and their ordering within it. Gazdar (1979) assumed that the mechanism in these suspending *if*-clauses was simply implicature cancellation by a general projection mechanism (whereby clausal implicatures cancel scalar ones inconsistent with them); for more recent commentary, see Hirschberg 1985 (118–120) and Atlas 1993a (211–217), who suggests that these concessive *if*-clauses do not have the semantics of full conditionals. In addition to these diagnostics, one may also note that the head of a scale (the A or E or topmost items in the square) can collocate with modifiers like *absolutely, barely, not quite* (as in *absolutely all* vs. ??*absolutely many, not quite all* vs. ??*not quite some*, etc.). One should note that these diagnostics establish scalar relations between expressions in a context, but they do not establish the GCI status of the scale (see the discussion of Hirschberg's scales in section 2.2.4.)

A summary of the points made so far is given in (58).

(4) a. *Positive Horn scales*

   A set of linguistic alternates $\langle x_1, x_2, \ldots, x_n \rangle$ such that $S(x_i)$ unilaterally entails $S(x_j)$, where S is an arbitrary simplex sentence-frame, and $x_i > x_j$, and where $x_1, x_2, \ldots, x_n$ are

   i. equally lexicalized items, of the same word class, from the same register; and

   ii. "about" the same semantic relations, or from the same semantic field.

   b. *Negative Horn scales*

   For each well-formed positive Horn scale of the form $\langle x_1, x_2, \ldots, x_n \rangle$, there will be a corresponding negative scale of the form $\langle \sim x_n, \ldots, \sim x_2, \sim x_1 \rangle$, regardless of the relative lexicalization of the negation.

   c. *Diagnostics for GCI scales*

   For any item x_j weaker than x_i on a scale, "x_j, in fact/if not/or even/or possibly x_i" should be a felicitous phrase in an appropriate sentence-frame.

Before attending to the issue of other kinds of scales, let us reap the harvest so far sown—for there are highly systematic generalizations to be made here.

2.2.2.1 Quantificational and Modal Operators: Horn's Arithmetic Square of Oppositions

I introduced in chapter 1 the traditional square of oppositions and reviewed Horn's (1973) argument that the subcontrary relation (between I and O corners of the square) is implicatural.[19] Further, the regularity that strong negative scalar items incorporate negation (*none*) whereas weak ones tend not to (*not all*) was attributed to the regular (i.e., generalized) implicature from *some* to 'not all'. Indeed I argued that this kind of regularity cannot be captured without a theory of default or generalized inference. This area is relatively well understood in English, and I provide just sufficient detail for those studying other languages to see how to proceed (much more will be found in Horn 1989).

A problem that has arisen in understanding the quantifiers is the exact relationship between midscale negative and positive quantifiers. For example, is *Few came* the negative counterpart of *Many came*, and are they contraries or subcontraries? And what is the contradictory of *Many came*? There are a great many quantifiers in English whose position in the square is not immediately self-evident (e.g., *several, a few, many, very many, most* or *very few, a minority, not many*). Clearly, if we are to understand quantification, we must understand the relationships between quantifiers that are midway on, or not at either end of, Horn scales. Diagrammatically, the problem is shown in figure 2.1.

What we seek is a general solution in terms of the square of oppositions to the problem of whether the negative counterpart of a given scalar item is a contrary or a subcontrary, and what its contradictory is. Then, the solution will carry over from the quantifiers to the modals, logical con-

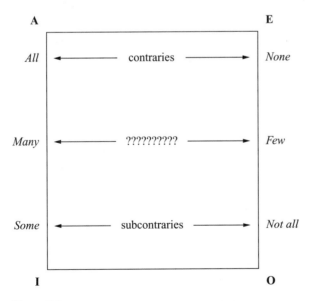

Figure 2.1
The problem of the location of midscale expressions

Table 2.1
Counterparts across the quantifiers, modals, and connectives within the square of opposition

	A-Corner	E-Corner	I-Corner	O-Corner
Quantifiers	all	none	some	not all
	both	neither	one	not both
	everything	nothing	something	not everything
	everybody	nobody	somebody	not everybody
	always	never	sometimes	not always
Modals				
alethic	necessary	impossible	possible	possible not
epistemic	certain	impossible	possible/ may	possible not/ may not
deontic	must/need to	must not	may/can	may not
	obligated	forbidden	permitted	permitted not to
Connectives	(both)...and	neither...nor	(either)...or	not both

nectives, and other domains. Following Jespersen (1917), Sapir (1930), and generations of philosophical and logical thought (all nicely summarized in Horn 1989), we may put into correspondence on the square the sets of notions given in table 2.1. The placement of scalar items on the square requires in the first instance a distinction between the positive (A-I dimension) scales and the negative (E-O dimension) scales. This may be established partly by reference to the well-known duals (repeated here from chapter 1):

(5) *The duals*

$$A \ldots = \sim I \ldots \sim \qquad \text{(e.g., } all \ldots \text{ implies } not\ some \ldots not \ldots)$$
$$I \ldots = \sim A \ldots \sim \qquad \text{(e.g., } some \ldots \text{ implies } not\ all \ldots not \ldots)$$
$$\sim A \ldots = I \sim \ldots \qquad \text{(e.g., } not\ all \ldots \text{ implies } some \ldots not \ldots)$$
$$\sim I = A \ldots \sim \qquad \text{(e.g., } not\ some \ldots \text{ implies } all \ldots not \ldots)$$

It may partly also be established by reference to Horn's "suspender" tests (1989: 235–236):

(6) *Using suspending clauses to*

    a. Establish ordering in positive scales

       i. "Some or even all came."

      ii. ??"All or even some came."

1.0	*all/every*	*none*	−1.0
		hardly any	
		very few	
		few	
	most/a majority		
		a minority	
0.5	*half*		−0.5
	very many		
	many		
	quite a few		
	several		
0.0	*some*	*not all*	0.0

Figure 2.2
Arithmetic scale for English quantifying phrases

    b. Establish ordering in negative scales
       i.   "Not all or even none came."
       ii. ??"None or even not all came."
    c. Disallow mixed positive and negative scalar items[20]
       i. ??"Some or even none came."
       ii. ??"None or even some came."

To establish a correspondence between items on the positive and corresponding negative scales, Horn suggests that, as a heuristic device, we arithmetize the square by assigning values in the range of 0 to 1.0 on the positive and 0 to –1.0 on the negative scale (in each case, in the direction weak W to strong S ends of the scale). Using tests to be discussed, Horn (1989: 237) gives figure 2.2 as the square for English quantifiers. The halfway 0.5 position marks the line above which positive items have negative items as *contraries* (e.g., "all came" entails 'not none came'); below that line, positive items have negative items as *subcontraries* (i.e., the relationship is implicatural; e.g., "some came" implicates but does not entail 'not all came'). How do we establish that, for example, *most* is above the line and *many* below it? First, we can show that *most* is higher on the positive scale than *many* by Horn's "suspender" tests: one can say "Many if not most of them came", but not ??"Most if not many of them came." Second, we can use Löbner's (1987) test for tolerant versus intolerant logical operators: logical contraries are intolerant of conjunction with their internal negations (i.e., an intolerant quantifier Q does not combine in an acceptable sentence of the form "Q(x) P(x) and Q(x) $\sim$ P(x)") , whereas implicated subcontraries are tolerant of such a conjunction.[21]

(7) *Löbner's tolerance test*
    a. Intolerant quantifiers
        i.   *"All of the boys came but all of them didn't."
        ii. *"Most of the boys came but most didn't."
        iii. *"A majority of the boys came but a majority didn't."
    b. Tolerant quantifiers
        i.   "Many of the boys came, but many didn't."
        ii. "Quite a few of the boys came, but quite a few didn't."
        iii. "Several of the boys came, but several didn't."

Putting the two tests together, Horn's "suspender" tests for order and Löbner's test for tolerance, we can order all the items on both the positive and negative scales, and place them correctly with regard to the crucial midway line establishing contrary versus subcontrary (implicatural) relations. Items aligned horizontally on the positive and negative scales are taken to be directly opposed as contraries (if above the midline) or subcontraries (if below it).[22] Using these methods, we can obtain the kind of model illustrated in figure 2.2, with the two scales (positive and negative) systematically related. Then we can predict not only the intrascalar GCIs (e.g., *Several x*φ*'d* will implicate 'Not many φ'd'), but the crossscalar inferences between the expressions near the I and O corners (e.g., *A few* φ*'d* will implicate 'Many didn't φ' and vice versa). The same procedures of course can be employed over various sets of logical operators. Readers may like to play with quantificational frequency adverbs of the type exemplified by *seldom, often*, and *rarely* and see if they can construct the positive and negative scales, the contrary versus subcontrary and contradictory relationships.[23]

2.2.2.2   Entailment Scales over Nonlogical Predicates

2.2.2.2.1   General Vocabulary   There are many entailment scales that cannot be arranged in a square of oppositions even though they come as paired positive and negative scales. Consider for example gradable adjectives ⟨*hot, warm*⟩ and ⟨*cold, cool*⟩; these form two scales linked by a (sub)contrary relationship rather than one unified scale, as shown by the usual tests. For example, one can say *It's warm, in fact quite hot*, but not *?It's cool, in fact quite warm*, because *warm* and *cool* belong to different scales. Moreover, the comparative *warmer* means 'further towards hot' (not, on analogy to, e.g., *redder*, 'more towards warm'), whereas *cooler* means 'further towards cold'—that is, the scales are headed in different directions (Horn 1989: 239–240). But the two scales form no square because such predicates allow no inner negations, and thus *hot* and *cold* are not related like *all* and *none* as A to E corners of the square (Horn 1989: p. 245, 548–549). The full scales in this case seem to be ⟨*boiling, hot, warm*⟩ and ⟨*freezing, cold, cool, lukewarm*⟩. Similar paired scales abound; for example, ⟨*excellent, good, all right*⟩ and ⟨*awful, bad, mediocre*⟩. Further examples are given in (62).

(8) a. i. "The handwriting is similar."
    ii. +> 'not identical'
    iii. ⟨*identical, similar*⟩
    iv. "The handwriting is similar, if not identical."
  b. i. "This is a partial solution."
    ii. +> 'not complete'
    iii. ⟨*complete, partial*⟩
    iv. "This is a partial solution, and indeed perhaps a complete one."

and similarly for ⟨*long-term, short-term*⟩ (or ⟨*permanent, durable*⟩), ⟨*huge, large*⟩, ⟨*ancient, old*⟩, and so on.

In addition to gradable adjectives, verbs form scales like ⟨*adore, love, like*⟩ and its negative counterpart ⟨*loathe, hate, dislike*⟩. Some scalar verbs like those in the scale ⟨*know, believe*⟩, which permit internal negations, have been of considerable philosophical interest: *knowing p* entails *believing p*, and indeed *not believing that not p*, but stating "John believes *p*" implicates 'John doesn't know *p*'. It is likely that our analysis of the lexical meaning of verbs has systematically failed to take scalar implicatures into account.

2.2.2.2.2 The Number Words One kind of scale that has exercised analysts is that formed by the infinite series of numbers words or numerical expressions in English, ⟨*. . . , five, four, three, two, one*⟩. Horn (1972) assumed that the numerical expressions should fall within his scalar approach, carrying the normal implicatures: thus an assertion "He has three children" should implicate but not entail that he has no more. In general, the reasons for assuming that there is such a scale with corresponding GCIs still seem good: the assertion of (9a) would have the semantic content paraphrased in (9b) (the lower bound 'at least three' is entailed)[24] and the GCI in (9c) (the upper bound is implicated, as in scales generally). The normal suspension tests apply as in (9d), showing that the content of (9c) cannot be entailed. Finally, in the right context, where an exact specification is irrelevant, the implicature is implicitly cancelled as in (9e)

(9) a. "John has three children."
    b. "John has at least three children."
    c. "John has at most three children."
    d. "John has three children, if not four/and perhaps more/or possibly five."
    e. A: "Does John qualify for the Large-Family Benefit?"
       B: "Sure, he has three children all right."

Despite these attractions, there are a number of difficulties with a scalar approach to number words. First, mathematics would be in danger: when we assert that the square root of 9 is 3 we do not mean that the square root of at least 9 is *at least three*, otherwise we could as well say the square root of 9 is 2 (Sadock 1984)—special conventions are in force of course, and we may want to distinguish sharply between natural language numerical expressions and cardinal numbers (Atlas 1993: chap. 2). Second, Horn (1972) himself drew attention to the fact that in certain specific circumstances the scales could be inverted, for example in tallying golf scores where the higher score is the lesser number one might felicitously say "He can do the round in seventy two, if not seventy." This possibility of scale-reversal does not appear to arise with other quantifiers (Sadock 1984: 143) and indeed otherwise seems restricted to pragmatically defined scales; this raises the general issue of the extent to which all scales are in the last resort pragmatic in nature, an issue addressed in section 2.2.4.

But this possibility of scale reversal, coupled with the fact that the implicature can evaporate in contexts like (9e), has led some analysts to abandon the scalar approach to numerical expressions. One position is to claim that the number words are just ambiguous between an 'exactly' and an 'at least' interpretation, perhaps disambiguated in specific linguistic contexts—for example, as 'exactly *n*' when acting as determiners (see Kempson 1975; this is Kamp's position as reported in Kadmon 1984).

But the prospect of infinite ambiguities not only here but then elsewhere too is very unattractive (especially compared to the scalar approach, where the two uses of numeral expressions follow from general properties of any scalar series whatsoever). Another approach is to assume that the meaning of, say, *three* is simply indeterminate at the semantic level between 'at least three' and 'exactly three' and is then further specified by a particularized conversational implicature in context as appropriate, or perhaps restricted by semantic constraints in particular constructions (thus Atlas (1983) suggests that collective NPs have the 'exactly' inter- .pretation). Kempson (1986) and Atlas (1993b) take this approach but for different reasons: Kempson because she wishes to reduce GCIs to PCIs compatible with Relevance theory,[25] and Atlas because he wishes to assimilate the unspecified nature of cardinal semantics to his account of *not*, which has a similar property. Carston (1985) took a similar line, arguing that *three* is semantically unspecified between three readings, 'at least three', 'at most three' (as in the reverse-scale cases), and 'exactly three', particular contexts being responsible for our understanding in each case.

The trouble with much of this argumentation is that it confounds general problems of the very existence of GCIs as a species of inference, pragmatic intrusion into truth conditions, the general nature of semantic representations before pragmatic enrichment, so-called metalinguistic negation, and the projection problem for implicatures—with the rather specific difficulties associated with the English number words. The specific difficulties boil down to the following facts.[26] First, in math-literate cultures, there will be possible confusion between English *three* and the numeral '3', with a consequent bias towards an 'exactly three' interpretation. Second, this may be associated with the fact that in some cases the number words are associated with upper-bounding specifications that are not easily defeasible (Kadmon 1984: 30ff; Horn 1989: 251). For example, compare "He has one child", which seems to stipulate only one, with "He has a child", where the upper-bounding implicature is more easily lifted. This may well be due however precisely to an M-implicature associated with that opposition. Similarly, "I have two hundred and three dollars" more strongly suggests an upper bound than "I have two hundred dollars", which can again perhaps be attributed to a Manner implicature: to bother to say "two hundred *and three*" where the shorter "two hundred" alone might be sufficient suggests that there is reason to be precise, and the speaker is acting in accordance with that reason. Third, as Horn (1989: 251–252) points out (see also Brown and Levinson 1987: 258ff), all implicatures are potentially subject to a process of conventionalization, and the number words may be under pressure to lexicalize the 'exactly' reading: where 'three' is lexically incorporated, as in *three-sided, triple, thrice, three-ply*, or *triumvirate*, no 'at least' reading is possible (Horn 1978, Atlas 1983), a fact already clear in the ordinals like *fourth prize*. Fourth, there are perhaps genuine differences in interpretive freedom between number words in different syntactic and thematic positions, as Atlas (1983), Kadmon (1987), Fretheim (1992), Van Kuppevelt (1996), and Scharten (1997) argue, which might be expected if the partial conventionalization account is correct.

These complicating factors and confusions are sufficient to make the number words *not* the correct testbed for the whole theory of scalar implicature (as, e.g., Kempson (1986: 86) seems to suppose). Horn (1992b: 172–175) indeed abandons the classic scalar approach to just the number words, pointing out a number of additional special properties. Still, when due allowance is made for the special role of number words in math-literate cultures, and consequent possible conventionalization of the 'exactly' readings, there are a number of reasons to hang on to a scalar interpretation of ordinary language numeral expressions in general. One central piece of evidence is provided by those languages that have a finite series of numerals. Many Australian languages, for example, have just three number words, which are glossed as 'one', 'two' and often 'three'. The scalar prediction is clear in these cases: we have a finite scale ⟨'three', 'two', 'one'⟩, where 'one' or 'two' will implicate *ceteris paribus* an upper bound; but because there is no stronger item 'four', the cardinal 'three' should lack this clear upper bounding by GCI. And this is clearly the case in, for example, Guugu Yimithirr: *nubuun* can be glossed 'one', *gudhirra* 'two', but *guunduu* must be glossed 'three or more, a few'.[27] And this is the general report (see Dixon 1980: 108). None of the other theories make this correct prediction. Finally, Cruse (1986: 69–70) points out that by certain tests for the better establishment of one sense over another, the 'exactly' interpretations of the English number words are psychologically more salient than the 'at least' interpretations, and by the same tests it can be seen that this corresponds with the favored interpretations of the quantifiers (those with doubts about the very existence of GCIs may find this bias interesting).[28]

2.2.2.2.3 *Closed-class Morphemes, Function Words* Entailment scales can be found among any restricted set of lexemes with semantic asymmetries of the right kind. One happy hunting ground, barely exploited to date, is the area of closed-class morphemes and function words, although not all of these are organized as entailment scales. Treating the quantifiers in this way has yielded, as we have seen, rich insights. The connectives were of course the original focus of Grice's (1967) theory, and GCI theory explains many of their properties—for example, the scalar relations of ⟨*and, or*⟩ explain the preferred exclusive reading of the disjunction, and the clausal implicatures of *if* and *or* rely on the availability if stronger locutions that entail their constituent sentences like *since* and *and*.

GCI theory makes a number of interesting predictions with respect to sets of closed-class morphemes or function words covering single semantic domains:

- On the whole, we expect sets of contrasting function words, because the pragmatic load can then be increased through pragmatic oppositions without further increasing the set of expressions;
- We can expect scalar oppositions due to informational asymmetries, in which case the usual scalar predictions should apply (e.g., for a scale ⟨*S, W*⟩, we do not expect lexicalization of 'not *S*');
- There are likely to be Manner contrasts due to the M-principle introduced in chapter 1 and further described below (where a set of marked/ unmarked expressions covering the same domain will tend to pick up complementary oppositions, the unmarked ones picking up the stereotypical state of affairs); for example, a contrast between simplex *on* and the compound preposition *on top of*.

Here, I concentrate on the scalar implicatures, returning at the end of the section to the prospect of handling closed classes in terms of multiple pragmatic principles.

An important example is provided by the articles, although Grice's (1975: 56) remarks here seem to have deflected proper analysis (including Atlas and Levinson 1981: 49; Carston 1988: 214). Grice noted the conundrum that "I went into a house" suggests that the speaker went into someone else's house, whereas "I cut a finger" suggests I cut my own finger. There is in fact no scale ⟨*my, a*⟩ because possession and indefiniteness are not "about" the same semantic relations; consequently, there is no GCI from "a NP" to 'not my NP', and nonscalar inferences of various kinds would seem to be involved. However, there is an inference from indefinite reference to the inappropriateness of definite reference, for the articles form a Horn scale ⟨*the, a*⟩ by the usual criteria:

(10) a. "I saw the man with a red hat."
        Entailed: 'I saw *a* man with a red hat.'
     b. "I saw *a* man with a red hat."
        Implicated: 'I saw someone who I would hesitate to describe as
        the man with a red hat.'
     c. "I saw *a* man with a red hat, in fact *the* very man with a red hat
        you saw yesterday."

Grice's examples are thus indirectly explained: when one says "I went into
a house" one Q-implicates 'I didn't go into the house', where the definite
suggests (I-implicates) my very own house. On the other hand, when I say
"I cut a finger" I merely implicate that it was no unique, otherwise salient
finger (say, the one I cut before) that suffered, and that interpretation is
compatible with the assumption that it was my own finger (which in turn
is a more stereotypical reading than one that involves the chopping of
other peoples' fingers).

   Hawkins (1991) has argued that if this analysis is adopted, many puzzles in the analysis of definiteness seem more tractable. He holds on to an
essentially Russellian analysis of the definite article, thereby explaining
the entailment relationship between *the X* and *an X* (the representation of
the contains the representation of *a* as a conjunct), supplemented with a
conventional implicature associated with *the* that specifies the kind of
mutually accessible set in which the referent must be unique. The semantic representation of *a* is simply the existential quantifier, and the baffling
range of uses that are associated with it follow in large part from the
Q-implicatures that derive from the contrast with *the*. In general, an
indefinite phrase *an X* seems to be associated with the presumption of
nonuniqueness (as in *A senator resigned*), but there are plenty of circumstances in which this presumption is defeated by background knowledge
or a constructional meaning, as in existential statements like *Nine has a
positive square root*, or *France has a capital*. The explanation would be
that *an X* picks up its nonuniqueness presumption by contrast to the
stronger definite article, in the normal scalar way, except where this is
overridden by background knowledge or semantic conditions.

   In those circumstances where the indefinite is read as referring to a
unique entity, a definite article is also grammatical, but it tends to force
the assumption of a different contextual set in which the referent is
unique. Consider (11), where one might expect only a definite article to be
possible, given the unique nature of the offices in question, but in fact
both the definite and indefinite article can be used.

(11) a. England has a prime minister, and America has a president.

   b. England has the prime minister and America has the president.

Hawkins (1991: 421–422) notes that we read the existential construction in (11a) as assigning types of constitutional leadership, offices with unique incumbents, to countries. In contrast, we read (11b) in a different way: the definite forces us to find some further contextual set in which the referent is unique (e.g., England is hosting the prime minister of France, whereas America is hosting France's president). The explanation seems to be that existential statements tend to take an indefinite object (whose uniqueness may be given by background knowledge), so that a definite NP encourages us to find another construal. These kind of complexities seem consistent with the pragmatic account but not with some more restrictive semantics for the indefinite article (e.g., specifying lack of uniqueness). Note that on this account, the anaphoric potential of the definite, as opposed to the indefinite, follows from the meaning (contrast discourse semantic accounts like Heim 1982). The range of data that can thus be explained by this approach far exceeds other existing accounts of the nature of the definite/indefinite contrast. Before we can fully appreciate this, I need to introduce some further types of implicature, and further observations about the articles are given later in this chapter (see, e.g., remarks on bridging inferences in section 2.3 and on the opposition between article and zero-article in section 2.4.1).

Lyons (1977) advances the view, well supported by diachronic evidence, that the definite article may in some respects be treated as a deictic determiner unmarked for the proximal/distal distinction expressed by *this* and *that*. Hawkins (1991: 415) suggests that the contrast is essentially that the demonstratives presume accessibility to perception or via discourse, whereas the definite article is neutral (although both presume uniqueness in some set). If this were correct, one might expect a scale ⟨ *{this, that}*, *the*⟩, such that by saying "Could you lend me the book?" one would suggest that the book is not perceptually available in the situation of speech (for then *this book* or *that book* would be more informative). Notice that there is indeed a contrast between (12a) and (12b), the first being sayable with my hand in my pocket, or on the telephone, whereas the second requires a demonstration or exhibit of the finger (ignoring for a moment the anaphoric uses of the determiners).[29]

(12) a. The index finger on my left hand is hurting.

   b. This index finger on my left hand is hurting.

More tentatively, we may note that the marked deictic determiners also come in closed classes and may be susceptible to a similar analysis. For example, there may well be a Q-contrast between ⟨*this, that*⟩, where *this* has more precise criteria of application than *that*: the proximal deictic is marked for proximity, the so-called distal deictic presumes accessibility (in space or discourse) but is unmarked for proximity, and thus picks up the complementary interpretation. This predicts that *that* has a wide distribution, potentially overlapping with *this*, as indeed seems to be the case. Thus for the same spatial arrangement of a book on a table I can say both *I wrote this book* and *I wrote that book*, but if there are two books, *that book* will suggest the one I would not describe as *this book*. This kind of opposition between deictically specified and unspecified has already been suggested by Wilkins and Hill (1995) for 'come' and 'go' verbs in various languages, and may carry over to other sets like ⟨*here, there*⟩.

I turn now to anaphoric uses of these determiners. Prince (1981) argues that there is a hierarchy of anaphoric expressions in English, according to the degree to which their referents are mentally activated, as it were. She argues that "the use of an NP representing a certain point on the scale implicates that the speaker could not have felicitously referred to the same entity by another NP higher on the scale" (1981: 245). Developing these ideas further, Gundel, Hedberg, and Zacharski (1989, 1993) outline a Givenness Hierarchy (see figure 2.3) along the following lines, where the stronger requirements are leftwards and the weaker ones rightwards, because any referent that is "in focus" (in central attention in the discourse) is also "activated" (previously referred to, etc.), "familiar," and so on. On the basis of quantitative textual evidence, they claim that the English anaphoric expressions pattern as shown in figure 2.3. But the use of a rightwards expression only *implicates* that a leftwards one does not

in-focus >	activated >	familiar >	uniquely identifiable >	type-identifiable
it	*that, this*	*that NP*	*the NP*	*a NP*
zero	*this NP*			indefinite *this NP*
unstressed pronouns				

Figure 2.3
Givenness Hierarchy (after Gundel, Hedberg, and Zacharski 1993)

apply (just as noted above for the use of the indefinite vs. the definite article), but this is sufficient to suggest a change of referent. For example, use of *that* signals a change of referent from *it* (Gundel, Hedberg, and Zacharski 1989: 94).

(13) He had to show *it* to the agency before he sent *it* to the newspaper, and when the editor asked for a change, he had to show *that* to the censors too.

Whatever the success of this particular analysis, implicature does seem to have a systematic role in signaling changes of referent, and this is addressed directly in chapter 4.

Grammatical morphemes, with their contrastive oppositions, may also frequently exhibit Q-contrasts parasitic on, and additional to, semantical contrasts. Consider tense in English.[30] Harnish (1976, 1991: 354) notes "the use of the past tense often carries the implication that the activity or state indicated by the verb no longer is present"; thus the pattern in (14a–b) (see also Comrie 1985: 24). Harnish might have gone on to suggest a scale as in (14c), where it is more informative to know if the event still holds rather than just that the event held at some previous time (because knowing the current situation gives us a unique known instance in time where the event is known to hold, whereas a past tense only assures us that there was some instant at which the event occurred).

(14) a. "John used to live in Rome."
      Implicature: 'John no longer lives in Rome.'
   b. "John used to live in Rome, and in fact he still does."
   c. ⟨PRESENT, PAST⟩
   d. "John lives in Rome."

Most formal treatments of tense reflect the asymmetry in informational specificity by stating in effect that the present tense of an event holds if the time of an event coincides with the designated utterance time, whereas the past tense holds if there is at least *some* time preceding utterance time at which the event occurred (e.g., Cann 1993: 242–243). Given the linear nature of time, it is also the case that any present event becomes a past event: the past is more event-populated than the present! These considerations, together with the tendency for present relevance of present events, suffice to ensure an informational asymmetry between the tenses even where no entailment relationship holds (strictly, of course, it does not follow from the uttering of *John is sleeping* at t_j that John *was* sleeping at t_i, the moment before, although it is likely, and indeed it is certain at t_k, the moment after the utterance, that he was sleeping before).

There are many other implicatures from tenses that need a proper pragmatic account (see Comrie 1985: 25, 71). Consider, for example, the perfect tenses, where the extra complexity of the perfect over the simple tenses suggests that a simple tense specification would not have been adequate (see Harder 1994: 73):

(15) a. "John had been living in London."
     Implicature: 'He was no longer living in London.'
   b. "John had been living in London, and in fact it turned out he still was."

(16) a. "John will have finished by tomorrow."
     Implicature: 'He has not yet finished.'
   b. "John will have finished by tomorrow, in fact he has already done so."

Languages that make do without tenses and temporal conjunctions like *after* or *before* often use oppositions between aspects to implicate sequence and anteriority. Bohnemeyer (1998) shows for example that speakers of Yucatec, a language without tense or temporal conjunctions, can systematically communicate temporal information through two kinds of generalized implicature: from aspectual unboundedness one can infer temporal overlap (as in "John came in. Mary was sleeping"), and from aspectual boundedness one can infer temporal nonoverlap (as in "John came in. Mary got up", with order then indicated iconically).

Another area that would be worth reexamining from an implicatural point of view are spatial expressions in closed sets, whether local cases, prepositions or post-positions. Here we can expect all our three pragmatic principles to be involved. For example, ⟨*at, near*⟩ form an entailment scale, such that *X is at the station* entails *X is near the station*; if one then asserts the weaker item, as in "John is near the station" one implicates 'not at the station' (Levinson 1995b: 192–194). To understand the full range of pragmatic oppositions between different spatial prepositions, one will need to bring in our other pragmatic principles. Thus, for example, {*on, on top of*} form an M-opposition, such that "on top of the desk" suggests a noncanonical placement (e.g., the object is not in contact with the desk, resting instead on other objects which are themselves directly on the desk) or a noncanonical viewing angle (e.g., the speaker is under the desk).

I know of no treatment of local cases along these kind of lines, although it is notable that the locative case, being normally unopposed to more specific local cases, tends to pick up stereotypical associations (in, e.g., Tamil) by the I-principle, so that 'Mango is table-LOC' suggests 'The mango is on the table', 'Mango is bowl-LOC' suggests 'The mango is in the bowl', which could have been more exactly specified by more prolix postpositional phrases. These latter do not constrain the interpretation of the locative because they are not in Q-contrast but rather in M-contrast relation with the simple case marker.

Other case contrasts, or contrasts between case and other constructions, should be susceptible to pragmatic treatment. For example, Levine (1990) examines the contrast in Russian between possessive forms of NP and dative NPs with possessive meanings, where the latter carry implicatures of noncanonical or special relationship. Heinämäki (1994: 213–214) notes that Finnish has the following contrast between partitive and accusative cases:

(17) a. Terttu luki kirjaa.
       Terttu read book-PART
       'Terttu was reading a (part of the) book.'
   b. Terttu luki kirjan.
       Terttu read book-ACC
       'Terttu read (all) the book.'
   c. Terttu luki kirjan   vain puoliväliin.
       Terttu read book-ACC only halfway-through
       'Terttu read the book only halfway through'

Heinämäki notes that the inference in (17a) to the effect that only part of the book was read is cancellable; and so is the inference in (17b) to the effect that all of the book was read. The partitive in conjunction with a durative verb like 'read' is specifically noncommittal about whether the event is bounded or not, whereas the accusative is specific that the event is indeed bounded. We then have in effect a meta-scale of the from ⟨BOUNDED, ±BOUNDED⟩, instantiated by the accusative and partitive cases respectively, such that the use of the unspecified partitive form suggests that a bounded event is not being referred to. The specific interpretations from boundedness to 'read all the book', and from unboundedness to 'read part of the book', can be attributed to the I-principle, which induces stereotypical interpretations; these can also be canceled as indicated in (17c), where the 'read all the book' inference is canceled by explicit indication that the bound of the reading was only half-way through the book.

These illustrations suggest that an implicature analysis of closed classes of morphemes may yield many important insights and resolve many puzzles that arise from the apparently elusive and variable content of these expressions.

2.2.3 Q-Contrasts Based on Other Kinds of Lexical Opposition

If Q-implicatures are based on the opposition between an informationally stronger and an informationally weaker expression, it is conceivable that there are other kinds of Q-implicature than those based on Horn scales or Gazdar's clausal oppositions. There may for example be lexical sets or semantic fields giving rise to similar inferences where however the criteria for Horn scales, for example, are not met. To the extent that such inferences are based directly on the structure of the lexicon, rather than ancillary knowledge about the specific context, one might expect them to have a generalized character. In this section, a number of putative kinds of such inference are discussed, but it should be borne in mind here that the phenomena are hardly explored and definitely not fully understood. This section is included only in the hope that it will spur further work.

It has long been clear that we can get scalar-like inferences from sets of linguistic expressions that fail the entailment criterion for Horn scales (see, e.g., Harnish 1976). Thus the pair of verbs *succeed, try* behave as if they belonged to a Horn scale, but as (18c) shows, there is no entailment from *x succeeded* to *x tried*.

(18) a. *Putative scale: ⟨succeed, try⟩*
     b. "John tried to reach the peak."
        Q-implicature: 'he didn't succeed.'
        Suspension: "John tried to reach the peak, and indeed/or perhaps he succeeded."
     c. "John succeeded without even trying."

The correct theoretical moves here are perhaps not clear. A Gricean argument based on Q is still applicable, because there seems to be an informational asymmetry between the expressions: trying involves trying to succeed, hence the listener may be expected to have an interest in the success of the attempt; the failure to supply information about success thus implicating that it was not achieved. Although *succeeding* does not entail *trying, a succeeded in φing* contrasts with the simpler *a φ'd* and thus perhaps M-implicates that *'a φ'd with directed effort'*.[31] The implicature from *try* to 'not succeed' is clearly generalized, so we cannot assign it to Hirschberg's (1985) solution for particularized scales discussed below. It is not presuppositional, as it is nondetachable—that is to say, the inference is attached to the semantical content not the lexical form, and thus the same inference appears from the more or less synonymous pair ⟨*manage, attempt*⟩. Tentatively, then we shall adopt the view that there are non-entailment scales, which nevertheless carry generalized conversational implicatures.[32]

We may be tempted by other putative scales, where the phenomena are actually rather different:

(19) *Pseudo-scale:* ⟨*mountain, hill*⟩
     "John can climb hills."
     Implicature: 'John can not climb mountains.'

Here there is not only no entailment relation between the items on the pseudo-scale (the one term excludes the other), there is no intrinsic informational asymmetry. Rather, we are in the domain of the assertion of one alternate implicating the inapplicability of the other, which is lower ranked in some way. This kind of implicature is taken up later, but it is at best marginal as far as generalized conversational implicature is concerned.

A more interesting marginal case is provided by deictic preemption: as Fillmore (1975) notes, we cannot, if today is Tuesday, say "Tuesday" meaning 'today' without danger of being mistaken to mean next Tuesday. In a similar way, *you* preempts the name of the addressee, *here* preempts the name of the place, and so on. One analysis is that whereas, in our way of reckoning, Tuesdays are multiple (this week's and next week's, for example), during this diurnal span there is only one today. Thus *today* is informationally richer—it uniquely refers, whereas *Tuesday* does not: there is a scale of referential determinateness with a genuine informational asymmetry, where asserting the weaker item implicates that the stronger does not apply:

(20) *Scale:* ⟨*today* = Tuesday, *Tuesday*⟩
     "Let's meet on Tuesday."
     Implicature: 'Let's not meet today, *this* Tuesday, but rather *next* Tuesday.'

I believe that this kind of referential asymmetry is crucial to the understanding of anaphora, as will be spelled out in chapter 4: determinate reference is informationally richer than potentially indeterminate reference, and scalar-like inferences are thus invoked by the use of the informationally weaker expression.

Still, it is clear that there are implicatures of contrast that have nothing to do with informational asymmetry. Harnish points out the following kind of inference based on lexical alternates, which he felt could be attributed to the first maxim of Quantity (Harnish 1976, 1991: 336):

(21) *Alternates:* ⟨*white, red, blue,...*⟩
    "The flag is white."
    Q +> 'The flag is not white and red.'
    "The flag is white and red" entails "The flag is white."

It is clear that, whatever our initial intuitions, the statement "The flag is white and red" must entail that "the flag is white", because if "the flag is white" is false, then the conjunction must also be false. One way of looking at this is to claim that nonranked alternates, in addition to the ranked scalar alternates, give rise to systematic implicatures: assertion of the one alternate will *ceteris paribus* imply the inapplicability of others unmentioned, otherwise by the Q-principle the speaker should have mentioned them.

Harnish (1976, 1991: 320) notes that, unlike the case where "the flag is white" implicates 'the flag is white all over', there is no corresponding 'all over' inference associated with such other adjectives as *spotted, stained, torn, dented*, and so on. On the other hand, it can be noted that there is indeed a corresponding inference with *smooth, rough, warm, cold, shiny, wooden, iron*, and so forth. One stain is sufficient to warrant the description *stained*, whereas one spot of white is not sufficient to warrant the description *white* (without further specification). It is notable that the adjectives without the 'all over' inference seem to lack underived alternates or contrastive terms: the best we can do are the contradictories like *unspotted, unstained, untorn (whole?), undented*. And that perhaps is the root of the difference: *white* belongs to a salient lexical set of alternates that are at most contraries[33] and may simultaneously apply to a single referent—the use of the one term then implicates that the use of the others, which could equally apply, are not applicable in this case.

These different kinds of example raise the possibility that there is a whole set of distinct but related types of Q-implicature, each bearing a family resemblance to one another, and each deriving from different kinds of contrast set provided by the structure of the lexicon. They would be related under the Q umbrella by the fact that in each case the inferences are (a) negative, (b) metalinguistic, in the sense that they depend on a contrast set of expressions, and (c) they rely on the fact that the unmentioned alternates are either more informative alone (the scalar case) or a conjunction of two or more of them would have been so (the alternates case).

It is worth looking back at the work of the structuralist semanticists (like Lyons, Lehrer and Lehrer, Haas, Cruse), those who have been especially interested in the way in which the lexicon can be seen to be organized into semantic fields, and the ways in which the semantic values of expressions are (at least partially) defined by the sense relations that hold between lexemes. In what follows, I make special use of the work by Cruse (1986) and confine myself to different kinds of contrast set (e.g., taxonomies, metonymies, chains, helices). Such an exercise does not appear to reveal simple generalizations, and indeed the remarks below are extremely tentative. The generalized character of these inferences is in general dubious. Nevertheless, looking through these types one can see some general tendency for implicature production of two types (similar, independent observations can be found in Hirschberg 1985: 60–61, 65, 108–113):

(22) a. *Type I:* use of a superordinate (more general) expression, (especially above the "basic level" of Rosch 1977), suggests that the speaker is not in a position to use a (more specific, more informative, "basic level") subordinate expression, or deems it irrelevant:
"I just saw a horrid animal in the larder."
+> 'speaker is not sure whether it was a rat, a shrew, a mouse, or what.'

b. *Type II:* use of an alternate from a contrast set suggests the inapplicability of another alternate, even when both could apply:
"He lectures on Wednesdays."
+> 'As far the speaker knows, he does not lecture on Thursdays.'

c. *Type IIb:* the denial of an alternate in a contrast set suggests that the other alternates may apply:
"He doesn't lecture on Wednesdays."
+> 'For all the speaker knows, he lectures on another day of the week.'

The form of the Type I implicature is a particularly weak, disjunctive implicature. Note, however, that it is based on an informational asymmetry, and this suggests a parallel to Q-inferences. The Type II implicatures, like those associated with the color terms, are more theoretically puzzling and indeed less systematic but are nevertheless regular in at least some cases. They seem to arise especially in connection with two kinds of lexical sets: sets of compatibles, like the color terms, where an expectation of exhaustivity is raised by the use of one term; and sets that exhibit some kind of intrinsic order (like the days of the week). The inferences in other cases may require special contexts (e.g., following a question: "Does he have pets?", "He has cats" implicates clearly that he has no dogs; see Hirschberg 1985), or special intonation (Ladd 1980; Horn 1989: 230f, 410; Ward and Hirschberg 1985), and thus lie beyond a theory of GCIs. They seem to have a secondary type (labeled Type IIb above), as suggested by Hirschberg (1985), where the denial of an alternate implicates the possible applicability of another. Type II inferences still seem to fall under the rubric of the Q-principle, or Grice's first maxim of Quantity, because they are based on the absence of specified information that one would expect to be provided if applicable.

The generalized nature of most of these inferences must be in doubt. Type I implicatures may lack a generalized status in part because of the potential depth of taxonomic structure in the vocabulary and thus an unclarity of opposition. Matsumoto (1995) suggests that it is choice of a term above the "basic level" terms that gives rise to the inference that the speaker cannot be more specific. He illustrates with kinship terms in Japanese, where, for example, the basic-level terms are more specific than English, so that use of the 'brother' term implicates that the speaker cannot specify 'younger-' or 'older-brother', which are the basic-level terms in Japanese. It is noteworthy that such inferences seem on occasion to have been sufficiently persistent to be a major source for diachronic shifts in lexical meaning. Thus where there are pairs of terms where one (the hyponym) is semantically marked for some feature, say +F, and the other (the superordinate) is unmarked, then the use of the unmarked term can come to implicate the alternative value for the feature (i.e., −F), the superordinate thus coming to function as its own hyponym, an "auto-hyponym" (Horn 1984: 32ff; Lyons 1977: 308–311). A thumb is a kind of finger, hence we have five fingers. But normally *finger* will denote 'digit other than thumb'. Similarly, *dog* can come to denote 'male dog' in contrast to *bitch* because the speaker by withholding the sex-marked term implicates that the other sex must be intended. Note that we can think of these inferences in a similar way to scalar implicatures: ⟨*thumb, finger*⟩ and ⟨*bitch, dog*⟩ form ordered pairs where the first member entails the second in a suitable sentence frame, and the use of the second member thus implicates that the speaker is not in a position to assert that the stronger expression holds (hence "I cut my finger" suggests the speaker knows he did not cut a thumb). Diachronically, implicated autohyponymy leads to systematic polysemy (Horn 1984; Kempson 1980).

Type II inferences seem, as mentioned, to have a generalized status in only a few cases, usually over sets of *compatibles* (i.e., sets of alternate, contrasting, terms that may be predicated of the same individual without inconsistency). The color terms are the prototype case here, as described above. In just the same way, if one asserts "The marble is smooth", one implicates that it is not also rough in some places (i.e., that it is smooth all over), although there is clearly no incompatibility between being smooth in some places and rough in others. The negative Type IIb inferences seem to arise rather reliably from the negation of one alternate to the suggestion that another applies. Here of course one needs to distinguish between the cases where such an inference is more or less necessary (as from "The flag is not white" to the conclusion that it must be another color), as opposed to cases where it is freely invited (as from "He doesn't lecture on Wednesdays" to the inference that he does lecture on other days).

It is clear that considerably more work is required before such inferences will be fully understood. They depend in part on the structure of the particular semantic fields. Thus "It will be ready on Wednesday" suggests 'it will not be ready on the prior Tuesday', due to the helical structure of the set of names for days of the week. Research is thus required into the distinct kinds of semantic fields (e.g., taxonomies, meronomies; see Cruse 1986) and the way in which they may set up a basis for specific kinds of inference. Many of the inferences that arise in connection with semantic fields are weak suggestions, which are only clearly attributable to the speaker as implicatures in particular contexts; for example, in the context of an answer to a question, as illustrated in (23) below. They thus lie at the borderline between GCIs and PCIs, because on the one hand they rely on the structure of the vocabulary, and on the other hand, they depend on specific contexts to emerge. This prompts a review of this borderline.

(23) a. A: "Did John climb a mountain?"
          B: "He climbed a hill."
             +> 'As far as the speaker knows, he did not climb a
             mountain.'
      b. A: "What did you see in the larder?"
          B: "I saw a horrid animal."
             +> 'speaker is not sure whether it was a rat, a shrew, a
             mouse or what.'

2.2.4   Residual Problems: Scalar Implicature, GCIs, and PCIs

The classic scalar implicatures considered so far derive from the structure
of the vocabulary, specifically from salient, contrastive alternates ordered
in informational strength. For example, the quantificational scalar implicatures have the systematic properties they have just because the set of,
for example, English quantifiers have the logical relations between themselves that are captured in the traditional square of oppositions. The
implicatures are parasitic on that structure. It is for this reason that they
have the default character they have: they are generalized conversational
implicatures because they depend on invariant salient properties of language structure rather than variable contexts.

But, from the outset of the development of the theory of scalar implicature, it was recognized that in various ways scales may be said to be
pragmatically defined. It has already been noted that the cardinal scale
can be inverted in special pragmatic contexts, although it appears to be
unique for vocabulary-defined scales in this respect. Fauconnier (1975)
pointed out that many scalar implicatures seem to be derived from scales
that depend on a structure of assumptions beyond the lexicon. To provide
a fresh example, the pattern in (24) suggests a scale of driving different-
sized trucks, but clearly this is not an entailment scale, nor one based on
lexical patterning of another sort, but on general assumptions about the
world (permits, or abilities, to drive large trucks normally permit driving
small ones, but not vice versa; but clearly the world could be otherwise).

(24) "He can drive small trucks."
     Implicature: 'He can't drive big ones.'
     ⟨Driving big trucks, driving small trucks⟩
     "He can drive small trucks, and indeed/if not big ones too."

Hirschberg (1985) offers a systematic generalization of these pragmatically given scales and the inferences they allow, but in so doing she

presumes that she can subsume, and thus reduce, all scalar GCIs to PCIs, an issue I will return to after introducing the theory. Hirschberg denies that there is any principled distinction between GCIs and PCIs (1985: 42) and offers instead a theory ranging both over scales given by the lexicon and those given by real-world or pragmatic factors. Consider for example Fred's marathon attempt to cycle from the West Coast to New York City: if we are told he has made it to Utah, we infer that he has not got further east.

(25) A: "How is Fred doing?"
     B: "He's got to Salt Lake City."
        +> 'not Chicago, New York' etc.
        Given the scale: ⟨New York, Chicago, Salt Lake City, Reno⟩

The inference depends on a nonce scale, a contextually given ad hoc scale, which I dub a *Hirschberg scale*. Similarly with the following example:

(26) A: "Did you get Paul Newman's autograph?"
     B: "I got Joanne Woodward's."
        +> 'not Paul Newman's.'
        Given scale of autograph prestige: ⟨Newman, Woodward⟩

She also independently notes that lexical sets of incompatibles can give interesting implicatures—affirmation of one implicates denial of another, whereas denial of one alternate implicates affirmation of another:

(27) A: "Do you speak Spanish?"
     B: "I speak Portuguese."
        +> 'I don't speak Spanish.'

She offers the following generalization. A set of expressions may act as a Hirschberg scale, providing there is *any partial ordering relation defined over them in a contextually salient way.* A partially ordered set, or *poset*, is any set of values V (items ranked)[34] associated with such a partial ordering O; a particular poset is defined by the set of values V and the specific ordering relationship O.[35] Because the ordering relation O might consist of an *is-a-kind-of* relation, we could get a partial ordering ⟨{oak, maple} tree⟩ or if O is the ordering relation *has-parts*, then ⟨book, {chapter 1, chapter 2, ...}⟩. We can accommodate the classical Horn scales as just the special case where O is the entailment relation.[36] Alternates (like {*black, white, red, ...*} are therefore distinctive by virtue of *not* being ordered by the ordering relation. The rules for implicature derivation are then:

(28) *For ordered items*
    a. *Stating* a lower ordered value L implicates the speaker doesn't believe a higher value H or doesn't know if H obtains (schematically "L" +> not-H)
       i. "Some came"
          +> 'not all' (O = entailment, V = $\langle all,\ some \rangle$)
       ii. "It's a tree"
          +> 'not sure which kind' (O = is-a-kind-of, V = $\langle$ {oak, maple, ...}, tree $\rangle$)
       iii. "I've read chapter 1"
          +> 'not the whole book' (O = has-parts, V = $\langle$ whole book, {chapter 1, chapter 2, ...} $\rangle$)
    b. *Denying* a higher ordered value H implicates that the speaker believes a lower one obtains or may obtain (schematically "not H" +> L)
       i. "Not all came"
          +> 'some did'
       ii. "It's not an oak"
          +> 'it is a tree'
       iii. "I haven't read the whole dissertation"
          +> 'I have read some parts'

(29) *For unordered items*
    a. *Affirming* an alternate L_1 implicates other alternates L_2 or L_n are false or unknown ("L_1" +> not-L_2)
       i. "I've read chapter 1"
          +> 'not chapter 2'
       ii. "You need a typhus shot"
          +> 'not cholera too'
    b. *Denying* an alternate L_1 implicates that other alternates L_2 or L_n may be true or unknown ("not L_1" +> L_2)
       i. "It's not an oak"
          +> 'it maybe a maple or ...'
       ii. "She doesn't have a boy"
          +> 'she has a girl'

Some further examples of the kind of pragmatically given partial orderings that one can find underlying particularized implicatures of these sorts follow (where O is the ordering relation):

(30) a. A: "Are you Greek?

      B: "I speak some Greek"

        +> 'I am not Greek.'

   b. O = *has-attribute*

     Poset = ⟨Greek, {Greek-speaking, Greek relatives, Greek
residency, Greek ancestry}⟩

(31) a. A: "So is she married?

      B: "She's engaged"

        +> 'she's not yet married.'

   b. O = *has-prior-stage*

     Poset = ⟨marriage, engagement, going-steady, dating⟩

(32) a. "Smoking is a misdemeanor."

        +> 'Smoking is not a felony.'

   b. O = *is-a-lesser-offense-than*

     Poset = ⟨tort, misdemeanor, felony, capital crime⟩

It must be conceded this is a good account of some elusive PCIs, like those in the immediately preceding examples. But there are a number of problems.[37] The most serious is that the theory will overgenerate implicatures because it offers no constraints on scalehood. One might try to limit the ordering-relations structuring posets in some way, but that is not in the spirit of the theory and it will not be sufficient any way. As we have seen, even the entailment relation will overgenerate if not restricted by our constraints on Horn scales: we do not implicate the negation of everything that entails what we said (if we did, then by saying "two plus two equals four" I would implicate 'It is not necessarily the case that two plus two equals four').[38] Hirschberg (1985: chap. 6) suggests that the relevant poset must be salient to both speaker and addressee, but the question then is how this comes about. Although she points to discourse context, prosody, and the like, it is clear that there is no general solution here.[39] All implicatures are made dependent on the contextually salient ordering relation, so we have no account of implicature generation without an account of how this is arrived at.

    Hirschberg thus sketches a theory under which scalar GCIs and scalar PCIs can be seen to be ultimately related: there are scalar implicatures based on the lexicon (GCIs) and ones based on salient-contrast-in-the-world (PCIs). I see no real conflict between GCI theory and her broader theory, and I do not think it establishes, as she claims (1985: 42), that "the traditional distinction between generalized and particularized implicature is a false one." The GCI theorist is simply claiming that speakers carry their lexicons on their backs as it were, from context to context, and it is mutual knowledge of this fact that elevates the Q-heuristic to a default mode of inference. And indeed Hirschberg (1985: 141) more or less concedes this:

> all other things being equal, a domain independent ordering will be more likely to be assumed salient for the purpose of supporting scalar implicature than will a domain dependent ordering.

2.2.5   Clausal Implicatures

As we saw in chapter 1, Grice was much concerned with the pragmatic inferences associated with the logical connectives. Among those he wished to account for are inferences of epistemic uncertainty that arise from both disjunctions and conditionals (see, e.g., Grice 1989: 8–10). For example, if I say "Sue is either in the attic or in the garden", I implicate that I do not know which. In such a case, the inference cannot be due to the scalar opposition between ⟨*and, or*⟩, because Sue can clearly not be in both places at once. In any case, the scalar inference would be to 'not both p & q', and the inference we are interested in here is to 'the speaker does not know whether p, or whether q'. The inference is general, but defeasible (as shown by "I hid the prize either in the attic or the garden, but I am not telling you which"), and thus has all the hallmarks of a GCI. Grice's explanation was that, if one knew p or knew that q, it would be uncooperative to utter "p or q", and therefore that the speaker must have some chain of reasoning in mind that concludes with $p \vee q$ and yet which does not involve as premises plain p or plain q.

Gazdar (1979: 59–62) has influentially advanced a different way of obtaining the inferences of epistemic uncertainty. He suggests that just as with the scalar implicatures, the inference rests on opposing alternative expressions but, in this case, of a constructional kind. Wherever there is a construction X-ϕ, such that X-ϕ entails ϕ, and an alternative of roughly equal brevity Y-ϕ which is otherwise semantically identical to X-ϕ but fails to entail ϕ, then asserting the weaker Y-ϕ will Q-implicate that the speaker does not know whether ϕ obtains or not. The Gricean reasoning is, of course, that if the speaker was in the position to utter the stronger X-ϕ he or she should do so by the first maxim of Quantity (my Q principle), and if the speaker utters instead the weaker Y-ϕ, he or she can be presumed to be in ignorance of the truth of φ. Gazdar (1979) proposed that the implicature from the weaker expression Y-φ should have the form $\{P\phi, P \sim \phi\}$ (i.e., 'for all the speaker knows φ, for all the speaker knows $\sim$φ'), but I gloss the implicatures informally with *perhaps* or epistemic *may*.

In the case of the connectives, neither *If p then q* nor *p or q* entail their constituent sentences. Moreover, there are contrasting constructions of equal brevity that entail their constituent sentences—for example, *Since p then q* is the entailing counterpart to *If p then q*, and *p and q* the more informative counterpart to *p or q*. Hence we obtain the clausal implicatures illustrated below where (33a) and (34a) carry the implicatures that immediately follow, and (33b) and (34b) are alternative phrasings that would avoid the implicatures (because the constituent sentences are entailed).

(33) a. "If eating eggs is bad for one, we should give up omelets."
        Q +> '(For all the speaker knows) eating eggs may be bad for one, or it may not be bad for one; we perhaps should give up eating omelets, or we perhaps should not.'
     b. "Since eating eggs is bad for one, we should give up omelets."

(34) a. "Sue is a linguist or an anthropologist."
        Q +> 'For all the speaker knows, Sue is perhaps a linguist, or perhaps not a linguist, perhaps an anthropologist, or perhaps not an anthropologist.'
     b. "Sue is a linguist and an anthropologist."

These implicatures capture the inference of epistemic noncommittedness associated with the conditional and the disjunction. Notice that there is a Horn scale ⟨*and, or*⟩ giving rise to an additional but distinct scalar implicature from the use of the disjunction, viz. that the speaker is not in a position to use the conjunction (an implicature which would be satisfied if the speaker knew one of the disjuncts to be false).

If this account is accepted (and not all find it plausible; see Atlas 1993a),[40] then it generalizes to all cases of embedding constructions where strong and weak constructions are both available. In particular, many verbs come in doublets of the appropriate kind. Consider, for example, the contrastive pair *know, believe*, where *know*-φ entails φ, but *believe*-φ does not entail φ or $\sim$φ. There are sentences of roughly equal brevity like (35a–b), which differ only in that one (35a) has a linguistic expression that entails an embedded sentence S, whereas the other (35b) has in the same slot a linguistic expression that fails to entail *S*. Then if one knew that *S* was true, one would be in breach of the first maxim of Quantity (my Q-principle) if one used (35b); hence the sentence in (35b) implicates that the speaker is not in a position to use the stronger sentence in (35a).

(35) a. "The doctor knows that the patient will not recover."
   b. "The doctor believes that the patient will not recover."
      Q +> 'The doctor may or may not know that the patient will not recover.'

There are many such pairs—for example, the verbs *realize, think* or *reveal, claim*, as illustrated in (36).

(36) a. "John realized that the accountant had made a mistake."
      Entails: 'The accountant had made a mistake.'
   b. "John thought that the accountant had made a mistake."
      Q +> 'The accountant may have made a mistake, or he may not have.'
   c. "The government revealed that the files had been destroyed."
      Entails: 'The files had been destroyed.'
   d. "The government claimed that the files had been destroyed."
      Q +> 'The files may have been destroyed, or they may not have been.'

In these cases, such paired expressions also form Horn scales and give rise to the corresponding scalar implicatures. But they are distinct. For example, from "John believes Sue came" we have, via the scale ⟨*know, believe*⟩, the scalar inference '(The speaker knows that) it is not the case that John knows that Sue came'. That implicature is compatible with the speaker knowing that Sue did not come. But the clausal implicature from "John believes Sue came" is 'For all the speaker knows, Sue came, or Sue did not come'. Thus the clausal implicatures indicate epistemic uncertainty about the truth of the embedded sentences, not the speaker's knowledge of (or belief about) the negation of the matrix clause as in scalar implicatures from the same construction.

The class of relevant verbs giving rise to clausal implicatures includes most of the verbs of propositional attitude (unless like *know* or *realize* they entail the truth or falsity of their complements) and most of the verbs of saying (again, unless like *disclose, divulge, admit* they entail the truth or falsity of their complements) (Gazdar 1979: 61). Table 2.2 gives some

Table 2.2
Verbal doublets giving rise to clausal implicatures

Weak verbs not entailing their complements	Strong verbs entailing their complements
say, claim, hold	disclose, divulge, reveal
deny, reject	disprove, refute
predict	foresee
believe	know

examples of relevant verbs, with the column on the left displaying verbs that do not entail their complements, and which will therefore in a frame of the kind *V that* φ give rise to clausal implicatures, whereas the column to the right contains more informative expressions (which do entail their complements) that might have been employed to avoid the implicature. Note that there are not the same strict conditions here on expression alternatives that there are in the case of Horn scales—the requirement simply is that there should be available some alternative expression of roughly equal brevity that due to its semantics would not carry the implicature.

It should be clear from these brief remarks that clausal implicatures have not been heavily researched since Gazdar (1979) proposed this distinction. Most researchers have acknowledged that these are a distinct subspecies of inference and that, by the Gricean argument sketched, they should fall under the first maxim of Quantity or, as here, the Q-principle (but see Atlas 1993b for doubts). Some though consider there is no reason at all to group them together with their scalar cousins (see Frederking 1996).

One issue I have left aside here is the relation of these implicatures to presuppositions. Most analysts hold that presuppositions cannot be reduced to matters of implicature and that presuppositions are attached to their lexical or syntactic triggers (and are thus not detachable in Grice's sense; see Levinson 1983: chap. 3 for review). On Gazdar's (1979: 59–60) theory whereby clausal implicatures cancel inconsistent presuppositions, it was therefore necessary to exclude the possibility that some expression of the form *X*-φ both presupposes and clausally implicates φ, otherwise φ would be inevitably canceled. This was achieved by stipulation in that theory (by blocking the troublesome clausal implicatures), but the relationship clearly requires further research.

2.3   EXPLORING I-INFERENCES

2.3.1   Formulating the Maxim or Heuristic

Recollect that Grice (1975) proposed two maxims of Quantity:

Q1: "Make your contribution as informative as is required (for the current purposes of the exchange)"

Q2: "Do not make your contribution more informative than is required." (Grice 1975)

Is the second maxim (which I abbreviate Q2) otiose? Grice (1975: 46) was unsure:

It might be said that to be overinformative is not a transgression of the CP [Cooperative Principle] but merely a waste of time. However it might be answered that such overinformativeness may be confusing in that it is liable to raise side issues; and there may also be an indirect effect, in that hearers may be misled as a result of thinking that there is some particular POINT in the provision of the excess information.

Perhaps the maxims of Relevance or Manner would handle these "indirect effects." And Grice (1989: 372) later repeated his doubts.

But the doubts seem misplaced, even from a strictly Gricean point of view. Thus he found no trouble imagining the correlate of such a principle in a nonverbal activity such as passing too many screws when one was required (1975: 47). Zipf (1949) has provided statistical data from many kinds of human activity, including language, that seem to support it. Two observations seem to have worried Grice. One was that Relevance might secure the same effects because too much information would surely be irrelevant (indeed, an infringement of the second maxim of Quantity may also constitute an infringement of the maxim of Manner). The other was that the principle did not, it seemed to him, yield the rich set of inferences one would expect in the category of flouted or exploited maxims (only one clear example being provided in Grice 1975: 52). But that, as it turns out, is the wrong place to look.[41] It is in the observance of the maxim that its effects are most apparent, for there is indeed strong evidence in favor of its interpretive corollary, which as a first approximation might be phrased "Don't provide unnecessary information, specifically don't say what would be obvious anyway" (for much crosslinguistic evidence in favor of such a heuristic, see Haiman 1985a). Such a principle might account for our tendency to interpret utterances in line with our knowledge about what is normal or typical, as in (37a). It is clear that providing too much information defeats this kind of interpretation, as in (37b), where the excess information does indeed lead the recipient to think "that there is some particular POINT in the provision of the excess information" as Grice imagined.

(37) a. "He opened the door."
          +> in the normal way by turning the handle.
      b. "He opened the door by turning the handle quickly anti-clockwise."
          +> not in the normal way.

The evidence for such a tendency towards economy is overwhelming. As Haiman (1985a: 150) puts it, "there is a powerful tendency in languages ... to give reduced expression to the familiar and the predictable," a correlation that is "one of the most well-attested in human language." But a tendency of this Zipfian sort could have sources other than the speaker's orientation to some maxim or heuristic.

There is in fact a great deal of evidence for the existence of a speaker's preference for minimal specifications, and its interpretive corollary, to be found in the extensive literature on the empirical properties of conversation (reviewed in Levinson 1987a: 79–98). I will cite just one general observation here. Researchers have noted that there is a decided preference for reference to persons to be achieved by the shortest expression, with the least descriptive content, that will do the job. That this has the status of a maxim, or expected procedure, is shown by the fact that when a speaker is in doubt about whether a brief form will do, the form is often produced with a distinctive rising intonation, and only when lack of response indicates that the recipient has not understood, is a fuller specification given, also with rising intonation; and so on recursively, until recognition is achieved. For example (from Sacks and Schegloff 1979: 19, where the question mark indicates the rising intonation):

(38) A: ... well I was the only one other than that that the uhm tch Fords?
          uh Mrs. Holmes Ford?
          You know uh the the cellist.
                          [
      B: Oh yes. She's she's the cellist.
      A: Yes.

Unless there is some kind of maxim in operation, it would be hard to understand why a speaker would not initially choose, or immediately escalate to, a descriptive phrase that he knew would be more than sufficient to achieve successful reference. Note that a parallel pattern can be observed in self-identifications on the telephone (Schegloff 1979), where (a) intimates expect their identity to be conveyed just by the sample of voice quality in their first "Hello", only escalating step by step, when overt recognition is withheld, with further examples of voice quality, then nicknames or firstnames: "Hello (.) It's me (.) Steve (.) Levinson";[42] (b) persons less intimate may escalate to self-descriptive phrases: "Hello. It's Les (.) Garston (.) the man who called about the plumbing." Those who doubt the existence of some maxim of minimization (e.g., Carston 1995: 223) must therefore find not only an account of the general tendencies for minimization but also an account of this apparent orientation of speakers to just such a principle.

I offer the following (after Levinson 1987b) as a first approximation to a characterization of the maxim involved (more elaborate formulations and discussions can be found in Atlas and Levinson 1981, Levinson 1987a,b). Following the practice initiated by Atlas and Levinson (1981), I call this rendition of Grice's Q2 maxim the *Principle of Informativeness*, or the *I-Principle* for short.

(39) *I-Principle*

Speaker's maxim: the maxim of Minimization. "Say as little as necessary"; that is, produce the minimal linguistic information sufficient to achieve your communicational ends (bearing Q in mind).

Recipient's corollary: the Enrichment Rule. Amplify the informational content of the speaker's utterance, by finding the most *specific* interpretation, up to what you judge to be the speaker's m-intended point,[43] unless the speaker has broken the maxim of Minimization by using a marked or prolix expression. Specifically:

a. Assume the richest temporal, causal and referential connections between described situations or events, consistent with what is taken for granted.

b. Assume that stereotypical relations obtain between referents or events, unless this is inconsistent with (a).

    c. Avoid interpretations that multiply entities referred to (assume referential parsimony); specifically, prefer coreferential readings of reduced NPs (pronouns or zeros).

    d. Assume the existence or actuality of what a sentence is about if that is consistent with what is taken for granted.

This characterization contains a number of undefined terms. The direction in which one would hope for clarification is mostly clear enough, but none of these are trivial notions. For now, I can offer only the following glosses:

1. *Specificity*: p is *more specific than* q if (a) p is more informative than q (e.g., p entails q); and (b) p is isomorphic with q (i.e., each term or relation in p has a denotation that is a subset of the denotations of the corresponding expressions in q). (For further remarks, see below.)

2. *Stereotype*: As Putnam (1975: 249ff) notes, a stereotype needn't have a close relation to reality or statistical tendency (e.g., "as fierce as a gorilla" or "absent-minded professor"). On Putnam's view, meanings are stereotypes that may fail to determine correct extensions; on my view, stereotypes are connotations associated with meanings, but not part of them, which nevertheless play a role in interpretation.[44]

3. *Informativeness*: p is *more informative than* q if the set of states of affairs that q rules out is a proper subset of the set that p rules out (Bar-Hillel and Carnap 1952; Popper 1959). This account makes a number of idealizations and thus can only be considered a first approximation (see discussion in Levinson 1987b: 404–406).

4. *Minimal*: One needs to distinguish *semantic generality* (crucial here; e.g., *building* vs. *hall*) from *expression brevity* (e.g., *hall vs. auditorium*). Zipf (1949) argues that these tend to conflate (e.g., a pronoun is both semantically general and brief). This follows from the conjunction of his Law of Abbreviation ('the more use, the shorter the expression') and his Principle of Economic Versatility ('the more semantically general, the more use'). Equally in the Prague School theory of markedness, the unmarked expression in an opposition is both formally less complex and semantically general, whereas the marked expression is formally more complex and semantically more specific (Jakobson 1939; see also discussion in Horn 1989: chap. 3).

This characterization is compatible with the original proposal in Atlas and Levinson (1981). We sketched there a two-level account: first, all the competing interpretations are generated; then the most informative is selected. The principles generating the set of competing interpretations were left open in that account, but clearly they should delimit the set of possible interpretations. In the sketch just given, the relevant principles are given a bit more flesh: they include the search for maximal cohesion, or temporal, spatial, causal, and referential connectedness, and the presumption of stereotypical relations and the actuality of referents. Again, in the earlier account, it was claimed that I-inferences:

> enrich 'what is said' by *reshaping* the range of possible states of affairs associated with 'what is said' to a narrower range of possible states of affairs associated with 'what is communicated.' 'What is communicated' is MORE PRECISE than 'what is said'." In contrast, Q-inferences were held "to *shrink* the range of possible states of affairs ... 'What is communicated is MORE DEFINITE than 'what is said', (Atlas and Levinson 1981: 35–36, italics added)

The contrast intended was the idea that I-inferences are not just more informative in the sense that they entail what is said (that is equally true of most Q-implicatures): they introduce semantic relations absent from what is said, and in that sense can be said to reshape the proposition expressed (whereas Q-implicatures of the scalar type only introduce a negative bound from within the same semantic field). I have tried to capture this notion by building into the concept of more specificity (replacing the earlier concept of more precision) the requirement that although the interpretation is (partially) isomorphic with the content of what is said, each constituent may have a more restricted sense and denotation. Thus the phrase *a spoon in the cup* may have the interpretation 'a metal spoon partially inside the ceramic teacup', *went and bought* may have the interpretation 'went and then bought', *took a drink* the interpretation 'imbibed an alcoholic drink', *she bit her nails* the interpretation 'she bit her own finger nails', and so on. The isomorphism holds of course not at the level of English phrases and glosses but at the abstract level of propositional representation: what is implicated is a specialization of one or more of each of the intensions of what is said.[45] It corresponds to the fact, noted below, that it is usually difficult to express an I-implicature as an unrelated proposition conjoined to 'what is said'.[46]

Now, under the I-Principle rubric, I want to collect a whole range of inferences that appear to go in just the reverse direction to that in which Q-implicatures tend. To emphasize the tension, we may say that I-implicatures are inferences from *the lack of further specification to the lack of need for it, whereas Q-implicatures are inferences from the lack of informational richness to the speaker's inability to provide it.*[47] Under the rubric of the I-Principle, we can gather a range of well-known phenomena, as follows (+> stands for 'implicates'; ++> stands for 'communicates', i.e., the sum of what is 'said' and the I-implicature in question):

(40) *Conditional perfection* (Geis and Zwicky 1971)
"If you mow the lawn, I'll give you five dollars."
I +> 'If you don't mow the lawn, I will not give five dollars' or perhaps 'If I give you $5, you will have mown the lawn.'
++> '(If and) only if you mow the lawn, will I give you five dollars.'

(41) *Conjunction buttressing* (e.g., Atlas and Levinson 1981)
An utterance of the form "p and q" where p and q describe events, such as "John turned the key and the engine started."
++> 'p and then q' (temporal sequence)
'p therefore q' (causal connectedness)
'A did X in order to cause q' (teleology, intentionality)

(42) *Bridging* (Clark and Haviland 1977)
"John unpacked the picnic. The beer was warm."
+> 'The beer was part of the picnic.'

(43) *Inference to stereotype* (Atlas and Levinson 1981)
"John said 'Hello' to the secretary and then he smiled."
++> 'John said 'Hello' to the female secretary and then John smiled.'

(44) *Negative strengthening* (Horn 1989: chap. 5)
"I don't like Alice."
+> 'I positively dislike Alice.'

(45) *Preferred local coreference*
"John came in and he sat down."
++> 'John$_1$ came in and he$_1$ sat down.'

(46) *Mirror maxim* (Harnish 1976: 359)
"Harry and Sue bought a piano."
+> 'They bought it together, not one each.'

(47) *Noun-noun compounds (NN-relations)* (Hobbs et al. 1993)
"The oil compressor gauge."
+> 'The gauge that measures the state of the compressor that compresses the oil.'

(48) *Specializations of spatial terms* (Herskovits 1986)
   a. "The nail is in the wood."
      +> 'The nail is buried in the wood.'
   b. "The spoon is in the cup."
      +> 'The spoon has its bowl-part in the cup.'

(49) *Possessive interpretations* (Sperber and Wilson 1986)
   a. "Wendy's children"
      +> 'those to whom she is parent.'
   b. "Wendy's house"
      +> 'the one she lives in.'
   c. "Wendy's responsibility"
      +> 'the one falling on her.'
   d. "Wendy's theory"
      +> 'the one she originated.'

It is immediately clear that by comparison to, say, scalar Q-implicatures, these inferences are heterogeneous, and the kinds of procedures involved in actually deriving the inferences in question may differ significantly. The claim therefore is not that the same mental algorithms compute this range of inferences but rather that there is a single overarching principle that *licenses* them, legitimating the application of any of the subprocesses involved, and that this by virtue of its overall relation to the Q- and M-Principles regulates the conditions under which the particular inferences are blocked or canceled. To belabor the point: the I-principle here operates as an instruction to find an interpretation that meets certain requirements (positive, stereotypical, highly specific interpretations).

Now a question that immediately arises is: in what sense are these I-inferences *generalized*? Most of these inferences interact with shared background presumptions, which might in principle vary, and thus the inferences might have none of the cross-context, even crosslinguistic, invariance that are the hallmarks of GCIs. But at a sufficient level of abstraction, it is quite clear that the kinds of inferences here collected— for example, conjunction-buttressing, negative-strengthening, preferred patterns of coreference—do hold as preferred interpretations across contexts and indeed across languages. And at a slightly higher level of abstraction, the different types collected can be seen to share the property of maximizing the informational load by narrowing the interpretation to a specific subcase of what has been said.

Perhaps the sense of commonality between the different subtypes of I-inferences can be reinforced by contrasting their properties with those of the Q-inferences:

(50) Q- vs. I-inferences
    a. Common properties of I-inferences
        i.   They are inferences to more specific interpretations: what is implicated is a specialization of what is said.
        ii. The inference is positive in character: the extension of what is implicated is a proper subset of the extension of what is said, the extension being restricted positively (not as with scalar implicatures, by complementarity).
        iii. The inference is typically guided by stereotypical assumptions; to spell such inferences out more fully would be both redundant and onerous, and perhaps (in the case of euphemism, etc.) socially undesirable.
        iv. The inference makes no essential reference to something else that might have been said but wasn't (call this the absence of a metalinguistic element).[48]
    b. Contrasting properties of the Q scalar implicatures
        i.   Q-inferences are inferences to more precise interpretations: e.g., the scalar inference 'Some and not all x are G' is a subcase of what was said: "Some x are G'.
        ii. The inference is negative in character: the extension of what is implicated is a proper subset of the extension of what is said because the complement of that proper subset is ruled out by the negative scalar implicature (e.g., "some" +> 'not all').
        iii. There is no reference to stereotypical or indeed any background (nonlinguistic) knowledge in the derivation of a scalar GCI (although such knowledge may cancel a scalar implicature).
        iv. The inference is metalinguistic: it makes essential reference to something else (the stronger scalar item) that might have been said but wasn't.

Before proceeding, I should pause to deal with some problems that have arisen with these observations. First, there are rival accounts of some, if not all, of these phenomena. Let us turn first to conditional perfection. Van der Auwera (1995, 1997) claims that much older accounts in the heritage of Ducrot offer a better explanation than the standard I-implicature one: conditional perfection is actually just a scalar Q-implicature; the scale is of the form $\langle((if\ p,\ then\ q)\ \&\ (if\ r,\ then\ q)),\ if\ p\ then\ q\rangle$, and by asserting the conditional, one implicates that there is no other conditional with consequent q. As he acknowledges, this runs afoul of my constraint on Horn scales requiring equal lexicalization,[49] but he jettisons that constraint and in general reanalyzes the nature of scales in favor of ranked propositions of arbitrary complexity. This is just a different theory of Q-type inferences, and I shall leave it to the reader to adjudicate (the theory seems interestingly allied to Hirschberg's PCI account of scalar implicature, which might subsume it). Carston (1995: 221–222) notes that the conditional perfection implicature is actually generalized to the point that it may run against stereotypical assumptions: "If you don't mow the lawn, I'll give you five dollars" now suggests that *not* mowing the lawn is a necessary condition for the speaker's gift. In fact, it is noteworthy that any form of words that suggests a *sufficient* condition is liable to enrichment to a *necessary* condition: "Mow the lawn and I'll give you five dollars", "Go on: earn five dollars and mow the lawn", and so on.[50] Thus the nature of the inference licensed by the I-principle must be to the necessary condition, provided that is consistent with what is taken for granted (in "If the door is locked, I have a key", the inference does not go through).

Second, some commentators have pointed out a failure of precision, at least in earlier formulations. Carston (1995) for example points out that whereas I have represented Q-implicatures as just the content implicated, not the conjunction of implicature with what is said, I have represented I-inferences in terms of the total signification of what is said plus what is implicated (Levinson 1987a). Correcting this, the conditional-perfection implicature from "If you mow the lawn, I'll give you five dollars" should read 'If you don't mow the lawn, I won't give you five dollars', with the total communicated content 'Iff you mow the lawn, will I give you five dollars'. Carston goes on to note that the implicature alone does not entail the content of what is said, as she thought I claimed, and moreover that as a result my distinction between Q- and I-inferences collapses.[51] The failure of precision was regrettable, and occasionally where it matters I use the symbol $+>$ (and the term *implicate*) for the pure implicated content, and $++>$ (and the barbaric **implicate*) for the total communicated or conveyed content (or at least for the sum of what is said and the relevant implicatures being discussed). But there is in fact a reason for the lapse: it is difficult, in probably most cases of I-implicature, to represent the implicature alone without that implicature entailing the content of what is said; for example, in the case of conjunction buttressing where utterances of the form *p and q* implicate something like '*p* and then *q*' (or 'after *p*, *q*'), the latter entails the content of what is said. This is not an accident: it follows from the nature of I-implicatures that they are enrichments of what is said, whereas Q-implicatures merely exclude something else that might have been said but wasn't. Thus we can often represent the Q-implicature as a conjunct which does not itself include the content of what is said, whereas I-implicatures are not so satisfactorily represented in this way. For this reason, I will normally cite I-*implicatures in their inclusive form without special typographical conventions.

However, the lapse has none of the dire theoretical consequences that Carston (1995: 220) hopes for. As stated (apparently not clearly enough) in Levinson 1987a and three paragraphs above, in the case of both Q- and I-inferences (and indeed in all implicatures other than flouts, exploitations, or tropes), the communicated content will entail what is said (otherwise, what would be the value-added content of implicatures?). The difference lies in the character of the value added to what is said: in the case of I-implicatures the inferences are positive strengthenings towards the stereotypical, which make no metalinguistic reference; in the case of Q-inferences they are inferences to the negation of statements employing stronger alternative linguistic expressions. I-inferences import rich assumptions about the world; Q-implicatures circumscribe what has been said by what else might have been said but wasn't. One would of course wish to be more precise, but the characterization seems to me intuitively clear.

The difference in character between Q- and I-implicatures can perhaps best be appreciated by considering how they might yield inconsistent implicatures. As mentioned, they appear to generate implicatures in opposite directions: informally the Q-principle specifies "What you haven't said you do not mean (otherwise you should have said so)", whereas the I-principle can be glossed "What you haven't bothered to say, you expect me, the recipient, to supply." Thus, if we permit a scale ⟨*since, and*⟩, which in fact is barred by the constraint that scalar items must be "about" the same semantic relations, then we would obtain implicatures that are not only inconsistent but actually contradictories:

(51) "John turned the key and the engine started."
      I ++> 'Since John turned the key, the engine started.'
      Pseudo-scale: ⟨*since, and*⟩
      no Q +> 'It is not the case that: Since John turned the key, the engine started.'

In this case the clash is averted by the constraints on Horn scales (see section 2.2.2). But there are cases where genuine clashes occur—that is, where the potential implicatures from Q- and I-principles are inconsistent. In these cases, it appears, as a matter of observation, that Q-inferences always take precedence (or cancel) I-implicatures. It will transpire that single sentences will often engender multiple implicatures. For example, in (52) the disjunction gives rise to a clausal Q-implicature that defeats the I-inference to conditional perfection.

(52) "If you come, he'll forgive you, or even if you don't come he may forgive you anyway."
Q-implicature: 'It's possible that even if you don't come he may forgive you anyway.' [clausal implicature from disjunction]
Potential I-implicature: 'If you don't come he will not forgive you.'
Q-implicature defeats I-implicature.

2.3.2   Some Prominent I-Implicatures

2.3.2.1   Conjunction-buttressing and Parataxis   Let us now review in a bit more detail some of these kinds of I-implicature. I have noted that conjunction is ripe for I-enrichment: when events are conjoined, they tend to be read as temporally successive and, if at all plausible, as causally linked.[52] There are many rival accounts of this phenomenon (see Lang 1984 for an attempt to embed this problem in the larger range of possible conjunction interpretations). Partee (1984) has suggested that the temporal succession reading works a bit like anaphora: a past-tense event description establishes a reference interval R (intuitively just after the event) that is picked up by the next past tense; if the succeeding clause describes an event, R includes the event; if it describes a state, the duration of the state includes R.[53] Similarly, Kamp and Reyle (1993: 521ff) note a presumption of temporal vicinity, which in the case of descriptions of states will be read as temporal inclusion and in the case of events as temporal succession. They observe that this seems not to depend solely on world knowledge and appear to conclude that the matter is semantic or that it at least must be captured in the semantic representation or DRS. The pragmaticist has in fact no quarrel with the representational ideas here but insists on the pragmatic character of the inference, with important implications for the role of pragmatics in the construction of semantic representations, an issue taken up in chapter 3. The formal-semantics tradition, incidentally, says nothing about the causal and teleological

implicatures from *p and q*, so in any case it needs supplementing with a pragmatic account. But what the pragmatist will insist on is that the succession inference is pragmatic, hence defeasible under conditions where the contrary is assumed, or where it is explicitly or implicitly canceled:

(53) a. "Hans wrote a novel and he sold the rights to Macmillan."
     I ++> 'Hans wrote a novel and then sold the rights
     to Macmillan.'
   b. "Hans wrote a novel and he sold the rights to Macmillan in advance." (implicature canceled by the interpretation of *in advance*)
   c. "Hans wrote a novel and sold the rights to Macmillan but not necessarily in that order." (implicature canceled by explicit denial)
   d. "Hans wrote a novel and made up the plot as he commuted to work." (implicature defeated by our knowledge that one must make up the plot while or before writing a novel).

Equally, of course, our knowledge of the world may defeat default interpretations. Thus sequentiality is overruled by assumptions of simultaneity in (54a–b) (Schmerling 1975: 214).

(54) a. The lights went off and I couldn't see.
   b. Joan sung a ballad and accompanied herself on the guitar.

Occasionally the very search for some rich connectedness may require the rejection of the 'and then' interpretation in favor of a reversed sequence (prosodic clues being important here):

(55) a. He got a Ph.D. and he only did a month's research!
   b. But *she* won an Olympic medal and she was born in a slum and undernourished as a child.

Most authors agree that although the inference to temporal sequence is defeasible, and in some conjunctions hardly seems to even arise, it is nevertheless crosslinguistically the default interpretation of two conjoined past-tensed event descriptions without special prosodic or other marking (see, e.g., Haiman 1985c; Lascarides and Asher 1993). Nonce-implicature theorists may want to insist that it all depends on content and context and that there is no such default interpretation, but Carston (1995: 232) points out that even when our knowledge of the world would suggest '*q* before *p*', still we attempt to read "*p* and *q*" as '*p* before *q*':

(56) He opened the door and she handed him the key.

Clearly there are language-specific semantic constraints on this sequential interpretation, arising from tense, aspect, and Aktionsart, gapping, and reduction, which are highly complex. Although *He researched the subject and gave some lectures* carries the normal implicature, there are no sequential implicatures associated with *He is researching the subject and he is giving some lectures, He was researching the subject and giving some lectures, He researches the subject and he gives some lectures,* or *He used to research the subject and he used to give some lectures,* which encode overlapping, ongoing activities. If the Aktionsarten of the verbs are mismatched, one suggesting a state the other a dynamic event, we tend to get an inclusion reading as in *He knew he was wrong and apologized,* or *He slept and fell off the chair,* or we may force an habitual simultaneous reading out of the dynamic verb as in *He lived in Cambridge and traveled to London.* As well, some sentences with *and* simply do not have an underlying conjunction semantics: *She went and spoiled her dress* or *I've got to try and find it* involve complex idiomatic expressions of the form *go/ try and VP* (Schmerling 1975). In fact, conjunction reduction in English seems often to grammaticalize specific interpretations (as Schmerling documents). All of these factors are well known, if not well understood, and I mention them simply to emphasize that the I-implicature can only go through when not blocked by this web of semantic factors.[54]

Now these same interpretive tendencies are observable in parataxis or the unmarked adjunction of clauses, which is as predicted: there is no possible Horn scale between nothing (i.e., sheer adjunction) and other linguistic expressions that might give rise to Q-implicatures that would block the I-inference to maximal connectedness (however, I will show that the possibility of a Manner contrast between explicit conjunction and parataxis does arise). Hence (57a) and (57b) suggest their respective implicatures, pretty much as the corresponding sentences with *and* would.

(57) a. "John turned the switch. The motor started."
    I ++> 'John turned the switch and then as an intended result the motor started.'

  b. "John lost his grip on the cliff. He fell and broke his leg."
    I ++> 'John lost his grip on the cliff and then as an (unintended) result he fell and broke his leg.'

  c. "John fell and broke his leg. He lost his grip on the cliff."
    I ++> 'John fell and broke his leg. The reason was he (had just before) lost his grip on the cliff.'

d. "John fell and broke his leg and he lost his grip on the cliff."
   No implicature: 'John fell and broke his leg. The reason was he
   lost his grip on the cliff.'

Some have even considered that parataxis, or more properly asyndetic conjunction, should be interpreted simply as elided conjunction (Lang 1984: 80). But the range of possible invited inferences is much wider with parataxis as shown by (57c) with the assumed temporal order reversed from the clauses, an interpretation not available to the same sentence with an explicit conjunction as in (57d) (Gazdar 1979: 44). In fact, sheer adjunction of clauses is often sufficient to invoke a diversity of complex interclausal relations, as in Bloomfield's "It's 10 o'clock, I have to go home" (see Matthews 1981: 32ff; Hobbs 1979). Indeed, many languages make do without the complex set of intersentential connectives available in English, using parataxis instead. For example, the Australian language Guugu Yimithirr lacks sentential disjunctions, indicative conditionals, and sentential conjunctions, which are all signaled paratactially (in the case of disjunctions and conditionals, with the addition of dubitative or emphatic particles). The following examples indicate how one would translate English sentences with connectives: [55]

(58) *English target:* 'Either he died or he didn't.'
     Nyulu biinii nguba,   nguba   gaari.
     he   died perhaps, perhaps not
     'Perhaps he died, perhaps he didn't.'

(59) *English target:* 'If you go, you'll get meat.'
     Nyundu budhu dhadaa, nyundu minha maanaa bira.
     You   maybe go   you   meat get   for sure
     'Maybe you will go, (then) you will certainly get meat.'

(60) *English target:* 'I came and he left.'
     Ngayu gaday; nyulu dhaday.
     I   came he   left
     'I came. He left.'

Although it may be unusual for the *main* way of expressing conditionals to be parataxis (plus or minus emphatic particles), many languages can optionally express conditionals through parataxis. In English, we do this by, for example, conjoining or adjoining an imperative and an indicative as in (61a–b), but in Vietnamese (as well as Chinese, Hindi, Hua, and in many other languages) two ordinary indicatives will do, as in (61c) (Haiman 1985a: 44–5).[56]

(61) a. Touch that chest and I'll scream.
    b. You're so smart, you fix it.
    c. Không có màn không chịu nổi.
       not   be net   not   bear can
       'If there's no net, you can't stand it.'

The basis for an I-implicature from an utterance of the form "*p. q*" to 'if *p*, then *q*' is not clear. But Haiman suggests that in both cases there is a relation between ordering and the way in which the second sentence is informationally processed (according to Greenberg's (1966a: 84) universal 14, conditionals in all languages tend to have a canonical order with the antecedent first). Thus in conditionals, the antecedent provides the context for the assessment of the consequent.[57]

Parataxis is an important instance of the tendency to find from minimal specifications maximally cohesive, rich interpretations. Some theorists, like Hobbs (1979), suggest that this kind of inference is possible because there is in fact a fixed taxonomy of possible clause relations, and the recipient need only select between the half dozen or so major relations in order to fix an interpretation.

We have noted that sentences joined by parataxis often invite the same inferences as conjunctions. But we have also noted that paratactic inferences are a broader class. In some languages, there is a clear opposition between explicit conjunction and sheer parataxis, with parataxis suggesting a closer more integrated sequence of events, and sentences explicitly conjoined suggesting that the events either took place at a different time, or were not connected, or involved different protagonists, and so forth (Haiman 1985a: 111–115). An account of this can be given in terms of the I- and M-principles, in a pattern that will shortly become familiar: minimal forms invite maximally rich interpretations, maximal forms defeat them.[58] Haiman goes on to suggest that there is a cline of the form *conjunction > parataxis > gapping/reduction* where the more reduced the form, the greater the suggestion that the two events are actually a single complex one.[59]

The classic cases of "bridging inferences" (Clark and Haviland 1977) occur in paratactic (asyndetic) constructions (but the inferences go through in explicit conjunctions too), and they seem to be forced by the attempt to find coherence across the two conjoined or adjoined clauses.

Note that although they may utilize background knowledge as in (62a) (where we all know that every car has a steering wheel), or activate frames as in (62b) (all dining rooms have windows and some dining rooms have French windows), they are completely independent of such information.

(62) a. "Harold bought an old car. The steering wheel was loose."
I +> 'The steering wheel of the car.'

   b. "Patience walked into the dining room. The French windows were open."
I +> 'The dining room had French windows'[60]

   c. "Hilda climbed into the capsule. The proton-thruster was attached to the console."
I +> 'The capsule had a proton-thruster.'

   d. "Hilda climbed into the capsule. A proton-thruster was attached to the console."
I +> 'The capsule had a proton-thruster.'

It is the presumptive quality of the inference, even in the absence of stereotypical information, that is a hallmark of I-implicature. Notice that the presumption doesn't seem to reside in the definiteness of the NP (as accounts in terms of accommodation presume), because both (62c) and (62d) carry the same I-implicature (but differ in inferences as to the uniqueness and normality of proton-thrusters in capsules; see Hawkins 1978, 1991).

2.3.2.2   Negative Strengthening

2.3.2.2.1   Gradable Antonyms   There are a large range of implicatures associated one way or another with negative statements (see Horn 1989). Negative scales, as we have already seen, are regular sources of Q-implicatures (thus "Not all of them came" suggests 'Some of them came'). Double-negatives, litotes (like *a not insignificant achievement*), and their implicatures fall under my third maxim, the M-principle. Sometimes, as we shall see in chapter 3, implicatures fall under the scope of negation (so-called metalinguistic negation).

But various kinds of negative strengthening are clearly attributable to the I-principle. As a first example, consider the gradable antonyms (Lyons 1977: 271ff) like {*hot, cold*}, {*large, small*}, {*good, bad*}, and so on, which allow explicit grading (as in *this is hotter than that*). Although these are clearly semantically contraries (something can be neither hot nor

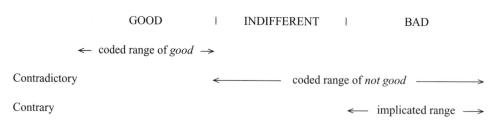

Figure 2.4
Contradictories implicating contraries

cold, neither good nor bad, etc.), it has long been noted that the negation of a gradable adjective tends to be interpreted *as if* the antonyms were themselves contradictory—that is, as if *not good* meant *bad* excluding middle ground (see Lyons 1977: 278, who suggests a Gricean account; and Horn 1989: 205ff). This amounts to the following (potentially confusing) conclusion: the negative of a gradable, which is in fact a weak contradictory including the middle ground, implicates the contrary, its antonym, excluding the middle ground. Figure 2.4 may help to clarify and show how this implicature informationally restricts, and thus strengthens, the negative predicate exemplified in (63).

(63) "It was not a good thing to do."
      I ++> 'It was a bad thing to do.'

The implicature appears to be restricted to the denial of the unmarked antonym (*good, tall, large* etc., as shown by the neutral question form, e.g., *How tall is he?* which does not presume that he is tall). The process is fairly, if not entirely, general. It may be partly motivated by the polite avoidance of disparaging antonyms or by euphemism. Thus Greenberg (1966b, cited in Horn 1989: 336) notes that many languages have no word for 'bad' because it is so routinely implicated by 'not good'. Note that, as discussed above under the Q-principle, gradable predicates of these sorts sometimes form scales, with associated implicatures from the assertion of the weaker expressions and from the denial of the stronger ones. One might therefore expect complex interactions between Q- and I-implicatures here, but on the whole they do not occur. This is because (a) the scales are split and never encompass both antonyms (there is no scale *⟨good, bad⟩ as there is ⟨excellent, good⟩) and (b) the unmarked pair of the gradable predicate (e.g., *good*) is usually the weaker item in a scale with an extreme value as the stronger (e.g., ⟨*excellent, good*⟩ with negative scale ⟨*not-*

good, not-excellent⟩) and because weaker items become the stronger item in a negative scale, they fail to generate Q-implicatures ("*not good*" has no scalar implicatures).[61] Additionally, gradable predicates like *like* appear to yield similar inferences, here to the contrary 'dislike', as in (64).

(64) "I don't like garlic."
      +> 'I dislike garlic.'

2.3.2.2.2   NEG-Raising (NR)   There is a tendency for negative main sentences with subordinate clauses to be read as negations of the subordinate clause:

(65) a. "I don't think he is reliable."
          I ++> 'I think he is not reliable.'
      b. "I don't think that the suspect wanted to believe it was a crime."
          I ++> 'I think that the suspect wanted to believe it was not a crime.'

The historical ruminations on this phenomenon go back at least to St. Anselm, as Horn (1989: 308ff) describes. The remarks in this section are based on Horn's excellent account. In the period of transformational grammar when it was assumed that there should be a direct relation between meaning and deep structure, it was proposed that this interpretation, whereby the sentence is read as if the negation occurred in the lower clause, should be explained by supposing that the negative was downstairs in deep structure and derivationally raised (hence the epithet Neg-raising [NR], which the modern reader may prefer to think about in terms of interpretive Neg-lowering). In that case, it was noted, the negative could be moved from arbitrarily low down in the sentence, providing the predicates over which it jumped were of a certain type (see (65b)). The relevant predicates governing this phenomenon appear to be verbs of mental activity or desire (*think, believe, want*) or impersonal verbs embedding sentences like *It doesn't seem likely* or *It is not to be expected that he'll come*. But why?

The syntactic analysis no longer fits with today's syntactic theories, and in any case it runs into trouble with the fact that allegedly raised negatives can be lexicalized as in "Nobody believes he'll do it", which implicates 'Everyone believes he won't do it' (Horn 1978). This leaves the possibilities of explanation in terms of semantic ambiguity or pragmatic enrichment. The essential semantic observations are as follows:

1. NR sentences have two interpretations:

(66) "I don't believe that he came"
  a. 'I believe that he did not come'
     (the NR-reading or narrow-scope interpretation)
  b. 'It is not the case that I believe that he came'
     (the 'literal' L-reading or wide-scope interpretation)

2. The NR-reading (or interpretation) entails the literal L-reading,[62] but not vice versa; the NR-reading is thus more informative than the L-reading. Or to put it another way, the NR-reading is the stronger contrary, whereas the L-reading is the weaker contradictory (see figure 2.5):

(67) "It's not probable that the Dow Jones will recover"
     $++>$ 'It's probable it won't recover.'

3. Only some verbs permit the NR-reading; many verbs of propositional attitude, or other verbs allowing internal negations of subordinate clauses, like *know, realize, be certain* do not (e.g., "I don't know that he came" cannot be read 'I know he didn't come'). In general, the class of verbs permitting NR seems to be a subset, in any language, of verbs of opinion, volition, obligation, probability, and perception (Horn 1978, 1989: 322–323).

(68) a. I don't believe the USA will put another man on the moon
        (contradictory: $\sim$Bp)
     b. I believe the USA will not put another man on the moon
        (contrary: B $\sim$ p)

Let us set aside the possibility that negated NR predicates could just be ambiguous in some way (in effect the claim that, e.g., *not believe* has an idiomatic, noncompositional reading equivalent to the meaning of *believe not*). There are intrinsic impediments to such a claim—fox example, *Nobody believes we can win a nuclear war* would require, on an idiom theory, another idiom linking *Nobody believes p* with the meaning of

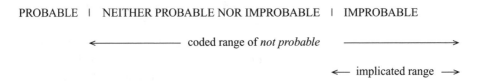

PROBABLE | NEITHER PROBABLE NOR IMPROBABLE | IMPROBABLE

←————————— coded range of *not probable* —————————→

←— implicated range —→

Figure 2.5
Neg-raising as implicated contraries (see example 67)

Everybody believes that not-p, and so on for every appropriate incorporated negative and every NR predicate. Second, there are generalizations
to be captured by taking the alternative, pragmatic approach that are
unavailable to the idiom/ambiguity approach. The assumption taken
here is that NR-interpretations are in fact I-implicatures (not, e.g., Q-
implicatures) for reasons that will become clear.

The central problem for understanding the phenomenon is understanding the third point above, why just some predicates allow the NR-
reading. The categories of predicates responsible have resisted any simple
semantic generalizations (indeed have baffled generations of linguists),
and the processes are indeed not entirely predictable. But there is a good,
if not exceptionless, overall generalization about which predicates allow
the NR-reading, which can best be stated in Horn's arithmetic scalar
model. Take the set of predicates indicating epistemic states, states of
knowledge, opinion, and the like: in English, these include *know, realize,
be certain, be evident/clear/sure, be odd/significant, believe, suppose,
think, be likely/probable, seem, appear*, and so on. Let us extract as a
coherent set that form a pair of positive and negative scales the epistemic
adjectives ⟨*certain, likely, possible*⟩ with corresponding negative meta-
scale ⟨*impossible, not likely, not certain*⟩. Then we can map these onto the
arithmetic square of oppositions as shown in figure 2.6 (from Horn 1989:
325), with the strong items in a contrary relation, the weak items in a
pragmatic subcontrary relation, and the diagonal lines across the square
(e.g., from *certain* to *not certain*) constituting contradictories.

By Löbner's test, *likely* and *not likely* are intolerant: **It's likely she'll go
and likely she won't*, so are placed above the 0.5 midline, whereas *possible*
and *not certain* are tolerant (*It's possible but not certain she'll go*) and
therefore belong below the midline. By the suspension tests *likely* is below
certain (*It's likely, and indeed certain ...* but *??It's certain, and indeed
likely ...*) and so should be placed just above the midline. Now it turns
out that it is predicates in this position, just above the midline like *likely*,
that permit NR-interpretations: thus "It's not likely that she'll come"
suggests 'It's likely that she'll not come'. Stronger intolerant predicates
generally do not ("It is not certain that she'll come" fails to implicate 'It is
certain she will not come'[63]). And weak, tolerant ones like *possible* likewise do not have NR-readings ("It's not possible she'll come" fails to
implicate 'It's possible she will not come').

Horn's generalization is that NR-readings can only occur with (a relatively weak) intolerant predicate P if both the contrary $P \sim$ and the

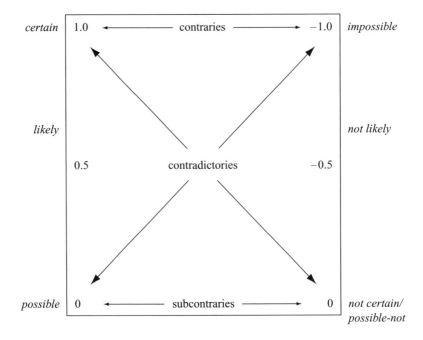

Figure 2.6
Epistemic predicates in the arithmetic square

contradictory $\sim P$ are close to each other and to the 0.5 midpoint, as illustrated in figure 2.7.

Another way of putting the same generalization is to say that NR-interpretations are, as noted above, from the statement of a *contradictory* (e.g., $\sim P$) to the inference of a *contrary* ($P\sim$). Because only tolerant predicates can have contraries (intolerant ones below the 0.5 line will have only subcontraries), it follows that only intolerant predicates (scalar items above the 0.5 line) yield NR-readings. Besides, the contradictory of a weak scalar like *possible* (namely, *impossible*) is informationally stronger than its subcontrary (*possible not*), so there can be no implicature to a stronger subcontrary. But why should strong intolerant predicates (e.g., *know, be certain*) be barred from NR-interpretations? The answer that Horn gives (1989: 326ff) is that the NR- interpretations are only possible when the difference between them and the literal L-interpretations carries minimal functional load: "a lower-clause understanding for higher-clause negation tends to be possible only when the two readings for the outer-neg

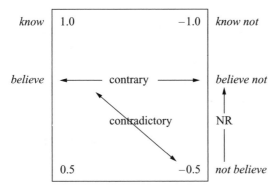

Figure 2.7
Restricted locale for Neg-raising within the square

sentence that would result are almost, but not quite, truth-conditionally identical" (Horn 1989: 329). Clearly this condition is not met in the case of a strongly intolerant, strong scalar item like *know*: there is an enormous informational gulf between the contradictory (*not knowing that p*) and the contrary (*knowing that not p*): NR-interpretation here would magically convert our ignorance into knowledge (would it were so easy)!

I return now to the question: what type of implicature is responsible for NR-understandings? It is immediately evident from the figure above that NR-interpretations cannot be due to the Q-principle. In fact, they work in exactly the reverse direction: they run *upwards* along the negative scale (here ⟨*know-not, not-believe*⟩). But this of course is just what the Q-principle in general disallows: if there is a stronger alternate expression on a scale, then the Q-principle enjoins you to use it if it is applicable. That is why there is no implicature from "I don't know that *p*" to 'I know that not *p*': if you had meant the latter, you should have said it. Inferences that do work in the reverse direction are I-implicatures, and NR-inferences must be I-implicatures. They have the necessary hallmarks: (a) they are inferences to a more informative proposition that would entail what is said (the implicature as usual for I-inferences not being representable as an independent proposition from what is said); (b) they do not impose an additional negation on the already negative understanding of the utterance; (c) they are not metalinguistic (there is no necessary reference to other linguistic items—the inference is from a contradictory to a contrary); (d) as in many other kinds of I-inference that invite a stronger interpretation from a weaker statement, they have extensive euphemistic uses (Leech 1983: 101f; Horn 1989: 330–337, 350–352).

In fact, NR-inferences are the one systematic class of exceptions that I know of to the generalization that that Q-implicatures block inconsistent I-implicatures. But they are the exceptions that prove the rule: they are a kind of minor, highly delimited creep up a Q-scale:

1. NR-interpretations are restricted to cases where they can carry only the smallest functional load, where the semantic differences between the asserted contradictory and the implicated contrary are at a minimum.

2. NR-interpretations, although they are not unmotivated idioms, are idiomatic or governed by conventions of use (see Searle 1975: 76 for the distinction; also Morgan 1978):

   a. One can find pairs of almost synonymous predicates where one allows NR-interpretations and the other doesn't: compare "I don't want to go" I++> 'I want to not go' with "I don't hope to go" with no implicature 'I hope to not go'.

   b. NR-interpretations are often signaled by the inclusion of negative polarity items that occur *as if* the negation was syntactically in the lower clause. Thus one can say *I don't think he knows anything at all*, but not **I think he knows anything at all*. Similarly *I don't want to go at all* is fine, but *?*I don't hope to go at all* is odd. These are the hallmarks of partial conventionalization or "short-circuited implicature" (Horn and Bayer 1984; Linebarger 1991).

In short, the systematic crosslinguistic tendency for NR-interpretations can only be explained in terms of a general pragmatic process like I-implicature.[64] No theory of nonce implicature can explain the regular tendency. On the other hand, its domain of application is strictly bounded by the other informational maxim, the Q-principle: in fact, the very occurrence of NR is a leakage in the blocking mechanism whereby the Q-principle bounds the I-principle. We can be grateful for the leakage because it makes clearly visible the antinomic character of the two principles (which some like Carston (1995) have doubted), even if it is a bit of a theoretical embarrassment. The embarrassment is lessened by noting that NR-inferences are protected from extinction by partial conventionalization. The full path of conventionalization can also be noted, whereby *not likely* becomes lexicalized as *unlikely*, which can then only have the contrary, 'likely not' reading associated with NR.

2.4   M-IMPLICATURES AND HORN'S DIVISION OF LABOR

Grice (1967, 1989: 27) introduced his final maxim thus: "Under the category of Manner, which I understand as relating not (like the previous categories) to what is said but, rather, to *how* what is said is to be said, I include the supermaxim—"Be perspicuous"—and various maxims such as:

1. Avoid obscurity of expression
2. Avoid ambiguity.
3. Be brief (avoid unnecessary prolixity).
4. Be orderly."

Most modern accounts reduce these in one way or another, by rejecting some and sweeping the remainder into a maxim of Relevance (Sperber and Wilson 1986) or by reassigning the first two submaxims to the Q principle and the last two to an R principle (Horn 1984, 1989: 194). As far as the present account goes, in so far as the second submaxim ("avoid ambiguity") is interpreted to include semantic generality, it will be partially accounted for under the Q-principle (because it will in general be less informative to express a general interpretation where it could have been avoided by choice of another expression). Genuine ambiguity is otherwise rather hard to avoid: the simplest sentences tend towards multiple ambiguities, as work in natural language processing has demonstrated. The fourth submaxim, "be orderly," relates to the larger issue of iconicity in language: because speech is linear, the main dimension of iconicity is order. I take this to be a natural cognitive propensity, whose implications have been explored elsewhere (Haiman 1985a,b), and I have some doubts that it has maxim status, because its effects may be largely achieved by the I-principle.[65] The third submaxim, "be brief," has both an informational and a formal aspect. The informational aspect is subsumed under the I-principle (maxim of Minimization), whereby semantically general expressions pick up specific reference, and I noted that by Zipfian principles, semantically general expressions also tend to be more frequent and thus briefer in form. Nevertheless, the formal aspects of "avoid unnecessary prolixity" (M3) and the first submaxim (M1), "avoid obscurity of expression," survive in my scheme as a single Manner principle. Manner elements survive in rival schemes, too, but not as independent principles. In Sperber and Wilson's (1986) Relevance theory, marked expressions require more processing effort and thus contribute to the estimation of Relevance; in Horn's (1984, 1989) scheme of Q- and R-principles, unmarked expressions are encouraged by R and marked ones signal that Q is in force. Horn thus conflates informational minimality and expression brevity within R, and informational maximality with expression markedness within Q. The underlying reason to resist this conflation in my scheme is that the three principles Q, I, and M are here considered heuristics, which are invoked by the kinds of linguistic expressions employed: just as the use of an item from a contrast set suggests that the contrastive items would be inappropriate, or the use of a minimal expression invokes a maximal interpretation, so the use of a marked expression signals an opposing interpretation to the one that would have been induced by the use of an unmarked expression. Each heuristic has its mode of invocation, and in the case of the M-heuristic, it is the *form* of the expression rather than its meaning that performs this service.

The version of Grice's Manner maxim that I favor is one that reduces it to a single simple principle that has been much commented on by analysts with other axes to grind, and in fact Haiman's (1985a: 147) formulation (grinding his own axe, the iconicity underlying much grammar) is quite similar to my (shamefully) independent formulation of the same era. He suggests, as a first approximation, that "Formal complexity corresponds to conceptual complexity." But a better rival formulation, "Morphological markedness corresponds to semantic markedness," he points out, is not quite a corollary because semantic markedness encompasses not only conceptual complexity but also unfamiliar, infrequent concepts. It is, then, this relation between formal markedness and semantic markedness that is the relation in question.

The M-principle was introduced in chapter 1 as a general heuristic, and needs only a little further elaboration here.

(69) *The M-Principle*

Speaker's maxim: Indicate an abnormal, nonstereotypical situation by using marked expressions that contrast with those you would use to describe the corresponding normal, stereotypical situation.

Recipient's corollary: What is said in an abnormal way indicates an abnormal situation, or marked messages indicate marked situations, specifically:

Where S has said "p" containing marked expression M, and there is an unmarked alternate expression U with the same denotation D which the speaker might have employed in the same sentence-frame instead, then where U would have I-implicated the stereotypical or more specific subset d of D, the marked expression M will implicate the complement of the denotation d, namely $\bar{d}$ of D.

The notion of *markedness* employed here is a generalization of the Prague School concept (as in Jakobson 1939; Greenberg 1966b; Horn 1989: chap. 3). On the formal side, marked forms, in comparison to corresponding unmarked forms, are more morphologically complex and less lexicalized, more prolix or periphrastic, less frequent or usual, and less neutral in register. On the meaning side, such forms suggest some additional meaning or connotation absent from the corresponding unmarked forms. The notion of *same sentence frame*, which needs further explication along structuralist lines, is intended to restrict the substitute U versus M expressions, so that, for example, the opposition between actives and passives will not come under this principle, which is of restricted scope.

2.4.1   Horn's (1984) Division of Pragmatic Labor

The M-principle as here stated builds in Horn's (1984, 1989: 197ff) "division of pragmatic labor," on which indeed the present idea is based (Horn in turn borrowing from McCawley 1978). For the record, Horn states the division of pragmatic labor in terms of his Q- and R-principles: his Q is pretty much equivalent to both my Q plus my M, whereas his R principle is roughly coextensive with my I-principle. Thus where the implicatures of unmarked alternates pick up the central, stereotypical subset of denotations by my I and his R, the marked expressions implicate the complementary extension by my M but his Q. (I hardly need to point out that the roots of these ideas are as old as structural linguistics: clear formulations of similar principles can be found in Bréal 1900, Saussure 1916, and Bloomfield 1933).

The central observation is that M-implicatures seem to be essentially parasitic on corresponding I-implicatures: whatever an *unmarked* expression U would I-implicate, the marked alternative (denotational synonym) M will implicate the *complement* of U's denotation. The Gricean reasoning, of course, is that the speaker seems to have gone out of his way to avoid using the unmarked expression and so must be trying to avoid whatever the unmarked expression would suggest. The following examples illustrate the potential range of the phenomenon.

(70) a. "John could solve the problem."
       I +> 'and he did.'
     b. "John had the ability to solve the problem."
        M +> 'but he didn't.'

(71) a. "John turned the switch and the motor started."
       I +> 'John intentionally caused the starting.'
     b. "John turned the switch and almost immediately thereafter the motor started."
        M +> 'the two events may have been coincidental.'

(72) a. "Sue smiled."
       I +> 'Sue produced a nice happy expression.'
     b. "The corners of Sue's lips turned slightly upwards."
        M +> 'Sue produced a smirk or grimace.'

(73) a. "Sally was knitting. Occasionally, *she* looked out the window."
       I +> *she* refers to Sally.
     b. "Sally was knitting. Occasionally, *the woman* looked out the window."
        M +> *the woman* does not refer to Sally.

2.4.1.1 Lexical Doublets and Rival Word Formations Let us begin by considering how this division of pragmatic labor might play out within the lexicon. Consider lexical pairs of the kind *drink* versus *beverage*: they belong to different registers (one colloquial, one primally written); the first is the more familiar, frequent, normal, friendly word. But *drink* is no longer neutral: "He bought a drink" suggests an alcoholic drink, it has become specialized by I-implicature towards the stereotypical extension (perhaps egged on by euphemism).[66] To avoid the connotations, chocolate-drink manufacturers extol the virtues of their *beverage* (historically, *beverage* was at least as contaminated!). Some further pairs of this sort follow:

(74) a. "He was reading a book"
       I ++> 'He was reading an ordinary book.'
     b. "He was reading a tome"
        M ++> 'He was reading some massive, weighty volume.'

(75) a. "Her house is on the corner"
       I ++> 'Her house, of the normal variety, is on the corner.'
     b. "Her residence is on the corner"
        M ++> 'Her immodest, pretentious house is on the corner.'

(76) a. "A missile struck the house"
   I ++> 'A rocket struck the house.'
b. "A projectile struck the house"
   M ++> 'Some brickbat other than a rocket struck the house.'

(77) a. "They had an argument"
   I ++> 'They had a disagreeable disputation.'
b. "They had a discussion/disputation"
   M ++> 'They had a gentlemanly debate.'

Cross-register doublets like these are numerous in English (*horse, steed; letter, missive; gift, donation*), but their interest is mainly historical: it is fairly clear that the process of narrowing by I-implicature (as with *missile* to 'rocket') not only allows a new life for worn-out (marked) words but, by M-implicature (to the complement of the I-implicature associated with the unmarked term), trims their meaning too. Horn (1984: 32–37) makes further remarks on the relation of diachronic studies of lexicography to Gricean principles.

A more interesting area for the synchronic study of the lexicon is derivational morphology. Often, there are two or more rival derivational routes, as from verb to noun: thus we have from *inform* both *informant* and *informer*. As Kiparsky (1982) points out, this can occur only if the two forms pick up different extensions, but otherwise an existing derivation preempts a new one: *to cook* is the source of the noun *cook*, 'one who cooks', and this blocks *cooker* with that sense, but not with the sense 'thing that cooks'. (Often blocking is complete: there is no *braker* 'thing that brakes' from *to brake* given the preexisting blocking noun *brake*, except in child language where it occurs; q.v. Clark 1993: 118.) Horn (1984: 26ff) relates this to his Q and R (here corresponding to my M and I) principles; the regular, unmarked formation picks up the stereotypical extension, often narrowed in the typical way—so *informer* becomes not only 'one who informs' but also 'one who informs against his own'; *informant* is the marked derivation and picks up an exclusive (if not complementary) denotation, as in the linguistics usage. (Historically, the *OED* entries suggest that *informant* may once indeed have picked up the complement, before itself becoming associated with betrayal, an association now lost.) By Kiparsky's generalization, "avoid synonymy," the outputs of derivational processes must be semantically contrastive, but they may be assigned rather different extensions: thus *sealer* is one who seals (documents or woodwork), but it may also refer to a layer of varnish; a *sealant* is then restricted to stuff that seals of some more gooey consistency, in short a mastic (*Webster's Dictionary*, 1991 edition).

This division of labor in word formation, between regular formations with stereotypical meanings, and irregular ones with specialized meanings, is of special interest in the study of child language acquisition. The gradual increase of lexical knowledge requires constant adjustment in the meanings of the already learned lexicon. If a learner doesn't know the verb *to row*, then on the analogy with denominal verbs like *sail*, he or she may coin the verb *to oar*; later discovery of the verb *to row* may not result in immediate blocking of *to oar*. Rather, the child may try to maintain the hypothesis of a contrast in meaning, by perhaps assigning the new verb *to row* a superordinate meaning over *to oar, to paddle*, or *to sail* (Clark 1993: 94). Similarly, children produce regular inflections like *goed* at the same age (or even after) they are correctly saying *went*, because they appear to have assumed that *went* is a different verb with a very similar, but contrastive, meaning, and this hypothesis may be maintained for years (Clark 1993: 103f). The prediction from Horn's division of pragmatic labor is that where the child has two words like *to oar* and *to row* not only will they be assigned distinct meanings by the Saussurean or Clarkian principle of contrast, but also that the more regular formation may initially (and often incorrectly) be assigned the more stereotypical, central denotation.[67]

2.4.1.2 Lexicalized Forms versus Periphrasis Often, an existing lexicalization may be in opposition to a periphrastic alternative. Take a simple example like *pink* versus *pale red* (McCawley 1978: 245–246, after Householder). *Pink* preempts the central values of that color; thus although one might well define *pink* as 'pale red', an utterance "The dress is pale red" would suggest (by M-contrast with *pink*) that the dress is not prototypical pink but somewhere between *pink* and *red*. Such observations have often been taken to be an argument against lexical decomposition, but of course they merely establish the existence of pragmatic contrasts. Note that *pale blue* carries no such implicature to 'not the prototypical value of whitish blue', because there is no contrasting lexicalization. Modal verbs often allow periphrastic alternatives, and the distribution of interpretations is then often in the predicted direction:

(78) a. "You may leave."
            I +> 'and please do so.'
      b. "You are permitted to leave."
            M +> 'but you may stay.'

It is presumably for this reason, Horn (1984) points out, that indirect speech acts with the lexicalized forms (like *Can you pass the salt?*) are idiomatic, whereas the periphrastic forms (like *Are you able to pass the salt?*) resist the richer interpretation.

The causatives are a *cause célèbre*.[68] McCawley (1978, in part following Shibatani 1972) pointed out that there is a regular association of the lexicalized causative with direct causation and the periphrastic one with indirect causation as in:

(79) a. "Larry stopped the car."
        I ++> 'Larry caused the car to stop in the normal way, by using the foot pedal.'
    b. "Larry got the car to stop." or "Larry caused the car to stop."
        M ++> 'Larry caused the car to stop in a nonstereotypical way, e.g., using the emergency brake.'

(80) a. "The Spanish killed the Aztecs."
        I ++> 'The Spaniards slaughtered the Aztecs directly.'
    b. "The Spanish caused the Aztecs to die."
        M ++> 'The Spaniards killed the Aztecs indirectly, e.g., by disease and hard labor.'

(81) a. "Sue moved the car."
        I ++> 'Sue moved the car by driving it, by using the engine.'
    b. "Sue made the car move."
        M ++> 'Sue moved the car in some abnormal way, e.g., by pushing it.'

The Gricean argument in these cases is clear enough: if the speaker has gone out of his way to avoid the simpler expression, he must be intending to refer to an event that contrasts to that which would have been describable with the simple lexicalized causative. But the proof of the pudding, McCawley noted (1978: 250), is that when there is no lexicalized causative, there is then no implicatural contrast and the periphrastic construction carries no extra meaning. Thus there is no causative verb 'to make laugh' or 'to make *x* drop *y*' (e.g., no *to *laughen*, or *to *droppen*), and the periphrastic forms here pick up stereotypical extensions:

(82) a. "Bill made Mary laugh."
        No implicature 'by some unordinary means, e.g., tickling her toes'
    b. "Bill caused Mary to drop her parcel."
        No implicature 'by some extraordinary means'

McCawley (1978: 257) concludes by noting the iconic relation, whereby "the syntactically unmarked causative constructions (i.e., lexical causatives) will be interpreted as referring to minimally marked causal relations (i.e., some kind of direct causation)." Thus the unmarked interpretation is not definitively coded in the lexical causative; rather the inference to the stereotype is itself implicated. Thus in (83), although (83a) suggests the stereotype and (83b) suggests the complement, there is no anomaly in (83c) despite the fact that the *by*-phrase cancels the assumption in (83a).

(83) a. "The outlaw killed the sheriff."

  I +> 'by direct means, e.g., gunning him down'

  b. "The outlaw caused the sheriff to die."

  M +> 'by some unusual means, e.g., spiking his gun, half cutting his stirrup-leather, poisoning his aperitif.'

  c. "The outlaw killed the sheriff by putting poison in his water bottle."

This phenomenon is widely attested across languages; for example, in Japanese (Shibatani 1972), Inuktitut (Allen 1994), and numerous languages cited by Haiman (1985a: 108ff). Many languages have lexical causatives and regular causative derivational morphology: in this case, the longer derivational form is restricted to human (or animate) causes, presuming the indirect causation of a verbal command: one says in effect 'He stopped the ball' but 'He made them come to a stop' (Haiman 1985a: 109–110). The marked derivational or periphrastic constructions may even carry magical connotations, roughly as in 'He raised the plate' versus 'He made the plate rise up.'

2.4.1.3 Litotes: When Two Negatives Don't Make a Positive Another area where lexicalized versus periphrastic constructions produce productive oppositions is the contrast between p and $\sim\sim p$. To understand this area, we need to understand the apparent irregularities of English affixal negations; this may seem to be a digression, but it also has pragmatic implications (see Horn 1989: 273–308, who discusses much antecedent work). We have already seen the pattern whereby "I don't like garlic" I-implicates 'I dislike garlic'; that is, where the contradictory gets strengthened to the contrary. There are many lexical items incorporating affixal negatives in English, like *impossible, unhappy, inhuman*, or *noncommunist*. The lexicographer's problem is to explain why these sometimes mean the contrary but sometimes the contradictory of the positive: *unhappy* means

the contrary 'sad', not the contradictory 'not happy (i.e., either sad or in-between'), but *unimpoverished* means the contradictory 'not impoverished', *unworthy* means just 'not worthy', and so on.

Horn's account of this forest of inconvenient and troublesome sememes goes as follows. There are constraints on the I-implicature from the contradictory of lexeme W to the contrary of W. Simplifying somewhat, the inference only goes through if:

1. the base expression W is a relatively weak positive scalar item, thus one notes the absence of **dislove* but the presence of *dislike*, and
2. W is affectively positive, so we have *unhappy* implicating '(nearly) sad', but *??unsad* if allowable at all, not implicating 'happy' (and so on for *impolite* vs. *??unrude, unhealthy* vs. *?unsick, unwise* vs. *??unfoolish,* etc.),[69] and
3. the negative form is relatively unproductive, i.e., not-W is relatively lexicalized. This is something of a gradient affair, along the scale from most productive to least productive: *non- > un- > in- > dis-* etc.

These conditions predict that we will get pairs of affixally negative lexemes like the following, where only the first of each pair can have the strong contrary reading: *immoral* vs. *non-moral, irrational* vs. *non-rational, unChristian* vs. *non-Christian, inhuman* (or *unhuman*) vs. *non-human.*

The third constraint, the more lexicalized the more likely to have a contrary reading, is actually a side effect of the fact, described in chapter 1, that the O corner of the square of oppositions tends not to lexicalize but is instead typically instantiated as the contradictory negation of the A corner (thus we have *not all* rather than the hypothetical **nall*, on the model of *none*). If the O-corner expressions do get their negatives fused, then they have to be interpreted as having moved up the negative scale towards the E corner.

We are now in a position to tackle double negations. Not every negative of a negative is equivalent to a positive. In particular, if W is a positive item, and $\overline{W}$ is the contrary of W, $\sim(\overline{W})$ will not be equivalent to W, as figure 2.8 makes clear. Thus *not unhappy* is logically compatible with both being happy and being neither happy nor sad, although it pragmatically suggests the latter. The two negatives in this case are not equivalent to the positive (*happy*) for logical reasons. On the other hand, saying "It's not true that he's not happy" is indeed logically equivalent to the statement that he is happy. For this reason, no pragmatic motivation is necessary for the use of negated contraries of the kind *not unhappy, not*

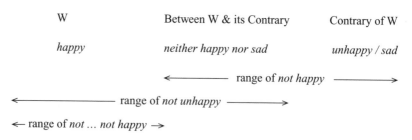

Figure 2.8
Logical range of different negatives

infrequent, or *not unintelligent*: speakers may use these forms to say what they logically mean (however, there is in fact a systematic pragmatic suggestion—more in a moment).

But it is quite different with the frequent use of the double negative $\sim(\sim W$ where $\sim W$ is a contradictory of W. For example, things are either possible or impossible; there's no middle ground. So, when someone asserts "It's not impossible" (i.e., it's not not-possible), logically he might as well have said "It's possible." Note that some of these negated contradictories have superficial similarity to the negations of contraries—for example, *not unuseful* is logically equivalent to *useful*, while we have seen how *not unhappy* is not equivalent to *happy*—so the analyst must beware. This frequent figure of speech (the negation of the contradictory) needs a pragmatic motivation, and it is of course given by the Hornian division of pragmatic labor: if two expressions have the same denotation, the marked one will pick up the interpretation complementary to the unmarked expression's. The pragmatic functions are intuitively clear in examples like the following, where the speaker appears to be withholding the positive term, because the situation does not quite match that extreme:

(84) a. "She's not incapable of exertion."
          M ++> 'She's less capable of exertion than "*capable*" would I-implicate.'
      b. "His record is not unblemished."
          M ++> 'His record is perhaps not exactly blemished, but nearly unblotted.'
          Alternatively: 'His record is not just blemished, it's atrocious.'
      c. "It took a not inconsiderable effort."
          M ++> 'It took a close-to-considerable effort.'

    d. "She was not unpleased by his efforts."
       M ++> 'She was less than fully pleased or ecstatic about his efforts.'
    e. "He's a not unjust man."
       M ++> 'He's a reasonably just man.'
    f. "A not unreliable service."
       M ++> 'A sort of reliable-ish service.'

Nevertheless, as Horn (1991a) documents, rhetoricians have long argued about both the meaning and the desirability of litotes, some (like Erasmus) suggesting that it is in fact an appropriately discreet and gentlemanly way to assert the extreme positive, as in "Your letter was no small joy." But the consensus (or at least that extracted by Horn) is that the inference may go either way: (a) it may suggest that the property described falls short of the positive or (b) that it exceeds the positive or that the positive needs emphasizing (as in "I was not unaware of the problem" suggesting that the speaker was indeed acutely aware). The learned commentary suggests indeed that the (b) use is parasitic on the (a) use: by asserting "I am not an ungenerous man" I might implicate that I am something less than fully generous, but because modesty would be reason for that, I may in fact implicate something less modest. Thus polite understatement may be a factor in the extreme value readings. The Hornian division of labor is of course neutral to the swing of interpretation one way or the other (which may well be conditioned by politeness or other factors; see Horn 1991a: 91), but it predicts that whatever is meant is complementary to what the plain positive would have meant.

    Let us return now to the cases first raised, the negation of the contraries, which I set aside as justified in use by their logical properties. Now the pragmatic division of labor suggests that even when justified by the logic of a negated contrary, such cumbersome forms as *not unhappy*, with all the compounded processing difficulties of negatives of (special) negatives, may also be justified by pragmatic specialization. Why not say the simple positive disjunction "He's happy or content"? It seems that "not unhappy" is used rather to suggest that something less than fully or extremely 'happy' holds: although not quite equivalent to 'content', it seems to exclude the extreme value of happy. For this reason, the rhetoricians seem to have swept these cases in with the denial of the contradictories: in many cases, they have a similar weakening force.

2.4.1.4 Grammaticalized/Morphologized versus Lexical Expressions
Consider *the child's picture* versus *the picture of the child*. The first suggests an intimate relation; the child perhaps painted the picture, or at least owns it. The second strongly suggests that it depicts the child (otherwise why not say *the picture by the child* or even, dialect permitting, *the picture of the child's?*). The *of* construction of course doesn't encode 'depiction of': *the best picture of the Louvre* clearly allows the possessive reading, and *the guns of the warship* has nothing to do with pictures at all. The generalization is just that the briefer, morphologized suffix of possession suggests by I-implicature a closer, more intimate relation between the NPs, and the choice of the lexical *of* construction discourages this by M-implicature. Note here a fact of some interest, which we can find elsewhere too: we sometimes find a double-marking, as in *the picture of the child's*, and this can have the effect of returning us to the interpretation associated with the unmarked form. If expression "X" I-implicates restriction to denotation D, and expression "Y" M-implicates restriction to the complement $\bar{D}$, then expression "Z" which M-contrasts with "Y", suggests the complement of $\bar{D}$, which of course is D.

Possessive constructions in many languages offer two forms, one associated with "inalienable" possessions (kin, body parts, etc.) and another associated with "alienable" possessions (houses, horses, etc.). Haiman (1985a: 130–136) points out that the inalienable relation is almost invariably expressed with a less prolix form, so that there is an iconicity between the reduced bulk of the expression and the intimacy of the relation. This might be taken to be a consequence of the I- and M-principles, now conventionalized and frozen in grammar.

2.4.1.5 Zero versus Nonempty Morphology Finally, there is an interesting, rather miscellaneous set of circumstances under which there is an opposition between a zero-morph, or a gap, and an explicit morpheme. Such an opposition, I pointed out, cannot arise under the Q-principle, where matching linguistic expressions of different informativeness are required to generate an implicature. Thus gaps and zero-morphs are open to I-interpretation and tend to engender rich interpretations to specific referents, stereotypical situations, or connected events. And these interpretations may be defeated or blocked by the insertion of lexical material instead.

Consider, for example, the opposition between *the N* and *N* in the following sentences (Horn 1993: 41):

(85) a. She went to school/church/university/bed/hospital/sea/town.
     Conventionalized I-implicature: 'She went to do the associated
     stereotypical activity.'
   b. She went to the school/church/university/bed/hospital/sea/town.
     M +> 'She went to the place but not necessarily to do the
     associated stereotypical activity.'

Notice that not all the relevant nouns in English permit this zero-article:
one can't say for example **She went to office*. Although this might tempt
one to claim that the whole pattern is purely a matter of idioms, one
should note that the underlying pattern of pragmatic interpretations is
essentially regular but constrained by the availability of the contraction.
Thus *She went to the office* I-implicates 'to do the associated activity (i.e.,
to work)' because there is no possibility of the shorter expression **to
office*, and thus no M-implicature can arise from *the office* to block the
I-enrichment.

Nominal compounds in English, and in many languages, have an
unmarked N-N form. Assuming that the semantic relation between the
nouns is no more than an existentially quantified variable over relations,
the exact relation must be inferred. Grammars of English give a dozen or
more patterns, with relationships like N_1 powers N_2 (*windmill*) or N_1 has
N_2, (*doorknob*), and so forth (see, e.g., Quirk, Greenbaum, Leech, and
Svartvik, 1972: 1021–1026). Note that the interpretation is not fixed: a
wood container could be a container for wood or of wood. A glance at any
technical manual shows that this is indeed a productive system, and the
relationship must be inferred in such novel compounds as *ferrule ring,
antenna coupler, standby memory, key protect indication, power lock*, and
so on. The I-induced interpretation, we have seen, is usually to a rich
relationship between the nouns, as fits most plausibly with stereotypical
assumptions. But if one tries to spell this out lexically, the resulting
utterance often has distinct implicatures: compare *matchbox* (the box),
box of matches (box containing matches), *box for matches* (nonproto-
typical box specially made for containing matches), and so on. Intuitively,
the N-N form suggests a dubbing or naming of a specific relation that the
recipient should be able to infer; any spelling out of the relation suggests
(by M-implicature) some other relationship between the nouns.

In the discussion of the I-interpretations of conjunction and parataxis,
we have seen that in English many of the same interpretations are available for sentences of the form "A and B" and "A. B", but not all. Thus

"He broke his leg. He fell" I-implicates 'He broke his leg because he fell', an interpretation that is blocked by the insertion of *and* in "He broke his leg and he fell." In English, the systematic opposition between *and* and zero is perhaps undermined by two factors, (a) the often obligatory requirement for *and* within a clause (*He came __ went, *Sue __ Mary came), (b) the tendency for the phonetic reduction of *and* to a single assimilated nasal as in "He came'n' got it." In other languages, more systematic oppositions have been observed: in Turkish, Ono, Fe?fe? Bamileke, and other languages, the absence of the conjunction between two actions by a single actor carries the meaning that they constitute one single complex action: saying in effect "He went to the market __ he bought yams" implies that the yams came from the market, whereas "He went to the market and he bought yams" may imply that the yams came from elsewhere (i.e., there were two independent actions) (Haiman 1985a: 111–115). In some languages, the effect is weak but discernible: in Sissala, for example, "When [the conjunction] *a* is left out, ... one would expect the event to happen exactly according to the stereotype or scenario. ... The addition of *a* ... might alert the hearer to some minor departure from stereotypicality" (Blass 1990: 250).

English conjunction reduction, though, fits the same pattern of interpretation. In this case, the gap is a grammatically conditioned reduction subject to constraints of various sorts, most obviously the identity of the subject across two clauses. Example (86a) strongly suggests a single complex action of store-going-in-order-to-whiskey-buy.[70] The sentence (86b) suggests some contrast with such a single-minded whiskey expedition; he may, weak soul, have gone to do the weekly shopping and been tempted by a bottle of whiskey. When the explicit conjunction is reinforced with *both* as in (86c) or with *in addition* as in (86d), we seem to be dealing with a list of actions and not a single expedition of any kind at all.

(86) a. "He went to the store and bought some whiskey."
       I ++> 'He went to the store and, there and then, he bought the whiskey.'
     b. "He went to the store and he bought some whiskey."
       M ++> 'He went to the store and he (perhaps elsewhere, perhaps incidentally) bought some whiskey.'
     c. "He both went to the store and he bought some whiskey."
       M ++> 'He did two separate actions: he went to the store and he bought some whiskey.'

    d. "He went to the store and in addition he bought some whiskey."
M ++> 'He did two separate actions: he went to the store and
he bought some whiskey.'

Conjunction reduction, of course, involves some sort of deletion of the
subject and thus raises the issue of alternative referring expressions.
Under the I-principle, I have already briefly reviewed evidence from conversation analysis for a maxim of the sort "choose the minimal referring
expression that will achieve identification" (after Sacks and Schegloff
1979; Schegloff 1972, 1979, 1996). In the same sort of way, many linguists
have noted a scale of referring expressions *zero > pronoun > name > description*, so that the more toward the left an item is, the more likely an
anaphoric interpretation is preferred. Although sometimes these choices
are grammatically specified, and thus their interpretations constrained,
sometimes there is a syntactic freedom of choice, as in English:

(87) a. "Susan went to the library and __ continued to read *Wuthering
      Heights.*"
    b. "Susan went to the library and she continued to read *Wuthering
      Heights.*"
    c. "Susan went to the library and the woman continued to read
      Wuthering Heights."
    d. "Her mother wanted to stay at home and finish her novel, and
      urged Susan to leave. Susan went to the library and she
      continued to read *Wuthering Heights.*"
    e. "Susan went to the library and the dreamy girl continued to
      read *Wuthering Heights.*"

In (87a) we are forced to the coreferential reading; in (87b) we prefer it,
unless the context biases an alternative as in (87d). But in (87c) we
strongly prefer a disjoint reading, although a coreferential reading can be
restored with additional material as in (87e). These issues, perennially
controversial, will be covered in depth in chapter 4. Here I simply note
that this pattern fits the general scheme of the pragmatic division of
labor: minimal forms will pick up maximally informative readings by the
I-principle, whereas contrastive maximal forms (*the woman* vs. *she*) suggest a complementary interpretation by the M-principle.

2.4.1.6 Repetition and Reduplication   One of the most straightforward
predictions from the M-principle is that repetitions and reduplications

should suggest interpretations distinct from the use of the unduplicated form. Any principle of contrast, however, will predict some meaning difference between the use of a form "X" and "X-X." The prediction from the division of pragmatic labor, however, is that where "X" I-implicates restriction to the subset of denoted entities D, "X-X" will pick out the complement $\bar{D}$; where "X" carries no clear I-induced restriction, or non-stereotypical exemplars are salient in the context, "X-X" should implicate a narrowing to, for example, an extreme or prototypical variant of D. Hence we have both *Oh we're just living-together living-together* (roommates, not lovers), and *I want a salad-salad* (a real lettuce salad, not a tuna salad, etc.) (Horn 1993: 48–51).

Two preliminaries: First, not every instance of a repeated form "X-X" is to be understood as a repetition or reduplication for pragmatic effect; it can be determined by good structural principles. For example, the phrase *a rich, rich man* is structurally ambiguous, as usually perhaps indicated in the prosody:

(88) a. "a [[rich][rich man]]"
       = 'a man rich among the rich'
     b. "a [[rich rich] man]"
       Implicates: 'a very wealthy man'

It is only the flat structure in (88b) for which we need a pragmatic account. Second, the linguistic terminology is here confused, with one author's *duplication*, another's *reduplication*, and so on. I follow Naylor's (1986) recommendation to follow Sapir (1921: 76) on a wide notion of reduplication:

Nothing is more natural than the prevalence of reduplication, in other words, the repetition of all or part of the radical element. The process is generally employed, with self-evident symbolism, to indicate such concepts as distribution, plurality, repetition, customary activity, increase of size, added intensity, continuance.

The term reduplication can nevertheless be restricted to a morphological process of word formation, repetition thus denoting word and phrase-level duplication. As Sapir (1921: 77) noted, "it can hardly be said that the duplicative process is of a distinctively grammatical significance in English ... we must turn to other languages for illustration" (cited in Naylor 1986: 177). However, before leaving English, it is worth noting the following patterns of repetition (partly from Quirk, Greenbaum, Leech, and Svartvik 1972: 618).

(89) a. Modifiers and intensification
     a very, very, very, steep path
     a deep, deep pool
     an old old church
     Run quickly quickly!
     a blue, blue sea
   b. Conjoined comparatives and increasing value
     He grew angrier and angrier.
     It became more and more apparent.
   c. Conjoined verbs and continued/repeated action
     He ran and ran and ran up the hill.
     She knocked and knocked on the door.
   d. Conjoined/adjoined nouns and distributed plurality
     He could see stars (and) stars (and) stars.
     There were kids (and) kids all over the place.
   e. Conjoined nouns and distinctions within the class
     There are doctors and doctors; some you can trust, some you can't.

All of these repetitions seem to have a similar structure to nonrepetitions, so that *he ran and ran* would have the same structure as *he ran and walked*. Semantically, the repetitions thus appear to be redundant. It is possible, as Naylor (1986) suggests, that one could adopt an analysis where the sequence of forms introduces a sequence of reference points, giving us an aspect-like characterization of *he ran and ran* or *he grew angrier and angrier* or, alternatively, an interpretation as a sequence of reference points along a time-line as suggested by Partee (1984) for different cases. But this will not give us an analysis of *blue, blue sea*, or *doctors and doctors*, and so on. Because this is a highly productive process (unreduceable to a small list of idioms), I am inclined to a pragmatic interpretation.[71] Note that the interpretations are richer than, for example, Quirk et al. (1972) suggest: *he ran and ran and ran* suggests not only continued action but intensity: he ran hard.

An M-implicature analysis suggests that the X(and)X form should pick up a complementary interpretation from the X form. In many cases, this seems correct. "He's clever" states that he is intelligent, but "He's clever-clever" implicates that he is trying too hard to be clever and is thus less than fully bright. Or consider the following contrasts:

(90) a. "He went to bed and slept"
     I +> 'he had a normal night's sleep'

b. "He went to bed and slept and slept"
   M +> 'he slept longer than usual'
c. "In Outer Mongolia, there are doctors."
   I +> 'in Outer Mongolia one can find useful general
   practitioners of medicine.'
d. "In Outer Mongolia, there are doctors and doctors."
   M ++> 'in Outer Mongolia, one can find useful general
   practitioners of medicine, on the one hand, and on the other
   so-called doctors who could not be called useful general
   practitioners of medicine.'

In the intensity readings of cases like *big, big dog*, the repetition seems to pick out the extreme value along the following lines: if *big dog* denotes the set of big dogs *D*, and I-implicates a stereotypical subset (e.g., Alsatian-size dogs), then *big, big dog* M-implicates that the speaker has in mind a distinct subset (e.g., St. Bernard-size dogs), within the set *D*.

Turning to other languages, one can find repetition in productive word formation—that is, full reduplication. In Tzeltal and Tzotzil, for example, whereas the use of nonreduplicated color terms picks out the prototypical, stereotypical hues, the reduplicated terms indicate that the color in question deviates from the relevant focal or prototypical hue (Berlin 1963: 216). In Australian languages (Dixon 1980), reduplicated verbs may have aspectual meanings (as in Dyirbal *gunbal-gunbal* 'cut repeatedly'), but we also find clear M-inferences to the nonprototype extensions as in Western Desert *wati-wati* 'kids pretending to be men' (vs. *wati* 'men'), or *kintha-kintha-la* 'little dog' (vs. *kintha* 'dog') in Dyari. Perhaps the most extended study of this kind of reduplication is that by Botha (1988) for Afrikaans, where root reduplication is a highly productive kind of derivational morphology. The traditional grammarians of Afrikaans list about 13 distinct kinds of meanings that result (Botha 1988: 92–95), many in opposed directions: thus *bakke-bakke* 'lots of bowls', but *ruk-ruk* 'a few times, occasionally'; or *dik-dik* 'very thick', but *skop-skop* 'tentatively kick'; or even *troppe-troppe* 'scattered flocks' versus *tien-tien* 'ten together'. Botha's valiant attempt to specify a single semantic rule of interpretation involving the notion of increased value is therefore less than fully convincing. Rather, some fairly complex pragmatic process of interpretation may be suspected, and the M-principle is certainly a candidate: if *dik snye brood* means 'thick slice (of) bread' and I-implicates a stereotypical generous slab, then *dik-dik snye brood* M-implicates something different from that (because *dik* rules out difference in the wafer direction, the suggested denotation is thicker than the normal generous slab). If *skop* 'kick' tends to I-implicate 'kick hard', then *skop-skop* will suggest 'less than hard'. Whether the inference goes in the intensity/increase direction or the attenuation/limited dimension seems to depend on the direction of I-inference from the unreduplicated form, the reduplication then picking up the complement.

There is much literature on partial reduplication, too extensive for review here. But it is worth pointing out that even in this area, often deeply built in to morphological processes and subject to all the vagaries of meaning associated with derivational morphology, there are some cases worth the pragmaticist's attention. Many languages have a means of giving a word sheer extra bulk. In Tamil, for example, there is a kind of reduplication known as echo-word formation, where the first syllable of a multisyllabic word is repeated after the word with the initial consonant altered by rule. The interpretation is always to shift the interpretation away from the prototype extension of the word (cf. Yiddish English *problem shmoblem*).

(91) *Echo-words in Tamil*
    a. kooma-sooma
       M +> 'medical coma or something like that'
    b. paittiyam giyttiyam
       M +> 'almost insanity'
    c. pooliis kiiliis
       M +> 'police or someone like them'

2.5   THE JOINT EFFECT OF Q-, I- AND M-IMPLICATURES

At the risk of redundancy, it is worth pointing out how these three principles converge to predict the inferences in slightly different sentences. Consider, for example, the coordinating connectives once again. We have already met all of the following kinds of inference:

(92) "John went to the library or he worked on his book."
    Q-scalar +> 'John did not both go to the library and work on his book.'
    Q-clausal +> 'I don't know whether John went to the library or whether he worked on his book.'
    No I-implicature from *p or q* [because Q-implicatures block

I-implicatures; see section 2.5.1]

No M-implicature from *either p or q* [bcause Q implicatures block M implicatures; see section 2.5.1]

(93) a. "John went to the library and he worked on his book."

I ++> 'John went first to the library, and then, as intended, worked there on his book.'

No Q-implicature from *p and q* because *and* is the strong member of the scale ⟨*and, or*⟩

No M-implicature from *p and q* because in English zero and *and* are not systematically opposed.

b. "John went to the library *and in addition* he worked on his book." or "John *both* went to the library *and* he worked on his book."

M ++> 'contrast with (a)., e.g., John did two independent actions, library-going and book-writing.'

Or consider the modals:

(94) a. "You may/can use the car."

Q scalar +> 'It's not the case that you *must* use the car.'

I ++> 'I offer you the use of the car.'

b. "You *are allowed to* use the car."

M +> 'Contrast with I implicature, e.g., this is not an offer, but a statement of fact.' [M-implicatures cancel I-implicatures, see section 2.5.1]

Q-scalar +> 'It's not the case that you are *obliged* to use the car.' [M-implicatures do not cancel Q-implicatures, see section 2.5.1]

Or consider the many implicatures due to negation:

(95) a. "Not all the girls are sporty."

Q-scalar +> 'Some of th girls are sporty.' [negative meta-scale ⟨*not-some/none, not-all*⟩]

b. "I *don't believe* all the girls are sporty."

I ++> 'I believe not all the girls are sporty.'

Q-scalar +> 'I believe some of the girls are sporty.'

c. "It's *not unlikely* that all the girls are sporty."

M ++> 'It's just slightly less than likely that all the girls are sporty.'

We have also considered the potential of the application of these principles to closed-class contrast sets like the prepositions or the articles (see Hawkins 1991 for close discussion):[72]

(96) a. "I bought a good novel. I talked to an author about it."
     Q-scalar $+>$ 'I talked to someone other than *the* author of the good novel.' [nonuniqueness is implicated by Horn-scale $\langle the, a \rangle$]

  b. "I bought a good novel. I talked to *the* author about it."
     I $++>$: 'I talked to the author of the good novel.'

  c. "I bought an old car. *A* wheel was loose."
     I $++>$: 'A wheel of the old car was loose.'
     Q-scalar $+>$ 'A nonunique wheel was loose, i.e., not the steering wheel but a road wheel' (otherwise the speaker should have said *The wheel*).

These examples merely illustrate that it is the intersection of the principles that yield the richest predictions, and it is this intersection that is exploited in the account of anaphora offered in chapter 4. For these predictions to be reasonably precise, however, it is essential to consider how the principles interact when inconsistent implicatures are generated. It is to that issue that I turn next.

2.5.1 The Projection Problem

Conversational implicatures are, by definition, volatile, defeasible inferences. Generalized implicatures are, of course, just as defeasible in the context of statements to the contrary, as they are to contextual assumptions that rule them out of court:

(97) "If you come, he'll forgive you, and in fact he'll forgive you anyway (regardless of whether you come)."
     Potential I-implicature of conditional perfection: 'If you don't come, he will not forgive you.' (or: I $++>$ 'if and only if you come will he forgive you.')
     Entailment of the second conjunct and the whole sentence: "and in fact he'll forgive you anyway (regardless of whether you come)".
     The entailment defeats the I-implicature.

But what happens if, by dint of multiple principles, we have multiple conflicting inferences or inconsistent potential implicatures?[73] We have seen that Q-inferences and I-inferences appear to work in opposite directions: I-implicatures are strong inferences, encouraged by minimal forms, to the likely intended stereotypical or more specific interpretation; Q-implicatures are bounding inferences from the use of a particular expression to the inapplicability of another, stronger one that has not been uttered. The antinomic tendencies of these two principles are well brought out in Horn's (1984) version of the story. Q-implicatures thus appear to induce the negation of the very sort of stronger interpretation that the I-principle encourages. Atlas and Levinson (1981), on whose principles Horn drew, suggested that this clash is in part resolved by constraining the Q-principle appropriately—in particular, by setting up two further constraints on scales: expressions can only form a ranked Horn-scale if they are (i) equally lexicalized and (ii) are "about" the same semantic relations, as reviewed above. Nevertheless, where genuine inconsistencies appear, it was suggested that Q-inferences have priority over I-inferences that are inconsistent with them.

Note, though, that I-inferences often come about through reduced forms, which are then outside the scope of the Q-principle. For example, I suggested that ⟨*the, a*⟩ form a scale, such that use of the indefinite suggests that the speaker is not in a position to use the definite. There is also a zero-article form for certain places and institutions, which is associated with an (at least partially conventionalized) I-inference to stereotypical associated activities. But because this has a zero realization, it fails the lexicalization constraint on scales and can play no role in the definiteness scale, and has an independent existence:

(98) a. "John went to university."
       (conventionalized) I +> 'to the institution.'
     b. "John went to the university."
       can be read as 'went to the campus' or 'went to that particular institution.'
     c. "John went to a university."
       Q +> 'not *the* university', thus suggesting the institutional rather than the location interpretation.

In this sort of way, clashes between the I- and Q-principles are often averted.

There is also a potential clash between the I-principle and the M-principle: the I-principle generates inferences to the rich, specific subcase, whereas the M-principle generates inferences in the precisely opposed direction. In this case, the M-implicatures take priority over the I-implicatures that would have arisen from the use of a corresponding unmarked expression, as described in Horn's division of pragmatic labor discussed earlier.

Thus we have three principles potentially producing incompatible inferences from a simple utterance: in general, utterances generate multiple potential implicatures. As sentences become complex, these inferences may arise from different clauses, and traffic rules will need to be established. In short, we have a *projection problem*: we need to be able to state the conditions under which a potential implicature generated from a part of a sentence is in fact inherited by the whole. In previous publications (Levinson 1987a,b), I suggested the following "resolution schema":

(99) a. Genuine Q-implicatures from tight Horn scales (and their meta-rule derived negative scales) and similar contrast sets of equally brief, equally lexicalized expressions "about" the same semantic relations, take precedence over I-implicatures;

   b. In all other cases, the I-principle induces stereotypical interpretations, *unless*:

   c. A marked expression has been used where an unmarked one could have been employed instead, in which case the M-implicature defeats the relevant I-implicature, by inducing the inference to the complement of the I-implicature that would have arisen from the unmarked expression.

This schema simply captures the two observations already made: that Q-inferences defeat I-inferences inconsistent with them, and that M-inferences do likewise (as in the division of pragmatic labor). It leaves the relation between M- and Q-inferences unresolved. There is some evidence that in fact Q-inferences defeat M-inferences inconsistent with them, and this would allow the simple statement that inconsistencies between potential implicatures are resolved by assigning priority first to Q-, then to M-, and only finally to I-inferences:

(100) *Resolution of inconsistent potential implicatures*
   Priority is assigned to inferences according to the principle under which they are generated:
   Q-implicatures > M-implicatures > I-implicatures
   Examples:

a. Q > I   see (101)–(103)
b. Q > M   see (105)–(106)
c. M > I   see (83)–(86), (104)

This still leaves much detail unresolved—for example, the resolution of potential implicatures of different subtypes arising under the same principle, or of inferences coming from different clauses. But first let me illustrate how this resolution schema works.

First, I want to illustrate the way in which Q-inferences seem to defeat I-inferences.[74] Consider a conjunction like "Bill entered the room and Harry left." As I have shown, we tend to interpret this, as licensed by the I-principle, along the lines 'Bill entered the room, and then, perhaps as a result, Harry left the room'.[75] Now the disjunction "Bill entered the room or Harry left" carries no such temporal and causal inferences. That is because the use of the disjunction carries two Q-implicatures: the scalar inference 'It's not the case that both Bill entered the room and Harry left' and the clausal inference 'For all the speaker knows, Bill may or may not have entered the room, and Harry may or may not have left it'. These Q-inferences are clearly inconsistent with the I-inference, which requires the conjunction of events, and it is an observable matter of fact that the I-inference simply is not associated with the disjunction.

Conditionals give rise (according to the account in Gazdar 1979) to (potential) clausal Q-implicatures, and it is these Q-implicatures to the speaker's epistemic uncertainty about the embedded clauses that account for the very general tendency for pragmatic inferences of a consequent to be suspended by mention in an antecedent. This pattern holds for scalar implicatures (as in *If not all of the boys came, some of them did*) and even presuppositions (as in *If there is a king of France, he is probably bald*), as reviewed in Levinson 1983 (pp. 142–145, 223–225). It also holds for I-inferences, as illustrated by the following (note that I revert to the explicit epistemic modification of implicatures, with all but the clausal implicatures embedded under a belief operator K, in order to bring out the inconsistencies):

(101) "John drank three beers and drove home, if not in the reverse order."
       Q-clausal inference from second clause: 'Possibly he did it in the reverse order', i.e., P(John first drove home then drank three beers)
       Potential I-inference from first clause: 'John drank three beers and then drove home', i.e., K(John drank three beers and then drove home)

Implicatures of the whole utterance: only Q-clausal inference from second clause, not I-inference from first clause.

A similar pattern holds for disjunctions: the whole disjunction lacks an implicature arising from one disjunct if the other disjunct entails its contradictory. Just as the potential scalar implicature in *Some of the boys came or all of them did* is suspended by the clausal implicature from the second disjunct, so we have the same phenomenon with I-inferences canceled when they are inconsistent with Q-clausal ones:

(102) a. "John drank the three beers and drove home, or first drove
     home and then drank the three beers."
     Potential I-implicature of first disjunct: K('John first drank the
     three beers and then drove home')
     Q-clausal implicature from the disjunction: P('John first drove
     home then drank the three beers.')

  b. "John and Marty bought a piano or they bought one each."
     Potential I-implicature from first clause (Atlas and Levinson
     1981, after Harnish 1976):
     K('John and Marty bought a single piano together')
     Q-clausal implicature from the disjunction: P('they bought one
     each.')

Consider now a slightly more involved case, where Q-inferences defeat the I-inference to "conditional perfection":

(103) "If they try again, they'll beat the landspeed record, or they've
     beaten it already and won't try again."
     Potential I-implicature of conditional perfection: 'If they don't try
     again, they won't beat the landspeed record', or K('if they will not
     try again at t_2, they have not beaten the record.')
     Q-clausal implicature from second disjunct: 'Possibly they've beaten
     the record already and will not try again.'
     P('they've beaten the record at t_1 and will not try again at t_2.')
     Q-implicature defeats the potential I-implicature.

The generalization over this and many other cases thus appears to be that Q-inferences have priority over I-inferences.[76] One class of systematic exceptions, I have noted, appear to be the Neg-raising I-inferences, which seem to be partially conventionalized and are restricted so that the informativeness of the inference only slightly exceeds the content of what is said (see section 2.3.2).

The priority of M- over I-inferences was detailed in the discussion of the M-principle and the division of pragmatic labor. For example:

(104) a. "Cortes killed Montezuma."
I ++> 'Cortes directly caused the death of Montezuma, e.g., strangled him with his own hands.'
  b. "Cortes caused the death of Montezuma."
M ++> 'Cortes indirectly caused the death of Montezuma, e.g., ordered him to be put to death.'

Now what happens if an M- and a Q-implicature are inconsistent? Consider the following example:

(105) a. "Cortes caused the death of Montezuma, or indeed he killed him outright with his own hands."
  b. "Cortes *caused the death of* Montezuma."
M +> K ('Cortes brought about the death of Montezuma indirectly, not with his own hands.')
  c. *p or q* Q-clausal +> {Pq; P ~ q}; instantiating: Q +> P('Cortes killed him outright with his own hands.')

Example (105a) clearly lacks the potential M-implicature of (105b) arising from the first clause, and this is obviously due to the content of the following disjunct. The M-inference would equally have been defeated by a conditional clause: "Cortes caused the death of Montezuma, if indeed he did not kill him outright with his own hands", because conditionals give rise to the same type of Q clausal implicature as disjunctions. Or another example:

(106) a. "It's not unlikely that Giant Stride will win the Derby, and indeed I think it likely."
  b. "It's not unlikely that Giant Stride will win the Derby."
M ++> 'It's less than fully likely that Giant Stride will win the Derby.' [from use of double negative *not unlikely*]
i.e., K('it's not likely that Giant Stride will win the Derby.')
  c. "and indeed I think it likely."
Q-clausal +> 'It is possible it is likely.' [from use of *think* which does not entail its complement]
i.e., P('it is likely that Giant Stride will win the Derby.')
  d. The Q-inference in (c) defeats the inconsistent M-inference in (b).

Again, other clausal inferences will do the same job: consider, for example, "It's not unlikely that Giant Stride will win the Derby, if indeed there's any uncertainty at all", which will Q-implicate 'It is possible that it is certain.'

As far as I can see, therefore, the proposed priority of Q > M > I appears to work. But why? It is fairly clear why both the Q- and the M-principles should have priority over the I-principle: they are both meta-linguistic principles that work by reference to what the speaker might otherwise have said but hasn't. In short, the speaker has gone out of his or her way to produce an utterance that suggests otherwise than the straight inference to the stereotypical or canonical subcase. The relative priority of the Q-principle over the M-principle is presumably attributable to the relative importance of informational content over expression modulation. This line of explanation is based on the idea that the I-principle legitimates the working assumption "enrich!" in the normal case, and the other principles serve to constrain that enrichment. Another way of looking at it is to compare the phenomena to blocking in morphology and syntax: the more specific rules block the application of more general rules. Thus inferences based on highly constrained sets of lexemes (Q-inferences) block those based on wider ranging contrasts in markedness (M-inferences), which in turn block those based on stereotypes about the world and the inference of maximal cohesion (I-inferences). The need for such blocking rules is clear in default reasoning systems: as Lascarides and Asher (1993: 444) note, "we want a defeasible logic to validate the inference in which the more specific rule is preferred."

Let us now turn to the question of subspecies of inference types. Gazdar (1979), as I showed earlier, made the distinction between clausal and scalar Quantity implicatures. One reason for this is that they appear to have different projection properties (but see Soames 1982 for critique, and Kay 1992 for response).[77]

(107) a. "If all of my friends don't earn more than me, then some of them earn more than me."
  b. "Some of them earn more than me."
     Q scalar $+>$ K('Not all of my friends earn more than me.')
  c. "If p then q" Q-clausal $+>$ {Pp, P $\sim$ p, Pq, P $\sim$ q}
  d. "If all of my friends don't earn more than me."
     Q-clausal $+>$ P('all of my friends earn more than me.')
     [from P $\sim$ ('all of my friends don't earn more than me.')]
  e. The clausal-implicature in (d) overrides the potential scalar implicature in (b).

Whether there are other such subspecies with ordered priorities has simply not been established at this stage. Indeed the whole issue of implicature projection has not been taken seriously hitherto, with the exception of Gazdar (1979). I have already noted Gazdar's (1979: 56–59) claim that implicatures should be blocked by any logical operators whose scope they fall within, and Hirschberg's (1985: 73) restriction of this blocking rule to negation (accepted by Kadmon 1987 and Horn 1989: 234). I pointed out that in fact no such blocking under negation is necessary, once the systematicity of negative scales is appreciated: thus, an utterance of the form "... not ... some ..." invokes the scale ⟨*not-some/none, not all*⟩, in which the offending expression is the strongest member and therefore generates no scalar implicatures.[78]

In fact, I shall take Gazdar's (1979) projection mechanism as a first approximation to what is required. Let us idealize a conversation in such a way that each utterance contributes its information to the context or the common ground—that is, that which is taken for granted by the speaker as shared assumptions. Now let each utterance be processed in such a way that its encoded and implicated content is added incrementally to the context in a fixed order.[79] The order suggested by the remarks above should be:

(108) Ordered incrementation of the context by the content C of an utterance U

    a. Each aspect of utterance content should be added to *C* only if it is consistent with what has already been added to *C* by *U* or preceding utterances, or is part of *C* by virtue of being assumptions taken for granted;

    b. Aspects of utterance content should be added to *C*, providing they are consistent, in the following order:

       i.   the entailments of *U*

       ii. (1) the potential clausal Q-implicatures of *U*

             (2) the potential scalar Q-implicatures of *U*

       iii. the potential M-implicatures of *U*

       iv. the potential I-implicatures of *U*

In such a system, all the potential implicatures are generated and are then filtered out by a process of incremental addition to the context only if consistency is satisfied. This process of generation plus filtering captures the essential notion of *default* inference. The process can be viewed simply as a technical solution, but it can also be viewed as psycholinguistic prediction of some interest. The important concept of *defeasibility* is thus modeled in terms of filtering by inconsistent, higher ordered assumptions. There would be other, more complex reconstructions of that concept, as discussed in chapter 1 under the rubric of nonmonotonic inference systems, and there are perhaps reasons to think one may have to escalate in that direction especially when we move outside the domain of GCIs (see, e.g., the fifth point in the next paragraph).

In various other ways that hardly need to be spelled out, this filtering system is an idealization. First, Gazdar's (1979: 130) model is a model of speaker's commitment, not actually a model of mutually accepted propositions as appropriate to conversation (in this respect, it borrows from Hamblin's (1971) model of a speaker's commitment slate), although that modification looks feasible. Second, the model cannot handle retraction, and more importantly it cannot handle implicature cancellation at arbitrary distance. The notion of utterance in Gazdar's model follows the Bar-Hillel (1954) concept of a sentence-context pairing, but in fact it is clear that implicatures can be canceled from across sentences, as in "I ate some of the biscuits. In fact, I'm dreadfully sorry, they were so delicious, I ate them all." For this reason, I propose in chapter 3 that implicatures must be kept distinct from other assumptions so that they can be later canceled from theoretically arbitrary distance.[80] Third, in the case of tropes (e.g., ironies and metaphors), what is entailed may sometimes be canceled by what is implicated (e.g., "Chomsky is never inscrutable", said ironically, might implicate 'he is always inscrutable'). Fourth, there are probably constructional differences in the order in which clauses are incremented—for example, in theories such as DRT the antecedents of conditionals contribute to the context before the consequent (Kamp and Reyle 1993: 147ff). Such construction-specific cumulative rules were employed in earlier models of presupposition projection (see Soames 1982 for a summary), and as I show in chapter 3, they may play a role in how GCIs are interpreted. Fifth, the central concept of addition under *consistency* runs into trouble with particularized implicatures attributable to the maxim of Relevance, which I assume to be centrally concerned with the relation of utterances to the presumed goal-structure of the ongoing activity to which the discourse is contributing.[81] Consider for example:

(109) A: "Well, what did you achieve today?"
      B: "Oh I went downtown and dealt with some bills."
         B's utterance potentially I-implicates: 'I went downtown and then dealt with some bills.' or 'I went downtown in order to deal with some bills.'

Here it seems that because the requirement set by local conversational goals is just to provide a list, the I-inferences to order and teleology are not firm (in contrast, for example, to the same response to "Where did you go?").

A further major difficulty will become clear in the chapter 3. Generalized implicatures can play a role in "fixing" the propositional content of statements and the entailments of that content. This of course threatens any such scheme as the one sketched above, where entailments cancel implicatures inconsistent with them, unless such pragmatic intrusion into truth conditions has a systematic basis (which, in fact, seems to be the case).

Despite these insufficiencies, the proposed model is a useful first approximation for the purposes of modeling just the kind of inferences we are concerned with here—namely, the generalized implicatures. And I shall presume that something along these lines is at least a productive research strategy to follow. Some theorists interested in GCIs seem to suggest a pessimism that any system of this kind will work.[82] Nonce-implicature theorists, who refuse to countenance the existence of GCIs, may look at these projection complications attending GCI theory as a giant *reductio ad absurdum*, the last epicycles of a Ptolemaic system. Surely a theory with less maxims or principles, a Copernican alternative, is to be preferred? It may seem that the fewer the principles, the fewer the clashes between rival inferences there are likely to be. But that is not the case: there will simply be fewer ways to classify the rival inferences, and so fewer ways to specify traffic rules between them. Similarly, nonce-implicature theorists (those who only grant the existence of PCIs) fail to attend to the problems of inconsistent inferences arising from different clauses. It may indeed be a general assumption in our conscious phenomenology of communication that "it is the first interpretation to occur to the addressee that is the one the communicator intended to convey" (Sperber and Wilson 1986: 169), but this uniqueness can only be achieved by a massive pruning, a veritable massacre, of lexical and structural ambiguities, pragmatic resolutions of deixis and anaphora, and the myriads of pragmatic inferences that arise. GCI theory, by suggesting default heuristics, greatly restricts the dimensions of the task, at least in this corner of utterance-meaning.

Chapter 3

Generalized Conversational Implicature and the Semantics/Pragmatics Interface

3.1 BACKGROUND

In the previous chapters, I outlined a theory of generalized conversational implicatures, sketched a tentative catalog of the phenomena that come under the theory, and explored some of the ways in which they may interact with one another. Grice developed a theory of implicature not because he had any overriding interest in, for example, conversational understanding, but because he saw correctly that a theory of preferred interpretations would make possible a reassessment of what aspects of the meaning of particular linguistic expressions are really semantically specified and which aspects come about through a process of interpretive enrichment. This program, when pushed through in the sort of way we have explored in the previous chapters, renders problematic and "up for grabs" the correct division of labor between semantics and pragmatics in the explanation of many aspects of meaning. These possibilities have hardly been explored. We have already seen, for example, that GCIs may be responsible for the assignment of scope—that was the import of the discussion of the Neg-raising examples in chapter 2 (see also Bach 1982, 1994: 129–130; Hobbs 1996). Similarly, GCIs seem to play a role in the fundamentals of reference, as noted in the discussion of the scalar implicatures associated with definite versus indefinite determiners; this is a theme further explored in this chapter,[1] but especially in the next. Many specific alleged ambiguities, of both a potentially structural and lexical kind, might succumb to an account in terms of monosemy (semantic generality) plus or minus implicatures (Ruhl 1989). There are perhaps specific historical reasons, but no good intellectual ones, for why the Gricean program in this direction has not been pushed further through.[2]

In this chapter, though, rather than develop the analysis of GCIs further, I wish instead to use the modest harvest gathered so far as a lever on the general theory of meaning. It turns out that GCIs have fundamental implications for the way in which we should construct an overall theory of meaning—in particular, for what we may call (somewhat grandiosely) its *architecture*. I shall assume that "meaning" is essentially composite—that is, that we need to carve up the semiotic pie much in the way that Grice envisaged, into the component entailments, conventional implicatures, presuppositions, felicity conditions, GCIs, and PCIs associated with particular expressions on particular occasions of use.[3] To describe and analyze these different aspects of meaning, we will need distinct bodies of principles (each constituting a component in the overall theory); for example, semantic inference is based on monotonic principles, but many aspects of pragmatic meaning are defeasible and nonmonotonic in character. We then have to ask: How do these elements or components of meaning interact? That I take to be a question about the architecture of a theory of meaning. Chomsky (1965) introduced a highly influential way of thinking about this: he suggested that the traditional levels of linguistic analysis (syntax, phonology, semantics) should be thought of as independent *components* or modules, with the interaction between components being conceived of in terms of *logical priority*—that is, the interaction being determined by what kind of *input* each module needs.[4] He was thus able to finesse the central interesting question of the control and flow of information between components by building a solution into the components themselves (each component transforming a specific type of input into a specific kind of output appropriate as input to another component, such that the logical ordering of components does not need to be stipulated).[5] In the theory of meaning, we seem to have inherited this thinking: semantics is normally held to be *logically prior* to pragmatics, and thus semantics is *autonomous* with respect to pragmatics in just the way that Chomsky imagines syntax to be autonomous with respect to semantics. This chapter attempts to demonstrate that this is simply not a tenable way of thinking in the theory of meaning.[6]

The crucial fact that I will try to establish is that generalized conversational implicatures seem to play a role in the assignment of truth-conditional content.[7] This may seem not only a distinctly odd idea but even definitionally impossible, because implicatures are often partially defined in opposition to truth-conditional content. Some scholars have therefore argued that any such inferences should be called something else (e.g., "explicatures" or "implicitures"), but calling them something else will not change the fact that they are the very same beasts. In the end, it will be seen, I think, to be an inevitable conclusion that GCIs play a role in truth-conditional content. Now if there is such a role for generalized implicatures, then it will have major implications for the architecture of the theory of meaning—we will need to drastically revise our understanding of the pragmatics/semantics interface and the flow of information between the components in a general theory of meaning.

A revolution of that order may not be prompted by the role of generalized implicatures alone—after all, energetic theorists may find some other way of accounting for the facts. However, there are convergent strands of thinking that are heading toward the same general conclusion—namely, that a rethinking of the pragmatics/semantics interface is in order—so that my particular thesis (that generalized implicatures can contribute to truth-conditional content) is merely one of a number of contributory arguments. Other arguments heading in the same direction can be found, on the one hand, in new pragmatic theories like Sperber and Wilson's Relevance theory and the artificial-intelligence work that goes under the rubric of "local pragmatics" (e.g., Hobbs et al. 1987); and, on the other hand, in new semantic theories like Situation Semantics (Barwise and Perry 1983) and the context-change theories of semantic representation (as in the Discourse Representation Theory [DRT] of Kamp 1981 or the File Change Semantics of Heim 1982). These trends, together with the evidence adduced here, do indeed suggest that the entire theory of meaning requires a radical new architecture that will integrate old insights in new ways. My purpose is to be brash about the implications, to try and force them onto the agenda of those engaged in formal semantics.

Although the arguments here can be taken as contributory to these general trends, they are also intended to favor some of them against others. Thus I believe the results favor a DRT conceptualist approach to formal semantics, where there is a specific kind of level of mental representation for meanings (Kamp 1981) over the realist position favored in Situation Semantics (Barwise and Perry 1983). I also believe that the results argue against Sperber and Wilson's (1986) Relevance theory by showing that generalized implicatures exist and play a systematic role in truth-conditional content. The facts also argue against the AI work in local pragmatics where scalar implicatures, for example, play no role in embellishing logical forms. In this sort of way, I hope to advance the search for the new architecture for the theory of meaning by placing further constraints on the solution.

In the end, the picture I advance is much less radical than some alternative possibilities (some of which will be considered below). To spill the beans: essentially, I argue that the theory of meaning has the components or levels we always thought it had—it is just that we have to reconstrue the kinds of relations that hold between them. Thus, semantics remains the familiar beast—it consists of two rather separate processes: one that cranks out a level of semantic representation (albeit much more abstract and underdetermined than used to be thought) from surface structure, and another process of semantic interpretation that interprets a richer level of representation (where truth conditions, entailment relations, or sense relations can be captured). Both levels of representation are closely related to linguistic structure, and they are intimately connected because the first level of representation is functionally constrained by the role it has to play in semantic interpretation. Pragmatics too encompasses more than one process: on the one hand, default inferences can be calculated on the fly, given fragments of semantic representation; on the other hand, further pragmatic inferences (of both a specific and default character) can be calculated given the results of semantic interpretation. The novel suggestion here is that *semantic and pragmatic processes can interleave, in ways that are probably controlled by the constructional types in the semantic representation*. Where pragmatic inferences end up embedded in semantic representations or their interpretations, I shall talk about *intrusion*; some kinds of intrusion are relatively uncontroversial, but the systematicity of GCI intrusion has not been properly appreciated, and it is this that requires a rethinking of the semantics/pragmatics interface.

Although this picture is relatively conservative, the interaction between pragmatic and semantic factors raises many terminological problems: what has happened to the distinctions between semantics and pragmatics, sentence-meaning and utterance-meaning, what is said and what is implicated? What do we mean by "semantic representation" when even the first level may involve pragmatic disambiguation and the second level is shot through with pragmatic contributions? I attempt no terminological reformation here, and this is largely because many of the old notions are good enough, *provided* we focus on processes or operations on representations rather than on the representations themselves. The representations are going to become strange, hybrid semantico-pragmatic entitities, but the processes that construct them and interpret them are perhaps just the familiar old semantic and pragmatic processes, with the addition of presumptive meanings. The picture will become clearer, I hope, as we proceed, so I ask the reader to bear with me.

One further caveat: because both pragmatic theory and semantic theory are undergoing rapid change at the moment, any proposals about the exact location of an interface are bound to be theory-dependent. There are enough new varieties of semantic theory, each constantly evolving, to make it well nigh impossible to predict how each would maneuver around every pragmatic shoal. It will often be the case that some semantic reanalysis might be able to absorb the particular example of what I am arguing to be implicatural content. My strategy is thus to try and foresee and deal with the counterarguments as far as this is possible but also to simply flood the opposition by showing that there is a vast range of data that would be simply explained by general pragmatic processes, but that would require an insuperable amount of ad hoc semantic reanalysis (if that were possible at all).

Once again, I will concentrate on just one, very large set of pragmatic facts—the generalized conversational implicatures (GCIs) that are the subject of this book. In certain respects, this may amount to an artificial restriction because the general theme to be explored is the extent to which pragmatic inferences in general contribute propositional content. But there are particular reasons to concentrate on GCIs. One is that (underexplored though they are) they are well understood in comparison to any other kind of pragmatic inference—there are clear predictions about what interpretations should arise in what conditions. Second, it is the default nature of GCIs that causes them to be deeply entangled in grammar and semantics—they are both hard to distinguish from encoded content, and they exert functional pressure on syntax, lexicon, and semantics (we have already seen for example, that there is a redundancy constraint: certain kinds of GCIs block grammatical and lexical encodings; see Horn 1989). Third, it is not clear that particularized conversational implicatures play the same kind of role in fixing propositional content (but see section 3.5.1.1 and, e.g., Bach 1994).

Let me summarize the kind of theory of GCIs that has emerged in the preceding chapters:

1. A rationale is provided, in terms of ways of overcoming the constraints of the narrow bandwidth of human speech, for three cross-cutting inferential heuristics that more or less amount to Grice's maxims of

Quantity 1, Quantity 2, and Manner (Relevance inferences can't be GCIs).

2. This partially motivates a typology of GCIs, into Q, I, and M types with subtypes.

3. A single utterance often gives rise to conflicting subtypes of GCI, and the clash (or projection problem) is resolved by a set of priorities, Q > M > I (with ordered subtypes).

4. GCIs can up to a point be formalized, and their defeasible behavior in complex sentences modeled, either in terms of an incremental addition of "all the news that fits" or perhaps in terms of some nonmonotonic logic (e.g., default or autoepistemic) of the kinds currently being explored in AI.

5. Finally, I made some observations that will be developed in this chapter: GCIs play a role in fundamental linguistic processes like reference resolution, generality narrowing, scope assignments, and so on.

I use the details of this typology of GCIs in the material that follows, but little depends on the details of my scheme—I simply use the typology to demonstrate the extensive range of pragmatic intrusions into semantics.

3.2   THE RECEIVED VIEW: SEMANTICS AS INPUT TO PRAGMATICS

Grice (1989: 25, 87f) made the distinction between saying and implicating, but his definition of what is *said* is complex and by no means clear (see Harnish, 1976: 332ff; Bach 1994). Roughly, though:[8]

(1) *U* said that *p* by uttering *x* iff:

    a. *x* conventionally ("timelessly") means *p*

    b. *U* speaker-meant *p* (this condition serves, e.g., to select one of a number of ambiguous readings)

    c. *p* = the conventional meaning of *x* minus any conventional implicatures (i.e., any non-truth-conditional but conventional aspects of meaning that 'indicate' but do not contribute to 'what is said').

There is a philosophical literature on Grice's notion of "what is said" that I will refer to in passing (but see especially Bach 1994, Recanati 1993). But linguistic commentators have on the whole been happy to take Grice's notion of "what is said" as mapping more or less onto truth-conditional content (an interpretation encouraged by Grice's treatment of the logical connectives). (Due allowance has to be made of course for the satisfaction conditions, rather than truth conditions, of nonassetoric speech acts, but here I abstract away from this additional problem.) However, as Atlas and Levinson (1981: 1ff) note, two utterances with the same truth conditions (e.g., *It's done* and *It's done and if it's done, it's done*) can have quite distinct implicatures (see also the discussion in of litotes in section 2.4.1.3, and why, in particular, $\sim\sim p$ does not have the same import as p). Atlas and Levinson (1981) proposed therefore that what is said, in Grice's sense, should be related to the level of semantic representation or logical form, and this is the position I take here.[9] (Such a level is almost certainly much more abstract and underspecified than was previously thought, but more of that later.)

Grice (1975: 44) also notes some essential prerequisites for an identification of what is said, and these will prove crucial:

"for a full identification of what the speaker had said one would need to know (a) the identity of [the referents], (b) the time of utterance, (c) the meaning on the particular occasion of utterance, of the phrase [uttered]."

In short, we need to have resolved reference, fixed indexicals, and disambiguated expressions before we can identify what a speaker has said on an occasion of utterance.

In contrast to what is said, and on the basis of what is said, a speaker may conversationally implicate further propositions. By saying p, utterer *U conversationally implicates q* if:

(a) *U* is presumed to be following the maxims,
(b) the supposition q is required to maintain (a), and
(c) *U* thinks the recipient will realize (b).

"To work out ... a particular conversational implicature the hearer will rely on ... the conventional meaning of the words ... together with the identity of any references involved" (1975: 50).

The central idea is simple and clear. What is *said* is the input to the pragmatic reasoning responsible for output of *implicatures*: what is implicated is calculated on the basis of what is said (together with aspects of *how* it was said, in the case of Manner implicatures). "What is said" seems to be designed to be equivalent to the proposition expressed by the use of a sentence or the truth-conditional content of the utterance, and is in turn dependent on reference resolution, indexical fixing, and disambiguation. Although it is impossible to provide a diagram that is neutral over all the different theoretical positions, I believe that the received

view of an abstract (competence) model of meaning assignment is more or
less accurately captured in figure 3.1 (this picture clearly doesn't capture
the view in Situation Semantics or DRT [more on this later] nor does it
incorporate theory-specific components of grammar). Here, there is a
logical ordering of operations, so that the syntax provides strings with
structural analyses, selected between by a disambiguation device of some sort
(usually not directly addressed in linguistic theory). The disambiguated
structure can then be associated with a semantic representation or logical
form, which in turn can then be associated with a model-theoretic interpretation, but only after the "fixing" of indexicals with the aid of a highly
restricted kind of pragmatic input—namely, the values of the pragmatic
indices obtaining in the speech situation. The interpretation is then taken
to provide a proposition expressed by the utterance on an occasion of use.
The output of the semantics is then the input to the pragmatics, where
Gricean mechanisms provide augmented (and occasionally, as in "flouts,"
altered) interpretations.

In this chapter, I examine two major kinds of problem for the received
view. The first problem, covered in section 3.2.1, is that even if we accept
Grice's rather restricted account of what is involved in fixing what is said,
namely the factors already mentioned (reference identification, deixis, and
disambiguation), implicatures can be seen paradoxically to play a role in
the establishment of what is said. This leads to an interesting chicken-and-
egg problem about the priority of what is said versus what is implicated.
At this point, it will prove useful to pause to consider possible responses.
The second problem, examined in section 3.3, is that the content of generalized conversational implicatures can fall within the scope of logical
operators and other higher level processes of semantic composition. In
section 3.4, I turn once again to reference fixing, now in detail, and show
that GCIs interact with some of the crucial philosophical distinctions in
reference. These three lines of evidence converge in requiring a rejection
of the received view of the semantics/pragmatics interface and point in the
direction of a new architecture for the theory of meaning.

3.2.1   Grice's Circle: Implicatural Contributions to "What Is Said"

An initial problem for the received view is just this: Grice gives three
preconditions to determining what was said: (a) identifying the referents,
(b) fixing the deictic parameters, and (c) disambiguating the linguistic
string in question. To these we may add at least the further preconditions
to determining the proposition expressed: (d) unpacking ellipses and (e)

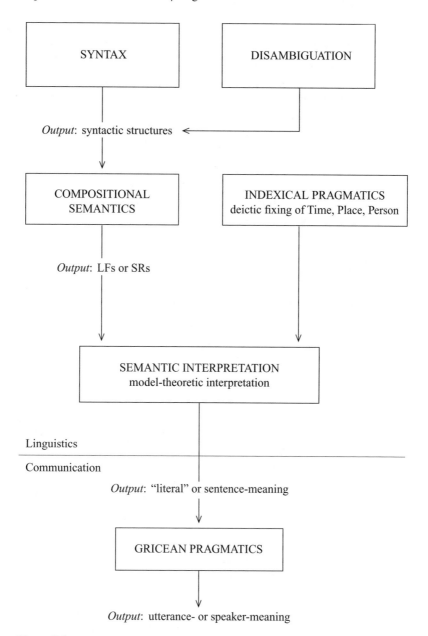

Figure 3.1
Received view of the semantics/pragmatics relation

narrowing generalities. But each of these turn out to involve exactly those inferential mechanisms that characterize Gricean pragmatics—that supposedly postsemantic (and perhaps nonlinguistic) process that maps literal meanings (the output of semantic interpretation) into speaker-meanings.

In the following subsections, I briefly illustrate this claim that Gricean inferences are involved in determining *what* proposition has been "literally" expressed. Note that no claim is being made that Gricean inferences are exclusively responsible for reference fixing, disambiguation, and indexical resolution—just that they sometimes, and quite plausibly often, are. Later I will return and substantiate some of these claims in much greater detail. The aim here is simply to make a prima facie case in order to elucidate the structure of the argument.

3.2.2 Disambiguation

It is uncontroversial that arbitrary amounts of world knowledge might be involved in disambiguation, as the following examples should make clear (example (2a) is after Hirst 1987 and (2c) is after Winograd 1972).

(2) a. The view could be improved by the addition of a *plant* out there. (lexical ambiguity of *plant*)

   a'. The view would be destroyed by the addition of a *plant* out there.

   b. Mary left [the book] [on the bus.]

   b'. Mary left [the book on the atom.] (structural ambiguity of PP attachment)

   c. The administrators barred the demonstrators because *they* advocated violence.[10]

   c'. The administrators barred the demonstrators because *they* feared violence.

   d. He looked at the kids [in the park] *with a telescope*.

   d'. He looked at the kids [in the park *with a statue*].

It's a more interesting claim that Gricean principles would be involved. For example, a moment's reflection will convince that the maxim of Relevance will be involved in selecting those readings that make possible "sequiturs" to a prior utterance (see also Sperber and Wilson 1986: 183ff). The following is a simple case (from Hirst 1987; note though that prosody would often disambiguate this sort of case):

(3) A: i. "What are they doing in the kitchen?"

      ii. "What kind of apples are those?"

   B: "They are cooking apples."

It is much less obvious that GCIs might be involved in disambiguation, but a few examples should make that plausible:

(4) a. "He's an indiscriminate dog-lover; he likes [some cats] and dogs."
    b. He likes [[some cats] and dogs]
       Interpretation: 'he likes some cats and dogs (in general)'
       GCI: 'he likes some-but-not-all cats'
    c. He likes [some [cats and dogs]]
       Interpretation: 'he likes some cats and some dogs'
       GCI: 'he likes some-but-not-all cats and some-but-not-all-dogs'

Example (4a) makes the point this way. Suppose we take the last NP of the sentence to have the structure: [[some cats] and dogs]. Then *he likes some cats* has the scalar (Q) GCI 'he doesn't like all cats'; this interpretation is compatible with the first clause, which implies that he likes all dogs. Now suppose instead that we take the NP to be structured this way: [some [cats and dogs]], with the interpretation 'he likes some cats and he likes some dogs'. Then there will be a GCI 'he likes some-but-not-all cats and some-but-not-all dogs'. But such an implicature is inconsistent with the first clause *He's an indiscriminate dog-lover*; if we then reject the syntactic analysis that gives rise to the inconsistent implicature, we'll arrive at the right bracketing of the NP.

This account has some plausibility and some generality. Consider:

(5) a. "He has a whole pack of dogs. He has three cats and dogs."
    b. He has [[three cats] and dogs].
       Interpretation: 'he has three cats and an indeterminate number of dogs'
       GCI: 'he has no more than three cats'
    c. He has [three [cats and dogs]]
       Interpretation: 'he has three cats and three dogs'
       GCI: 'he has no more than three cats and no more than three dogs'

Just as before, the structural analysis that has a semantic interpretation that induces an implicature consistent with the context will be preferred over another analysis that induces an inconsistent implicature. Note that, on the assumption that the "exactly" interpretation is only implicated, the semantic content alone cannot account for the favored readings.

Another example with structural ambiguity might be:

(6) a. "She heard some of the firecrackers in the kitchen."
    b. She heard [some of the firecrackers] [in the kitchen] (but others while she was in the sitting room).

    c. She heard [some of the firecrackers in the kitchen] (but some of
       them must have been quieter).

    d. *Gloss of literal content:* 'She heard at least some of the firecrackers
       in the kitchen.'

    e. *GCI:* 'She heard some but not all of the firecrackers in the kitchen.'

    f. She heard [some but not all of the firecrackers] [in the kitchen]
       (but others while in the sitting room).

A PP like *in the kitchen* in (6a). can often be attached high (here to the
VP) or low (here to the object NP), as clarified in (6b) and (6c). The literal
content of (6a), roughly glossed in (6d), does not predispose us one way or
the other. But the GCI in (6e) biases us toward the (6b) reading, as in (6f),
because otherwise it will take special circumstances (e.g., variable hearing
loss, uneven quality of firecrackers) to explain why the protagonist only
heard some but not all of the (presumably equally loud) firecrackers that
went off in the kitchen.

GCIs may participate in the disambiguation of lexical ambiguities,
especially perhaps through the I-inference to stereotypical extensions.
Thus the kind of disambiguations often attributed to brute encyclopedic
knowledge may be mediated by Gricean procedures: the speaker must
presume that the addressee will use the same salient stereotype (regardless
of its factual probabilities) to resolve the ambiguity (as in *He took another
drink*, where *drink* is interpreted as the alcoholic variety).

If the observation that GCIs can select between ambiguities is correct
and fully general, it is perhaps not self-evident why. GCIs are cancelable;
thus given a context inconsistent with them, they quite routinely evaporate. The answer must be that the recipient works on the assumption that
the speaker would so design his utterance that, other things being equal,
the predictable GCIs would go through.[11] Thus given the option of pre-
serving the implicatures, an interpreter generally chooses that interpretation that will do so.

These examples are less than fully natural because they attempt to isolate just one kind of pragmatic inference at a time—in many, more natural, examples, GCIs of many different kinds collaborate, as it were, to
favor one reading among a set of ambiguous ones:

(7) a. "She submitted an uneven article. Some of the paper was
      excellent." (I, Relevance, Q)

    b. *article*$_1$: 'thing'
     article$_2$: 'short academic treatise'

$paper_1$: mass noun 'stuff for writing on'
$paper_2$: count noun 'academic treatise'
$uneven_1$: 'bumpy'
$uneven_2$: 'variable quality'

  c. GCIs:

    i. "Some of the paper" Q +> 'not all of the paper'

    ii. the referent of *an article₂* = the referent of *the paper₂*
       (I-preference for local coreference)

    iii. *uneven article* should be read 'variable quality academic
       treatise' rather than 'bumpy academic treatise' (attributable to
       an I-inference to the stereotypical interpretation)

Without specifying all the inferential mechanisms, it seems likely that a global process of inference to the best interpretation will seek an interpretation consistent with all the GCIs (Atlas and Levinson 1981). Such an interpretation will minimize the entities and properties postulated, as suggested by the I-principle. In many cases, that interpretation will select between ambiguous meanings and structures.

3.2.3 Indexical Resolution

It is uncontroversial that certain pragmatic factors—namely, pragmatic indices or deictic parameters—are input to semantic interpretation. But it has been supposed that these indexical factors are of a limited kind and may be swept within a truth-conditional apparatus.[12] There are a number of distinct assumptions here, each of which can be challenged:

1. *Indexical expressions are few in number and limited in kind.* (But in fact there are many different kinds of covertly indexical expressions; see Enç 1981, Barwise and Perry 1983, Mitchell 1986);

2. *The indexical parameters or indices are a fixed, small set* for e.g., speakers, addressees, times of utterance, places of utterance, and indicated objects (see, e.g., Lewis 1972). (But crosslinguistic studies show that many more parameters may be required—for example, Kwakiutl forces a choice between "visible/nonvisible to participants" on most NPs in the same way that English forces a choice of tense on most verbs; see the catalogs of exotic deictic parameters in Fillmore 1975, Levinson 1983, Anderson and Keenan 1985).

3. *The assignment of an indexical value to an indexical expression is a simple process of a direct mapping between context and expression.* There is a look-up table as it were, that assigns the expression *I* to the

current speaker, the expression *here* to the place of utterance, *now* to the time of uttering, and so on.

It is this last assumption that I challenge here: that indexicals require no inferential resolution and, in particular, that the assignment of indexical values has nothing to do with pragmatic inference in general, and thus nothing to do with GCIs. The assumption is undermined by examples like the following, organized under the major traditional dimensions of deixis—namely, place, person, and time (Levinson 1983: chap. 2):

(8) *Place*
   a. "Take *these three* drinks to the three people over there; take *these four* to the four people over there."
      Q ++> 'Take the drinks that are exactly three in number over there, take the drinks that are exactly four in number over there.'
   b. "Some of those apples are ripe; *those ones are for you*, the other ones are for Bill."
      Q ++> 'Some but not all of those apples are ripe; just the ripe ones are for you ...'
   c. "This sofa is comfortable; come over *here*" vs. "California is beautiful; come over *here*."
      I-principle: delimits *here* by anaphoric resolution.

(9) *Person*
   a. A: i. "He said you did it?"
         ii. "He confessed?" (alternative possible question)
      B: "He said *I* did it" (maxim of Relevance)
   b. "*Some of you* know the news; I'm not talking to *you*; I'm talking to the rest of you."
      Q-principle: delimits *to you* to 'to some but not all of you'

(10) *Time*
   a. "I *used to* have a car like that."
      Q-implicates: 'I no longer have a car like that'
   b. "The meeting is on *Thursday*."
      Q-implicates: 'not tomorrow' when tomorrow is Thursday.

Consider the use of example (8a) in the absence of gestural indication (on the phrase *these three* drinks) and in a context where the speaker is pouring wine into two sets of glasses: one set has exactly three glasses, the other exactly four. Given that the numeral words in English can be argued to only implicate an upper bound, *three* glosses as 'at least three' at the level of semantic content, although it normally carries a GCI 'at most three'. Thus the expression *these three glasses* has the semantic content 'these glasses of cardinality no less than three'. It follows that, in the absence of gesture, the expression might equally designate either set of glasses. Yet the utterance would be perfectly felicitous in the circumstances sketched, because any interpreter would use the GCI 'at most three' to resolve the indexical reference. (Without such pragmatic resolution, the utterance ought to be anomalous; because it isn't, we must assume that GCIs play a role in fixing indexical reference.)

Consider now example (8b). The expression *some of those apples* is consistent with all of those apples but is delimited by a GCI to 'some but not all of those'. It is the pragmatically delimited set, a proper subset of the apples, that is introduced as a discourse referent by *some of those apples*. This is shown by the fact that the following demonstrative pronoun *those ones* must refer to a subset of the apples (cf. similar observations for nonindexicals by Kadmon (1987)). If the phrase *those ones* is both anaphoric and deictic, which I believe is the right analysis, then the truth conditions for *those ones are for you* are dependent on the GCI that restricts the set of apples to less than all. The point may be sharpened by the subsequent contrastive referring phrase: without the pragmatic restriction on *those ones*, *the other ones* has no clear denotation.

Example (8c) makes a simple but very general point. Indexical parameters are not alone sufficient, on the whole, to give one a reasonably circumscribed denotation (the one clear exception is the pronoun *I*, which is individuated by the speaker parameter alone; but see (9a)). For example, *here* denotes some region inclusive of some part of the speaker's immediate location; *bring it here* might mean 'bring it to my fingertips' (imagine the surgeon, in need of a scalpel, to the nurse) or 'bring it to Los Angeles' (perhaps we are talking about something that needs no exact location, like an advertising blimp). Suppose A is in Los Angeles and B is in New York and the following exchange takes place:

(11) A: "Where's the conference being held?"
     B: "It's being held here."

If *here* means 'some space inclusive of the speaker's location', then would B have told the truth if the conference is being held in Princeton? Surely not. But without further pragmatic restriction of the extent of *here*, what B said was true (a proper account of such restrictions can be found in Schegloff 1972). In the cases in (8c), it is clear that pragmatic restriction of the extent of *here* is made by anaphoric linkage to antecedents, a process that comes under the I-inferential category: *here* is essentially indexical but anaphorically restricted.

Person deixis might be thought to be immune from pragmatic resolution, but this is not the case. After all, even *I* can be interpreted as referring to the speaker of directly quoted speech (as in (9a), where a Relevance implicature would be instrumental in selecting interpretations according to alternate prior utterances). *You* clearly may refer to more than one addressee, or parties not addressed at all, or even some subset of the parties just previously addressed as in (9b). Here only if *some of you* implicates 'not all of you' will *the rest of you* have denotation.

Temporal deixis is in fact especially permeated by Gricean mechanisms, because temporal reference is normally made more precise by opposition to other temporal expressions that were not used—that is, by Q- and M-implicature. Thus *used to V* in (10a), where V is verb, will normally implicate 'no longer V' by opposition to the simple present (yet there's no inconsistency in "I used to love swimming, and in fact I still do"; see chap. 2). Or more simply, *Thursday* said on Wednesday will Q-implicate 'not tomorrow', because *tomorrow* would be the more informative expression and was not used (there are many Thursdays, but only one tomorrow, given a today!).

There can be little doubt then that GCIs, along with other pragmatic processes, are involved in the resolution of indexical expressions, without which, of course, no exact proposition will be expressed.

3.2.4 Reference Identification

There are two ways in which reference might be said to fail: (a) cases where there is nothing in the domain of discourse that fits the descriptive content of the referring expression—variously analyzed as yielding sentences that are false (Russell 1905) or unspecified for truth or falsity (Strawson 1950); and (b) cases where there are more than one entity in the domain of discourse (or more than one discourse referent in the sense of Karttunen 1976) that fit the descriptive content—cases of referential ambiguity as it were.[13] Both are critical to the establishment of "what is said": we can hardly be sure what proposition is expressed if we are unsure what the arguments of a predication denote (or, sometimes, which other discourse referents they are identical to).

In section 3.4 below I provide a detailed argument for the role of GCIs in nonanaphoric reference determination. Here I indicate briefly how

GCIs may be claimed to have a role in anaphoric reference determination. First, recollect that it is uncontroversial that pragmatic factors are involved in the resolution of discourse anaphora (see, e.g., the case of the anaphoric reference to *administrators* or *demonstrators* in (2c)).

Anaphoric expressions are regularly less prolix and more semantically general than the expression with which the discourse referent was first introduced (by an indefinite or sometimes a definite descriptive phrase). This, I have argued (Levinson 1987a,b) is a natural by-product of the I-principle (Grice's "Don't say more than necessary"). Thus if you intend coreference, you should make the referring expression short or semantically general. The recipient's corollary is: "From a semantically general, minimal reference form choose the interpretation that maximizes informative content," which will generally amount to a preference for local coreference. On this account, example (12a) has a preferred reading (more or less regardless of how many competing prior antecedents for *he* there may be) in which *he* is coidentified with *John*.

(12) a. "John came in and *he* sat down."
    I-induced coreference preference

   b. "John came in and *the man* sat down."
    M-induced disjoint preference

   c. "Felix voted for *him*."
    Q-induced disjoint reference

   d. "Only Felix voted for *him*."
    Can be coidentified, because "Only Felix voted for *himself*" would mean something different.

The identification can be avoided by choosing a definite referring expression that is not maximally semantically general, as in (12b). Here the speaker's use of the longer expression *the man* will only be warranted by an assumption that the speaker wishes to avoid what the natural interpretation associated with the pronoun would be, as in (12a). By the M-principle, there is a preferred interpretation under which *the man* and *John* are identified with different individuals.[14]

More controversially, Reinhart (1983) has suggested that (contrary to Chomsky's binding conditions) the object pronoun in (12c) is only interpreted as disjoint from the subject because of a Manner GCI (see also Horn 1984). My own analysis (Levinson 1987a,b) is that this is a Q-opposition: given the choice of the coindexing reflexive form or the free pronoun, the use of the latter suggests that the former is not intended via a metascale ⟨REFLEXIVE, NONREFLEXIVE PRONOUN⟩. This predicts that disjoint reference in sentences like (12c) should be defeasible (cancelable in context). Thus in the right circumstances, the pronoun may be coidentified with the subject as indicated in (12d). Reinhart's account is controversial because it yields up much of what has been supposed to be grammar to pragmatics; nevertheless the defeasibility of noncoreference assignments seems to make better empirical predictions. I return to these issues in chapter 4.

But whether this pragmatic account of the disjoint reference of nonreflexive clausemate NPs is correct or not, the I- and M-implicatures would seem to play a crucial role in reference determination, as sketched in (12a,b). By the same token, I-inferences would seem to be responsible for "bridging" inferences, legitimating the inference to the best interpretation in cases like the following:

(13) a. "The bridge collapsed. The wood was rotten."
      I ++> 'The wood of which the bridge was made was rotten.'
   b. "The bridge collapsed. A wooden strut was rotten."
      I ++> 'A crucial wooden strut of the bridge was rotten.'
   c. "Every old car needs to have the battery checked."
      I ++> 'Each car needs to have the battery which belongs to
      that car checked.'

The first example seems to require that we suppose that the bridge was made of wood. But we only need to make that supposition in order to find a coherence relation holding between the two clauses. The supposition that there is a causal relation requires the supposition that the bridge was made of wood; a specific mass of wood is then available for definite reference. The inference is supported by the I-induced submaxim "Don't state what can be inferred" and is line with our stereotypical expectations of the kinds of materials bridges can be made of. (Some theorists [Heim 1982, Kadmon 1987] have supposed that the inference is motivated only by the "accommodation" of the definite referring expression (*the wood*) which requires a familiar or given antecedent; but the bridging inference in the indefinite version in (13b) shows that more global I-principle processes are involved.)

The second kind of example in (13c) (due to Kempson 1986) is interesting because it shows that definite expressions acting as variables under explicit quantification may still require pragmatic bridging: the assumption must be made that each car has one battery. The general form of the

I-inference in these cases is: given a definite description with no obvious antecedent, make that minimal assumption that will tend to the best (maximally informative) interpretation (often, that 'the x' is part of, or associated with, a previously mentioned 'the y').

3.2.5 Ellipsis Unpacking

If A says "Who came?" and B replies "John," has B said something that can be true or false? Surely; he has expressed the proposition that John came. Just as the second maxim of Quantity ("Don't say more than necessary") or my I-principle motivates minimal expressions like pronouns, so, together with a maxim of Relevance, it motivates ellipsis. The corresponding pragmatic principle of construal is (very crudely): supply the missing predicates (here marked between angled brackets, as in (14a)) from the preceding discourse context. Ellipsis and anaphora are of course closely linked, with the interpretation of the "unsaid" governed by the I-principle, in tandem with a Relevance maxim (as discussed in chap. 1), as in example (14b).

(14) a. A: "Who came?"
         B: "John" ⟨came⟩ (Relevance and I-implicature)
     b. "Over to 41, there's a nice move. Gets fouled by number 35 of the Spartans."
     c. A: "Which side got three goals?"
         Q-implicates: 'Which side got three-and-no-more goals?'
         B: "Tottenham Hotspurs" ⟨got three-and-no-more goals⟩
     d. "Our team got three goals and theirs did ⟨get three-and-no-more-goals⟩ too; so it was a draw, three all." (Q)
     e. A: "They won't visit Mary's parents."
         B: "Old grudge."   (from Barton 1988)

Now notice that the interpretation of a gapped or elided constituent carries the implicatures of the antecedent. Thus in (14c), if the predicate of A's utterance carries a scalar implicature, B's ellipsis over the same predicate does too. As for (14d), does the conclusion follow from the first sentence and the rules of soccer? Only if our team got exactly three goals and no more, and their team got exactly three too. But that is the proposition, amplified by implicatures, that is indeed expressed (see section 3.3.).

In many structural loci, ellipsis is a fundamentally linguistic, rule-governed process, so that recovery of elided material can in fact be thought of as guided by syntactic and semantic principles. But it is clearly not true for examples like (14e), where complex reasoning and not rule application is involved in proposition recovery. It would take us too far afield to explore ellipsis in any depth, but it is self-evident that the recovery of the proposition expressed will depend in these cases often on substantial Gricean inference (see Barton 1988 for detailed explorations). The consequence is this: the pragmatics is involved in the recovery of the elided linguistic material, which must then be semantically interpreted, at which point we apparently need another pragmatic processing stage to recover the implicatures of the elided material.

3.2.6   Generality Narrowing

A central and persuasive tenet of Radical Pragmatics has been that what had previously been interpreted as ambiguity was better treated as generality plus implicatures—hence the claims that despite appearances *or*, *not*, *possible*, *some*, and so on are univocal, not ambiguous. If correct the corollary is that many natural language expressions are maximally general, to the point of bordering on vacuity (see Ruhl 1989). Consider the following examples:

(15) a. "Fixing this car will take *some time*."
     b. "I've eaten breakfast."
     c. "The flag is white."
     d. "The British flag is white."
     e. "If the flag is white, then it can't be blue."
     f. "John is tall."
     g. "Since the surgeon came quickly, he cannot be blamed."

Without pragmatic restrictions (Sperber and Wilson 1986: 189f point out), (15a) will border on the tautological, whereas (15b) will always be true of any ordinary breakfast-eater, even before he gets out of bed.[15] Similarly, if (15c) only means 'the flag is at least partially white' (Harnish 1976), then (15d) will be true but just grossly misleading and (15e) will be false. At an extreme, it is not totally implausible to suggest that gradable adjectives only predicate of their arguments that the entity in question has the relevant property to some (unspecified) degree (Sadock 1981). Thus the content of (15f) might be little more than 'John has height'! But the truth of (15f) is judged against some implicit category that John is assigned to (tall for a seven-year-old is not tall for a basketball player). (Alternatively, all degree adjectives may be treated as implicit comparatives containing a covert indexical-like argument place.) As for manner adverbs like *quickly* in (15g), they too will hardly restrict the interpretation of their predicates unless some implicit standard is taken into account. Suppose we have an emergency in the hospital, and the surgeon started jogging from his home when he should have jumped in his car; no judge would judge (15g) true.

One should distinguish two possible views here. On the original Gricean or standard Radical Pragmatics view, the lexical content of such expressions is taken to be their weakest exhibited meaning, with the assumption that the pragmatics supplements the expressions to give their stronger interpretations. Thus, for example, one takes *or* to have as lexical content the specific meaning of inclusive disjunction, strengthened to exclusive disjunction by the GCI based on the scale ⟨*and, or*⟩, which yields a 'not both' implicature from the failure to use *and*. Let us call this the *weak univocality* view. On another view, energetically purveyed by Atlas (1979, 1989), the lexical content of expressions may be indifferent, or semantically general over, both the weak and strong interpretations. On this view, the lexical content is also weak, but it is not specific. For example, Atlas (1993a) maintains that the semantic content of *three* encompasses both the weak interpretation ('at least three') and the strong one ('exactly three'), and is specialized in context. He dubs this the *semantic generality* view. However, because both views involve semantic generality (either based on the weak interpretation or on an overarching abstraction), I use the phrase to cover both kinds of analysis.

GCIs play a systematic role in generality narrowing. Horn (1984) notes in particular that both Q-narrowing and I-narrowing are frequent enough to play a systematic role in semantic change. Here are some examples of implicature-based narrowing:

(16) a. "I ate a few of the cookies"
    +> 'not all of them.' (Q-narrowing)
 b. "He hurt a *finger*"
    +> 'not a thumb.' (Q-narrowing)
 c. "It's a *big* city"
    +> 'not enormous.' (Q)
 d. "I put the *warm* pot on the table and left the hot one on the stove."
    ++> 'I put the warm-but-not-hot pot on the table.' (Q)
 e. "He had a drink"
    I +> 'alcoholic drink.' (I-narrowing)

    f. "This is a bread knife"
      I +> 'for slicing bread.' (I)
    g. "This is a steel knife"
      I +> 'made of steel.' (I)
    h. "Larry's book is about negation"
      I +> the book Larry wrote. (I)
      (cf. "Larry's book is a thriller he got from the library.")

If pragmatic narrowing of semantically general predicates is not taken into account, the proposition expressed by many sentences will be general to the point of vacuity. Intuitions about truth conditions are very much more specific: surely when we say *Larry's book is about negation* the proposition expressed depends on the implicit pragmatic narrowing of the generality associated with the possessive. The possessive encodes that there is *some* intimate relation between Larry and the book, but it is an inference guided by Gricean principles on the one hand and contextual information on the other that gives a specific content to that relation (see also Sperber and Wilson 1986), and thus plays a role here in reference determination. It is worth pointing out that all the oblique cases in Case-marking languages have this kind of semantic generality (as with Latin Ablative, which expresses source, cause, agency, instrument, deprivation, or direction from), so that no reasonably circumscribed proposition will be expressed without pragmatic resolution of the semantic content.

3.2.7 Some Interim Conclusions: Responses to Grice's Circle

The argument so far is this. Grice's account makes implicature dependent on a prior determination of "the said." The said in turn depends on disambiguation, indexical resolution, reference fixing, not to mention ellipsis unpacking and generality narrowing. But each of these processes, which are prerequisites to determining the proposition expressed, may themselves depend crucially on processes that look indistinguishable from implicatures. Thus what is said seems both to determine and to be determined by implicature. Let us call this *Grice's circle*.[16]

It should be clear that this is not a minor point in Gricean exegesis. It is a circle that equally afflicts any theory that seeks to make a semantics/pragmatics distinction play a crucial role in the general theory of meaning. The "said" can be taken to be truth-conditional content—the proposition expressed, the output of the process of semantic interpretation; the proper domain of a theory of linguistic meaning. The "implicated" can be taken more generally than I am taking it here, to include all the processes of pragmatic inference; it is the proper domain of a theory of communication. Then truth-conditional content depends on most, perhaps all, of the known species of pragmatic inference; or the theory of linguistic meaning is dependent on, not independent of, the theory of communication. Starkly: general pragmatic inference (not just the—supposedly—limited phenomenon of indexicality) is crucial input to semantic interpretation. Those who hope that a theory of linguistics will be a theory of a closed mental module (à la Fodor) will have to yield up semantic interpretation to another module or mental process. These conclusions have already been reached and stoically accepted by Sperber and Wilson (1986, 1995: 257–258) and their followers on the grounds of partially different but parallel arguments.[17]

Grice's circle seems to require at least two applications of Gricean pragmatics. Not only will we need the Gricean inferences to determine truth-conditional content, but we will also need the inferential mechanisms in just the way that Grice imagined, namely to give us postsemantic pragmatics. This is because we still need an account of the double-barreled flavor of ironies, indirections, and other tropes—two propositions are expressed: the so-called literal meaning and the full speaker-meaning. And the only way to get two levels is to have the literal proposition fixed prior to a second batch of pragmatic processing. Figure 3.2 makes the point graphically, with two layers of semantic processing interleaved with two layers of pragmatic processing. (Once again, such a diagram is not to be mistaken for a processing model—it just indicates which kinds of information are prequisites to which kind of assignment of meaning. The two boxes labeled "pragmatics" are here presumed to constitute one and the same component or kind of process.[18]). Grice's circle is the dilemma I wish to focus on here. Does it require a rethinking of the relations between semantics and pragmatics, perhaps even of the whole nature of modular interaction as currently envisaged in linguistics? Or are there ways to resist the conclusion that semantics and pragmatics are interleaved?

Let us consider possible ways to resist the conclusion, and if that fails, to contain the damage.

3.2.7.1 Denial of the Evidence   The first line of defense is the challenge: the evidence is simply not good enough. Let us create an imaginary (although not entirely fictional) character whom we may call *the Obstinate Theorist* and who will recur throughout what follows (he may be identi-

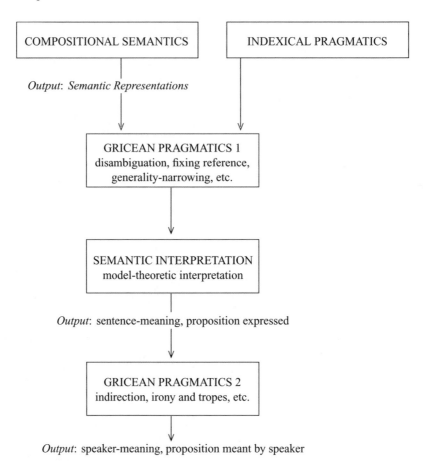

Figure 3.2
Presemantic and postsemantic pragmatics

fied with a number of eminent theoreticians, e.g., the author of Kripke 1977; see also Bach 1994). The Obstinate Theorist (affectionately OT) is principally an old-fashioned Gricean, assuming postsemantic pragmatics, although he is willing (we'll assume) to reanalyze pragmatic phenomena as semantic wherever they threaten to upset the cozy picture by intruding on the semantics. So how will he respond to our threats to the traditional picture?

The traditional picture can be maintained in part by simply letting the semantics provide highly general meanings (as envisaged originally in Radical Pragmatics), later pragmatically restricted. I will call this the

Generality-plus-implicatures move (covering both the "weak univocality" and "nonspecific semantic generality" views, as distinguished in Atlas 1989). Implicatures of course have truth conditions too; and (it may be claimed) the intuitions about truth conditions of sentence-tokens are simply being mixed with the intuitions about truth conditions of utterance-tokens. Thus in the cases of generality narrowing and indexicality narrowing reviewed above (sections 3.2.6 and 3.2.3, respectively), the Obstinate Theorist can simply claim that the proposition expressed has indeed a near-vacuous semantic content, triggering pragmatic narrowing.

In the case of disambiguation, OT can simply opt to resolve ambiguities postsemantically; that is, for each *n*-ways ambiguous string, the semantics must provide *n* propositional contents, which can be selected between by a later pragmatic process. As for ellipsis, we need to distinguish two kinds of cases: (a) the cases that are rule-governed (as in VP deletion) and for which a semantic interpretation can be algorithmically provided; and (b) the cases that are pragmatically construed. For the latter, we need a theory of subsentential phrasal semantics that will give us satisfaction conditions for sentence fragments. The satisfaction conditions can then be the input to the pragmatic component, which will yield a full proposition, the one elliptically expressed.

But the Obstinate Theorist has an Achilles heel—namely, the cases where reference is determined by implicature (these will include some of the I-narrowings, as in *Larry's book*, and some of the indexical resolutions, as in *some of you*, as well as the cases in section 3.2.4). For if the extensions of the parts are partially determined by implicature, the extension of the whole expression cannot be calculated without pragmatic input. Thus in these cases, insistence on postsemantic pragmatics will yield no propositional content at all, and thus no grist for the postsemantic pragmatic mill: without something to work on, the pragmatics cannot rescue the semantics (in the way that it may be held to in the cases of semantic generality approaching semantic vacuity).

The main purpose of this chapter is to show that the Obstinate Theorist's position is simply not tenable however attractive it may seem at first sight. Thus the bulk of my arguments will be aimed at his retort that the evidence for Grice's circle is simply not good enough, with special attention paid to the Obstinate Theorist's Achilles heel, the argument from reference.

3.2.7.2 Damage Limitation: Restricted Presemantic Pragmatics   A second move we can make is to admit that there is pragmatic intrusion but

claim that the kind of pragmatic intrusion prior to semantic interpretation is of a special limited kind, even though it may be derived by Gricean mechanisms. Thus Sperber and Wilson (1986) and Kempson (1986) make a distinction between *explicatures* and *implicatures*—explicatures explicate logical forms, which are then input to interpretation yielding propositional contents, which in turn are then input to the implicature-deriving process. This distinction will only be of interest if the range of explicatures is somehow of a special restricted kind, a disjoint type of inference or at least a distinct subset of the processes called implicature. For example, it would be an interesting (although, it will transpire, a probably false) claim that only GCIs, rather than particularized implicatures, can play a role in proposition determination. This move limits the damage, as it were, by entertaining the hypothesis that I call *restricted presemantic pragmatics*.

3.2.7.3 Semantic Retreat   The London School (Sperber and Wilson, Kempson, Carston, and colleagues, so dubbed by Horn (1984)) couple this claim about two distinct kinds of pragmatic inference to a logically independent claim of Fodorean modularity: a semantics (or more generally linguistics) module is by definition a closed processing system. It follows that semantics stops before any pragmatic processing begins. Thus linguistic semantics has nothing directly to do with propositions: it characterizes a level of logical form or semantic representation that is algorithmically derived from syntactic information. Semantic representations are syntactical objects; their *interpretation* belongs to the Fodorean central processor, where a theory of communication belongs.[19] Let us call this move *semantic retreat*.

Notice that semantic setreat has characterized Chomsky's thought all along apart from a brief and uncharacteristic flirt with the feature-based semantics of Katz and Fodor in the mid 1960s. The level of LF is not only syntactical (uninterpreted) but actually just a slightly modified level of syntax. Curiously, even Katz's position is also a kind of semantic retreat because his markerese is an uninterpreted syntactical level of representation, supposedly algorithmically derived from syntactic input. The greater richness of Katzian Semantic Representation over Chomskyan LF, and the correlated claim that semantic inferences can be captured by markerese, is just an expression of the greater optimism on Katz's part that pragmatic intrusion is minimal! In fact, the new evidence of pragmatic intrusion will be sufficient to make Katz's position untenable: one simply cannot fully capture the semantic relations of synonymy, antonymy, entailment, and so on at a preintrusive level.

The strategy of semantic retreat leaves semantic representations as incomplete formulae without determinate interpretation. Consequently, none of the traditional notions of semantics, like entailment relations, sense relations, or any other kind of necessary meaning relations, hold at this level at all. There can be no principled objection to the setting up of such a level of representation if it solves important problems (and in fact I assume a similar level below). But clearly, the burden is then on the theorist to complete the picture and reconstruct the notions of traditional semantics on another level.

3.2.7.4 Enlarged Indexicality   A fourth move we can make is to treat pragmatic intrusion of the type illustrated above as a kind of enlarged indexicality. For example, Sag (1981) outlines a way in which metonymic shifts of reference (e.g., from *Plato* to 'Plato's works') may be captured using Kaplan's *character/content* distinction. In essence, an expression has an intension only relative to context, which fixes the intension (and thus the extension) in that context. I discuss this proposal in more detail later, but I believe it cannot work in the cases presented here, given the defeasibility of implicatures.

A similar strategy would seem to be the preferred move in Situation Semantics (Barwise and Perry 1983), although in this framework in addition to the utterance situation providing indexical parameters, there may also be resource situations (i.e., other contextually pertinent situations) that serve to fix contextual variables. In contrast to the Generality-plus-implicatures approach, this approach must assign to apparently general predicates some kind of implicit but built-in placeholders for indexical or contextual material. For example, just as *behind* in "John is behind the tree" is, despite appearances, really a three-place predicate (BEHIND (John, tree, reference-point)) so *tall* in "John is tall" is really a two-place predicate (TALL (John, reference-value)). Because meaning is, on the Situation Semantics view, a relation between the utterance-situation and the described-situation, the utterance-situation (along with resource-situations) provides the implicit reference values.

On this view, many natural language expressions are covertly quasi-indexical or, to coin a term, are *contextuals*. They contain within their semantic representation variables requiring contextual identification.

There is no doubt that such covert indexicality is more widespread than normally recognized, as in the definition of *local* in *local pub* (see, e.g., Enç 1981). It is also clear that constructions that are often treated in terms of semantic-generality-plus-implicatures, like the genitive in *Larry's book*, may be reanalyzed as encoding an indexical variable that has to be contextually specified (see Recanati 1993: 235ff). But the approach being discussed here, best represented by Situation Semantics, is to assume that *all* cases of pragmatic intrusion are in fact kinds of indexical resolution in a broad sense. It is thus hoped that a proper treatment of semantics along these lines will accommodate pervasive context dependency while eradicating the threat of more disorderly kinds of pragmatic intrusion. It is important to see, though, that this framework has no place for other kinds of pragmatic determination of propositional content and therefore that the arguments developed in this chapter—to the effect that implicatures help to fix propositional content—would appear to undermine the Situation Semantics approach to context dependency.

3.2.7.5 "Pragmantics"   One response to pragmatic intrusion into semantic interpretation is to take it as evidence against the possibility of any principled distinction between semantics and pragmatics in the first place. Lakoff (1972, 1987) has been a consistent advocate of the abolition of the distinction, and others too (e.g., Baker and Hacker 1984, Jackendoff 1990: 18) have seen the semantics/pragmatics distinction as an unfortunate corollary of the tactic of treating natural languages with the mechanisms developed for the analysis of formal languages.

Here, we can only make a few elementary points against this response. First, in the perspective advocated here, pragmatic inference is fundamentally *nonmonotonic*, semantic inference is *monotonic*. Thus it is simply not possible to conflate two fundamentally different kinds of reasoning without doing violence to the essential nature of one or the other of them. The "pragmantics" cocktail that results would lose the predictive power that the modular account provides (entailments will end up defeasible, or implicatures will end up nondefeasible, or both). Second, although the abolitionists may gain succor from the evidence for pragmatic intrusion, the intrusive phenomena discussed here do not directly support their position: all they show is that semantics and pragmatics must be more intimately related than had been thought. Our arguments will provide no evidence for "pragmantics" as long as there are alternate models that will preserve modularity and accommodate the facts (one of which we now turn to).

3.2.7.6 Discourse Representation Theory: A Common Slate for Semantic and Pragmatic Contributions

The final position we consider here just bites the bullet: let pragmatic information intrude into semantic representations and consequently into their interpretation. Pragmatic intrusionism can be construed in different ways. Some theories of semantics already countenance it. In many ways, this is the route taken by Discourse Representation Theory (Kamp 1981) and its relatives (e.g., Heim's (1982) File Change semantics). For, despite talk of deriving discourse semantic representations (DRSs) by algorithm from syntactic input, DRSs in fact incorporate the results of pragmatic resolution (most obviously, anaphoric linkages). This is clearest in a series of works where it is explicitly proposed that implicated material is entered into DRSs or File cards (Landman 1986, Kadmon 1987, Roberts 1987). To adopt a metaphor, in these proposals there is a common slate, a level of propositional representation, upon which both semantics and pragmatics can write— the contributions may be distinguished, let's suppose, by the color of the ink: semantics in black, pragmatics in red. Semantics and pragmatics remain modular "pens" as it were: they are separate devices making distinctively different contributions to a common level of representation. The slate thus represents the semantic and pragmatic content of accumulated utterances, and it is this representation as a whole that is assigned a model-theoretic interpretation. We shall explore this model below (see especially section 3.5.4), and although it raises many questions it also appears to offer a simple, perfectly coherent way of conceiving of modularity with intrusion.

3.2.7.7 Taking Stock

In this chapter, I can only respond to some of these moves. First, I shall try to pile on the evidence for pragmatic intrusion to make the denial of the evidence as difficult as possible. Second, I argue briefly against the enlarged indexicality and restricted presemantic pragmatics positions. Third, I consider the different kinds of moves that are open to the Pragmatic Intrusionist and offer a proposal about how to think about the relation of between semantic representations, their pragmatic enrichments, and truth conditions (which incidentally is a constructive alternative to semantic retreat).

Let us take stock. It appears from the evidence (and more will be presented shortly) that semantic representations (i.e., semantic structures algorithmically decodable from syntactic structures) are indeed subpropositional: it takes pragmatic resolution of the full Gricean sort to fix the proposition expressed. The proposition expressed is the entity that participates in the normal semantic relations of entailment, sense relations with other expressions, and so on. But that proposition may then receive further pragmatic enrichments of the standard kind, including additional implicatures. This leaves us with terminological difficulties: what is semantics, what is pragmatics, what is said, what is implicated, and so on?

Although recognition of the problem is relatively new, the difficulty has already been compounded by rival recommendations for terminology. Some want to retain Grice's label "what is said" with a narrow application, so that it corresponds to a semantic representation, disambiguated with indexicals resolved, but not necessarily yet expressing any determinate proposition (Bach 1994: 144). Others want to expand the notion to cover something much broader, closer to the everyday concept of "what is stated"; on this account, any kind of pragmatic resolution or implicatural strengthening up to a level corresponding to a conscious, commonsensical notion of what has been claimed counts as "what is said" (Recanati 1989). On this account, GCIs belong entirely to the domain of "what is said" (for response, see Horn 1992a,b). Some have tried to isolate out a middle ground between what is given by the semantic representation, perhaps after disambiguation and indexical resolution on the one hand, and full-blown Gricean implicatures on the other hand. Thus Sperber and Wilson (1986) call explicatures the informational enrichments of semantic representations necessary to achieve not only minimal propositions but also ones of sufficient informational content to count as conversational contributions (thus "Fixing your watch will take some time" expresses a proposition, but one too vacuous as it stands to count as the proposition expressed). On this account, GCIs are explicatures and lie outside the scope of a theory of implicature (which was I think the intention). Carston (1988) has tried to clarify this view, suggesting that the notion "implicature" should be reserved for propositions that are not in any way enrichments of what is said but rather "functionally unrelated" (see Recanati 1989 for critique). Bach (1994) offers the new term "impliciture" (with an *i*) for the middle ground but he views this in a different way, covering only completions and expansions of the semantic content that are in line with the structure of the sentence (and, as mentioned, prag-

Table 3.1
Terminologies in the domain between "what is said" and "what is implicated"

Author	Semantic Representation	Deictic & reference resolution	Minimal proposition	Enriched proposition	Additional propositions
Grice 1989	"What is said"			"Implicature"	
Sperber & Wilson 1986	"Semantics"	"Explicature"			"Implicature"
Carston 1988	"Semantics"	"Explicature"			"Implicature"
	"What is said"				
Recanati 1989	"What is said"				
	"Sentence meaning"	"Explicature"			
Levinson 1988b	"What is said"				
	"The coded"	"Implicature"			
Bach 1994	"What is said"		"Impliciture"		"Implicature"

matic resolutions of indexicals and ambiguities count for him not as implicitures but as what is said). Table 3.1 attempts to display in a crude fashion the mismatching alignments of terms and concepts (it should be interpreted as showing the maximal extent of notions like "implicature" and "explicature" according to different authors).

Let us discuss the explicature/implicature distinction in a bit more detail. Both explicatures and implicatures are pragmatic inferences, derived by the same mechanisms, with the same context dependence and defeasibility (Carston 1988: 158). The idea is that there is a sharp distinction between the fleshed-out logical form attributed to an utterance (its explicature), and fully implicit, unrelated but pragmatically conveyed propositions (the implicatures; see Sperber and Wilson 1986: 181–182). Carston (1988: 173) hopes that explicatures will correspond with the set of pragmatic inferences that fall within the scope of logical operators or intrude into the truth conditions of "what is said." The problem is then to identify by independent criteria what an explicature is (see Recanati 1989, 1993: chap. 13–14 for helpful discussion). The following criteria have been suggested: (a) the representations of explicatures contain the semantic representation attributed to the utterance as a proper subpart (Sperber and Wilson 1986: 181); (b) explicatures express unique and complete propositions (Sperber and Wilson 1986: 179; Carston 1988); (c) explicatures express the *minimal* complete proposition—that is, they are the minimal enrichment of a semantic representation sufficient to make it truth-evaluable (rejected by Sperber and Wilson 1986: 189; Carston 1988; Recanati 1993); (d) explicatures have a "functional independence" from implicatures and must support distinct inferences (Carston 1988: 158); (e) explicatures fall within the scope of logical operators (Recanati 1989: 321–325); and (f) explicatures correspond to a pretheroretical intuition about what a speaker said (Recanati 1993: 246–250).

These criteria in fact fail to make any clear distinction between explicature and implicature. Criterion (a) is partly just a matter of how the analyst phrases the pragmatic inference: after all, any implicature can be added as a conjunct to "what is said." Take the utterance *John's three children came to the party*—the corresponding scalar inference can be phrased as 'The totality of John's children of cardinality 3 came to the party' or as a separate proposition 'John has no more than three children', and so on. Criterion (b) is taken as a necessary but not sufficient criterion, and in particular the rather promising criterion (c) is rejected, so that an explicature is not just the minimal expansion of an utterance until it reaches propositional explicitness but rather an expansion until it reaches sufficient informational specificity to play a role in further pragmatic inference. (Criterion (c) would have left the bulk of GCIs as implicatures, whereas Recanati (1993: 249) and Carston (1995: 237) presume that these are essentially explicatures.) This leaves any distinction between explicatures and implicatures completely unresolved. Hence the suggestion of criterion (d), functional independence, which in effect requires that implicatures do not entail explicatures, or what is implicated does not entail what is said. But as we saw concerning criterion (a), this is essentially a matter of how the analyst phrases the implicature (see also Recanati 1989: 317 n 11).[20] Moreover, Recanati (1989: 318–320) points out that this criterion cuts across the proposed distinction, because there are clear cases where an implicature entails what is said. There are also cases where what is explicated fails to entail the sentence meaning (as in "I haven't eaten breakfast" with the explicature 'I haven't eaten breakfast today'; see Bach 1994: 134). Recanati therefore proposes to shift the burden to two further criteria (e) and (f). The first states that implicatures cannot fall within the scope of negation or other logical operators—any such pragmatic inferences that do so are really explicatures. But Recanati (1993: 269–274) came to recognize that there are substantial difficulties with such a scope test—as we shall see in section 3.3.3, the very same scalar inference may or may not fall within the scope of negation (cf. "John doesn't have three children, he has two" vs. "John doesn't have three children, he has four"), and many other aspects of an utterance may be "metalinguistically" negated. He therefore places the burden on the pretheoretical intuition about what has been said (Recanati 1993: 246–250), claiming that this is always consciously accessible. A consequence, he notes, is that GCIs will normally be explicatures, part of what is said (yet, as Horn (1992b: 176–178) notes, the history of linguistic thought tends to demonstrate the contrary intuition). This is shaky ground indeed: as Bach (1994: 137–139) points out, judgments are likely to depend on how one elicits the intuitions. Moreover, in noncooperative circumstances like cross-examination in a court of law, what would normally taken to be part of what the speaker is committed to—but has not literally said—is routinely queried, indicating that our pretheoretical notions of what has been said are dependent on the mode of talk (Levinson 1983: 121). Thus at the moment we have no reliable distinguishing criteria for the explicature/implicature distinction even for terminological purposes, and there is certainly no indication that any such distinction would substantially help us understand the nature of the inferences in question.

Bach (1994) offers us a different way to cut the pie: we should recognize a middle ground between "what is said" (including indexical resolution and reference fixing) on the one hand, and what is implicated on the other. In the middle stands "impliciture", what is implicit in what has been said. What is implicit involves both "completion" (getting us from "what is said" or proposition-radical to a minimal proposition) and "expansion" (which gets us from the minimal proposition to what is implicitly meant). An example of a completion would be the inference from "This suitcase is too heavy" to 'This suitcase is too heavy for cabin baggage', and an example of an expansion would be the inference from "I have nothing to wear" to 'I have nothing appropriate to wear to the wedding'. GCIs will, at least in many cases, be *implicitures* (with an *i*) on this account (see Bach 1994: 135).[21] Although the distinctions seem clearer and perhaps more helpful than the Relevance theory distinctions, Bach (1994: 140) equally fails to give us a clear boundary between impliciture and implicature, saying only that "an implicatum is completely separate from what is said and is inferred from it." But as we have

seen, this is in large part a matter of how the analyst phrases the inferences.[22] Bach is not proposing any special kind of inference exclusive to
implicitures, and thus the issues are essentially terminological.

My own view is that all such terminological efforts are fruitless: Grice's
circle ensures that there is no consistent way of cutting up the semiotic
pie such that "what is said" excludes "what is implicated." None of the
authors here consider that the processes involved in deriving explicatures
or implicitures and so on are essentially different in kind from those used
in deriving implicatures.[23] Merely relabeling pragmatic inferences that
play a role in fixing the intended proposition something other than
"implicature" hardly alters the nature of the problem. Rather, I shall
presume that we want to define the types of content by the *processes* that
yield them and the important semantical properties they have (e.g.,
default presumption, defeasability under distinct conditions).[24] The
search for "what is explicated" or "what is implicited" betrays a failure
to grasp the dimensions of Grice's circle; nevertheless I will return to the
issue of the middle ground between the "said" and the "implicated" at
the end of the chapter.

3.3 INTRUSIVE CONSTRUCTIONS

We have established a prima facie case for the existence of Grice's circle,
the idea that implicatures may play a role in fixing what is said. But we
will need more evidence before we will be willing to reorganize our whole
way of thinking about semantic theory. What we seek is some incontrovertible evidence that implicatures contribute essentially to truth conditions. One method would be to search for evidence that, in some cases,
assignment of truth conditions without prior assessment of implicatures
will give us the wrong truth conditions. In particular, I shall attempt here
to find a set of constructions, dubbed *intrusive constructions*, that have the
following property: the truth conditions of the whole depend in part on
the implicatures of the parts (for an early collection of such observations,
see Gazdar 1979: 164–168). Cohen (1971) was the first to pursue this
strategy; however his goal was the reverse of ours—he sought to establish
that Grice's arguments about the implicatural overlays on the logical
connectives had to be wrong by showing that the consequence of accepting them was that pragmatics was intrusive. If we no longer take this as a
reductio ad absurdum, the arguments have a new interest.

3.3.1   Comparatives

Wilson (1975: 151) provides the following kind of example:

(17) "Driving home and drinking three beers is better than drinking three beers and driving home."

   I++> 'Driving home and then drinking three beers is better than drinking three beers and then driving home.'

Sentences of the form "A is better than B" will be anomalous, indeed contradictory (necessarily false), unless the proposition expressed by A is distinct from that expressed by B. But if A has the form 'p and q' and B has the form 'q and p', and *and* is equivalent to the truth-functional connective & (and thus $p \; \& \; q \equiv q \; \& \; p$), then "A is better than B" will be necessarily false. But example (17) has this form; and such an assertion seems, let us agree, just plain true!

What makes "p and q is better than q and p" noncontradictory is the inference from *and* to 'and then'; "p and then q is better than q and then p" is a perfectly sensible proposition capable of being true. But if the inference to 'and then' is pragmatic (and the Gricean arguments seem perfectly sound), then our assessment of such comparatives involves pragmatic intrusion: the truth conditions of the whole construction are calculated taking into account the implicatures of the parts. The inference from *and* to 'and then' is on Grice's scheme a Manner implicature, and on my scheme an I-implicature.

But perhaps Cohen (1971) is right that this is just evidence for the semantic nature of temporal sequentiality. For example, given a sequence of tensed clauses like *John came in and sat down*, Grice's position with respect to *and* could be maintained, while the truth-conditional nature of the 'and then' inference could be attributed to the implicit indexical sequence of reference times in the two verbs.[25] This account is more difficult to maintain with untensed gerunds or other infinite verb forms as in example (17), but nevertheless it raises the possibility that some reanalysis along semantic lines (some semantic escape hatch, as it were) might be found for these cases of apparent pragmatic intrusion.

So the critical question is: how general is the phenomenon? In particular, can other implicatures (perhaps less amenable to semantic reanalysis) intrude in the same way? It is at this point that our typology of implicatures (GCIs) comes back into play; what we can attempt to do is run the different types of GCI through each type of intrusive construction to see if there is a general tendency towards intrusion in these constructions.

The evidence will show, I believe, that there is such a tendency. To reduce the need for discussion, I will build into the examples some minimal context suggestive of the intended interpretation. Let us turn first to Q (scalar) implicatures within comparative constructions. Consider the following, which on a purely semantic basis should be self-contradictory; if they are not felt to be self-contradictory and seem rather to express a plausible proposition, then that can only be the result of a strengthening of the underlined expressions by a Q implicature.

(18) a. "AIDS vaccination will cause significant mortality: but losing *some* of the population is better than losing at least some and perhaps all of it."

     a'. "AIDS vaccination will cause significant mortality: but losing *some* of the population is better than losing *at least* some of it."

     b. "You shouldn't continue to gamble; I know you've already lost two hundred dollars, but losing *two hundred* dollars is better than losing at least two hundred dollars and possibly more."

     c. "You should get out of stocks: I know you've already lost a lot, but a *large* loss is better than a large and possibly enormous one."

     d. "It's best to know where you stand: to be charged with reckless driving *or* manslaughter is better than being charged with one or the other and possibly both."

Some brief notes: in (18a) the semantic content of *some* (roughly, 'at least one' or 'some, not excluding all') is perfectly compatible with *all*; thus the two expressions on each side of the comparative (*some, at least some and perhaps all*) are approximately synonymous or extensionally equivalent.[26] What makes the sentence noncontradictory is simply the scalar implicature from *some* to 'not all' (an implicature explicitly canceled in the phrase *some and maybe all*).[27] Thus taking the sentence to be of the form 'A is better than B', A is distinct from B only in having that additional implicature. Similarly for (18b): *two hundred* has the semantic content 'at least two hundred' (two hundred and possibly more), but Q-implicates 'no more than two hundred'; only on the assumption of that implicature is (18b) other than contradictory. In the case of (18c), we have a scale ⟨*enormous, large*⟩ such that use of *large* implicates 'not enormous' but is semantically compatible with *enormous*; again only if the implicature is used to strengthen the first clause is the sentence as a whole capable of being true. In (18d), there is a scale ⟨*and, or*⟩ such that use of *p or q* implicates 'not both p and q' (for discussion see Gazdar 1979; Levinson 1983: 133ff); again, only if the implicature goes through will the content of A and B be sufficiently distinct to avoid a contradiction.

Intrusive Manner implicatures are somewhat harder to find, but nevertheless the following examples seem to be reasonable candidates:

(19) a. "It's better to eat your meat than to ingest it."
     b. "It's better to be a long way from one's friends than a long long way."
     c. "You need to train harder: running and running and running is better than running."
     d. "Legible handwriting is better than not illegible handwriting." (or: "You are more likely to get the job if your handwriting is legible than if it's not illegible.")
     e. "Linguists should use clearer examples: citing a grammatical example is better than citing a not ungrammatical one."

Possible cases of I-intrusion (other than those based on *and*) in comparatives are the following:

(20) a. "Ivan and Penny driving to Chicago is better than Ivan driving to Chicago and Penny driving to Chicago."
     b. "If Steve and Jay write a paper there's a better chance of truth than if Steve writes a paper and Jay writes a paper."
     c. "Hammering the nail into the wood is safer than hammering the nail some way into the wood."

There's a prima facie case, then, that pragmatic intrusion in comparatives is not limited to cases (like those based on the implicatures of *and*) where an analysis in semantic terms is an alternative.

However, readers may find some of the examples given in (18)–(20) somewhat strained. This is a point then to reconsider the structure of the argument and see whether it can be made more general. The case we are making is based on the assumption that to establish pragmatic intrusion in the construction "A is better than B" we must find two clauses A and B which are logically equivalent but pragmatically distinct, such that substitution in the construction yields an intuitive truth where a necessary falsehood would be predicted on purely semantic grounds. The reasoning is based on the assumption that, whatever the semantics of the comparative construction are exactly, the semantics must at least meet the following condition: the comparative relation ϕ-*er* is necessarily *irreflexive*, thus in *A is φ-er than B, A* and *B* must be distinct. Now, our examples are open to objection because it is a little hard to come up with cases where A and B are semantically equivalent but pragmatically distinct, and yet will still fit happily into the construction. But given the irreflexivity of the construction, I think weaker requirements can be met and still be sufficient to establish pragmatic intrusion. As far as I can see, the semantics of the comparative *A is φ-er than B* requires that not only must the two clauses be semantically distinct, but also that the two clauses must not be related in such a way that B encompasses what A denotes (e.g., A and B should not be privative opposites). More exactly, if B entails A, and B is "about" the same semantic relations as A (e.g., B is not a conjunction of the form 'A and C'), then a comparative of the form "A is φ-er than B" will be necessarily false, unless rescued by pragmatic intrusion. For example, "Having a child is better than having a son" seems false or nonsensical (unless we can somehow pragmatically intepret *child* as excluding 'male child'). So if we can find examples of this kind where in fact the utterance is intuitively true or potentially true, we should be able to find that the acceptability is due to the implicatural strengthening of A so that it is no longer entailed by B. For example, if I assert "Eating some of the cake is better (for my health) than eating all of it", what I say is false unless *some* is construed as 'some and not all' (i.e., is strengthened by the scalar implicature).[28] Without the pragmatic strengthening, I have asserted that one state of affairs (eating at least some) is better than another state of affairs (eating all) that guarantees the very state of affairs I claim is preferable. Moreover, the state of affairs I claim to be preferable is completely compatible, in no way precludes, and may indeed be embedded within the state of affairs I claim to be less preferable.

Thus if example (21a) has the semantic content in (21b), we can see that (21a) should (on semantic grounds alone) be nonsensical: any situation in which one has four children will also be one in which one has at least three children, so how could one prefer a situation (having at least three children) to another which guarantees that same situation? It is a bit like saying "It is better to be a woman than to be a queen" (which if it makes sense at all, requires forcing an unwomanly interpretation of *queen*). We can then go on to make parallel arguments for (21c) and (21d) and indeed for cases parallel to all those above.

(21) a. "Having three children is better than having four children."
   b. 'Having at least three children is better than having at least four children.'

    c. "Eating some of the cookies is better than eating all of them."
    d. "Drinking warm coffee is better than drinking hot coffee."

Clearly, rather a lot depends here on the correct analysis of comparatives, on which we will momentarily digress. Existing accounts (to the best of my knowledge) only deal with comparison of individuals, not propositions as in these cases. In the existing accounts, *a is taller than b* is analyzed variously as follows: a sentence of this form asserts that there is some comparison class relative to which *a* is tall and *b* is not tall (Klein 1980); or the sentence asserts that there is some measure *m* of tallness such that *a* exhibits *m* and *b* does not (Seuren 1974); or there is some measure of tallness *m* exhibited by individual *a* that is greater than all the measures of tallness exhibited by *b* (Atlas 1984b: 362ff; n. 11). By analogy, *A is better than B* might be analyzed as asserting that there is some situation in which A is good and B is not good; or (on Atlas's account) that there is some degree of goodness that A has that is greater than all degrees of goodness that B has.[29] On that analogy, a comparative "A is ϕ-er than B" where there is an entailment relation between A and B (specifically, where B $\vdash$ A and the representation of A explicitly encompasses the possibility of B) should self-destruct (be incapable of being true), because any situation in which B holds will contain the situation described by A. Thus the following sentences are predicted correctly to be semantically anomalous:[30]

(22) a. ?"Being a bachelor is better than being an unmarried person."
    b. ?"Having a vehicle is better than having a car."
    c. ?"Having a child is better than having a male child."

If this is correct, then all the examples in (21a–d), for example, which do not seem anomalous, must be rescued by the pragmatic intrusion of Q-implicatures.

    Perhaps the issue can be clarified by reverting to cases where individuals are being compared. Suppose we assert a sentence of the form '*a is better than b*' in conditions where as a matter of linguistic fact any *b*-individual must also be an *a*-individual, then on any reasonable account of comparatives we should, I think, get an anomaly (cf. ?"A woman is better than a queen", ?"A vehicle is better than a car", ?"A child is better than a boy", etc.).[31] It follows that examples like those below ought to be anomalous. For example, the literal content of (23a) amounts to (23a′) but (23a′) is indeed clearly anomalous, because any woman with at least four children will also be a woman with at least three children. However, contrary to the semantic prediction, sentence (23a) is perfectly felicitous and capable of being true—but it can only express a coherent proposition if *three* is strengthened to 'exactly 3'. Indeed, (switching to a clearly extensional predicate like *smaller*) I take (23b) to be unequivocally true, even though the semantics alone will render it false (since the family with three children is only semantically specified as having at least three children!). Lest this be thought to be a property of the numerals (and thus reliant on a possibly mistaken scalar analysis there), note that the same argument will go through for the other cases:[32]

(23) a. "Any mother with three children is happier than any mother with four."
     a'. Any mother with at least 3 children is happier than any mother with at least 4 children.
     b. "A nuclear family with three children is smaller than a nuclear family with five children."
     c. "A student who cheats on some exams is better than one who cheats on all."
     d. "A teacher who is sometimes late is preferable to one who is always late."

There are still some semantic points that need at least some minimal clarification. For example, I take it that these sentences are, disregarding implicatural enrichments, clearly literally false (assuming the 'at least' semantic analysis of the relevant scalar predicates) on the assumption that there is at least one entity in the domain of discourse that satisfies the stronger conditions (e.g., in (23a) that there is a mother with four children); that will ensure that these implicitly universally quantified indefinite NPs range over some individual *b* such that one is asserting '*b* is φ-er than *b*', which will be necessarily false. It is a separate question (one about which I am at present unclear) whether a sentence of the form '*a* is φ-er than *b*' where every *b* is an *a* actually entails '*a* is φ-er than *a*' and thus entails a necessary falsehood.[33] But we cannot pursue these matters here.

The point of this digression is to try to establish that the argument for pragmatic intrusion into comparatives can be made on a much wider basis than on examples of the form "A is better than B" where A is semantically equivalent to B. However, regardless of the success of my foray into the semantics of comparatives, and thus my extended list of examples, there is no doubt that examples of the more restricted kind can be found, and that these appear to constitute knock-down evidence for the role of pragmatic strengthening in semantic interpretation. It is a truth that the reader may appreciate that reading a book is easier than reading a tome.

3.3.2   The Conditional

The conditional provides some of the strongest apparent evidence for pragmatic intrusion. It is generally conceded that there is still no adequate semantic analysis of the natural language conditional, but that existing accounts agree on the following conditions on such an analysis:

If A then B is true if and only if "every one of a number of ways in which A can be true constitutes, or carries with it, a way of B's being true" (Kamp 1981: 11). On Kamp's specific version of this analysis, *if A then B* will be true iff each way of verifying A carries with it a verification of B (i.e., each embedding of the discourse representation of A in a model M can be extended to an embedding of the discourse representation of B in M as well). Thus we only assent to the truth of the whole conditional if every way in which A can be true guarantees the truth of B.

With this semantic analysis in mind, we can now turn to consider cases where the semantics will predict a falsity, but our intuitions nevertheless declare a plausible truth. In these examples, the conditional as a whole is assessed on the assumption that the *implicatures* (as well as the entailments) of the antecedent are satisfied by the model: thus in these cases it seems that *if A then B* is intuitively true iff every way of verifying the entailments *and* the implicatures of A carries with it a verification of B.[34] The clearest examples are once again provided by Q-implicature intrusions:

(24) a. "If each side in the soccer game got *three* goals, then the game was a draw."

    a'. *Gloss of the semantic content:* If each side in the soccer game got at least three goals, then the game was a draw.

    b. "If you ate *some* of the cookies and no one else ate any, then there must still be some left."
(or "If the USA won some of the Olympic medals, other countries must have got the rest.")

    c. "If the chair *sometimes* comes to department meetings that is not enough; he should come always."

    d. "If you earn *forty thousand* dollars and have no capital, you can't buy a house in Palo Alto."

e. "If John owns *three* cars, then the fourth outside his house must belong to someone else."

f. "If you think John has *three* children, you're wrong; he has four."

If you feel inclined to assent to any of these, then you are interpreting them in such a way as to strengthen the antecedent by a Q-implicature (e.g., in (24a) *three* must be interpreted as '3 and no more', in (24b) *some* must be interpreted as 'some and not all', in (24c) *sometimes* as 'sometimes and not always', and in (24d) *forty thousand* as 'forty thousand and no more'). Otherwise, there are no grounds for acceding to the consequent. To see this, let us consider just (24a) in detail: if *three* has the semantic content 'at least 3', then (24a) has the literal content glossed in (24a′). But given the rules of soccer, (24a′) is clearly (contingently) false: there are ways of verifying the antecedent (e.g., one team got exactly three goals and the other got exactly four goals) that do not guarantee the truth of the consequent. If however the antecedent is strengthened by the scalar implicature so that the antecedent reads 'each side got 3 and at most 3 goals', then (given the rules of soccer) the whole will be predicted to be true. Because our intuitions are quite clear that the sentence is true, it seems evident that the truth conditions of the whole depend on taking into account the implicatures of the antecedent.

We can also find I-implicature intrusions: thus the following are only reasonably interpreted as truthful claims if *and* is strengthened to 'and then'.

(25) a. "If you have a baby *and* get married, then the baby is strictly speaking illegitimate."

b. "If he turned on the override switch *and* the reactor overheated, he's responsible for the disaster."

c. "If they declared a Republic *and* the old king died of a heart attack, then they're responsible for his death; but if the old king died of a heart attack *and* they declared a Republic, they cannot be blamed for the old king's death." (after Cohen 1971)

d. "If you reconnect the battery *and* turn the ignition key, the car will probably start."

To see that *and* is not a special case, consider other I-inferences:

(26) a. "If Bill and and Penny drive to Chicago, they can discuss sociolinguistics in the car for hours."

a'. "If Mandy and Rick drive to New York, they'll end up with two cars and no parking in Manhattan."

b. "If you hammer the nail into the door, you can hang things on it."

b'. "If you hammer the nail into the door, no one will scratch themselves on it."

c. "If Bill's book is good, he will get tenure."

c'. "If Bill's book is good, he'll never return it to the library."

In each of these cases, it has been argued, there is a strengthening implicature attributable in our scheme to the I-principle. Thus a predication of two agents usually carries a 'together' implicature (Harnish 1976, Atlas and Levinson 1981) as in (26a); the GCI can be overridden as illustrated in (26a'). In (26b) the spatial relation *in* merely specifies at least partial inclusion; the interpretation of partial versus full inclusion is a matter of stereotypical knowledge and inference, as sketched in (26b) versus (26b') (see, e.g., Herskovits 1986). In (26c), the relation indicated by the possessive is semantically general; the semantics of *Bill's book* presumably only specifies that there is some (more or less intimate) relation between Bill and a definite book—the relation might be a relation of writing, reading, owning, borrowing, editing, and so forth as given by an I-inference in the context (see Kay and Zimmer 1976, Sperber and Wilson 1986). Without having previously talked about Bill's book, we can indicate the relation we have in mind, as in (26c) versus (26c'). But (26c) will only be true, let us suppose, if the book Bill wrote is good. (Clearly, the inference here involves a matter of reference determination; see section 3.4.)

Finally, M-implicatures may also perhaps intrude in conditionals. The following may be cases, but I concede that they are less than wholly clear:

(27) a. "If it's a long way to your place, we can make it; but if it's a long, long way, we may not be able to."

b. "If he hit and hit and hit the victim then he's more culpable than if he hit him."

b'. "If the surgeon tried and tried and tried to save the patient, then he did more than try."

c. "If the President is not ignorant of the facts, he doesn't really know them either."

d. "If we're not unwelcome, then we are hardly welcome."

e. "If he caused Marlene's death, he'll get a manslaughter charge; if he killed her, he'll get second-degree murder."

Thus in (27a), if it is conceded that the reduplication of *long* is not semantic modification, then *long, long* merely suggests (M-implicates) a greater distance than *long*; in which case (27a) will be contradictory unless the M-implicature is used to strengthen the antecedent of the second conditional. Similarly, the repetition in (27b) arguably adds no semantic content, in which case there will be ways of verifying the antecedent that do not verify the consequent—so the conditional should be false, even though it is arguably true. In this case, as noted above, if past tenses are not treated as quantifications over past times but rather as enforcing a sequence of reference times (as in Partee 1984), then perhaps there is a semantic account of the possible truth of (27b). Where repetition suggests intensity, as in (27b′) not repeated action as in (27b), then the case for semantic intrusion would be better, but perhaps (27b′) is not too clear. In (27c) the double negative *not ignorant* logically implies *knows* (because ignorance and knowledge are contradictories) but suggests (M-implicates) something less than full cognizance. Thus what ought to be a contradiction comes out as an intuitive truth; we can account for this if the M-implicature is taken into account in the assessment of the whole conditional. Similarly for (27d). In (27e) the periphrastic causative *cause x's death* suggests indirect or unintentional causation by reference to the complementary I-implicatures from the use of the less-prolix lexical causative *kill*, which suggests direct or intentional causation. Assuming that manslaughter and murder are inconsistent charges, the two conditionals in (27e) should be contradictory with respect to one another, because the two antecedents with identical semantic conditions are paired with inconsistent consequents. But intuitively, that is not the case—(27e) seems like a perfectly consistent and sensible assertion. Again, the problem evaporates if the M-implicature (of indirect causation) of the first antecedent and I-implicature (of direct causation) of the second antecedent play a role in the truth-conditional assessment of each conditional.

Unfortunately, as noted above, a good semantic analysis of conditionals still eludes us. So it may be possible to claim that somehow the semantics of conditionals makes special allowance for pragmatic factors. For example, Barwise (1986) argues (following Goodman) that conditionals have a built-in *ceteris paribus* condition, such that if you say, for example, "If I strike this match it'll light" we want to maintain that the utterance is true even though various *ceteris paribus* conditions (e.g., the matches are not damp) have not been spelled out. So it may be said that our intrusive implicatures are merely part of the *ceteris paribus* conditions: "If each side has three goals, then it is a draw" is true relative to the condition 'each side has at most three'. I do not think Barwise's account could as it stands handle this kind of intrusion, because such intrusions are systematic inferences that are conveyed by the utterance itself, not independently existing background assumptions (not, for example, antecedent "resource situations"). Nevertheless, we should attend to the possibility that some better account of the semantics of the conditional might eliminate these apparent pragmatic intrusions.

To deal with this objection it is worth making a few further observations. First, some of the same intrusions take place in *disjunctions* where there are no *ceteris paribus* conditions on any analysis ((28a) from Wilson 1975: 151):

(28) a. "She either got married *and* had a child, or had a child and got married; but I don't know which."
  b. "According to the prosecution, the victim was either shot *and* thrown in the lake or thrown in the lake and shot, but not both (i.e., not shot, thrown in the lake, and shot again)."
  c. "If you believe his weak alibi, he cannot have been responsible for all the crimes. But one thing is certain: he either committed *some* of the crimes or he committed some and possibly all of them. I don't know which."
  d. "Marcos either owned *three* Swiss bank accounts or *at least* three Swiss bank accounts; only on the first assumption can we be sure that all the embezzled money has been recovered."

Some brief notes: in (28a) the speaker's assertion of ignorance over two possibilities will be inconsistent or anomalous with the disjunction if each disjunct has the same semantic content. Plausibly the inconsistency is pragmatic rather than semantic, because it amounts to Moore's paradox: the speaker of (28a) is asserting "p or p and I don't know that p."[35] But the point is that we have no intuitions of any such oddity. The only way to account for the lack of such intuitions is to suppose that the I-implicature from *and* to 'and then' has strengthened the disjuncts. The second example is similar except that here a contradiction rather than a pragmatic paradox would result if the semantics were not strengthened by the same pragmatic intrusion from *and*. In (28c), if *some* has semantic content 'at least some' and only Q-implicates 'not all', then *some and possibly all* is an approximate gloss of the semantic content. Again, we can only account for the intuitive absence of the pragmatic paradox if the

Q-implicature plays a role in the truth conditions. In (28d) we have an assertion of the form "*p* or *q*; only if *p* and not *q*, *r*" where *p* is semantically equivalent to *q*; again only a Q-implicature from *three* to 'no more than three' will rescue the speaker from an absurdity that is not felt in fact to arise.

A second argument against the possibility of accounting for pragmatic intrusion in conditionals by a Barwise-type semantics is that the kind of pragmatic intrusion in conditionals is not limited to informative GCIs that might conceivably play a role in *ceteris paribus* conditions. Tropes of various sorts can also intrude:

(29) a. "If you appoint a little Chomsky, all the sociolinguists will resign."
  b. "If the smog is so adorable, that explains why the mansions in Beverly Hills are deserted in the summer."
  c. [Sun shining] "If it continues to rain like this, I'll come to England more often."

Finally, most of the intrusions that can be found in conditionals can also be found in *because*-clauses, which are (I assume) semantically remote from the antecedents of conditionals since *because*-clauses are entailed.[36]

(30) a. "Because he drank three beers *and* drove home, he went to jail."
  b. "Because he turned on the override switch *and* the reactor melted, he's responsible for a thousand deaths."
  c. "Because he earns *forty thousand* dollars, he can't afford a house in Palo Alto."
  d. "Because he has *one* child, Huang is permitted to have an academic job in Beijing."
  e. "Because the police recovered *some* of the missing gold, they will later recover it all."
  f. "Because he's *such a fine friend*, I've struck him off my list."[37]
  g. "Because they appointed another *little Chomsky*, the sociolinguists all resigned."

3.3.3 Metalinguistic Negation and Other Negatives

It has been noted for some time (see Wilson 1975: 149ff; Horn 1985; Kempson 1986) that there are uses of negation where what is negated is only an implicature. Here are some cases where what is negated is a Q-implicature:

(31) a. "John doesn't have three children, he has four."
   b. "I'm not happy, I'm ecstatic."
   c. "He didn't lose a finger, he lost an arm."
   d. "It's not possible, it's certain."
   e. "It's not true that either the President or the Vice-President must sign the treaty; they both must."
   f. "He's not good-looking, he's downright handsome."
   g. "I didn't do it once or twice, I did it once only."
   h. "Some men aren't chauvinists, all men are."

The analysis of these cases is controversial. Kempson (1986; see also Kempson and Cormack 1981, 1982) claims they provide evidence that truth conditions must be stated over explicated logical forms—that is, that these cases prove that some limited pragmatic intrusion (of explicatures) takes place. Thus Kempson's claim is that a sentence like (32a) can be thought of as negating two positive contents—the implicated and the entailed, as detailed in (32b). Thus negation ranges over both the implicated and the entailed as in (32c), with the consequence that (32d) (where the positive implicature is false and the positive content true) is one set of conditions under which (32a) will be true.

(32) a. "John doesn't have three children, he has four."
   b. *Positive content p:* 'John has at least 3 children.'
      Positive implicature q: 'John has at most 3 children.'
   c. *Content of whole:* $\sim(p \ \& \ q) \equiv \sim p \vee \sim q$
   d. *Verifying circumstance:* $p \ \& \ \sim q$
      Instantiating: 'John has at least three children but not at most three children.'

In contrast to Kempson's claim, Horn (1985, 1989: chap. 6) argues that these are not true logical negations; what is involved is a metalinguistic operator, a denying of the appropriateness of an utterance. Thus (32a) is shorthand, as it were, for "You can't appropriately describe John as having three children; you should describe him as having four." He provides persuasive evidence for the existence of a metalinguistic negation—for example, no logical analysis is possible of utterances like "It's not a [təmeɪtəʊ], it's a [təmɑːtəʊ]." So the only question is whether these pragmatic intrusions are cases, in which case we are not dealing with pragmatic intrusions into semantic negations.

Horn provides a set of diagnostics for metalinguistic negations and concludes that these implicatural cases conform to the type: (a) metalinguistic negations typically occur with a special intonation contour; (b) they are typically followed by a rectifying clause ("he has four" in (32a); (c) they do not permit negative polarity items (cf. "He didn't eat some of the cookies; he ate all of them" vs. *"He didn't eat any of the cookies, he ate all of them"); and (d) they do not allow negative incorporation (cf. "John doesn't have three *or* four children; he has four" vs. *"John has neither three nor four children; he has four.") However, most if not all of these properties follow from the fact that metalinguistic negations are retorts to prior utterances, and as we shall see, these implicature-denying negations must also be responses to prior positive assertions.

Horn's (1989: 384) motivation for defending the metalinguistic account of examples like (32a) is that (following Kempson) he thinks that otherwise scalar inferences would have to be part of the semantic content of the scalar expressions. By assimilating these cases to a nonlogical use of negation, the pragmatic account of the scalar inferences is preserved. Horn's position would be worth defending if these were the only otherwise convincing examples of pragmatic intrusion into truth-conditions. But if, as argued here, pragmatic intrusion can occur in many constructions, there may be little motivation to resist the intrusion account here too. Besides, Kempson (1986) provides some evidence that the negation in this kind of sentence doesn't have the properties associated with unequivocally metalinguistic negations.

These cases are truly puzzling for a number of reasons. First, Kempson is right to insist that unlike some uses of metalinguistic negation (as in "It's not a [vɑːz], it's a [veɪz]") where no proposition is being denied, these implicature-denying negations are logical in character: a proposition (the implicature) falls under the scope of a one-place truth-functional operator indistinguishable from the familiar one we call negation! On the other hand, Horn is right to insist that what is being denied is the assertability of the positive sentence that would have carried the implicature that is being explicitly canceled. But there is a further wrinkle to the problem that does not seem to have been noticed, because of the prevailing inadequate theory of implicature projection. This is simply that, under the prevailing theory, implicatures do not arise under negation (Gazdar 1979, Hirschberg 1985, Horn 1989). Thus, at least if the negation in question is the ordinary truth-functional operator, there could be no implicature to deny! This theory of the blocking of implicatures under negation is in fact not correct (as pointed out in chapter 2), but the correct theory yields equally odd results: the implicatures that will arise from negative sentences will not be the same as the ones that arise from their positive counterparts. Thus, for example, "John doesn't have three children" cannot induce the implicature 'John has no more than three children', which is therefore not available for cancellation by the negation, metalinguistic or logical. Below we will see that if we adopt a general account of pragmatic intrusion, all these puzzles evaporate together, and this conceptual mopping-up itself recommends both the thesis of pragmatic intrusion in general and its role in these implicature-denying negations in particular.

Note that implicature-denying uses of negative expressions are not limited to explicit negations. Consider the *rather than* construction as below:

(33) a. "He has three children rather than four."
      Entails: 'He has three children and he does not have four.'
      Conventional implicature: 'It has been suggested that he has three-children-and-no more.'
    b. "He has four children rather than three."

Here (33a) would naturally be used to correct an erroneous presumption in the discourse, and *p rather than q* may be held to have a conventional implicature that p, together with its conversational implicatures, has been previously erroneously asserted or assumed. Now note that we can invert p and q as in (33b); in this case what is negated can only be the conversational implicature of *three*, viz. 'only three'. Or in Horn's terms, what is being negated is the felicity of asserting *three* given that it carries the 'only three' implicature. This "metalinguistic" use of the construction must be involved in the following examples:

(34) a. "He is brilliant, rather than clever."
    b. "She had a baby and got married, rather than got married and had a baby."
    c. "The meal was delicious, rather than edible."
    d. "His reprieve is not impossible, rather than definitely possible."
    e. "It is a long way, rather than a long, long way."
    f. "John prefers cars with six cylinders, rather than those with four."

3.3.4   Conclusions Regarding Intrusive Constructions

I have argued that there are a number of constructions, dubbed intrusive constructions, where the truth conditions of the whole expression depend on the implicatures of some of its constituent parts. Perhaps the case is better made on some of these constructions than on others. There will always be doubts about whether a better semantic analysis of the relevant construction might not accommodate the apparent pragmatic intrusions in some other way. Further, there are unclarities in the data: for example, some of the comparative examples may seem marginally acceptable because of the unnatural repetition of the implicature-inducing expression. (More natural-sounding paraphrases would beg too many questions about the synonymy of the paraphrases; but if we shift the argument to cases where A entails B in utterances of the form "A is better than B" we can get clearer examples, although we raise further queries about the semantics of the comparative.) Others examples, especially those based on Manner intrusions, may seem like metalinguistic or quotative uses that ought to be treated exceptionally. Nevertheless, despite these difficulties, the clearest cases—like the Q- and I-implicature intrusions in conditionals —seem close to knockdown cases for the intrusive role of pragmatic factors in truth-conditional content. It would seem quite counterintuitive to deny the truth of utterances like "If John ate some of the cookies but no one else ate any, there must still be some left."

Yet the argument from these intrusive constructions (good as it has seemed to Cohen 1971, Wilson 1975, Gazdar 1979, and Levinson 1983) is in fact vulnerable to a simple alternative—namely, the traditional account in terms of a postsemantic Gricean pragmatics. Here is an example of how the alternative account might go. Suppose the speaker has said "Having to study and take an exam is better than taking an exam and having to study." What she has said is of the form 'A is better than A', which is necessarily false, a contradiction. But to utter a contradiction is not only to flout the maxim of Quality, it is also to flout the first maxim of Quantity ('Provide sufficient information'). Therefore, on the assumption that the speaker is being cooperative at some underlying level, that is not what she means; for the utterance to have some informative content it must amount to 'A is better than B' where B is distinct from A. To obtain such an interpretation all that needs to be supposed is that the speaker means 'Having to study and then take an exam is better than having to take an exam and then belatedly do some studying'. So that is what the speaker intends the hearer to infer.[38] In a similar way, Bach (1987a: 71– 74, 78; 1994: 153–154) takes the line that, taken literally, metalinguistic negations like "John doesn't like Mary; he loves her" are just contradictions, so cooperative interlocutors understand them charitably, as nonliteral utterances short for related, expanded propositions (like 'John doesn't *merely* like Mary, he loves her').[39]

In short, for every case that we put forward as a case of semantic intrusion in a complex construction, the traditional (postsemantic pragmatics) theorist (our Obstinate Theorist) can always counter that what is literally said is contradictory, false or sufficiently empty that it will constitute a flouting of the maxims of Quantity and Quality. The infelicity of what is said is sufficiently blatant that it will induce an implicature to preserve the underlying assumption of cooperation. What could be a better trigger to a Gricean inference than (for example) a categorial falsehood?

But against this, one should note that not all of our cases provide literal contradictions as potential triggers for a flouting interpretation. Although case (35a) below provides a necessary falsehood, case (35b) provides on this analysis merely a contingent falsehood given the rules of soccer (but still, arguably enough to constitute a flagrant violation of Quality).

(35) a. "Having to study and take an exam is better than taking an exam and having to study."
    Anti-intrusion hypothesis: this is patently false, and a flouting of the maxim of Quality.
  b. "If each side gets three goals, it'll be a draw."
    Intrusion hypothesis: this is a very dubious flout.
  c. "If it costs twenty dollars, I have enough money to get in."
    Content: 'If it costs twenty dollars or more, I have enough money to get in.'
  d. "In the ancient Toltec sacred ball game, if each side got three goals, the game was a draw."

But (35c) is more difficult: there is no particular reason to think the sentence is false even on the literal analysis (i.e., without the implicature stengthening the antecedent); the speaker may have a thousand dollars in his pocket. Still, it may be objected, the conditional will be false under some verifications of the antecedent (say, if it costs not only $20 but another $1000), and that is sufficient to render it generally false and thus capable of triggering a flouting interpretation. This seems highly dubious. But, supposing we concede, consider (35d). We have no idea what the rules of the ancient Toltec ball game were; we may be quite open to the idea that the aim was to stop the other side getting three goals, after which goals were no longer determinative of victory. But that is not how one reads the assertion: the speaker of (35d) is surely committed to stating that a draw results if each team gets exactly three goals. Yet this interpretation cannot be based on a flouting of the maxim of Quality, because no known falsehood has been stated. Thus there are serious problems for a flouting analysis of these intrusive cases. An account in terms of the intrusion of default GCIs, on the other hand, predicts that the implicaturally strengthened reading should be available even when it is not required or coerced in order to obtain a cooperative interpretation.[40] In contrast, the flouting analysis suggests that the implicaturally strengthened interpretations should only arise to rescue an utterance from absurdity, falsity, or some other uncooperative infelicity. It seems to me that the GCI account is correct in cases like (35d) and the flouting account makes incorrect predictions.

But perhaps the main objection to the flouting account is that it is simply not in line with our intuitions. The comparative and conditional cases simply do not give rise to intuitions of exploitation in the way that, say, ironies or fresh metaphors do; there's no sense of violation and inferential repair. To refresh the intuitions, consider what is being claimed: comparatives like (36a) must be treated as overt flouts of Quality in the same way that obvious contradictions like (36b) are. Similarly, conditionals like (36c) must be treated as obvious contingent falsehoods exactly on a par with the ironic interpretation of (36d). But intuitively there is no such parallelism. Although we may have few intuitions about most linguistic processes, the mechanisms involved in processing flouts do seem capable of being made conscious—witness the great body of ancient learning on the tropes. Thus (36b) and (36d), but not (36a) and (36c), intuitively require double processing, as it were.

(36) a. "Getting drunk and driving home is much worse than driving home and getting drunk."
     b. "Clinton is both the President and not the President."
     c. "If each team gets three goals, it's a draw."
     d. "If you want a theory-neutral education in linguistics, you should go to MIT."

A final response I shall save in detail for later, but in a nutshell it is this. The flouting account is invoked in our intrusive cases simply to obviate the claim of pragmatic input to semantics. It amounts to insisting on prepragmatic semantics. But if the account is pursued, it will turn out to have the very consequence it is trying to avoid—namely, a presemantic pragmatics (or pragmatic input to the compositional semantics of the complex constructions we have been focusing on).

Despite these severe difficulties for a flouting account of these intrusive constructions, we nevertheless have to concede that these kind of examples are simply not as knockdown as has sometimes been thought. And we can assume that our Obstinate Theorist, determined to preserve a pragmatics-free semantics, will obstinately hang on to the flouting analysis (and for a spirited defense of this position, see Bach 1987a: 71–74, 78–82, 1994: 135–136). Let us therefore pursue a different tack that is not so easily countered, and in particular let us attack the Obstinate Theorist's Achilles' heel—reference determination.

3.4   THE ARGUMENT FROM REFERENCE

3.4.1   How Implicatures Can Determine Definite Reference

The idea that pragmatic factors play an important role in reference determination has been quite widely explored in the philosophy of language (one has only to think of Strawson's (1950) presuppositions of definite descriptions, of Searle's (1969) account of referring as a speech act, of Donnellan's (1966) referential/attributive distinction between uses of referring expressions, of Nunberg's (1978) indirect ostension). Nevertheless, the fiction that (Carnapian) intensions, given just a world and a time, *determine* extensions has been quite largely maintained in formal semantics (and this despite Putnam's demonstration of the implausibility of the idea; see Putnam 1975: chap. 12). Still, the ground is well prepared for the idea that Gricean inferences might play a decisive role in reference, although the idea has scarcely been explored.

I have already argued briefly that anaphoric resolution is guided in part by the play between I-inferences (favoring local coreference and other cohesive connections) and M-inferences (favoring the complementary interpretations; see also Levinson, 1987a, b, and chapter 4 in this book). Thus anaphoric pronouns, whether these are thought of as referring expressions or variables, are linked to antecedent referring expressions at least partly by implicature.

In this section I argue that GCIs can play a systematic role in the determination of the reference or extension of definite descriptions, including deictic or exophoric uses thereof, and I shall go on to make some further remarks about indefinite referring expressions. The theoretical significance of this claim that implicatures can determine extensions will depend on one's theories about the nature of reference and the role that it plays in meaning. There are certainly general implications for the theory of reference—for example, this claim, if substantiated, seems to me to be one of the best empirical arguments against the just-mentioned view that intensions determine extensions.

However, we are only interested here in the theory of reference as it bears on the main task: showing that pragmatic factors are prerequisites to semantic interpretation. So here is what I am going to attempt to show. Suppose we can find those very Gricean inferences, which are supposed to operate only postsemantically, involved in the determination of the reference of canonical referring expressions. Then, given the principle of the compositionality of reference (as in, say, Martin 1987: 88), it follows that the extensions of the maximal expression cannot be determined without determining the extensions of each of its constituent expressions, which in turn may depend *ex hypothesi* on implicature. Thus we can cannot obtain a truth value (a maximal extension) without *first* doing the pragmatics. In short, if we can find cases of implicaturally determined reference, then we show that the whole semantic apparatus that recursively defines intensions and extensions is reliant on pragmatic input.

It may be objected in advance that theories divide on what happens when reference is semantically ill-defined (as in cases where implicature determines reference). In Strawsonian theories (now in the ascendant, in the modern guises of Situation Semantics and DRT), without reference determination semantic interpretation cannot get off the ground (we get null interpretations). In Russellian theories, we can get an overall extension in such circumstances, namely a truth value False. Thus, on the first kind of theory, pragmatic determination of reference will be essential input to semantics; but on the second kind of theory, the ability to produce truth values for these cases will, I shall demonstrate, be more of an embarrassment than an asset. So the demonstration that implicatures play a role in the determination of reference is as near to a knockdown argument for intrusion that we are likely to find.

Here is a sample of the argument. Consider the following, where (37a) is said in a context where (37b) is mutually evident to speaker and addressee:

(37) a. "The man with *two* children near him is my brother; the man with *three* children near him is my brother-in-law."

    b. *Context:* Two men are clearly visible, one has two children near him (and he's the speaker's brother) and the other has three children near him (and he's the speaker's brother-in-law).

    c. *Content:* 'The man with *at least two* children near him is my brother; the man with *at least three* children near him is my brother-in-law.'

    d. "You should buy the car with four doors rather than the one with two; it's more useful and the price is good."[41]

Has the speaker successfully referred? Surely. Yet what he has 'said' amounts only to (37c); thus the referring expression *the man with two children near him* applies equally to the speaker's brother and to the speaker's brother-in-law. Thus on any theory of definite descriptions (from Russell 1905 to Kadmon 1987) that builds in a uniqueness condition, the expression will either fail to denote (Strawson), or render the utterance false (Russell).[42] But, of course, in practice it would felicitously denote. The reason is that a Q-scalar-inference will, by perfectly regular process, amplify the content to 'the man with at least two children and no more than two children near him'.[43] To belabor the point: what could be a more felicitous referring expression and a truer utterance than the use of sentence (37a) in the context (37b)? Yet on a Strawsonian account, the speaker will have failed to make any (true or false) statement at all, whereas on a Russellian account the statement he made will be false.

    It takes only a moment to see that there is nothing special about the example—(37d) above is perhaps a more natural example. Nor does the observation rest on a particular analysis of ordinary language numerals (which, as we have already seen in chapter 2, is contentious). Consider the following examples of referring expressions whose referents can only be individuated by Q-implicatures based on other scales:

(38) a. "I don't like sitting in the *hot* tub, but I like sitting in the *warm* one."
       (Scale: ⟨*hot, warm*⟩)

    b. "The student who cheated on *some* of the exams should be pardoned, but the one who cheated on *all* of the exams should be expelled."
       (Scale: ⟨*all, some*⟩)

    c. The man who *tried* to assassinate the President was arrested, but the man who *succeeded* in assassinating the President was never apprehended."
       (Scale: ⟨*succeed, try*⟩)

    d. "The senator who is *possibly* implicated in the scandal is the bald man over there; the senator who is *certainly* implicated is the one who looks like Al Capone."
    (Scale: ⟨*certainly, possibly*⟩)

    e. "Drosophila mutants are of two sorts: The mutant that has a left wing *or* a right wing is not viable; but the mutant that has both a left *and* a right wing is perfectly viable."
    (Scale: ⟨*and, or*⟩)

    f. "For once there were two reasonable finalists. But true to form, the committee gave the prize not to the *excellent* one but to the *good* one."
    (Scale: ⟨*excellent, good*⟩)

(39) *Generalization:* given a scale ⟨S, W⟩, where S is the "strong" expression, W the "weak" one, *the W* cannot (by virtue of W alone) be distinct from *the S*, since anything that satisfies S will satisfy W. But in fact *the W* is felicitous in these cases, because *the W* is pragmatically strengthened to exclude *the S*.

To run through these examples briefly. In (38a) *the warm one [tub]* won't single out a referent given its semantic content alone; there are two tubs, one hot and one warm, but the meaning of *warm* is only 'at least warm (and possibly hot)'; but the use of the weaker expression scalar-implicates that the stronger expression (expressing the more extreme property, hotness) would have been inappropriate. Thus *the warm tub* implicates 'the warm-and-not-hot tub'. In (38b), there are two students mentioned who would satisfy the condition *cheated on some of the exams*, for someone who cheats on all certainly cheats on some. Again, only if *some* is strengthened to 'some-and-not-all' will *the student who cheated on some of the exams* pick out a unique referent. In (38c), the property of being the one *who tried to assassinate the President* must equally apply to the one who succeeded (assassination is an intentional, effortful activity). But normally, when we use the expression *try* we implicate lack of success; that this is only an implicature is clear from the noncontradictoriness of a sentence like 'He tried and finally succeeded'. Again, the inference is due to a scalar opposition between *try* and *succeed*; thus, *the man who tried to assassinate the President* is uniquely described only if *tried* is strengthened by Q-implicature to 'tried-and-didn't-succeed'.[44] In (38d), one who is certainly implicated in a scandal is also possibly implicated in a scandal; and one who is possibly implicated in a scandal may indeed be certainly implicated as shown by the noncontradictoriness of a sentence like 'He is possibly, and in fact certainly, implicated in the scandal'. Thus again the expression with the weaker scalar item, *the senator who is possibly implicated*, will fail to uniquely denote unless it is strengthened by scalar implicature to 'the senator who is possibly-but-not-certainly implicated'. In (38e), the description *with a left or a right wing* will apply equally to an entity with both wings; for the semantics of *or* is inclusive, only strengthened to the exclusive interpretation by a scalar Q-implicature. So only when we have the implicature 'with a left or a right wing and not both' in place, as it were, will the description succeed in denoting. Finally, in (38f), the description *good finalist* does not semantically preclude that the finalist is excellent; however, given the scale ⟨*excellent, good*⟩, there is an upperbounding implicature that resolves the description to 'the good but not excellent finalist', thus establishing a unique description. In all of these cases, a default conversational implicature will arise by perfectly general mechanisms to render the referring expression felicitous, but the reference can only succeed with the help of such pragmatic strengthening (see the generalization in (39)).

We can find similar examples from the other two major categories of GCI. Here are some examples with I-implicatures:

(40) a. "The men who drank beer *and* drove home are in jail; the men who drove home *and* drank beer are free."
      b. "The couple who started saving *and* bought a house are now worse off than the couple who bought a house *and* started saving: real estate values just took off."
      c. "The students who *don't like* math are going to fail this course; the students who like it and even the students who [are not fond of it but] don't mind it are going to pass."
      d. "The boss came in and said hello to the *secretary*; *she/the unflappable woman* smiled."
      e. "The woman *at* the desk is the secretary; the woman *near* the desk is her boss."
      f. "The man *reading* is my brother-in-law; the man working is my cousin."
      g. "John admires the book he's reading; but *John's* book is in fact better."

In (40a–b) the implicated asymmetry of *and* comes up again: only on the pragmatically strengthened 'and then' interpretation will definite

[LIKERS   ]   [INDIFFERENT   ]   [DISLIKERS   ]

[.......................*not likers*..........................]

[......................*not minders*........................]

[*not-fond-&-not-minders*]

Figure 3.3
Contradictories before pragmatic strengthening to contraries

references of the form "The *X* who did *U* and *V*" be distinct from "The *X* who did *V* and *U*." In (40c), not liking math is compatible with not minding it; it is, literally, simply the state of not being fond of it, which encompasses both the haters and those indifferent to it. But by a perfectly general I-mechanism whereby contradictories are strengthened to contraries (Horn 1989), *the students who don't like math* is interpreted as 'the students who positively dislike math' (cf. "He doesn't like garlic"). Only when strengthened in that way (to the set of dislikers) is the set of not-liking students distinct from (not overlapping with) the set of students not-fond-of-but-not-minding math (the indifferent ones), as required by the inconsistent predicates *fail* and *pass*. Figure 3.3 shows the overlapping nature of the sets as literally stated and may help to show how in interpretation the sets have to be pragmatically delimited. Note that if we change the example slightly so that the material in square brackets (*are not fond of it but*) is omitted, we then have a three-way nonoverlapping distinction set up by implicature: (a) the don't-likers are pragmatically restricted to the dislikers by I-strengthening from contradictory to contrary, as before; (b) the students who like math (stated); and (c) the students who don't mind math, which is strengthened by a Q-implicature to the students who don't-like-but-don't-mind (due to the scale-like opposition between the strong 'like' and the weak 'not mind' there's an inference from *not mind* to 'not positively like' even though 'not minding' is consistent with 'liking').[45]

Examples (40d–e) are perhaps less clear, but they are candidate cases where I-inferences to the stereotype (see chapter 2 and Atlas and Levinson 1981) might play a role in referential determination. In (40d), assuming that *she* (or an anaphoric epithet like *the unflappable woman*) is understood to be anaphoric to one of the prior NPs, there is a tendency to interpret it as coreferring with *the secretary* based on our stereotypical assumptions about the sex of secretaries and bosses. Given this, the speaker ought to have used a different set of NP expressions if the speaker had intended otherwise, and this gives sufficient warrant for the inference (thus the inference is an implicature, warranted by cooperative assumptions, and not a mere probability about the world that aids one to understand a misleadingly ambiguous utterance). In (40e), the two descriptions *at the desk* and *near the desk* are almost truth-conditionally equivalent (that is, anything that satisfies the one, might be claimed to satisfy the other); but I shall assume that *at* specifies a closer relation (i.e., a smaller boundary area) than *near*. But if the terms are distinct in this way, they are certainly overlapping in descriptive content: one who is at x, is certainly near x. Thus the definite description *the woman near the desk* will be equally satisfied by either woman (provided there are two women in the immediate vicinity of the desk). Yet if one woman is sitting down with knees under the desk and the other standing in front of it, even though either woman might be described truthfully as *near the desk* or *at the desk*, there is little doubt who, given pragmatic principles, should be so described. The reason is that *at* (no doubt owing to its 'very immediate vicinity' meaning) tends to induce additional stereotypical assumptions— someone who is *at a desk* is typically sitting down and working on it, someone who is *at the church* is typically worshipping in it, someone who is *at the door* is typically waiting to be let in, and so on (see Herskovits 1986). Thus given these stereotypical I-enrichments, the definite descriptions in (40e) will be unambiguous and felicitous. Similarly in (40f), given the generally prevailing assumption that reading is more likely to be done for pleasure than profit, and given an opposition between *the man reading* and *the man working* which will only be resolved by assuming that the man reading is not thereby working, a speaker will I-implicate 'the man-reading-&-not-working'. Finally, (40g) will be false unless *the book he's reading* is distinct from *John's book* (recall sentences of the kind 'The book John is reading is better than John's book'). Thus we tend to assume that the relation between John and the book in *John's book* is the other stereotypical person-to-book relation, namely authorship.

Finally, we can construct (perhaps somewhat less clear) examples where a definite referring expression will only succeed in denoting if an M-implicature strengthens the descriptive content. Consider:

(41) a. "The tall man is my brother; the *tall, tall* man is my uncle."
     b. "The large building is CSLI; the *large, large* building is the medical school."

    c. "She doesn't mind the teacher who teases her; but she hates the teacher who teases and teases and teases her."

    d. "True to form, instead of appointing the clever candidate, they appointed the *clever clever* candidate."

    e. "She made the fruit salad; I made the *salad salad*."

    f. "There are two routes to the summit: the possible one and the *not impossible* one."

    g. "The boss always used a hit man. In the dock, the man who *caused her death* is the man to the left, the man who killed her is the man to the right."

    h. "The California Code makes a distinction between ordinary vehicles and special purpose ones. So, in the lot there, the car has to conform to vehicle emissions, but the *vehicular device* doesn't have to."

In (41a–c) repetition suggests a heightened quality to the predications in question, sufficient to achieve unique reference by the referring expressions. Clearly, the assumption here (justified in chapter 2) is that the kinds of repetition used in these examples is not semantic modification. Thus, on this assumption, the repetitive descriptions add no truth-conditional content, but the use of the more prolix expressions implicates a distinction from the unrepetitive descriptions—namely, one in which the action or property is intensified (as suggested iconically).[46] In (41d–e) the reduplications clearly take on special meanings by M-implicature (as suggested to me by Larry Horn). In (41f), the opposition between the simple positive *the possible one* and the double negative *the not impossible one* suggests that one route is markedly more passable than the other, and thus again an M-implicature allows two referring expressions with identical semantic content to refer uniquely to different referents. In (41g), the use of the periphrastic causative (as before) suggests indirect causation by M-implicature calculated in contrast to the lexical causative *kill*, which suggests direct causation by I-implicature; thus we can identify the indirect killer with the boss, the direct killer with the hit man. Similarly in (41h), the periphrastic *vehicular device* suggests some very un-car-like vehicle.

    I have already mentioned further examples of M-determination of reference that are of a rather different kind and involve a preference for disjoint reference invoked by the use of a more prolix or informationally nonredundant NP (Levinson 1987a, b and chapter 4 of this book). This has to be understood against the I-heuristic for anaphoric linkage: wherever a following NP has a semantic content properly included in the content of a preceding NP (and thus the following NP is more semantically general than the preceding NP), there is a strong preference for coreference or, more strictly, an anaphoric relation. This is illustrated in (42a–b). Note that this preference for coreference is discouraged where a subsequent referring expression contains semantic conditions not contained within the potential antecedent as illustrated in a' (where not all ships are ferries) and b' (where not all Johns are adult males).

(42) a.   "The ferry$_1$ hit a rock. The ship$_1$ capsized."
    a'.   "The ship$_1$ hit a rock. The ferry$_2$ capsized."
    b.   "John$_1$ entered the room. He$_1$ walked over to the window."
    b'.   "John$_1$ entered the room. The man$_2$ walked over to the window."

This pattern will be explored further in chapter 4, but the point here is simply that it appears that implicature is often the linking principle that makes one NP referentially dependent on a specific prior referring expression.

   If this account of all these cases of pragmatic determination of reference is roughly on the right lines, then it would seem that our job is done. Recollect that our aim was to find knockdown arguments to the effect that Grice's circle is a genuine dilemma: The Gricean 'what is said', upon which basis implicatures are supposed to be calculated, is itself partly determined by implicatures that help fix reference. The theoretical implication is that Carnapian intensions (together with worlds and indices) do not alone determine extensions. Instead, there is crucial pragmatic input to semantic interpretation, and the pragmatic principles in question are identical to those thought to operate only as postsemantic principles of Gricean utterance interpretation. Yet the battle with the Obstinate Theorist is still not quite over.

3.4.2   Implicaturally Determined Reference and Donnellan's Referential/Attributive Distinction

The examples I have given are meant to establish that implicature calculation is often a prerequisite to establishing reference. Can our Obstinate Theorist escape this conclusion? I don't believe so, but we know he's going to try. Here is what he might say:

You've made an implicit distinction between implicaturally determined reference and pure (semantically) determined reference. Actually, this is just the identical distinction to Donnellan's (1966) *referential* versus *attributive* distinction. Quite respectable people (Donnellan (1978) himself, Barwise and Perry (1983)) think that this distinction is *semantic*. Other, even more respectable people (like Kripke (1977)) think that the distinction is one between semantic correctness on the one hand and pragmatic success with semantic error on the other—more precisely, that it's a distinction between a proper semantic use and an improper but occasionally successful use of referring expressions. Either way, there's a perfectly good account of the *referential uses* (alias implicaturally determined references) that is quite compatible with the received view that all Gricean pragmatics is postsemantic.

Could the Obstinate theorist be right, that our distinction between pure reference and implicaturally fixed reference is the very same distinction as Donnellan's? Recollect Donnellan's examples of the kind:

(43) a. "The man over there drinking champagne is happy tonight."
      b. *Context:* the man the speaker has in mind is holding a champagne glass in fact full of seltzer.
      c. *Kripke's alternate context:* same, but there's also another man over there (whom the speaker does not have in mind) who has a nonvisible glass of champagne and is gloomy.
      d. "Smith's murderer is insane."
          Referential: That chap, Smith's murderer, is insane.
          Attributive: Whoever is Smith's murderer is insane.

The puzzle associated with the utterance of (43a) in the context (43b) is: if the fake-champagne drinker is indeed happy, we're inclined to think what was said was true, even though on a Russellian analysis (given context (43b)) it should be false, and on a Strawsonian analysis of definite descriptions it should be neither true nor false. If we change the context, as suggested by Kripke (1977), to that in (43c), then on either analysis what is said ought just to be false.

Donnellan's suggestion: in some cases, we use the description to get to the referent and then throw away the description as it were; then if the predication holds of the referent, what was said was true. Thus there are often two interpretations of definite NPs as sketched in (43d), where the referential interpretations treat the description merely as a route to the referent, but the attributive interpretations require that whatever meets the description has the predicated properties.

Are our cases instances of the very same referential use of definite descriptions? Consider again the prototype example:

(44) a. "The man with two children near him is my brother; the man with three children near him is my brother-in-law."
   b. *Context:* Two men are clearly visible, one has two children near him and the other has three children near him. The first is the speaker's brother, the second his brother-in-law.
   c. *Russellian analysis:* (a) is false
      Strawsonian analysis: (a) is truth-valueless
      Intuitively: (a) is true! (stronger than Donnellan's cases)

On a Russellian analysis, the first definite description applied to its predication will be just plain false—it fails to meet the uniqueness specification. But again, just as in the Donnellan cases, reference may succeed nevertheless, and we'd be loath to call the sentence false in context (44b). So this suggests an immediate identification of implicaturally fixed reference and speaker reference (Donnellan's *referential* uses). The other term of the correspondence would identify implicature-free reference determination with Donnellan's attributive uses. The parallel between the two distinctions may seem quite exact, as comparison of examples (43) and (44) above should make clear.

But there's an *insuperable problem* with this identification of the two distinctions. Implicaturally fixed references exhibit within themselves the very same Donnellan ambiguity (if that is what it is). Consider:

(45) "The man who has two children is prudent; the man who has three is a fool."
   Referential use: in a context where two men are visible, one with two children near him, the other with three.
   Attributive use: gloss 'whoever has two children and no more is prudent; whoever has three is a fool.'

In the referential use, note that the man who visibly has two children may in fact have three (one hiding behind a tree); the fertility of the two men has nothing to do with the predications because the number of the children is simply a route to the referents. But in the attributive use, the description "occurs essentially" as Donnellan puts it, just as in his prototype cases.

Thus we cannot assimilate the implicaturally fixed versus pure reference distinction to the Donnellan distinction; it is orthogonal. So the Obstinate Theorist is just wrong. But, he may retort, the distinctions may be related, even if not identical, in which case the semantic machinery or pragmatic arguments developed to handle the Donnellan distinction might be redeployed, *mutatis mutandis*, to handle our distinction. So let us examine Kripke's pragmatic account and Barwise and Perry's account to see what succor there may be for the Obstinate Theorist.

Kripke points out that, with a clear distinction between speaker-meaning and linguistic-meaning, it seems perfectly possible to just maintain that the Donnellan referential uses are, where strictly false, just plain false at the level of linguistic-meaning while being true at the level of speaker-meaning. That is, Donnellan's distinction is not a semantic one and we may distinguish between:

1. Semantic reference: "Where the speaker has a designator in his idiolect, certain conventions of his idiolect (given various facts about the world) determine the referent in the idiolect."
2. Speaker's reference: "That object which the speaker wishes to talk about, on a given occasion, and believes fulfills the conditions for being the semantic referent of the designator."

Note one mismatch between our implicature-determined reference and Kripke's speaker-reference: in our cases, the speaker has no intention of conforming to the semantical rules. That is, the speaker is under no mistaken illusions about the relation between his words and the world; he knows perfectly well that his semantic reference will be inadequate or inapplicable without implicatural strengthening. When a speaker refers to the man as *the man with two children*, even though there are two men who fit the semantic content by having at least two children and even though the addressee can see that the semantic content is not individuating, he does so with intention aforethought. And even though a Russellian analysis requires that what our speaker said was false, the speaker has no false impressions and by any reasonable account (I would think) is speaking truly (assuming the predication holds). That is what gives our cases interest—they are not odd quirks of odd circumstances. They are intentional and routine uses of expressions where the semantic conditions for use are not met.[47]

Kripke concedes that there's just one circumstance under which he might admit that Donnellan's distinction is semantical—namely, if the successful (but condition-failing) reference was clearly intuitively true. Donnellan's cases arguably fail this test, but the implicaturally determined cases seem to pass it.[48] Nevertheless, I am not advancing the distinction as a semantic ambiguity; it's a truth-conditional "ambiguity" only because semantic conditions are routinely enriched by pragmatic conditions prior to truth-conditional assessment. Thus we can agree that our implicaturally determined references involve pragmatic factors while still insisting that the truth conditions of the utterance are as they intuitively are.

At the risk of repetition let me sum up so far: our distinction between pure and implicaturally determined reference is orthogonal to Donnellan's referential versus attributive distinction. Nor is it accommodated by Kripke's semantic-reference versus speaker-reference, because of the mismatch between speaker-reference and implicaturally determined reference: (a) In speaker-reference there must be a (possibly erroneous) belief that the semantic conditions are met, but in implicaturally determined reference this is not so (uniqueness conditions for example may be obviously infringed); (b) In speaker-reference it is sufficient that the speaker believes that the semantic conditions are met; in implicaturally determined reference that is not necessary but in any case not sufficient—the implicated conditions must also be met; (c) Implicaturally determined reference meets at least the prima facie condition Kripke puts on a genuine semantic ambiguity, namely that one has the clear intuition that such a statement is true (even when, in our cases, *qua* semantic-reference it is false)—yet nevertheless it is obviously not a semantic ambiguity because it is introduced by Gricean mechanisms. The solution to that dilemma is simply to admit that implicatures contribute to truth conditions.

Kripke's (1977) tack is to treat the referential/attributive distinction as corresponding to a pragmatics/semantics distinction and thus to dismiss the cases where there is conflict as usable falsities. Another approach is to take the distinction as indeed a semantic distinction as Barwise and Perry (1983) do in Situation Semantics. Perhaps that treatment might be able to accommodate our distinction between (pure) semantic reference and implicaturally determined reference, and we should consider it briefly. In that theory, the meaning of an expression is a relation between various contextual factors and described situations. Therefore, the Donnellan distinction can be captured by letting the referential use of definite description *the F(x)* (to use an informal notation) only have the denoted *individual a* in the described situation, whereas attributive uses have the *describing condition F* itself (indirectly) in the described situation (Barwise and Perry 1983: 146ff). Thus in the referential use of, say, *the man drinking champagne*, the describing condition is used to obtain the referent, but is thrown away as it were. It does its job by constraining another situation, the *resource situation*, which is some accessible situation (e.g., the immediate view, in which there is a man drinking what appears to be champagne). The meaning of the referential use of definite NPs can then be thought of as a function that has as argument the 'resource situation' and as value the referent (here the salient apparent champagne drinker, let's call him Joe). Thus the interpretation of *The man drinking champagne is happy* is a described situation in which Joe is happy.

Can we apply the same analysis to implicaturally determined references like *the man with two children* (in the context of a man with exactly two and a man with exactly three children), and if so would it help? The answers are yes and no, respectively. The idea that the resource situation, once it has done its individual-selecting job, can be discarded has something right about it for these cases too. But the mechanisms of resource situations will not help us. That would only shift the problem to another situation (from the described to the resource situation), and in that other situation we still have the identical conundrum, namely that these definite descriptions fail to describe uniquely without implicatural strengthening. Thus, without that strengthening, the function taking us from resource situations to individuals will be ill-defined (it will have two values— the man with exactly two and the man with exactly three children—for one argument). A second reason for not looking to this analysis for succor is simply that if the same mechanism gives a good analysis of the Donnellan cases, then it cannot do so for this distinction because, as we have seen, it is orthogonal. Indeed, our cases of implicaturally determined reference can have both the attributive and the referential reading—which shows that the resource situations simply can't be involved in our distinction (because they are invoked on one reading, gone on the other). In any case, although the general apparatus of Situation Semantics has many impressive ways of handling those aspects of contextual determination of interpretation that are indexical or quasi-indexical, there is no place for elaborate pragmatic reasoning of the Gricean kind.

I conclude that implicaturally determined references are not some semantic distinction in disguise (as they might be on some analyses if they conflated with the Donnellan distinction). They are what they appear to be: cases where implicatures play a crucial role in determining truth-conditional content.

3.4.3 The Obstinate Theorist's Final Retort on Reference

In the case of intrusive constructions, we admitted that the Obstinate Theorist who insists on a postsemantic pragmatics can just require what seems felicitous to be false or contradictory and then treat the intuitive content as a Gricean inference from a flout. Can't the Obstinate Theorist do that in these cases, too? *The man with two children G's*, said where there are two individuals one with two and one with three children, is false (Russell) or undefined (Strawson); to get some cooperative proposition, the speaker must intend the hearer to push the sentence through the pragmatics (cf. Bach 1987a: 82–85)!

Two objections:

1. Methodological: if this tactic is pursued willy-nilly, in violation of our intuitions about truth and falsity, why not claim that any other sentence for which the proponent's semantic theory makes the wrong predictions is in fact patched up by the postsemantic pragmatics and thus is after all correctly analyzed by his unlikely theory?

2. Substantive: on some accounts of definites (e.g., Russell's), the negative will be true just when it is intuitively false, and the positive false just when it is intuitively true, which is too absurd to be rescued by Gricean maneuvers!

To see this consider the informal Russellian analysis in (46d) of the negative sentence in (46a), which states that one or more of three conditions are not met. In the context (46c), there's an individual satisfying the conditions of being my brother and having at least two children; but the middle condition requiring that there be no other individual with at least two children is not met—therefore the denial of the positive sentence will be true. Thus the semantic prediction is that (46a) will be true just when it is intuitively false, and (46b) will be false just when it is intuitively true. The Obstinate Theorist's attempt to hang on to a postsemantic pragmatics will thus have quite absurd consequences.

(46) a. "It's not the case that the man with two children is my brother."
  b. "The man with two children is my brother."
  c. *Context:* There is a man with exactly 2 kids who is my brother, and another with exactly 3 kids who is not my brother.
  d. $\sim [\exists x \; HAS \; (x, \; at\text{-}least\text{-}2\text{-}children) \; \& \; \sim \exists y \; (HAS \; (y, \; at\text{-}least\text{-}2\text{-}children) \; \& \; y \neq x) \; \& \; my\text{-}brother(x)]$
  e. *On a Russellian analysis:* (a) = True   (b) = False
     Intuition: (a) = False   (b) = True!

The conclusion, I would hope, is that implicaturally determined reference must be accepted, and we must turn to consider the consequences for an overall theory of meaning. But first we must give the Obstinate Theorist the *coup de grace*.

3.4.4   Presemantic Pragmatics versus Postpragmatic Semantics

What (I hope) we have established so far:

1. We need some presemantic Gricean pragmatics—to do disambiguation and indexical resolution, not to mention ellipsis unpacking and generality-narrowing.

2. We seem to need substantial presemantic Gricean pragmatics to handle the intrusion examples in complex constructions like the comparative and the conditional.

3. Even in simple sentences, we find Gricean intrusion in reference-determination—if we resist the Gricean analysis, we predict bizarre truth conditions (e.g., *the man with two children* case, where on the Russellian analysis we get a falsehood where there's an intuitive truth and a truth where there's an intuitive falsehood).

All these difficulties disappear if we accept that Gricean processes can be input to truth-conditional content (although further puzzles arise, naturally).

But let's return to our Obstinate Theorist, the one who insists on maintaining a pure semantics and a wholly postsemantic pragmatics. None of the conclusions listed above seem totally insuperable at first sight to such a die-hard. Here would be his responses:

1′. We don't attempt contextual *disambiguation* prior to semantics; we just give a single distinct semantic interpretation for each reading. Likewise, we don't do presemantic indexical resolution or any other generality narrowing; we just end up with extremely general truth-conditional content ("Bill was here" will be true just in case Bill was within some unspecified area, possibly of limitless extent, which includes the speaker!).

2′. In the *intrusion constructions*, we Obstinate Theorists may just take these to be "Gricean flouts:" thus our intuition that *If each side got three goals, it was a draw* is true is simply based on assessing the truth of the statement-plus-implicatures—it is an assessment of speaker-meaning, not sentence-meaning.

3′. In the *reference* cases, we need to distinguish different kinds of cases:

a. In the cases where what is said is literally false according to the Obstinate Theorist (as on a Russellian analysis of our case of *the man with two children*) we can adopt a flouting analysis, which gets us a truth for the statement-plus-implicature (the speaker-meaning).

b. Where reference is undefined, the account is more tortured. (For example, the Strawsonian analysis of *the man with two children*; the "bridging" anaphora cases where no unique referent has been previously established, as in *The bridge collapsed. The wood was rotten.*) Here the semantics gives us nothing (null interpretations); so the pragmatics can give us nothing. Here the Obstinate Theorist will have to gesture to some theory of *accommodation* (cf. Lewis 1979) whereby the use of an undefined reference is reinterpreted *as if it had been the use of some other referring expression that would have been well defined* had it been used. The important point here is that this invoking of *accommodation constitutes an admission of presemantic pragmatics in these cases.*

c. In the cases where we have competing antecedents—as in my account of preferred interpretations of pronouns versus lexical NPs—we can just have the semantics give the interpretation for each potential antecedent (i.e., treat the sentence as *n*-ways ambiguous).

Let us indulge the Obstinate Theorist and see what his theory would be like—what would the consequences be? Well, one surprising consequence has been pointed out to me by Ivan Sag: namely, the result of having no presemantic pragmatics will be to have a *postpragmatic semantics*! In which case, we come back to more or less the same picture: a semantic component with Gricean input.

Let us trace through Sag's argument. Our Obstinate Theorist will deny that the example (47a) below is true—because without intrusion it is necessarily false. But the semantics will compute the pragmatics-free interpretation, namely the contradiction, by (say) treating *worse than* as a two-place predicate which can be true only if the extensions of the two arguments are distinct. The semantics now sends the results to the pragmatics.[49] The pragmatics will now reject the interpretation as a cooperative assertion, and seek to patch it up, e.g., by computing the 'and subsequently' implicature of each *and* in the schema '(event$_1$) *and* (event$_2$)'. But now what? We need to compute the meaning and extension of the whole sentence over again, but this time with an alteration in the meaning and extension of two of its parts. To do that kind of recomputation for any arbitrary sentence we need the whole apparatus of compositional semantics. But by hypothesis, the semantics is free of pragmatic input: so this recomputation cannot be done by the "pure" semantics. Equally, the recomputation can't be done in the pragmatics: the pragmatics is part of a theory of communication, built on nonmonotonic principles quite different in character than those operative in semantics. So we will need a second semantics component, a *postpragmatic semantics*, which, unlike the "pure" semantics does accept pragmatic input but is in all other ways identical!

So we need to send our sentence with its pragmatically retooled parts back to a second semantics component to get the semantic content of the whole: we apply the predicate *worse than* to two altered arguments (as in a′) and derive a set of truth conditions and an extension in our world (say, a truth).

(47) a. "Having a baby and getting married is worse than getting married and having a baby."

   a′. 'Having a baby *and then* getting married is worse than getting married *and then* having a baby.'

   b. "If each side gets three goals, then it's a draw."

   b′. 'If each side gets *three-and-no-more* goals, then it's a draw.'

In more or less exactly the same way, the conditional in (47b) will come out false (contingently, given the rules of soccer), and the semantic content (the proposition expressed) will be sent to the pragmatics for first-aid treatment. If the addressee knows the rules of soccer, the falsehood will be self-evident; the content of *three* (namely, at least three) can undergo the normal scalar strengthening. But now we want to know the truth conditions (and the truth) of the whole, recomputed by combining the intensions and extensions of the retooled parts. We need a semantics again, a postpragmatic semantics.

Thus the only alternative to a presemantic pragmatics is a postpragmatic semantics. Let us now assess these two alternatives. The following subsections detail what is against the Obstinate Theorist's scheme.

3.4.4.1   Violation of Intuitions   The Obstinate Theorist's scheme makes the wrong predictions about intuitions of truth and falsity (as in all the intrusive construction examples); we are told to discount these intuitions as really intuitions about the truth value of the proposition expressed at the level of speaker-meaning, not at the level of sentence-meaning. Additionally, it discounts our intuitions about the distinction between floutings or exploitational implicatures and ordinary GCIs. To repeat an earlier point, the intrusive comparative constructions are supposed to have the flouted quality we associate, for example, with patent contradictions (thus there should be a close parallel between (48a) and (48b)), and the conditional intrusive examples should feel parallel to ironies.

(48) a. "Getting drunk and driving home is much worse than driving home and getting drunk."

    b. "Clinton is both the President and not the President."

    c. "If each team gets three goals, it's a draw."

    d. "If you want a theory-neutral education in linguistics, you should go to MIT."

The sentences in (48b,d) seem transparently to require the reprocessing one associates with flouts; example (48a) is certainly less clearly in this category, and (48c) intuitively doesn't belong at all. It's hard to say how much weight should be put on such intuitions, but surely some.

3.4.4.2 Exceptions There seem to be exceptions to the Obstinate Theorist's position that he must concede. These are the cases where reference is undefined, so no overall extensions can be computed by the semantics. If the semantics provides nothing at all in the way of interpretation, the pragmatics will have nothing to work on. Cases include the definite reference examples on a Strawsonian analysis, the bridging examples and other cases of so-called accommodation; also perhaps examples of indexical resolution where without narrowing we can get no extension (perhaps, examples like *Some of you come here. You can be on this team, you others on that.*) In these cases, we need the pragmatics to give us something in the way of an extension as input to the semantics, in order to get any interpretation at all.

3.4.4.3 Lack of Economy The Obstinate Theorist makes us recalculate the semantic content after pragmatic resolution; thus we get double the semantic processing. We also need, by hypothesis of the purity of semantics, two semantic components—the pure one, and one that takes input from the pragmatics to recalculate more sensible intensions and extensions. And it follows as an additional oddity of this position that we will need *yet another* pragmatics! Consider the following:

(49) a. "In China, if you have a small family with two children, you are deified."

    b. [Said of inebriated lecturer] "At least we are all agreed that in future we'll have the reception before the lecture: having plenty of port and giving a lecture produces better results than giving a lecture and having plenty of port."

Here, after passing through the pure semantics, we need to do the Gricean pragmatics, so that in (49a) *two* is restricted to 'at most two' and in (49b) the two *and*s get amplified to 'and then'. Then we need to recompute the semantics (in the postpragmatics semantics) with these new extensions. But now that we have the propositions expressed by the utterances, we find they are obviously false (given what we know about China and deification, and what we know about giving lectures on plenty of port). So we send them off again for pragmatic processing, to the pragmatics that follows the postpragmatic semantics!

Thus the overall picture proposed by the Obstinate Theorist has the character that obstinacy unfortunately tends to have: unattractive repetition. His theory has two more or less identical components doing semantic interpretation, and he has at least two applications of Gricean pragmatics (three if he acknowledges the force of the accommodation examples mentioned above). We end up with a simpler picture with less exceptions on the view that allows a presemantic pragmatics—or more generally does not insist on a position where semantic interpretation accepts no pragmatic input. But above all, when we examine the consequences of the Obstinate Theorist's position, we see that he cannot avoid the very result that motivates his theoretical contortions—namely, an interleaving of pragmatic and semantic processes. Thus in the critical respect, both our theory and the Obstinate Theorist's do not in the end differ!

3.5   SOME IMPLICATIONS

3.5.1   Disposing of the Existing Responses

I outlined above a number of existing or potential responses to Grice's circle (see section 3.2.7). In light of the further evidence adduced we may return to them and see if we can now dispose of at least some of them.

3.5.1.1   Lack of Evidence   This response, personified in our Obstinate Theorist, has been the direct target of most of the remarks above. If doubts still remain about intrusion phenomena, then that may be because we have restricted ourselves to the intrusion of GCIs only. If particularized implicatures are also taken into account, the range of evidence widens immensely, because many cases of disambiguation, narrowing, and other kinds of pragmatic resolution depend on Relevance implicatures (as argued in Sperber and Wilson 1986). As well, we have already noted the case of metonymic transfers (Nunberg 1978, Sag 1981, Fau-

connier 1985). The following examples make the point that semantic and syntactic intrusion occurs in these cases:

(50) a. "James Joyce liked to read *himself*."
   b. "If *this painter* [pointing at a painting] was more abstract, *he* would sell well."
   c. "If you can't find a copy of *Chomsky* over in *Philosophy*, I will lend you mine."
   d. [Pointing at old car] "*That* was when I was a kid."

If the net is widened to take into account the intrusion of background knowledge generally (as licensed by the I-principle or a maxim of Relevance), then all the pragmatic resolution that goes under the rubric of *local pragmatics* in AI work provides directly relevant data (see Hobbs et al. 1987). This includes the role of knowledge in resolving metonymies, generality narrowing in nominal compounds, pronominal resolution, quantifier scoping, disambiguation, and so forth. Detailed studies like that by Herskovits (1986) of the pragmatic resolution of spatial descriptions are further grist.

   Also, we now need to go back and look at many of the apparently trivial facts that were adduced in favor of generative semantics and that were given burial without autopsy (the literature on indirect speech acts, negative polarity items, and so on all come to mind). For example, we reviewed in chapter 2 Horn's (1978, 1989) argument that Neg-raising is actually an I-inference (R-implicature in his terms) whose availability is systematically determined by scalar strength of predicate (among other things); because the distribution and interpretation of negative polarity items depends on the availability of this inference, we have a systematic intrusion of pragmatics into semantics and grammar (although this clearly involves ongoing conventionalization). Also, work on nonce uses of nouns as verbs, and the like (as studied by Clark and Clark 1979) are directly pertinent (see Sag 1981). A renewal of interest in encoded subjectivity and point of view in language (Lyons 1981, Kuno 1987)—whether in logophoric reflexives (Sells 1987, O'Connor 1987), free indirect style and metapragmatics (Lucy 1993), evidentials (Chafe and Nichols 1986), or more generally in the lexicon (Mitchell 1986)—suggests that the signaling of point of view exploits generalized pragmatic inference (this is explored in chapter 4). All in all, there appears to be a wealth of data (in need, it is true, of detailed reassessment) that demonstrates not only the

intrusion of pragmatic inference in semantic interpretation but how that
intrusion can also influence the distribution of syntactic elements.

3.5.1.2 Restricted Presemantic Pragmatics This approach allows that
Gricean pragmatics might provide input to semantics but requires that it
be of a limited and restricted kind. Thus, as mentioned, Relevance theorists propose that there is a special kind of implicature, an explicature,
that embellishes logical forms in limited ways. We have reviewed the criteria for explicatures that have been suggested by Sperber and Wilson
(1986), Carston (1988), and Recanati (1989, 1993), and we found that
they remain unclear. The hypothesis is not well circumscribed, but the
general idea is clear enough: contextual input should first be used to
extract a sufficiently informative proposition. It is an idea shared with
the AI community, who make much the same assumption and call the
restricted amplifications of logical form "local pragmatics" (see, e.g.,
Hobbs et al. 1987).

For the existence of explicatures to be more than a terminological issue,
they must have some specific, identifying properties. The difficulty is to
see how and why certain restricted kinds of pragmatic inference should
alone have presemantic application and, if so, why they should be derived
by the identical apparatus that derives postsemantic implicatures (the principle of Relevance in Relevance Theory). In fact, the best candidates for such
presemantic inferences might be GCIs. By hypothesis, they are default
inferences driven by (potentially fragmentary) semantic representations,
but Relevance theory recognizes no such special class of default inferences.

One way to test the hypothesis that explicatures are essentially different
in kind from implicatures is to take those implicatures that look most
postsemantic—namely, the tropes and flouts that seem to presuppose the
prior establishment of a literal meaning—and see whether they can intrude in semantic interpretation or play a role in reference determination.
Unfortunately for the hypothesis in question, they do seem to have that
ability. Let us just focus on the ability of such tropes to determine reference (because from that ability, it will follow that tropes will intrude in
our intrusive constructions).

(51) *Metonymic particularized transfers:*
   a. "John took the book to Philosophy."
      Context (i): in a bookstore, *Philosophy* might refer to a certain
      stretch of shelving;

Context (ii): in a university, *Philosophy* might refer to a
department)
b. "Pearl Harbor remembers Pearl Harbor." (newspaper headline)[50]

(52) *Ironic reference:*
 a. "If you need a car, you may borrow my Porsche" (referring to
    speaker's VW).
 b. "I had the choice between a career in linguistics and a career in
    domestic economy; and bless me, I went and chose the easy
    option."

(53) *Metaphoric reference:*
 a. "Come and meet our resident Greenberg" (said of Bernard
    Comrie).
 b. "Pass the vintage vinegar" (said of a bad wine).

(54) *Reference by indirection:*
 a. "I need to go to the you-know-where."
 b. "I was most sorry to hear of Fred's passing."

The same kind of reference-by-trope can then be embedded in an intrusion construction, as in the now familiar "If you want a theory-neutral
education in linguistics, you should go to MIT", or "Even if you take my
Porsche, you'll still get there in time", or "If you like this vintage vinegar,
you will be pleased to hear you can buy it for one dollar a bottle at your
local Tesco Superstore." Note that ironies, on the Sperber-Wilson theory
of Relevance, are implicatures interpreted as "echoes" of what someone
might have said: they are distinctly not explicatures. Yet they may play a
role in determining the proposition expressed by the antecedent of a conditional, against which the consequent should be assessed.

   The idea that some implicatures are essential to the determination of
the propositional content of an utterance, whereas others are further
embellishments or exploitations, may well be correct. But it does not
follow that these two roles are necessarily occupied by pragmatic inferences of different natural classes. As we have seen, the evidence does not
directly point in that direction. However, caution is in order. It could be,
for example, that there are distinct types of intrusion: some, like those
associated with our GCIs and perhaps the metonymic transfers above,
may be genuinely presemantic (in the sense that they can be calculated
without access to the full propositional content of the utterance), whereas
others (like the cases of ironic reference) may require double processing—

being sent back for pragmatic readjustment after the "literal meaning" is computed (much as our Obstinate Theorist has argued for all the intrusion cases). There is some intuitive support for this (see Horn 1992b: 184–188). But single versus double processing would seem to be a dimension orthogonal to the explicature/implicature distinction: we may be forced to compute an irony by double processing to obtain a proposition (an explicature) relevant enough for the kind of processing envisaged in Relevance theory.

The position adopted here is therefore that—for reasons spelled out below—GCIs constitute a genus of pragmatic inference especially able and likely to intrude into semantic representations, but whether they do so will depend in part at least on the position of GCI-inducing expressions in constructions. In short, on particular occasions, GCIs may or may not be explicatures: they crosscut the Relevance-theory distinction between explicatures and implicatures, as do other kinds of pragmatic inference.

3.5.1.3 Semantic Retreat: Semantics as Syntax The strategy of semantic retreat is to yield over matters of (what is normally called semantic) interpretation entirely to pragmatics (or other general reasoning abilities), while assigning to semantics only the job of computing an LF or semantic representation from the syntactic input and lexical content. As mentioned, a number of theorists who hold very different ideas about the nature of semantic representations may be tempted by such a position. For example, not only Relevance theorists (Sperber and Wilson 1995: 257–258) may fit in here, but also those who hold that linguistic semantics is exhausted by the level of LF in Chomskyan theory (a level that consists of "those aspects of semantic structure which are expressed syntactically" (May 1987: 306)). Even those conceptualists like Katz, who think of semantics as essentially computations over an extremely rich syntax of "markerese" or the like, may wish to hand over matters of the interpretation of such representations to pragmatics.

On such a strategy, we escape semantic intrusion by yielding up all aspects of utterance interpretation to pragmatics. Few theorists would, I think, deny that such an abstract, underspecified level of semantic content should play an important role in a semantic theory (see e.g., Ruhl 1989, Pustejovsky 1995, van Deemter and Peters 1996). The question is whether this is all there is to linguistic semantics. It is therefore important to see that what one is left with is an extremely impoverished level of representation. Kempson (1986) recognizes this: on her account, logical forms will have undecided scope, meta-variables for pronouns, vacuously general terms, in short, subpropositional status. The consequence is that such a level of semantic representation or logical form is no longer a level over which the traditional sense relations can be stated—it simply cannot be as rich as Katz (1987) imagines. That is because, if we are correct about pragmatic intrusion, the intuitive concept of entailment, in terms of which all the sense relations (synonymy, antonymy, converseness, etc.) are defined, cannot be stated over semantic representations alone. If one thinks of entailment in terms of truth conditions, the reason for this is obvious: truth is a property of utterances (complete with intrusive implicatures), and entailment is the concept of inference-while-preserving-truth. But equally, if one thinks of sense relations as primitive, such relations must still relate well-defined propositions, not underspecified propositional schema of the kind that we may be able to algorithmically extract from syntactic structures. (Given indexicality, Katz's position is already threatened—for example, synonymy relations can't really be stated except by holding indices constant—but given pragmatic intrusion the position is overwhelmed.[51])

Semantic retreat therefore has the consequence that semantics does not look like either of the familiar, conventional, rival enterprises: it is not about truth-conditional content on the one hand, nor about the relations of sense that hold between sentences on the other hand. Instead, it is exclusively about a new, strange level populated by semantic wraiths—a level of fragmentary structures, underspecification and half-information, even archi-sememes (Atlas 1989: 146). The recognition of the existence of this level is one of the important sea changes in the history of semantics—it is real enough, but it is relative *terra incognita*.

But one can recognize the actuality of this level of underspecified semantic representations without subscribing to semantic retreat. There are two reasons to resist such a limited scope for linguistic semantics. The first is conservative: what little we know about the properties of semantic representations is based on their abilities to support logical inference—indeed without taking inferential properties into account, there are more or less no known constraints on semantic representations. Underspecified semantic representations do not constitute a level on which notions of semantic inference can be based. To retain the insights of the long tradition of research about semantic inference, we need to find another level at which these insights hold, and it will be a level to which pragmatic information has contributed. Second, the position of semantic retreat presumes that there is nothing especially *linguistic* about the inferences derived from utterances or the processes by which they are derived—it is just in effect *thinking* (or processing general conceptual structures). This view hugely underestimates the gap between linguistic and nonlinguistic cognition: linguistic representations (whether pragmatically enriched or not) have many special properties like linearity, generality, indexicality, and culture-specific lexicons which would seem to be quite remote from a "language of thought" (Levinson 1997). There is every reason then to try and reconstrue the interaction between semantics and pragmatics as the intimate interlocking of distinct processes, rather than, as traditionally, in terms of the output of the one being the input to the other.

3.5.1.4 Enlarged Indexicality This approach, typified by Situation Semantics but attractive also to more conservative logical models of semantics, seeks to treat contextual dependence as limited to the resolution of preexisting variables, built in to the semantics of specific expressions ("contextuals" in the terminology suggested above). The radical pragmatics approach of generality-plus-implicatures (i.e., lexical or constructional weak univocality) is often in direct opposition to this indexical approach to the analysis of particular constructions and lexical items. Sophisticated tests are needed to distinguish between such implicit variables (fixed either by the utterance situation or resource situations) and generality (narrowed by implicatures). The study of indexicality by Enç (1981) provides some tools for this. For example, once indexicals are fixed, they are "rigid" under negation, intensional contexts, and anaphora; if the enlarged class of contextuals also must have this property (which I think it must), then we have a whole battery of tests for contextuals versus generality-plus-implicature.[52] With such tests, we can expect the phenomena to divide: we can expect some cases to be better analyzed one way and some the other. For example, it is conceivable that the narrowing of degree predicates or the asymmetric temporality of *and* may ultimately be better analyzed in this way than as I-induced generality-narrowings (although the existing tests strongly suggest otherwise). But we can be assured, I think, that GCI intrusion as a whole and the intrusion of general background knowledge as explored in AI local pragmatics cannot be handled by this enlarged indexicality approach.

There is another approach that might also come under the rubric of "enlarged indexicality"—namely, Sag's (1981) proposal that we treat lexical and phrasal categories as generally capable of behaving quasiindexically (see also Enç 1981). He suggests that Kaplan's machinery for handling indexicals can be naturally extended to deal with many kinds of pragmatically determined shifts of intension and extension. I discuss (and reject) the applicability of this approach to GCI intrusion in section 3.5.3 below.

3.5.1.5 "Pragmantics"   As noted previously, some may take pragmatic intrusion as evidence against the possibility of any semantics/pragmatics boundary, and positive evidence for what I have called *pragmantics*, a horrid cocktail of semantics and pragmatics, popular in the days of Generative Semantics (Lakoff 1972) and still popular with many Cognitive Linguists who see no role for a semantics/pragmatics distinction (Langacker 1987: 154; Jackendoff 1983: 105–106, 1992a: 32). This is of course not the conclusion I wish to draw, and although such a view may seem consistent with the intrusion data, it doesn't follow from any of the evidence we have collected. What is lost on such a view is the crucial distinction between semantic entailment and pragmatic defeasible inference, which itself is part of the critical data.

Pragmantics can be avoided if we can find a way of accounting for pragmatic intrusion into truth conditions while maintaining the modularity of a distinct pragmatics (built on nonmonotonic principles) and semantics (built on monotonic principles). Conceptually this is not as difficult as it seems at first sight. But we might ask for more—namely, evidence that by maintaining modularity, and by defining exactly how the semantics and pragmatics interact, we can predict exactly how, when, and why pragmatic intrusions take place; and especially if we can show that intrusive constructions have the properties they do just because of a principled interaction between two distinct components. It is to this we must now turn.

3.5.2   Modularity and Control[53]

Linguistic theory has, through its presiding genius, come to have a particular architecture. A theory, in this tradition, consists in a set of components (A, B, C, etc.), each of which can be thought of as a function that relates an input to an output. Component A can thus be thought of as a function A that takes an *a* and gives us a *b* as value; component B as a function that takes a *b* as argument and gives a *c* as value; component C as a function that takes *c* as an argument and gives us *d* as value; and so on. (Thus A might be syntax issuing surface structures, B might be phonology taking surface structures into phonetic representations, etc.) Within components we can have levels that meet the same requirements. Then the overall structure of the theory is given to us by the nature of its parts: the output of A feeds B, whose output goes to C, and so forth. The components or modules (in a non-Fodorean sense) themselves define a logical order of the passing of "control" (to use programming parlance).

This Chomskyan picture is not though in any way inevitable or intrinsic to the subject matter. It is elegant precisely because it frees us from the need to have a theory of "control"—an independent theory that specifies how components may interact. But if pragmatic intrusion is indeed established, this picture cannot easily be maintained (at least for the relation between the components or modules that do semantic interpretation and pragmatic processing). The obvious proposal is to change the unidirectional monologue between components into a bidirectional dialogue—to let the components talk more freely to one another. For example, semantic processing could proceed up to some point, pragmatic processing then be called in the way that a subroutine can be called in a program, and semantic processing can then proceed further. The result: the effects of pragmatic intrusion. This picture is decisively *not* the same as the pragmatics cocktail rejected above. The reason is that each component continues to be built, exactly as on current assumptions, as a homogeneous system of rules or principles of an *essentially different kind* from those in other components (that's what justifies the split into components). Thus semantics might continue to operate on the basis of logical principles, whereas pragmatics might operate on an system of abduction and default rules. (This methodological justification of "modularity" has nothing to do with the psychological justifications of Fodorean "vertical" modularity, or faculty psychology; it is a method of making a simpler theory by a policy of divide and conquer, in the ultimate hope of course that a simple theory of the mind is more likely to be correct than an unmotivatedly complex one.)

But once we have abandoned the Chomskyan architecture for a theory of meaning, now we do indeed have a new task: namely, a theory of modular control. Indeed, much of the theoretical interest in a theory of meaning now moves to that theory. What might it look like? Let us briefly explore some ways in which we can get some constraints back in by considering two different kinds of existing proposal for incorporating pragmatic information in semantic representations.

3.5.3   Sag's Proposal and Possible Amplifications

First, let us consider a very tightly constrained theory of the control between the semantics and pragmatics components. Suppose that each constituent of a sentence is processed from the bottom up. Suppose too that for each constituent we retain *semantic priority*—that is, for each syntactic unit, the semantics is called first, the pragmatics second. Thus for the sentence *The man with two children is a rocket alarm specialist*, we might start with the semantic interpretation of lexical items and begin to build them into the interpretation of phrases. Whenever we process a lexical item, we check in a semantic network or lexicon for possible stronger scalar items; if we find one, we call the pragmatics to calculate the scalar implicatures, which then get combined with the lexical content, which then contributes to the interpretation of the phrase. Similarly, whenever we hit a construction like nominal compounding as in *rocket alarm*, the pragmatics will be called to calculate an I-implicature to the most probable inference. Thus on this account, the semantic processor or the control structure must locate triggers that invoke the pragmatics, and the semantics also has the overall responsibility, as it were, of constructing the framework for the overall interpretation, using the compositional mechanisms for building intensions and extensions as classically assumed in formal semantics. On this view, which I take it is close to, or at least consistent with, Sag 1981, the main change from classical assumptions is simply that intensions (and correspondingly extensions) may be partially determined by pragmatic information.

Let us briefly review Sag's original proposal. He considered cases originally brought up by Nunberg (1978) where metonymic transfers of sense and reference are involved (on (55g) see Fauconnier 1985, Jackendoff 1992b).

(55) a. "The ham sandwich is getting restless."
   b. "Every ham sandwich at table 9 is still waiting."
   c. "I like this painter" [pointing at a picture]
   d. "*The Financial Times* is saying sell IBM and buy Apple."
   e. "Stanford swims to win."
   f. "Chomsky takes up three feet of my bookshelf."
   g. "Norman Mailer likes to read himself."

Sag argues that rather than treat these as postsemantic Gricean inferences from absurdities, we should consider ways of allowing denotations to be shifted within the semantics. For example, we can use the Kaplan

	Constant character	*Variable character*
Constant content	rigid designators	indexicals
Variable content	nonindexicals	Nunberg metonyms and other pragmatic reconstruals

Figure 3.4
The possible place of pragmatic reconstruals in Kaplan's scheme

distinction between *character* and *content* (intension), where a Kaplan character is a function from contextual indices to intensions or contents, which are in turn thought of in the usual way as functions from world/ time pairs to extensions. As Enç (1981) points out, Kaplan's scheme gives us a typology as in Figure 3.4. Sag's point is that expressions used with Nunbergian metonymic shifts could have both variable character and variable content (a cell unused in Kaplan's scheme), so that context could fix the intension (from, e.g., *ham sandwich* to 'ham sandwich orderer'), and the intension could then pick out the relevant denotation in the relevant world.

That way we preserve the compositional effect, whereby having "coerced" (in the parlance of artificial intelligence) *ham sandwich* into 'ham sandwich orderer' in example (55a), we get the normal compositional effects of preposing *the* or *every* (as in (55b)). The phrase *ham sandwich* is just a normal N′ with a shifted denotation; and the shifted denotation behaves compositionally just as the denotation of any N′. It is hardly surprising that the classical machinery of formal semantics could absorb such changes in the meaning of constituents—after all, it is largely indifferent to lexical content, from which indifference it derives the generality of the compositional mechanism. Hence augmenting or changing the lexical content does not essentially damage the mechanism.

The question now arises, could our GCI intrusions be treated in exactly this same way? For example, could scalar lexical items be treated as having systematically variable Kaplan characters—sometimes contributing implicatures, sometimes not. (Thus *three* could have the intension 'at least 3' or 'exactly 3', as the context dictates.)

Although the Kaplan-style analysis may be fine for the metonymic conversions that Sag was considering, it will be difficult to adapt for implicatural restrictions on denotation for the simple reason that implicatures are subject to cancellation by systematic projection rules as shown by (56a–d), and by contextual assumptions, as in (56e).

(56) a. "The man with two *or more* children over there is the Dean."
     b. "The man with five *if not six* children over there ..."
     c. "The man with two *and perhaps three* children ..."
     d. "The man with two, *in fact three*, children ..."
     e. "Only the single man with three children should bother to apply for food stamps" (attributive 'at least' interpretation).
     f. "The man with three children is my brother; actually he has four but the other is hidden behind him from this angle."

The cancellation may be done at arbitrary distance in the discourse (as illustrated in (56f)), so our Kaplanesque noncancelable system will be in trouble. The problem is that once expressions plus their implicatures have been converted into Kaplan contents (intensions) they would be just as monotonic (nondefeasible) as entailments. What we need instead is some model where we can keep a record of implicatural contribution so that, unlike entailed content, it can be annulled by later parts of the same sentence (or other parts of the discourse, or general background assumptions). This is an argument instead for the intermediate kind of semantic representation used in, for example, Discourse Representation Theory (Kamp and Reyle 1993); we may need to be able to get back to implicated conditions and erase them.

Another problem is the size of constituent that is processed at a time; if the pragmatic processing operated automatically and irrecoverably at the lexical level it would make the wrong predictions: a GCI cannot convert every occurrence of *two* into 'two and no more' because immediate collocations may make the decision one way (as with *at least two*) or the other (*exactly two*); and indeed while *all* is not an implicature inducing item, the collocation *not . . . all* is (where *all* may be at arbitrary distance from *not* but must be within its scope). But if we retreat to the next level up, say the two-bar constituent level, collocations at the *next* level up may be immediately relevant (as in *a minimum sentence of two years* vs. *costs two dollars*), and so on, all the way up to the clause, the sentence, and ultimately the discourse. If we hold off until we have all the information possibly required, we end up with a postsemantic pragmatics (which, we have argued, cannot alone handle intrusion and pragmatic resolution of reference failure).

This is of course a problem for any suggestion for incorporating implicatures into truth conditions; what is difficult is that we sometimes seem forced to incorporate implicatures by intrasentential context (as in the intrusive constructions), but as a general strategy need to be able to hold off commitment, or at least need to be able to cancel them. Here suggestions within the Discourse Representation Theory framework by Kadmon and others are of special interest.

3.5.4   Kadmon's DRT Proposal and Possible Extensions

3.5.4.1   Background   Discourse Representation Theory (Kamp 1981, Kamp and Reyle 1993) is one of a family of recent semantic theories that build on the insight that utterances are interpreted incrementally in the context of prior utterances. Although its protagonists often talk as if there was an algorithm that converts syntactic strings into semantic representations of a discourse (Kamp and Reyle 1993: 85), in fact contextual parameters intervene in various ways, most obviously in resolving anaphora (p. 67) or specifying background information (p. 85). Thus DRT is in fact a hybrid pragmatico-semantics, where truth conditions are stated not directly on representations derived solely from syntactic structures but on a level of representation that is only partially determined by the syntactic structure of a single sentence. To start with, a DRS (discourse representation structure) is a representation of a sequence of assetoric sentences (a so-called discourse), so that prior sentences can offer antecedents for anaphoric items in a sentence whose representation is under construction as it were. Kamp's (1981) theory has nothing to say about how choices between competing antecedents are resolved: this is clearly a pragmatic matter except for gender constraints, or grammatical constraints like the Binding Conditions (Chomsky 1981; pragmatic versions of these are described, e.g., in Reinhart 1983 and explored in chapter 4). But a DRS records a choice—and in that way incorporates pragmatic resolution.

Heim (1982, 1983a) independently developed a similar system, File Change Semantics, which contains more explicit suggestions about the incorporation of pragmatic information.[54] Very sketchily, here are the central ideas. Each discourse referent introduced is assigned a new file card, upon which any predications of the discourse referent are added as conditions. A file is a set of file cards, and it represents the state of the discourse at any point; each file can be assigned truth conditions. The content of an utterance amounts to the file-updating it achieves; sentences (or the logical forms associated with them) do not have truth conditions—their truth-conditional content is captured only by their potential to update files. Definite NPs carry felicity conditions, namely that a file card for their referents already exists (this captures the existence presuppositions of definites). A corollary of the claim that a definite can only be used felicitously if it is familiar, is that definites licensed by common knowledge (*the President*) or by the visual field (*that cat over there*) must be admitted into the file (Heim 1982: 309ff). And to deal with the use of definites *not* overtly licensed in any of these ways (as in *I am sorry I'm late; the car wouldn't start*), Heim has to appeal to accommodation: they are processed as if they had a preexisting file (1982: 370ff). These cases include "bridging" definites. Thus, pragmatic processes like bridging inferences (I-implicatures in our scheme) are incorporated in files, and it is upon files that truth conditions are stated. Thus pragmatic intrusion is explicitly accepted in this model.[55] Because definite-description felicity conditions behave like classical presuppositions with regards to presuppositional projection, Heim has to relativize the existence implications to particular constructions: in effect, temporary ("local") file cards are introduced in some cases to handle presuppositional denials (*The king of France didn't come; there isn't one*; but see Heim 1983b). Both DRT and File Change Semantics thus have an explicit representation of "the common ground"; but unlike Stalnaker's (1972) original proposal, the common ground contains not only a set of propositions but also a set of designated variables, discourse referents.

3.5.4.2 Kadmon's Proposal   Kadmon (1987) however takes the matter of pragmatic intrusion somewhat further. She takes the DRS to be a complete record of the common ground including all that is implicated. She assumes that implicatures are generated and canceled by a mechanism separate from DRS processing, but that the content of implicatures are recorded in just the same way as entailed content, but in a designated "color" as it were (my metaphor rather than hers), so that they are marked as cancelable.[56]

Let us briefly review her suggestions about scalar implicatures. She suggests that indefinites with numeral determiners and common nouns (*n CNs*) like *three boys* in *Three boys ran away* should have the same form of semantic content as *a boy* in the Heim/Kamp proposals—that is, the phrase should introduce a new discourse referent with the conditions of being a set of boys of cardinality 3. But because discourse referents in general only have to have their conditions satisfied by *some* entity in the model,[57] it does not follow that there are no other boys. Thus the semantic content amounts to that assumed in standard pragmatics, namely 'at least three boys' (Kadmon defends this position against Kamp's 'exactly three' proposal).[58]

Kadmon is particularly concerned with arguing, against Heim's conditions on definites based exclusively on familiarity, for a resuscitation of the uniqueness condition. Accepting her argument for current purposes, it follows that anaphoric definites should also require unique antecedents, and thus that *n CN* indefinites (e.g., *three dogs*) should only be possible antecedents if the 'at most' implicature has strengthened them. Her examples are telling (p. 82ff), but I try some of mine:

(57) a. A: "The toll plaza is up ahead. Do you have three dollars?"
     B: "Sure, I've got over ten."
     A: "Okay, have *it* handy."
   b. "Three men walked in. They were a rough lot. ??A fourth was wearing a beret."
   c. "At least three men walked in. They were a rough lot."

Here in (57a) I suggest that, despite a preference for local coreference, *it* refers most naturally to the exactly three dollars that we assume is required; above all, it could not refer to the *over ten*. It might refer to another unique entity, such as the wallet containing the collection of more than ten dollars; or even just to that collection in its entirety, however big it is, but not just to the ten that were included in it. Example (57b) illustrates that anaphora seems to force the scalar implicature (which being a GCI would of course tend to arise anyway); whereas the interpretation of *they* in (57c) must apply to the total collection, not the three mentioned.

Kadmon gives some indication of the role of implicature cancellation in this account. Consider the following example (Kadmon 1987: 117, 167f, 172ff):

(58) "I have to show this document to three colleagues. *They* are in a meeting right now. I also have to show it to two other colleagues, but they have already left."

Here the first *they* will force a scalar-implicature interpretation of *three* as 'exactly three'. The admission in the third sentence that there are two other relevant colleagues will cancel this implicature. Therefore the felicity condition on *they*, which requires a unique maximal set as antecedent, now needs to be satisfied some other way. Kadmon suggests (p. 174) that an antecedent is accommodated—namely, the set of three colleagues in a meeting (rather than, as prior to the cancellation, the maximal set of three colleagues who must be shown the document).

To Kadmon's arguments for pragmatic intrusion of scalar implicatures into anaphoric reference, we may add examples of different kinds. Consider for example the following (from what has been said above, readers may proliferate examples for themselves):

(59) a. "Some of the students passed the exam. *They* were the lucky ones. *The others* have to retake it."

b. "If the Princess had a baby and got married, then doing *so* is clearly now more fashionable than getting married and having a baby."

c. "If some of the students passed the exam, then *that* is not as good as all of them passing the exam."

Thus in (59a) the truth conditions for *They were the lucky ones* must identify *they* as referring to a proper subset of the students (as required by the scalar implicature 'some but not all'); otherwise *the others* will be undefined. In (59b) the VP anaphora clearly picks up the I-implicature from *and* to 'and then', whereas (59c) shows that sentential anaphora with *that* must be construed as picking up the implicatures of the antecedent sentence.

DRT is specifically set up to capture anaphoric relations, so if Kadmon is correct about these observations, then DRSs not only *may* be thus enriched with scalar implicatures, they *must* be if the original motivation is to be met. Thus there is a strong argument from anaphora for the intrusion of GCIs into truth conditions, and DRT seems to be the theory best able to handle this intrusion.

3.5.5 Some Future Directions: DRT and Intrusive Constructions

This way of representing pragmatic intrusion seems extremely promising.[59] But DRT would be especially attractive if it provided predictions about just which constructions would naturally be interpreted with intrusive implicatures. In fact it does indeed seem to make some predictions in the right direction. I discuss here just two problems: the intrusion in conditionals and in metalinguistic negation.

Most obviously, the conditional intrusions may have a natural account in terms of the sequence of interpretation. Thus Kamp's (1981) scheme for the truth conditions of "If A then B" (where m(A) is the DRS for A and m(B) that for B) reads thus: the conditional *If A then B* will be true iff every proper embedding of m(A) can be extended to a proper embedding for m(B). Thus A is assessed prior to B, and B is understood as a conditional assertion dependent on A: hence the intrusions of the implicatures of A into the conditions under which one can expect the consequent to hold.

Now, Heim (1983b) has already noted that this treatment of the conditional gives a natural account of presupposition projection: the sequential updating of the context, first by A, and then by B, predicts that where B has a presupposition entailed by A, the presupposition is itself conditional as it were. Because presupposition projection is intrinsically linked to negation, before turning to see how DRT might give a natural account of the metalinguistic negation cases (i.e., intrusion in negative sentences), it will be helpful to examine briefly the problem of *implicature projection*. Indeed the viability of the DRT approach to pragmatic intrusion is likely to depend on the projection properties of conversational implicatures, which have hardly been studied and about which there are currently erroneous assumptions (owing to under-critical acceptance of Gazdar 1979).

A first point to note is that the projection properties of scalar Q-implicatures look surprisingly similar to those of classical presuppositions (e.g., factives, definite descriptions), as pointed out by Levinson (1983: 223–225). Compare, for example, the lifting of a scalar implicature (here 'no more than three') to the suspension of the factive presupposition due to *regret* (namely, that its complement is true) in the following contexts:

(60) a. "John has *three* children, if indeed not more."
     a'. "John doesn't *regret* doing it, if indeed he did it."
     b. "Either John has *three* children or he has more."
     b'. "Either John doesn't *regret* doing it or he didn't do it."
     c. "John doesn't have *three* children."
     c'. "John doesn't *regret* doing it."

Thus the "filtering" in conditionals and disjunctions looks exactly parallel, suggesting that whatever the correct treatment is for presuppositions, it should carry over to implicatures. Where the differences emerge is under negation: example (60c) does not share with its positive counterpart the implicature 'John has at most three children', whereas (60c′) does indeed (by definition of course) share the presupposition 'John did it' with its positive counterpart. Because there is a natural account of at least some aspects of the presuppositional projection problem in DRT and File Change Semantics (see Heim 1983b, Landman 1986), there is every reason to pursue this parallelism and see whether we can't find an independent explanation for the failure of implicatures under negation.

With this background, let us now turn back to the other kind of intrusive construction—namely, the metalinguistic-negation intrusions, as in:

(61) a. "John doesn't have three children, he has four."
     b. "John has three children."
     c. NOT (John has at least three children & *John has at most three children*).

The intuition is that the kind of sentence in (61a) could only be used where it is supposed in the context that John has three children. One way of construing this is that an assertion has been previously made in the discourse, viz. (61b), "John has three children". In that case, the scalar implicature 'at most three' would have been added distinctively 'in red ink' into the DRS. (As suggested before, let us imagine that semantic conditions are written into the DRS with black ink, but defeasible pragmatic conditions with red ink, so that they can be canceled at arbitrary distance.)

Against this background, (61a) is construed as a *denial of the assertion* of (61b). In the DRT framework there is a natural way to represent that denial, namely by treating example (61a) as quasi-anaphoric to the preceding positive assertion in (61b) so that all the semantic conditions of (61b) are copied over into the DR of (61a).[60] Thus (61a) and (61b) have identical representations except that (61a) has an external negation that ranges over both the entailed content (black ink) and the implicated (red ink) as informally represented in (61c) as italics. The overall DRS already contains entailed commitment to John having at least three children (due to the prior assertion of (61b)), so only the implicated commitment in (61c) (carried over from (61b)) is cancellable. Hence the metalinguistic negation interpretation of (61a) follows naturally, and there is no contradiction (at the level of entailments).

The elegance of the DRT analysis may not immediately strike the reader. However, it combines the best parts and avoids the worst parts of two incompatible accounts of metalinguistic negations of implicature, those by Horn (1985) and Kempson (1986). On Horn's account the negation in these cases is not logical (not reducible to a truth-functional one-place connective with the familiar truth table), but "voices an objection to a previous utterance (not proposition) on any grounds whatever." I take this to be a bad part of the analysis, because the negation is in fact in this case behaving exactly like the normal truth-functional operator—it simply ranges over different (nonentailed) content. The correct part of Horn's analysis is that these utterances do indeed "voice an objection to a previous *utterance*" (i.e., to the utterance-meaning, replete with implicatures), and not just to the sentence-meaning, of some previous utterance in the discourse. It is because of that quasi-anaphoric relation between the prior positive sentence (61b) and its later denial in (61a) that these implicature-denying negations share certain properties with nonlogical metalinguistic negations (as in "It's not a [vɑːz], it's a [veɪz]"). As mentioned, metalinguistic negations in general do not permit negative polarity items nor the incorporation of negatives, because they echo the utterances to which they are retorts (Horn 1989: 392–402; see also Carston 1996). Horn mistakenly assimilates implicature-denying negations to the nonlogical class of metalinguistic negations because of these shared properties, whereas in fact the properties follow from the shared function as retorts.[61]

Turning now to Kempson's account, the good part is the insistence that these negations just are our familiar one-place truth function. The bad part is the assumption that negation could ordinarily range over explicatures. The only case in which implicatures come within the scope of negation is where the negative sentence is a denial of a prior assertion (as Horn insists). The reason that this must be so is that *the implicatures in question would never arise directly under negation*: the implicatures being denied belong to the prior positive assertion.

Let us expound this point carefully (at the risk of redundancy with the exposition in chapter 2). According to the pragmatic theory developed here so far, for each and every positive Q-scale of the form $\langle S, W \rangle$ where S is a strong scalar item entailing (in an arbitrary simplex sentence frame) the weak scalar item W (in the same sentence frame), there is a corresponding negative scale $\langle not\text{-}W, not\text{-}S \rangle$ where '$not\text{-}S$' (or '$not\text{-}W$') is a shorthand for S (or W) occurring within the scope of negation, and $not\text{-}W$ entails $not\text{-}S$ (in the same sentence frame).[62] Thus for example, given the positive scale $\langle all, some \rangle$, there is a corresponding negative scale $\langle not\text{-}some$ (i.e., $none$), $not\text{-}all \rangle$, and the following kinds of implicature are therefore predicted—where only the weak items induce scalar implicatures:

(62) a. "Some of the men came" +> 'Not all of the men came.'
    b. "All of the men came" (no scalar implicature).
    c. "Not all of the men came" +> 'Some of the men came'.
    d. "None of the men came" (no implicature).

If we now return to the relevant example, repeated in (63a), we can see that where the plain negative (63d) is asserted, and asserted without the background of a prior assertion of the positive (63b), we do not have the positive scale ⟨..., *four, three, two, one*⟩ to induce the implicature 'not four'. Indeed 'not four' is entailed by the assertion *not three* (which means 'not three or more'). Instead, we have a negative scale running the other way: ⟨*not-one, not-two, not-three*⟩. The prediction is that when you say (63d), you implicate that John has at least one child and you assert (entail) that he has less than three.[63]

(63) a. "John doesn't have three children, he has four."
    b. "John has three children."
    c. NOT [John has at least three children & *John has at most three children*].
    d. "John doesn't have three children."

Now we see also the answer to the one apparent difference between the projection properties of presuppositions and implicatures. According to Horn (1972, 1985, 1989), Gazdar (1979), and Hirschberg (1985), scalar implicatures are simply blocked (i.e., do not arise) under negation. This is an erroneous assumption based on the correct observation that the *same* implicatures are not shared by positive and negative counterparts of the same sentence (utterance-type). As we have seen, the apparent blockage is due to the fact that negatives reverse scales (because negation effects the strength of scalar items) and so we get different implicatures, which themselves survive negation just as presuppositions do. This opens the way for a fully general account of presupposition and implicature projection—and if Heim (1983b) is right that File Change/DRT–type semantics gives a natural treatment of the former, it should also give a natural treatment of the latter.

To return to the claims about metalinguistic negation: the DRT treatment can now be appreciated as unifying prior accounts. The negation is ordinary negation (Kempson), the utterance is a denial of a previous positive assertion (Horn), and the implicature that is canceled by the negation is not an implicature of the negative sentence itself (contra

Kempson), it is the implicature of the prior positive assertion. All of this is obtained by existing DRT machinery.

This kind of result lends substantial prima facie support to the DRT treatment and requires further exploration. Apart from getting the cancellation aspects of the projection problem for implicatures right, the DRT treatment must also be able to explain the fact that just like some presuppositions, implicatures pass through "holes" that would block entailments. Thus in nonentailed clauses, like the antecedent and consequent of conditionals, both implicatures and presuppositions can get entered permanently into the DRS *as if* asserted, even though neither the antecedent nor the consequent leave unconditional information.

(64) a. "If John has any conscience, he'll regret he did it."
       Presupposes: 'John did it'.
    b. "If John has a low income, his three children will suffer."
       Implicates: 'John has three and no more than three children'.

Just as presupposition projection has been seen to be one of the cardinal attractions of DRT, so implicature projection may be an interesting test ground for that theory and its ilk.

3.5.6   A Residual Problem: How to Get from Semantic Representations to Propositions

On all theories of semantics, pragmatic resolution—at least the fixing of indexical reference, and disambiguation—is required before a semantic representation expresses a proposition or describes a situation. In the newer semantic frameworks, like DRT and Situation Semantics, the range of kinds of pragmatic resolution is enlarged: anaphora resolution, the filling in of contextual parameters and *ceteris paribus* conditions, all need to be taken into account. None of these models sketch any mechanism for pragmatic resolution; indeed they are often misleadingly phrased in terms of an algorithm deriving semantic representations from syntactic representations.

But the new Gricean pragmatic theories appear to be in no better shape. In fact Radical Pragmatics programs, which reassign much that had been thought semantic to pragmatic resolution (Cole 1981: xi), only serve to increase the essential problem. Atlas (1989) persuasively argues for the Strawsonian dictum that sentences express no propositions—only statements, or pragmatically interpreted utterances, can do so. The same sentiments have been expressed and argued for by the London School

(Kempson 1986, Sperber and Wilson 1986, Carston 1988). For these theories the essential problem, quite unacknowledged by the way, is this: a Gricean mechanism is supposed to get us from a level of semantic representation, now impoverished to a subpropositional schema of some sort, to a representation capable of specifying propositional content, a level of logical form as it were. But Gricean mechanisms are *reasoning* mechanisms, and they presuppose propositional input as well as propositional output. In this respect, owing to its explicit commitment to deductive reasoning, Relevance Theory appears especially incoherent: "no assumption is simply decoded [from an utterance], and ... the recovery of any assumption requires an element of inference" (Sperber and Wilson 1986: 182). But how are we to get from nonlogical forms to further contextual implications that will enrich them by a deductive process that can only handle logical forms? Theories that are abductive or inductive in character, or that are phrased in terms of an inference to the best explanation, may not face this theoretical incoherence, but of course that does not erase the *computational* problem. Thus Atlas (1989: 146) states "Gricean inference is not restricted to mapping propositions ('what is said') into propositions ('what is implicated'). It also maps Lockean, 'abstract' sentence-meanings into propositions (utterance-meanings)." He goes on to point out that the intrusion phenomena cataloged here (or rather in Levinson 1988b) are evidence for precisely this claim.

What kind of a computation is it that would take us from under-specified semantic representations to logical forms capable of expressing propositions? Much depends on the form of the input semantic representation, and here Radical Pragmaticists have offered us only the sketchiest of ideas. We might think in terms of logical formulae with unbound variables, or semantic representations with contextual parameters to be instantiated. But clearly, Radical Pragmaticists of all persuasions have in mind representations that are much further divorced from logical forms than this. Even Fodor (1983: 135 n. 29, cited in Atlas 1989: 148) concedes that scope may be indeterminate at this level and that "perhaps the specifically *linguistic* processes in the production/perception of speech deploy representations that are *shallower* than logical forms." Atlas (1989: 146) views the indeterminacy in terms of semantic generality and offers various analogies, including the archi-phoneme. Sperber and Wilson (1986: 181) talk of the "development" of a logical form "by using contextual information to complete and enrich this logical form into a propositional form." The notion of explicature, or Bach's notion of impliciture, might have been employed to denote the inferences that map a semantic representation into a proposition, but in fact both Sperber and Wilson's explicature (and Carston's (1988) or Recanati's (1989) versions) and Bach's impliciture take us well beyond the minimal proposition expressed, closer to some intuitive notion of 'what is said' as what is effectively stated.

The notions developed in this book have some bearing on these issues, which constitute it seems to me by far the most pressing problem in an overall theory of meaning. First, we have presumed that an ampliative reasoning system must be involved (i.e., a kind of reasoning that, unlike deduction, expands the information given). Just as we may from a few shards guess the outlines of an ancient pot, so we seem to make the ampliative enrichment from a subpropositional to a propositional representation. Deduction can only map determinate logical forms into logical forms. But abduction and induction can map any data format into propositions (e.g., shards into the date they were made). Second, the theory of GCIs offers us a glimpse of how we may constrain this inference to the best interpretation (Atlas and Levinson 1981), namely by using heuristics to warrant *presumptive solutions*.

Let me develop this last point in a little more detail. It has long been noted that humans can coordinate on a single joint solution where the problem involved in fact offers no unique solution, and they can do this in the absence of communication. For example, two people told that they will each get $100 if they think of the same number will beat the infinite odds and think of the same number, often enough at least to make this an expensive experiment (Schelling 1960). Humans solve these problems by considering what each would think the other would think that each would think was the most salient solution. On the Gricean account of communication (Grice 1957), this is exactly the intentional context in which an utterance is offered for comprehension—as a clue to a salient solution to a coordination problem (see Clark 1996: chap. 3). The mutual knowledge that communicator and recipient are mutually oriented to heuristics of the kind proposed here—that is, the Q-, M-, and I-principles—provide extra, highly salient constraints to the solution of the problem. The problem of course is: how should the speaker frame his utterance so that the proposition the recipient attributes to it has exactly the properties that the speaker intended it to have? Our heuristics recommend to the speaker the selection between forms that might invoke the relevant relations, so that, for example, minimal forms will pick up stereotypical or otherwise more specific interpretations, maximal forms will discourage this, and forms that are weaker than others on a scale of informativeness will implicate that the stronger forms may not hold.

The Gricean intentional umbrella, coupled with the Schelling saliency principle, provides inferences arising under our heuristics with their default, presumptive character. Now, the importance of GCIs is that they offer some partial solution for how to get from fragmentary semantic representations to fulsome, proposition-bearing representations or logical forms. Because they are presumptive, and because they depend in the first instance on the recovery of the meaning and form of the particular expressions that give rise to them, the inference can be made without complete access to the logical form of the whole utterance. This has both procedural and psychological aspects. Procedurally, the expression *some of the boys G'd* can be immediately associated with the default assumption *some but not all of the boys G'd* even when some indeterminate aspect of the predicate *G* has not yet been resolved. Psycholinguistically, in the stream of incoming speech during comprehension, the phrase *some of the boys* can invoke the default assumption 'not all of the boys' even before the predicate has been heard. The default presumption must of course be held separately from the other recovered content because once the predicate is resolved it may be defeated by higher-ordered assumptions (e.g., entailments in the discourse or antecedent assumptions).

Thus the default properties of GCIs account for their intrusive abilities: such inferences can and will be made on the fly and, if not canceled by the mechanisms sketched in this book, will end up within the propositional content of complex sentences whose parts are semantically evaluated with respect to each other (as in comparatives and conditionals, and in the case of denials, evaluated with respect to the corresponding affirmative).

3.6   CONCLUSIONS

In this chapter, I have pursued an idea that at first seems nonsensical—namely, the notion that implicatures could play a role in truth conditions. I hope to have made a prima facie case for that view. Indeed, I hope to have shown that the view is inevitable.

Our natural reluctance to accept a view that entails such far-reaching overhaul of the current theory of meaning is unlikely to be overcome without some prospect of some alternative, no less-coherent overall picture. I believe that a theory like DRT, which provides a level of representation to which both pragmatic and semantic processes can contribute and which is the level at which semantic interpretation is defined, does in fact offer such a picture. I will have to leave it to others with more competence in that area to develop or reject these suggestions. Meanwhile, I should record that Grice (1987: 375) claimed in his "retrospective epilogue" to have foreseen from the beginning the problems we have here been grappling with: "It certainly does not seem reasonable to subscribe to an absolute ban on the possibility that an embedding locution may govern the standard nonconventional implicatum rather than the conventional import of the embedded sentence." He gives conditionals and negations as examples of such embedding locutions and goes on to add: "But where the limits of a license may lie which allows us to relate embedding operators to the standard implicata rather than to conventional meanings, I have to admit I do not know." Knowing the answer to that question will be to have a new and profoundly different understanding of the semantics/pragmatics interface.

Chapter 4

Grammar and Implicature: Sentential Anaphora Reexamined

4.1 GRAMMAR AND IMPLICATURE

In the previous chapter we explored the quite far-reaching consequences that the phenomena of generalized conversational implicature may have for our conception of the semantics/pragmatics interface. In this chapter, we shall explore another interaction, namely the relation between grammar and pragmatics, and ask how we may be forced to reconstrue this division of labor given the phenomena of GCIs.[1] In both cases, the underlying questions are the same: given the existence of preferred interpretations, and as a corollary, preferred ways of putting things (i.e., expression types associated with preferred interpretations), aspects of interpretation that we have in the past thought of as stipulated by the lexicon or the grammar may in fact be attributable to pragmatic principles of preferred interpretation. This chapter focuses on just one area, anaphora, where plausibly such misattributions have been made.

It may seem that a theory of implicature or preferred interpretation would be remote from any theory of grammatical well-formedness. Indeed, the relation between syntax and pragmatics is of a fundamentally different kind than the semantics/pragmatics interface, for it is indirect. It is only through effects on meaning, broadly construed, that implicature can impose distributional or collocational constraints. But we should remind ourselves that distinctions between syntactic, semantic, and pragmatic phenomena are not given to us by direct intuition in advance of theoretical development: "On the contrary, the problem of delimitation will clearly remain open until these fields are much better understood than they are today" (Chomsky 1965: 159). With the development of a theory of generalized, default inference, these border discriminations become considerably harder. For example, we may think we are blessed with access to specifically syntactic intuitions that rule out *The boys is funny*; but consider the sentence *The french fries is impatient for his bill*, which at first seems to violate the same basic agreement rule of English, but becomes acceptable on the construal that *the french fries* metonymically refers to a singular customer who ordered french fries at a restaurant (Nunberg 1978). The theoretical moves over such cases are not so easy, but they do suggest that verb agreement is after all determined by something more complex and contextual than the inheritance of syntactic features of plurality.[2] Thus we cannot accept, in lieu of argument, hunches and presumptions that such and such phenomena have an "unmistakable syntactic flavor."[3]

If we are willing to keep an open mind, it does seem fairly clear that there are intimate connections between distributional constraints and implicature or, more generally, between utterance-form and utterance-type meaning (i.e., the third level of meaning, concerned with favored means for expressing certain meanings, as discussed in chapter 1). There are connections both on the synchronic and diachronic axes. On a synchronic basis, the connections are in principle straightforward: a particular utterance-type or form has a range of semantic interpretations, which are in turn correlated with default implicatures of various types. Such implicatures then preempt alternative expressions, which would instead implicate something else by contrast (as in the familiar play between I- and M-implicating expressions, e.g., in the direct vs. indirect suggestions from *kill* vs. *cause to die*).[4] Implicatures thus restrict collocations of expressions *relative to interpretations*, as many syntactic principles (e.g., the Binding Conditions) are also held to do. They are much less likely to yield impossible collocations on any interpretation (as other syntactic principles, e.g., movement constraints, may do) because of their defeasible nature (e.g., *immediately, intentionally, directly* collocate better with *kill* than *cause to die*, but they can override the implicature of indirect causation associated with the periphrastic expression). Where such strong collocational constraints exist, they are probably due to an additional 'standardization' (Bach and Harnish 1979: 192–195; Bach 1995) or 'short-circuited implicature' (Morgan 1978, Horn and Bayer 1984), as in the licensing by implicated Neg-Raising of negative polarity items in positive subordinate clauses (e.g., "I don't think he has *any* money"; see Linebarger 1991).[5]

Once we turn to a diachronic perspective, the relation between grammar and implicature can be shown to be rather fundamental. Implicated meanings are a major source of grammatical change, as shown by the literature on grammaticalization, which explores the diachronic processes whereby grammatical elements and constructions are recruited from previously available expressions and constructions. For example, many modals and auxiliaries seem to have acquired their special grammatical status through the implicatures of their prior main-verb usages (Bybee, Pagliuca, and Perkins 1991). Thus the grammatical reanalysis of *be going to V*, from a verb of motion together with a purposive clause to a future auxiliary, may plausibly be claimed to be based on the combined temporal implicatures of *go* and the purposive construction (Hopper and Traugott 1993: 82ff). There is a main-verb reading of *go* in (1a) below, followed by a purposive clause, the whole glossable as in (1b). On this (the original) interpretation, implicatures arise that the subject will indeed reach the destination in the future, and that he will carry out the intended course of action. It is these strong future implications that have been grammaticalized into a new structural pattern with a fixed interpretation—namely, *be going to* analyzed as an auxiliary constituent with future time reference, roughly with the gloss in (1d) (intentional implications perhaps persisting).

(1) a. "He is going to join the army."
    b. 'He is on his way to join the army.'
    c. I +> 'at some later point he will have arrived and will have joined the army.'
    d. 'He will join the army.'

Examples of such diachronic processes can be found throughout the grammaticalization literature (see Traugott and Heine 1991; Heine, Claudi, and Hünnemeyer 1991; Bybee, Pagliuca, and Perkins 1991; Hopper and Traugott 1993), although they are rarely analyzed strictly in neo-Gricean terms (but see Traugott and König 1991, Traugott 1998; see also Levinson 1979, where a sequence from particularized through generalized to conventional implicature was proposed). One major source for new grammatical constructions is what we have called I-implicatures; for example, the evolution of causal *since* from an earlier purely temporal connective with the meaning 'after' is nicely documented by Traugott and Heine (1991). Similarly, M-implicatures seem to play a systematic role in deriving, and rederiving, emphatic reflexives (Langacker 1977, Faltz 1989), a point to which I will return. This cyclical process, whereby implicatures become conventionalized and then acquire further implicatures, which can in turn conventionalize, gives us a deep diachronic layering of "fossilized" and partially conventionalized implicature that can be attested in various domains, especially perhaps in areas like euphemism and honorifics, where there is a functional pressure on innovation (Brown and Levinson 1987: 258ff). In this chapter, this diachronic layering will play an important role in our attempt to understand crosslinguistic patterns of anaphora in implicatural terms. In short, the historical evidence points to systematic relations between grammar and implicature that ought to be more carefully explored as an interesting test ground for different theories of implicature.

If we may take as granted that grammaticalization often involves the codification of a new construction out of an expression plus its generalized implicatures, then there are some general consequences for the analysis of grammar:

1. That a pattern of interpretation is now rule-governed and fully grammaticalized does not preclude the relevance of a pragmatic analysis as an hypothesis about diachronic origins.
2. We might have very similar patterns in two languages, but in one language find the pattern grammaticalized and in the other merely a preferred pattern of interpretation.
3. We might find that such a match between a grammatical pattern and its implicatural origins plays a role in language learning and language change through reanalysis: what adults treat as implicature-based, children may treat as rule-based (and vice versa).
4. We might catch the process halfway, as it were, and find rule-governed aspects and implicatural fringes to a construction-in-the-making.

A useful symptom of grammaticalization in progress is the existence of morphosyntactic reflexes of an inference, as explored in the literature on "short-circuited" implicature (see Horn and Bayer 1984) . Thus we must embrace the possibility of pragmatic explanation without pragmatic reduction.

We may find ourselves genuinely in doubt about whether we are dealing with what is fundamentally a grammatical or a pragmatic pattern. Where we have rival accounts of the same phenomenon in terms of grammatical principles or in terms of pragmatic principles, both kinds of account could have substance. But in a number of fundamental ways, they may be incompatible:

1. Insofar as the grammatical account is supposed to follow from universal principles that are too abstract to be learned, the existence of a pragmatic account in terms of general principles of usage undermines the alleged unlearnability essential to this type of grammatical hypothesis.

2. And insofar as the constructional meanings are *indefeasible*—that is, the interpretations are inflexible and can be specified by exceptionless rule, we may confidently attribute the interpretation to a grammatical source; but insofar as they are *defeasible* and show all the hallmarks of nonmonotonic inference that we associate with pragmatic inference, we should attribute the pattern of preferred interpretation to pragmatics.[6]

In this chapter, we shall focus on the pragmatics of intrasentential anaphora. This choice is not fortuitous. Anaphora has been the focus of a tremendous amount of work over 30 years of the generative tradition, and especially within the Government and Binding (GB) or Principles and Parameters framework (Chomsky 1981, 1986, 1995: chap. 1), and thus also within its direct competitors. In the GB framework, the Binding Conditions governing the interpretations of different kinds of overt referring expressions were also intended to hold for covert nominals (NP traces, *pro*, PRO, and variables). Thus the Binding Conditions had a central position within syntactic theory, effectively controlling both anaphora and movement. Since then there has been a tendency to handle movement constraints in other ways (by chain theory) and restrict the Binding Principles to the handling of anaphora. Still, in Chomsky's Minimalist Program, the Binding Conditions still play a crucial role, and remain essentially the same, except that they are recast as interpretive conditions holding at the level of LF (Chomsky 1995: 211). Intrasentential anaphora thus continues to be a focus of current work within the generative framework (see, e.g., Reinhart and Reuland 1993, Koster and Reuland 1991, Hornstein 1995, Harbert 1995). Here then are a series of closely argued proposals about syntactic constraints on the interpretation of anaphoric expressions. If we could successfully show that at least some of these constraints are in fact not syntactic in origin, but follow from patterns of preferred interpretation, it would amount to a substantial redistribution of the division of labor between grammar and pragmatics. I shall make tentative proposals along these lines, trying to attribute to our existing apparatus of inferential heuristics some of the patterns of interpretation that have been thought to be syntactically specified. Again, this is the classical Gricean strategy, now applied to the syntax/pragmatics relation rather than the semantics/pragmatics one: suspect any alleged grammatical stipulation that fits a Gricean pattern to be a pattern of preferred interpretation (possibly under varying degrees of grammaticalization).

Such attempts at pragmatic reduction can be misunderstood, and we shall need to steer away from possible misinterpretations of the goal of the enterprise. But briefly, the goal has nothing to do with wholesale functional reductionism. It has rather to do with introducing an additional tool—a rival line of explanation that has been grossly underestimated, largely because pragmatic inference has been thought to be largely contextual and thus not systematic. Once the very notion of a preferred interpretation based on highly general principles is accepted, it opens up the possibility of a radical redivision of labor between grammar and pragmatics. The possibility ought to be welcomed by grammarians, because once recalcitrant phenomena with the hallmarks of preferred defeasible interpretations are removed from what is to be explained, much cleaner syntactic theories may become available. Because GCI theory is in its infancy, worked on by only a handful of scholars, we cannot expect these first attempts to handle all of the complexities. If first indications are even at all promising, however, it ought to indicate that more work should be diverted in this direction.

Often, the reactions of syntacticians to such attempts to renegotiate the division of labor are of the form "a miss is as good as a mile," with the provision of a few apparent counterexamples; but all syntactic theories, in the domain of anaphora at least, are also replete with counterexamples (and indeed Chomsky (1995: 19f) himself sees the need for fairly radical idealization). Because the pragmatic theory, in a way to be explained, is in crucial cases essentially parasitic on the syntactic theory, the apparent counterexamples for the pragmatic theory may actually reflect inadequate syntactic analysis. Indeed, one of the special properties of pragmatic analyses is that they are simple, direct instantiations of enormously general, crosslinguistic tendencies—you cannot tinker with them to get the right result in a particular language in the same way that you can fine-tune a syntactic analysis. In the long run, when such pragmatic principles are better grounded, we may even be able to use the pragmatic theory predictions to help in the fine-tuning of the syntactic analysis: because the pragmatics operates on the syntactically specified interpretations to yield further preferred interpretations, if the latter are incorrectly predicted it may indicate that the former have been misanalyzed.

4.2 IMPLICATURE AND COREFERENCE

4.2.1 The Pragmatics of Local Anaphora

Anaphora is the phenomenon whereby one linguistic expression (the *anaphor*), lacking clear independent reference, can pick up reference or interpretation through connection to another linguistic expression (usually an *antecedent*). (Incidentally, the special Chomskyan sense of *Anaphor*—reflexives, reciprocals, and their like—will be distinguished by a capital letter; the unmodified term *pronoun* will be used in the Chomskyan manner to exclude reflexive pronouns.) Not every anaphoric expression has a referential interpretation. In *Everybody has his foibles*, for example, the pronoun *his* is usually thought to be equivalent to a logical variable, whereas in *John has his foibles*, the pronoun *his*—when its referent is coidentified with John—is usually thought to be parasitically referential, through linkage to *John*. Some of these decisions are theory-dependent, and I shall loosely talk about coreference and disjoint reference without necessarily presuming that the anaphoric elements in question are strictly referential. I am concerned here only with NP-anaphora, but there are many other kinds (see Webber 1979: chap. 1 for a catalogue).

Despite the preoccupation with anaphora in the syntax and semantics journals, there are good prima facie reasons to think that anaphora is primarily a pragmatic matter. Anaphora is, after all, basically a cross-sentence ("discourse") phenomenon and thus quite largely outside the domain of intrasentential processes. Now it would be odd if cross-sentence patterns of interpretation were entirely unrelated to intra-sentential patterns; and of course they aren't. Consider for example the parallel between (2) (so-called discourse anaphora) and (3) (sentential anaphora).

(2) a. "John came in. *He* sat down."   (preferred coreference)
    b. "John came in. *The man* sat down."   (preferred disjoint reference)

(3) a. "John likes *his* father."   (preferred coreference)
    b. "John likes *the man's* father."   (disjoint reference)

There is an obvious pattern here (let us call it the *general anaphora pattern*): reduced forms (less prolix, more semantically general) favor co-referential readings, prolix full forms favor noncoreferential (disjoint) readings (the pragmatic vs. grammatical status of the disjoint reading of

(3b) will exercise us) . Now it is clear that the pattern does indeed go across the pragmatics/grammar border—that is, that what is in essence a pragmatic preference for local coreference induced by minimal forms can become a matter of grammatical stipulation leaving no room for other interpretations:

(4) a. "John came in and *the man* sat down."   (disjoint reference preferred)

b. "John came in and *he* sat down."   (coreference preferred)

c. "John came in and __ sat down."   (coreference required)

But that, as we have already noted, is part of the importance of the pragmatic preferred interpretations—that they tend to become grammaticalized, providing a diachronic source for grammatical stipulations of interpretation. Not all grammar is "frozen pragmatics" of course, but some undoubtedly is. From a diachronic perspective, there is thus no necessary incompatibility between a grammatical and a pragmatic analysis. From a synchronic perspective, on the other hand, we clearly want just one analysis. In trying to decide whether we are dealing with grammatical stipulation or mere preferred interpretation, we inevitably appeal to our litmus test of defeasibility—in (4b) coreference is preferred but not necessary, and in (4c) there is only one interpretation.

Another, more fundamental reason for thinking of anaphora primarily in pragmatic terms has to do with the essence of anaphoric expressions: they are semantically general, and require additional contextual resolution or inferential specification. Anaphora consists in the *referential dependence* of one NP on another, rather than simply in the matter of coreference. (One might have accidental coreference—as when a speaker forgets that he has already mentioned some protagonist or is unaware that Cicero was the same man as Tully.) That referential dependence can only arise if an NP fails on its own to achieve reference, generally through underspecification. That is why pronouns are the primary type of anaphoric expression in many languages; they are minimal nominal expressions with maximal semantic generality (usually encoding only some subset of person, number, gender, and case features). Although languages may generally (but apparently not universally) have specialized expressions that are *necessarily* referentially dependent, like *himself* in English, just about any semantically general expression can function anaphorically. To see this, consider the following pairs:

(5) a. "The ferry hit a rock. The ship capsized."
   b. "The ship hit a rock. The ferry capsized."

(6) a. "The bus overturned. The vehicle was completely wrecked."
   b. "The vehicle was completely wrecked. The bus overturned."

(7) a. "The professor rubbed his eyes. The man looked weary."
   b. "The man looked weary. The professor rubbed his eyes."

(8) a. "Their Boeing 727 is relatively new, but the aircraft is of an old design."
   b. "The aircraft is relatively new, but their Boeing 727 is of an old design."

(9) a. "I like London. My wife likes it there."
   b. "I like it there. My wife likes London."

In these pairs, the two referring expressions in subject position in the (a) examples can easily be read as coreferential, but it is much harder to get the coreferential interpretations in the (b) examples; instead we tend to read them as lists (e.g., a list of shipping disasters, or vehicle crashes, or tired gentlemen, or aircraft; see Sanford and Garrod 1981, Garnham 1989 for experimental verification of these tendencies). Yet the only difference is that in the (a) sentences a semantically more specific (less general) description precedes a compatible one that is semantically less specific (more general), whereas in the (b) sentences the order is reversed. This shows, I think, that semantic generality is at the heart of anaphora; it is the essential property for an anaphoric expression. Now notice that semantic generality is also the essential property inducing I-implicatures—for example, it is the semantic generality of "I don't like garlic" that invites the inference 'I dislike garlic', and the semantic generality of conjunction that suggests causality in "He threw the switch and the engine stopped." There is a prima facie case that the same principle is involved.

Thus although it is tempting to think of pronouns as semantically specialized anaphoric devices, it seems likely that they play such a prominent role in anaphora simply through their semantic generality; in English, for example, the third-person pronouns merely restrict their referents to third-person entities that are, as required, singular or plural, and if singular (and human or closely associated animal) male, female, or neuter. In many languages, even those restrictions are missing (e.g., in many Australian languages, a single third-singular pronoun will cover any animate entity indiscriminately). Pronouns are often held to be ambiguous between

variable, referentially dependent, and deictic uses (and yet other senses
have been proposed); but the fact that in language after language all three
functions can be performed by the same pronominal expressions suggests
that their semantic character simply encompasses all three.[7] The examples
in (5)–(9) make the point that anaphoric potential is a matter of semantic
generality *relative* to the antecedent. Anaphoric potential is, on the whole,
a property not of expressions but of uses of expressions. Nevertheless, the
more semantically general an expression is, the greater the likelihood that
it will be descriptively inadequate for reference identification, and thus the
greater the chance that it must be referentially dependent (hence the tendency to the anaphoric use of pronouns even though they are capable of
supporting in many circumstances a directly referential use).

In perhaps the majority of languages (including the Australian ones
again) NP-anaphora is also expressed through an NP-gap—by dropping
the NP altogether. Such a device gives us the limiting case—NP-gaps are
of course at the extreme limit of semantic generality, with no intrinsic
content features of their own. Many languages thus provide their speakers
with a scale of semantically reduced NPs that includes at least the following kinds of expressions:

lexical NPs > pronouns > NP-gaps

where a choice towards the right increases the likelihood of an anaphoric
reading.[8]

Thus an anaphoric NP is dependent by virtue of being semantically
general to the point that it fails to adequately refer; it is only by being
linked to some other, usually prior, NP that has fuller semantic specification (or is linked to one that does) that reference is achieved. But that
linkage is nearly always pragmatic and inferential and scarcely ever a
matter of grammatical specification—it is generally agreed that (besides
any gender restrictions) the only information that a grammar provides (if
any) is some specification of the domain in which a search for an antecedent can be made. (Sometimes it will turn out, of course, that there is
only one possible antecedent in the specified domain, but that is a matter
of accident.) Although the grammars of some languages (but not all, as
we shall see) provide forms that are *necessarily* referentially dependent
within some domain (*Anaphors* in the GB sense, or reflexives and reciprocals in particular), the linkage process itself nearly always remains
firmly outside grammar in pragmatics and is often, as we know, a matter

of probabilities, of likely interpretations, or as I shall prefer to call it "an inference to the best interpretation" (specifically an I-inference).[9]

That pragmatic principles are involved in the picking out of ante-cedents for anaphoric expressions is uncontroversial; what principles are involved, on the other hand, is much disputed. But it is clear that much "encyclopedic" knowledge and other contingent factors are involved, as the following sort of example (after Winograd 1972: 33) shows:[10]

(10) a. "The police$_1$ barred the demonstrators$_2$ because they$_2$ advocated violence."
     b. "The police$_1$ barred the demonstrators$_2$ because they$_1$ feared violence."

Here the reference of *they* depends crucially on assumptions about who would most likely be advocating or fearing violence. In the same way, reflexives too can often have competing antecedents, where a choice be-tween them is made on the grounds of background assumptions:

(11) a. "The benefactors$_1$ gave the faculty$_2$ a clubroom for themselves$_2$."
     b. "The benefactors$_1$ gave the faculty$_2$ a portrait of themselves$_1$."

However, in addition to these ad hoc, case-by-case factors, I want to claim that general pragmatic principles—and in particular, GCIs—play a role in restricting and delimiting the search for antecedents. They do this by suggesting that antecedents can be found locally, or alternatively, by contrast, outside a local domain. To be succinct: the use of a relatively semantically general expression (like a pronoun) will I-implicate local coreference, and the use of a more semantically specific expression (like a definite description) will M-implicate the complementary interpretation (i.e., disjointness from the reference of local NPs).[11] In the case of cross-sentential anaphora, the relevant concept of a local domain will be given to us by a theory of discourse (as for example sketched in Fox 1987, where the local domain amounts to a single conversational sequence). In the case of intrasentential anaphora, local domains are given to us by the syntax. In addition to the role of the I- and M-principles, the Q-principle will suggest that if a less informative, less restrictive expression (like a pronoun) is used just where a contrastive more informative expression (like a reflexive) could have been used instead, then the reading that would have come about through the use of the more informative ex-pression is *not* intended. These are very simple, switch-like operators:

M-inferences cancel the I-tendency to local coreference, Q-inferences
cancel restrictive reflexive interpretations (or logophoric ones to be discussed later). It should be immediately clear that GCIs could at most be
just one of many factors determining the choice of particular antecedents
for an anaphor. My claim will be only that GCIs provide some additional
simple, but nevertheless crucial, semiotics that help the addressee compute
the intended anaphoric link-up.

To summarize: there are at least three reasons to think that anaphora is
fundamentally pragmatic. First, the essential patterns are cross-sentential,
as well as intrasentential. Second, the necessary semantic property for an
anaphoric expression is not some specialized semantic feature—any
semantically general expression will do the job (i.e., any expression that is
more general than the intended antecedent). Third, virtually all anaphora
involves pragmatic resolution between alternatives, which may themselves
be constrained by many other factors, including syntax.

Let us return to what we called the *general anaphora pattern*, illustrated
in (2)–(3) and repeated here:

(12) a. "John came in. *He* sat down."   (preferred coreference)
     b. "John came in. *The man* sat down."   (preferred disjoint
                                                reference)

(13) a. "John likes *his* father."   (preferred coreference)
     b. "John likes *the man's* father."   (disjoint reference)

It should already be more or less clear how our preexisting pragmatic
apparatus can give an account of this pattern. The explanation will go like
this: I-implicatures predominate in the absence of countervailing Q or M
implicatures, so in the (a) sentences there will be a general preference for
local coreference encouraged by the use of semantically general forms. On
the other hand, where, as in the (b) sentences, a marked, more prolix expression has been used, we obtain an M-implicature that is complementary to that which would have arisen by I-implicature from the use of the
simple expression—in other words, we will now obtain the preference for
noncoreference in a local domain. (Note that the reading in (13b) is normally assumed to be stipulated by grammatical principle, but it is also
predicted by the pragmatic pattern.) The reader is owed an account of
exactly how the I-principle yields this preference, which is provided in the
next section, 4.2.2.

These principles can be seen at work in discourse (see Levinson 1987a),
but we cannot expect to find such preferred interpretations flawlessly

predicted, for there are many conflicting processes involved in the interpretation of texts or conversation. Our principles are just one component
in a full account of how reference tracking takes place. Much work has
been done on the empirical study of tendencies in various kinds of discourse, and it is clear that many complex factors are at work (see, e.g.,
Fox 1996). One should note that the GCI contribution to a full account of
reference tracking in discourse is intended to be modest (the critique in
Ariel 1994 mistakes it for an exhaustive theory of anaphora). A full account will certainly involve topic and "paragraph" units and other measures of textual distance to antecedents, thematic and syntactic saliency,
cognitive saliency and mutual accessibility, encyclopedic associations, and
so on (see, e.g., Kibrik 1996). Second, modest though the contribution is,
it is essential: GCIs provide vital semiotic signals about roughly where to
look for antecedents—it is, unlike many of the other factors, *part of the
signal* itself, a kind of meaning that piggybacks on the central coded significance, as sketched in the Introduction and chapter 1.[12]

4.2.2   Inferring Coreference[13]

I have claimed that the basic anaphora pattern is for a relatively semantically general NP to pick up coreference locally and a marked or prolix
one to indicate that that would be inappropriate. It is important to show
that there is some natural way in which the preference for locally co-
referent interpretations of semantically general expressions is a by-product
of the I-principle. What must be shown in particular is that where a
coreferential interpretation is available it will generally provide an informationally richer, more informative, stereotypical, and "better" interpretation in line with the general direction of that principle.[14] It is possible to
show that, in general, coreferential interpretations will indeed be more
informative than noncoreferential ones. There are a number of distinct,
but mutually compatible, arguments.

First, there's an argument at the level of reference—an argument to the
effect that the presumption of a minimal domain of reference increases
the informational load an utterance may bear. Let us adopt, for lack of
serious alternatives, the analysis of informativeness due to Bar-Hillel and
Carnap (1952; see also chapter 1 above), which is one way of operation-
alizing the Popperian idea of informativeness-relative-to-falsifiablity: the
greater the number of possible state descriptions that are ruled out by (are
incompatible with) a proposition, the more informative it is. This will
have as a consequence (Bar-Hillel and Carnap, 1952: 227ff) the simple

entailment analysis of informativeness that underlies the Horn scales
involved in the Q-implicatures.

Now, the method of state descriptions suggests one way in which we
might derive, or theoretically predict, the empirically observable preference for coreferential interpretations that was stated as condition (c) of
the I-principle in (39) in chapter 2. (Without such a theoretical argument,
linking the preference for coreferential interpretations to the I-principle,
we will have to state condition (c) as an independent pragmatic principle.)
The argument would go as follows: a coreferential interpretation reduces
the number of entities required in the domain of discourse—that is, the
interpretation can proceed on a smaller domain of discourse than it
could on a noncoreferential interpretation. But if the set of entities in the
domain of discourse is smaller, so too will be the number of state
descriptions *compatible* with the assertion in question.[15] Thus the assertion will be, from an extensional point of view, less "general" (i.e., compatible with fewer possible states of affairs) and thus more specific and
informative on the assumption of the minimal possible domain of discourse. Assuming coreference rather than introducing further entities into
the domain of discourse will thus increase the informativeness of a statement—and hence, it may be argued, the preference for coreferential
interpretations can be seen to be properly a part of the I- principle.[16]

Popper (1959: 68ff) independently offers another argument leading in
the same direction. Existential statements are weak—they are not falsifi-
able by any single observation; consequently, the fewer existential commitments the stronger the "theory" (read "assertion" for our purposes).
Consider, for example, the two interpretations of the same sentence indicated below:

(14) a. "John$_1$ loved his$_1$ father."

   b. "John$_1$ loved his$_2$ father."

On Popper's view the logical forms would be something like the following, respectively:

(15) a. $\exists x \ [\text{LOVE}(x, \imath z \ (F(z, x))) \ \& \ x = \text{John}]$
   There's an x such that x loves the unique z which is father of x,
   and x is John.

   b. $\exists x \ \exists y \ [\text{LOVE}(x, \imath z \ (F(z, y))) \ \& \ x \neq y \ \& \ x = \text{John}]$
   There's an x and a y such that x loves the unique z who is father
   of y, and y is distinct from x, and x is John.

Given the principle, "the more existential quantifiers, the less informative the statement," the interpretation in (15a) is clearly to be preferred by the I-principle to the interpretation in (15b). Thus the preference for coreferential interpretations can also be seen to follow naturally from the I-principle on this alternative Popperian account.[17]

Some differences between these two accounts are worth pointing out. Notice that the Carnapian argument is at the level of reference; it is an argument favoring the assumption of parsimony in reference—it might be glossed "for interpretation, choose a domain (D) or world (compatible with all one knows) that makes a statement most specific and thus maximizes D-informativeness." The Popperian argument assumes that the domain of discourse is held constant, and offers an evaluation for alternative statements that a sentence might have been used to make—it might be glossed "choose the logical form (or set of truth conditions, or proposition expressed) that minimizes existential commitment and thus maximizes P-informativeness." It is thus an argument essentially at the level of logical form, although because it involves the referential apparatus of existential quantification, it is also an argument at the level of reference.

There may be other ways in which to derive the preference for coreferential readings from the Principle of Informativeness. If both of the above arguments are partially at the level of reference, another argument is at the level of sense. In 'John came in and he sat down', regardless of the domain of discourse, the coreferential reading is obviously more informative *about John*. Indeed the coreferential reading is more informative about John than the noncoreferential reading would be about either referent if distinct; it is likely therefore to be a better, more informative interpretation.[18]

Recently, and largely independently of the philosophical tradition, notions similar to these have been explored in AI approaches to "common-sense reasoning." For example (as mentioned in chapter 1), some nonmonotonic reasoning systems employ the notion of circumscription (see Ginsberg 1987, sect. 3), which limits the model in which formulae are proved. The idea is to capture common-sense reasoning of the kind "Assume the car will start unless one knows it is broken" by adding specific conjectures about the data base to the reasoning system. One such conjecture is: if the system can't prove that certain entities satisfy a predicate (e.g., the battery is flat), then assume they do not satisfy it (i.e., the battery is not flat). Another is: if the system doesn't know about certain entities, then assume they don't exist (e.g., don't even consider that the *a* might be broken, if one doesn't know whether the car has an *a*). Assume then that, for the domain in question, "the known entities are all there are." McCarthy (1980) calls this *domain circumscription* and notes that it is closely related to communicational presumptions, which turn such a conjecture into something more like a reliable rule of inference. Minimizing the domain of discourse is informative, on this account, because it allows us to make many additional inferences.

Yet another argument would make the preference for coreference a mere side effect of the search for strong I-induced connections across clauses. For example, by identifying *John* and *he* in (16) we can interpret the two VPs as describing a single complex action, here the action of entering in order to sit down:

(16) a. "Bill was waiting. John came in. He sat down."
     b. *Single complex action:* coming in & sitting down

Such an interpretation would not be available if less local coreference (e.g., of *he* with *Bill*) was assumed. There is a great deal of crosslinguistic evidence, nicely surveyed by Foley and Van Valin 1983, that supports the view that coreference assignment is intimately connected to cross-clause linkage. They claim that, looking at multiclause constructions in general, the tighter the encoded semantic linkage, the greater the degree of syntactic bonding, and the more tendency to coreference across clauses (see also Haiman 1985a, Lehmann 1988). Again, working from the point of view of computational pragmatics, Hobbs (1979, 1982) argues that it is the assumption of a specific kind of conceptual linkage between clauses that determines coreference rather than the other way around. The presumption (by the I-principle in our scheme) is that any two clauses *will* be linked by one of a number of restricted conceptual ties (causality, instantiation, etc.) and in general this will require coreference across the clauses. There is much to be said for this alternative conceptualization of the problem, but it is surely a complementary perspective. In any case, here we will tend to idealize away from this more global view of the nature of coreference assignments.

I shall assume that at least one of these arguments, and most probably a conjunction of a number of them,[19] is sound and that we may thus derive the preference for coreferential readings from the general I-principle, rather than stipulate it. And in any case, we may take that preference to be an empirical fact, whatever the success of this theoretical account.

4.2.3 Inferring Disjoint Reference

If the I-principle induces inferences to coreference, such inferences are blocked in a straightforward manner by the M-principle. As I noted in chapter 2, the I-principle is triggered by expressions that are either *brief* or *semantically general*, the two generally being correlated by Zipfian principles (see Levinson 1987b for further discussion). The corollary is that, by the M-principle, if a speaker wants the addressee to avoid such a co-referential interpretation, the NP in question should be marked in form or semantically specific in content. Thus (to partially repeat earlier examples) we have the patterns in the following contrastive pairs of utterances (preferred readings marked with the appropriate indices):

(17) a. "The car ferry$_1$ hit a rock. The vessel$_1$ capsized."
          I +> coreference
      b. "The vessel$_1$ hit a rock. The car ferry$_2$ capsized."
          M +> disjoint reference
      c. "The car ferry hit a rock. It capsized."
          I +> coreference

Although the signal is gradient, the interpretation is a switch between local coreference or local disjointness: the "heavier" (in semantics or form) a succeeding NP, the more likely an addressee will read it as disjoint. Now, implicatures being defeasible, there are systematic counterexamples. If the succeeding "heavy" NP can be seen as motivated by expressing an attitude of the speaker (as in epithets), or expanded to add a piece of further descriptive or explanatory information, it may nevertheless be read as coreferential:

(18) a. "The car ferry hit a rock. The whole bloody thing capsized."
      b. "The car ferry hit a rock. The badly overloaded vessel capsized."

I take it that this much is straightforward. Less obvious is that the Q-principle might also be involved in generating disjoint interpretations. Q-inferences typically (but not exclusively) operate over *privative opposites* (Horn 1989: 317ff), where two expressions differ only in that one of the pair has additional semantic specification. Arguably, pronouns and reflexives have precisely this property: thus *himself* and *him* both have reference to singular, male entities whose identity is recoverable from context. They differ in that the reflexive has an additional property, which one may conceive of in different ways: one could hold that *himself* must be bound (syntactically coindexed) in a local domain, whereas the pronoun is free; or one could hold that the essential difference is that *himself* is necessarily referentially dependent on a prior NP, whereas *him* may pick up its reference in other ways (deictically or contextually). In either case, in a straightforward way, the reflexive is more informative than the pronoun: it fixes reference much more narrowly. Even where the pronoun is presumed to be referentially dependent, while the reflexive must find an antecedent in a limited domain, the pronoun may pick up an antecedent in a much wider domain. A reflexive thus effectively rules out many more referential possibilities and by the Bar-Hillel and Carnap metric must be judged more informative than a corresponding pronoun. The Popperian metric, whereby the less existential commitments the stronger the statement, will also give the same result.[20]

Now, expressions that are paradigmatically contrastive (can occur in the same syntactic slots), that are in privative opposition within a semantic field, and that are both lexicalized ought to form a Horn scale. If ⟨*himself, him*⟩ forms such a scale, asserting an utterance with the less informative *him* in a slot where the expression *himself* could have occurred should implicate that the speaker is avoiding the more informative statement. In effect, by utilizing a pronoun where a reflexive could have been used, the speaker Q-implicates disjoint reference. This gives us an alternative, and perhaps at first sight implausible, account of the following familiar pattern:[21]

(19) a. "John₁ admires himself₁."   (coreferential by grammatical stipulation)

b. "John₁ admires him₂."   (disjoint by Q-implicature)

Most readers will feel that both sides of this pattern are grammatically stipulated and thus that *him* simply cannot refer to John. This is not however invariably the case. A crucial fact in the plausibility of this account is that the reading is, despite being a strong default interpretation, nevertheless a defeasible inference: as Evans (1980) and Reinhart (1983: 168ff) point out, the interpretations indicated by the referential indices below are entirely natural if unusual:[22]

(20) a. "No one else voted for Marcos₁, but Marcos₁ voted for him₁."

b. "Ronald₁ and Nancy₂ have one thing in common: Nancy₂ adores him₁ and Ronald₁ adores him₁ too."

c. "Everyone despises poor William₁. Mary despises him₁. Joan despises him₁, why, even poor William₁ despises him₁!"

The conditions under which the pronoun can be read as coreferential despite being clause-bound are admittedly limited—in the examples at hand, for example, the discourse sets up as topic a property predicated about an individual (e.g., voting for Marcos), and then this predicate is predicated of the same individual. Further kinds of examples are where the pronoun is employed coreferentially but deictically, or in statements of identity:

(21) a. "I didn't hurt you$_1$, you$_1$ hurt you$_1$."
     b. "[The man who did it]$_1$ is him$_1$."
     c. "He$_1$ became the first chairman$_1$ of the department."

Yet another case is where the reflexive would have a bound-variable interpretation that the speaker wishes to avoid. Thus (22a) does not mean the same as (22b). In (22a), everyone may have voted for the chairman, but no one except the chairman voted for themselves; whereas in (22b) the chairman got only one vote. Thus (22b) is freed from pragmatic restrictions to allow the expression of the referential interpretation.

(22) a. "Only the chairman$_1$ voted for himself$_1$."
     b. "Only the chairman$_1$ voted for him$_1$."

These sorts of examples would seem to establish that the strong preference for disjoint reference of a pronoun where a reflexive could have appeared is not a matter of entailment or grammatical stipulation (unless we are willing to abandon the litmus test of defeasibility discussed above).[23] Let me remind the skeptical reader that it is not given to us by direct intuition whether a pattern of interpretation is specified by grammar and lexicon or by generalized implicature—witness the millennia of controversy about the correct semantic analysis of the Square of Oppositions reviewed in chapters 1 and 2.

Those readers who nevertheless continue to find implausible the idea that in *John hit him* disjoint reference is just implicated, not grammatically stipulated, should bear with me for two reasons. The first reason is that I noted at the beginning of the chapter that GCIs induce interpretations so reliably associated with expressions that they tend to grammaticalize. It may be that we are dealing here with a partially or generally grammaticalized pattern in English (although the limited defeasibility then needs some explanation). Note that the diachronic rather than synchronic status of an implicatural analysis would not lessen its importance. For these patterns would no longer follow from deep, unlearnable and thus innate principles of Universal Grammar, as Chomsky has proposed, but rather owe their generality to the universality of usage principles that are not essentially linguistic, everywhere exhibited, and thus intrinsically learnable.

The second reason for begging patience is that we shall see in the later part of this chapter that there are indeed indications that there may be additional principles behind the presumption that in *John hit him* the subject and object are distinct in reference. One piece of evidence (to be discussed at length in section 4.3.3.1) is that there are languages without any overt marking of reflexivity (contrary to the many confident claims that no such languages exist—see, e.g., Reinhart and Reuland 1993: 662). If the preference for reading statements of the kind 'John hit him' was only due to Q-implicature from the availability of a reflexive that was not used, it would be hard to understand the patterns in these languages, where the same (if much weaker) preference persists. Later, I shall attribute this to a background presumption that co-arguments of a verb are distinct in reference. Such a principle might be grounded in various ways. Indeed, I shall entertain the idea that the presumption of clausemate distinctness is simply an I-principle induced preference for the stereotype, where the stereotypical actions that humans are preoccupied with are irreflexive. If so, it should be easily canceled by Q- or M-inferences, which, as we have noted, always take priority if inconsistent (this raises one set of problems, which I discuss in section 4.3.3). In the English case, then, this I-inference to disjointness would be overridden by the semantics of the reflexive and reinforced by the Q-implicature to noncoreference by the use of a pronoun where a reflexive could have been used to refer to what a co-argument refers to. This double implicature in the case of nonreflexive pronouns will not prove totally redundant: often, reflexives encode more than just referential identity, so that avoiding a reflexive may be motivated by other considerations; but the I-presumption of co-argument distinctness will help to focus the contrast between pronoun and reflexive on reference alone just when antecedent and anaphoric expression are co-arguments of the same verb.

4.3 BINDING THEORY AND PRAGMATICS

4.3.1 Introduction

Let us turn now to intrasentential anaphora, the area where we expect to find competing grammatical and pragmatic accounts of constraints on the interpretation of referentially dependent expressions. We will take Chomsky's (1981: 188) Binding Theory as the point of departure:

(23) *Binding Conditions*

   A: An Anaphor is bound in its governing category.[24]

   B: A pronominal is free (not bound) in its governing category.

   C: An R-expression (lexical NP or variable) is free everywhere.

This set of conditions relies on a series of definitions which have been varied from time to time, but which at their simplest are of this kind (Chomsky 1981; see Radford 1981: chap. 11 for elementary exposition):

1. An argument is *bound* iff is it coindexed with a c-commanding argument, otherwise it is *free*.
2. A constituent X *c-commands* Y iff the branching node over (dominating) X dominates Y, but neither X nor Y directly dominate one another.[25]
3. The *governing category* or *local domain* for an expression X is the minimal S or NP that contains whatever constituent (e.g., verb or preposition) governs X (and also contains, in more recent formulations, such as Chomsky 1986: 169, other specified constituents, for instance a subject).

Despite many efforts to improve the empirical coverage of the theory by altering the conditions or tinkering with the constituent definitions, Chomsky himself still adheres in the Minimalist framework to a set of conditions that as far as we are concerned are more or less equivalent (Chomsky 1995: 211):

(24) *Interpretive version of the Binding Conditions*

   A: If α is an Anaphor, interpret it as coreferential with a c-commanding phrase in the relevant local domain D.

   B: If α is a pronominal, interpret it as disjoint from every c-commanding phrase in D.

   C: If α is an R-expression, interpret it as disjoint from every c-commanding phrase.

What has changed is that the Conditions are now held only to hold at LF, the syntax/semantic interface, where they filter interpretations, and further, as mentioned earlier, they no longer play the same role as constraints on movement.

The empirical coverage of the Binding Conditions is reasonably good, but there exists a large catalogue of well known counterexamples even within English to the classical formulations (see the useful summary in Zribi-Hertz 1989). Particularly worrisome, though, is the crosslinguistic evidence that points to substantial differences, especially with regards to Anaphors that can be bound at seemingly arbitrarily long distances. The response has been a flurry of attempts to come up with better formulations. It would be impossible here to review the many alternative formulations that have been proposed. Suffice it to say that there are a number of critical ways to fine-tune the predictions. First, one can employ different notions of c-command or, more radically, seek to replace it altogether with other notions less directly configurational (theta-hierarchies or obliqueness hierarchies, see, e.g., Jackendoff 1972 or Pollard and Sag 1994). Second, one might rethink the basic classification of NPs in three types (Anaphors, pronominals, and R-expressions): one could deny that everything that looks like a reflexive is an Anaphor, or one could insist on different kinds of Anaphors, and so on. Third, and this has been the major focus of research, one can play with the definition of the domain D in rather different ways: (a) one can, like Chomsky, attempt to hold onto a universal definition but so arrange things that the D for Anaphors is effectively slightly different than the D for pronominals, so handling one class of counterexamples where the general complementary distribution of pronominals and anaphors breaks down; (b) one can abandon universal constraints and specify, for example, a domain D according to each language; or one can allow that some languages may have more than one kind of Anaphor, each with different relevant domains. On the whole, the preferred solution is to parameterize D or the notion of governing category—that is, to handle the variation needed both across languages and within languages with different kinds of Anaphors, by expanding or contracting the local domain D by specifying that it must also contain some other element, such as a subject or an agreement feature (see Reuland and Koster 1991: 2, and other papers in Koster and Reuland 1991, Harbert 1995). We will return to these complexities later.

The reader will recollect that the Binding Conditions were developed to predict, inter alia, the following kinds of interpretive constraint (as before, I use coindexing simply as an expository device to indicate referential dependency where the indices are identical, referential independence where different):

(25) a. "John$_1$ admires himself$_1$."   (coindexing stipulated by
                                                Condition A)

   b. "John$_1$ admires him$_2$."   (coindexing forbidden by
                                                Condition B)

   c. "John$_1$ admires the professor$_2$."   (coindexing forbidden by
                                                Condition C)

   d. "John$_1$ said he$_1$ would come."   (coindexing permitted by
                                                Condition B)

   e. "John$_1$ said the professor$_2$ would   (coindexing forbidden by
      come."   Condition C)

Let me now outline how I shall proceed to suggest that much of this simple pattern, together with many of the further complex details, is in great part pragmatic in origin. First, I will outline one kind of approach that I developed in Levinson 1987a,b. For expositional purposes, we may consider a series of approximations to the data. Initially, this kind of account was developed to deal with data in an Australian language, where the patterns are rather clearly pragmatic, but I shall give only the briefest indication of that here (see Levinson 1987a). This first line of approach has the following general properties:

1. Binding Condition A is taken to be grammatically specified, as in the GB accounts.
2. Conditions B and C are then reduced to pragmatics by showing them to be the consequence of applying GCI theory to Condition A.

This account relies heavily both on Chomsky's original (1981) formulation of the problems and the data and on Reinhart's (1983) own proposals for pragmatic reductionism. I dub this the *A-first account* because it derives the rest of the anaphora patterns from Condition A of the Binding Theory.

   However, it has become clear that the original formulation of the problem is not quite correct; in particular, it ignores the following aspects of the problem that have filled the linguistics journals between 1982 and the present:

1. Reflexives and pronouns are not quite in complementary distribution (on a given indexing) even in the familiar languages; but in many other languages—especially those exhibiting *long-range reflexives*—the complementarity breaks down fundamentally.

2. Just where the complementarity in coreference possibilities breaks down, another kind of contrast can be seen to take its place—namely, a contrast in *logophoricity*, or subjective point of view (long-range reflexives generally suggesting the point of view of their referents).

3. The whole semantic apparatus—indexing, the notions of disjointness and coreference—needs revising in the light of Evans's (1980) fundamental insight that coreference must be distinguished from referential dependency.

I will extend my original 1987 account to handle some of these facts, but in the end I concede that for some languages the account remains unsatisfactory.

So in the second half of this chapter I want to propose a much revised pragmatic reductionism of the Binding Conditions, which in many ways is rather more radical because it does not accept the unreducable nature of Condition A. The crucial ingredients of the new account are:

1. Most of the ideas of the old account;
2. Three additional ingredients:
   a. a pragmatic treatment of what GB theorists have assumed are different Binding Domains for Conditions A and B; this is gotten by introducing a pragmatic analogue of Condition B;
   b. a pragmatic account of logophoricity contrasts;
   c. a sensitivity to Evans's distinction between coreference and referential dependency.
3. Some overview of new data from other languages that suggests that a more wholesale reductionism will in some cases be unavoidable.

I dub this alternative account the *B-first account* (Levinson 1991) because it gives pride of place to the anaphora pattern sometimes attributed (but not here) to Condition B of the Binding Theory and makes the rest of the patterns derivative from that.

Finally, I will suggest that rather than replacing the old account with the new one, the two should be seen as complementary. For some languages the A-first account works well, for others the B-first account is essential. However, in many languages, it seems that some amalgamation of the two accounts is required. This is to be explained, I suggest, by taking a diachronic perspective, in which A-first patterns derive from B-first patterns of anaphora; thus many A-first languages have B-first residues. This evolutionary (or *B-then-A*) account seems to provide a unified explanation for many facts, including the association of long-range reflexives with logophoricity.

4.3.2   The A-First Account: Pragmatic Reduction of Binding Conditions B and C

4.3.2.1   English: A First Approximation   We have noted what I have called the *general anaphora pattern*: the more semantically general or reduced an NP is, the greater the tendency to read it as locally corefer-ential. In those languages that permit zero-anaphora (e.g., the so-called *pro*-drop languages like Italian, or many nonconfigurational languages, like most of the Australian ones) we can extend the scale of reduction, from lexical NP, to pronoun, to NP-gap. And our pragmatic principles can now be seen to predict the general anaphora pattern along the fol-lowing lines.

First of all, the I-principle will tend to favor locally coreferential inter-pretations wherever feasible, but especially where an NP tends towards semantic generality. Second, this tendency will be tempered by the M-principle, for by the Hornian division of labor wherever an I-implicature would lead to a coreferential interpretation, the use of a marked or pro-lix expression will M-implicate the complementary disjoint interpreta-tion. By our projection principles, M-implicatures defeat incompatible I-implicatures; therefore, the use of a marked expression will overrule the tendency to coreferential interpretations.

(26)   *The general anaphora pattern*
      lexical NP > pronoun > NP-gap
      ⟵―――――― M-implicates noncoreference
      I-implicates coreference ――――⟶

An interesting prediction here is that where a language permits anaphora by NP-gap, the use of a pronoun despite its semantic generality will M-implicate some contrastive interpretation, and quite often a contrast in local noncoreference. Usage in many languages seems to support this prediction (e.g., in Chinese, Guugu Yimithirr, Tamil, Korean, Turkish, Greek)[26] although the contrast is by no means invariably interpreted on every occasion as a contrast in intended reference (but rather, sometimes in terms of emphasis, topichood, etc.).[27]

So far, we have employed only part of the pragmatic apparatus devel-oped here. Let us now bring in the third kind of implicature in our scheme by suggesting that the opposition between reflexives and ordinary pronouns is essentially a matter of scalar (Q-) implicature. In section 4.2.3 I suggested that reflexives and pronouns are in the kind of privative opposition typical of Horn scales, of the form ⟨*himself, him*⟩ and thus that the use of the pronoun can Q-implicate that the reflexive situation does not obtain. The use of a reflexive will indicate coreference by semantic stipulation (in the A-first theory). But wherever a nonreflexive pronoun is used in a locus where a reflexive is structurally permitted, the I-inference will be overruled by a strong scalar Q-inference to disjointness (recollect that Q inferences always take priority over I-inferences). Both M- and Q-principles thus constrain I-inferences to coreference.

This much seems to follow directly from the theory outlined in chapters 1 and 2—nothing more needs to be stipulated. We turn now to the predictions for intrasentential anaphora in English. Let me illustrate how we can put these ingredients together to get a first approximation to an account of the binding patterns in English (a more adequate account will follow in section 4.3.2.2). Our target, initially anyway, can be taken to be the simplest version of Chomsky's conditions as below (Radford 1981: 367; Koster and May 1982: 137):

(27) *Binding Conditions*
    A: Anaphors (reflexives and reciprocals) must be bound in their
        governing category.
    B: (Nonreflexive) Pronouns must be free in their governing
        category.
    C: A lexical NP must be free everywhere.

The constitutive concepts may again for the purposes of argument be taken to have their simplest specification: *bound* means coindexed with a c-commanding argument, *free* means not bound, and *governing category* can be taken to be the minimal domain, S or NP, containing the governor of the constituent in question.

Here is how a partial pragmatic reduction of the Conditions might go. First, no attempt is made to reduce the pattern of interpretation in Condition A of the Binding Theory—that is, we take the interpretation of reflexives and reciprocals to be stipulated by specification of the local domain (S or NP) in which an antecedent must be found (but see section 4.3.2.2). Then, taking Condition A as given, we can derive Condition B and C along the following lines:

First, where the syntax permits a direct coding of referential dependency, and thus of coreference with another NP in a restricted domain (by the use of an Anaphor), a speaker intending such coreference should use such a reflexive or reciprocal. Otherwise a speaker would be in breach of the Q-principle that enjoins the speaker to avoid the use of a statement that is informationally weaker than his knowledge of the world allows. This warrants the recipient to infer from the use of a nonreflexive pronoun that the speaker intended some reference distinct from that which would have been coded by the use of a reflexive.

Second, where a semantically general expression (e.g., a pronoun) is used, the use of the semantically general expression will I-implicate local coreference unless: (a) a reflexive could have been used in that locus, in which case the pronoun will Q-implicate locally disjoint reference (as explained in the previous paragraph); or (b) a still more semantically general expression might have been used than was in fact employed, in which case the use of the more prolix or semantically specific form may M-implicate the complement of the I-implicature to coreference, that is, disjoint reference with NPs in the local domain (as explained in the discussion of the general anaphora pattern).

To see how this gives a pragmatic reduction of facts normally attributed to Conditions B and C, consider the following sentences, where the preferred interpretations are indicated by referential indices:

(28) a.   "John$_1$ likes *him$_2$*."
      a'.   "John$_1$ likes *himself$_1$*."
      b.   "John$_1$ told her$_2$ that *he$_1$* gave her$_2$ a valentine."
      b'.   *"John$_1$ told her$_2$ that *himself$_1$* gave her$_2$ a valentine."
      c.   "John$_1$ told her$_2$ that *the man$_3$* gave her$_2$ a valentine."

Let me spell out the account. First of all, the use of the sentence in (28a) contrasts with the use of the reflexive as in (28a'). The alternates ⟨*himself, him*⟩ form a clear contrast set, one member more informative than the other, as in a Horn scale, such that the use of the weaker *him* Q-implicates the inapplicability of the stronger *himself*.[28] Second, Q-implicatures can only arise where there is a possible alternation between a stronger and weaker expression, such as a reflexive versus nonreflexive pronoun. There is no such possibility for the subject pronoun in (28b)–(28b') is ungrammatical. In the absence of any Q-implicatures to block I-enrichment, the I-principle will induce coreference in order to achieve parsimony in reference; any semantically general expressions, minimized in an informational sense, are (given the I-principle) ripe for such I-enrichment (unless the Q-principle intervenes). Therefore, where person/number/gender features permit, pronouns should be interpreted as locally coreferentially where possible, as in (28b). (There is of course no account of this preference within the GB framework, but within our pragmatic framework it is correctly predicted.)

Finally, however, expressions of roughly equal semantic generality may contrast on the level of markedness of linguistic form (they may be periphrastic phrases, complex in derivational morphology, or nonidiomatic terms). Where there is such a set, and a marked form is employed, an M-implicature will arise to suggest the complementary interpretation to the I-implicature that would have arisen from the use of the unmarked alternate. Thus the use of *the man* in (28c) induces an M-implicature to noncoreferentiality, just where the pronoun *he* would induce an I-implicature to coreferentiality.

It should be clear from the analysis of the sentences in (28) that we now have a partial pragmatic reduction of the Binding Conditions themselves. At the risk of redundancy, let me spell it out:

1. We accept Condition A as a rule of (English) grammar.

2. Condition B is then predicted (and rendered unnecessary) by the Q-principle as follows: wherever a reflexive (the semantically stronger expression) could occur, the use of a pronoun (the semantically weaker expression) will Q-implicate the inapplicability of a coreferential reading. We will thus obtain the complementary distribution of Anaphors and coreferentially interpretable pronouns, without invoking a separate Condition B. Where reflexives cannot occur, pronouns, being semantically general, will I-implicate preferred coreferential interpretations (a pattern for which there is, quite properly, no GB account, it being clearly a matter of preferred interpretation).

3. The pattern described in Condition C is the outcome of two pragmatic principles: the one applied to Condition A, the other to the pattern normally labeled Condition B. The Q-principle, just as in the case of pronouns, will induce a noncoreferential interpretation wherever a lexical NP is used where a reflexive might have occurred (this alone would predict a similar distribution for pronouns and lexical NPs). Additionally, however, the use of the more prolix or marked lexical NP where a reflexive could not have occurred, and thus where a pronoun would normally be subject to I-induced coreferentiality, will M-implicate disjoint reference (thus distinguishing lexical NPs from pronouns in terms of distribution on coreferential interpretations). Schematically:

(29) *Partial reduction of Binding Conditions*
  Condition A:
  Content: "Anaphors (reflexives and reciprocals) are bound (coindexed with a c-commanding NP) in their minimal governing category."
  Pragmatic account: Nil
  Condition B:
  Content: "Pronouns must be free (not coindexed with a c-commanding NP) in their minimal governing category."
  Pragmatic account: Given the scale ⟨*himself, him*⟩, use of the weaker, less specific *him* will Q-implicate disjoint reference (if you had meant the stronger, more specific coreferential subcase, you should have used the form that encodes coreference, namely *himself*).
  Condition C:
  Content: "Lexical NPs must be free (not coindexed with a c-commanding NP) throughout the sentence."
  Pragmatic account: Two parts:
  i. Just as in B, there will be a Q-opposition between ⟨*himself, the man*⟩, such that wherever you could have used a reflexive you should have, if you intend coreference.
  ii. Unlike in B, there will be a further opposition between the potential use of the pronoun and the use of lexical NP: {*he, the man*} are opposed by the Hornian division of labor: *He*, being a minimal form, will encourage an I-inference to local coreference; *the man* (etc.) will M-implicate disjoint reference, because the speaker would seem to be avoiding the I-implicatures induced by the pronoun.

Thus a case can be made for the elimination of both Condition B and Condition C from principles of (universal) grammar—their effects seem to be predicted by independently motivated pragmatic principles. Note in particular how the argument depends not only on the details of our three interacting pragmatic principles but also on the projection principle for implicatures given by the hierarchy $Q > M > I$. It is certainly of interest that these anaphoric patterns should be predicted by a relatively structured, independently motivated pragmatic apparatus that is sufficiently constrained to make sharp predictions.

Such a reduction is, of course, far from wholly original: the mirror-image relation between Conditions A and B of the Binding Theory invites a grammatical explanation of Condition A and a pragmatic explanation of the complementary pattern in Condition B.[29] An early attempt was made by Dowty (1980: 32ff) using a maxim of ambiguity-avoidance, and another more carefully constructed account is made by Reinhart (1983), which can be combined closely with the present proposals and is thus discussed below (see also Sadock 1983, Horn 1984). In addition, there has been a growing body of counterexamples not only to the original Binding Conditions but also to the successive revisions developed to account for class after class of problems. This in turn has led some authors to acknowledge that much that had been thought to be grammatically stipulated is in fact better handled by a pragmatic or discourse theory. These retreats naturally open up an acknowledged space for a pragmatic account.

Now, there are some significant residual problems for such a first approximation to a pragmatic reduction of Binding Conditions B and C. Three major problems are the following:

1. First, the pragmatic account appears to be in trouble wherever the complementary distribution between Anaphors and (nonreflexive) pronouns breaks down. This in fact happens in English in a number of well-studied contexts, for example certain prepositional phrases:

(30) a. "John$_1$ saw a snake near him$_1$/himself$_1$."
     b. "John$_1$ didn't like Sue being promoted above himself$_1$/him$_1$."

Attention to this central problem will be postponed till we have first considered a second approximation to the English patterns.

2. Arguably, the unacceptability of *He_1 thinks John$_1$ is a genius* is far too strong to be accounted for just by the M-principle. We may point to the fact that the ban on the coreferential interpretation is in fact defeasible—for example, the sentence becomes acceptable when the context sets up a special relevant property of, say, thinking-John-to-be-a-genius as in *Everybody thinks John is a genius, why, even he$_1$ thinks John$_1$ is a genius*. Still, there is a contrast in acceptability between *John$_1$ thinks John$_1$ is a genius* (relatively acceptable) and *He$_1$ thinks John$_1$ is a genius* (relatively unacceptable), and this is not so easily explained by the M-principle alone. This issue will be addressed directly in the second approximation to English below.

3. The pragmatic account given so far relies on an implicit unmarked order of antecedent and anaphoric expression. This order effect was

demonstrated in section 4.2.1, where two NPs, one semantically specific and one more general, resist a coreferential reading unless they are in the order: specific NP > general NP. Some rule of the sort, often mentioned in studies of anaphora, seems to be in play: 'First introduce your referent by a full specification, thereafter use a reduced form' (see, e.g., Fox 1987: 18). But in fact here structural position rather than sheer order matters, as shown by the following pairs, where it appears that it is the c-command relation between *John* and *him* that matters, not the order:

(31) a.   "John$_1$ saw a snake near him$_1$."
     b. *"He$_1$ saw a snake near John$_1$."
     c.   "Near him$_1$, John$_1$ saw a snake."
     d. *"Near John$_1$, he$_1$ saw a snake."

Thus at the very least a pragmatic account would have to have some sensitivity to marked phrase orders. That alone would also be insufficient because of the following kind of example, where on the syntactic account the absence of any c-command relation between the NPs and pronouns makes coreference possible either way:

(32) a.   "John's$_1$ friends admire him$_1$."   (coreference preferred but optional)
     b.   "His$_1$ friends admire John$_1$."   (coreference optional)

In short, we appear to need either some configurational constraints on pronominal reference, or some analog to them in the form of semantic or functional concepts. In the second approximation, we'll consider one kind of solution to getting more structure into the account. An alternative, pragmatic approach may be possible using the notions of *theme* and *rheme*: essentially, the main reference of the theme may not be referred to with a full form in the rheme (Bolinger 1979).

   In what follows, I attempt to provide solutions of different kinds to each of these problems. But before proceeding, the reader should bear in mind that the moves taken in an A-first pragmatic analysis, which takes a Condition A for granted and gets the B and C patterns partly by mirror image from A, depend critically on the exact specification of Condition A. Thus the kinds of move that the pragmaticist should make here are very much determined by the choice of a syntactic or semantic account. Let us focus first on an approach particularly intended to interact with a pragmatic account. Later, however, we will return to consider some other approaches drawn from some of the many different contemporary kinds of syntactic analysis of binding constraints, and consider how well these might interact with the kind of pragmatic apparatus developed here.

4.3.2.2 A Second Approximation: Enlisting Reinhart's Account As just noted, there appears to be more configurational structure involved in constraining anaphoric linkages in English than can be predicted from any simple pragmatic ordering rule for the introduction of pronouns. Note though that on an A-first account, most of the configurational constraints in the Binding Theory are not lost. Rather the constraints in Conditions B and C are now in part obtained by pragmatic reflection from the syntactically specified Condition A pattern, such that a pronoun in any structural location where a reflexive could have occurred, will be implicated to be free (unbound) in that locus. But further specific constraints on the occurrence of full NPs and pronouns seem now to have no account, as for example the just noted pattern where a c-commanded pronoun may be coreferential even if fronted (as in *Near him₁, John₁ saw a snake*) whereas a pronoun c-commanding a lexical NP may not be, even if fronted (**Near John₁, he₁ saw a snake*). We clearly need some additional machinery, either in the way of constraints on full coreferring NPs in the rheme, or in terms of something like c-command. In this section, we explore the possibilities of building in more configurational constraints into the A-first account.

Reinhart (1983) develops an interesting account of the English binding patterns which makes a fundamental distinction between grammatical coindexing and mere coreference, an account since extended in various ways (Reinhart 1986, Grodzinsky and Reinhart 1993). On this account, only grammatical coindexing comes within the Binding Theory, and grammatical coindexing is invariably semantically interpreted as variable binding. Reflexives get grammatically coindexed, and interpreted as variables, as is usually assumed. Moreover, a reflexive or nonreflexive bound by a quantifier also of course has the variable interpretation. But nonreflexive pronouns also can get coindexed just in case they are c-commanded by an NP outside their local domain, in which case they must also be interpreted as variables. Thus there are parallels among (33a–c), shown in the corresponding (informal) logical forms in (33g–i), respectively.

(33) a. "Oscar admires himself."
      b. "Everyone admires himself."
      c. "Oscar thinks he is a genius."
      d. "Everyone thinks he is a genius/they are geniuses."

    e.   "Oscar thinks he is a genius and so does Humphrey."

    f.   *"Oscar$_1$'s father thinks he$_1$ is a genius and Harry$_2$'s father does too" ⟨sc. think Harry$_2$ is a genius⟩.

    g.   Oscar (λx (x admires x)).

    h.   Everyone (λx (x admires x)).

    i.   Oscar (λx (x thinks x is a genius)).

On this analysis, the *he* in (33c) can be read as a variable, just as the pronoun *he* (or as some dialects prefer, *they*) undoubtedly is in (33d). This is demonstrated by the optional sloppy-identity reading of the ellipsed VP in (33e), where Humphrey thinks Humphrey, rather than Oscar, is a genius. Reinhart points out that in most circumstances a referential versus variable reading of (33c) amounts to an "equivalence" in interpretations (Reinhart 1983; Grodzinsky and Reinhart 1993: 74). The structures that allow these interpretations seem to be just the ones where a pronoun is c-commanded by an NP, matching in person, gender, and number, and where Condition B is met (the pronoun's antecedent is outside the minimal governing category). Thus in (33f), where *Oscar* does not c-command the pronoun, the bound-variable reading for the pronoun appears to be ruled out (although coreference is always possible in these structures).

Now on this analysis *only* bound-variable structures (i.e., reflexives generally and pronominals c-commanded by compatible NPs) come under the Binding Conditions, and these alone can be syntactically co-indexed. Any other kind of coreference is just that, reference to an entity that happens to have been referred to before (such NPs will thus have distinct syntactic indices, although they may be interpreted as coreferring for other reasons). This leaves the following central "ungrammatical" patterns entirely unaccounted for at a syntactic level, although they would be ruled out by the classical Binding Conditions B (for (34a)) and C (for (34b–d)). To avoid confusion with grammatical coindexing, I use italics to indicate the relevant coreferential readings:

(34) a. ??"*John* admires *him*."

         Avoided structure: John admires himself.

   b. ??"*He* thinks *John* is a genius."

         Avoided structure: John thinks he is a genius.

   c. ??"*He* admires *John*."

         Avoided structure: He admires himself.

   d. ??"*John* admires *the guy*."

         Avoided structure: John admires himself.

To explain these constraints, Reinhart appeals to pragmatics. She proposes (Reinhart 1983: 167) a pragmatic principle, a Manner maxim, "be as explicit as conditions permit." When applied to the structures in consideration, this amounts to the following addressee's strategy of interpretation: If the speaker avoids the bound-anaphora options provided by the structure he is using, then, unless he has reasons to avoid bound anaphora, he did not intend his expressions to corefer. Thus we have a specific explanation for why *He thinks that Oscar is brilliant* resists a coreferential interpretation: the speaker has avoided the parallel structure *Oscar thinks that he is brilliant*, which would have allowed the strong semantic interpretation. But because the source of the ban is pragmatic, defeasibility is permitted—especially where the bound-anaphora interpretation would in fact imply something different (Grodzinsky and Reinhart 1993: 79). Thus in apparent violations of Binding Conditions B and C, as in the following examples, these cases are not coindexed, merely coreferential, and further, they are interpretable as coreferring just because alternatives with reflexives (which would receive the bound-variable interpretation) would not be what the speaker meant:

(35) a. "His wife despises Oscar, his children despise him, even *Oscar* despises *him*."
  b. "Even *Oscar* despises *Oscar*."

Reinhart's pragmatics may account for the above patterns but will leave many other patterns unexplained—namely, wherever there is a preferred pattern of coreference or disjoint reference not associated with a c-commanding antecedent:

(36) a. "*John* came but *he* left quickly."   (coreference preferred)
  b. "*John* came but the man left quickly."   (disjoint reference preferred)
  c. "*His* father admires *him*."   (coreference preferred)
  d. "*His* father admires the Ajax goalkeeper."   (disjoint reference preferred)

If we replace Reinhart's ad hoc pragmatic maxim with our principles of entirely general application, we obtain a more encompassing account with no specially crafted pragmatic principles. We already have an account of the normal unacceptability of *John$_1$ admires him$_1$* in terms of the Q-opposition between the stronger, more informative reflexive and the pronoun. In the same way, we can assimilate to the Q-principle the opposition between bound-variable pronouns and other referring expressions: given that the structure *NP c-commanding Pronoun* allows a bound-variable interpretation, if the speaker uses a structure *Pronoun c-commanding lexical-NP*, which does not permit bound anaphora but would allow other coreference, then no such coreference is intended. Reinhart's account thus gives us two kinds of possibilities for syntactically encoding coreference: either through reflexives or through c-commanded pronouns. As a result, we get two pragmatic reflections of syntactic constraints on interpretation: the first, which we may call the *first mirror-image rule*, gives us a strong disjoint reading wherever a reflexive could have occurred (an approximation to Condition B as sketched above), and a second inference, the *second mirror-image rule*, gives us a strong disjoint reading for the pattern *Pronoun c-commanding lexical-NP*. The mirror image is given to us in both cases by the Q-principle: if you have not used an informative expression where you could have, then such an informative interpretation is not intended (italics in the example sentences indicate once again readings where the italicized NPs are coreferential):

(37) a. "John admires him."
        Q-implicates: disjoint reference (first mirror-image rule)
    b. "He thinks John admires Bill."
        Q-implicates: disjoint reference (second mirror-image rule)
    c. "*Sue* thinks *she* is adorable."
    d. ??"*She* thinks *Sue* is adorable."
    e. "Everybody loves *Sue*. Her husband thinks *Sue* is adorable, *her* parents think *Sue* is adorable, why even *she* thinks *Sue* is adorable."
    f. "*He* just couldn't believe that *the Führer* could lose the war."
    g. "*Her* parents think *Sue* is adorable."
    h. John (λx (x admires x))
        [logical form for "*John* admires *himself*."]
    i. Sue (λx (x thinks x is adorable))
        [logical form for "*Sue* thinks *she* is adorable."]

The strong resistance to reading (37d) as containing coreferential NPs is now explained on two grounds. First, there is a (relatively weak) M-implicature from the use of *Sue* where *she* might have been used. Second, there is a Q-implicature that, because a bound-variable structure might have been used but wasn't, leads one to suppose that coincidence of reference was not intended. Despite its robust character, this inference is defeasible, thus pragmatic, as shown by (37e, f) (after Bolinger 1979: 307). And the Q-implicature does not occur in structures where bound-variable interpretations are excluded, as in (37g), thus allowing coreference here despite the order of pronoun before lexical NP.

Reinhart phrases these two bound-anaphora rules as a Condition A (governing reflexives) and a highly restricted Condition B governing just the *NP c-commanding Pronoun* case. But a novel way of thinking of Reinhart's analysis—not one she promotes, by the way—is that it really amounts to claiming that English has something a bit like long-distance Anaphors (LDAs) disguised as ordinary pronouns: these are the pronominals under the bound-anaphora reading. The semantics is essentially the same for both reflexives and bound pronominals (her informal logical forms are shown in (37h, i)), but they must find their antecedents either within the local domain (for reflexives) or outside it (for pronominals acting as bound variables). LDAs indubitably exist in many languages, where an analysis in terms of features both pronominal and Anaphoric are sometimes proposed, as we shall see below. In any case, the central fact captured by Chomsky's Condition B, namely the unacceptability of interpretations like *John$_1$ admires him$_1$*, is on Reinhart's account (like ours) a pragmatic fact. Consequently, we can think about Reinhart's approach as requiring a boosted Condition A, in line with A-first pragmatic account proposed here, which now has two syntactic/semantic components: a rule of interpretation for reflexives (just as in the classical Condition A), and a rule of interpretation for pronouns c-commanded by NPs.[30]

The skeptic will raise various doubts about both Reinhart's analysis and the proposed interaction with our three GCI principles. Let us deal with the latter first. How exactly does the pronominal variable case (or rather the pattern *Pronoun c-commanding lexical-NP*) come within our Q-principle? Two doubts might be raised: (a) it cannot participate in a Horn scale because the pattern is an opposition between structures, not between expressions; and (b) the construction that would have to be held to be the informationally strong one, is in fact rather weak because it is ambiguous (between a variable and referential interpretation). In answer to the first doubt, we have already noted various systematic oppositions between structures, capable of yielding Q-inferences. For example, we considered in chapter 2 Gazdar's (1979) analysis of clausal implicatures, where it is proposed that there is an opposition between such structures as *Since p, q* and *If p, q*: the use of the less informative conditional, which does not entail its embedded clauses, will implicate that the speaker is not in a position to use the more informative *Since*-construction, which does so entail its embedded clauses. In a similar way, a speaker who uses the structure *Pronoun c-commanding lexical-NP* where he might have used the alternative *lexical-NP c-commanding Pronoun* (thus permitting grammatical coindexing), appears to wish to avoid that stronger interpretation. Let us turn now to the question of how an *ambiguous* construction or expression could be held to be the stronger term in a Q-opposition of this kind. In fact it seems quite generally to be the case that if the most precise, concise way to say that *p* is *U*, even where *U* is semantically ambiguous or general over *p* and *q*, and the speaker instead chooses to say *W*, which is semantically or formally distinct from *U*, then he will suggest that he is avoiding *U* and its implicatures. Take for example the M-opposition between *kill* and *cause to die*: the lexical causative does not entail direct causation but is instead semantically general over direct and indirect causation. Nevertheless, *kill* comes to be pragmatically specialized by I-implicature to direct causation, so that *cause to die* suggests indirect causation by M-implicature. More closely parallel, *most* is a quantifier that has a certain generality of meaning—specifically, it does not semantically exclude 'all'; otherwise *Most, in fact all, of the boys have scarlet fever* would be a contradiction. Still if one says *Many of the boys have scarlet fever*, one implicates 'not most', thus showing that the semantic generality of *most* is not inhibitive of Q-implicatures. Similarly, the quantifier *some* may be held to be actually ambiguous between the scalar quantifier in opposition with *all* versus a weaker indefinite determiner (usually unstressed as in *I want some beer*; see Milsark 1974; Gazdar 1980: 64; Horn 1997), but this does not inhibit its role in a Horn scale.

Another kind of reservation may be directed squarely at Reinhart's account. There are long-recognized difficulties with the c-command analysis, so that Reinhart's predictions about the general unacceptability of coreference when pronouns c-command lexical NPs are not correct in all cases (see Kuno 1987: 53–55; Pollard and Sag 1994: 246ff), and nor it is the case that all Anaphors must be c-commanded (Zribi-Hertz 1989). These problems are exacerbated when one comes to look at nonconfigurational languages, or languages with flat sentence structures, where the c-command analysis will generally fail (see, e.g., Levinson 1987b). For these reasons, the pragmaticist would be well advised to search for explanations for universal patterns that may be linked to machinery that appears less language-specific, and I shall discuss in section

4.3.2.4 proposals that replace c-command with functional sentence perspective notions like theme/rheme (Bolinger 1979) or with more semantic notions like thematic hierarchies (Jackendoff 1972, 1992a).

The pragmaticist may remain agnostic about this syntactic/semantic analysis. The point is that it is the kind of analysis many syntacticians think is reasonable. And if so, we can see that by adopting both a standard Binding Condition A plus an additional analysis of the pattern *NP c-commanding Pronoun* as a bound-variable structure similar in interpretation to reflexives, we can obtain all the rest of the patterns by means of our pragmatic rules. The substantial change from our first approximation to English, sketched above, is that now configurational structures play a role not only in the interpretation of pronouns where reflexives could have occurred (by the first mirror-image rule) but also (by the second mirror-image rule) in the interpretations of pronouns where reflexives could not have occurred (e.g., as subjects of subordinate clauses). Configurational patterns then play a role in the pragmatic interpretations, but they do so only by reflection (i.e., by an inference from a structure that might have been employed but wasn't). What is of interest to the pragmaticist is the general strategy pursued here: build in to the syntax just as much structure as you need, so that when it interacts with the independently motivated pragmatics the overall account has two desirable features: it is hugely economical, and it predicts defeasibility just where it is allowable. For the syntactician, it ought to be reassuring that the kind of pragmatic apparatus that would be needed to ground Reinhart's proposals is already independently motivated.

4.3.2.3   Could Condition C be Syntactic After All?   The second approximation given above goes some way to dealing with two of the three problems we foresaw for the A-first account: Reinhart's account gets a crucial element of further configurational structure into the account of pronoun interpretation, thus accounting for some of the asymmetries of interpretation that cannot be explained by the sheer order of pronoun and antecedent. At the same time, it accounts for the robustness of the ban on coreference in *Pronoun c-commanding lexical-NP* structures, now attributed to a Q-inference reinforced by an M-implicature. The third problem, the occasional overlap in distribution between Anaphors and pronouns, is still unaccounted for, but we will consider this shortly.

Despite the enormous volume of work that presupposes the three Chomskyan Binding Conditions, there has been very little attempt to defend them against the threat of pragmatic reductionism that goes back at least to Dowty (1980) and Reinhart (1983).[31] One exception is Lasnik (1991), who explicitly defends Condition C against Reinhart's account and pragmatic reductionism in general. Lasnik argues that Reinhart's pragmatic rule, which enjoins a speaker to use the most explicit means at his disposal, would predict that *$John_1$ thinks that I admire $John_1$ should be preferred over $John_1$ thinks that I admire him_1. And if one wishes to include extra information in an epithet, that too should license the full NP, as in $John_1$ thinks that I admire the $idiot_1$. These complaints ought to evaporate given our more explicit pragmatic apparatus, where the inference to conjointness is based on the I-principle and disjointness inferences are produced by Q- and M-inferences. Even if the repetition of full NPs were more explicit in some sense than a resort to anaphora, the systematic semiotics of GCIs would give rise to marked interpretations, including disjoint reference. GCIs constitute a market economy of forms engendering default interpretations; one cannot freely innovate without semiotic consequences (see the conclusions to this chapter). Nor is there anything very vague about the notions employed: Q-inferences are based squarely on semantic informativeness (à la Bar-Hillel and Carnap), whereas M-inferences based on markedness and prolixity give one the complement of I-inferences from corresponding unmarked forms. Thus the account goes schematically as follows (here italics indicate the NPs whose coreference is in question):

(38) a. "*John* thinks that I admire *him.*"
          I +> coreference
      b. "*John* thinks that I admire *John.*"
          M +> disjoint reference
      c. "*Howard Lasnik* admires *the author of 'Essays on anaphora.'*"
          Q +> disjoint reference by virtue of the Q-opposition ⟨*himself, the author*⟩
          M +> disjoint reference by virtue of the M-opposition {*himself, the author*};
          But both inferences will be overridden by world knowledge, if one knows that Lasnik is indeed the author of *Essays on anaphora.*
      d. "*Howard Lasnik* is *the author of 'Essays on anaphora.'*"
          Q and M-implicatures to disjointness overridden by semantic entailment, the stated identity

e. "*Lasnik* thinks that I admire *the Lasnik of 'Essays on anaphora'*, while in fact I admire *the Lasnik of 'Lectures on binding and empty categories.'*"
M-implicatures to disjointness overridden by the semantics/syntax

f. "*The man who can pull the sword out of this stone* is *King Arthur.*"

Hence, where a pronoun could have occurred and would have I-implicated conjoint reference (see (38a)), the use of a lexical NP (as in (38b)) will M-implicate that disjoint reference is intended if that fits our background knowledge. Where a reflexive could have occurred (as in (38c)), that would have restricted the referential interpretations further and would, *ceteris paribus*, have been more informative; its avoidance thus Q-implicates disjoint reference, reinforcing an M-implicature to the same effect. Note however that names rigidly refer and that descriptive phrases may also uniquely refer to the same individual; then naturally the referential semantics of *Scott admired the author of Waverly* overrides any implicature to disjoint reference (and similarly in (38c). If Condition C of the Binding Theory was really a rule of grammar, then (38d) would be ungrammatical, as indeed would all identity statements.[32] However, because the Condition C effects are mere implicatures, they evaporate in the face of the conflicting semantics of asserted identity. Pronouns in English (unlike in some languages) do not permit determiners, relative clauses, modifiers, or complements, especially in the accusative—one cannot (alas) in modern English say things like *Him of the lion heart*, so additional commentary will require a prolix head noun (as in (38e)). In example (38f), we have another identity statement, which can be read either referentially or attributively; but either way it is grammatically fine, so it is not possible to explain away these Condition C violations in terms of attributive *versus* predicative uses.

Lasnik's second line of attack is that a pragmatic account should be universal, whereas a syntactic account can be parameterized. Given which, the facts of a language like Thai should be problematic to the pragmatic account, for in Thai one can say sentences that are glossed as 'John₁ thinks that John₁ is smart' or even 'John₁ likes John₁'. However, a pragmatic account depends on the total local economy of NP types, for full lexical nouns can only implicate, on our account, by opposition to zeros, pronouns, and reflexives, and such implicatures fall away in the face of conflicting semantic factors. Chinese is another language that freely permits full NP repetition, and we are fortunate to have a careful study of the whole system from a pragmatic point of view (Huang 1994). In Chinese, for example, one must repeat lexical NPs to express a bound-variable interpretation (as in 'Every mother-in-law has mother-in-law difficulties'), but where the choice is free, there are implicatures, but not necessarily ones of disjoint reference (Huang 1994: 199ff). But Lasnik's argument here is on soft ground anyway. English has registers that permit, nay require, lexical-NP repetition instead of pronouns, notoriously for example in legal documents: on Lasnik's line of argumentation we would need a different parameterization of the Binding Conditions not just for each language but for each discourse genre. Crosslinguistic and cross-genre variation is not the stuff of syntactic universals. A pragmatic theory of the kind developed here, on the other hand, uses general principles interacting with language-specific conventions to predict both unmarked crosslinguistic tendencies and language-specific effects, while allowing for marked types of genre without grammatical violations.

Lasnik claims that Condition C should be split into two subconditions: (a) R-expressions (full lexical NPs) may not be bound by R-expressions, this held to be parameterized crosslinguistically; and (b) R-expressions may not be bound by pronouns, this holding universally. Both are supposed to hold in English, but we have already glimpsed exceptions. At the risk of repetition, let us lay out the scope of the many kinds of counterexamples.

4.3.2.3.1 Where a Lexical NP C-Commands Another Lexical NP   Here counterexamples are easy to find (Reinhart 1983):

(39) a. "Only Felix voted for Felix."
     b. "Margaret's husband is Dennis."
     c. "Dennis and Margaret have one thing in common: Dennis thinks Margaret terrific and Margaret thinks Margaret terrific."
     d. "Clinton said the President was not informed."
     e. "Frog went to Frog's house; Toad went to Toad's house."

On our analysis, the reason why repetition of lexical NPs with intended coreference is not generally found is always (at least) a matter of M-implicature: if a shorter, pronominal, or reflexive form can be used to I-implicate coreference, it should be. In some cases, such as those where a reflexive could have been used, there will also potentially be a strong

Q-implicature to disjoint reference (as in (39a,b)). The point to be made about these counterexamples is that in each case we can see why a reflexive or a pronoun has in fact not been used. In (39a) substitution of the second Felix with *himself* would have different truth conditions; in (39b) the substitution would make the identity statement functionless; in (39c) what is being discussed is the property of thinking Margaret terrific (not oneself terrific); in (39d) the choice of the lexical NP *the President* is understood to indicate that Clinton was speaking in an official capacity; in (39e) (from a children's book) the marked genre of "motherese" clearly embodies an assumption that pronominal reference tracking can be difficult for children.[33]

4.3.2.3.2 *Where a Pronoun C-Commands a Lexical NP*   This constraint is much more robust crosslinguistically, although some languages seem to exhibit it at most weakly.[34] English counterexamples are perhaps a little harder to find (compared to the preceding pattern), as we'd expect if Reinhart's account is right, but they certainly exist:[35]

(40) a. "Napoleon was endowed with supreme self-confidence. *He* never doubted that *Napoleon* was what France needed."

   b. "Clark Kent hurried. *He* realized that *Superman* was urgently needed."

   c. "*She* thinks *the wife* knows best; *he* thinks *the husband* knows best."

   d. "*He* thinks *the only reliable teacher of linguistics* is himself."

   e. "*She* thinks it unfair that *the Chair of the Department* always has to be her."

   f. "*She* says *the youngest member of the family*, i.e., herself, should choose the holiday."

   g. "*He*'s doing what *John* always does."

   h. "*He* talks the way that only *the author of the Pisa Lectures* could possibly do."

   i. "*She*'s called *Madonna*."

   j. "*He* became known as *Napoleon*."

   k. "*He* succeeded his father as *James Ist of England*."

   l. "*He* managed to become *the President of the USA*."

   m. "*He* is *the very man you first dated*."

   n. "*She* thought *Oedipus' mother* was someone else."

   k. "*She* knows what *Joan Bresnan* currently believes, because *she* is *Joan Bresnan*."

It is thus quite easy to get the pronoun–c-commanding–NP coreferential reading under certain semantic/pragmatic conditions[36]—for example, where the NP expresses an identity relation that is not obvious either to the addressee or to the subject, or where the NP makes explicit a double identity, or where what is relevant is the identity of the same referent under a second description, and so on.[37] Any attempt to hang on to a syntactic version of Condition C runs straight into the morass of these many kinds of exceptions. A pragmatic account on the other hand specifically allows for defeasibility under principled circumstances.

4.3.2.4 Nonconfigurational Approaches to Binding

We have so far taken for granted the view that binding consists in the coindexing of a c-commanding antecedent with an Anaphor. C-command is defined over phrase structure, and the Binding Theory relies on the hierarchical nature of phrase structure as a crosslinguistic universal. However, it is well known that this view is problematic with respect to languages that either have flat-sentence structure (i.e., with no VP constituent; see, e.g., Kiss 1991), or worse, have little overt constituent structure altogether, as in languages with not only free phrase order but free word order (see Hale 1983). Therefore it is worth looking for alternative accounts phrased in terms of other grammatical or semantic notions that may have greater crosslinguistic currency. In this section, let us first consider a nonconfigurational language and how it reinforces the need for a pragmatic account, and then turn to alternative concepts that might be employed to explain the patterns currently explained in terms of configurational notions.

4.3.2.4.1 Binding in a Nonconfigurational Language

Guugu Yimithirr, a language spoken in northern Queensland (see Haviland 1979), may serve to remind us of the difficulty of extending the standard Binding Theory to nonconfigurational languages. Like many of the Australian languages, it does not exhibit the structural properties that are the basis for a Chomskyan account. For example, there seem to be only two rather weak arguments for any kind of constituency at all in Guugu Yimithirr (Levinson 1987b); this makes the application of notions like c-command and structural domain for binding impossible to define in a configurational manner. Many other notions central to such accounts either fail to apply or are counterexemplified (like the θ-Criterion, which forbids two arguments to have the same semantic role).[38] Even the contrast between pronouns and lexical NPs in Guugu Yimithirr seems to be essentially different from the contrast between pronominals and R-expressions in GB theory (pronouns in Guugu Yimithirr being more like nominals in various ways, like permitting modifiers). In all these properties it is by no means unique; Guugu Yimithirr may stand as one of a large class of languages where the application of such concepts is essentially problematical.

Guugu Yimithirr has no unequivocal reflexive construction; reflexivity is expressed by use of what is often called the antipassive in Australian languages—that is, a verbal affix that converts a transitive verb (with an ergative subject) into an intransitive verb (with an absolutive subject). The interpretations of this construction are potentially very wide, ranging from indefinite or accidental agency to reciprocal or reflexive action of an agent upon itself:

(41) Bama   gudhiira gunda-dhi.
     people-ABS two-ABS hit-ANTIPASSIVE
     'Someone hit the two people accidentally.'
     'The two people hit themselves.'
     'The two people hit one another.'

Interestingly, the reflexive or reciprocal interpretations are much strengthened if the emphatic particle -:gu is added to the subject (a point we will take up in connection with a B-first pragmatic account). This construction therefore offers a way of expressing reflexive action of a subject upon what would, without the antipassive affix, be expressed as a direct object:

(42) John-ngun nhangu   gunday.
     John-ERG him+ACC hit+past
     'John hit him.'

No other kinds of arguments, such as adjuncts or oblique NPs, can thus be reflexivized, unlike in the English sentence *John gave Mary the book about herself.* The issue of having to find an antecedent within a specified domain (as with English Anaphors) is thus irrelevant—there is no Anaphor (only an indication that one argument is missing) and the "antecedent" must be the subject.

Thus not only is the coding of reflexivity not directly explicit (but rather semantically general over reflexivity and unknown agency, etc.), it is also restricted to the relationship between what in a transitive sentence would be core co-arguments, specifically subject and direct object. The pragmatic account that we have developed therefore predicts less certainty of disjoint reference between a subject and an overt object of a normal (nonantipassivized) transitive verb and, further, no presumption of disjoint reference between NPs in other positions. This prediction seems to be generally correct; sentences glossing as 'John hit John', while having a preferentially disjoint intepretation, would seem more freely to allow coreferential interpretations than in English, and English *John gave Mary the book about herself* would have to be translated as 'John gave Mary the book about Mary'. Further, in Guugu Yimithirr, just as in English, we express 'John$_1$ asked his$_1$ father' with a possessive pronoun, there being no way to reflexivize the possessive; but the possibilities of coreference here, which on the Binding Theory would follow under Condition B from the pronominal being free in the NP *his father*, are clearly due to the absence of a pragmatic contrast (as, on our account, they are in English). Similarly, under Condition C we would expect sentences glossing 'His$_1$ father told him$_1$ that John$_1$ should make it' to be out; but in fact they appear to be fine, which indicates that we have no strong inference here against coreferring lexical NPs with pronominal antecedents.

What is striking therefore is the association of a preferred disjoint interpretation of pronouns and NPs just where the antipassive might have been used to code a missing argument (and thus, inter alia, coidentity of the arguments) but was not. This can be neatly accounted for by Q-inference. There is no evidence that the GB apparatus of binding domains and disjoint reference conditions are in any way involved. Referential dependence is indicated by a construction that signals a necessarily omitted argument (all arguments in Guugu Yimithirr in any position whatsoever can be optionally omitted).

In fact Guugu Yimithirr offers much further evidence for the operation of principles of pragmatic cohesion and contrast. The general anaphora pattern is nicely exemplified in a system where zero-anaphora is general, and thus a three-way contrast in semantic generality is available (lexical NP, pronoun, NP-gap). NP-gaps induce coreferential interpretations where possible but indefinite reference where there is no available appropriate antecedent, whereas the use of a pronoun where a gap may have been expected is often sufficient to suggest (via M-implicature) locally disjoint reference. But the reader is referred to Levinson 1987a and 1987b for further discussion. The point here is that in languages of this sort, the *grammar* of anaphora appears reduced to a minimum. Without a pragmatic account of the anaphora patterns, we have no account of the clear preferences in interpretation at all.

4.3.2.4.2 Alternatives to C-Command Nonconfigurational concepts, like hierarchies of grammatical relations or thematic relations, have been explored from time to time as alternatives to c-command conditions on binding. One candidate often proposed is a hierarchy of thematic relations (Jackendoff 1972, Wilkins 1988, Reinhart and Reuland 1991, Kiss 1991). Suppose we have a thematic hierarchy Agent > Goal > Theme, and a constraint that the antecedent must outrank the Anaphor on this hierarchy; then we can understand the following sort of pattern:

(43) a. John talked to Bill$_1$ (Goal) about himself$_1$ (Theme).
     b. *John talked about Bill$_1$ (Theme) to himself$_1$ (Goal).

The predictions from a thematic hierarchy are in many cases the same as from the grammatical relations hierarchy, but Pollard and Sag (1992: 297–299) argue that where they diverge a theory based on grammatical relations does better. Pollard and Sag (1992, 1994) therefore advance an account in a configuration-based theory of grammar, HPSG, in which nevertheless configurational constraints are (ironically enough) supplanted by a hierarchy of obliqueness across grammatical relations (see also Hellan 1991). Clearly, for this to work, genuine Anaphors have to be restricted to those whose antecedents are co-arguments, and thus antecedents that also bear a grammatical relation to the same predicate. Their theory simply requires that an Anaphor must be bound to an antecedent that is a *less oblique* complement of the same head. Thus we obtain not only the standard examples as in (44a), but also where a verb subcategorizes for both a primary and more oblique object, the former may perform as antecedent for the latter.

(44) a. John$_1$ likes himself$_1$.
     b. Mary described John$_1$ to himself$_1$.
     c. Mary talked to John about himself.
     d. Mary talked to John about herself.

In (44c), where both prepositions are nonpredicative and share their features with their objects, the acceptability is predicted because *to*-phrases are held to be less oblique than *about*-phrases (Pollard and Sag 1994: 264). Similarly (44d) is acceptable; the subject *Mary* is less oblique than the Anaphor in a subcategorized PP that shares the features of its object.

This theory does not cover the full distribution of English reflexives (many of which are not co-arguments with their antecedents), holding that the residue (and by implication the long-distance Anaphors of other languages) are pseudo-Anaphors (see discussion in Section 4.3.2.5.3). Because these pseudo-Anaphors overlap in distribution with pronouns on a coreferential reading, Pollard and Sag (1994) can adopt a Binding Condition B that requires a nonreflexive pronominal to be free in just the domain where an Anaphor must be bound, thereby predicting a complementary distribution between true Anaphors and pronouns.[39] We could therefore without problems apply an A-first pragmatic account to this theory, and reduce their Condition B to implicature, along the lines sketched in our first approximation.

Such grammatical alternatives to configurational accounts are not the only possibilities. At the outset, it was shown how linear order seems to play a crucial role in cross-sentential anaphora, presuming some rule of the kind "first introduce your referents with full forms, thereafter use reduced forms." Intrasententially, however, this conflicts with many an example, as noted—there are exceptions in both marked phrase orders (*Near him, John saw a snake*) and in cases where the pronoun is embedded in the subject (*His children admire John*). In early transformational grammar, these observations gave rise to the "precede and command" analysis, which was observationally fairly good (see Kuno 1987: chap. 2 for review) and which preserved the ordering requirement, arguably an essentially pragmatic or discourse element, later lost in the c-command account, which makes the ordering facts epiphenomenal. It would seem worthwhile to explore the possibility of reversing the argument, thus making the configurational facts epiphenomenal from discourse principles. Something very near to the right principle is given by Bolinger (1979: 306), using the notions theme and rheme, and *reidentification* (i.e., the use of a full form after a referent has already been introduced in the discourse): don't reintroduce the topic of the theme in the rheme (or "the topic may be reidentified easily in the theme, but in the rheme only if the theme lacks a normally topical form"). As Reinhart (1983: 97) notes, this gives a good account of many apparently configurational constraints, but she notes that it would need extending to handle cases where both antecedent and pronoun are in the rheme (e.g., *Rosa locked him in Ben's room* where *him* cannot be identified with *Ben*). My own suggestion (Levinson 1991: 114–115) was that there is also a gradient within the rheme, where thematic role hierarchies would restrict coreferential possibilities (this ties into Jackendoff's (1972) observations). It is not at all clear that such an account could not be made to work, but we should concede that it needs further exploration (see also Van Valin 1990: 178–183).

4.3.2.5   Where Complementary Distribution Fails: Long-Distance Anaphora and Related Phenomena   Our pragmatic machinery nicely produces the very generally attested complementary distribution of pronoun and Anaphor (by the Q-principle) and of pronoun and lexical NP (by the M-principle). But our approximations to English appear to fail in a crucial way: it is well known that there are marginal, but systematic, contexts in which the pronoun and the Anaphor overlap in distribution. How can the account be generalized to cover these cases? In the literature, there are four main classes of context where this overlap between Anaphor A and pronoun P has been noticed in English (Zribi-Hertz 1989: 698f):

1. So-called picture-noun reflexives:
    a. A or P embedded within the subject of a subordinate clause:
        They thought that pictures of themselves/them would be on sale.
    b. A or P are embedded objects in an existential subordinate clause:
        They said that there are pictures of themselves/them in the post office.
2. Genitives (pronouns/reciprocals):
    They love their/each other's wives.
3. Certain locative prepositional phrases:
    They hid the money behind themselves/them.
4. So-called emphatic contexts, involving contrast, comparison and restrictions of predication:
    He thinks Mary is taller than himself/him.
    He believes that men like himself/him are rare.
    He believes that it was not sent to either him or her/either her or himself.
    He thinks Mary loves him/himself, not Peter.
    He thinks Mary hates even him/himself.

Enormous ingenuity has gone into seeking a way to reconcile these facts with the Binding Conditions. Four main tacks have been taken:

1. One can try to find ways in which what appear to be the same contexts are in fact distinguished (e.g., there is an empty subject in the small clause [*e pictures of them*] but not in the NP [*pictures of themselves*], as in Chomsky 1986: 173);
2. One may hold that emphatic or other pseudo-Anaphors fall outside the theory (see Zribi-Hertz 1989 for discussion, also Bouchard 1983, Baker 1995);
3. One may hold that "downstairs" Anaphors are raised in LF, where the Binding Conditions apply (see Harbert 1995: 203–208 for review);

4. One may tinker with the domains in the Binding Conditions A and B so that just the right overlap is predicted (as in Chomsky 1986).

The last approach has been the most popular because it seems independently motivated by the phenomenon of long-distance anaphora in other languages. However, Chomsky's own response was directed squarely at handling English examples like the following:

(45) a. They$_1$ read [their$_1$ books].
   b. They$_1$ read [each other's$_1$ books].
   c. The professors$_1$ thought that [books about themselves$_1$] would be on sale.
   d. The professors$_1$ thought that [books about them$_1$] would be on sale.

To handle these, Chomsky (1986) suggested revising the Binding Conditions utilizing the notion of a "Binding Theory compatibility requirement," which effectively extends the range of Anaphors slightly by requiring that there is an actual binder or potential antecedent within the domain D. Thus in the first two sentences above, both an Anaphor and a pronoun can occur in the same slot bound to the same antecedent. This is because, on the 1986 account, *each other* simply cannot be coindexed within the bracketed NP domain; therefore the actual domain is the matrix sentence. The pronoun however must be free in its domain; therefore the issue of an obligatory potential binder doesn't arise. The pronoun is thus free in the NP which is its domain, and can be coreferential with the subject of the matrix sentence just like the Anaphor. A similar analysis can then be given of (45c,d): in (45c) the compatibility requirement for a potential binder within the governing category (marked with square brackets) is not met, so the Anaphor may be bound by the matrix subject, but in (45d) the pronoun must still be free within the same domain.

A pragmatic account is not the slightest embarrassed by the failure of a contrast between (45a) and (45b) in coreferentiality. This is because the reciprocal and the possessive pronoun do not mean the same—the pairing of books and readers in (45a) is unconstrained, but in (45b) each reader must read the books owned by the other. If one means the latter, one will have to say it. There may be as consequence a (Q-based) assumption that the plain possessive does not denote that particular reciprocal situation, but in both cases the anaphoric link-up is the same. The reasons then are entirely general: where two Q-contrasting expressions (or constructions) differ in meaning on two dimensions (here (i) necessary vs. optional referential dependency, (ii) reciprocal vs. unspecified distribution), the use of the informationally weaker expression is justified if one is seeking to avoid at least one of the stronger meanings. Many languages (e.g., Norwegian) have possessive reflexives that will contrast on just the one dimension with the reciprocal, and on the other dimension with the possessive (non-reflexive) pronoun, which will then tend to be read as disjoint (Hellan 1991).

But the overlap in (45c,d) is more problematic for the simple A-first pragmatic account developed so far. In fact, however, the pragmatic explanation, which presumes some extension of the range at which reflexives can be bound, will turn out to be exactly the same in kind as that given for the reciprocal versus possessive pronoun: the reflexive here contrasts with the pronoun on two dimensions, necessary referential dependency and a subjective perspective called *logophoricity* in the literature. The general nature of this second dimension of contrast becomes clearer when we look at other languages, which we shall shortly do.[40] Meanwhile, note that Chomsky's (1986) emendation of the Binding Conditions will not in fact achieve any generality of coverage. Reciprocals can occur deeply embedded from their antecedents (as in *They$_1$ feared that the prosecutor would reveal that Noriega had contributed to each other$_1$'s campaign funds*; see Pollard and Sag 1994: 257), and even the nonreflexive pronoun in *They$_1$ put the books [beside them$_1$/themselves$_1$]* escapes the account, because it ought to be free throughout the sentence (the bracketed PP not constituting a binding domain on this theory; Harbert 1995: 192). Within the GB framework there have been many attempts to find different kinds of solutions to the empirical inadequacy of the classical Binding Theory (see Harbert 1995 for review). In fact, as we shall see, English reflexives are routinely long-distance bound, as are reflexives in many other languages. The patterns in these other languages, to which we now turn, also give us a better idea of how to develop a pragmatic account that can handle the kind of neutralization between disjoint/conjoint reference that we find in the above contexts in English.

4.3.2.5.1 *Long-distance Anaphora and Logophoricity* It has been clear almost from the outset that the Binding Theory runs into difficulties with so-called long-distance Anaphors in many languages (see, e.g., Maling 1984). Long-distance anaphora involves the occurrence of referentially dependent anaphors which are just like Anaphors in that they must be

bound, and yet violate (the classical) Condition A of the Binding Conditions by having antecedents that lie outside of their minimal governing
categories. Pretheoretically we may coarsely distinguish between different
kinds of referentially dependent Anaphors: those locally bound reflexives
that require co-argument antecedents (like prototypical cases of English
reflexives), those that require binding within the clause but can occur in
adjuncts (like English reflexives embedded in PPs), and those (so-called
non-clause-bound reflexives [NCBRs]) that may be bound outside the
immediate containing clause altogether (like Icelandic *sig*, Chinese *ziji*).
The last are of course particularly challenging to the theory, and a great
deal of work has gone into trying to understand the phenomena. The
distribution of such long-distance Anaphors may include the following,
as indicated by the English glosses with *self* standing for the Anaphor
(although the European languages tend to lack a nominative long-
distance Anaphor as in (46b)).

(46) a. 'John hit self.'
     b. 'John said that self would come.'
     c. 'John said that Bill would hit self.'

Unfortunately, on close examination the patterns are fairly heterogenous,
even within the European languages (see the useful survey in Reuland and
Koster 1991). Thus in the Germanic languages (Icelandic, Norwegian,
Dutch, etc.) the long-distance Anaphors are simplex morphemes (like *sig*,
seg, *zich*) which may occur clause-bound, and prefer subject antecedents;
when bound outside the clause they are not necessarily in complementary
distribution with pronouns (i.e., pronouns can be conjoint with the same
antecedent). But despite the commonalities, even here the details vary in
intricate ways, according to such factors as the finiteness or the subjunctive nature of higher clauses, and according to the availability of other
(often compound) reflexives in clause-bound contexts. Thus although
Icelandic, Danish, and Gothic allow structures in English gloss like (47a),
Icelandic exceptionally allows binding across a tensed-clause boundary as
in (47b) (Harbert 1995: 193–194).

(47) a. 'John$_1$ asked Peter to shave self$_1$.'
     b. 'John$_1$ said that I had (subjunctive) betrayed self$_1$.'

Once we turn to languages further afield, the phenomena look rather different. For example, Chinese has long-distance reflexives that can be "bound"
from an arbitrary distance by an antecedent that is not necessarily in a

c-commanding position;[41] such LDAs can be either simplex or compound (both *ziji* and *ta ziji*), and if compound the antecedent need not be a subject (Huang 1994: 76–78, 196–199). The Japanese LDA *zibun* also exhibits a great freedom in the circumstances under which it must be bound (Mazuka and Lust 1994).

Despite the substantial variation, LDAs do show certain similarities: (a) when they are simplex, they lack (person, number) agreement features;[42] (b) when they have local antecedents, they contrast in reference with pronouns,[43] but when they have long-distance antecedents, they do not necessarily contrast in reference with a pronoun (i.e., complementary distribution with respect to coreference fails);[44] (c) nevertheless, wherever both a pronoun and a long-distance Anaphor could occur in a grammatical slot with the same reference, the Anaphor always contrasts in meaning with the ordinary pronoun, the associated meanings having something to do with emphatic contrast, empathy, or protagonist's perspective, subjective point of view, and so on.

The first fact, the tendency to lack concord features, is presumably a reflex of the fact that LDAs are (by definition) necessarily referentially dependent on a discourse antecedent, unlike pronouns which may have independent reference and with which LDAs contrast. But it is the second and third facts that are crucial here: the complementary referential possibilities between pronoun and reflexive break down conclusively in these long-distance environments, permitting (in gloss) both 'John said self would come' and 'John said he would come' for the coreferential reading (or for languages without nominative Anaphors, 'John said Bill loves self' and 'John said Bill loves him'). This neutralization of the referential contrast between Anaphor and pronoun is of course problematic for the classical Binding Theory, and it has become the focus of intensive research and a substantial literature (see, e.g., Harbert 1995: 193ff; Huang 1994: chap. 4, in preparation; and Koster and Reuland 1991 for review and references).

There are at least three major responses within the framework. First, one can reclassify LDAs as something other than the Anaphors of Binding Theory (Bouchard 1983). Or, one can assume that in underlying LF the Anaphor is actually locally bound just as presumed in the classical theory (and is thus raised at LF; Pica 1987). Finally, one can parameterize Anaphors, so that they have distinct binding domains in different languages, allowing that even different Anaphors within a language (e.g., complex vs. simplex ones) might have different binding domains (Wexler and Manzini 1987).

All of these responses have their own problems (see, e.g., Huang 1994, chap. 4). The first option requires, for example, that one treats homophonous expressions as distinct lexical items (e.g., Anaphors when locally bound, referentially dependent pronominals elsewhere), and that one minimizes the difference between pronominals (with their exophoric and deictic potential) and LDAs (which have only referential dependence and distinct distribution). The second option, using a raising at LF analysis, has been applied ingeniously to some of the Germanic languages (see Harbert 1995: 203ff), but it runs into overwhelming problems with languages like Chinese (on which there has also been considerable work; see Huang 1994: chap. 4 for review). The last option gives the best hope of empirical coverage, but at the expense of an ad hoc variation of domains which lacks the system-wide implications that parameters are supposed to have in the Principles and Parameters framework. Some analysts are optimistic that we may need just three kinds of domains: one for clause-bound reflexives (like the prototype English exemplars) as in classic Binding Condition A, one for LDAs consisting of the first finite clause to be stated as a variant Condition A, and one for homophonous pseudo-reflexives that are subject to discourse conditions rather than the Binding Conditions (Reuland and Koster 1991). The admission that many LDA look-alikes escape the Binding Conditions is unavoidable because they often seem to be "bound" by non-c-commanding antecedents, sometimes outside the sentence altogether. But it is damaging because it makes the claim that the Binding Conditions have, say, just two alternate domains pretty unfalsifiable. Most commentators would concede that despite the energetic exploration of these three different ways in which the Binding Theory might be reconciled with the phenomena of long-distance anaphora, we have at present no convincing overall theory from a syntactic point of view.

Now a pragmatic account of the (A-first) kind developed here would at first sight appear to be in just as much trouble from the failure of the complementarity of LDAs and pronouns as the Binding Theory accounts. Clearly, this is the same kind of problem we found with the English reflexives, which turned out to overlap in distribution (on a coreferential reading) with pronouns in a few special contexts; but here in the case of LDAs the overlap is not marginal, but systematic, and for most of the relevant languages holds for all the long-distance loci. But the LDA facts very clearly signal the direction in which the pragmatic theory can be rescued: as mentioned, even where the Anaphor and the pronoun can have the same reference, they always contrast in meaning in some other dimension. And the way in which they contrast is similar to the contrast in reference: the Anaphor is necessarily referentially dependent, whereas the pronoun may or may not be; the Anaphor carries additional perspectival information, which the pronoun is unmarked for. In short, in both the referential and nonreferential contrasts, the Anaphor is informationally richer than the pronoun. This opens up the possibility that just as we have a Q-inference contrast from the use of the pronoun to the absence of conjoint reference that would have been signaled by an Anaphor in some loci, so we have a Q-inference in other loci from the use of the pronoun to the assumption that the perspective associated with the Anaphor is not intended. Let us examine the meaning difference in a little more detail.

The relevant meaning distinctions associated with LDAs were first noticed in connection with the logophoric pronouns and clitics of West African languages (Hagège 1974). Logophors are special expressions used in subordinate clauses to indicate coreferentiality with a matrix subject, but under specific conditions: usually the matrix verb must be a verb of saying or a verb of mental state, and thus the prototype context is of the sort 'John$_1$ said that *logophor*$_1$ would come', where the logophor may in some cases actually have evolved from a first-person pronoun. Hagège noted that the logophor encodes the subjective perspective of the participant, and noted the parallel to long-distance anaphora in languages like Japanese. In fact, recent work has shown that the similarities are far-reaching (Sells 1987; Stirling 1993: chap. 6), and we will return briefly to consider the distinctions between switch-reference systems, LDAs, and logophors. Logophors are licensed by specific semantic contexts—typically a verb, or complementizer associated with a verb, of communication, epistemic or mental state, or perception and what is clearly signaled is the perspective and subjective state of the protagonist, the so-called logocentric NP or antecedent, not the current speaker. Sells (1987) analyzes these semantic contexts in terms of three features: whether or not there is an internal, reported speaker or *source* of communication, whether or not there is an internal *self* whose mental state is described, and whether or not there is an internal *pivot* or relativized deictic center. The strongest logophoric contexts are those in which there is a text-internal source, self, and pivot, and the weakest are those in which there is only an internal pivot; intermediate are contexts in which there is an external source, but internal self and pivot (i.e., the external speaker reports the mental state and perspective of a protagonist). These contexts are forced by, respectively, verbs of communication, verbs of psychological attitude, and constructions (like verbs of perception) forcing the perspective of an internal protagonist. Logophoric languages appear to allow logophors progressively down this implicational scale (Stirling 1993: 259–260).

Just as in LDA, logophors and pronouns are not necessarily in complementary distribution with regards to reference: whereas the logophor must be coreferential with its antecedent (the so-called logocentric NP) a plain pronoun may or may not be. As Stirling (1993: 266–267) puts it:

In all languages in which such a contrast is possible, it is associated with a meaning distinction of a remarkably consistent kind: if the ordinary pronoun is used, it indicates that the speaker has assimilated the proposition being reported into her own scheme of things, and accepts its truth and/or approves of its content. If the logophoric pronoun is chosen, it indicates that the speaker has not assimilated the proposition into her knowledge base, and does not necessarily accept its truth or approve of its content: in some sense, responsibility for its truth, content or linguistic characterization is distanced, and left to the referent of the logophoric pronoun.

Not surprisingly, then, there are collocational constraints with evidentials (O'Connor 1993: 225f) and with mood (Stirling 1993). The subjective point of view associated with the logophor can be thought of as a complex feature [+logophoric] which is imposed by, or in concord with, such a feature associated with logophoric verbs, the feature being in turn characterized in terms of the atomic features source, self, and pivot mentioned above (Sells 1987; for a simpler alternative, see Stirling 1993: 282ff).

Long-distance Anaphors and logophors have a great deal in common, as was already noticed by Hagège (1974). First, the semantic constraints on LDAs and logophors appear to be very closely similar. For example, in Icelandic, the LDA *sig* occurs especially in subjunctive clauses, where the mood signals that the point of view is not the speaker's but that of the subject of the relevant verb, as evidenced by the deniability of the truth of the proposition (Stirling 1993: 268). Second, the perspectival distinctions associated with logophors versus pronouns also correctly predict many aspects of the distribution of LDAs versus pronominals (see, e.g., Kuno 1987, Sells 1987, Hellan 1991, and references therein for studies of Japanese, Korean, and Germanic long-distance anaphora). For example, the

Chinese LDA *ziji* appears to be very closely linked to logophoric contexts (Huang 1994: 187ff), occurring especially under verbs of saying and thinking or feeling, and just like the West African logophors, sometimes being triggered by complementizers derived from verbs of saying. Indeed, so close is the parallel that one may ask whether they are not in fact the same basic phenomenon, the main differences apparently being that whereas LDAs may usually be locally bound, logophors are usually in complementary distribution with locally bound reflexives (Stirling 1993: 259). Scholars in the Binding Theory tradition have also noted the parallels, but their reaction has been, for example, to distinguish between different uses of LDAs: (i) those uses of LDAs, subject to the Binding Theory, that have antecedents within the first finite clause, and (ii) those so-called logophoric uses that occur beyond this maximal extent of syntactic binding and are controlled by discourse factors (Reuland and Koster 1991: 22–24).[45] This retreat from a global structural theory is motivated by the fact that both LDAs and logophors can have their antecedents outside c-commanding positions, even outside the sentence altogether, and thus elsewhere in the discourse (see examples in Stirling 1993: 262–263; Huang 1994: 195; Mazuka and Lust 1994).

Let us return then to the pragmatic account. The proposal (which originates with O'Connor [1987]1993) should now be clear. Long-distance Anaphors have two essential semantic properties: first, they are always referentially dependent; second, they are logophoric. That these are conjunctive conditions is clear, from Kuno's (1987: 141) analysis of Icelandic LDAs, for example:

A reflexive pronoun can be used in a complement clause in Icelandic if it is coreferential with a [+logo−1] NP of the main clause *and* if the complement clause is an expression of the logophoric NP's point of view rather than the speaker's rendition of it

(where Kuno's [+logo−1] feature marks the source or self in Sells's terms). Both semantic features contrast with ordinary pronouns, which are unmarked for referential dependency and unmarked for logophoricity, or schematically:

(48) **LDAs**   **Pronouns**

  [+referential dependency]   [±referential dependency]
  [+logophoric]   [±logophoric]

We now have a privative opposition on two dimensions, and the use of the pronoun will indicate that the more informative LDA is being avoided, because one or the other of the features associated with the LDA does not apply—in other words, the conjunctive definition of the LDA yields a disjunctive Q-inference from the use of the pronoun. We may thus maintain the A-first analysis in all its essentials; we simply recognize that a Q-based contrast should be a contrast in informativeness, but it need not be a contrast in reference. Where the stronger item contrasts with the weaker expression in more than one way, then the use of the weaker form will be associated with avoidance of one or more of the contents of the stronger expression. Schematically, using English glosses where *self* stands for the LDA and *him* for the nonreflexive pronoun:

(49) a. i. 'John$_1$ likes self$_1$.'
           Coreference required by Condition A within an enlarged
           binding domain.
      ii. 'John$_1$ likes him$_2$.'
           Q-contrast with the LDA in reference
    b. i. 'John$_1$ says that self$_1$ will come.'
           Coreference required by Condition A within an enlarged
           binding domain.
      ii. 'John$_1$ says that he$_{1/2}$ will come.'
           Q-contrast with the LDA in logophoricity, plus or minus
           contrast in reference.

Such an account will also hold for genuine logophors, where the pronoun may implicate either disjoint reference or the adoption of the speaker's, rather than the protagonist's, point of view, thus exhibiting the pattern in (49b) (the pattern in (49a) is usually preempted by alternative short-range reflexives). It may also hold for switch-reference markers, which are again closely related to both logophors and LDAs.[46] Switch-reference systems are systems of (normally) verbal suffixing that indicate whether a (usually subordinate) clause has the same or different subject as the main clause; they are found in areal clusters in North America, Africa, New Guinea, Australia, and a few other locations (see Haiman and Munro 1983 for a collection of case studies, and Stirling 1993 for analysis and survey). In fact, a Gricean account of disjoint reference in switch-reference systems was independently proposed by O'Connor (1993) for Northern Pomo, which also has long-range reflexives. O'Connor noted that the long-range reflexives overlap in distribution with coreferentially interpreted pronouns, and she proposed the analysis we have just adopted, viz. that pronouns implicate a contrast either in reference or in logophoricity; but she went on to extend the account to switch-reference systems.

The reason to suspect pragmatic factors in switch-reference systems is that the different-subject marker (DS) often contrasts with the same-subject marker (SS) in ways other than just reference, and in these cases conjoint reference is possible with DS marking. Quite typically, the SS marker is associated with a sequence of actions performed by the same actor in proximate locations, so that it can be seen as one complex action (as in the gloss 'He went to the store and he bought-SS some whiskey'), following a pattern we have already associated with the I-principle—coreference is associated with cohesive interpretations. In line with this expectation, SS markers tend to be the relatively unmarked morphological option (sometimes zero) associated with sequentiality, whereas the more marked (morphologically complex) DS markers are associated with simultaneous actions by different actors (see Stirling 1993: 30–32). So far we have the familiar I- versus M-inference pattern, discussed at length in chapter 2, but apparently here fully grammaticalized. But there is also evidence in some switch-reference systems with overt SS marking for a privative opposition, with the DS marker actually unspecified for disjointness, but picking up that presumption by Q-inference. So we would have an opposition of the following kind (where the "single complex action" feature may be variously interpreted in different languages to involve same degree of agency, or close spatio-temporal cohesion):

(50) **SS marker**   **DS marker**
      [+referential dependence]   [±referential dependence]
      [+single complex action]   [±single complex action]

If this is correct, we would expect the disjointness of the DS marker to be defeasible, and in many languages this seems to be the case. Further, we would expect that there would be two main reasons to avoid the SS marker: either the two subjects are disjoint in reference, or the two actions do not form a single complex action, one action being less intentional or separated in space or time from the other. DS markers then implicate a disjunction, either disjoint reference or two distinct actions. Again, such cases of DS markers unexpectedly allowing coreference coupled with a contrast in action-coherence seem to be well attested, although the details are complex, and depend of course on the exact specification of the features built into the SS marker in particular languages (see Stirling 1993: 33–34, 50, 98–114, 150–153). In short, for some switch-reference systems with systematically opposed overt SS and DS markers, we may be able to maintain just the same kind of analysis as for LDAs and logophors—coreference is stipulated by the SS marker (in line with the A-first pragmatic analysis) and the DS-marker, which is semantically general, picks up its disjoint reference implications by pragmatic opposition (see O'Connor 1993 for a case, Nichols 1983 for discussion).

There are thus similarities between LDAs, logophors, and SS markers in switch-reference systems. This reopens the fundamental question, raised by Dowty (1980) and Reinhart (1983), but at first sight closed by the very existence of switch-reference systems, concerning whether we can state an important linguistic universal that holds that disjoint reference systems are never fully grammatically specified whereas coreference systems may be so. It seems in fact unlikely that this is an interesting property of Universal Grammar, unpredictable on other grounds. Rather, it is probably a tendency that follows on Zipfian grounds of functional economy: given a grammatical specification of the informationally richer pole, namely coreference, disjoint reference can be signaled by avoiding that grammatical construction.[47] Just as the fact that *some*, by Q-contrast to *all*, default implicates 'not all' and thus effectively blocks by redundancy the lexicalization of a new form **nall*, so the grammaticalization of Anaphors, logophors, and SS-markers may tend to make redundant the grammaticalization of systematic, specialized disjoint-reference mechanisms—existing terms in the privative opposition (between conjoint-reference marker and unspecified default) will do the job.[48] This is the logic of the A-first pragmatic account. On the other hand, given that these disjoint inferences from the weaker term of a privative opposition are generalized, this existing expression may well come to have its GCIs conventionalized over time, as arguably in switch-reference systems or indeed even in the Condition B behavior of English pronouns.

4.3.2.5.2   The Long-distance Uses of English Reflexives   Let us now return to the puzzles of English reflexives. Can we find meaning differences, similar to those associated with LDAs and logophors, between reflexives and pronouns when they can both occur in the same locus with a coreferential meaning (as in *John hid the book behind him/himself*)? Kuno (1987), marshalling a large number of earlier observations by Ross (1970), Cantrall (1974), and others, has argued vigorously that we can. For example, we noted above three classes of much examined cases where reflexives and pronouns have overlapping distribution (leaving aside the overlap of reciprocals and pronouns): locative PPs, picture-noun reflexives, and various emphatic contexts.[49] In each of these cases, Kuno points out that there are reasonably clear if subtle meaning differences between the corresponding sentences with pronouns or reflexives. For example, in those locative PPs that allow this alternation, the reflexives set up a protagonist's perspective on events, which is intuitively clear enough in (51a) but even makes a difference to truth conditions in (51b) (after Cantrall 1974, cited in Zribi-Hertz 1989: 704; see also Kuno 1987: 153).

(51) a. i. "He$_1$ pushed the brandy away from him$_1$."
            Gloss: observer "camera-angle"
      ii. "He$_1$ pushed the brandy away from himself$_1$."
            Gloss: protagonist's "camera-angle"
  b. i. "The women$_1$ were standing in the background with the children behind them$_1$."
            Gloss: observer's perspective, with children beyond the women
      ii. "The women$_1$ were standing in the background with the children behind themselves$_1$."
            Gloss: women's perspective, with children at their backs

Similarly, the picture-noun reflexive cases also reveal a clear meaning difference between the reflexive and the pronoun (Kuno 1987: 126, 174), often rather subtle consequences of the subjective point of view associated with the reflexive, as in (52a). Consequently there are collocational constraints, where the sentential context makes it difficult to take the perspective of the protagonist referred to with the reflexive, as in (52b).

(52) a. i. "John$_1$ heard some strange gossip about him$_1$ on the radio."
            Gloss: "strange" in the estimation of the speaker
      ii. "John$_1$ heard some strange gossip about himself$_1$ on the radio."
            Gloss: "strange" in the estimation of John
  b. i. "Mary told John that there was a picture of himself in the post office."
      ii. ??"Mary said about John that there was a picture of himself in the post office."

The so-called emphatic reflexives reveal a similar pattern (see Zribi-Hertz 1989: 698f for further examples and references), with the protagonist perspective associated with the reflexive often engendering presumptions of restrictive exclusivity:

(53) a. "John₁ believes the letter was sent to him₁ and Mary."
     Gloss: observer perspective: the letter was also perhaps sent to
     others

   b. "John₁ believes the letter was sent to himself₁ and Mary."
     Gloss: participant perspective: letter not sent to others

To see that these rather subtle semantic factors are robust enough to
engender collocational constraints with other perspectival indicators,
consider the following pairs:

(54) a.   "John is happy that Anne has come so far to see himself."
   b. ??"John is happy that Anne has gone so far to see himself."
        Deixis not relativized to John's point of view.

(55) a.   "According to John, the paper was written by Anne and
          himself."
   b. ??"Speaking of John, the paper was written by Anne and
          himself."
        Antecedent embedded in observer-perspective phrase.

(56) a.   "John said frankly that Anne was infatuated with himself."
   b. ??"John said apparently that Anne was infatuated with himself."
        Observer-perspective associated with evidential *apparently*

(57) a.   "The Prime Minister₁ was worried that *The Sun* would publish
          that damn compromising memo about himself₁."
        Reflexive collocates with positive psych-verb and expletive
        determiners

   b. ??"The Prime Minister₁ was unaware that *The Sun* would publish
          the compromising memo about himself₁."
        Negative psych-verb and absence of other perspectival markers
        suggests observer perspective

Note too that, because a portion of discourse must maintain only *one* internal, subjective viewpoint, we have a natural account of why we cannot
easily have two Anaphors with distinct reference in the same sentence
(Zribi-Hertz 1989: 713ff; Pollard and Sag 1992: 275) as in ??*John traded
Mary pictures of herself for pictures of himself.*[50]

   Zribi-Hertz (1989), utilizing a textual database, shows that there is little
reason to resist the conclusion that English reflexives exhibit LDA behavior. The intuitions of clause-boundedness for English Anaphors come
about, she claims (1989: 722–723), because a clause is the minimal point-
of-view domain, and when we present an isolated clause we assume that

this corresponds to such a domain. Hence although *Jane is speaking only to himself* is ungrammatical in isolation, it is fine when embedded with an appropriate antecedent, as in *John hopes that Jane is speaking only to himself*. Anaphors must be bound in this point-of-view domain and may occur long-distance bound only if the antecedent is the closest "subject of consciousness"—that is, the protagonist from whose subjective point of view affairs are presented (only when locally bound can Anaphors combine with an objective point of view, on this account). Zribi-Hertz seems to presume that these semantic conditions exhaust the constraints on the long-distance uses. She also points out that there is an intrinsic connection between the endophoricity, or obligatory referential dependency, of reflexives and logophoricity (1989: 724): "reflexive pronouns serve the *internal* narrative point of view and they are bound *within* some structural domain" in which this point of view is systematically maintained.[51]

If we then assimilate the English cases of overlapping distribution of pronoun and reflexive to the same kind of phenomenon exhibited in LDA generally, we have most of the basic ingredients of an implicatural account of the patterns.[52] The A-first account gives us the complementary distribution of pronouns and reflexives by Q-implicature where it occurs, essentially where antecedent and reflexive are co-arguments, or at least clausemates. To account for the long-range uses of English reflexives, Condition A of the Binding Theory would need to be extended; Kuno (1987) offers many rather specific structural conditions that could be added to Condition A with a wider domain, whereas Zribi-Hertz, as just mentioned, offers rather simple semantic constraints on logophoricity which can be set up to override the restrictions of Condition A. Either way, a syntactico-semantic set of constraints could predict the long-range occurrences of the reflexive.[53] Once again, then, wherever we can have a reflexive in these long-distance environments, the use of a pronoun will contrast; but because the reflexive is marked for both referential dependency and logophoricity (or internal perspective), the contrast need not be in terms of reference. And in the long-distance uses, the contrast is now between a subjective versus objective point of view, or schematically:

(58) *Q-contrast in coreference, rather than logophoricity*
   a. "John was speaking to himself."
      Coreferential by Binding Condition A
   b. "John was speaking to him."
      Disjoint by Q-implicature

(59) *Q-contrasts in logophoricity, rather than reference*
   a. "John hoped that Anne would speak to himself."
      Coreferential and logophoric by an extended Condition A
   b. "John hoped that Anne would speak to him."
      Nonlogophoric by Q-contrast
      Coreferential by presumptive I-inference

It is clear that there is one major residual problem for the pragmatic account of LDA generally. It is to explain why, given that the reflexive encodes both coreference and logophoricity, the contrast in reference is dominant where the pronoun could have a clausemate antecedent, and the contrast in logophoricity is dominant elsewhere.[54] If reflexives with LDA uses are in general marked [+logophoric, +referential dependence], then avoidance of the reflexive with a pronoun should be interpreted as either a contrast in reference, or logophoricity, or both. Yet in the clause-bound cases, the contrast always seems to be one of reference *simpliciter*, and with long-distance antecedents, the contrast generally seems to be one of logophoricity (although it may be one of reference, too).

There seem to be essentially two lines of possible explanation here. On the one hand, one may claim, in a line following Bouchard (1983) through to Pollard and Sag (1994), that true reflexives are restricted to those with clausemate antecedents, whereas all long-distance bound reflexives are essentially pronouns of a special contrastive sort that happen to be homophonous with real Anaphors; we turn to this view in section 4.3.2.5.3. On the other hand, one may attempt to find an additional pragmatic factor that would explain the overriding concern with reference within the clause. In the second half of this chapter, I will show that such an additional factor (to be labeled the DRP) is independently motivated by the existence of languages without conventionalized Anaphors at all: such languages exhibit a preference for the reading of clausemate (co-argument) NPs as disjoint. But because such languages have no grammatical Anaphors, this can only be a default presumption, and thus a pragmatic principle and not a reflex of a universal Condition B. It turns out that these languages are also relevant to understanding languages like English that conform to the A-first pattern—English indeed is diachronically derived from such a language. This additional pragmatic principle, of presumed disjointness of arguments, ultimately involves superseding the A-first approach with a more complex, diachronically laminated account of the pragmatics of anaphora. Meanwhile, one can see that the existence of such a principle is exactly what is needed to complete the above account: clausemate NPs will be presumed disjoint in reference unless marked as reflexive, and a pronoun will therefore be interpreted as motivated in order to Q-contrast in reference; whereas outside the clause of the antecedent, an LDA can more openly be interpreted as either contrasting in logophoricity or reference or both. Before pursuing this, however, we turn initially to the first option given above.

4.3.2.5.3 *LDAs as Homophonous with, but Distinct from, Real Anaphors*

Condition A of the Binding Theory, in any of Chomsky's formulations, requires that the Anaphor be bound by an antecedent at close range. It follows that all sorts of reflexives in English, like the following, are simply not Anaphors on this approach:

(60) a. "John said the paper was written by Ann and himself."
   b. "John wanted the photo taken with Ann in front of himself."
   c. "The college president thought that Bacon's picture of himself was unattractive."
   d. "The picture of himself in the commonroom bothered the college president."

Some go further and think that true Anaphors are more restricted still, so that picture-noun reflexives, as in *John found a picture of himself*, are really pseudo-Anaphors (Pollard and Sag 1992, following, e.g., Postal 1974) and thus that Chomsky's (1986) efforts to extend slightly the binding domain for Anaphors were mistaken. True Anaphors, on this line, are co-arguments with their antecedents, and all other uses of reflexives are homophonous pseudo-Anaphors ("exempt anaphors" in Pollard and Sag's terminology). The reason for abandoning the line, for example, that picture NPs are real Anaphors is that acceptability appears to be governed by gradient pragmatic or processing factors—subjects intervening between the antecedent and the anaphor are acceptable the less animate and referential they are:

(61) a. ??"Bill$_1$ remembered that John saw a picture of himself$_1$ in the police station."
   b. ?"Bill$_1$ remembered that *The Times* carried a picture of himself$_1$."
   c. "Bill$_1$ remembered that nothing could make a picture of himself$_1$ look respectable."

Pollard and Sag (1994: 269) attribute this to processing factors, but equally we have an explanation in terms of the I-principle preferring the most local plausible antecedent. A second factor governing the occurrence of pseudo-Anaphors is the logophoricity requirement already reviewed in detail. An increasing number of scholars seem prepared to consider LDAs to be in general pseudo-Anaphors, subject to pragmatic constraints rather than the Binding Conditions (see, e.g., Koster 1994, Mazuka and Lust 1994)—but they do not develop the pragmatic analysis that would then be required.

If this line is correct, we have a natural explanation of the way that the Q-inferences from pronouns divide into disjointness-inferences for co-arguments and a wider disjunctive inference, to either disjointness or antilogophoricity, in long-range uses of reflexives. The clausebound, co-argument (nonreflexive) pronouns are in Q-contrast with true Anaphors, which must be bound by a coargument; pronouns elsewhere may be in Q-contrast with quite different lexical items, namely pseudo-Anaphors, with referential dependence and logophoric implications. Such a line would also have some support (unnoted by Pollard and Sag) from languages where reflexivity is indicated by a marked verbal form that indicates that two of its arguments are coreferential (see Faltz 1985)—here reflexivity must be about co-arguments. The whole Pollard and Sag (1992, 1994) approach, which is based on a nonconfigurational version of the Binding Conditions within a different grammatical framework (HPSG), can be made to dovetail with the pragmatic account just as well as those more directly in the Chomskyan tradition.

However, there are some good reasons to resist this approach to English. The first is methodological: as Zribi-Hertz (1989: 721) puts it, considering the same option, "First-year students in linguistics already know, however, that the homonymy solution should be regarded as a last resort—a bad solution per se, a 'desperate' strategy." Why should there be two sets of reflexives, with exactly the same members, the same obligatory referential dependency, but different binding constraints? The second reason for skepticism is that long-distance-bound reflexives occur also in core argument positions, not just adjuncts, so that the distinction between real and pseudo-Anaphors becomes more definitional than observational. Indeed, Pollard and Sag (1992: 278–279) are forced to suggest that many well-attested uses of such reflexives are just ungrammatical, but acceptable in prose.[55] Clearly, if this line is to be pursued, we need independent evidence for the distinction between real and pseudo-Anaphors (i.e., good tests that rest on other than binding-domain factors). Meanwhile, we shall continue to explore the alternative line that attempts to unify an account of reflexives and seeks a further pragmatic factor to explain the special concern with coreference versus disjointness within the clause.

4.3.2.5.4 *Conclusions to the A-First Pragmatic Analysis* In the first part of this chapter we explored the idea that grammatical principles need only state the conditions for the binding of Anaphors. Nearly all systematic disjointness conditions, specifically the sort of constraint specified in Binding Conditions B and C, would follow by pragmatic "mirror image" from the kind of binding principle exemplified in the various versions of Condition A. This would follow by principles of economy: unmarked pronouns pick up the disjoint meaning by Q-contrast to reflexives wherever they might have been employed. Meanwhile, pronouns and full lexical NPs tend to contrast in reference because of the I-inference to coreference from minimal expressions associated with pronouns, and the M-contrast to disjointness that then arises where a pronoun might have been used but a full referring expression was used instead. Hence the general contrastive behavior of reflexives, pronouns, and lexical NPs with respect to anaphoric linkage.

Such an approach has none of the inexactness of most functional explanations: whatever syntactic and semantic conditioning there is on the occurrence of Anaphors will get reflected into the pragmatic account of the behavior of pronouns. If the distribution of Anaphors was accounted for solely in terms of their lexical properties (and their necessary referential dependence in particular), there would be little motivation for maintaining an A-first account (for some languages, this may be the case; see Huang 1994 on Chinese). But insofar as there are three terms involved—antecedent, Anaphor, and binding domain defined in syntactic or semantic terms—an A-first account is well motivated (see Hellan 1991 for an interesting typology of different kinds of domain constraints). On the other hand, while making precise predictions, the pragmatic account does allow for principled defeasibility, which a syntactic account of the Binding Conditions variety will never be able to explain.

The A-first style of account is not restricted to any specific kind of grammatical framework. Modern approaches vary in various profound ways: some theories aim for maximum coverage of reflexive distributions whereas others distinguish real from pseudo-Anaphors (which are then disregarded); some theories presume configurational constraints whereas others argue that they are based on hierarchies of thematic or grammatical relations; some theories cut the pie differently, into bound-variable anaphora versus referential dependencies, for example, rather than into Anaphors versus pronouns; some theories bring meaning differences (like logophoricity) into the account, others do not. Pronominalization and anaphora were among the earliest subjects to be explored in generative grammar, and after 40 years of intensive research there is still no adequate explanation of all the phenomena nor any consensus about where it may yet be found. I believe that the failure to take into account the systematic contribution of a theory of generalized pragmatic inference is a substantial reason why further progress has not been made. A theory of GCIs can interdigitate with any of these frameworks, reapportioning some predictions from the syntax to the pragmatics and offering some handle on the unexplained residue of defeasible patterns. In each case, however, the corresponding pragmatic predictions will be different and worth investigating as indirect evidence for or against the different syntactic approaches. The overall power of the resulting theory, with the syntax and the pragmatics working in tandem, is certain to be considerably better than any of the purely syntactic accounts taken on their own. I have sketched in passing how for each of the discussed frameworks the pragmatics might be put to work.

The major challenge to an A-first account is undoubtedly the failure of complementarity of pronouns and reflexives (i.e., their overlap in certain loci as potentially linked to the same antecedent). We have gone to some effort to establish that the pragmatic account does not necessarily break down on account of this. Pragmatic contrasts can be on various dimensions, and where an Anaphor encodes perspectival information as well as referential dependency, the contrast with a pronoun can as well be in terms of the logophoric dimension. However, unless we buy the distinction between Anaphors and pseudo-Anaphors, we clearly do need an explanation of why the contrast is nearly always in terms of reference just in the clausebound cases, whereas in the long-range binding cases the contrast is either in terms of logophoricity or reference or both.

4.3.3   The B-First Account, with a Pragmatic Reduction of Binding Conditions A and C[56]

Let us now explore a radical alternative to the preceding account which has taken Condition A of the Binding Theory as a basic rule of grammar, and has developed pragmatic reductions of Conditions B and C as parasitic on Condition A. In this alternative, we shift the center of the account and make the Condition B pattern basic and derive Conditions A and C as pragmatic derivatives. Such an alternative account seems better suited to certain languages, and because the account uses the same pragmatic apparatus, there is no theoretical inconsistency between our *A-first* and what we may call a *B-first* account. In either case, any one language (now being thought of as a sociolinguistic entity) should be treated as having stabilized a particular pattern of anaphoric interpretation as basic, as the conceptual anchorage for the rest of the system. This stabilized core (whether Condition A-like or Condition B-like) is then subject to our familiar Q-, I-, and M-inferences, yielding "for free" the rest of the system. What determines this kind of pragmatic parametrization is historical process, and in the end I shall argue that A-first languages tend to exhibit residues of a B-first stage, thus showing that there is no radical discontinuity between these types.

Here is how a B-first account might be developed. The starting point is a stabilized pattern of interpretation where clausemate NPs are preferentially interpreted as distinct in reference. This could be thought of as a matter of grammatical stipulation—Condition B or C as part of Universal Grammar surfacing as an inferential presumption. Against that, whereas Condition A is often thought to display parametric variation in the size of the binding domain, there is little evidence that Condition B behaves in the same way (specifically, the exclusion domain tends to remain strictly local; see Harbert 1995: 194–195). Second, as we have seen, the B-pattern is defeasible. Thus the core B-like pattern could itself be pragmatically motivated. Farmer and Harnish (1987), for example, advance a pragmatic presumption as the basic datum for pronominal anaphora; they propose a pragmatic Disjoint Reference Presumption (DRP), which holds that "the arguments of a predicate are intended to be disjoint, unless marked otherwise" (1987: 557). The origin of such a pragmatic presumption is left unclear on their account, but we may perhaps be able to relate it to the GCI framework. Under a classification of actions of central human interest, agents normally act upon entities other than themselves; the prototypical action—what is described by the prototypical transitive clause—is one agent acting upon some entity distinct from itself. If that is how the world stereotypically is, then an interpretation of an arbitrary transitive sentence as having referentially distinct arguments is given to us by the I-principle, which encourages and warrants an interpretation to the stereotype. Note that this is not some kind of behaviorist presumption that the statistical preponderance of nonreflexive states of affairs, or even linguistic statements, is inductively learned and then reflected unwittingly in pragmatic presumption. The I-principle is a principle of default interpretation, which capitalizes on the underspecification of linguistic meaning together with mutual beliefs about regularities in the world to yield rich interpretations as hypotheses about utterance-meaning. It thrives on mutual assumptions of mutual orientation to stereotypes (i.e., on complex mental constructs), not behaviorist response.

In language typology, crosslinguistic tendencies are used to suggest, for example, a universal markedness hierarchy, so that Agents are prototypically animate and Patients inanimate—the *Ur*-act, as it were, is somebody doing an action to something—with deviations from these expectations progressively marked (Comrie 1981: 120ff). The same reasoning applied to reflexivity would set up a universal prototype or tendency where Agents doing things to disjoint referents is the unmarked expectation, any deviations being marked either by formal or pragmatic means (cf. a similar presumption in Reinhart and Reuland 1993). Because this tendency is not reflected in all languages by special morphology or syntax, but in some languages may be merely reflected in patterns of use, it is plausible that it is due to extralinguistic principles rather than innate ideas or Universal Grammar.

There will be those who are skeptical. As Zribi-Hertz (1995) puts it, criticizing the use of the DRP by Huang (1994), "What criteria do we have to decide what is 'more 'natural' than what? If we don't have any independent test for 'naturalness,' the DRP is nothing but a clone of Principle B." But there are signs of naturalness—namely, the fact that it is reflexive statements, not the nonreflexive ones, that are the linguistically marked alternative in all languages that mark reflexivity at all. Second, the DRP is only a defeasible tendency, so it is distinct in kind from a grammatical stipulation like Condition B. Still, the critic may point to the fact that some actions are stereotypically reflexive, like brushing one's teeth, bathing, and so on. But here, interestingly, languages often do recognize the special character of such stereotypically reflexive actions. In Frisian, for example, it is just these predicates that allow the use of the normal pronoun for self-reference rather than the reflexive or emphatic form (thus one says *Willem*₁ *wasket him*₁ not **Willem*₁ *wasket himsels*₁ for 'William washes himself', Reuland 1994: 239; the same was true in

Middle English, see Faltz 1985: 242). In this case the unmarked pronoun indicates the stereotypical situation, irrespective of whether one or two agents are involved. However, because the DRP is the normal presumption, languages more often indicate stereotypical reflexive (or so-called introverted) predicates in a way that signals both their departure from the DRP and their stereotypical status: as a strong crosslinguistic tendency, introverted predicates occur with a null or reduced reflexive marking (Haiman 1985a: 168–174), as in English "He put a coat on __" (or as in the "weak" reflexives of the Germanic languages, discussed below). Here the reduced form picks up the stereotype in line with the I-principle, and the special marking indicates deviation from the DRP. This special treatment of such exceptional predicates as shaving, bathing, dressing, adorning, and so on—in accord with their stereotypical expectations of reflexive action but in contrast to the DRP—is interesting indirect evidence in favor of the pragmatic nature of the DRP, as based on stereotypical expectations for disjoint arguments with regard to the majority of transitive predicates.

Still, the critic may point out that reflexivity in many languages is not confined to core arguments of transitives, as in so-called raising contexts like *John revealed himself to be a Mason*. The response here is that the DRP is only a small part of an explanatory apparatus, which cannot predict all the loci that a specific language will treat as requiring reflexivization. In English, the DRP plays only a small part in explaining the patterns (namely, it predicts where pronoun and reflexive firmly contrast in reference), which at least as far as Anaphors are concerned are firmly grammaticalized.

Huang (1991, 1994: 130) notes that there are potential problems for the neo-Gricean theory if the DRP is taken to be given to us by the I-principle. Although there are good reasons, already reviewed in chapter 2, for taking the priority of $Q > M > I$ inferences to regulate implicature projection, there are no worked out principles regulating, say, the relative priority of subtypes of I-inference. But if the DRP follows from the I-principle, and the preference for local coreference of reduced forms also follows from the I-principle, the two will often be in conflict, unless we recognize that the preference for coreference operates only beyond the clause. Huang therefore entertains the conjecture that the DRP should be thought of as part of our background presumptions about the world, which would then, as always, override default implicatures. That, however, has problems of its own: as we shall see, the origin of many reflexives lies in the use of emphatic particles, presumably because these are a natural way of M-implicating that the DRP doesn't obtain. In that case, the DRP itself must be cancelable by a higher-ranking inference type, and all this fits with the assumption that the DRP is I-implicated, with M-implicatures taking priority over I-implicatures in the usual way.[57]

But whatever the exact source of the DRP, once we presume it, we can then derive the Condition A pattern this way. First note that reflexives are marked forms; if they are pronoun-like in grammatical category, they tend to be longer, more morphologically complex than ordinary pronouns (cf. *himself* with *him*); if reflexivity is encoded on the verb, then the verbal morphology is marked (Faltz 1985). Thus, what the marked, prolix forms indicate is that the normal, stereotypical scenario associated with a transitive clause does not in fact obtain—notice is served by M-implicature that the I-inference to the stereotype is not intended. If the stereotype is disjoint reference for arguments, then the M-implicature is (by Horn's 1984 division of pragmatic labor) to the complement of that interpretation, namely to coreference. Hence (given that, by our projection rules for implicatures, M-implicatures cancel any rival I-implicatures) we derive the Condition A-like pattern for marked pronouns, so-called Anaphors.

It remains to account for the Condition C-like pattern. Here the account is familiar. Where a pronoun is in a lower clause and thus not a clausemate with another NP (thus the pragmatic Condition B-like DRP is not in play), as in *He thinks that he should come*, there will be nothing to prevent the I-implicated tendency to coreference (assuming matched agreement features, etc.). But if, just where such a pronoun would so implicate coreference, a marked form (in this case a lexical referring expression) is employed instead, as in *He thinks that John should come*, then again we get the complementary M-interpretation, this time to disjoint reference.

Thus, to recapitulate: the sentence in (62a) below is interpreted with disjoint arguments in line with the (I-induced) stereotype "clausemate arguments are distinct"; the marked form of the pronoun in (62b) warns (M-implicates) "contrary to stereotype," and because M-implicatures override I-implicatures, we obtain a conjoint interpretation. The pronoun in (62c), on the other hand, does not fall under the presumption of clausemate disjointness because the only potential antecedent is in another clause; the pronoun is unmarked, so there is nothing to stop the I-preference for coreferentiality of reduced forms going through. In (62d), by contrast, the use of a full lexical NP suggests (M-implicates) that whatever might have been implicated by the use of the pronoun is being avoided and thus that the complement of the interpretation in (62c) (now disjointness) is intended.

(62) a. "John likes him."   (disjoint by DRP)
     b. "John likes himself."   (conjoint by M)
     c. "John said he went."   (conjoint by I)
     d. "John said the boy went." (disjoint by M)

There is considerable evidence of different kinds in favor of a B-first pragmatic analysis of this kind for at least certain languages. One kind of support comes from typological evidence for a widespread association of reflexives and emphatics—in language after language, the reflexive seems to be homophonous with an emphatic particle or affix (Moravcsik 1972, Langacker and Munro 1975).[58] For example, just as in English we have the emphatic use of the reflexive pronoun in (63a), compared to the reflexive use as in (63b), so in, for example, Tamil we have the emphatic particle in (63c) homophonous with the root of the reflexive pronoun in (63d).

(63) a. "She herself will come."
     b. "She hit herself."
     c. Ava-taan   varuva.
        she-EMPH will come.
        'she herself will come.'
     d. Ava taan-e   aicca.
        she   self-ACC hit.
        'she hit herself.'

The B-first account predicts this of course; on that account, "anaphors" are just pronouns marked in such a way that they will trigger an M-implicature to the complement of the normal interpretation—if clausemate co-arguments are normally disjoint, a marked pronoun will M-implicate coreference. The contrastive, emphatic particle or affix does the job nicely. Note that many languages have two or more reflexive Anaphors—for example, the Germanic languages typically have two reflexive forms, cognate with German weak reflexive *sich* and strong reflexive *sich selbst* (see Reuland and Koster 1991). It is the strong reflexives that tend to occur with clausemate antecedents, and the weak ones with long-distance antecedents, except that they also occur locally bound with inherently reflexive (introverted) verbs. Note that this fits the DRP-based prediction rather well: emphatic reflexives occur intraclausally where a marked alternative to the DRP-based assumption of disjoint reference is required; where in fact there is a stereotypical presumption of an agent acting on himself (as in many inherently reflexive verbs), the emphatic reflexive may not be required.[59]

What is being offered here is, of course, a very simple explanation for the oft-noted overlap between reflexive and emphatic forms. That overlap is sufficiently salient that there have been a number of attempts to try and explain it. In the heyday of Generative Semantics there were attempts for example to derive *John himself came* from *John, he came* (Moyne 1971) or *John—John's own self—came* (Cantrall 1973; see Jayaseelan 1988 for a revival). There have also been careful and interesting attempts to characterize the exact semantic/pragmatic import of the intensifier use of reflexive forms; thus Moravcsik (1972) distinguishes a head-bound use (as in *John himself came*) from an adverbial use (*John came himself*), and Edmondson and Plank (1978) suggest the first has to do with a pragmatic scale (in the sense of Fauconnier 1975) of unexpectedness, the second with a scale of direct agency or experience.[60] Philosophers, too, have speculated on the meaning of phrases like *He himself*, Hintikka (1970) for example claiming that the intensifier rules out an intensional (or attributive) interpretation, Geach (1972) that it translates a first-person pronoun into a form appropriate for indirect speech (cf. the discussion of logophoricity above). All of this is usefully reviewed by Edmondson and Plank (1978) and König (1991), but summarizing the semantico-pragmatic effects of the intensifier uses of reflexive forms, we may note that (a) there is a contrastive, contrary-to-expectation element; (b) there is a natural negative gloss, of the sort 'and not anyone else', 'and not the more expectable persons', and so on; (c) the intensifier often plays a role in reference, by forcing a particular coreferential interpretation of a pronoun;[61] (d) the intensifier could often be replaced with like effect by stress; and (e) issues of scope arise according to placement. All of these features are compatible with, indeed explained by, an account in terms of M-implicature and Horn's (1984) division of pragmatic labor (i.e., in my terms, the complementarity of I-implicatures and M-implicatures). M-implicatures, by picking out the complementary interpretation to the stereotypical I-based interpretation that would have been generated by the use of simple unmarked form, naturally give rise to contrary-to-stereotype, negative interpretations. It is left open on this account that the contrast intended may be either one of unexpectedness or point of view, on the one hand, or one of reference, on the other. That contrastive stress might do exactly the same job is likewise explained—for all the intensification of the NP is doing is warning of a marked interpretation. Thus simple though it is, the B-first account of the overlap between reflexive pronouns and emphatic intensifiers modifying pronouns has much to recommend it.

There is more general evidence for the use of marked forms to indicate marked, reflexive, interpretations. In those languages, like many Australian ones, where the reflexive is signaled by a special verb form, that verb form is a marked form. In languages like Guugu Yimithirr (Haviland 1979, Levinson 1987a, b) this special verb form does not directly encode reflexivity but only indicates directly that one argument is missing. There is a pragmatic inference in many cases to the reflexive. But this can be further reinforced by the use of an emphatic affix which then makes the reflexive or reciprocal reading central:

(64) Bama-gu   gunda-dhi.
     the people(ABS)-EMPH hit-ANTIPASSIVE
     'The people hit each other.'
     'The people hit themselves.'
     'Someone hit the people.'

Thus in languages which currently lack, but which seem to be in the process of acquiring, fully grammaticalized, unequivocal Anaphors, we can find the same association between markedness and reflexive readings.

A third closely related kind of evidence for the B-first account is the diachronic fact that reflexives seem in many cases to have derived from emphatic or contrastive forms, even if there is no longer a homophonous corresponding emphatic particle or affix. This seems to be the case with Tamil *taan* or Chinese *ziji*, for example, and I discuss the history of English reflexives in detail. But the most persuasive kind of evidence for the B-first analysis comes from consideration of languages that lack Anaphors altogether. As noted, such languages obviously cannot support an A-first analysis. It is therefore crucial to see what patterns of anaphora they exhibit.

4.3.3.1 Languages without Reflexives   There are scattered reports from around the world of languages that do not directly code reflexivity. Such languages seem to have been largely ignored by grammatical theorists even though they would appear to be crucial evidence against the centrality of the binding apparatus.[62] It is not yet clear just how common the

are distinct in reference; any marked form raises some possible doubt about this, and so it is the normal way to express coreference if intended. Apparently, the same holds for the expression of the reciprocal relationship, although there are also intransitive roots and so on that can also be used to express this.

Kilivila, another Austronesian language, is a clear example of a language without dedicated reflexives; again a normal transitive verb is used, but with one of a series of emphatic pronouns in addition to the subject (Senft 1986: 54ff, personal communication):[64]

(67) m-to-na   e-wai titole-la.
     Dem-CPman-Dem 3-beat self–3.Poss.ProIV
     'This man beats himself' or 'This man beats (someone).'

The emphatic pronoun *titolela* (or equally from another series *alama-guta*), built on a possessive pronoun suffix *-la* (or possessive prefix *ala*) plus an emphatic particle, is construed as referring to the subject, but either as an emphatic adjunct to the subject or as object of the verb. There is no formal means to distinguish the readings. Yet another, distantly related, Austronesian language, Tahitian, apparently follows the same sort of pattern (Tryon 1970: 97). To express the reflexive, one can only use the pronoun:

(68) 'ua ha'opohe 'oia 'iana.
     was kill   he   him
     'He killed himself' or 'He killed him.'

But there is an emphatic affix *iho*, which when added to the pronoun seems to be the standard way to express the reciprocal meaning.

An Austronesian language that has been the subject of some detailed GB work is Chamorro (Chung 1989). Chung notes (1989: 148ff) that Anaphors and pronominals are morphologically identical just as in Fijian, although the reflexive interpretation can be forced by an optional adverb *maisa* (glossed as 'by oneself'). However, she goes on to argue that two grammatical constraints are sensitive to the coindexing of NPs within minimal governing categories, and therefore that Chamorro quasi-pronominals are in effect ambiguous ("morphologically syncretic"), distinguished into Anaphors and pronominals at the syntactic level. However, it is hard to see how this can be made an empirical proposition, given that whenever a proform is locally bound, it can be claimed to be a covert Anaphor, and where not, a pronominal. Additionally, a peculiar consequence of taking these constraints to be syntactic criteria for covert Anaphors is that the same criteria then identify NP-trace and PRO as non-Anaphors (p. 173ff). It seems to me then that it may be preferable to treat the special constraints on Chamorro pronominals construed reflexively as semantic. For example, there seems to be a syntactic filter banning any third-person-plural subject of a normal transitive clause, unless subject and object are coreferential. But the exception is surely based on the natural semantic conception of reflexive clauses as quasi-intransitive, as shown in the worldwide association of middle verb forms with reflexivity both synchronically and diachronically (see, e.g., Geniušienė, 1987). The second constraint likewise gives no real support to a syntactic distinction between Anaphor and pronominal.[65] In any case, Chamorro is clearly a language where a single set of pronominals does double duty as a set of reflexive and nonreflexive pronouns, as seems to be so often the case in the Austronesian family.

4.3.3.1.3 Creoles[66]   A third and diverse group of languages that seem to generally lack Anaphors are the pidgins and creoles of all origins. These languages have recently been surveyed by Carden and Stewart (1986, 1988, 1990) to see to what extent the Binding Conditions adequately describe their anaphoric patterns. They point out that the issue is rather interesting from the point of view of the Bioprogram hypothesis advanced by Bickerton (1981); if the Binding Conditions are innate, and if pidgins upon creolizing should reveal the essential stripped-down properties of human language, then we might expect to find the Binding Conditions rapidly instantiated upon creolization. This is not, however, at all what was found in the survey. Instead, the evidence seems to show both that pidgins and creoles tend to lack Anaphors and that they tend to lack a grammaticalized Binding Condition B (pronouns obligatorily disjoint with clausemate antecedents). I repeat a selection of their findings.

Carden and Stewart (1986, 1988) report that in the Northern dialect of Haitian Creole the ordinary pronouns may be used as reflexives:

(69) a. Emile dwe   ede li.
        Emile₁ should help him₁/₂ (can be coreferential)
        'Emile should help him/himself.'
     b. Emile dwe   ede tèt-a-li (*or* kò-a-li).
        Emile should help himself (must be coreferential)
        'Emile should help himself.'

They note that the literal meanings of *tèt* ('head') and *kò* ('body') play a role in the choice between these reflexive forms and that *tèt* is used as an emphatic focusing particle as in *tèt-Emile* ('it was Emile himself'). They conclude from this that the Northern dialect of the creole can be treated as an earlier, less grammaticalized stage of the creole. Historical data seems to support this—the earliest materials provide plenty of evidence for the use of the plain pronouns as reflexives but little or no evidence for the specialized reflexive forms. The implication is that the earliest forms of Haitian Creole (pre-1800) had no reflexives; the later reflexives based on body-part metaphors may be due either to ultimate (African) substrate sources or just as likely to independent invention.

Other creoles also evidence no reflexive forms, such as the Spanish-based Palenquero (Carden and Stewart 1986: 24, 199), French-based Guadeloupe, and Arabic-based KiNubi, not to mention various pidgins including Chinese pidgin English and early Chinook Jargon (Carden and Stewart 1990: 5). Moreover, perhaps half of all Creole lects allow the reflexive use of clausemate pronouns (1986: n. 58; Carden and Stewart 1987: 23ff exemplify from, e.g., Martinique Creole, Chinook Jargon, Bislama, KiNubi, Negerhollands). Corne (1988) shows that Mauritian Creole uses the ordinary pronouns as reflexives in the unmarked case, even though it has reflexive forms (although Corne believes this use of pronouns to be a post-creole innovation, Carden and Stewart (1989) reanalyze the historical material to argue that this use of the pronouns is derived from the original pidginization process).

Comparison leads Carden and Stewart to hypothesize a diachronic sequence in creole languages (I here generalize from their 1986 discussion of Haitian Creole):

(a) *Stage 1:* no encoded reflexives; plain pronouns used reflexively
(b) *Stage 2:* gradual emergence of morphological reflexives (e.g., based on body-part metaphors) with a clausemate, subject-antecedent condition, coexisting with but encroaching upon the use of ordinary pronouns as reflexives
(c) *Stage 3:* the loss of the reflexive use of the ordinary pronouns

One point that they draw special attention to is that the tolerant treatment of pronouns as possible reflexives is not a feature that is by any means lost abruptly (surviving some hundreds of years in some dialects of the Haitian Creole), as might be expected if Condition B were part of the Bioprogram that would assert itself immediately upon the acquisition of native speakers, in other words upon creolization of the original pidgin. The gradual nature of the change towards a typologically unmarked system (with reflexives and Condition B-like patterns) argues either against Bickerton's (1981) idea that creolization should reveal the Bioprogram in the raw as it were, or against the idea that the Binding Conditions are core elements of that Bioprogram.

Carden and Stewart also note the parallels in language acquisition, pointing out that this supports the idea that creole patterns are tied closely to patterns in first-language acquisition. Studies by Solan (1987), Jakubowicz (1984), and others (see Lust 1986 and Kaufman 1994 for review) show that while the clausemate restriction on the interpretation of reflexives (in languages that have them) is acquired early, the Condition B nonreflexive use of pronouns is much more uncertainly acquired, with sometimes as many as 50% of four- to six-year-olds finding a clausemate coreference between an NP and a nonreflexive pronoun perfectly possible (Solan 1987). As Carden and Stewart point out, this finding is surprising in the light of the apparent rarity of languages that permit the reflexive use of ordinary clausemate pronouns.

In any case, the conclusion that we may draw here from the creole studies is that there is distinct evidence in favor of a B-first analysis in such languages, both synchronically in that many creoles just use a marked or emphatic pronoun to indicate a reflexive, and diachronically in that creoles that do seem to have Anaphors also seem to have passed through a B-first stage with no Anaphors in the cases for which we have data.[67]

4.3.3.1.4 *Old English* As the diachronic sequence hypothesized for creoles makes clear, a B-first analysis clearly projects a diachronic sequence: Anaphors should develop out of marked pronouns that are used to M-implicate conjointness in opposition to the I-based presumption of disjoint clausemates. In that case, an A-first language, at least one that codes reflexivity through reflexive pronouns, should develop out of a B-first language (at least that should be one likely source). English is then an interesting test case, because it was clearly at one stage, the earliest recorded stage of Old English, a B-first language without encoded Anaphors.

According to Visser's (1963: 420–439) compendious treatment of Old English, *self* was not originally a reflexive element:

in the earliest Old English texts *self* could be added to the personal pronouns in the nominative whenever this was thought necessary for the sake of emphasis.... It seems however to have taken some time before *self* was added to the reflexive pronouns [i.e., ordinary pronouns used reflexively] ... that already from the beginning of the Old English period were widely used as objects without the addition of *self*. (p. 420)

Thus *self* clearly began as an emphatic adjectival adjunct to nominative pronouns "with the purpose of emphasizing the identity of the person or thing denoted by the object and the subject" (p. 425), and at the time of Beowulf a reflexive object could only be expressed by the normal accusative pronoun, as in *ic me clænsie* ('I washed me').[68] By the time of King Alfred both that mode of expression and its counterpart with *self* (as in *ic me selfne clænsie*) seem to have been current: thus both *hie forseoð hie selfe* and *hie forseoð hie* (p. 421). Indeed the use of the simple pronoun as a reflexive continued right through the Middle English period, although during that period (say 1200–1500):

there is a distinct change in the relative frequency of the two forms: the simple pronouns, which in the beginning are numerically predominant, are gradually, and to an ever increasing extent, encroached upon by the compound pronouns (= pronouns + *self*), with the result that by the second half of the fifteenth century they are more or less in the minority in most writings. (p. 432)

Throughout this period then "such a phrase as *he ofsticode hine* might mean either 'he stabbed him' (someone else) or 'he stabbed himself'" (Visser 1963: 433, citing Sweet). Visser suggests that the emphatic was increasingly used to avoid such possible ambiguities.[69]

It is tempting, of course, for modern commentators to make a sharp distinction between the emphatic and reflexive uses of self,

but to import it into OE is to follow a false native informant. As I see it Quirk and Wrenn are on the right track when they say...: 'For the most part, *self* was used in OE simply to emphasize and was not, as in Mod. E., associated with being a reflexive sign or a pronoun-enclitic'." (Mitchell 1985: 189)

The essential fact about Old English is that both the plain pronoun (e.g., *hine*) and the corresponding emphatic pronoun (e.g., *hine selfne*) could be used either reflexively or nonreflexively in, for example, object position (op. cit. p. 115).[70] Thus the reflexive uses indubitably grew out of the emphatic uses, and not the other way around. Nevertheless, text counts show that "potentially reflexive uses are *one* typical context for use of an emphatic" (Faltz 1989: 328). Faltz (1985: 242) notes a further piece of evidence for the evolution of reflexives from the use of emphatics to mark nonstereotypical interpretations. The hypothesis suggests that where a reflexive interpretation might in fact be stereotypical, as with predicates like 'wash' and 'dress', the emphatic pronouns would not in fact be used. And this seems to have been the case in Middle English: one said *he cladde hym as a poure laborer* rather than *he cladde hym self*. In these stereotypically reflexive actions one can see a tension between the global stereotype reflected in the DRP ("presume no coarguments corefer") and the specific stereotype ('one washes, etc., oneself') and consequent instabilities in their treatment. Thus the progression from *ic me clænsie > ic me selfne clænsie > ic clænsie*—that is, the loss of the reflexive object with verbs like *wash*, *dress*, *shave*, and so on—has been much commented on (see, e.g., Jespersen 1927: 325f; Visser 1963: 145ff). The endpoint of the development, the correlation of the omission of the object with the stereotypical reading (as predicted by the I-principle), is of course striking. The history of English thus seems to provide excellent evidence for an evolution of reflexives out of emphatics. The point at which the emphatic became grammaticalized as a reflexive can perhaps be equated with the point at which it lost its inflection, at the transition of Old to Middle English. But as just indicated, this long preceded the acquisition of indefeasible (or grammaticalized) Condition B-like patterns outlawing the reflexive use of ordinary pronouns, a practice that survived well into Shakespeare's time and beyond (Visser 1963: 435; Haiman 1995).

However, regardless of the diachronic progression, there is little doubt that Old English was a classical B-first language, at least in the earliest period: it lacked Anaphors entirely, operating with a presumption of clausemate NP disjointness, a presumption that could be defeated by the use of a pronoun with an emphatic adjunct. The history of Dutch (and no doubt other West Germanic languages) might have been similar had it not been for the relatively recent influence of German: before then just as in Old English there were no reflexives, with pronouns doing double duty.[71] But, according to Everaert (1986: 3), "in the fourteenth and fifteenth centuries the eastern dialects of the Dutch language area started to use a *sich*-reflexive (which later developed into *zich*) under the influence of Middle Low German dialects involved in a process of *sich* adoption from Middle High German. If we look at the present-day non-standard dialects we can observe that the use of *zich* is still limited to the eastern dialects (Ureland 1981)." Everaert notes that West Flemish (1986: 43) and Afrikaans (1986: 39–40) continue to operate without morphological reflexives.[72]

There is no doubt, then, that there are languages without Anaphors or reflexives of any kind. The most interesting thing about such languages from the current point of view is that *the opposition between coreference and disjoint reference in such languages can only be achieved pragmatically*—it can only be suggested, indeed implicated, by the choice of a specific kind of referring expression. If there are general pragmatic processes that can be reliably employed to make such referential distinctions in such languages (and there must be), then there is every reason to think that the same pragmatic processes operate in other languages to support partially grammaticalized oppositions of the same kind. Thus the very existence of languages of this sort is evidence in favor of the fundamental role that we are attributing to generalized conversational implicature in the interpretation of anaphora.

4.3.3.2 Interim Conclusions: The B-First Account   There is, then, distinct evidence in favor of a B-first analysis. First, as we have seen, there is evidence that there are languages that have no way of coding reflexivity at all. This makes an A-first analysis impossible, of course, because the A-first analysis predicts all the patterns of anaphora as pragmatically derived from a grammatical core—something like Condition A of the Binding Theory. It goes without saying that such B-first languages are even more serious challenges to theories like that of Chomsky (1981, 1986), where Condition A is claimed to have no basis in experience and is held to govern NP-movement as well as Anaphor construal. We can then ask whether in languages with an ill-developed or zero-coding of reflexivity, we can nevertheless find a grammaticalized Condition B. But the question suggests its own answer—if nonreflexive core arguments of transitive verbs were stipulated to be necessarily disjoint (as in Conditions B and C), how could reflexivity be expressed at all when there is no direct coding of reflexivity? Nonreflexively marked NPs in such languages must be construable, under the right circumstances, as coreferential with a co-argument antecedent. So, in such languages, the assumption of disjoint clausemate arguments can only be a tendency—in short, a pragmatic inference to the stereotype. What we do see in such languages is the development of some device to suggest the nonstereotypical coreferential interpretation; the theory of GCIs predicts that such a device would be merely a matter of marking the NP or the verb emphatically or contrastively, so suggesting a marked situation—that is, M-implicating conjoint reference against an I-based assumption of disjoint clausemates.

Thus we obtain Condition A-like patterns of interpretation of marked pronouns as a pragmatic inference from a preestablished B-like pattern.

A B-first analysis therefore requires that Condition B-like patterns of interpretation cannot have a deep grammatical or innate basis. Yet Reinhart for one thinks that at least the disjoint pattern in bound-variable anaphora as in *Everybody likes him* does indeed have an innate basis (Grodzinsky and Reinhart 1993; see also Chien and Wexler 1990). But the language-acquisition facts even in A-first languages like English, where adult intuitions about locally disjoint pronouns are very strong, do not support an innate Condition B. As mentioned, these studies seem to show that children learning A-first languages learn the clausemate restriction on reflexives relatively early (as early as 3 years old) and relatively exceptionlessly (up to 95%); but the assumption that a nonreflexive pronoun in object position is disjoint from the clausemate subject is learned relatively late (as late as 5 or 6 years old) and applied only some of the time (in some experimental conditions as little as 36%—see Solan 1987; also Jakubowicz 1984, Read and Hare 1979). Surveying these studies, Kaufman (1994: 182) concluded that "taken together, these studies demonstrate that children's performance with pronouns is sometimes poorer and often more variable than their performance with reflexives," nor did she find the recent tests of bound-variable disjointness to support Reinhart's assumption that at least that aspect of Condition B was more robust (see also C. Koster 1994). These particular investigations in A-first languages support our A-first analysis, by suggesting that children must first learn, or learn to apply, Condition A, and only then would be able to slowly appreciate the pragmatic implications of that pattern (i.e., Condition B and C patterns), often not before middle childhood (C. Koster 1994: 201). They also clearly indicate that Condition B is not as natural and robust as it seems to the intuitions of adult speakers of A-first languages.

We seem to be left then with the possibility that there are two rather radically different kinds of languages: those that have a grammaticalized Condition A (or similar principle), and those that lack it but have a pragmatically based Condition B-like assumption that clausemate arguments are distinct unless otherwise indicated. The A-first languages are numerically in the ascendant, and there is historical evidence that the B-first languages tend to develop into A-first systems. In both cases, though, our theory of GCIs gives some account of how the rest of the anaphora patterns can be derived.

4.4   THE B-THEN-A ACCOUNT: SYNTHESIS OF THE A-FIRST AND B-FIRST ACCOUNTS

Let us sum up so far. We have reviewed the earlier A-first account of binding patterns, which makes the anaphoric patterns often attributed to Conditions B and C of the Binding Theory pragmatically derivative from grammaticalized Anaphors. We have shown how certain difficulties with this may be circumvented. In particular, the most prominent problem, the overlap in distribution between (especially long-range) reflexives and pronouns, was shown to not necessarily be an overwhelming difficulty at all. Instead, by bringing the subtle logophoric aspects of long-distance reflexives into the picture, we can maintain the Q-based contrast between pronoun and reflexive. Thus we end up with a natural extension of the A-first account into languages and phenomena (like switch reference) beyond those for which it was originally developed. We can now say that there is a large class of languages (those we have been calling the A-first languages) that seem to fall within the scope of such a partial pragmatic reduction of the Binding Conditions.

But the reader will recollect that one problem remains with the A-first account, sufficient to suggest that we are still missing an essential ingredient—namely, the fact that the reflexive and the pronoun seem to be in a different kind of opposition where there is a clausemate, co-argument antecedent within the clause, compared to where the antecedent is more remote. In the first case, the opposition is nearly always one of reference; in the second case, it is either one of reference or one of logophoricity— hence the pronoun can often occur with the same reference but opposed in logophoricity. On the face of it, this fact in many languages with long-range reflexives predisposes us once again to a grammatical account, taking the reflexive and the pronoun to have different binding domains. But once the wider facts about distribution of such reflexives are considered (like the fact that the antecedent can be far removed, even beyond the sentence, or deictically implicit in the case of first- and second-person antecedents), the grammatical account of long-distance Anaphors no longer looks so attractive (see, e.g., Mazuka and Lust 1994, J. Koster 1994). The basic fact—a semantic fact—is that the reflexive is necessarily referentially dependent, the pronoun only optionally so; the search for an antecedent seems to be guided by matters of preferential interpretation, not grammatical principles (for an extended justification of this for

Chinese, see Huang 1989). Besides, a grammatical account would leave the logophoric contrasts unaccounted for.

But if we bring our B-first analysis back into the consideration of A-first languages, we can now find an answer to this rather central puzzle. Suppose we assume that in A-first languages we can find the same presumption that is central to the anaphoric operations of B-first languages—namely, the presumption that core arguments of a single clause are disjoint (the DRP). Additionally, of course, we have the Q-implicated contrast between reflexive and pronoun, which in a language without long-distance reflexives is sufficient explanation of the tendency to read the pronoun as disjoint with a clausemate antecedent. Thus in languages without long-distance reflexives, the presumption that core arguments are disjoint is redundant, which is why it never figured in our original A-first account. But in languages with long-distance reflexives, although the two pragmatic principles will be largely overlapping and reinforcing, in the case of the long-distance use of the reflexive there will be a Q-contrast outside the scope of the clausemate-disjointness presumption. In those long-distance locations, the Q-contrast need not be interpreted as a contrast in reference (although it may be); it may instead be interpreted as a contrast in logophoricity, along the lines that O'Connor (1993) suggests.

To summarize the argument, then, we have two pragmatic principles at work underlying the different patterns of interpretation for pronouns in opposition to locally bound reflexives on the one hand, versus pronouns in opposition to long-range reflexives on the other:

1. The presumption of clausemate co-argument disjointness, the DRP, a stereotypical presumption that can be attributed to the I-principle.
2. A scalar Q-implicature contrast between reflexive and pronoun, based on the differential semantic strength of the reflexive and the pronoun, the one being necessarily referentially dependent, the other only optionally so; the one suggesting subjective perspective and emphasis, the other lacking such suggestions.

Where the two presumptions overlap (i.e., where antecedent and anaphoric items are co-argument clausemates), the first pragmatic presumption will ensure there is always a contrast in reference. And the contrast in reference will be sufficient motivation for the use of reflexive versus pronoun, thus exhausting the pragmatic import. Outside these positions, a long-range reflexive is contrastive but not necessarily contrastive in reference. Such a synchronic account goes some of the way toward answering our central puzzle. But it still leaves aspects of the puzzle unexplained. In particular, it is still not clear why the reflexive in long-range positions should have a logophoric interpretation that is not prominent in the clausemate use. Where does the deictic markedness come from?

The problem is only fully resolved, I believe, by taking a diachronic perspective, by looking at the anaphoric patterns that languages exhibit as accretions of pragmatic practices. We have already seen, in the review of the facts about Creole languages, and more especially in the detailed facts about the history of Old English, some reason to believe that B-first systems evolve into A-first systems. I would now like to propose that this is the general evolutionary route by which the familiar A-first languages have arisen. Restricting ourselves to the languages that mark reflexivity by NP type, on such a diachronic account, Anaphors arise as marked pronominal NPs M-implicating contrast with the clausemate-disjointness presumption. But the use in a B-first language of emphatics to encode the marking, as is so often the case, is obviously consistent with a much wider use of such forms. In particular, because a deictic perspective is the perennial unmarked presumption, a marked or emphatic form may always suggest a contrastive perspective, such as one where (as Stirling 1993 puts it) the "validator" is not the current speaker (see also Levinson 1988a). So here we have the explanation of the association of logophoricity with reflexives: both conjoint reference within the clause and a marked deictic perspective are perennial possibilities of interpretation of the use of a marked form in a B-first language, because it will suggest by M-implicature an interpretation complementary to the stereotypical one that would arise from the use of the corresponding unmarked form.

Putting these ingredients together, we may schematize the diachronic progression from B-first languages to A-first ones as follows (where English glosses sketch the various language patterns):[73]

(70) *Stage 1: No reflexives; core-arguments tend to be disjoint*
Sentences of the form 'John hit him' will I-implicate disjoint reference, via the DRP;[74] only ad hoc means such as the use of an emphatic or marked intonation can be used to M-implicate the complementary interpretation of exceptional coreference; the same means are likely to be used to M-implicate a marked deictic perspective.

(71) *Stage 2: Emphatic core-arguments may be conjoint*
  a. The exceptional coreferential interpretation of 'John hit him' is now regularly reinforced by the use of a particular focus or emphatic particle: "John hit him-EMPH" M-implicates 'John$_1$ hit himself$_1$.'
  b. An established usage of this sort reinforces the contrast with the simple pronoun without the emphatic, so "John hit him" I-implicates more strongly 'John$_1$ hit him$_2$.'
  c. But because the marking of pronouns is by a focus particle with general uses, other contrasts (beyond reference) may be intended; one such contrast being the point-of-view contrast called logophoric, especially relevant outside the scope of the DRP: "John said he will come" expresses the unmarked deictic point of view, whereas "John said he-EMPH will come" M-implicates a marked point of view.

(72) *Stage 3: Emphatics become reflexives (A-first system)*
  An established system emerges: grammaticalized reflexives encoding necessary referential dependence within some domain (i.e., Anaphors) have evolved. So now:
  a. *Co-argument positions:* the pronoun in "John hit him" is not only presumed disjoint by the DRP, uncanceled by any M-implicature, but also Q-implicates disjoint reference by the scale ⟨Anaphor, Pronoun⟩. Hence the strong inference to disjoint core arguments from the use of a pronoun.
  b. *Where antecedent and anaphoric expression are not clausemate co-arguments:* here we are outside the domain of the DRP, so the inference to disjointness doesn't obtain; there is still a Q-contrast between pronoun and Anaphor, but now a contrast in reference is not the only possible one. The marked Anaphor may still carry the marked-point-of-view meaning (from Stage 2):
  ⟨Reflexive,   Pronoun⟩
  +coreference   unmarked
  +logophoric   unmarked
  The consequence is that use of the pronoun Q-implicates that the speaker is not in a position to use the Anaphor because either he intends disjoint reference or he intends nonlogophoricity.

So far, for this hypothetical diachronic progression we have adduced evidence only from Old English and the various mentioned Creoles. But the hypothesis seems to be largely, if not entirely, compatible with the diachronic hypotheses about the origins of reflexives that Faltz (1985) advances on the basis of typological reviews of reflexivity encoding. His findings are worth reviewing in detail. Faltz suggests (1985: 48ff) that the main typological distinction is between languages that have true, underived, pronominal reflexives (like Russian *sebja* and German *sich*[75]) and those with compound reflexives. Compound reflexives are of different types: (a) nominal head reflexives, usually modified by a possessive pronoun, as in Turkish *kendi-me* ('self-mine');[76] (b) adjunct reflexives, based on a pronoun modified with a reflexive adjunct as in Old English *hine-sylfne* '3msg-ACC + REFL' or Irish *é féin* 'him + REFL'; and (c) fused adjunct reflexives, like modern English where *himself* can no longer be analyzed simply as head + modifier.

In addition to all these types, there are verbal reflexivizers, often derived from cliticized pronominal or nominal reflexives (e.g., French *se* + Verb from Latin *se*), but which end up as true verbal affixes (like Russian middle -*sja* from pronominal *sebja*). Diagrammatically:

(73)

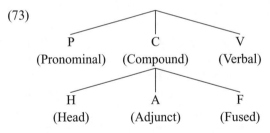

Certain properties are said to be restricted to each of these types. For example, P (pronominal) reflexives require subject antecedents, strictly require all coreferential clausemates to be encoded with the P form, but may have long-distance uses; whereas C reflexives tend to allow nonsubject antecedents, allow some oblique nonreflexive coreferential clausemates, but don't permit long-range uses. (It's clear, in fact, on the basis of more recent information that these could be at most systematic trends.)

Faltz (1985: chap. 6) then suggests that the following kinds of diachronic progressions may be hypothesized:

1. All verbal reflexives come from NP reflexives via cliticization, thus: P > V or C > V, together with an associated tendency for later semantic

bleaching of the V-reflexive verb form to a middle (or generalized intransitivizing) verb form; reverse progressions do not occur,[77] and it is hypothesized that there are no progressions *P > C or *C > P (p. 233ff).

2. Perhaps all C reflexives come from emphatic adjuncts on pronouns —for example, Old English *self*, French *même* (from late Latin **met-ipsimum*),[78] Dutch *zelf*, Papago *hijil*, and so on (1985: 243ff); some of those based on forms glossing like 'his head/body' also clearly derive from emphatics (Biblical Hebrew), whereas others may possibly have been directly coined to encode reflexivization.

3. More speculatively, P pronouns derive from subordinate reflexives (long-range-only reflexives)—that is, nonreflexive pronouns used coreferentially with nonclausemate antecedents, like the logophoric African pronouns discussed in section 4.3.2.5.1.[79] These subordinate reflexives in turn derive either from stressed pronouns or from a first-person pronoun used in direct reported speech.[80]

Thus, if in broad outline Faltz is right, nearly all reflexives ultimately arise from emphatic or stressed pronouns.[81] As to why this might be the case, he advances what is in effect a brief and informal version of our B-first account: "an emphatic is added to an NP as a warning to the hearer that the intended referent of that NP is unusual or unexpected" (p. 240); "in the absence of a reflexive strategy, it is natural for an emphatic to be used to signal that the more highly marked, less expected situation is present, namely that the NP (argument) in question has the same referent as another one in the same predication" (p. 242). In addition to Old English, Faltz cites Dutch, French and Spanish secondary reflexives (*même* and *mismo*), Papago, Hebrew, among other languages, as providing clear evidence for reflexives derived from emphatics.[82] The German secondary reflexive *selbst* is also interesting here; cognate with English *self*, it remains an intensifier used to mark reflexivity with nonsubject antecedents (the primary reflexive *sich* requiring a subject antecedent) as in:

(74) Hans sprach mit Fritz über   ihn (selbst).
     Hans spoke with Fritz about him (self)
     'Hans spoke with Fritz about him (himself).'

Here, without the addition of *selbst*, the reference of *ihn* is likely to be taken to be a third party, but with the addition, the referent is taken to be Fritz (Faltz 1985: 240). But *selbst* is also synchronically an intensifier:

(75) Der Präsident selbst wird kommen.
　　 the President self   will come
　　 'The President himself will come.'

and a focus particle:

(76) Selbst der Präsident wird kommen.
　　 self   the President will come
　　 'Even the President will come.'

the different scopes perhaps being responsible for the meaning differences in these usages (Edmondson and Plank 1978; König 1991: chap. 8). Diachronically, the NP intensification use seems to be prior to all the others (König, op. cit.).

　　Although Faltz's account antedates the great upsurge of work on binding, it seems still to be the most comprehensive crosslinguistic survey of reflexivization available (although see also Geniušiene 1987; Sells, Zaenen, and Zec 1987; Koster and Reuland 1991; Huang in prep.; and references therein); and it suggests that the account we are advancing may have some real crosslinguistic generality. Nevertheless, the diachronic evidence is still relatively thin and still relatively biased by data from Indo-European languages. Clearly we need much more work on the history of reflexives in those languages, like Tamil, Chinese, and Japanese, that provide long continuous records. In the history of all three of those languages, we can find evidence for at least a precondition for the reflexives-from-emphatics hypothesis—namely, evidence for overlap in function of the same morpheme(s) for both emphasis and reflexivity. Thus Classical Chinese *zi* clearly had both reflexive and emphatic uses like modern Chinese *ziji*.[83] Ancient Japanese had a range of reflexives that also functioned as subject intensifiers or emphatics;[84] modern *zibun* or *jibun* (the *ji-* morpheme is written with the same Chinese character as Classical *zi* and is obviously borrowed) clearly maintains the emphatic adjunct function (Mazuka and Lust 1994: 152).[85] Modern Tamil has the same telltale overlap in function of the morpheme *taan* as an indeclinable NP intensifier and a declinable (long-distance) reflexive; in Classical Tamil, the intensifier was a declinable postposition (Andronov 1969: 108). The tendency to pronominalize is continuing in the more recent use of *taan* as a nonreflexive honorific second- (or sometimes third-) person pronoun. Even in the present language, the emphatic and the reflexive are more than mere accidental homonyms: "with regard to the emphatic marker *taan*, one might wish to say that there is some semantic overlap with the reflexive pronoun *taan*," with another emphatic affix, *-ee*, sometimes also being used to indicate reflexivity (Asher 1985: 86). As Caldwell (1961[1865]: 401) noted over a century ago, Dravidian *taan* "must, I think, have originated from some emphatic demonstrative base," a conclusion supported by later comparative Dravidian studies (e.g., Gondi *tanaa* is "only used in the third person and in the nominative" (Burrow and Emeneau 1961: 207); that is, I suspect, purely as an emphatic adjunct).

Still, whatever the current empirical basis, the hypothesis seems plausible enough, and it is certainly open to empirical refutation. It clearly makes interesting predictions about the evolution of anaphoric patterns generally; it suggests, for example, that languages with long-distance reflexives may be midway between A-first and B-first patterns, and if so, we might expect a greater flexibility in interpretation in such languages than exists in English. Chinese is an interesting case in point, and it is worth seeing how the facts might be incorporated into an account of this sort.

In a thorough reexamination of Chinese anaphora, Huang (1991, 1994) claims that no grammatical account of the Chomskyan type will be able to handle the observed flexibility of interpretation associated, in particular, with the pronominal *ta* and the long-range reflexive *ziji*. He thoroughly reviews the many recent attempts to bring Chinese within the fold of the Binding Theory predictions—for example by means of (a) expanding the binding domain for *ziji*, (b) postulating movement at the level of Logical Form, and (c) reclassifying *ziji* as a special kind of pronominal. Each of these simply makes the wrong predictions. The essential facts (Huang 1994: 76–78) are that Chinese has two candidate reflexive Anaphors, simple *ziji* and complex *ta ziji* (or pronominal + *ziji*), which distribute in mostly the same ways: they can be both short- and long-distance bound (i.e., their antecedents can be local or indefinitely distant), and their antecedents need not be in c-commanding positions. They differ in that *ziji* requires a subject antecedent and *ta ziji* does not; and *ziji*, which is (unlike pronominal + *ziji*) unmarked for person, assumes the nearest possible antecedent is of the correct person (i.e., long-distance linking is ruled out by a "blocking rule" if the distant antecedent is of a different person than a local candidate). Rather than invoke the Binding Theory apparatus, an accurate account of the behavior of these reflexives can be obtained, he claims, simply by the interaction of their lexical or semantic content (referential dependency in particular) with pragmatic principles of a neo-Gricean kind.

However, Huang (1991, 1994) argues that the A-first account (as in Levinson 1987b) does not properly engage with Chinese, largely because on that account there should be a strong tendency (via Q-implicature) for the complementary interpretation of Anaphors and pronominals, whereas in Chinese this is not the case. Instead, he argues that to account for the patterns in Chinese one needs only M- and I-implicatures (with that order of priority), together with a presumption of intraclause argument distinctness (the DRP). Note that this is closely related to the B-first account already described (which was partly prompted by his work): on a B-first account, the DRP is the foundation, and M-implicatures invoked by emphatics are used to indicate coreference, whereas simple pronouns are I-implicated to be closely coreferential beyond the clause. In a B-first account, the Q-principle is otiose, because until a privative opposition between pronoun and reflexive has developed, there is no basis for scalar (or Q-based) implicature. However, Huang (1994: 130) does not invoke the M-principle to explain clausemate conjointness with *ziji*, which is rather semantically explained: *ziji* is clearly lexically specified as referentially dependent and thus can override the pragmatic assumption of the disjointness of co-arguments. The B-first account is tailored to a rather different situation, where there is no such stabilized semantic encoding, as in Old English. A schematic comparison between the accounts may help to make the contrast clear (where > signifies "overrides" and where "I-coreference" indicates an inference to conjointness induced by the I-principle, "semantics" indicates specified referential dependency, M+> indicates M-implicates and so on):

(77)		*B-first account*	*Huang's account of Chinese*
a.	'John blames him'	DRP>I-coreference[86]	DRP>I-coreference
b.	'John blames (him)self'	M>DRP	Semantics>DRP
c.	'John says that he will come'	I-coreference	I-coreference
d.	'John says that self will come'	M+>logophoricity I-coreference	M+>logophoricity Semantics & I-coreference

Huang's (1994: 128–147) account of Chinese appears to work well to explain both unacceptable and preferred interpretations of anaphoric elements. There is, in effect, a global tendency to locally coreferential readings of both the reflexive *ziji* and the nonreflexive pronoun *ta*, a tendency defeated in the case of *ta* with a potential clausemate antecedent by the presumption of co-argument distinctness. Contrasts between *ta* and *ziji*, which may be expected by M-implicature, tend outside the domain of the DRP to be interpreted as contrasts in emphaticness or logophoricity rather than reference. Both *ta* and *ziji* contrast with lexical NPs, which discourage coreferential interpretations by M. Because Chinese permits zero-anaphora, this has to be brought into the picture too: except in special circumstances, *ta* and zero tend to contrast in the expected way, with the pronoun suggesting more distant coreference than the zero-anaphor (p. 134ff).[87]

Chinese therefore differs from a prototype B-first language like Old English in having, in the form of *ziji*, a conventionalized pronominal that is obligatorily referentially dependent but without a clear syntactic specification of a binding domain. It is tempting to think of Chinese as transitional between a B-first language and an A-first one, with *ziji* being in the process of acquiring the Q-contrasts so typical of A-first languages. Unfortunately, there seems to be no history of pronominals and reflexives in Chinese easily accessible to the nonspecialist. Perhaps some speculation may be forgiven in the hope that specialists may be goaded into supplying us with the facts. As already mentioned, *ziji* already in Classical Chinese had both emphatic and reflexive uses, and it continues to be used as an intensifier (e.g., in collocation with a subject; Li and Thompson 1981: 138f). Thus, on the hypothesis that *ziji* was in origin an emphatic, we can hypothesize an earlier B-first state of the language with the following properties:

1. *Intraclausal anaphoric patterns:* use of the pronominal *ta* would tend to I-implicate local coreference, except with clausemate antecedents where the DRP would block coreference; this presumption being overruled by the use of a marked, emphatic *ta ziji* or *ziji* that would M-implicate the complementary interpretation, here coreference.

2. *Cross-clause anaphoric patterns:* here, where there is no presumption of disjoint reference, *ta* would tend to pick up a local antecedent; the use of (*ta*) *ziji* will M-implicate a contrastive interpretation but not necessarily a contrast in reference (no longer especially salient, outside the scope of the DRP)—the contrast may be on the dimensions of unexpectedness, sole agency, or nondeictic (logophoric) point of view.[88]

Later, through intraclausal anaphoric usage, *ziji* must have acquired specific semantic content, viz. necessary referential dependence, but it still retains the unexpectedness or logophoric implications associated with its original emphatic uses.

To what extent can we see the modern language as in diachronic progression from a B-first to an A-first language? First, let us see to what extent Chinese can be seen as conforming to A-first predictions. We might look at it this way: given that *ta* encompasses both deictic and anaphoric uses, there is now an ordering of semantic informativeness over the two expressions and thus the makings of a Horn scale $\langle ziji, ta \rangle$, with the use of the weaker *ta* suggesting that the use of *ziji* would be inappropriate. But *ziji*, even in the present language, is not an Anaphor in the Binding Theory sense, because it carries no specification of the domain in which it must be bound (Huang 1994: 88ff). The Q-opposition between *ziji* and *ta* is thus rather weak—*ziji* is no more informative about where to find an antecedent, and, after all, most pronominal uses are anaphoric and thus referentially dependent in any case. What strengthens the opposition is the encoding of contrast or unexpectedness, emphasis, and logophoricity associated with *ziji*. The use of *ta* therefore Q-implicates that either the speaker wishes to avoid referential dependence or that he wishes to avoid the logophoric or contrastive associations of *ziji*. Where reference is the salient issue (especially, where there is a potential intraclause antecedent such that the presumption of intraclausal argument distinctiveness is pertinent), the use of *ta* will strongly suggest disjoint reference,[89] but elsewhere it is just as likely to suggest noncontrastiveness or nonlogophoricity. So we obtain the following patterns of preferred interpretation (from Huang 1989: ch. 3, 1994: 125):

(78) a. Lao Wang piping   le   ziji.
      Lao Wang criticize PFV self
      'Wang$_1$ has criticized self$_1$.'
   b. Lao Wang piping   le   ta.
      Lao Wang criticize PFV 3sg
      'Wang$_1$ has criticized him$_2$.'

(79) a. Lao Wang shuo ziji shi ge gongchengshi.
      Lao Wang say   self be CL engineer
      'Wang$_1$ says that self$_1$ is an engineer.'
   b. Lao Wang shuo ta   shi ge gongchengshi.
      Lao Wang say   3sg be CL engineer
      'Wang$_1$ says that he$_1$ is an engineer.'

Thus disjoint versus conjoint reference is the most salient opposition between *ta* and *ziji* within the clause, because the DRP makes reference the salient issue there, whereas the subjective, logophoric contrast is the most salient opposition outside it. To this extent, an A-first account is compatible with the facts.

As discussed above, Huang's (1991, 1994) account of all this is simpler: in (79b) the presumption of clausemate argument distinctness overrides the I-preference for local coreference, whereas the latter in turn is over-ridden by the semantics of referential dependency in (78a). In (79a) the preference for coreference goes through unchecked. But Huang's account leaves questions unanswered—for example, why the *ta/ziji* opposition fails to form a Q-implicating Horn scale. It also, perhaps, hides the crosslinguistic generality of these patterns: if we bring the subjective (logophoric) meaning contrasts back into the picture we can see why we can have a pragmatic contrast without a change of reference. These contrasts, subtle though they are, are surely a prominent part of these systems, partially eclipsed by the focus on referential potential in grammatical theory but correctly emphasized in recent work by O'Connor (1993), Kuno (1987), Sells (1987), Stirling (1993), and others. The contrast between *ta* and *ziji* is therefore often interpreted nonreferentially, as acknowledged by Huang (1991), where *ziji* is claimed to carry an "unexpectedness message" indicating either logophoric viewpoint or contrastiveness, when used in positions where a pronoun or zero-anaphor could have the same reference. He has since gone on to document the logophoric implications of *ziji* in detail (Huang 1994: 184–199), suggesting that the logophoric implications of *ziji* are at least in part conventionalized. One piece of evidence (op. cit. p. 196) in favor of this is that, for example, a third-person antecedent cannot be searched for over a more local first-person antecedent, because the first-person reference defines a perspectival domain (hence, in gloss, *'John₁ thinks that I trust self₁ too much'). In short, if we consider *ta* and *ziji* to constitute an emerging privative opposition (with *ziji* necessarily referentially dependent and logophoric, *ta* unmarked), we have an account of the Chinese patterns that fits the crosslinguistic spectrum of systems, as intermediate between A-first and B-first.

Such an intermediate position would also help to explain some rather striking parallels between modern Chinese and the B-first Old English. Consider, for example, the surprising possibility of the following anaphoric links:[90]

(80) a. Wang Xiaojie feichang xinshang ta   ziji.
        Wang Miss   very   admire   3sg self
        'Miss Wang₁ admires herself₂ very much.'
    b. Moyses, se ðe   wæs Gode   sua weorð ðæt he oft   wið hine
       Moses   he who was to-God so   dear   that he often with him
       selfne spræc.
       self   spoke
       'Moses₁, who was so dear to God₂ that he₁ often spoke with
       [God] Himself₂.'

The seeming paradox of these usages, where we find apparent "reflexives"
associated with disjoint interpretations, is very hard to understand except
on a pragmatic account of a B-first kind. On a B-first account, an emphatic form may be used to implicate disjointness, overriding the DRP.
Double emphasis, though, may itelf override that interpretation in turn.[91]
As Huang (1994: 197–198) notes, both *ziji* and *ta ziji* continue to have
emphatic meanings: if *ziji* can implicate conjointness, then *ta ziji* can by
double contrast implicate the complementary interpretation (i.e., disjoint
reference). In some respects, then, Chinese appears to behave in the
manner of a B-first language like Old English, with *ziji* and *ta ziji* operating just like emphatics. This M-like behavior of *ziji* and *ta ziji* can also
be seen in the logophoric implications: example (81a) below (conforming
to the alleged "blocking rule" mentioned above) must be interpreted with
ziji linked to the first-person antecedent, because this introduces a subjective point of view, but the double form *ta ziji* in (81b) can override this
(Huang 1994: 196).

(81) a. Xiaoming₁ renwei wo₂ tai xiagxin ziji₂ le.
        Xiaoming₁ thinks I₂   too trust   self₂ CRS
        'Xiaoming thinks that I trust myself too much.'
    b. Xiaoming₁ renwei wo₂ tai xiagxin ta   ziji₂ le.
        Xiaoming₁ thinks I₂   too trust   3sg self₁ CRS
        'Xiaoming thinks that I trust him(self) too much.'

To this extent, then, Chinese looks rather like a B-first language, contrary
to the earlier discussed evidence for an emerging Q-opposition between *ta*
and *ziji*. These lines of evidence together converge to suggest an intermediate, transitional state for Chinese. Note too that Old English with
its emphatic "reflexives" could achieve long-distance anaphora just like
Chinese:

(82) a. Xiaoming   yiwei mama yao zeguai ziji le.
        Xiaoming think mom   will blame self CRS
        'Xiaoming$_1$ thinks that Mom$_2$ will blame self$_1$.'

     b. He [Gregorius] Ælmihtigne God bæd   þæt
        he   Almighty   God prayed that
        'He$_1$ prayed to Almighty God$_2$ that

        he hi   mid his gife   gescylde:
        he to-them with his grace should-bestow
        He$_2$ should bestow His$_2$ grace upon them:

        7 þæt he him   seolfum forgeafe   þæt
        and that he to-him self   would-grant that
        and that He$_2$ to himself$_1$ would grant that

        he moste ðone wæstm heora   gewinnes
        he might the   fruits   of-their labors
        he$_1$ might see the fruits of their labors

        in heofona rices   wuldre geseon.
        in heaven's kingdom's glory   see
        in the glory of the Kingdom of Heaven.'

In the Chinese, the search for an antecedent for *ziji* very naturally leaps over a clausemate subject, finding an antecedent in a matrix clause (Huang 1989: 50, 91ff). Similarly, Mitchell (1985: 194) argues that *him seolfum* in this extract from Bede "refers to Gregorius, the subject of the main clause, and not to God, the subject of the clause in which it stands." Thus the passage glossed 'He$_1$ prayed to Almighty God$_2$ ... that He$_2$ to himself$_1$ would grant ...' has the same pattern of anaphora as the Chinese sentence. Mitchell (1985: 194) points out that often the *-self* form in Old English "is in effect reflexive, though not grammatically so" in just this way.

These are surely striking parallels across time and linguistic phylogeny. In both Old English and Chinese, we seem to be dealing with a flexible system of anaphoric interpretation, with only very partial coding of Anaphoricity (i.e., referential dependency within a restricted domain), where the referentially dependent pronominal clearly has primordial emphatic or intensification functions that continue to affect its use. In the case of English, we know the further direction of development, toward true Anaphors with restrictive binding domains; it may not be entirely fanciful to imagine that Chinese is heading in the same direction, towards an A-first system. But regardless of that, the categories A-first, B-first, and transitional may provide a useful, if crude, first step towards a cross-linguistic typology of anaphoric systems, providing that they are taken together with the pragmatic principles that generate the patterns and severely restrict the possibilities of preferred interpretation.

4.5   CONCLUSIONS

4.5.1   Summary

This chapter has examined one crucial area, intrasentential anaphora, where syntax and pragmatics seem to closely interact to generate patterns of interpretation. I began by exploring the A-first account (Levinson 1987a,b), which attempts to reduce Binding Conditions B and C to matters of generalized conversational implicature using an apparatus independently motivated by much work in pragmatics. This analysis can be extended to subsume Reinhart's theory that holds that only bound-variable anaphora is grammatically specified. I also noted that the pragmatic theory could be made to engage with other approaches, such as those with nonconfigurational theories of binding, but in each case precise predictions will be made which are a further constraint on theory construction. Now, the A-first account runs into a number of difficulties, notably the failure of complementarity between pronouns and Anaphors. It was shown, however, how this could be handled by the observation that pronouns and reflexives are in other kinds of contrast in these positions. In developing this account, we also saw how it could be extended to cover some of the facts about long-distance reflexives, logophoric anaphoric expressions, and even perhaps switch reference.

But there is one crucial piece of data that has been ignored by all the work on Anaphors—namely, the existence of languages that lack reflexives altogether. Here an A-first account is clearly inapplicable. So for such B-first languages (Levinson 1991) I have shown how the same Gricean pragmatic principles can be used to predict a rather different strategy for indicating coreference and disjoint reference. While the A-first account explains how anaphoric patterns are projected by Gricean principles applied to grammaticalized Anaphors, the B-first account shows how grammaticalized Anaphors might arise in the first place. The B-first approach makes basic the DRP (i.e., the presumption of co-argument disjointness) and explains proto-Anaphors in terms of the use of marked expressions to indicate a marked message, namely co-argument coreference.

Thus it seems natural to suppose that all A-first languages have derived from B-first ones. If we take this diachronic perspective, linking our A-first and B-first accounts, we are then provided with a plausible explanation of the persistent association of logophoricity (marked perspective) and long-range reflexives. The DRP, inherited by A-first systems from B-first ones, explains why long-distance Anaphors are contrastive with pronouns over reference inside the clause but may be contrastive over point of view or logophoricity beyond the clause. Thus the third approach, a diachronic A-from-B account, seems to offer a detailed explanation of many of the facts of intrasentential anaphora across a broad spectrum of languages. The fact that independently motivated Gricean principles, with reasonably intricate projection rules, should happen to offer explanations in the right directions over the details of, say, English or Chinese is quite encouraging. Consider too that they throw light on such matters as why English-speaking children should start learning Condition A before learning Condition B, or why emphatics and reflexives so often have the same morphological form, or how English reflexives evolved, or why the typological facts about reflexives seem to be the way they are.

All three of the pragmatic accounts are of course compatible: the A-first and B-first accounts handle the synchronic patterns in different types of languages, and the diachronic A-from-B account connects them historically. But because the diachronic account gives a functionally motivated account of Condition A, it further undermines the idea that even this residue of the Binding Conditions is a direct reflection of innate predispositions, or Universal Grammar. Clearly, on this account, anaphoric patterns are layered accretions of practices motivated by rational functional principles, but which in becoming conventionalized make available yet further pragmatic exploitations. The patterns are learnable on the basis of evidence for the use of language taken together with the rational principles underlying language use. The time scale for evolution of one system into another (e.g., a B-first system into an A-first system), or of the emergence of true Anaphors, may be measured in hundreds of years. All this, of course, seems clearly at variance with a Chomskyan perspective, where anaphoric patterns are instantiations of mental templates and are considered to be in principle unlearnable, and where parameter switching can only take place within the space of a single generation. Because the conclusions are radical, it is worth briefly reviewing other evidence against the view that the Binding Conditions are a deep part of our intellectual makeup.

4.5.2   Pragmatics versus Parameters in Language Learning and Language Change

If the Binding Conditions were part of UG, the child's native endowment for language acquisition, one might expect them to fit well with the kind of language-learning model associated with the Principles and Parameters perspective, where the child's primary task is to select the correct settings (for the local language) from a small, pregiven set of parameters. To restrict the possibility of unknowing overgeneralization (given the absence of explicit information about the grammatical/ungrammatical boundary), the child must, it seems, prefer parameter values that generate the "smallest" language consistent with the data, the so-called subset principle (Wexler and Manzini 1987). Applied to the Binding Conditions this has the result that the child should always opt for the smallest domain D for Anaphors consistent with the data, and the largest D for pronouns (assuming that Anaphors and pronouns may have distinct Binding domains, as with LDAs). In effect, children should always opt for the most restrictive language. But as we have already noted, this does not fit the data for child speakers of languages like English, at least, where children allow nonreflexives to have more unrestricted interpretations (Solan 1987, Kaufman 1994). Nor do children learning LDA systems seem to go for a clause-bound interpretation initially (see, e.g., Sigurjónsdóttir, Hyams, and Chien 1988 on Icelandic, and discussion in Lightfoot 1989: 370–371). And B-first languages like Old English would be predicted to be highly marked, because the one set of pronouns can be interpreted unrestrictively as either Anaphors or nonreflexive pronouns.[92] Yet the evidence we reviewed showed that pidgins and creoles, which one would expect to exhibit unmarked parameter settings, are also in initial stages very likely to be B-first languages (Carden and Stewart 1988).

Compare now a pragmatic account of the learning of such systems. The evidence for the Q- and I-principles abound in many aspects of language data (see, e.g., Atlas and Levinson 1981; Levinson 1987a,b; Horn 1984, 1989). True, it is not clear exactly how the learner comes to formulate such principles, some like Sperber and Wilson (1986) presuming that something like these principles derives directly from innate predispositions to process information in certain ways, and others like Grice and those who follow him more closely (like the present author) imagining that they arise from some complex interaction between native rationality and the demands of the communication setting (see Levinson 1989). Be that as it may, such inferential principles (or something like them) indubitably exist and are clearly utilized (to growing extents) by the language learner, as are many other, not specifically linguistic, inferential procedures. Patterns of anaphora will then be inspected to see whether they can be treated as instantiations of Q- or M-oppositions to the I-based tendency to stereotypical and coreferential readings. If anaphoric patterns are learned this way, then there are clear predictions for acquisition based on the fact that the patterns arise from contrastive opposition. For example, in an A-first language, where Condition B patterns are parasitic on Condition A patterns, Condition A patterns would have to be learned first. And so in fact they seem to be.[93]

The parameter-setting model also has clear implications for how one would expect language change to occur. Lightfoot (1989: 325) suggests such change should happen because a structural reanalysis by the language learner of some syntactic patterns (a parameter switch) may force certain data to be ignored as 'impossible data', not part of the 'trigger (parameter setting) experience'. Vincent (1989a: 361) comments that one would then expect a certain special kind of obsolescence, notable for "the relatively sudden disappearance from attested sources." For example, once a *himself* form is analyzed as an Anaphor bound within a minimal domain, one might expect rapid loss of homophonous forms bound further afield; or once *him* is analyzed as a pronominal free in a domain, one would expect rapid squeezing out of the use of *him* as a reflexive. The loss should take place in transmission across one generation, and although one must allow for sociolinguistic diffusion across a population, individuals' usage should be consistent (Lightfoot 1989: 370).[94] But again, none of these predictions seem true of the history of anaphora in English, or indeed other languages, where the establishment of, for example, Condition B–type patterns of usage began in Anglo-Saxon times but were not complete in Shakespeare's. All this suggests that if language learning does indeed generally proceed by the setting of parameters, the view that Binding domains are candidate parameters does not have obvious empirical support from the facts of acquisition or the indirect effects that modes of acquisition might have on language change.

4.5.3   Pragmatics and the Generative Program

There are striking crosslinguistic parallels in anaphoric patterns. There are also some striking exceptions to what we have come to expect (e.g., the B-first languages). Finding a satisfactory explanation of both the deep parallels and the anomalies is going to be difficult. It will clearly involve a universal theory of construal tendencies and the way this interacts with language-specific details. One model for such an explanation is a parameterized Binding Theory interacting with other parameters in an innate language-learning device. Another model, the one being suggested here, is a universal pragmatic theory that covers the anaphoric tendencies, interacting with language-specific details that are partly historical accretions of practices.

The observations in this chapter, if correct, would seriously undermine the view that the Binding Conditions are part of the native endowment of human language. The A-first account suggests that all disjoint reference conditions belong to pragmatics, with only Condition A as a plausible candidate for a language universal; even here, the linguistic variation suggests that perhaps we are dealing primarily with the semantics of necessary referential dependency. The B-first account, though, suggests that Condition A emerges from usage conditions. The nativist hypothesis, in the absence of direct genetic evidence, can only be an argument from the absence of any alternative plausible account, so the very possibility of a pragmatic account of the core patterns of anaphora must raise doubts about whether the Binding Conditions play as central a role in our innate linguistic endowment as so much linguistic theorizing has presumed.

There is of course no general challenge here to some concept of a rich, restrictive innate linguistic ability or Universal Grammar—only an argument that we need to look elsewhere. Equally, there is no suggestion here that the current patterns of anaphora in, say, English, are entirely pragmatic—rather that the central facts can be seen to have functional motivation, that diachronic explanations might refer more to pragmatic principles than to principles of UG, and that defeasibilities of interpretation, at the margins as it were, are the stigmata of the functional origin of currently grammaticalized patterns. Thus the presumed inability of a pragmatic account to predict, for example, the details of reflexives in raising (or Exceptional Case Marking) contexts like *John believes himself to be ill* does not undermine the thrust of the argument—once a language has grammaticalized an A-first system, such a system will have to treat such weakened clause boundaries one way or the other, as permeable or impermeable barriers to binding.

An important question is whether other well-researched areas of grammatical analysis might not turn out to allow pragmatic analyses. One such possible target is the theory of Control, especially concerned with the study of infinitival complements, and the anaphoric linkage of the understood subject (PRO) of that complement. On the classic analysis, the anaphoric linkage is determined by the subcategorization of the verb as subject-controlling (as in (83a)) or object-controlling (as in (83b)).

(83) a. Max$_1$ promised Mary PRO$_1$ to come.
     b. Max asked Mary$_1$ PRO$_1$ to come.

But as has long been noted, there are indications that the interpretation depends also on pragmatic factors (e.g., the most probable scenario):

(84) a. Max asked Mary$_1$ PRO$_1$ to leave.
     b. Max$_1$ asked PRO$_1$ to leave.
     c. John appealed to Bill$_2$ PRO$_2$ to leave.
     d. John$_1$ appealed to Bill$_2$ PRO$_1$ to be allowed to leave.

In other languages, like German and Russian (Comrie 1984), Guugu Yimithirr (Levinson 1987b), or Chinese (Huang 1994), the pragmatic nature of these patterns is manifest, and the GCI apparatus applies with considerable success to predict the correct outcomes (see especially Huang 1994). But even in English one can note that the patterns, which are at least partially grammaticalized, conform to the pragmatic expectations. Consider for example Chomsky's (1981: 65) Avoid Pronoun principle, which specifies a preference for PRO over an overt pronoun to indicate coreference where both are allowable, as in:

(85) a. He$_1$'d prefer PRO$_1$ going.
     b. He$_1$'d prefer his$_2$ going (disjoint reference preferred).

But this is of course nothing but Horn's division of pragmatic labor (as Horn (1984: 23) points out), whereby an I-inference to local coreference arises from a gap but is defeated by an M-inference from the more prolix pronoun.[95] In short, there are many other areas where a syntactic analysis is generally presumed, but where a pragmatic analysis might predict the crosslinguistic patterns from entirely general principles.

Sometimes, as in anaphora, rather far-reaching pragmatic reductionism of allegedly syntactic principles may be feasible. But GCI theory in general should be seen as complementary to syntactic theory, as part of the explanatory theory for distributional patterns. The division of labor between syntax and pragmatics ought to be constantly in question in the analysis of phenomena. If a pattern appears to be general but defeasible, and explicable in terms of the general behavior of GCIs without any further apparatus, the presumption must be that it does not belong to syntax. If such a pattern is so explicable, but appears firm and not defeasible, we can suspect frozen pragmatics—that is, grammaticalized GCIs—with consequent further pragmatic inferences made available (as in A-first systems). Otherwise, we assume we are dealing with either general or language-specific syntactic specifications. A pragmatic account working in tandem with syntactic principles (as in the A-first account) can give us a better overall explanation on three counts: (a) it is economical, because it reduces what needs special, language-specific or arbitrary specification; (b) it accounts for restricted areas of defeasibility in interpretations just where they occur; and (c) it further constrains the syntactic part of the account by making predictions about further inferences from each syntactic specification of interpretation. That is the ultimate attraction of bringing GCI theory into the overall explanatory apparatus.

However, even grammarians sympathetic to pragmatic explanations have wondered whether pragmatic accounts, given their defeasible nature, can ever play a significant role in linguistic analysis and discovery: as Zribi-Hertz (1995) puts it, "The pragmatic approach thus leads to fuzziness and fuzziness is not heuristically productive." We have tried to show that a system of interacting pragmatic principles, with well-defined interactions between them, could in fact be heuristically valuable. Although the default nature of such principles indeed raises methodological problems by the standards of exceptionless syntactic principles, major pragmatic principles in turn have a signal methodological advantage over syntactic principles—they apply crosslinguistically across the board.[96] Such pragmatic principles make us question, for example, any proposed grammatical stipulation of disjoint reference, make us suspect any opposition between gaps and pronouns (or more generally simplex and complex morphemes) as a potential case of Horn's division of pragmatic labor, and make us scrutinize any privative opposition for its predicted Q-implicatures. The I-principle suggests systematic links ought to be found between clause-connectedness and coreferential interpretations, of the kind represented by PRO-structures, but not sufficiently explored crosslinguistically (see Foley and Van Valin 1983). Such principles also suggest typological distinctions, like those between A-first and B-first systems of anaphora (or systems with greater and lesser syntactic core; see Huang 1994: 259–260). They make rather detailed predictions about diachronic trajectories, as in our B-first to A-first transition, from emphatics to reflexives, thus explaining the associations of reflexives with logophoricity. It has to be conceded that these heuristics are still relatively broad and crude, but then the detailed study of pragmatic principles has hardly begun.

Chapter 5
Epilogue

In this book I have tried to champion the notion of a presumptive meaning or preferred interpretation. The idea is simple but crucial to a theory of communication: when we say something, we find ourselves committed to much more, just by virtue of choices between all the ways we could have said it. There is nothing new in the idea, but the notion has never been pushed to the forefront of the theory of meaning where it belongs, together with the other, more familiar cast of characters—the entailments, presuppositions, metaphors, and so forth. One genus of such presumptive meanings is the category of GCIs, with the now-familiar species of Q-, I- and M-inferences. Together with other principles governing idiomatic use of language, these constitute our third level of utterance-type meaning, sitting between the coded meanings of linguistic expressions on the one hand, and nonce-inferences to speaker-meaning on the other.

Because of the interstitial position of this third level of meaning, reductionists will forever be tempted to assimilate it to either the level of coded meaning or the level of nonce-inference. But this is a mistake, not only because the interstitial nature of the phenomena with its defeasible regularities will resist such a move, but because this third level interacts so deeply with the structure of language that we will never build an adequate linguistic theory without paying proper attention to it.

I hope to have been reasonably successful in making a case for GCIs as an important kind of linguistic orphan. But why, one may ask, are such pragmatic factors so relatively neglected in current linguistic theory? One general source of resistance to incorporating pragmatic factors into linguistic theory is the continued feeling that pragmatics is not well-enough developed to yield any kinds of prediction.[1] Second, the view that pragmatics is concerned only with nonce-inference and with post hoc accounts of speaker-meaning discourages the search for any systematic interrelation between pragmatics and core linguistic theory. Third, the idea that pragmatics concerns itself with nonlinguistic reasoning that happens to be applied to linguistic objects suggests that the essential principles, insights, and goals lie far from those of linguistic theory. Fourth, resistance to the invasion of pragmatic explanations into areas erstwhile thought of as semantic or syntactic may be linked to a mistaken view that such explanations go together with an extreme functionalism that attempts to reduce all structure to use. Such reasons may add up to a feeling that syntax, phonology, and semantics must go it alone.

GCI theory is very clearly not related to this perception of pragmatics. Let me address the points above one by one. The theory makes clear predictions, as I have tried to detail throughout this book (and I will return to the point in a moment). It is not about nonce-inferences nor about post hoc explanations about what a speaker may in full context have meant: it is about what any reasonable interlocutor would understand by a certain way of putting things. The theory is not about reasoning *simpliciter*: it is about special modes of inference that come into play on the basis of our heuristics and their role in the special coordination problems posed by meaning$_{nn}$—indeed, as suggested in chapter 1, the kind of reasoning involved may be the Ur-type of default reasoning. Nor should it be misconstrued as a kind of radical reduction of structure to function: GCIs are inferences from structure and meaning to further presumptive meanings. The role of the theory of GCIs in linguistic theory is as an additional tool in the explanatory armory. It is not likely to replace any of the alternative tools, but it offers to shrink their domains of application to more manageable proportions.

Let us pursue a few of these issues in a little more detail.

5.1 PREDICTIVE POWER OF THE THEORY OF GCIS

GCI theory in its current state is a set of generalizations about the interrelations of linguistic expressions, the extra inferences that these interrelations give rise to, and the conditions under which these default inferences do not go through. These generalizations give us clear expectations about inferences that ought to arise from particular expressions, and in this sense the theory is predictive.[2]

GCI theory makes predictions about language structure at different levels of generalization. At the lowest level, it makes predictions about the presumptive meanings arising from individual morphemes and lexical items in their respective semantic fields. For example, unmarked lexemes will have specializations by I-inference to the stereotype, whereas their marked doublets will pick up complementary interpretations; informationally asymmetric sets of items in the same field will form scales, inverted under negation, with regular scalar inferences; weak scalar items will be in privative opposition with their stronger counterparts, with compatible extensions excluded by implicature. GCIs do not of course predict exactly what is lexically or grammatically coded—that is quite largely a language-specific matter. But they do constrain what is lexicalized, and they do govern the likely relations between such codings. Notice that the theory predicts multiple inferences even from quite small semantic fields, as exemplified by the "logical" connectives with their Q-, M-, and I-inferences (e.g., the scalar inference from *or*, the marked interpretation of double negation, conditional perfection of *if*) and the complex interactions between them governed by the projection rule. Notice too that the theory makes predictions not only about content but about form/meaning relations: unmarked forms pick up I-inferences; marked ones the complementary M-inferences.

At the next higher level, the theory makes general predictions about constraints operating over the lexicalization patterns in such fields. Here, for example, lies the crosslinguistic generalization that O-corners of the square of opposition generally resist lexicalization, while blocking rules in syntax and morphology (Aronoff 1974, Williams 1997) are arguably merely specific instantiations of Horn's (1984) division of labor between I- and M-inferences. At a still higher level, it makes predictions about the interaction of semantics and pragmatics—for example, the intrusion of pragmatic inferences into syntactic constructions where one constituent is evaluated against the interpretation of another. Similarly, it suggests economy in the syntactic component, with, for example, no need for stipulation of disjoint-reference conditions. Putting these different levels of abstraction together, we have clear predictions about pragmatic constraints on language structure—in effect, predictions about possible languages. These predictions arise because the Q-, M-, and I-heuristics operate across the board, generating presumptive inferences that insert themselves willy-nilly into the interpretations of utterances. They thus play a decisive role in structuring lexical fields and syntactic constructions, especially by redundancy constraints: what is implicated need not be coded.

In addition to predictions about synchronic structure at these different levels of abstraction, GCI theory clearly ought to make predictions about process. But here the predictions have not yet been worked out in any detail. Take online utterance comprehension: the prediction clearly is that GCIs should be available early, before full sentence-meaning is computed, because of their association with linguistic expressions and their alternates. There is very little psycholinguistic work directly addressed to implicature, and still less of this concerns online processing, but one may hope for rapid progress here.[3] One might also expect Gricean inferences to play a significant role in hypothesis formation about the meaning of linguistic expressions during language acquisition. The hypothesis would be that children would have the principles early but apply them incorrectly because of incomplete control of the relevant semantic fields (and this seems generally correct; see Jackson 1981; Jackson and Jacobs 1982; Clark 1993, 1997). Finally, GCI theory should make interesting predictions about language change (as in the hypothesis in chapter 4 about the evolution of A-first from B-first anaphoric systems). Because GCIs are regularly associated with linguistic expressions, they may easily be misanalyzed by both theorist and language learner as part of the coded content. On the other hand, the general redundancy constraint (i.e., what is implicated need not be coded) may be expected to put a brake on such tendencies for GCIs to end up as part of the conventional meaning of expressions. The present theory suggests that I-inferences might be primary engines of change, because inferences to the stereotype will reflect changes in sociocultural environment. M-inferences to the complement of I-inferences would then consequently be shifted also. But Q-inferences might be less likely to become conventionalized on the grounds that they arise from constrained sets of salient alternates, where change in the meaning of one member would have immediate implications for the understandings of the other members, the whole set acting as a constraint on change within. These tendencies seem consistent with what is known (see König and Traugott 1988, Traugott 1998).

In sum, GCI theory makes widescale predictions about the association of presumptive meanings with specific forms, and thus crosslinguistic predictions about a myriad of such particulars as lexicalization constraints on quantifiers, the kinds of predicates allowing Neg-raising, the semantic generality of anaphoric expressions, the tendency for switch-reference systems to lack strict coding of disjoint subjects, the rhetorical import of periphrasis or double negations, and so on.

5.2 PRESUMPTIVE INFERENCE AND GENERAL REASONING

It may perhaps be useful to contrast the present approach with some rival assumptions in Relevance theory. Wilson and Sperber (1986, 1991: 583) have argued that pragmatics amounts to nothing more than central reasoning processes applied to linguistic stimuli: "Grammar is a special-purpose modular system; pragmatics is not a cognitive system at all. There are no special-purpose pragmatic principles, maxims, strategies or rules; pragmatics is simply the domain in which grammar, logic and memory interact." They go on to suggest that "many linguists have assumed without question that speakers of English know a pragmatic code, analogous to a grammar, which enables them to recover the intended interpretation.... They have assumed in other words that pragmatics is a module, an extension of the grammar" (1991: 584). There is little doubt that they had Gricean theories of the present sort in mind as the target of these remarks.

The present theory has indeed proposed "special-purpose pragmatic principles," but even here, just as Grice did with his maxims, we hope to show that such principles follow from rational design characteristics (as outlined in chapter 1). Regardless of our success in that, the other charges certainly miss the target. GCI theory does not confuse inference under heuristics with decoding (indeed the Relevance-theory claim that interpretation involves the recovery of a single message under deduction seems closer to a decoding view). Nor is there any assumption that pragmatics is a module in the Fodorean sense of an encapsulated processing module. However, GCI theory does suppose that there is a body of knowledge and practice concerned with the *use* of language. This knowledge crucially involves metalinguistic knowledge about the structure of the lexicon—specifically, knowledge about the structuring of semantic fields, the availability of alternate expressions, subjective assessments of frequency and markedness of specific expressions, knowledge about the stereotypical associations of linguistic concepts in the speech community, mutual assumption of principles for resolving conflicts between inferences, and so on. It also involves mutual awareness of the central heuristics and a crucial understanding that recovering meaning$_{nn}$ involves solving coordination problems under those heuristics. These background assumptions about the nature of communication radically change the nature of the reasoning: if I see a man moving a hand in front of his face, the kind of reasoning involved in trying to guess what he is trying to hit versus what

he is trying to communicate seem very far apart, even though both inferences are in the domain of intention-recovery (Levinson 1995b). The
essential difference is that the mutual assumption of meaning$_{nn}$ and the
heuristics warrant the presumptive inferences that the theory tries to spell
out.

None of this amounts to anything like a module in the Fodorean sense.
But it does suggest that there are specific kinds of inferential analysis done
on the decoded content of utterances that are not applied to our analysis
of other things in the world, including any other noncommunicative
aspect of human behavior. Because (as I have argued) this special mode of
reasoning yielding default, defeasible inferences must interdigitate with
another kind of reasoning that yields monotonic inferences, pragmatic
reasoning of this sort must be organized in such a way that it can interact
with the results of semantic processing. We can, if we like, think about
pragmatic processing as specific kinds of subroutines that are called from
time to time. To that extent, pragmatics can be said to be a component in
an overall theory of grammar, without claiming that all the processes
involved have exclusively linguistic uses.

Sperber and Wilson also assume, along with many cognitive linguists,
that the semantic component outputs (possibly fragmentary) representations that are directly in the "language of thought." This is improbable,
even assuming there is one such thing (most cognitive scientists assume
with good reason that there are multiple conceptual representational
systems). Semantic representations are going to be much too closely tied
to the properties of language in general (e.g., the linearity due to the
medium) and to the structure and content of specific languages (e.g., specific grammatical categories and constructions) to make this plausible.
Rather, it seems that semantic representations are likely to be intermediate formats, which interface with linguistic form at one end and general
conception (and indeed further specialized formats) at the other (Bierwisch
1996; Levinson 1997; see Jackendoff 1996a: 546–547 for discussion). If
pragmatic inferencing is working on semantic representations rather than
conceptual structures (which must, after all, include imagistic representations and the like), then that is another reason to think that pragmatic
reasoning is language-specialized. But, all of this is admittedly speculative.

Despite the close relationship between the inferences discussed in this
book and those that were the ultimate target of Grice's theory, many
researchers may feel that the notion of implicature has here been stretched

too far. First, there is the issue of how GCIs relate to the classical Gricean scheme. In Grice's scheme, speakers implicate, but in my parlance, utterance-types carry generalized implicatures (and the talk of heuristics suggests a comprehension perspective): does this signal a category mistake? Not at all: rational speakers mean$_{nn}$ both what they say (except in non-literal uses of language) and what that saying implicates; different levels of meaning all come under the umbrella of meaning$_{nn}$. Grice (1989: 88–91, 117–137) himself made a number of distinctions within meaning$_{nn}$—for example, the distinctions between the *applied timeless meaning of an utterance-type* (capturing disambiguations), the *occasion-meaning of an utterance-type* (capturing what the speaker means by the use of the words), and *utterer's occasion-meaning* (capturing what the speaker intended). Although the distinctions are tortuous, I think that GCIs would fall somewhere between the first two distinctions (Grice indicates that idioms would be part of applied timeless meaning, and what the words are used to mean falls within occasion-meaning). Because GCIs are associated with utterance-types, they can be accessed without considering the utterer's occasion-meaning, and it is thus legitimate to view them neutrally, both from the speaker's and addressee's perspectives.

A second issue concerns whether GCIs are just too subliminal, as it were, to count as implicatures. In chapter 3, I discussed possible terminological distinctions (of the implicature, implicature, and explicature sort) in the area between what is said and what is not said at all but implicated only. I concluded that boundaries are here hard to draw, precisely because of the way in which the very same inferences may or may not "intrude" into the meanings of complex constructions, and can be phrased in different ways by the analyst. All the authors there surveyed presume that the inferential mechanisms would be essentially the same in all cases, and I have made the same assumption, and argued therefore that there is no clear way to make such distinctions. This may be wrong. It may be, for example, that the inferential procedures underlying I-inferences are sufficiently distinct to belong to an entirely different genus—after all, compared to the M- and Q-inferences they are much less metalinguistic in character, and much more dependent on common presumptions about the world (i.e., stereotypes). We may expect that future research will expose a much more detailed typology of pragmatic inference than we currently have at our disposal. But such a typology should be based precisely on the underlying inferential procedures and corresponding distinctions between the properties of inferences.

5.3 ROLE OF GCIS IN LINGUISTIC THEORY

In chapter 4, I developed a pragmatic account of anaphoric patterns, in partial competition with current syntactic accounts. The idea is that anaphoric potential relies crucially on semantic generality, in line with the I-principle, and that the intricate division of labor between NP-types in different loci is explained by the complex interactions of Q-, M-, and I-inferences, governed by their projection properties. Such moves have been suggested before, but in general the attempts have been rejected by syntacticians on the grounds that they simply don't get down to a sufficient level of detail to be interesting. I have tried to show that the detail both intralinguistically and crosslinguistically, synchronically and diachronically, fits the broad outlines of a pragmatic account. At the same time, different possible analyses, with different degrees of pragmatic reduction, have been sketched to show that the general promise of such an approach does not lie in a particular analysis but in the general way in which it interdigitates with semantic and syntactic accounts.

Chapter 4 suggests a reanalysis of phenomena that have been thought about as purely syntactic—that is, a shifting of the burden of explanation. In the same way, many of the inferences discussed in chapter 2 have been thought to be semantic—that is, part of the coded content of expressions; here, an attempt is made to shift the burden off the coded semantics into pragmatics. These are issues about the division of labor between explanatory devices, and of course there will be plenty of room for further argumentation. What I hope to have established is that GCIs have just the right properties to assume part of this burden.

Chapter 3 introduces more radical issues about the relation of this branch of pragmatics to linguistic theory. I have argued that GCIs force a reconstrual of the semantics/pragmatics interface. Instead of a simple feed-out, feed-in model of the interface, which continues to be assumed in much work that is close to GCI theory (like Relevance theory), I have argued that something more complex is required. But not much more complex: what I have suggested is that we divorce the issue of representation from the issue of what processes or components contribute to that representation.[4] In that way we have a level of representation, say as in DRT, to which the semantics contributes entailed conditions, whereas default inferences contribute pragmatic content marked as subject to later cancellation, and the whole structure can be semantically interpreted in the normal way and can then be further enriched by additional pragmatic inferences based on propositional content. Such a model seems to escape with ease the chicken-and-egg problems (of pragmatic contributions to semantic content) that assail the classical input/output model of the relation of semantics to pragmatics. At the same time, it keeps separate the two crucially distinct kinds of information—the defeasible and the indefeasible content.

There would be other ways to think about this model. One could equally view it in the following way: GCI pragmatics is a theory that inter alia maps (coded) semantic representations onto (enriched) semantic representations. Semantics is now understood to do two things: map syntactic structures onto (coded) semantic representations, and (enriched) semantic representations onto propositions. Pragmatics likewise not only maps initial semantic representations into enriched ones, but (if one likes) propositions into additional propositions. And the two processes, each masters of their own (indefeasible or defeasible) mode of inference, interleave. Thus the general picture is simple enough, although we cannot rule out additional interactions—for example, the role of pragmatics in extracting disambiguated (coded) semantic representations out of syntactic structures in the first place.

This picture though does change the way we think about (coded) semantic content. The more power there is in the pragmatic theory, the less rich such coded content has to be (a point well made by Sperber and Wilson 1986). Other work in pragmatics and semantics is now converging on the idea that such coded content may be abstract in the extreme and may fail to determine anything like a logical form. This opens up intriguing questions about what exactly the shape of such representations is. There are questions both about what we may call structural factors (the syntax, as it were, of semantic representations), and content factors (representations of lexemes in the object language). Many have assumed that the structural properties of semantic representations are logic-like. But there are reasons for doubt. Atlas (1989) argues persuasively that logical negation is not part of our representation of meaning and that negation is scope-indeterminate. Scope-free semantic representations have been proposed by a number of authors (e.g., Bach 1982), and the motivations are obvious. Hobbs (1996: 58) notes that a sentence like (1) has 120 possible scopings:

(1) In most democratic countries most politicians can fool most of the
     people on almost every issue most of the time.

Yet we seem to understand it instantly, and it seems unlikely that speakers or addressees actually compute even a small proportion of the possible readings and then discard the irrelevant ones. Similar problems assail other kinds of structural ambiguity (e.g., PP-attachment as in *Look at the man with a telescope*), and rather than posit a combinatorial explosion of readings, it makes good sense to consider the possibility that the structure is indeterminate or underspecified (see Matthews 1981, Van Deemter and Peters 1995). The need for a pragmatically informed way of building structure is particularly clear in the case of ellipsis (Kempson 1996).

Encoded lexical meanings may also be skeletal. Some authors have arrived at this conclusion just by considering the apparently limitless range of uses of lexemes, often crossing various syntactic categories (Ruhl 1989), or by documenting our ability to create what are clearly nonce uses (Clark 1983, Clark and Clark 1979, Nunberg 1995). It has also been long noticed that senses get specialized in verbal context, which argues against both polysemy and classical conceptions of compositionality. Ross (1981), for example, showed how the meanings of lexemes in construction with one another alter each other's senses (consider the meanings of *on* in *barnacles on the hull*, *soap opera on TV*, *opinion on the matter*, *man on the moon*, *cars on the move*, and so forth). More recently, these issues have come center stage in computational linguistics. Pustejovsky (1995), for example, shows how "co-compositional" effects can be achieved by having semantically general specifications in one lexical item be filled in by semantic specificity in another, supplemented with pragmatic presumptions (so that *John is enjoying the book* suggests that the enjoyment comes from reading it, whereas *John is enjoying the ice cream* suggests another kind of pleasurable activity). As a consequence, we need semantically general senses that will often be specialized by contextual or pragmatic factors rather than intratextual ones. But not every combination of words and background understandings can be forced into a meaningful collocation (compare *a sad day* vs. *an afraid day*). Consequently, Pustejovsky (1995) argues that we have to find a middle ground between sense-enumerative lexicons on the one hand, and fully unconstrained pragmatic determinations of sense on the other.

Current work on semantic generality and underspecification is generally conservative, modifying and relaxing older logical formalisms and sense-representations in the direction of more open structures. But we cannot rule out the possibility that much more radical rethinkings of the concepts of semantic representation are in order (Atlas 1989). These are surely among the most important current questions in the theory of meaning. Here a developed theory of presumptive meanings may play a crucial role: the more that can be said about default pragmatic inferences, the more we can guess about the nature of the semantic representations that must support them. Thus we can make significant progress on these issues only if we work simultaneously on both semantic and pragmatic theory. The central contribution of GCI theory is to suggest specific ways in which, given an underspecified or indeterminate semantic representation of a sentence-meaning, the possible interpretations are not equipollent—there is systematic biasing of interpretations, even before specific contextual influences have come into play. It is because of this predicted biasing that GCI theory, unlike nonce-theories of inference, puts systematic constraints on a theory of underlying representations.

It was Grice's personal goal to try to build a synthesis between the formalist and functionalist views of language (with Russell and Strawson, respectively, as prototypes). He noted that the kind of phenomena surveyed in this book are wrongly ignored by the formalists who fear weeds in their tidy gardens, or as he more memorably put it, "Like Cyrano de Bergerac's nose, they are features which are prominent without being disfiguring" (1987: 373). I have tried to advance this same goal on more thoroughly linguistic, and weedy, turf. The theoretical synthesis may or may not be successful, but that is not ultimately the most important issue, which is to keep those prominent pragmatic features in theoretical play. For as Grice (1987: 379) remarked in a somewhat different context, "The continuation of progress depends to a large extent on the possibility of 'saving the phenomena'."

Notes

Note to Students

1. The only careful collation of versions of Grice's texts that I know of is Arundale 1997.

Introduction

1. Let me emphasize: this is *not* a general theory about the nature of communication. As far as I can see, such a theory will be a composite of many different factors and considerations, including especially interactional factors almost totally ignored in the present work. Most of the resistance to the theory of Generalized Conversational Implicatures is based on a failure to understand its very limited ambitions.

2. Parts of the manuscript have been in circulation for a long time and have their own citation history (a version of chap. 3 in particular has gone the rounds since 1987, a version of chap. 1 since 1989, and a version of chap. 4 since 1991). In the meantime, a number of younger scholars have written pertinent material, sometimes independently drawing attention to the same phenomena, and I have tried to update all references correspondingly; apologies are due if I have overlooked some recent work.

3. The problem is that, whereas the speaker reasoned from an intention to a verbal means of achieving that intention, one can never reason back from conclusions to the premises that produced them—for the simple reason that there are always infinite candidates. Because, as a matter of fact, we do seem to make correct inferences of this kind, there has to be some heuristic limitation of the problem space. I believe that these heuristics are of distinct kinds: the sort explored in GCI theory, for example, as well as the different kind explored in the sequential analysis of discourse, which yields PCIs. All this is developed in chapter 1.

4. There are many suggestions about how to avoid this regress; in some version's of Grice's theory of meaning it is avoided by a reflexive (self-referring) intention—the speaker intending the recognition of that very intention. See, for example, Bach 1987b.

Chapter 1

1. Some authors think that this second version threatens an infinite regress of conditions (Schiffer 1972), and thus some think it much better to stick to the original account in terms of a single self-referring intention. See Harman 1974 (discussed in Avramides 1989: 56–58) and Bach 1987b, 1990: 391–393 on the merits of accounts in terms of reflexive versus iterated intentions.

2. An important departure from the classical Gricean account is sketched in Atlas and Levinson 1981, where it is pointed out that it is the structure of the semantical representation as well as the truth conditions that are the basis for the calculation of implicatures. Manner implicatures can also generally be read off the semantical representation (e.g., p and $\neg\neg p$ will have the same truth conditions, but $\neg\neg p$ will M-implicate that the stereotypical exemplication associated with p is not intended), although in some lexical/morphological oppositions sheer markedness is the operative factor.

3. The typographical emphasis is removed in the reprinting (Grice 1989: 37f).

4. This construal of Relevance (quite unlike the Sperber and Wilson (1986) informational version) correctly captures our pretheoretical intuitions that relevance is about connectedness and collaborative activity, as I outlined in Levinson 1987a. It is also along the lines that Grice intended: the tying of relevance to particular plans and goals is very clear in Grice 1989 (p. 222), hence his objection (p. 371–372) to the Sperber and Wilson conception. Plan-reconstruction accounts of particularized implicature are now standard in the AI literature (see, e.g., Cohen, Morgan, and Pollack 1990, Green and Carberry 1993).

5. Compare for example these recent comments: "His best known examples are particularized implicatures; the discussion of generalized implicatures is restricted to a few cases; and there is no evidence that he saw the distinction as theoretically significant" (Sperber and Wilson 1987: 748) and "The traditional distinction between generalized and particularized implicature is a false one, an artifact of the inventiveness of analysts—or lack thereof" (Hirschberg 1985: 42). Yet Grice's work on implicature opens with the issue of whether there is a way to account for the *systematic* divergences between the logical connectives and natural-language connectives (the issue which motivated his further development of the theory of implicature; see Grice 1989: 374). In addition, there is every reason to think that he was especially interested in the GCIs because they offered some kind of evidence for the way in which utterer's meaning might become associated with expression-meaning (the theory of implicature was a preamble to *that* theory; see Grice 1989: chap. 5 and 6).

6. This makes remarks like the following inapt: "The distinction between 'generalized' and 'particularized' conversational implicature is not represented in this diagram [presented in Neale's paper] because it is theoretically inert (for Grice)" (Neale 1992: 524, note 18).

7. For example (7), see Grice 1961 (1983: 251–252); 1978: 188; 1989: 44–46, 63f, 68. For example (8), see Grice 1981: 186; 1967: Lecture I, 10; 1989: 27, 68. For example (9), see especially Grice 1989: chap. 4.

8. The classical Gricean or Radical Pragmatics tradition took this semantically broad meaning to be identical to the weaker or less specified of the meanings exhibited by the expression in question (e.g., *some* would have a lexical content glossable roughly as 'at least some', which is overlayed by the GCI '(and) not all'. Atlas 1984a, and following him others, have argued that we should not presume this uniformly: we need to entertain the possibility that the lexical content is not to be equated with the weaker meaning but indifferent between the weaker and the stronger. On his account, we need to distinguish, as candidates for the lexical content, between a semantically broad but weakly specific meaning on the one hand, and a semantically general meaning on the other.

9. Of course there are exceptions, notably neo-Griceans such as Bach (1984, 1995) in philosophy of language or Horn (1989) or Huang (1994) in linguistics.

10. Speaker-meaning is here understood exclusively—that is, as speaker-meaning minus sentence-meaning (of course in Grice's theory of communication, both "what is said" and "what is implicated" are *ceteris paribus* part of meaning$_{nn}$, and thus included in speaker-meaning). Similarly, I shall use utterance-type-meaning as a shorthand for meaning that is not conventional meaning and not *just* speaker-meaning (although following the Gricean scheme the speaker means it) but is suggested by the utterance structure.

11. For Austin (1962), the perlocutionary act was a residual category that he was keen to detach from the illocutionary act, the main focus of his interest, and it was certainly broader and less well-defined than speaker-meaning. Nevertheless, this is the Austinian category into which Gricean particularized implicatures would fall: his prototype was an intended effect on an audience which relates to what is said at most obliquely (1962: 101), so that one can say "by saying x, I did y" (even the terminology shows the kinship between Austinian and Gricean thought; see Grice 1986). Searle (1986: 210) for one holds that "Grice argued that the intended effects of meaning were what Austin called perlocutionary effects."

12. Bach developed the notion specifically to account for explicit performatives being primarily constatives while standardly (but indirectly) performing the action they named. Later Bach and Harnish (1979) suggested various generalizations to, for example, indirect speech acts.

13. Following a suggestion of John Lyons.

14. There is nothing easy, of course, about the notion of sentence-meaning. Most formal semanticists operate with a notion of restricted utterance-meaning, assuming deictic and, often, anaphoric resolution. See chapter 3.

15. I owe this observation to Rob van der Sandt.

16. Interestingly, it is not easy to find all this spelled out in the textbooks. On the special kind of processing of speech versus non-speech sounds, and other neuro-physiological specializations, see Lieberman and Blumstein 1988: 148ff. On the perceptual match between auditory acuity and speech sounds see Lafon 1968: 81, fig. 2.

17. Uncontroversial it might seem, but Chomsky of course differs. He has argued (in, e.g., the 1981 Darwin lecture on "Language and communication," or *The Minimalist Program*, 1995: 18) that the mismatch between syntactic structures and parsing strategies points to a more haphazard history of our communicational abilities.

18. A range of measurements for different languages from different authors has been given by Laver (1994: 541–544). Not all the estimates are in agreement. But for English at least, the following facts look solid: in 20 hours of spontaneous English, the fastest rate was 5.4 syllables/sec. or 13.4 segments/sec. Practiced maximal rates for English peak, on optimal segments, at 8.2 syllables/sec., estimated to be a physiologically conditioned maximum.

19. The basis for the calculation, which was kindly made for me by Bill Poser at Stanford, is the following:

(a) the maximal normal speech rate is something like 7 syllables per second, with each syllable consisting on average of 2.5 segments, making a rate of 17.5 segments per sec.;

(b) the information-theoretic content of each segment is taken to be log to base 2 multiplied by n (where $n =$ the number of the phonemes in the language); thus for English (assuming that $n = 40$) we get 5.5 bits per phoneme;

(c) so the data-transfer rate will be the number of segments encoded per second multiplied by the information-theoretic value of each, thus $17.5 \times 5.5 = 96.3$ bps.

Bill Poser tells me that there are specialists who wrangle over how exactly this measure should in fact be computed for human speech. But the general point being made here is that such measures do not accurately calculate the rate of actual human information transfer; only what the rate would be on the counterfactual assumption that interpretive heuristics of various sorts were not in fact employed.

20. Calvert (1986: 178) notes a normal speaking rate of 10 sounds (segments) per second, with an effective maximum of 15 sounds/sec., and adds: "While we typically produce speech at 10 sounds/second, we can understand it at as much as 30 sounds/second when paying careful attention" (quoted in Laver 1994: 543).

21. This kind of argument from design was a favorite device of Grice's, most evident in his seminars (see Grandy and Warner 1986: 31ff). The term *pirot* may have been an oblique doff of the cap to Chomsky's (1957: 104) nonsense example "Pirots karulize etalically."

22. Even from a recipient's perspective, inference seems cheap—for example, there is no time advantage for resolving unambiguous pronominal anaphora over "ambiguous" zero-anaphors (Marslen-Wilson and Tyler, 1980). There may be additional virtues of inference: inferred messages often seem to have greater impact than coded ones, as long noted in traditional rhetoric. Green (1987) notes that this runs counter to Relevance-theory metrics.

23. For example, information is informative relative to goals: we expect a route description for a walker to be different than a route description for a driver, and both to differ from a description of the same landscape for other purposes.

24. The information-theoretic value of such a heuristic can easily be appreciated by comparing it to the compression algorithm based on the idea "only describe what has changed" with the decompression corrollary "what isn't mentioned hasn't changed." The heuristic may also be related to the closed-world assumption used to reason in AI databases: if there's no information about whether x is a P, assume that x is not a P (Reiter 1978).

25. These are not equivalent formulations of course, but here I am just interested in sketching the range of possible domains for such a heuristic.

26. The information-theoretic value of this heuristic can be seen by comparison to frames or data structures with inheritance by default, much used in AI (whereby, e.g., if x is a bird, and birds generally fly, x can be assumed to fly). Such inferences are potentially hazardous because they may be wrong, but where there is a tacit communicational convention to speak in such a way that they can be assumed to be true unless there is explicit warning to the contrary, the danger is removed. Various formalizations of such default reasoning systems may be found in Ginsberg 1987.

27. In the simplest case, ranked informativeness can be characterized in terms of unilateral entailment. Thus in an arbitrary simplex sentence frame like __ *the boys came, All of the boys came* entails *Some of them came*, provided the domain of discourse contains at least one boy.

28. Conflicting inferences would not alone justify the designation "projection problem," which has come to refer to how the inferences of complex expressions may not just be the sum of the inferences due to the parts. But GCIs of complex expressions involve just this kind of problem. See Levinson 1983: 142–144, 224–225, and chap. 3 and 4 in this book.

29. Simplifications include: (i) Q inferences may be based on sets other than informationally asymmetrical ones, (ii) I inferences may have other than stereotypical bases, (iii) the overiding or canceling of GCIs probably depends also on the incremental order of clauses, and certainly Relevance PCIs may override all GCIs. All of these issues are explored in chapter 2.

30. Some philosophers (e.g., Harman 1986: chap. 1), Kent Bach points out to me, insist on a distinction between reasoning and argument (in the sense of proof in a system), but those interested in capturing properties of human reasoning inevitably think about reasoning in terms of systems of inference, which are the only tools we have in which to model reasoning. Still, if one insists on this distinction, defeasibility is a property of reasoning and nonmonotonicity is a property of argument systems. Further, the exercise in this section may then be beside the point: reasoning is an activity that may employ fragments of argument, jumps of intuition, violent revisions of belief. Reasoning is an activity, not a system, and different modes of reasoning cannot be captured in terms of distinct systems.

31. These properties of implicature are well known (see, e.g., Levinson 1983: chap. 3), so those who want to hold onto a deductive account must, to preserve monotonicity, argue that the apparent defeasibility of implicatures is not in fact a matter of cancellation through the addition of a premise but rather through the

replacement of the entire set of premises. Implicature cancellation would then be exactly like having taken the wrong horn of an ambiguity, and being jolted by a later context into backtracking and taking the other horn. But there is no evidence for this and rather a lot against it, including the absence of garden-path phenomena in implicature resolution (compare, e.g., the cancellation of the implicature in "John stole some of the money, and possibly all of it," where there is no garden-path phenomenon, to "John didn't steal some of the money, he stole ALL of it," where there is). Another problem for the premise-swapping account is that there is in fact no contradiction in an utterance like "The facts are that John stole some of the money, if not all of it. In fact, my own belief is that he didn't steal it all," where a scalar implicature is generated, then suspended by a clausal implicature, but then the very same suspended inference is asserted. No serious attempt has ever been made to explain all these well-known problems by the few (like Sperber and Wilson 1986) who continue to maintain a deductive account (see Levinson 1989).

32. Some philosophers (e.g., Harman 1986: 4–5) think that the very notion of an "inductive logic" is a category mistake, arising from a confusion between reasoning and inference system.

33. Peirce (1932: 150–156) writes:

"The surprising fact, C, is observed;
But if A were true, C would be a matter of course;
Hence there is reason to suspect that A is true"

34. Thanks to Doug Edwards for pointing this out to me.

35. See, for example, Pople 1973, Reggia and Nau 1984, and Charniak and McDermott 1987.

36. Actually, this account departs slightly from Gazdar's characterization. For one thing, his model was concerned with a single speaker's commitment slate rather than with a model of what is mutually taken for granted (Gazdar 1979: 130).

37. This tagging approach is in fact the one adopted in chapter 3, where a DRT-type representation of utterance content is suggested, with both semantic and pragmatic conditions represented, but the pragmatic ones kept demarcated so that they are later erasable.

38. Perhaps this is what McCarthy (1980, 1986: 147) had in mind when he wrote of his theory of nonmonotonic reasoning using circumscription: "In puzzles, circumscription seems to be a rule of inference, while in life it is a rule of conjecture" (where by "puzzle" he meant a linguistically posed problem).

39. Bach (1984) has, for example, suggested that default reasoning in general (e.g., about the physical world) might be based on rather simple rules of thumb— for example, 'if it seems that p, infer p, *unless* a reason to the contrary occurs to one'. Here the weight of keeping reasoning reasonable falls on some special, yet to be elucidated, detection procedures for counterexamples (p. 45). But where tacit coordination and the mutual presumption of heuristics are operative this gets transformed: 'if the speaker seems to mean p, (he knows that we'll mutually

assume that) he does mean *p*, unless he signals otherwise'. The onus has been transferred to the speaker. It seems to me that quite a few types of fallacy in human reasoning can be attributed to confusing noncommunicational situations with communicational ones (Levinson 1995b).

40. Some authors (e.g., Searle 1979) doubt that there is much value in a notion of utterance-token meaning, on the grounds that an utterance-token has the same semantic content as its type, and its import as a token is best captured in terms of psychological notions (i.e., in terms of speaker-meaning).

41. GCIs are of course not untypical at all, if the phenomena surveyed in chapter 2 are anything to go by, and as I have argued they were certainly the ultimate targets of Grice's investigations. Nevertheless, it should be emphasized that GCI theory was never intended to replace the need for a theory of PCIs, although it may give clues to how such a more general theory might be usefully developed (see Hirschberg 1985). A great deal of misunderstanding has been generated by the failure to see the need for the third level in the theory of communication—namely, a theory of utterance-type meaning—and the failure to appreciate the very limited ambitions of GCI theory.

42. The critiques of Relevance theory center on getting any kind of predictive measure out of the theory (for a sympathetic attempt, which ends up adopting an account Sperber and Wilson (1986: 130) reject, see Poznanski, 1992: 129–44). The essence of the problem was given by Zipf's (1949: 3–4) maxim of the "singleness of the superlative"—maximizing the inferences while minimizing the effort is a double superlative that "renders the problem completely meaningless."

43. There are special controversies concerning the implicature analysis of cardinals; see chapter 2. Those who prefer other scalar predicates can substitute examples of the type *John stole some of the books, if not all of them*, and similar examples.

44. See Horn 1972, 1973; Gazdar 1979; Levinson 1983.

45. This holds except when the contradiction is read as a self-correction, as is perhaps possible in (42b).

46. Thomason credits his student McCafferty with many of the central ideas here; see McCafferty 1987.

47. Such accounts can be elaborated in various ways. For example, one can distinguish different kinds of accommodation (Thomason 1990: 352; see also Heim 1982: 381–384 and Soames 1989: 577–579), but these details are peripheral to the present discussion.

48. However, I will not concede that their accounts are adequate even here; for one thing, the concept of appropriateness or felicity on which the accounts rest is problematic (see Levinson 1983: 24–27).

49. Heim (1982) did not accept the uniqueness condition; but see Kadmon (1987) for a defense of it within a Kamp/Heim-type framework.

50. The entailments from A to I and E to O only go through, in modern standard quantificational logic, if we assume existential import for the universals (i.e., if there are some individuals quantified over in the universe of discourse).

51. Horn (1989: 260) discusses a principled exception: *needn't* is indeed interpreted as 'not obligatory', but this is because *need* is a negative polarity item that cannot be interpreted with internal negation as 'obligatory not'. Thus there is not the same pressure to interpret *needn't* in the same way that we interpret *musn't*, as at the E corner of the square.

52. The prediction is thus that, for example, the Sheffer Stroke (|, equivalent to $\sim(p \,\&\, q)$) will not appear as a surface lexical item in languages. For an extended discussion of Gricean constraints on logical connectives, see Gazdar and Pullum 1976 and Gazdar 1979: 74–87.

53. Herb Clark has suggested to me that these lexicalization facts might be accounted for without recourse to a theory of GCIs (which he is resistant to, being himself a nonce-implicature theorist), along the following lines:

(a) what is infrequently used, fails to lexicalize;
(b) negative expressions are infrequently used;
(c) ergo, "not all" etc. fail to lexicalize.

The reasons this argument fails is precisely because of the asymmetry between the lexicalization of the E corner ("none", "impossible", etc.) and the absence of lexicalization of the O corner.

54. The need for a theory of preferred interpretation in the theory of communication is perhaps just a reflex of a need for a new kind of theoretical object in the social sciences generally—namely, the maxim, the preferential mode of behavior. Bourdieu (1977) has argued eloquently for this kind of construct (his "habitus"), distinct from the notion of norm or rule (with its strict complementarity between permitted/prohibited or grammatical/ungrammatical), but capable of generating regularities in behavior. It is the *preferred ways* of making bread, of cooking leeks, of talking at dinner, or of marrying kin, passing on property, making a living, and so on, that constitute a culture, just as much as the jural rules that have been the major focus of anthropological research. I am chagrined to have to acknowledge that John Haviland pointed this out me almost a decade ago before I could see any sense at all in it.

Chapter 2

1. Thus Gazdar (1979: 46–47) argues that uttering "*p*" implicates in general that the speaker knows that, or is committed to, *p*—thus accounting for Moore's Paradox (the oddity of asserting "*p* but I don't believe that *p*"). Atlas 1993a elaborates Grice's (1989: 42) objection—namely, that this amounts to nothing more than a restatement of the maxim. In Grice's scheme, Quality plays an important part in the generation of PCIs like irony and sarcasm.

2. The reference (Grice 1989: 26) is to Kant's *Critique of Pure Reason* (1781: 70; 1933: 107). Irrespective of Kant, the four central Aristotelian categories of Quantity, Quality, Relation, and Action (Manner or Modality) have long been central in English philosophy of language. See, for example John Wilkins' 1641 *Essay towards a real character, and a philosophical language* (Eco 1997: 240).

3. I have phrased the principles in terms of a speaker's maxim and an addressee's corollary for reasons of perspicuity. They could be phrased more neutrally as heuristics to which both speaker and addressee are mutually oriented, as I sketched in chapter 1. There is however a special onus on the speaker: he or she will be understood *ceteris paribus* to have meant what (to employ the legal jargon) "any reasonable man" would have meant by the choice of expression that he or she used under these heuristics.

4. Assuming the domain of discourse to be non-empty.

5. As already mentioned, "U" $+>$ 'p' designates that uttering U implicates p, or more exactly an utterance of the type U engenders *ceteris paribus* the generalized conversational implicature p. I shall however be loose for the sake of brevity and reduce clauses to the relevant expressions; thus whereas one should say: 'a sentence of the form "Some φ'd" $+>$ 'Not all φ'd', I will sometimes reduce this to the statement: "Some" $+>$ 'Not all'. This is indeed loose talk. Where important, I distinguish between the implicated content alone (designated by $+>$) and the (relevant) implicated content together with what is 'said' (designated $++>$).

6. These utilize the epistemic logic formulated by Hintikka (1962). Readers may find it helpful to think of this as essentially related to an S4 Modal Logic; thus $Kp \equiv \sim P \sim p$, and so on.

7. For example, whereas "John has three children" may have the weaker implicature 'the speaker doesn't know that John has four', "I have three children" clearly carries the stronger 'the speaker knows he doesn't have four'. First-person statements can then often be expected to carry the stronger inference.

8. There are however one or two distinct signs that the weak epistemic modification is not correct for the scalar implicatures. For example, from the perhaps rather special scale ⟨*know, believe*⟩, an utterance of the form "I believe that p" will then generate an implicature 'The speaker doesn't know that/whether the speaker knows that p', which is incoherent or incorrect (whereas the stronger form 'The speaker knows that it is not the case that the speaker knows that p' is fine).

9. But Hirschberg (1985: 81) represents this as $\sim \text{BEL}(S,$ 'All came') in a three-valued logic (so $\sim \text{BEL}(S, p)$ ranges over cases where S believes p *false* and where S does not know whether p is true).

10. Jay Atlas clarified the point to me thus: asserting a weak scalar "A(W)" implicates $\sim A(S)$ because the addressee infers from "A(W)" that the speaker is not in an epistemic position to assert "A(S)." The speaker intends that $\sim A(S)$ is recognized to be consistent with what the speaker knows, this to be the grounds for adding plain $\sim A(S)$ to the common ground.

11. The essence of the problem is that we need a wider range of distinct epistemic commitments than are offered by duals of K and P. The Horn-scale inferences are in fact among the strongest commitments that can be implicated; much weaker suggestions also arise, as I show later on.

12. Here the *ceteris paribus* clause allows of course for the defeasibility of implicatures. Gazdar (1979) made a distinction between potential implicatures and

actual (uncanceled) implicatures, the output of the projection procedure, but I will leave this implicit. It is in fact required for his projection solution, adopted in part later on.

13. Thus Kp can be read 'The speaker believes p', and $Kp \equiv \sim P \sim p$, where $\sim P \sim p$ is read 'it is not consistent with what the speaker believes that not-p'. K and P are thus related like $\square$ and $\lozenge$ in, on Gazdar's 1979 formulation, an S4 modal logic.

14. See Gazdar (1979: 57–58) for more careful definition.

15. Van der Auwera (1995) attacks this lexicalization constraint because he wishes to enlarge the scope of scalar implicature to account, for example, for conditional perfection, (in the current framework, this will be given a completely different account in terms of the I principle). In fact, the degree of lexicalization of scalar items is crucial for understanding the complexities of scalar interpretations. The point is made clearly by Horn (1989: 497–499), who notes that it is precisely because there is no lexicalization of, for example, 'not everybody' that "Everybody didn't come" has an ambiguity of scope. Matsumoto (1995: 45) also attacks the lexicalization constraint in order to extend the scope of scalar implicature, even though his own theory of the bounding of scalar implicatures by a "conversational condition" (to the effect that there should be no *other* reason why the speaker might have avoided a stronger statement) is in fact more in line with the account given here and the brevity condition of Levinson (1983: 135). (These remarks are prompted by an unpublished note of Horn's.)

16. In dubbing this the "aboutness" constraint, Atlas and Levinson (1981: 42f) gesture at the theory of "aboutness" developed by Putnam (1958); see also Atlas 1989: 100ff.

17. The phenomenon of scale reversal under negation was clear early on (see, e.g., Fauconnier 1975, 1979), but the fact that this *solves* the projection problem without blocking under negation was apparently lost on later commentators.

18. Horn (1989: 169–170), reviewing the psychological literature, notes that the latencies are best accounted for on the assumption that negatives are converted into affirmatives.

19. An early application of Gricean or proto-Gricean ideas to the analysis of the Square is given by Fogelin (1967). For a review of the history of approaches here, see Horn 1990. For interesting recent extensions in the analysis of modals, see Van der Auwera 1996.

20. This is related to the restriction noted by Barwise and Cooper (1981) that monotone-increasing and monotone-decreasing quantifiers may not be conjoined, thus *Few students and most faculty came*, a constraint that can be described alternatively as 'Do not mix quantifiers from positive and negative scales' (see Horn 1989: 245ff).

21. The facts here are in fact underdescribed: many of the quantifiers have specific semantic constraints on their application. Thus *most* (as in *Most of the men came*) requires at least three members in the domain of discourse, and *many* is not tol-

erant in small domains (e.g., if many, say five, of seven men came, then one could not assert *Many didn't come*).

22. How do we determine this horizontal alignment? Partly in terms of which side of the tolerance line they fall. But partly by Horn's stipulation that a quantifier Q and its internal negation Q... $\sim$ are linked by a horizontal line. Suppose then we wish to know whether *most* has as a (sub)contrary *few*: we know that *most* is intolerant, so can only have a contrary; so if *few* is to be a candidate, it must be intolerant, which in fact it is (**Few of them came but few did not come*). *Most men came* has as contrary *Most men did not come;* so we can use the suspension tests to see whether *few* is ranked higher or lower on the negative scale than *most...not*, and what we find is that we can say *Most men didn't come, and in fact few came* but not ?? *Few came and in fact most men didn't come*, which suggests that *few* is higher on the scale and thus not a true contrary for *most*. In fact, on Horn's arithmetic model (sub)contraries Q and Q... $\sim$ should be so arranged that they sum to zero (i.e., are linked by a horizontal line).

23. If a hint is required: the positive scale is (or at least includes) ⟨*always, almost always, usually, often, sometimes*⟩ and its negative counterpart is ⟨*never, hardly ever, rarely/seldom, not always*⟩; see further hints given by Horn (1989: 238–239).

24. Such a paraphrase is not of course an analysis of the relevant semantic representation, which might be formalized in various different ways.

25. Kempson also introduces the issue of examples like "He doesn't have THREE children, he has four", rejecting Horn's account in terms of metalinguistic negation. I take up these issues in chapter 3.

26. Some scholars consider that there are a number of other fatal flaws in the implicature account of numeral expressions. For example, Seuren (1998: 409) thinks that *exactly three* would then incoherently mean 'exactly at least three'; but the solution is given by Kadmon (1987: chap. 4), who shows how an 'at least' semantics is compatible with modifiers like *exactly* (and nonredundant with *at least*) within a DRT framework. Essentially the solution works by treating *three men* like an indefinite phrase: *three* introduces an exact cardinality, but there is no commitment that that the set of three men is exhaustive. She points out that such a view is compatible with any further constraints on interpretation that may arise from predicative uses or rhematic positioning (an observation that has led other scholars, like Scharten (1997), to abandon the implicature account).

27. These data are from my own field notes, but independent confirmation can be found in the glosses of Haviland (1979: 176).

28. Compare (i), where in B's utterance the cardinal has the normal GCI, which thus contrasts rhetorically with A's utterance which lacks it; with (ii) where B's utterance still has the GCI despite the fact that an 'at least' interpretation would contrast better rhetorically but is obscured by the GCI:

(i)   A: I could earn at least ten dollars there.
      B: Well, you will earn ten dollars here.
          +> no more than ten dollars

(ii) A: I could earn only ten dollars there.
    B: Well, you will earn ten dollars here.
        +> no more than ten dollars

A similar pattern holds for the classic scalar implicatures:

(iii) A: He stole at least some of the money there
     B: Well, he stole some of the money here
        +> 'not all'

(iv) A: He stole only some of the money there
    B: Well, he stole some of the money here.
        +> 'not all'

Thus although in these discourse contexts an implied contrast is required, the 'at least' interpretation fails to come to mind for both the cardinal and the quantifier case, where it would be most relevant. This suggests that in both cases there is a GCI biasing interpretations in the same direction, regardless of the different discourse biasing (a pattern impossible to account for in a nonce-inference account like Relevance theory).

29. This may be an over-simple analysis for English. Hawkins (1991: 414–416) suggests *the* and *that* carry conventional implicatures that share the uniqueness specification but differ in the domains in which uniqueness is required, hence they are not in a relationship of privative opposition.

30. The typology of tense systems is not well worked out. There are systems of apparently six true tenses in Papuan languages, where the implicatural relations can be expected to be rather different.

31. Alternatively, Larry Horn suggests to me, one could claim that in the stereotypical case one does not succeed without trying, and thus *succeed* I-implicates 'try'. But just how the generalized implicatures of expressions should play a principled role in the construction of scales has never been worked out (indeed for arguments against the transitivity of implicatures, see Atlas 1984b: 359, 372–373). For remarks on the PCIs of context-dependent scales see Hirschberg 1985.

32. Another possible analysis, suggested by Kent Bach, is to hold on to the entailment analysis by denying that (18c) is a literal use of language.

33. See Horn 1989: 268ff. The problem of the compatibility of distinct color predicates is as old as the hills; see Frege 1884 (1953: 22) quoted in Harnish 1991: 316.

34. It is left unclear whether it is the linguistic expressions themselves that are ranked or the entities they denote.

35. The classical theory of scalar implicature had also assumed partial orderings (Gazdar 1979: 58, n. 22). Incidentally, to bring out the parallels with Horn scales, I will display Hirschberg scales in the same (arbitrary) manner with the strongest expressions to the left.

36. Hirschberg however indicates that on this theory, which attempts to reduce all scalar implicatures to PCIs, some Horn scales will be reanalyzed. For example,

Horn splits the temperature scale to give us two entailment scales $\langle hot, warm \rangle$ and $\langle cold, cool \rangle$; by contrast, Hirschberg (1985: 131) takes a single *is-warmer-than* relation over both sets.

37. Another problem is that the unification of phenomena that is one of the most attractive parts of the theory is in fact partially illusory: we need in fact separate rules for the generation of implicatures from unordered sets.

38. Burton-Roberts (1984) offers a serious account of the pseudo-scale $\langle necessarily\ p, p \rangle$. It was the need to rule out such absurdities that led Atlas and Levinson (1981) to propose the lexicalization and aboutness constraints, which require salient lexical alternates about the same relations.

39. An especially relevant cue may be a fall-rise intonational pattern indicating focus within a given set. See Ladd 1980: 145–162; Horn 1989: 230–231.

40. At first sight it seems that these clausal implicatures might be reduced to scalar implicature, especially if (as argued, e.g., by Soames (1982)) one abandons for scalar implicatures the strong epistemic modification $(K \sim p)$ in favor of the weaker modification $(\sim K \sim p)$ associated by Gazdar with clausal implicatures. But intuitively, from the assertion of *p or q* more is (generally) implicated than uncertainty about the applicability of the conjunction—namely, uncertainty about both individual propositions *p* and *q*. So alternatively (as Horn has suggested to me) we could claim that it is the opposition between the assertion of *p* alone and the disjunction that is responsible for that further inference. But this cannot be achieved by a scalar inference because a scale of the sort $\langle p, p\ or\ q \rangle$ would fail the lexicalization constraint—essential to fend off other pseudo-scales like $\langle \Box p, p \rangle$. What the concept of a clausal implicature captures is indeed this opposition between the assertion of *p* and the assertion of something that fails to entail *p*, but the account relies on a constructional asymmetry between constructions that entail *p* and those that fail to do so. Overall, I still find Gazdar's concept essential.

41. This is because an overt violation of the second maxim of Quantity is also likely to simultaneously infringe the maxim of Relevance or the maxim of Manner, just as Grice foresaw.

42. The symbol (.) indicates a short pause.

43. M-intention is Grice's (1989: 105) shorthand for the complex reflexive intention involved in speaker's meaning—namely, the speaker's intention to cause an effect in the recipient just by getting the recipient to recognize that that was his/her intention.

44. For example, because of the stereotype that gold is yellow, *white gold* or *blue gold* suggests a substance other than gold (cf. *black gold* for 'oil'), although jewellers in fact deal in both, and pure gold is white, uncontaminated with copper (see also Putnam 1975: 250).

45. A formal machinery that might be adapted for characterizing such a notion was explored originally in Carnap's (1947) concept of *intensional isomorphism*: to capture the fact that say $\sim (\sim p)$ and *p* have the same intension but not the same meaning, we need a notion of structured intensions in which they may be seen to be nonisomorphic (see, e.g., Lewis 1972: 182–186).

46. Those who believe in notions like explicature (Sperber and Wilson 1986) or impliciture (Bach 1994) will find in these characterizations of I-implicature further reason for suspicions that many GCIs are really instances of these preimplicatural enrichments of conventional meaning into something closer to what the speaker intended. This is perhaps mostly a harmless terminological matter. However, if it is thought that these notions will rescue us from serious dilemmas about the interaction of semantics and pragmatics, then see chapter 3.

47. An inability based either on the speaker's knowledge that a more informative proposition would be false, or on his or her lack of knowledge that it would be true.

48. Horn (1984) dubs this the "transderivational" property, in reference to the long-defunct rules in Generative Semantics that licensed a derivation only by comparison to another parallel derivation.

49. Van der Auwera notes rightly that, in earlier formulations of the constraint, Atlas and Levinson (1981) required *equal* lexicalization of expressions in a scale and that negative scales (like ⟨*none, not all*⟩) are then counterexamples. The correct formulation of the constraint is that the stronger element must be *equally or more lexicalized* than the weaker element. The properties of negative scales are now correctly accommodated. But for the psychological reasons I discuss in section 2.2.2 above, it may be better anyway to think of negative scales as introduced by meta-rule from the positive scales. Either way, the lexicalization constraint now escapes his strictures. However, in an interesting observation (1995: 5), he claims that Chinese does lexicalize 'iff' and 'if' to approximately the same degree, and if this is indeed so, the current theory predicts that the consequent Q-implicature from the *if*-expression should defeat conditional perfection, because if one meant the biconditional one should have said it.

50. Exactly how these utterances get read as conditionals is another matter; it has much to do with the illocutionary force of advice/suggestion associated with this use of the imperative, constituting a minor sentence-type (see Sadock and Zwicky 1985).

51. What I said was if *p* I-implicates *q*, then *q* must entail *p*, but that in both Q- and I-induced implicatures this is only one of the conditions (Levinson 1987a: 74). What I should have said is "If *p* I-*implicates *q*, then *q* must entail *p*. However, in neither the Q- nor the I-induced *implicatures is it [this necessary condition] anything like a *sufficient* condition." I would have thought that the second sentence made it sufficiently clear that the entailment condition between *implicatures and what is said holds for both species of *implicature. The reason that Carston (1995) attaches so much importance to this is that she hopes to make a distinction between *explicature* and *implicature* that hinges on implicatures not entailing explicatures. In fact, that distinction fails anyway, as I discuss in chapter 3.

52. This phenomenon was one of the first to receive Gricean treatments by linguists (see citations in Schmerling 1975).

53. An obvious problem with the generality of this account is that the phenomenon of implicated temporal succession occurs with untensed verbs. Consider

"Drinking a gallon of beer at the pub and driving home is wicked", a type of example made much of in the next chapter.

54. Most of Carston's (1995) supposed counterexamples to the proposed I-implicature are therefore beside the point.

55. Guugu Yimithirr does not lacks complex clausal relators entirely; it is simply that others are encoded. Guugu Yimithirr has three kinds of apprehensional clause connectors that current English lacks entirely (Haviland 1979), for example:

(i) Yuba-aygu dhadii   bidha buli-igamu.
    near-EMPH go + IMP child fall-PRECAUTIONARY
    'Go up close *lest the child fall.*'

56. Larry Horn points out to me that two indicatives can have a conditional in-terpretation in English, too, as in *You want it, you got it* (especially with a rising intonation on the first clause). But the imperative plus indicative construction clearly has (as he points out) more conventional conditional force, as indicated by the negative polarity forms in, for example, *Take any of that money and you're dead.*

57. This form of incremental processing is incorporated into formal semantic models like DRT. Note too that presuppositions of the consequent can be asserted in antecedents but not vice versa (as in *If John has children, John's children must have black hair too*; cf. *John has children. John's children must have black hair too.*)

58. Why is this contrast between *and* and nothing (parataxis) not obvious in English? It is obscured by a number of factors, such as prosodic marking, which can turn a paratactic association into an unrelated list, and syntactic gapping and reduction, which take the place of parataxis to suggest close association between events.

59. However, verb omission or gapping proper in English actually inhibits a causal reading (Levin and Prince 1986; Levin 1987): *A man was shot and a woman was arrested* can be read as a causally related sequence, but *A man was shot and a woman arrested* suggests a mere list. Clearly, gapping is restricted to sentences with parallel structure and thus suggests parallel, perhaps simultaneous, events.

60. French windows in British English denote glass-filled doors, or door-length windows.

61. There are exceptions like *hot*, which participates both in the scale ⟨*hot, warm*⟩ (and its negative corollary ⟨*not-warm, not-hot*⟩) and in the I-implicature from its negation to its antonym *cold*. The prediction from my theory is that "It is not hot" should Q +> 'It is warm', for this should defeat the inconsistent I-implicature 'It is cold'. This seems to be the case.

62. Assuming the subject is a rational thinker. Incidentally, I use the term "read-ing" here for conciseness, without conceding that the construction is ambiguous. Like Horn, I assume that there is in fact only one (semantically contradictory, rather than contrary) reading and two understandings or interpretations.

63. Although it does of course Q-implicate 'It is possible that she'll come'.

64. For much crosslinguistic information, see Horn 1978, 1989.

65. In general, iconic factors enter into the present account in two ways: simple, brief, unmarked expressions warrant maximally cohesive, stereotypical readings, by virtue of mutual attention to the I-principle; and marked expressions indicate the complementary interpretations by the M-principle that is about to be explained. Iconicity itself is *sui generis*, but the exploitation of it by virtue of mutual orientation to such licensing principles converts it into a matter of communicative expectation and thus a pattern of generalized conversational implicature. Hence it should occasion no surprise that many of the factors detailed in Haiman's (1985a) notes on the iconicity of grammar surface again in a theory of GCIs.

66. The intoxicating I-implicatures of *drink* are now long conventionalized and recognized in dictionaries as a separate sense, an autohyponym. In contrast, the sexist I-implicatures of *secretary* or *nurse* are, argues Horn, matters of social rather than linguistic convention. Certainly, I-implicatures seed the crystalization of semantic change, and one can expect to see gradations of conventionalization. But the distinction may not be so easy, because by changing social conventions one can change linguistic ones: in British English *vicar* and *vicaress* meant, respectively, male priest in the Church of England and his spouse, until the recent innovation of female priests.

67. If this is so, notice that the child's task is greatly complicated by the tendency for common vocabulary items to have irregular or suppletive forms instead of regular derivations, as in the strong verbs in Germanic, with *went* instead of *goed*.

68. Like many observations useful to the GCI theorists, these derive from Generative Semantics, which attempted to "syntacticize" many acute observations about meaning. The orphans of that theory, including the one discussed here or Neg-raising discussed previously, can in many cases be happily adopted within GCI theory. Newmeyer (1980), Harris (1993), and Seuren (1998: 502–526) offer accounts of the Generative Semantics movement and reference to central works.

69. Note that the prior existence of *sad*, following the blocking principle mentioned earlier, requires that *unhappy*—despite being read as a contrary of *happy* —somehow means something different from *sad*; the solution with this (and other cases like *unintelligent*) is to associate the derived form with a slightly less extreme value on the scale (see Horn 1989: 279–280).

70. Schmerling (1975) discusses these cases and points to a number of significant syntactic differences between the reduced and unreduced forms. For example, (i), but not (ii) and certainly not (iii), seems to allow a violation of Ross's coordinate structure constraint:

(i)   "Here's the whiskey that he went to the store and bought ____"

(ii)   ??*"Here's the whiskey that he went to the store and he bought ____"

(iii)   *"Here's the whiskey that he both went to the store and he bought ____"

From this she concludes that the first is not a real conjunction but more like a complex VP of the *He went and broke it* kind. Note however that the implicature of (i) is not fully grammaticalized or conventionalized to the point of non-defeasibility: "He went to the store and bought some whiskey on the way home" seems fine. An alternative possibility is that extractions of this kind are sensitive to the full Gricean import of the conjoined VPs, the sort of heretical thought entertained by Gordon and Lakoff (1971).

71. This is not to deny that such patterns can become conventionalized in constructions of the kind studied in Construction Grammar, a candidate being *There are Ns and (there are) Ns*, which suggests constrastive subsets of N.

72. A further wrinkle is the different possible phonetic realizations of the articles. Thus *the* is normally reduced to [ðə], but sometimes occurs with the close front vowel as in [ði:]. As one might expect from the 'division of pragmatic labour', [ðə] signals 'business as usual' (by I-implicature), whereas [ði:] signals warning (by M-implicature) of problems in production. See Fox Tree and Clark 1997. For other examples of markedness signaling interactional problems, see Levinson 1987a.

73. Gazdar (1979) was careful to distinguish *actual* from *potential* implicatures—that is, inferences that may arise but be discarded as candidates for part of what the speaker meant. I have been terminologically less exact, but I trust harmlessly: a presumptive inference will have the status of a generalized implicature if there is no reason to discard it.

74. For the reasons mentioned, it is relatively hard to find cases where I-inferences and Q-scalar inferences are in conflict. A puzzling case is discussed by Atlas and Levinson (1981: 44–45), involving a negative scale and conjunction-buttressing:

i. "It is not the case that John turned the switch and the motor started."
   Q-scale: $\langle \sim(p \text{ or } q), \sim(p \& q) \rangle$
   Q-inference: 'p or q' i.e., 'John turned the switch or the motor started'
   I-inference: 'It's not the case that John turned the switch and then as a result the motor started'
   Overall import of utterance:
   Reading (a): (can be forced by stress on *and*); Q defeats I:
   'Either John turned the switch or the motor started.'
   Reading (b): I-inference survives (where prosody indicates the conjunction is one complex event): 'It's not the case that John turned the switch thereby causing the motor to start', i.e., the whole complex event did not occur.

The proper explanation of reading (i-b) is not clear. One possibility, explored in chapter 3, is that the implicature here falls within the scope of the negation because it is, in a sense to be explored, incorporated within 'what is said', or intrudes into the truth conditions.

75. I have actually said little about ellipsis, but where, as here, the syntax does not resolve the missing constituents, the I-interpretation to maximal cohesion and coherence may supply them.

76. Another instance: in "He was able to solve the problem and it's possible he did so", the first clause carries an I-inference to 'He did so'; but the Q (clausal) inference from "it's possible he did so" to 'for all the speaker knows he didn't do so' defeats the I-inference.

77. As mentioned, Soames (1982) suggests that both scalar and clausal implicatures should have the weak epistemic modification, of the form $\neg K p$. Then inconsistencies between scalars and clausal implicatures do not seem to arise and one could dispense with the relative ordering of incrementation. But in fact this proposal doesn't capture the intuitive difference in epistemic content between the two types—it is the epistemic uncertainty that is precisely the content of the clausal inferences but not the scalars, which is why I have not followed him here.

78. This does remove one of the outstanding differences between presupposition projection and implicature projection, presuppositions by definition not being blocked by negation. In the case of scalar implicatures, the reversal of the scale comes to the same thing as blocking, but in the case of other implicatures, their behavior can now be seen to be the same as presuppositions.

79. Gazdar (1979) added also presupposed content; in fact, he was especially interested in the interactions between implicatures and presuppositions. But I leave all this aside here.

80. Theoretically arbitrary distance has to be tempered by performance facts. In fact, psycholinguists know well that conversationalists store only the gist of utterances long term, not the form, and thus presumably not the distinction between information coded and information implicated.

81. Such a notion has no relation to the Sperber-Wilson (1986) theory of Relevance, which is in fact an informational principle like my I-principle, bounded by effort, or something like my M-principle.

82. Horn (1989: 145), having specified antinomic Q- and R-principles of his own, notes briefly in a column detailing the properties of conversational implicata "Projection properties unclear, since conversational implicatures 'may be indeterminate' (Grice); but cf. Gazdar 1979, Hirschberg 1985." Kent Bach points out to me that one might hold that it is not the job of the GCI theorist to resolve the projection problem anyway. The GCI theorist's job might be complete when the *default* inferences are predicted, the rest of the story being left to the PCI theorist, because projection properties will be a story about particular constructions and usages. And as pointed out in chapter 3, some aspects of the projection problem ought to be solved by a better understanding of the intrusion of pragmatic inferences into the truth-conditional content of certain constructions.

Chapter 3

1. This chapter was, in an earlier form, widely circulated as a mimeo in 1987/1988, and responses to that paper can be found in the literature; since then a number of authors have taken up these themes and I have tried to incorporate responses to them. The ideas were developed in lectures to the 1987 Linguistic Institute of the LSA, and I am grateful to Larry Horn, who co-taught the course, for much interaction over them. In the following year at Stanford, I benefited from much discussion over these issues with Ivan Sag, and I am conscious of having absorbed many ideas, references and ways of looking at issues from him, which I have not acknowledged at every step. Also at Stanford, I gained much

from discussions with Jerry Hobbs, Herb Clark, Stan Peters, Jon Barwise and others; Craige Roberts put me in touch with then recent developments in DRT, without which this chapter would have a lame ending. I thank Jack Hawkins, Murvet Enç, Irene Heim, Ed Keenan, John Searle, Chuck Fillmore, and Paul Kay for most useful comments on oral versions given at USC, UCLA and Berkeley. The ideas have also benefited immensely from long discussion with Jay Atlas.

2. One such historical reason was the attrition of the "wars of presupposition," between those who held that presuppositions were essentially pragmatic, and possibly implicatural, in character, and those who held that they were essentially semantic. The battles seem to have come to an end from mutual exhaustion without final resolution. Another such reason was the attempt to derail the Gricean program by developing the theory of particularized implicatures at the expense of the generalized, a program that arguably has little strictly linguistic interest.

3. I consider this discovery of the different components of meaning to be the fundamental advance in modern semantics. Of course, it may happen that (as I myself have suggested) specific concepts like "felicity condition" and "presupposition" may in the end be reducible to others; but the point is that the observations of apparently distinct processes constitute the advance. Those who, like Jackendoff or Sperber and Wilson, assume that there is no such variety of phenomena, display, I think, a disregard for the fine-grained texture of linguistic meaning in the hope of getting a simple macroscopic picture. Out of focus photographs can have a certain charm, but out of focus X-rays are of no scientific use.

4. The notion of a component or level in linguistic theory has been thought about both in terms of a distinct type of representation for each level and a distinct set of operations over those representations. Defining the relations between levels as input/output relations requires that representations at the interface are compatible, indeed essentially the same. Another way of thinking has it that there are special mapping rules between levels, allowing much more significant mismatches between representations at the interface (Sadock 1991, Jackendoff 1997). Chomsky (1995: 27) himself uses the term "module" in a special way of course, referring to distinct sets of syntactic constraints (binding theory, Case theory, etc.) which interact in more complex ways to yield, it is supposed, the observed and complex patterns of grammatical well-formedness. Neither my use nor Chomsky's has anything to do with Fodor's (1983) notion of module as a distinct mental faculty.

5. Any overall model of the theory of meaning could be construed in either an abstract ("competence") or a processual ("performance") way. We shall be concerned here primarily with an abstract perspective, essentially with what kinds of information must be available to what processes, rather than the *order* in which such processes might actually operate in speech production or comprehension. As Bach (1994: 154–156) points out, despite noises to the contrary, we are in no position to provide processing models at this stage.

6. The claim that semantics is not autonomous with respect to pragmatics could easily amount to no more than an equivocation on the term "semantics" (Kent

Bach points out to me). Indeed I assume that we need to distinguish one sense of semantics, call it *semantics*$_1$, referring to a process that extracts an impoverished level of semantic representation from surface structure and lexical content, from another, call it *semantics*$_2$, which is a set of procedures that operate over a richer level of semantic representation to compute sense relations, entailment relations and truth conditions. The level of representation extracted by semantics$_1$ may perhaps be relatively autonomous, but even here we have to allow for pragmatic resolution of ambiguities. However, semantics$_2$ computes over a level of representation to which pragmatics has contributed in fundamental ways. My claim is that semantics$_2$ is essentially linguistic and cannot be equated with conceptual structure or thinking in general (as Sperber and Wilson 1986 or Jackendoff 1992a suggest). It is the properties of semantics$_2$ representations (not those of semantics$_1$) that are described in semantic textbooks (under the rubrics of sense relations, entailments, meaning-postulates, truth conditions), so that the claim that *this* level is not autonomous with respect to pragmatics is not a vacuous claim.

7. The truth conditions of sentences or utterances? If utterances, so what? So asks Kent Bach. But on the views developed below (and indeed in Bach 1982, 1987a, 1994), sentences don't have truth conditions, only utterances do. The interesting question then becomes: what kinds of inferential process get us to the minimal proposition-bearing entity, and my claim is that these are just the same kinds of process, with the same kind of product, that elsewhere may take us from a proposition expressed to something else the speaker meant, which is more obviously an implicature.

8. Bach (1994: 143) points out that a slightly unfortunate consequence of this definition is that 'saying that p' then entails 'meaning that p' (in Grice's sense of meaning$_{nn}$), so that Grice is forced to say that a speaker who intends a nonliteral interpretation of, for example, a trope has not 'said that *p*' but merely 'made as if to say that *p*'. One cannot in pure Gricean terminology then talk about 'saying one thing but meaning another instead'. (Grice's concept of meaning$_{nn}$ has itself been endlessly discussed; see, e.g., Schiffer 1972, Avramides 1989.)

9. Compare, for example, Bach (1994: 142, citing Grice 1989: 87): "Let me suggest that ... for Grice the contents of what is said are *structured* propositions associated with syntactic forms," so that, for instance, active-passive pairs with the same truth-conditional content will not count as 'saying the same thing'. Earlier, Bach and Harnish (1979: 29ff) had pointed out that the formula '*U* said that *p*' must be taken opaquely; that is, what *U* said depends not only on the extension but the intension, the sense, of the expressions used. Grice's own views about how finely the contents of what is said are to be individuated beyond the level of truth conditions are, it must be admitted, not clearly articulated.

10. It is a much discussed point whether anaphoric linkages should be thought of as syntactic ambiguities (resolved by grammatical coindexing) or semantic ambiguities (resolved at the level of denotation assignment) or, as I argue in section 3.24 and in chapter 4, as semantic generality requiring pragmatic resolution (except in the case of syntactically specified coreference, as in reflexives).

11. Thus in example (4), if the utterance is interpreted with the bracketing "He likes [some [cats and dogs]]", then the implicatures will include 'He like some but not all dogs'. If this is canceled by the preceding context, then we will have as interpretation of the whole utterance 'He likes some but not all cats and at least some dogs', which does not seem to be what is conveyed.

12. Thus in the context of Montague's treatment of pragmatics as the study of indexicality, Thomason (1974: 64) says "the close similarity of pragmatic and semantic theory raises the question of whether they are separate subjects at all."

13. The two problems are obviously connected on some accounts; for example, on the Russellian account of the uniqueness implications of definite descriptions, referential "ambiguity" amounts to falsity.

14. Principled exceptions are of course epithets, like *the bastard*, where a more prolix form that would otherwise encourage a disjoint reading is clearly warranted by the additional attitudinal information that can only be encoded in the fuller nominal.

15. But because a tensed sentence usually follows another, it may pick up a reference time from the context; see discussion of conjoined or adjoined sentences in chapter 2 and Partee's (1984) theory of implicit reference times involved in the use of past tenses.

16. This is my appellation. Grice (1989: 138–139) himself identified another circle, possibly related, of this sort: can we give an account of the (timeless, literal) meaning p of expression C in terms of people normally meaning$_{nn}$ (intending) p by C, where what they intend or mean$_{nn}$ by C will surely make reference to the timeless, literal meaning of C? Incidentally, the phrase "Grice's circle" is not meant to suggest that he had unwittingly tied himself in knots; Grice (1989: 375) indicates that he was entirely cognizant of the problems treated here.

17. Other theorists of many different persuasions seem to have come to parallel conclusions. Lewis (1979) supposed that accommodation (a kind of pragmatic presumption) is involved in many uses of definite descriptions, in the narrowing down of modal meanings to deontic versus epistemic, and so forth. Moore (1986) in an AI context states "the only way to hold fast to the position that the construction of logical form precedes all pragmatic processing seems to be to put in "dummy" symbols for the unknown relation," and so concludes that "a theoretically interesting level of logical form will have resolved contextually dependent definite references, as well as the other 'local' pragmatic indeterminacies" (1981 (1986: 286)).

18. Whether that pragmatic process itself is peculiar to language interpretation is a separate issue (I presume at least partially so; Wilson and Sperber 1986 presume not).

19. A convergent thought is Stalnaker's (1972) contention that semantics, *qua* the theory of propositions, is essentially independent of linguistics: "the subject has no essential connection with languages at all, natural or artificial" (1972: 382).

20. Recanati in that footnote reports a defense from Dan Sperber: the inference from "John has three children" to 'John has at most three children' should not be

considered the relevant inference, as opposed to 'John has exactly three children', which entails what is said and is therefore an explicature. But this seems entirely circular: we know the inference is an explicature, so we phrase it so it meets our criteria!

21. Even though the notion of impliciture encompasses both the minimal proposition expressed and the fuller enriched implicit proposition, Bach (1994: 157–160), in contrast to Carston and Recanati, holds that the minimal proposition plays a distinct and important functional role in getting to the expanded proposition. This is surely correct. But then why did he include the "expansions" beyond the minimal proposition in the category of impliciture?

22. He adds that an implicature "is a conceptually independent proposition, a proposition with perhaps no constituents in common with what is said", and gives the example of an utterance of "It's after 10" implicating 'the restaurant is closed'. But we could have phrased the implicature as 'The restaurant closes after 10', in which case there is a constituent in common with what is said, and the inference must be reclassified as an impliciture.

23. Explicatures are derived just like implicatures by the monadic principle of relevance (Sperber and Wilson 1986: 183–193), while "both [completion and expansion aspects of impliciture] involve basically the same sort of pragmatic process as in implicature proper" (Bach 1994: 144).

24. This point is not, it seems, easy to get across. Thus Carston (1995: 239) berates me for not supplying "any coherent distinction between those implicatures which contribute to what is said and those which function as independent assumptions communicated by the utterance." But there is none. That is why I don't subscribe to the terminological exercises surrounding "explicature," "implicature," and so on.

25. This would be the line favored in some recent treatments of tense; see, for example, Partee (1984: 257ff) who proposes "if the main clause is an event-clause, the last step in its processing is the resetting of the reference time to a time 'just after' the main clause event." Note though that not all sequences of simple past tenses get interpreted this way:

(i)   "He read a book and made copious notes"

(ii)   "He played the pipes with one hand and he hit the drum with the other"

and that these other ways are various (in (i) the note-taking was not contemporaneous with the reading, as the playing of pipes and hitting of drums was in (ii)). These look more like a case of generality-plus-implicatures than a case of multiple ambiguity (which would still involve resolution by implicatures).

26. It may be argued that there is some slippage here: *some x are P* can't be intensionally equivalent to *some and perhaps all x are P* because only the latter involves a modal notion; and in circumstances where 'some but necessarily not all x are P' is true, the first will be true and the second false. However, I think the objections are immaterial: the simpler nonmodal paraphrase as in (a') (with stress on *some* and *at least*) would seem to give the same result. Despite the

nondetachability of Q-implicatures, paraphrases with the same implicatures as the target expression are hard to find because periphrastic glosses generate M-implicatures, thereby obscuring semantical equivalence. Granted that guaranteeing the truth-conditional equivalence of an implicature-lifting paraphrase is difficult, the fact that pretty much regardless of the exact paraphrase the sentence is rescued from contradiction suggests that the only substantial difference between the A and B clauses in these 'A is better than B' cases is that A has a scalar implicature that B lacks.

27. Levinson (1983: 142–144) offers an account of implicature cancellation in cases like these.

28. Atlas (1993a: 171) discussing this argument of mine suggests a counter-example: "Eating some of the cake is better for my health than eating all of the cake and drinking arsenic", which has the structure *A is better than B* where B entails A, and where the whole is clearly true without depending on implicatural strengthening. Hence my additional constraint that the semantic structure of B should not explicitly encompass A, as in privative opposites like *horse* versus *stallion*. This is intended to capture the following kinds of cases, which seem to me clearly anomalous without pragmatic strengthening:

(i) a. "Eating some of the cake is better than eating all of it."
   b. *Semantic gloss:* 'Eating at least some of the cake and perhaps all of it is better than eating all of it'.

(ii) a. "Owning a vehicle is better than owning a car."
   b. *Semantic gloss:* 'Owning a vehicle, possibly a car, is better than owning a vehicle which is a car'.

29. I take it in fact that the existential quantification in all these accounts is too weak.

30. Atlas (1993a: 171) complains that utterances of the form "A is better than B" show no anomaly when A is equivalent to B because these are intensional contexts. However, we can make all the same arguments with extensional predicates like *bigger than*. For example, if the semantic content of "A family with five children is bigger than a family with two children" can be glossed 'A family with at least five children is bigger than a family with at least two children', then what is *said* would seem to be far from self-evidently true; the whole achieves its plausible interpretation through upper-bounding implicatures on the cardinals.

31. For example, consider Atlas's (1984b) account of comparatives. The logical form for 'y is ϕ-er than x' is as follows, where x* stands for the measures of ϕ-ness that x exhibits,
y* for measures of ϕ-ness that y exhibits:

$$(\exists y^*)(\forall x^*)(x^* < y^*)$$

That is, there is some measure of ϕ-ness that y exhibits such that for all measures of ϕ-ness that x exhibits, those measures are less than the y-measure. For example, a stick y is longer than a stick x if there's some part of y that exceeds in length every part of x.

32. Note that in (23c) we need to make the auxiliary assumption that the domain of discourse contains some exam that was cheated on, in order to get the entailment relation between *all* and *some*. The logical form of such a sentence, Atlas suggests, might be thought of as follows:

[∀x∀y (Student(y) & ∃u (exam(u) & cheats(y, u)) &
(Student(x) & ∀v (exam(v) → cheats(x, v)))]
→ better(y, x)

On this analysis, where there are no students who cheat on every exam the sentence will be true (because the falsity of the antecedent will guarantee the truth of the whole conditional); where there is a student who cheats on all exams, the sentence will be false (because it is asserted that he's better than himself).

33. Jay Atlas claims that there is no such entailment, and this follows from his (1984b) account.

34. This kind of phrasing looks like a category mistake, Kent Bach points out to me: traditionally, sentences entail and speakers implicate. But we are moving steadily away from this picture. First, utterance-types carry with them presumptive meanings (GCIs, to which the speaker is committed of course); second, sentences in the abstract are (at least in general) much too underspecified to entail anything. Thus in the new picture, it is utterances that both entail and implicate propositions. The idea that it is only *statements*, not sentences, that entail or carry truth, is of course not really new at all (see, e.g., Austin 1950).

35. Moore's paradox is of course the anomaly of the assertion "*p* and I don't believe that *p*." Grice (1978: 114) noted that this would follow from his maxim of Quality but held that uttering "*p*" did not *implicate* 'The speaker believes/knows that *p*' on the grounds that such a presumption only expresses the maxim itself. Others have been less cautious (see, e.g., Gazdar 1979: 46–48; Levinson 1983: 105) but have noted that unlike most implicatures this inference is not deniable (hence the paradox), indicating perhaps additional reinforcement through a sincerity condition on assertion. See Atlas 1993a for further discussion.

36. In fact, Irene Heim points out to me, Lewis's account of *because*-clauses relates them to counterfactuals; but there is no suggestion of such a move from Barwise's camp.

37. An example of Ivan Sag's.

38. The argument was put forcefully by Greg Ward to Ivan Sag, who passed it on to me, about the time that Bach (1987a) was putting it in print.

39. Bach argues that many uses of sentences are *nonliteral*: taken literally, they express an absurdity or untruth and must be understood as expressing a related, more explicit, more plausible proposition (Bach being in this regard, an incarnation of our Obstinate Theorist). Thus, if I say "I haven't eaten breakfast", I mean 'not yet today' although the literal meaning of the sentence might entail 'never' (cf. "I haven't eaten sheep's testicles"). On this account, we go around expressing falsities, charitably interpreted as closely related propositions. Bach's account and my account differ in that, using the mechanism of default interpretations, I think

that many of these cases are pragmatically enriched before any truth conditions are computed. I think my account fits better with intuitions about literality and truth and falsity, but he thinks these can't be trusted.

40. In contrast, a PCI account of the numeral terms (as advocated by, e.g., Carston 1988, and reluctantly toyed with by Horn 1992b) under these circumstances of doubt should make no prediction at all.

41. A spontaneous textual example:

(i) "I would've liked the two-cupboard cabinet; it's a three-cupboard one" Rah: P: 1: JMA p. 76.

A textual example of intrusion in the conditional is the following:

(ii) "Imagine the difficulty of understanding this information if it were presented one word at a time" (from Ford and Thompson 1986: 359).

42. Of course, we here historicize: neither Russell (1905) nor Strawson (1950) yet held the views of Grice (1967).

43. In some ways, the example is weakened by the presence of the second referring expression; given three visible children near the brother-in-law, he is (we suppose) the only referent describable as *the man with three children*, so by elimination the speaker's brother must be the other man. But the second referring expression is only there for expository reasons; the example stands without it.

44. The scale ⟨*succeed, try*⟩ is not quite prototypical; arguably, 'he succeeded in finding the solution' doesn't entail that he tried; see chapter 2 and Horn 1972, Hirschberg 1985, and Kay 1990 on Q-scales not based on entailment.

45. The hedge "scale-like" merely points to the fact that the opposition ⟨*like, not mind*⟩, although it has all the logical properties of a Horn scale, would seem to fail the lexicalization constraint posited by Atlas and Levinson (1981) and Levinson (1987b). A less stringent constraint, posited by Horn, only requires that the stronger item on a scale is *more* lexicalized than the weaker item (as in this case), as discussed in chapter 2.

46. Note that *The very tall man is even taller than the tall tall man* should be contradictory (or truth-valueless)—in short unusable—on the treatment of *tall tall* as *very tall*. But it seems to me that it could make good sense in the right context. A related possibility is of course that the first *tall* is a modifier of the second *tall*, or more exactly of the N′ *tall man*, with a structure like:

[N′[ADJ tall] [N′ [ADJ tall] [N man]]]

and an interpretation that takes the set of tall men into a taller proper subset. But we would then need an account of *a red red sunset, a deep deep blue, an honest honest man, the purest, purest honey, the tallest tallest building*, and so on, where intuitively the implicated content has less to do with objective qualities than it has to do with speaker certainty. We'd also lose the intuitive distinction between *a [rich [rich]] man* (rich among the rich) and *a rich, rich man* (rich, I assure you). Note also that it is not only modifiers that can be reduplicated; thus in American English *a dog dog* or *a salad salad* implicates a prototypical dog and a real (not, e.g., fruit) salad, respectively. And there are contexts where one could say *I gave away the (ordinary) dog but kept the dog dog*. But see the text for further examples.

47. Incidentally, Kripke's definition of speaker reference won't quite do even for cases close to those he considers. His example:

i. "Her husband is kind."

said of a man who is in fact her kind lover (and distinct from her wicked husband). But suppose the speaker says:

ii. "Her lover is kind."

where the speaker knows full well that the doting man in question is in fact her husband. What the speaker says is true if the man (her husband) is her lover and there are no other lovers in the wings—there is surely no incompatibility between being a husband and being a lover. But (ii) would be grossly misleading, of course, to someone not apprised of the marital bond between that woman and that man; example (ii) suggests that the man is not her husband by a Quantity implicature (cf. Grice's (1975) discussion of *his wife* vs. *a woman*). Suppose further that the addressee knows that the woman has a husband; then he will conclude that the man being talked about is *not* her husband. Thus the proposition expressed will be something like 'That man is her lover rather than her husband and he is kind'.

In this second case, we intuitively want to say that the semantic reference results in a true statement, and the speaker's reference results in a false or misleading one. The point is that Kripke's definition of speaker-reference needs to be patched up to allow for two further kinds of cases: (a) those (like the man with two children discussed in the text) where the semantic conditions are knowingly not met but successful speaker-reference takes place; and (b) those where the semantic conditions are met but the pragmatic conditions of a nonmisleading referring expression are not met (as in our *Her lover is kind* said of her doting husband) and speaker-reference is (arguably) not successful.

48. The passage is worth quoting:

If Donnellan had possessed a clear intuition that "Her husband is kind to her", uttered in reference to the kind lover of a woman married to a cruel husband, expressed the literal truth, then he would have adduced a phenomenon that conforms to the ambiguous D-language [where referential and attributive references are truth-conditionally distinct] but is incompatible with any Russell language [any language with the Russellian definite descriptions]. (Square brackets embrace my explications.)

49. Note that what the semantics alone will provide, in the case of contradictions, is singularly uninformative because every contradiction will have the same intension and extension. Not much semantic grist is thus provided for the pragmatic mill.

50. Example from Jerry Hobbs.

51. For example, Katz specifically argues for a full semantic determination of the modifier relation, which we have taken to be given by I-inference: according to him *good knife* can only mean 'good for cutting with' (1987: 203ff), because there's a 'cutting' marker waiting as it were for modification. This doesn't seem to

be true: a good pocketknife may be good by virtue of its many accessories, and indeed the Swiss Army knife company makes good business out of different knives good for different purposes.

52. Consider for example the negative sentence:

i. "I did not take some of your money"

and its positive counterpart:

ii. "I took some of your money."

The pronoun *I* is directly referential, and, given the same speaker, designates the same entity in (i) and (ii)—it depends on no other element in the sentence and falls outside the scope of negation or any other logical or modal operator. But the quantifier *some* falls of course under the scope of the negation in (i), and the scale upon which any scalar implicature would depend is likewise sensitive to the negative scope. Instead of the scale operative in (ii), viz. ⟨*all, some*⟩, we have in (i) the scale ⟨*not some, not all*⟩, and in fact therefore no scalar implicature at all (unless the utterance is interpreted as a denial of a prior assertion). In short, implicatures have none of the direct referential character that marks out indexicals. See Enç 1981: chap. 1.

53. In this discussion, I will argue that pragmatics should be considered a component in a theory of meaning, not of course in the Fodorean sense (Fodor 1983) of a specialized, encapsulated module, but in the sense (more normal in linguistics) of a set of distinct principles (I continue to use the term *module* only because *component* fails to yield an adjective like *modular*). Wilson and Sperber (1986) argue explicitly against this (although there may be some confusing conflation here between the notion of a linguistic level or component and a Fodorean module proper). But their arguments are based on the assumption that Gricean mechanisms are not inferential principles specialized to communication, and more particularly on the assumption that there are no GCIs. It should be clear that I make neither of these assumptions: maxims like the I-, Q- and M-principles are, on my account, specific heuristics adapted to the narrow bandwidth of human speech (or other forms of human communication), and rely on metalinguistic reasoning. And perhaps GCIs, by virtue of their resident default nature, have specific memory requirements and thus need some mental home base, as it were. However, even if pragmatic principles belong to no specialized linguistic component, but are free-floating in a Fodorean central processor, none of the arguments below about the interrelation of semantics and pragmatics seem to be weakened in any obvious way.

54. Heim (1983a: 171ff) does not map from syntactic structures directly to file cards and their updating; rather she proposes an intermediate level of logical form modeled on GB LF, at which level scope is disambiguated and anaphoric relations assigned by coindexing.

55. Thus Heim notes in her conclusion (1982: 401):

We have derived considerable benefit from permitting accommodation to be "interspersed" with interpretation.... This seems to me to add plausibility to the idea of a level of analysis like our files, which are, so to speak, generated simultaneously by rules of diverse components. The precise implications of this idea, and what it means for the relation between semantics and pragmatics, remain to be explored.

56. Kadmon notes (1987: 52f) that the cancellation mechanism introduced by Gazdar (1979) and generally assumed correct, viz. cancellation by inconsistent prior background knowledge, cannot handle backwards cancellation as in *I went into a house; it was my house.*

57. This is because within Kamp/Heim theories discourse referents are unbound variables unless they occur within the scope of an explicit quantifier or quantifier-inducing construction (like the conditional), and the rule of interpretation has the effect of an unselective existential quantification over all unbound variables. This peculiarity of the theory, whereby an assertion of the cardinality of x as n in the DRS does not restrict the cardinality of x in the domain to exactly n, has the benefit that it is possible to get semantics for *at least three* distinct from that for *three* (a problem that had always baffled me). In effect, *at least three* specifies in the DRS that the cardinality is equal or greater than three, thus not permitting an upper-bounding implicature (Kadmon 1987: 80). *Exactly three* specifies in the DRS that any set in the domain that meets the conditions for that discourse referent is a member of the self-same threesome (p. 62).

58. An exception is made for numeral-determiner indefinites in predicative position that are claimed to have the semantic content 'exactly three'; this is supposed to be achieved automatically by Partee's type-shifting semantics (Kadmon 1987: 64).

59. However, let me record here one obvious inadequacy. The DRT treatment looks as if it will work quite well for those implicatures we may call *additive* (i.e., GCIs and particularized implicatures that add pragmatic content to semantic conditions). But there is another class of implicatures, which we may call *subtractive*, which remove, coerce, or replace semantic conditions. (The terminology comes via Sag from, I believe, Sadock.) Examples of subtractive implicatures are ironies, and Lakoff's (1974) "amalgams" as in "I saw *you'll never guess how many* people at the party" (where *you'll never guess how many* acts like a quantifier). Clearly these subtractive implicatures need to modify or replace semantic conditions rather than merely add additional constraints. The problem is that this process apparently requires semantic conditions to be defeasible. It may be that we will need to insist that these apparent intrusions are indeed postsemantic, but I am concerned by some evidence to the contrary (in part reviewed in section 3.5.3).

60. Copying operations are quite fundamental to DRT—that is what is involved in anaphoric resolution. Various complex kinds of copying operation have also been explored by, for example, Craige Roberts in unpublished work on the pragmatic accommodation required to understand modal subordination.

61. Horn would no doubt respond that a generalization is being missed by this account—we now appear to have three kinds of negation: ordinary descriptive negation, implicature-denying negation, and metalinguistic negation. In a sense, this is correct: implicature-denying negations share one crucial property with the descriptive cases (i.e., the meaning of negation as a truth function), but the retort properties with the true metalinguistic cases. But in fact the DRT treatment suggests that implicature-denying negation is just the intersection of descriptive

negation with the echoic properties of retorts—nothing special needs to be said, unlike in the case of nonlogical metalinguistic negation. Geurts (1998) also holds the view that metalinguistic negation is not in fact a unitary phenomenon.

62. This generalization just follows from the nature of implicature-inducing scales. However, there are some reasons to think that negative scales should be introduced by metarule over positive scales, as discussed in chapter 2.

63. If the process was entirely regular with the numerals, one might expect the implicature 'John has two children'. However, the numerals do seem weaker in this regard. Yet Horn (1972) claims that it is quite general of scales that the middle values are less strongly implicated.

Chapter 4

1. In this chapter I have drawn on material published in Levinson (1987a,b, 1991) and the acknowledgements made therein are inherited here. However, I would particularly like once again to thank Larry Horn for crucial initial ideas and Nigel Vincent, Peter Matthews, and Yan Huang for early encouragement of heretical views.

2. For discussion of so-called pragmatic agreement, see Pollard and Sag 1994. Note that for some such cases one might hope for a semantic account. Consider:

(i) a. The ham sandwiches has left without paying.
        +> The man who ordered the ham sandwiches has gone without paying
    b. His family are coming to dinner.
    c. Five children in a car is the worst thing imaginable for any driver.
    d. Two eggs every morning is bad for your health.
    e. Vous êtes le professeur.

In (ia) we seem to have a syntactic reflex of pragmatic inferences associated with an expression. In (ib) real-world number (optionally) overrides grammatical singularity, and in (ic) construal of *five children in a car* as a singular situation permits singular verb agreement, and in (id) *two eggs* functions as a singular menu. One might hope to account for (ib–d) in terms of some general ambiguity of plural NPs between, say, plural and singular collective readings. But this will not do—we should then be able to say *The men is coming in* and we can't. Inevitably, some process of pragmatic construal seems to be involved. Implicature proper is more clearly involved in other cases, for example, honorific plurals may collocate with singular predications, as in (ie), where the plural form originally merely implicated respect, and in some languages continues to do so rather than being fully conventionalized (Brown and Levinson 1987: 198ff).

3. I have borrowed the phrase, not entirely fairly, from Saleemi's (1997) review of Huang's (1994) attempt to reduce anaphoric patterns in Chinese to pragmatic principles.

4. Various syntactic alternates have been proposed to differ in just this way. For example Steever (1977) argues that raised structures like *John believes Sue to be honest* implicate subjective access or judgment (I-implicatures from reduced

structures in our terms), compared to their unraised counterparts (M-implicating the complement). Chomsky (1981: 65) points out that the Avoid Pronoun alternations in *John would prefer going* (coreferential) versus *John would prefer his going* (preferably disjoint) might be related to Gricean factors, a point taken up by Horn (1984). Levinson (1987b: 417–420) argues that Control structures fit the same pattern and are not fully grammaticalized—see Comrie 1984 on Russian and Huang 1994: 149–158 on Chinese. I return to this point in section 4.5.3.

5. This and related issues are discussed by Horn (1989: 345–353). Indirect speech acts are another class of cases where collocational constraints are associated with standardized or short-circuited presumptive inferences. Thus preverbal *please* is associated with indirect requests, but only those that have idiomatic status (Lakoff 1973; see Levinson 1983: 272ff for references):

(i) a.   Please open the window.
   b.   Would you mind please opening the window?
   c.   ?Wouldn't you mind please opening the window?

In a similar way, honorific particles will not collocate happily with implicated disrespect (Brown and Levinson 1987). Another interesting class of cases involve sentential amalgams (Lakoff 1974), where whole clauses can slot into modifier positions on the basis that those clauses would have implicated the relevant modifier:

(ii) a.   "John invited you'll never guess how many people to his party."
    b.   +> 'John invited a lot of people to his party'
    c.   "You'll never guess how many people John invited to his party."
    d.   +> 'John invited a lot of people to his party'"
    e.   ?John invited Bill will never guess how many people to his party.

Here the sentence in (iia) is interpreted to mean roughly (iib), by virtue of the fact that uttering (iic) (but not, e.g., (iie)) would have implicated (iid). Thus the nonce modifier seems licensed by an implicature. The appropriate theoretical moves here are not so clear, but the phenomena certainly support the idea broached in chapter 3 that implicature can play a role inside the process of semantic interpretation, and that an incremental construction of a construal can play a role in licensing grammatical processes like agreement, or treatment of a sentence fragment as an NP as in (iia).

6. Perhaps the last point requires a further word. Defeasibility has to be, as far as I can see, the litmus test for a grammatical versus pragmatic account of linguistic patterns. Chomsky (1981: 227 n. 45) for one will not agree. He would rather suppose that pragmatics may override grammatical stipulation. It is true, of course, that under special conditions (e.g., a noisy environment), anything goes that works. But the greater the range of interpretations, and the more normal defeasible interpretations seem, the less plausible the grammatical account becomes. Let us concede though that the big picture counts too. If we have perfectly general principles, which work across language and provide deep insights into the workings of specific languages, and which would give us an account of the phenomenon in question "for free," then naturally we want to hang on to that explanation.

However, both pragmatic principles and principles of Universal Grammar may be of this kind, and in seeking to adjudicate between rival accounts we may then be forced to consider the essential character of the phenomena to be explained. Are they grammatical stipulations or merely preferred interpretations? It is this which brings us back to defeasibility as the test.

7. The hypothesis is that any language with deictic pronouns will allow these to be used both anaphorically and as variables. Certainly, there are also specialized referentially dependent expressions, like long-distance anaphors to be discussed in section 4.3.2.5.

8. Although semantic generality is clearly intrinsically connected to referential dependence, the former does not of course automatically engender the latter. It is quite possible to have a semantically general definite description like *the man* serve as a referentially independent expression as well as (on some other occasion) a referentially dependent one. Even though reflexive pronouns *encode* referential dependency in a certain domain (and are therefore in that respect not semantically general), nevertheless in many languages they are interestingly stripped of number/gender features and thus conform to this general pattern (for an interesting reanalysis of GB theory which makes this generality central, see Burzio 1991).

9. A possible exception is switch reference, in which a subordinate or coordinate verb may indicate that its subject is identical to that of a prior matrix or coordinate verb; in that case, perhaps the linkage is itself grammatically specified (see section 4.3.2.5.1). Another kind of exception would be local subject-oriented Anaphors, those reflexives or reciprocals that require an immediate subject as antecedent.

10. Here and throughout, subscript indices merely serve to pick out the relevant reading (same subscript indicating coreference) and have no theoretical status.

11. I use the term *disjoint* to mean *local* noncoreference or lack of anaphoric links to immediately preceding NPs. Obviously, such locally disjoint NPs may be coreferential with still earlier NPs (see Fox 1987 for empirical tendencies).

12. See Vonk, Hustinx, and Simons 1992 for experimental confirmation of this signaling function of choice between anaphoric expressions.

13. Kent Bach has objected to this kind of phrasing: addressees are not in the business of inferring coreference or its complement—rather, they are in the business of determining reference. That I think is true. GCIs, on the account developed in this chapter, at most help to signal *how* the addressee is to find the reference; just as often (as in the case of I-inferences) the assumption of coreference will be a side product of a larger inference (e.g., finding a maximally cohesive interpretation).

14. In a critique of my earlier papers (Levinson 1987a,b, 1991), Ariel (1994: 20) suggests that I am deeply confused about informativeness: "If anything, then, nonstereotypic interpretations are more informative than stereotypic ones, in that they eliminate from consideration a more deeply engrained belief. In other words, the I-principle cannot both be informativity and stereotypy." In fact, however,

she is herself confusing two very different notions: (i) the Shannon information-theoretic measure, which defines informativeness as inversely related to the statistical probability of signals; and (ii) the Bar-Hillel/Carnap measure, which relates informativeness to the discrimination power of message contents. The former is syntactic and probabilistic and plays absolutely no role in the theory here; the latter is semantic and structural and is the relevant theoretical foundation to this work. See Cherry 1966: 238ff for elementary exposition.

15. To illustrate: given two predicates M and Y, and one entity a, $M(a)$ will be compatible with just two state descriptions or states of affairs—namely, (i) $M(a)$ and $Y(a)$, and (ii) $M(a)$ and $\sim Y(a)$. But if we add another entity b, $M(a)$ will now be compatible with eight different state descriptions, as the reader may verify. Enlarging the domain to three individuals will yield 16 state descriptions compatible with the assertion M(a), and so on.

16. Bar-Hillel and Carnap (1952) did not themselves explore the effects of relative size of domain of discourse on this concept of informativeness. (There appear to be interesting theorems in this area, such as: the proportion of compatible to incompatible state descriptions for a given assertion stays constant whatever the size of the domain.) This concept of informativeness thus makes the informativeness of a statement relative to a domain of discourse a three-place relation: statement S is more informative in domain A than in domain B. It is a concept of the informativeness of a statement relative to a world. I owe these clarifications to Jay Atlas.

17. I am grateful to Jay Atlas for pointing out the force of the Popperian analysis to me.

18. This argument I owe, once again, to Jay Atlas. He adds that if it is objected that a particular addressee might prefer having a little information about two referents to having a lot about one, then one must concede that of course that is possible. But this is to invoke yet another notion of informativeness, namely informativeness-for-a-person in a context, which is of course a matter entirely relative to context. Such a notion of informativeness is of course not relevant to the business at hand—finding a default preference for interpretation.

19. Incidentally, we shall make use of yet further arguments about the relative informativeness of coreferential versus noncoreferential readings in section 4.3.2. These are notions at the level of sense, rather than extension. I shall claim that a sentence with a reflexive or other Anaphor is more informative than the corresponding sentence with a nonreflexive or non-Anaphor, because the former entails coreference where the latter at most permits it.

20. Sentence (ib), on a noncoreferential interpretation, requires an additional existential quantifier to (ia), as indicated by the associated logical forms.

(i) a. John likes himself.
         $\exists x [x = j \, \& \, L(x, x)]$
     b. John$_1$ likes him$_2$.
         $\exists x \exists y [x = j \text{ and } x \neq y \text{ and } L(x, y)]$

The reflexive is thus more informative than an ordinary pronoun on a disjoint reading.

21. A similar line of argumentation goes back to Dowty (1980), Reinhart (1983), Sadock (1983), and others. The only novel element here is the employment of the specific pragmatic machinery developed in this book (this too prefigured in Horn 1984: 24–25).

22. Further examples will be given immediately below. See also sections 4.3.2.4 and 4.3.3.1.

23. Some pragmatic inferences are undoubtedly stronger than others—that is, they are defeasible in fewer contexts, and alternative interpretations are intuitively less salient, or even hard to conceive. It should be an aim of GCI theory to account for at least some of these gradient effects, but there will inevitably be many other factors to do with functional sentence perspective, discourse structure, and so on. On the current theory, we can account for gradient strengths only along the following lines:

(a) Some kinds of implicatures are intrinsically "stronger" than others—in our theory Q-implicatures cancel both inconsistent I-implicatures and M-implicatures, whereas M-implicatures only cancel inconsistent I-implicatures. That the inference (if ungrammaticalized) from *John hit him* to the disjointness of the arguments is due to a scalar Q-inference helps to explain why it might be stronger than the I-inference to coreference of *John* and *his* in *John hit his children*, where coreference is only a suggestion. The strength of Q-inferences is in turn due to their meta-linguistic character, which unlike M-implicatures is not gradient in kind (markedness of expression being upgradable in various ways).

(b) Implicatures from different sources may reinforce one another—this would be one explanation of why *John hit him* is so strongly disjoint: not only is there a Q-implicature as just noted, but on the theory sketched below that there is also an I-inference to disjoint co-arguments, the two consistent implicatures would reinforce each other.

(c) Finally, we may decide that some pattern like the disjoint reference in *He thought John could do it* is an especially robust inference and handle it, as Reinhart (1983) proposes, by building extra grammatical machinery that assigns to *John thought he could do it* a strong variable interpretation, so that we have an additional Q-inference from the failure to use the strong structure.

24. I remind the reader that I am indicating the special Chomskyan sense of Anaphor with a capital letter.

25. In fact, to handle preposed constituents, one needs a more complex formulation: X c-commands Y iff either (i) the first branching node α dominating X also dominates Y, or (ii) the node α' immediately dominating α is of the same category as α and α' also dominates Y. See Kuno 1987 for the history of these notions.

26. See, for example, work by Huang (1994) on Chinese, Cho and Hong (1988) on Korean, Levinson (1987a) on Guugu Yimithirr, Enç (1986) on Turkish, and Dimitriadis (1995) on Greek.

27. Ariel (1994) complains that such a scale from lexical NP to pronoun to zero is far too crude, because there are many kinds of intermediate types. But this was never intended as a full scale, and the account can be extended as required, according to the NP types in the language (see remarks in chapter 2 with respect to Gundel, Hedberg, and Zacharski 1989).

28. Incidentally, as it has long been noted (e.g., Dowty 1980), there is no such contrast in English between *his own* and *his* (as in *He loves his/his own mother*) as one might at first expect. This follows from the lexicalization constraint on Horn scales, which requires the stronger expression (here *his own*) to be equally or more lexicalized than the weak expression (*his*), a condition clearly not met in English. In some languages, in contrast (like Norwegian) it is met, and then there is indeed a Q-contrast of the predicted sort. See the discussion of example (45).

29. An obvious objection is that the mirror-image relation is not a perfect reflection—this issue of the noncomplementarity of pronouns and Anaphors is discussed at length in section 4.3.2.5. A less obvious objection is that Conditions A and B appear to have independent existence, as shown by the fact that in certain loci they overlap and exclude both pronoun and Anaphor. For example, both *They hate him* (Condition B) and *They hate himself* (Condition A) seem ill-formed when *him* or *himself* is understood as one of *They* (Safir 1992: 38, after Lasnik). But in fact the Condition B–type case seems fine under the right contextual conditions. Consider *The Board must elect its own chairman unanimously and without abstentions—The bishop volunteered, so they elected him*; or *Renaldo was their best player—the whole team relied on him*; or under cultural conditions where all must drink to a toast, *They toasted him.*

30. Of course it does not matter at all whether one prefers, as Reinhart does, to think about her account as absorbing Condition A, together with a fragment of Condition B, with the rest of Conditions B and C obtained pragmatically. This is terminology only, as long as we acknowledge that Condition B has not been wholly reduced to pragmatics, because the NP–c-commanding–pronoun rule of interpretation requires that the pronoun is not in the same domain as the NP.

31. Reuland and Koster (1991: 2) even suggest, counterfactually, that everyone has given up on Condition C.

32. Larry Horn suggests to me that there has always been a tacit presumption that the Binding Conditions or their predecessors hold only for presupposed, not asserted or denied, coreference. But it is not clear why configuration-based principles should be sensitive to such semantic, or indeed, as it turns out, pragmatic content (Safir 1992). An account in terms of defeasible pragmatic conditions is attractive: asserted identity will automatically override pragmatic default inferences to disjointness, and no special exceptions have to be stated.

33. More may be involved here, as Larry Horn points out to me: this kind of use may depend on a parallelism of structure and thus a contrast in the frame *X went to X's house.*

34. For example, in Guugu Yimithirr one can relatively easily break this constraint, as in:

(i) Nhangu-gu   John-bi   biiba   nyulu   gunday.
    he-GEN + ABS-EMPH John-GEN + ABS father-ABS he-NOM hit
    'He₁ hit John₁'s father.'

See discussion in Levinson 1987b.

35. Such usages are positively common in first and second person, where mis-communication is unlikely. Larry Horn kindly provides me with the following textual examples:

(i)   Dole is asked if he intends to stress the character issue in the campaign: "I don't think so," Dole said, "My view is that *I* am going to talk about *Bob Dole.*" (ABC "Nightline" show, March 1996)

(ii) "'*I* gave Pittsburgh every opportunity to sign *Neil O'Donnell*,' O'Donnell said." *Hartford Courant*, March 1, 1996.

(iii) "*I*'m just doing what *Neil O'Donnell* can do," O'Donnell, quoted in *New York Times*, November 3, 1997.

(iv) "*I* just want to go to a place where *Howard Johnson* is going to put up some big numbers," Howard Johnson in radio interview after he signed with the Colorado Rookies following 1993 baseball season.

36. It is worth noting that Kuno (1987: 109) proposes an independent prag-matic constraint that may help to explain the general rarity of coreference in the pronoun–c-commanding–NP pattern. The constraint is partly a matter of linear order but partly a matter of *logophoricity*, a concept reviewed in section 4.3.2.6.

37. To these examples it may be objected that the coreferential lexical NP is not referentially dependent on the pronoun, even though it may be coreferential (thus invoking Evans's (1980) distinction again). Thus if the Binding Conditions were recast in terms of referential dependency rather than referential identity, these examples, it might be claimed by, say, Higginbotham (1983), would not be coun-terexamples. Even this though is not so clear in examples like:

(i)   *He* is doing what *John* always does.

(ii) *He* it was who became *King James Ist of England.*

(iii) *He* who lifts the sword out of this stone is *King Arthur.*

For example, in (iii) the pronoun must be interpreted as a bound variable (as in *Whoever lifts...*).

38. The θ-Criterion specifies that "each θ-role is assigned to one and only one argument" (Chomsky 1981: 36) or that "every NP must be taken as the argument of some predicate; furthermore it must be so taken once" (van Riemsdijk and Williams 1986: 243). On the face of it at least, the Guugu Yimithirr antipassive construction (to be reviewed below) is a direct counterexample; it indicates that single absolutive subject of the verb is to be taken twice, first in agent role than in patient role. And pleonastic pronouns in Guugu Yimithirr also violate this con-dition (see Levinson 1987b: 391, n. 19).

39. In this theory, there is also a Condition C, two versions of which are consid-ered, one of which makes use of a configurational notion and one of which does not. Again, pragmatic reduction seems straightforward.

40. In English there is a phenomenon that indicates the essential flavor of the pragmatic solution. Horn (1984: 24) notes that with first- and second-person pro-nouns, where reference is fixed, a contrast is exploited between reflexive and plain pronoun:

(i) Just go on home. *I*'ll worry about *me*.

In this textual example (from forthcoming work by Horn), the nonreflexive is used to avoid the logophoric or subjective associations of the reflexive (cf. the introvert *I'll worry about myself* with the extrovert or macho *I'll worry about me*; see also Haiman 1995: 229). This indicates that the reflexive in English does indeed carry these logophoric associations, in addition to stipulated referential dependency, as argued by Kuno (1987) and discussed further in this chapter.

41. I have put "bound" in scare quotes because technically, of course, within Binding Theory an expression can by definition only be bound by a c-commanding expression, but I shall not always be so careful.

42. In the literature it is often stated that LDAs are invariably monomorphemic (following Pica 1991); this is in fact not necessarily the case, as just noted for long-range uses of Chinese *ta ziji* (Huang 1994). There are also the LDA usages of English reflexives like *himself*, as discussed by Zribi-Herz (1989) and Horn and Lee (1995).

43. In nearly all cases, the LDA also has local, clause-bound uses, but the degree to which these are marginal clearly differs (see, e.g., Huang 1994: 111).

44. The complementarity of pronouns and LDAs does apparently persist systematically in a few languages, as in Gothic, and up to a point in Icelandic (see Harbert 1995: 194). In general, the pattern in the European languages is for the complementarity to evaporate once the reflexive is outside the classical Binding Theory domain (minimal governing category including a subject)—see the tabular presentation in Reuland and Koster 1991. For Icelandic the complementarity persists when the LDA *sig* is bound within the first containing finite clause but is lost beyond that (ibid. 12–13).

45. The term "logophoric" is thus sometimes, confusingly, used to imply non-Anaphoric.

46. The similarities and differences between these systems may be tentatively summed up thus (see Stirling 1993: 54–55, 259, Huang, in preparation):

	LDAs	Logophors	Switch reference
Clause-bound uses	+	−	−
Logophoric contexts only	+	+	−
Referential overlap	−	+ (limited)	+

where "referential overlap" indicates that logophors may refer to a set of which the antecedent is a member. Switch-reference systems allow not only this, but the converse, and intersecting reference. It seems clear that there are family-resemblance relations between these kinds of system, with intermediate cases. See Stirling 1993, passim. Recent reports (e.g., Culy 1997) suggest that the African logophoric systems in fact reveal considerably more diversity than previously realized.

47. A tendency because, as about to be noted, grammaticalization processes may partially "freeze" disjointness presumptions, and because there are isolated cases

where disjoint-reference markers seem to exist in isolation, such as the famous Dogrib anti-anaphor (see Harbert 1995: 214 for references).

48. DS markers remain the best systematic candidates for specialized disjoint-reference devices. However, they have for the most part perspicuous diachronic origins (see, e.g., Stirling 1993: 5, 144 for references).

49. There may perhaps also be cases of English LDA where there is no such overlap of pronoun and reflexive, especially where predicates of identity are involved as in *Frankenstein wants to produce a monster similar to himself/?him*. Safir (1992) presents a discussion in a framework that introduces pragmatic effects on Conditions A and B.

50. Interestingly, observes Larry Horn, this constraint is less clear with first- and second-person pronominals as in *Will you trade me those pictures of yourself for these pictures of myself*, but perhaps that is explained by the fact that the protagonists share the same perspective in the current speech event.

51. Baker (1995), also utilizing textual data, casts some doubt on Zribi-Hertz's (1989) logophoric analysis of English LDA. He suggests a systematic dialect difference between British and American English, with only British English systematically employing reflexives as "intensive" NPs. An "intensive" NP is not only contrastive but also refers to a central protagonist, a bit like Algonquian proximate (vs. obviative) pronouns. If he is correct about the dialects, this will certainly help to explain the muddied intuitions. But the "intensive" content analysis can be accommodated within the approach being developed here, although there are reasons (given below) to think that the range of meanings associated with the reflexive tend to be related to deictic markedness.

52. Zribi-Hertz (1989: 703) herself rejects a Gricean approach, apparently because she sees the principles involved as belonging to a systematic realm of their own, namely discourse grammar, from which sentence grammar is ultimately derivative (p. 724).

53. As Zribi-Hertz (1989: 705, n. 12) points out, there has been an unjustified reluctance by workers in the Binding Condition framework to consider English an LDA language. Consequently, such structural conditions as there are in long-range uses of the reflexive have been largely unexplored within this framework (but see Kuno 1987 and review in Van Valin 1990; Parker, Riley, and Meyer 1990).

54. There is an interesting set of exceptions to this tendency in English. Horn (1984: 24, and forthcoming work) notes that with first- and second-person pronouns, where reference is fixed, nonreflexive pronouns may be used with clause-mate antecedents to signal the avoidance of the subjective, logophoric associations of the reflexive, as in (Horn's textual examples):

(i)   I'm not looking at you, *I*'m looking at *me*.

(ii) Take good care of yourself. *You* belong to *you*.

(iii) Well, I'm employed by them but *I* am working for *me*.

These are the exceptions that prove the rule: in the clausemate case, pronouns usually contrast with reflexives primarily on the reference dimension—but where reference is fixed by first- or second-person reference, the referential contrast is neutralized and the logophoric associations come to the fore. Burzio (1991) presents similar patterns in Romance languages.

55. Pollard and Sag (1992: 279) suggest that "grammatical constraints can sometimes be relaxed by writers who exercise certain license with their language," basing their argument on the fact that in isolation native speakers find literary sentences like *Its burden did not rest upon herself alone* unacceptable. But as Zribi-Hertz (1989) points out, this is exactly the wrong test—isolated sentences are analyzed as micro-discourses, and long-range Anaphors must be bound within the discourse. See also Baker 1995 on dialect differences.

56. These sections contain material published in the last part of Levinson 1991, with modifications and bibliographical updates.

57. Huang is right that puzzles remain. If *John hit him* I-implicates disjoint reference by the DRP, why doesn't *John hit the man* M-implicate the complement, given that R-expressions often M-contrast with pronouns? The observable fact is that the DRP is strong and holds over all NPs unless the contrary is signaled by grammar (reflexivity, special marking of introverted predicates) or by marked or emphatic forms (in languages without any reflexive marking). Additionally, the opposition between pronoun and lexical NP arises in loci where coreference is at issue, and the pronoun is a minimal form suggesting coreference; but here disjoint reference is at issue, and if the pronoun is disjoint, then certainly the less minimal form will be too, unless specially marked by, say, emphatics in languages without Anaphors.

58. The term "emphatic" is (as Faltz 1985: 239 remarks) regrettably vague. Without attempting any careful analysis, we may note though that what we have in mind are, for example, the various uses of the English "reflexive" as illustrated in:

(i)   The Queen herself said so.

(ii)   He cut the lawn himself.

(iii) He flogged the Bishop himself.

The effect in these cases may be glossed 'and not anyone else', 'not through the agency of a third party', and so on. The effect is thus to insist on the exact reference, to rebut a contrary suggestion or a stereotypical presumption, and so forth. The scope of such particles can be complex, as indicated by the ambiguity of (iii) (*He himself flogged the Bishop* vs. *The Bishop himself was flogged by him*). For a most useful exploration of the semantics/pragmatics and scope of such particles, see König 1991. He notes (pp. 87–96) that a general phenomenon is the fact that scalar additive particles often take the same form as the so-called emphatic reflexive pronouns or intensifiers: German *selbst*, Dutch *zelfs*, Norwegian *selv*, French *même*, Irish *féin*, and so on. Thus he relates scalar *even* to the emphatic uses of *himself* (cf. French *même*, German *selbst* cognate with English *self*)—

both, to follow Edmondson and Plank (1978), "associate a pragmatic scale with propositions graduated in terms of the speaker's expectations of the involvement of certain individuals in the relevant states, process and events." See also Kay 1990.

59. It is thus the weak reflexives that (especially) participate in long-distance binding and its associated logophoricity (see, e.g., Everaert, 1986: 212f; Hellan 1988: 87ff, 95). The strong reflexives have not had the same intensive study as the weak ones (Hellan 1988: 87), so perhaps the facts are not so clear. For example, the strong reflexives in Dutch, Norwegian, and Icelandic also have long-range uses if they are stressed (Everaert 1986: 218f, 253 n. 4, 254 n. 12; Hellan 1986: 104), an observation in line with the current theory. But clearly the main factor here is the relative antiquity of the weak reflexive (from proto-Indo-European *s(w)-, lost from West Germanic and then reborrowed later in, for example, Dutch), which may itself derive from an emphatic (see below). The strong reflexive form in all these languages seems to retain the pure emphatic functions (e.g., as a modifier of a subject) and to be in the process of extending its functions in the way predicted by the argument here. For some generalizations about weak/marked versus strong/unmarked reflexives, see Faltz 1985 and Yang 1983. For an attempt to predict their respective distributions, see Pica 1984, 1987; Everaert 1986: chap. 8; among others. Rizzi (1989) treats the association of weak (morphologically simple) reflexives and long-range binding (and conversely, compound reflexives and local binding) as so universally strong that it would suffice for "degree–0 learnability"—a child would not even need access to subordinate clauses to know what the binding domain of a specific lexical Anaphor was! But Chinese, for example, allows long reflexivization with both simple *ziji* and compound *ta ziji* (Huang 1994: 77f). The tendency for weak (morphologically simpler) reflexives to have long-distance uses is attributed by Faltz (1985: 256ff) to their diachronic origins as stressed pronouns in subordinate clauses, as with the African logophoric pronouns and perhaps proto-Indo-European *s(w)-. If the association between weak reflexives and long-range uses does turn out to be a language-family wide generalization, there is a direct potential explanation from our theory. The very fact that clausemate reflexivity is indicated by what was originally an emphatic form, which in long-range uses may be indicating merely a contrast in perspective rather than reference, may motivate double emphasis in the clausemate cases. In fact, there is direct diachronic evidence for this process in the origin of many strong reflexive forms as double or triple emphatics. For example, Homeric Greek reflexive *he-* (from Proto-Indo-European *s(w)-) was later fused with *autós* (a form used like English *-self* to form compound reflexives) to yield Classical *heautón* in the third person, this in turn becoming Modern *eaftós*, now further modified with a possessive pronoun indicating person, as in *eaftó tu*, 'self his'. Proto-Romance *met-ipsimum* is an even clearer case of triple emphatic derivation. See also Langacker 1977 on Amerindian languages.

60. Edmondson and Plank (178: 386) in fact suggest that there is a third *himself* in English that indicates a reversal of semantic roles, as in *Bill hit Sue and was himself hit by Ann.*

61. For example, after Edmondson and Plank (1978: 380):

(i) John is a hippie. John's brother is a banker, happily married with three children. He/He himself/HE is very much admired by people of his own type.

The tendency is to take the unadorned pronoun to refer locally to John's brother (as predicted by the I-principle), but a marked pronoun (with the intensifier *himself* or intonational/stress prominence) suggests coreference with *John* (by Horn's 1984 division of labor whereby a marked form M-implicates the complement of the I-implicature that would have arisen from the unmarked form).

62. An anonymous referee, commenting on Levinson 1991, held that the existence of languages without Anaphors is no more embarrassing to the Binding Theory than the existence of languages without nasal consonants, although it might be interesting to see whether such languages invariably fail to have NP movement processes, as GB-theory might predict. Such a correlation is almost certainly missing; for example, one can find passives in most of the languages under consideration. There is in fact one detailed GB-style analysis of a B-first language by Chung (1989), which describes Chamorro as without overt morphological Anaphors but with canonical NP-traces in raising and passive constructions. Chung in fact is driven to the reluctant conclusion that Chomsky's parallel between movement and bound anaphora may have to be abandoned. See discussion in section 4.3.3.1.2. More recently, there have been moves to think of the Binding Theory as simply failing to apply to languages that at first sight seem to have good long-distance Anaphors, like Japanese (see Mazuka and Lust 1994).

63. This could function like the optional English *own* in *John admires his own book* (Larry Horn suggests to me), but much more likely it is just an emphatic. Either way, it is clearly not an Anaphor.

64. The subject is composed of demonstrative affixes flanking a classifier for men (marked 'CPman'). This expression is semantically general with anaphoric uses, so it could equally be translated as 'he'.

65. The other syntactic reflex of the supposed Anaphors in Chamorro is a "subject effect" whereby coreference is exceptionally ruled out where an antecedent precedes a subject with an embedded pronominal (in general, Chamorro seems to allow coreference wherever an antecedent precedes or c-commands a pronominal). This is because, it is claimed, in these structures c-command is impossible, but real Anaphors require it. It is unclear though, on this explanation, why a pronoun—which would look identical—should not be able to be bound in this location. In short, other factors seem involved. Chung (1989: 162–164) therefore considers an alternative pragmatic explanation, that this disjointness is due to a pragmatic opposition of the kind used by Reinhart (1983) or in our Q-based account of A-first languages, preferring the use of the Anaphor (with a passive or active transform if necessary). Overall, the attempt to distinguish pronominals from covert Anaphors masquerading in the same form seems an almost-impossible task.

66. I am most grateful to David Perlmutter for putting me in touch with this work on Creoles, not to mention useful discussions with him, conducted partly on the jog.

67. See also Carden 1989 on Guianese for diachronic evidence.

68. Mitchell (1985: 189) concurs with Visser's observation that:

emphatic self is found in the earliest texts in the nominative ... its use with an accusative reflexive pronoun appears to come later. It is not found in Beowulf, Genesis, Exodus, Christ and Satan, Deor or even Juliana, although it is evident in the prose of King Alfred's time.

69. Visser (1963: 439ff) documents the same "ambiguity" with the reciprocal meaning: *hi gecyston hi* could mean either 'they kissed them' or 'they kissed each other', this usage surviving into Middle English but being supplanted by various means of reciprocal marking, such as by adverbs glossed as 'mutually', and the *each...other* forms already utilized in Old English.

70. Mitchell (1985: 115) gives the following kind of example of the nonreflexive use of the form *hine selfne*:

(i) Moyses, se ðe wæs Gode sua weorð ðæt he oft wið hine selfne spræc
    'Moses₁ who was so dear to God₂ that he₁ often spoke with Him-self₂'
    (from King Alfred's West Saxon version of Gregory's Pastoral Care 131.11)

The example is discussed further in section 4.4.

71. Thus, according to grammars of the seventeenth and eighteenth centuries, a sentence like *Hij beschuldight hem* ('He accuses him/himself') was ambiguous. See Everaert 1986: 3ff and references therein.

72. A reflexive based on an emphatic, as in *hem zelf*, is also still current in standard Dutch, see Koster 1986: 344f, Koster 1994.

73. The evolution in the other direction (i.e., by the loss of Anaphors) is not of course inconceivable; indeed this seems to be what exceptionally happened in the West Germanic languages which are presumed to have lost the reconstructed Proto-Germanic reflexive **sik* (see note 75). But the diachronic processes here would be of a quite different kind, Nigel Vincent points out to me, perhaps owing to phonetic change or language contact. The bidirectional possibilities should not be confused with some natural cycle; for example, Vincent (1989b) insists, the apparent synthesis-analysis-synthesis cycle in some Romance verbal inflections disguises quite different underlying mechanisms. The historical change of B-first to A-first systems would seem in accord with the kind of grammaticalization of analytic into synthetic grammatical systems.

74. With introverted or inherently reflexive predicates like 'wash', 'shave', 'dress', one may expect the pronoun to be ommitted (I-implicating coreference) or if present to be understood in line with the stereotypical reflexive action.

75. From Proto-European **s(w)-*, proto-Germanic **sik*, a form lost in the development of English (Faltz 1985: 210).

76. This leaves reflexives like Japanese *zibun*, a nominal head without modifier, somewhat stranded; Faltz (1985: 49) suggests that they must either be assimilated to the true pronominal reflexives or analyzed as head+zero modifier.

77. Faltz rejects (1985: 278 n. 6) the idea that intransitivizing verbal affixes might specialize to become reflexives; actually, though, this seems to be happening in the

case of Guugu Yimithirr antipassive or middle (see Haviland 1979, Levinson 1987b), with reflexive specialization of the intransitivized verb being currently marked by an additional emphatic on the single NP. Of course, the Guugu Yimi-thirr antipassive might already have passed through a reflexive stage, with sub-sequent semantic bleaching; but some evidence against this is that some verbs (see Haviland 1979: 126f) that obligatorily take antipassive inflection (by some frozen, and thus presumably old, process) simply have an intransitive meaning (e.g., 'explode', 'shine').

78. Nigel Vincent tells me that the Proto-Romance formation *met-ipsimum* must be a case of threefold emphasis: *met* was an emphatic (as in *egomet* 'I myself'), *ipse* was the standard Latin emphatic pronoun with case inflection, and *-imum* was the superlative suffix as found in *maximum*. He adds that Italian *stesso* derives from *iste-ipse*, a double pronoun combination. Langacker (1977) also discusses the evolution of Uto-Aztecan reflexives.

79. Faltz (1985) does not appear to have been aware of Hagège's work and makes no reference to the subjective point-of-view phenomena associated with long-distance reflexives, although he discusses some of the classical logophoric languages, like Ewe (p. 252).

80. Of course, the derivation of a long-distance pronoun from a first-person pronoun in a language that has no system of indirect reported speech (i.e., from a form glossing as "John said I will come" to a form "John said self would come") would make immediate sense of the logophoric associations of such pronouns. But Faltz (1985: 263ff) notes a number of problems for such a development, although it seems eminently plausible for some of the African languages (like Ewe). However, it is quite clear that this cannot be the source of all such long-distance reflexives with associated logophoricity, because these are (as Faltz notes, p. 257ff) often (as in Igbo) clearly third-person in origin.

81. The exceptions will be those derived from first-person long-range-only "reflexives" and any C forms of the 'body-his' kind that may have been directly coined. For the record, Baker (1995: 94–95, n. 33) doubts this historical analysis on semantic grounds—he thinks that the two functions (reflexivity, emphasis or discourse prominence) are "conceptually independent" and the diachronic relation between them involves drastic reanalysis, but he owes us an account of why the two conceptually independent functions so repeatedly get marked with the same morphemes.

82. The evidence is of different kinds. The weakest is mere overlap in function between emphatics and reflexive morphemes. Stronger evidence, as in the case of Papago, is where this is reinforced by comparison with related languages where the morpheme only has a reflexive function. Best of all, of course, as in the rest of the cited languages, is where there are records showing increased grammaticalization over time of the emphatic into a reflexive.

83. Harbsmeier (1981: chap. 3) contains some interesting material on Classical Chinese reflexives. He claims that pronominal *ji* was a contrastive reflexive pronominal (related to, but distinct from the nominal *ji* referring to the Taoist 'Self';

p. 178) with clausemate antecedents, but also a noncontrastive long-distance reflexive requiring coreference with the subject of the highest clause (p. 187); whereas *zi* clearly had emphatic functions of many sorts, just like the adverbial uses of modern Mandarin *ziji* (Li and Thompson 1981: 138).

84. For example, Syromiatnikov (1981: 81f) notes both reflexive and emphatic adjunct uses for *onöre* and *midukara* in Ancient Japanese (cf. Modern Japanese *mizukara*, an alternate to *zibun*; Hinds 1986: 116). These seem to be bleached head nominals (e.g., *kara* means 'body'), a common reflexive source classified by Faltz (1985) as a kind of C pronoun.

85. Although rarely mentioned in the recent theoretical literature on *jibun/zibun* (e.g., in neither Kuno 1973 nor Hinds 1986 nor Sells 1987), the emphatic functions figure prominently in traditional pedagogical grammars (e.g., Vaccari and Vaccari 1948: 358ff list uses similar to English 'He himself came' and 'I bought it myself'; they even note the double emphatic use of *jibun jishin* to translate 'you did it yourself' [lit. *ji-bun* 'self-part', *ji-shin* 'self-body']). See also Mazuka and Lust 1994: 152.

86. It may be preferable, as previously mentioned, simply to assume that the I-preference to coreference only operates outside the scope of the DRP.

87. Incidentally, Huang (1994: 144) wonders in fact whether his account might not be generalized to languages like English, making an A-first account generally unnecessary. But there are at least two basic differences between the languages which motivate holding on to an A-first account. Firstly, sentences of the form 'He$_1$ hit him$_1$' with the coreferential interpretation have a different status in the two languages, being traditionally accepted by the grammarians as grammatical in Chinese (Huang 1994: 130) and rejected in English—thus we need an explanation (given by the Q-principle) of why the DRP is not so easily overruled in English. Second, reflexives in English (but not it seems in Chinese) have (it is argued) grammatically specified binding domains, and there are other signs of con-ventionalization (as in the bound-anaphora patterns), which then in turn have pragmatic implications, as modeled in the A-first account.

88. It is notable that in modern Chinese there is often a contrast in preferred ref-erential interpretation of embedded pronominals that favors a local antecedent for *ta* and a more distant one for *ziji*. For example, Huang (1989: 91) notes of the following kind of example that the favored interpretation coidentifies *Wang* (rather than *Li*) and *ziji*:

(i) Lao Wang yiwei Lao Li bu zhidao ziji qu guo Meiguo.
    Lao Wang think Lao Li not know self go EXP America
    'Wang thinks that Li doesn't know that self has been to America.'

This tendency for *ziji* linkage to skip over a good candidate antecedent that would have been the favored link with *ta* may therefore be partially explained by this pragmatic theory (specifically, the M-contrast between *ta* and *ziji*). Huang (1989: 106 n. 6) points out that a similar pattern has been noted for Japanese. However, our account cannot be the full explanation because even where there is no contrast with *ta*, *ziji* still prefers a more distant antecedent. In a sentence with only one embedded clause glossing, say, as 'Wang thinks Li has fallen in love with *ta/ziji*' the nearest antecedent, *Li*, is a clausemate disfavoring identification with *ta*, but *ziji* would still naturally refer to *Wang*.

89. That this is only a suggestion was clear, Huang (1994: 130) points out, to traditional grammarians of Chinese; he quotes Wang Li: "As for *ta ma ta* ('He rebukes him'), it is ambiguous: it can mean either 'he rebukes himself' or 'he rebukes another person'."

90. The Chinese example is from Huang (1989: 96), and the source of the Old English example is cited in note 70 (see Mitchell 1985: 115). I am grateful to April McMahon for help in interpreting the Old English examples.

91. The logic is as follows: If an unmarked utterance U I-implicates p, and a marked utterance M M-implicates the complement $\bar{p}$, a doubly marked utterance MM often implicates the complement of $\bar{p}$, that is, p (most often with some additional restriction; see chapter 2).

92. For an attempt to construe the pronouns of a B-first language as systematically ambiguous between Anaphor and pronoun, see Chung 1989. More generally, some theorists, like Koster (1986: 341ff, 1994), consider that pronouns are ambiguously Anaphors and pronominals, while reflexives may equally be Anaphors or pronominals (as in *John himself came*).

93. Apart from the delayed acquisition of Binding Condition B patterns found by Solan and others mentioned above, Reinhart (1986: 140–142) notes that findings about children's use of backward anaphora favor treating Condition B patterns as pragmatic. She argues that the data support her particular A-first analysis, with all types of bound anaphora collectively distinguished from pragmatic anaphora (but see C. Koster 1994). Her argument, like mine, is based on the presumption that innate predispositions should show up earlier in acquisition than pragmatically determined patterns.

94. Consider, for example, Platzack's (1987) consideration of the time scale for the parameter switch from null subjects to realized subjects in Swedish. Platzack argues that there are a number of syntactic reflexes of this parameter (e.g., subject-verb agreement, expletive pronouns vs. gaps, *that*-trace filter violations) and that the historical record shows that "these changes occurred together during a relatively short space of time—more or less within the seventeenth century" and that this supports "the hypothesis that they are all reflexes of a single parameter in the grammar" (p. 397f). The statistics he produces for frequency of null subjects might support a slightly more gradual account, in terms perhaps of a 200-year process; and there were also special sociolinguistic factors during this period of major state formation (as he points out). Nevertheless, there is a rather striking contrast in timescale between this Swedish case, with relatively rapid linked changes, and the history of English anaphora with the very slow acquisition of Anaphors and the apparent lack of linkage between the acquisition of something like Condition A, on the one hand, and Condition B–type patterns on the other. Kroch (1989) takes a more skeptical view, maintaining that most linguistic change is likely to be gradual and that language learners may happily operate with two

slightly inconsistent grammars, which makes rapid parametric change unlikely. See also the much more gradual loss of *pro*-drop in Old/Middle French analyzed by Adams (1987).

95. Chomsky (1981: 65) was perfectly aware that a pragmatic analysis might be in order here, saying that the Principle "... might be regarded as a subcase of a conversational principle of not saying more than is required, ... but there is some reason to believe it functions as a principle of grammar." Although in recent work Chomsky (1995) has stressed economy and lack of overdetermination within the linguistic system itself which maps phonological form onto logical form, he now concedes that "we do expect to find connections between the properties of the language and the manner of its use" (p. 168).

96. That is, we do not expect a Gricean principle to simply not apply to some specific language, in the way that it has been supposed that syntactic principles (especially outside the "core") might admit of marked exceptions. A claim to this effect has indeed been made by Elinor Ochs for Malagasy (then E. O. Keenan [1976] 1998), but Brown and Levinson (1987: 9, 288–289 n. 27) point out that the data do not substantiate this but rather point to specific social taboos overruling direct speech in limited circumstances. Brown and Levinson (1987) develop a theory in which the signaling of politeness works precisely by foregrounding such departures against a Gricean background. In the same way, against such a firm background of Gricean expectations, exceptional practices will be found in specific discourse genres. In these cases, Gricean principles are not even in limited suspension—the practices take their semiotic value from the departures from Gricean expectations.

Epilogue

1. Gazdar (1979: 11–13) documented this sentiment 20 years ago, and in the interim it has diminished perhaps only slightly. The complaint is often made that pragmatics "has found it difficult to achieve the degree of formal precision considered desirable in the linguistic sciences today" (Seuren 1998: 407). Note that formalization and prediction are not necessarily related; most predictions in the empirical branches of linguistics (e.g., psycholinguistics or language typology) are not formalized but are clear enough. Because pragmatics is, more or less by definition, not concerned with *rules* or with *monotonic inference*, any formalization is going to have an unfamiliar appearance—it is just not going to look like formalization in syntax and semantics (good examples can be found in the work on AI or natural language processing; see, e.g., Hobbs et al 1993). Large-scale formalization is also likely to be premature and involve fundamental fudges because we simply do not fully understand the underlying kinds of reasoning involved. This is not to say that fragmentary formalizations (as in Gazdar 1979, Wainer 1991, or Lascarides and Asher 1993) may not be extremely helpful. GCI theory, because of its limited scope and because of the existence of models of default reasoning, is a particularly promising area. Meanwhile, if the thesis of chapter 3 is roughly correct, much of what is currently done in formal semantics is the formalization of the pragmatically enriched semantic content of utterances.

2. Admittedly, because the inferences arise under our heuristics from the underlying semantic representations as well as the form of expressions, precise predictions depend on the semantic analysis of the relevant expressions. Note that because the conditions under which default inferences are defeasible are reasonably clear, defeasibility itself should not greatly weaken the predictions.

3. For off-line effects of Gricean inferences, see, for example, Moxey and Sanford 1993, Newstead 1995 on scalar inference; Dulany and Hilton 1991, on scalar inferences; Politzer and Noveck 1991, on Gricean effects on the conjunction fallacy. For on-line processing of anaphora, ambiguity, and so on, which may involve Gricean effects, see the reviews in Garrod and Sanford 1994 and Singer 1994. For a model of comprehension where pragmatic principles are involved early in on-line processing and before general knowledge of the world, see Ni, Crain, and Shankweiler 1996.

4. This is to depart from the otherwise attractive proposal of representational modularity by Jackendoff 1996b; see Bierwisch 1996: 41 for additional motivations.

References

Adams, M. 1987. From Old French to the theory of pro-drop. *Natural Language & Linguistic Theory* 5:1–32.

Allen, J. 1983. Recognizing intentions from natural language utterances. In M. Brady and R. C. Berwick (eds.), *Computational models of discourse* (pp. 107–166). Cambridge: Cambridge University Press.

Allen, S. 1994. *Acquisition of some mechanisms of transitivity alternation in arctic Quebec Inuktitut*. Ph.D. dissertation, McGill University, Montreal.

Anderson, S., and Keenan, E. 1985. Deixis. In T. Shopen (ed.), *Language typology and syntactic description*. Vol. 3, *Grammatical categories and the lexicon* (pp. 259–307). Cambridge: Cambridge University Press.

Andronov, M. 1969. *A standard grammar of modern and classical Tamil*. Madras, India: New Century Book House.

Ariel, M. 1994. Interpreting anaphoric expressions: A cognitive versus a pragmatic approach. *Journal of Linguistics* 30:3–42.

Aronoff, M. 1974. *Word formation in generative grammar*. Cambridge, MA: MIT Press.

Arundale, R. B. 1997. 'Studies in the way of words': Grice's new directions in conceptualizing meaning in conversational interaction. Mimeo, Department of Communication, University of Alaska, Fairbanks. (Paper presented at the International Communication Association, Chicago, May 1991.)

Asher, R. 1985. *Tamil*. London: Croom Helm.

Atlas, J. 1979. How linguistics matters to philosophy. In D. Dinneen and C.-K. Oh (eds.), *Syntax and semantics*. Vol. 11, *Presupposition* (pp. 265–281). New York: Academic Press.

Atlas, J. 1983. Comments on Horn (1985). Ms., Pomona College, Claremont, CA.

Atlas, J. 1984a. Grammatical non-specification: The mistaken disjunction theory. *Linguistics and Philosophy* 7:433–443.

Atlas, J. 1984b. Comparative adjectives and adverbials of degree: An introduction to radically radical pragmatics. *Linguistics and Philosophy* 7:347–377.

Atlas, J. 1989. *Philosophy without ambiguity*. Oxford: Clarendon Press.

Atlas, J. 1993a. The implications of conversation: The 1990 Leuven lectures. Ms., Pomona College, Claremont, CA.

Atlas, J. 1993b. The importance of being 'only': Testing the neo-Gricean versus neo-entailment paradigms. *Journal of Semantics* 10:301–318.

Atlas, J. (in press). *Pragmatic analysis: Logic, meaning, and conversational implicature*. Oxford: Oxford University Press.

Atlas, J., and Levinson, S. 1973. What is an implicature? Part 1: Kenny Logic. MSSB mimeo.

Atlas, J. D., and Levinson, S. C. 1981. *It*-clefts, informativeness, and logical form: Radical pragmatics (revised standard version). In Cole 1981: 1–61.

Austin, J. L. 1950. Truth. *Proceedings of the Aristotelian Society*. Supplementary vol. 24. [Reprinted in J. L. Austin, 1970, *Philosophical papers*, pp. 117–133. Oxford: Oxford University Press.]

Austin, J. L. 1962. *How to do things with words*. Oxford: Oxford University Press.

Austin, P. 1981. *A grammar of Diyari, South Australia*. Cambridge: Cambridge University Press.

Austin, P. 1987. Cases and clauses in Jiwarli, Western Australia. Ms., La Trobe University, Melbourne.

Avramides, A. 1989. *Meaning and mind: An examination of a Gricean account of language*. Cambridge, MA: MIT Press.

Bach, K. 1975. Performatives are statements too. *Philosophical Studies* 28:229–236.

Bach, K. 1982. Semantic nonspecificity and mixed quantifiers. *Linguistics and Philosophy* 4:593–605.

Bach, K. 1984. Default reasoning: Jumping to conclusions and knowing when to think twice. *Pacific Philosophical Quarterly* 65:37–58.

Bach, K. 1987a. *Thought and reference*. Oxford: Oxford University Press.

Bach, K. 1987b. On communicative intentions: A reply to Recanati. *Mind and Language* 2:141–154.

Bach, K. 1990. Communicative intentions, plan recognition, and pragmatics. In Cohen, Morgan, and Pollack 1990: 389–400.

Bach, K. 1994. Conversational implicture. *Mind and Language* 9:124–162.

Bach, K. 1995. Standardization and conventionalization. *Linguistics and Philosophy* 18:677–686.

Bach, K., and Harnish, R. M. 1979. *Linguistic communication and speech acts*. Cambridge, MA: MIT Press.

Bache, C., Basbøll, H., and Lindberg, C. E. (eds.) 1994. *Tense, aspect, and action: Empirical and theoretical contributions to language typology*. Berlin: Mouton de Gruyter.

Baker, C. L. 1995. Contrast, discourse prominence, and intensification, with special reference to locally free reflexives in British English. *Language* 71:63–101.

Baker, G. P., and Hacker, P. 1984. *Language, sense, and nonsense*: *A critical investigation into modern theories of language*. Oxford: Blackwell.

Bar-Hillel, Y. 1954. Indexical expressions. *Mind* 63:359–379.

Bar-Hillel, Y., and Carnap, R. 1952. An outline of a theory of semantic information. MIT Technical Report 247. [Reprinted in Y. Bar-Hillel, 1964, *Language and information*, pp. 221–274. Reading, MA: Addison-Wesley.]

Barton, E. 1988. *Base-generated constituents: A theory of grammatical structure and pragmatic interpretation*. Pragmatics and Beyond Series, Amsterdam: John Benjamins.

Barwise, J. 1986. Conditionals and conditional information. In E. Closs-Traugott, A. ter Meulen, J. Reilly, and C. Ferguson (eds.), *On conditionals* (pp. 21–54). Cambridge: Cambridge University Press.

Barwise, J., and Cooper, R. 1981. Generalized quantifiers and natural language. *Linguistics and Philosophy* 4:159–219.

Barwise J., and Perry, J. 1983. *Situations and attitudes*. Cambridge, MA: MIT Press.

Berlin, B. 1963. Some semantic features of reduplication in Tzeltal. *International Journal of American Linguistics* 29:211–218.

Bickerton, D. 1981. *Roots of language*. Ann Arbor, MI: Karoma.

Bierwisch, M. 1996. How much space gets into language? In Bloom, Peterson, Nadel, and Garrett 1996: 31–76.

Blakemore, D. 1992. *Understanding utterances*. Oxford: Blackwell.

Blass, R. 1990. *Relevance relations in discourse*. Cambridge: Cambridge University Press.

Bloom, P., Peterson, M., Nadel, L., and Garrett, M. (eds.) 1996. *Language and space*. Cambridge, MA: MIT Press.

Bloomfield, L. 1933. *Language*. New York: Holt, Rinehart, and Winston.

Bohnemeyer, J. 1998. *Time relations in discourse: Evidence from a comparative approach to Yukatek Maya*. Ph.D. dissertation, Tilburg University, The Netherlands.

Bolinger, D. 1979. Pronouns in discourse. In T. Givón (ed.), *Syntax and semantics*. Vol. 12, *Discourse and syntax* (pp. 289–310). New York: Academic Press.

Botha, R. 1988. *Form and meaning in word formation: A study of Afrikaans reduplication*. Cambridge: Cambridge University Press.

Bouchard, D. 1983. *On the content of empty categories*. Dordrecht: Foris.

Bourdieu, P. 1977. *Outline of a theory of practice*. Cambridge: Cambridge University Press.

Bréal, M. 1900. *Semantics*. [Trans. Mrs. H. Cust]. New York: Henry Holt.

Brown, P., and Levinson, S. C. 1978. Universals in language usage: Politeness phenomena. In E. Goody (ed.), *Questions and politeness: Strategies in social interaction* (pp. 56–289). Cambridge: Cambridge University Press.

Brown, P., and Levinson, S. C. 1987. *Politeness*. Cambridge: Cambridge University Press.

Burrow, T., and Emeneau, M. 1961. *A Dravidian etymological dictionary*. Oxford: Clarendon Press.

Burton-Roberts, N. 1984. Modality and implicature. *Linguistics and Philosophy* 7:181–206.

Burzio, L. 1991. The morphological basis of anaphora. *Journal of Linguistics* 27:81–105.

Bybee, J., Pagliuca, W., and Perkins R. 1991. Back to the future. In Traugott and Heine 1991: 17–58.

Calvert, D. R. 1986. *Descriptive phonetics*. 2d ed. Stuttgart: Thieme.

Caldwell, Bishop R. 1961 [1856]. *A comparative grammar of the Dravidian or South-Indian family of languages*. Madras, India: Madras University Press. [Originally London: Harrison.]

Cann, R. 1993. *Formal semantics: An introduction*. Cambridge: Cambridge University Press.

Cantrall, W. R. 1973. Why I would relate own, emphatic reflexives, and intensive pronouns, my own self. *Proceedings of the regional meeting of the Chicago Linguistics Society* 9:57–67.

Cantrall, W. R. 1974. *Viewpoint, reflexives, and the nature of noun phrases*. Janua Linguarum, Series Practica 210. The Hague: Mouton.

Carden, G. 1989. Reflexives constructions in Atipa and other early Guyanese texts. In M. Fauquenoy (ed.), *Special issue of Textes, Etudes, et Documents 7–8* (pp. 1–21). Paris: L'Harmattan.

Carden, G., and Stewart, W. 1986. Binding theory, bioprogram, and creolization: Evidence from Haitian Creole. Paper presented at Linguistic Society of America annual meeting. [Published as Carden and Stewart 1988.]

Carden, G., and Stewart, W. 1987. Mauritian Creole reflexives: An alternative historical scenario. Ms., University of British Columbia.

Carden, G., and Stewart, W. 1988. Binding theory, bioprogram, and creolization: Evidence from Haitian Creole. *Journal of Pidgin and Creole Languages* 3:1–67.

Carden, G., and Stewart, W. 1989. Mauritian Creole reflexives: A reply to Corne. *Journal of Pidgin and Creole Languages* 4:65–101.

Carden, G., and Stewart, W. 1990. Clefts, topicalization, and coreference in Haitian Creole: Implications for models of creolization based on L1 acquisition. Paper presented at the Conference on Focus and Grammatical Relations in Creole Languages, University of Chicago, May 1990.

Carnap, R. 1947. *Meaning and necessity*. Chicago: University of Chicago Press.

Carston, R. 1985. A reanalysis of some 'quantity implicatures'. Ms., University College London.

Carston, R. 1988. Implicature, explicature, and truth-theoretic semantics. In R. Kempson (ed.), *Mental representations: The interface between language and reality* (pp. 155–181). Cambridge: Cambridge University Press.

Carston, R. 1995. Quantity maxims and generalised implicature. *Lingua* 96:213–244.

Carston, R. 1996. Metalinguistic negation and echoic use. *Journal of Pragmatics* 25:309–330.

Chafe, W., and Nichols, J. (eds.) 1986. *Evidentiality: The linguistic coding of epistemology*. Norwood, NJ: Ablex.

Changeux, P. 1994. Art and neuroscience. *Leonardo* 27:189–201.

Charniak, E., and McDermott, D. 1987. *Introduction to artificial intelligence*. Reading, MA: Addison-Wesley.

Cherry, C. 1966. *On human communication*. Cambridge, MA: MIT Press.

Chien, Y.-C., and Wexler, K. 1990. Children's knowledge of locality conditions in binding as evidence for the modularity of syntax and pragmatics. *Language Acquisition* 1:225–295.

Cho, Y. Y., and Hong, K.-S. 1988. Evidence for the VP constituent from child Korean. In E. Clark and Y. Matsumoto (eds.), *Proceedings of the Annual Child Language Forum: Papers and reports on child language development* (pp. 31–38). Stanford, CA: Stanford University.

Chomsky, N. 1956. Three models for the description of language. *IRE Transactions on Information Theory* IT2: 113–114.

Chomsky, N. 1957. *Syntactic structures*. The Hague: Mouton.

Chomsky, N. 1959. On certain formal properties of grammars. *Information and Control* 2:137–167.

Chomsky, N. 1965. *Aspects of the theory of syntax*. Cambridge, MA: MIT Press.

Chomsky, N. 1975. *Reflections on language*. New York: Pantheon.

Chomsky, N. 1981. *Lectures on government and binding: The Pisa lectures*. Dordrecht: Foris.

Chomsky, N. 1986. *Knowledge of language*. New York: Praeger.

Chomsky, N. 1995. *The Minimalist Program*. Cambridge, MA: MIT Press.

Chung, S. 1989. On the notion "null anaphor" in Chamorro. In O. Jaeggli and K. Safir (eds.), *The null subject parameter* (pp. 143–184). Dordrecht: Kluwer.

Clark, E. 1993. *The lexicon in acquisition*. Cambridge: Cambridge University Press.

Clark, E. 1997. Conceptual perspective and lexical choice in acquisition. *Cognition* 64:1–37.

Clark, E., and Clark, H. 1979. Where nouns surface as verbs. *Language* 55:767–811.

Clark, H. H. 1983. Making sense of nonce sense. In G. B. Flores D'Arcais and R. Jarvella (eds.), *The process of language understanding* (pp. 297–332). New York: Wiley.

Clark, H. H. 1996. *Using language.* Cambridge: Cambridge University Press.

Clark, H. H., and Clark, E. V. 1979. When nouns surface as verbs. *Language* 55:797–811.

Clark, H. H., and Haviland, J. 1977. Comprehension and the given-new contract. In R. Freedle (ed.), *Discourse production and comprehension* (pp. 1–40). Hillsdale, NJ: Lawrence Erlbaum.

Closs-Traugott, E., ter Meulen, A., Reilly, J., and Ferguson, C. (eds.) 1986. *On conditionals.* Cambridge: Cambridge University Press.

Cohen, L. J. 1971. The logical particles of natural language. In Y. Bar-Hillel (ed.), *Pragmatics of natural language* (pp. 50–68). Dordrecht: Reidel.

Cohen, P., Morgan, J., and Pollack, M. 1990. *Intentions in communication.* Cambridge, MA: MIT Press.

Cole, P. (ed.) 1978. *Syntax and semantics.* Vol. 9, *Pragmatics.* New York: Academic Press.

Cole, P. (ed.) 1981. *Radical pragmatics.* New York: Academic Press.

Cole, P., and Morgan, J. (eds.) 1975. *Syntax and semantics.* Vol. 3, *Speech acts.* New York: Academic Press.

Comrie, B. 1981. *Language universals and linguistic typology.* Oxford: Blackwell.

Comrie, B. 1984. Subject and object control: Syntax, semantics, pragmatics. *Proceedings of the annual meeting of the Berkeley Linguistic Society* 10:450–464.

Comrie, B. 1985. *Tense.* Cambridge: Cambridge University Press.

Corne, C. 1988. Mauritian Creole reflexives. *Journal of Pidgin and Creole Linguistics* 3:69–94.

Cruse, D. A. 1986. *Lexical semantics.* Cambridge: Cambridge University Press.

Culy, C. 1997. Logophoric pronouns and point of view. *Linguistics* 35:845–860.

Davis, S. (ed.) 1991. *Pragmatics: A reader.* Oxford: Oxford University Press.

Dimitriadis, A. 1995. When pro-drop languages don't: On overt pronominal subjects in Greek. *Penn Working Papers in Linguistics*, 2:45–60.

Dixon, R. M. W. 1980. *The languages of Australia.* Cambridge: Cambridge University Press.

Dixon, R. M. W. 1981. Wargamay. In R. M. W. Dixon and B. Blake (eds.), *Handbook of Australian languages*, Vol. 2 (pp. 1–143.). Canberra, Australia: ANU Press.

Dixon, R. M. W. 1983. Nyawaygi. In R. M. W. Dixon and B. Blake (eds.), *Handbook of Australian languages*, Vol. 3 (pp. 430–525). Canberra, Australia: ANU Press.

Dixon, R. M. W. 1988. *A grammar of Boumaa Fijian.* Chicago: University of Chicago Press.

Dixon, R. M. W., and Blake, B. (eds.) 1983. *Handbook of Australian languages.* Vol. 3. Canberra, Australia: ANU Press.

Donnellan, K. S. 1966. Reference and definite description. *The Philosophical Review* 75:281–304.

Donnellan, K. S. 1978. Speaker references, description, and anaphora. In Cole 1978: 47–68.

Dowty, D. 1980. Comments on the paper by Bach and Partee. In J. Kreiman and A. Ojeda (eds.), *Proceedings of the Chicago Linguistics Society: Parasession on pronouns and anaphora* 16:29–40.

Dulany, D., and Hilton, D. 1991. Conversational implicature, conscious representation, and the conjunction fallacy. *Social Cognition* 9:85–110.

Eades, D. 1979. Gumbaynggir. In Dixon and Blake 1983: 244–361.

Eco, U. 1997. *The search for the perfect language.* London: Fontana.

Edmondson, J. A., and Plank, F. 1978. Great expectations: An intensive self analysis. *Linguistics and Philosophy* 2:373–413.

Enç, M. 1981. *Tense without scope: An analysis of nouns as indexicals.* Ph.D. dissertation, University of Wisconsin, Madison.

Enç, M. 1986. Topic switching and pronominal subjects in Turkish. In D. Slobin and K. Zimmer (eds.), *Typological studies in Turkish linguistics* (pp. 195–208). Amsterdam: John Benjamins.

Evans, G. 1980. Pronouns. *Linguistic Inquiry* 11:337–362.

Evans, N. 1995. *A grammar of Kayardild.* Berlin: Mouton de Gruyter.

Everaert, M. 1986. *The syntax of reflexivization.* Dordrecht: Foris.

Faltz, L. M. 1977. *Reflexivization: A study in universal syntax.* Ph.D. dissertation, University of California, Berkeley.

Faltz, L. M. 1985. *Reflexivization: A study in universal syntax.* [Revised version of Faltz 1977.] New York: Garland.

Faltz, L. M. 1989. A role for inference in meaning change. *Studies in Language,* 13:317–31.

Farmer, A., and Harnish, M. 1987. Communicative reference with pronouns. In Verschueren and Bertuccelli-Papi 1987: 547–565.

Fauconnier, G. 1975. Pragmatic scales and logical structure. *Linguistic Inquiry* 6:353–375.

Fauconnier, G. 1979. Implication reversal in natural language. In F. Guenthner and S. Schmidt (eds.), *Formal semantics for natural language* (pp. 289–301). Dordrecht: Reidel.

Fauconnier, G. 1985. *Mental spaces: Aspects of meaning construction in natural language.* Cambridge, MA: MIT Press.

Fillmore, C. 1975. *Santa Cruz lectures on deixis.* Mimeo, Indiana University Linguistics Club, Bloomington, IN. [Reprinted as Fillmore, C. 1997, *Lectures on deixis.* Stanford, CA: CSLI Publications.]

Fodor, J. 1983. *The modularity of mind*. Cambridge, MA: MIT Press.

Foley, W., and Van Valin, R. D. 1983. *Functional syntax and universal grammar*. Cambridge: Cambridge University Press.

Fogelin, R. 1967. *Evidence and meaning*. Atlantic Highlands, NJ: Humanities Press.

Ford, C. E., and Thompson, S. A. 1986. Conditionals in discourse: A text-based study from English. In Closs-Traugott, ter Meulen, Reilly, and Ferguson 1986: 353–372.

Fox, B. 1987. *Discourse structure and anaphora*. Cambridge: Cambridge University Press.

Fox, B. (ed.) 1996. *Studies in anaphora*. Amsterdam: John Benjamins.

Fox Tree, J., and Clark, H. 1997. Pronouncing "the" as "thee" to signal problems in speaking. *Cognition* 62:151–167.

Frederking, R. 1996. Grice's maxims: "Do the right thing." Paper delivered at the AAAI Symposium on Computational Implicature. Stanford, CA, March 1996.

Frege, G. [1884] 1953. *The foundations of arithmetic*. New York: Harper and Row.

Fretheim, T. 1992. The effect of intonation on a type of scalar implicature. *Journal of Pragmatics* 18:1–30.

Garnham, A. 1989. Integrating information in text comprehension: The interpretation of anaphoric noun phrases. In G. Carlson and M. Tanenhaus (eds.), *Linguistic structure in language processing* (pp. 359–400). Dordrecht: Kluwer.

Garrod, S., and Sanford, A. 1994. Resolving sentences in a discourse context. In Gernsbacher 1994: 675–698.

Gazdar, G. 1979. *Pragmatics: Implicature, presupposition, and logical form*. New York: Academic Press.

Gazdar, G. 1980. Pragmatic constraints on linguistic production. In B. Butterworth (ed.), *Language production*, Vol. 1 (pp. 49–68). New York: Academic Press.

Gazdar, G., and Pullum, G. 1976. Truth-functional connectives in natural language. *Proceedings of the Chicago Linguistic Society* 12:220–234.

Geach, P. T. 1972. *Logic matters*. Oxford: Blackwell.

Geis, M., and Zwicky, A. 1971. On invited inferences. *Linguistic Inquiry* 2:561–565.

Geniušienė, E. 1987. *The typology of reflexives*. Berlin: Mouton de Gruyter.

Gernsbacher, M. (ed.) 1994. *Handbook of psycholinguistics*. New York: Academic Press.

Geurts, B. 1998. The mechanisms of denial. *Language* 74:274–307.

Ginsberg, M. (ed.) 1987. *Readings in non-monotonic reasoning*. Los Altos, CA: Morgan Kaufman.

Gordon, D., and Lakoff, G. 1971. Conversational postulates. *Proceedings of the Chicago Linguistic Society* 7:63–84.

Grandy, R., and Warner, R. 1986. *Philosophical grounds of rationality*. Oxford: Clarendon Press.

Green, G. 1987. Some remarks on why there is implicature. *Studies in the Linguistic Sciences*, 17:77–92.

Green, N., and Carberry, S. 1993. A discourse-plan-based approach to a class of particularized conversational implicature. *ESCOL'93*: 117–128.

Greenberg, J. 1966a. *Universals of language*. 2d ed. Cambridge, MA: MIT Press.

Greenberg, J. 1966b. *Language universals, with special reference to feature hierarchies*. The Hague: Mouton.

Grice, H. P. 1957. Meaning. *Philosophical Review*, 67:377–388.

Grice, H. P. 1961. The causal theory of perception. *The Aristotelian society: Proceedings, supplementary*. Vol. 35 (pp. 121–153). [Reprinted in S. Davis (ed.) 1983, *Causal theories of mind* (pp. 245–70).] Berlin: Mouton de Gruyter.

Grice, H. P. 1967. Logic and conversation. William James Lectures. Ms., Harvard University.

Grice, H. P. 1969. Utterer's meaning and intentions. *Philisophical Review* 78:147–177. [Reprinted in Grice 1989.]

Grice, H. P. 1975. Logic and conversation. In Cole and Morgan 1975: 41–58.

Grice, H. P. 1978. Further notes on logic and conversation. In Cole 1978: 113–128.

Grice, H. P. 1981. Presupposition and conversational implicatures. In Cole 1981: 183–198.

Grice, H. P. 1986. Reply to Richards. In Grandy and Warner 1986: 45–106.

Grice, P. 1989. *Studies in the way of words*. Cambridge, MA: Harvard University Press.

Grodzinsky, Y., and Reinhart, T. 1993. The innateness of binding and coreference. *Linguistic Inquiry* 24:69–101.

Gundel, J., Hedberg, N., and Zacharski, R. 1989. Givenness, implicature, and demonstrative reference in English. *Proceedings of the Chicago Linguistic Society. Part 2: Parasession on language in context* 25:89–103.

Gundel, J., Hedberg, N., and Zacharski, R. 1993. Cognitive status and the form of referring expressions in discourse. *Language* 69:274–307.

Hagège, C. 1974. Les pronoms logophoriques. *Bulletin de la Société de Linguistique de Paris* 69:287–310.

Haiman, J. 1985a. *Natural syntax*. Cambridge: Cambridge University Press.

Haiman, J. (ed.) 1985b. *Iconicity in syntax*. Amsterdam: John Benjamins.

Haiman, J. 1985c. Symmetry. In Haiman 1985b: 73–95.

Haiman, J. 1995. Grammatical signs of the divided self. In W. Abraham, T. Givón, and S. Thompson (eds.), *Discourse grammar and typology* (pp. 213–234). Amsterdam: John Benjamins.

Haiman, J., and Munro, P. (eds.) 1983. *Switch reference and Universal Grammar*. Amsterdam: John Benjamins.

Hale, K. 1983. Warlpiri and the grammar of non-configurational languages. *Natural Language & Linguistic Theory* 1:5–47.

Hamblin, C. L. 1971. Mathematical models of dialogue. *Theoria* 37:130–155.

Harbert, W. 1995. Binding theory, control, and *pro*. In G. Webelhuth (ed.), *Government and binding theory and the Minimalist Program* (pp. 177–240). Oxford: Blackwell.

Harbsmeier, C. 1981. *Aspects of classical Chinese syntax*. London: Curzon Press.

Harder, P. 1994. Verbal time reference in English: Structure and functions. In Bache, Basbøll, and Lindberg 1994: 61–80.

Harman, G. 1974. Review of Stephen Schiffer's *Meaning*. *Journal of Philosophy* 71:224–229.

Harman, G. 1986. *Change in view: Principles of reasoning*. Cambridge, MA: MIT Press.

Harnish, R. 1976. Logical form and implicature. In T. Bever, J. J. Katz, and T. Langendoen (eds.), *An integrated theory of linguistic ability* (pp. 313–392). New York: Crowell.

Harnish, R. 1991. Logical form and implicature. In S. Davis (ed.), *Pragmatics* (pp. 316–364). Oxford: Oxford University Press.

Harris, R. A. 1993. *The linguistics wars*. Oxford: Oxford University Press.

Haviland, J. 1979. Guugu Yimidhirr. In R. M. W. Dixon and B. Blake (eds.), *Handbook of Australian languages*. Vol. 1 (pp. 27–182). Canberra, Australia: ANU Press.

Hawkins, J. 1978. *Definiteness and indefiniteness: A study in reference and grammaticality prediction*. London: Croom Helm.

Hawkins, J. 1991. On (in)definite articles: Implicatures and (un)grammaticality prediction. *Journal of Linguistics* 27:405–442.

Heim, I. 1982. *The semantics of definite and indefinite descriptions*. Ph.D. dissertation, University of Massachusetts, Amherst.

Heim, I. 1983a. File change semantics and the familiarity theory of definiteness. In R. Bäuerle, U. Egli, and A. von Stechow (eds.), *Semantics from different points of view* (pp. 164–189). Berlin: Springer.

Heim, I. 1983b. On the projection problem for presuppositions. *West Coast Conference on Formal Linguistics* 2:114–125. [Reprinted in Davis 1991: 397–405.]

Heinämäki, O. 1994. Aspect as boundedness in Finnish. In Bache, Basbøll, and Lindberg 1994: 207–233.

Heine, B., Claudi, U., and Hünnemeyer, F. 1991. *Grammaticalization: A conceptual framework*. Chicago: Chicago University Press.

Hellan, L. 1986. On anaphora and predication in Norwegian. In L. Hellan and K. K. Christensen (eds.), *Topics in Scandinavian syntax* (pp. 103–124). Dordrecht: Reidel.

Hellan, L. 1988. *Anaphora in Norwegian and the theory of grammar*. Dordrecht: Foris.

Hellan, L. 1991. Containment and connectedness anaphors. In Koster and Reuland 1991: 27–48.

Herskovits, A. 1986. *Language and spatial cognition: An interdisciplinary study of the prepositions in English*. Cambridge: Cambridge University Press.

Higginbotham, J. 1983. Logical form, binding, and nominals. *Linguistic Inquiry* 14:395–420.

Hinds, J. 1986. *Japanese*. London: Croom Helm.

Hintikka, J. 1962. *Knowledge and belief*. Ithaca, NY: Cornell University Press.

Hintikka, J. 1970. On attributions of 'self-knowledge'. *The Journal of Philosophy* 67:73–87.

Hirschberg, J. 1985. *A theory of scalar implicature*. Moore School of Electrical Engineering, University of Pennsylvania, Technical Report MS-CIS–85–56. [Reprinted as Hirschberg, J. 1991. *A theory of scalar implicature*. New York: Garland.]

Hirst, G. 1987. *Semantic interpretation and the resolution of ambiguity*. Cambridge: Cambridge University Press.

Hobbs, J. 1979. Coherence and coreference. *Cognitive Science* 3:67–90.

Hobbs, J. 1982. Towards understanding of coherence in discourse. In W. Lehnert and M. H. Ringle (eds.), *Strategies of natural language processing* (pp. 223–244). Hillsdale, NJ: Lawrence Erlbaum.

Hobbs, J. 1987. *Implicature and definite reference*. Stanford, CA: CSLI Report 87–99.

Hobbs, J. 1996. Monotone decreasing quantifiers in a scope-free logical form. In Van Deemter and Peters 1996: 55–76.

Hobbs, J., and Martin, P. 1987. *Local pragmatics*. Technical Memo, SRI International, Menlo Park, CA.

Hobbs, J., Croft, W., Davies, T., Edwards, D., and Laws, K. 1987. Commonsense metaphysics and lexical semantics. *Computational Linguistics* 13:241–250.

Hobbs, J., Stickel, M., Appelt, D., and Martin, P. 1990. Interpretation as abduction. Technical Note 499, SRI International, Menlo Park, CA.

Hobbs, J., Stickel, M., Appelt, D., and Martin, P. 1993. Interpretation as abduction. *Artificial Intelligence* 63:69–142.

Holdcroft, D. 1987. Conversational relevance. In Verschueren and Bertuccelli-Papi 1987: 477–496.

Holland, J. J., Holyok, K. J., Nisbett, R., and Thagard, P. R. 1989. *Induction: Processes of inference, learning, and discovery*. Cambridge, MA: MIT Press.

Hopper, P., and Traugott, E. 1993. *Grammaticalization*. Cambridge: Cambridge University Press.

Horn, L. R. 1972. *On the semantic properties of logical operators in English*. Mimeo, Indiana University Linguistics Club, Bloomington, IN.

Horn, L. R. 1973. Greek Grice: A brief survey of proto-conversational rules in the history of logic. *Proceedings of the Chicago Linguistic Society* 9:205–214.

Horn, L. R. 1978. Remarks on Neg-Raising. In Cole 1978: 129–220.

Horn, L. R. 1984. Toward a new taxonomy for pragmatic inference: Q- and R-based implicature. In D. Shiffrin (ed.), *Meaning, form, and use in context* (pp. 11–42). Washington, DC: Georgetown University Press.

Horn, L. R. 1985. Metalinguistic negation and pragmatic ambiguity. *Language* 61:121–174.

Horn, L. R. 1989. *A natural history of negation*. Chicago: University of Chicago Press.

Horn, L. R. 1990. Hamburgers and the truth: Why Gricean inference is Gricean. *Proceedings of the Berkeley Linguistic Society* 16:454–471.

Horn, L. R. 1991a. *Duplex negatio affirmat...*: The economy of double negation. *Proceedings of the Chicago Linguistic Society: Parasession on Negation* 27:80–106.

Horn, L. R. 1991b. Given as new: When redundant affirmation isn't. *Journal of Pragmatics* 15:305–328.

Horn, L. R. 1992a. Pragmatics, implicature, and presupposition. In W. Bright (ed.), *International Encyclopaedia of Linguistics*, Vol. 1 (pp. 260–266). Oxford: Oxford University Press.

Horn, L. R. 1992b. The said and the unsaid. *SALT II: Proceedings of the second Conference on Semantics and Linguistic Theory* (pp. 163–192). Columbus, OH: Ohio State University Linguistics Department.

Horn, L. R. 1993. Economy and redundancy in a dualistic model of natural language. *SKY 1993: 1993 Yearbook of the Linguistic Asssociation of Finland*, pp. 33–72.

Horn, L. R. 1996b. Presupposition and implicature. In Lappin 1996: 299–320.

Horn, L. R. 1997. All John's children are as bald as the King of France: Existential import and the geometry of opposition. *Papers from the 33rd Meeting of the Chicago Linguistic Society* 33:155–179.

Horn, L. R., and Bayer, S. 1984. Short-circuited implicature: A negative contribution. *Linguistics and Philosophy* 7:397–414. [Reprinted in A. Kasher (ed.), 1998, *Pragmatics*, Vol. 4 (pp. 658–675). London: Routledge.]

Horn, L. R., and Lee, Y.-S. 1995. Progovac on polarity. *Journal of Linguistics* 31:401–424.

Hornstein, N. 1995. *Logical form: From GB to Minimalism*. Oxford: Blackwell.

Huang, Y. 1989. *Anaphora in Chinese: Towards a pragmatic analysis*. Ph.D. dissertation, University of Cambridge.

Huang, Y. 1991. A neo-Gricean pragmatic theory of anaphora. *Journal of Linguistics* 27:301–335.

Huang, Y. 1994. *The syntax and pragmatics of anaphora: A study with special reference to Chinese*. Cambridge: Cambridge University Press.

Huang, Y. 2000. *Anaphora: A cross-linguistic study* (Oxford Studies in Typology and Linguistic Theory). Oxford: Oxford University Press.

Jackendoff, R. 1972. *Semantic interpretation in generative grammar*. Cambridge, MA: MIT Press.

Jackendoff, R. 1983. *Semantics and cognition*. Cambridge, MA: MIT Press.

Jackendoff, R. 1990. *Semantic structures*. Cambridge, MA: MIT Press.

Jackendoff, R. 1992a. *Languages of the mind*. Cambridge, MA: MIT Press.

Jackendoff, R. 1992b. Mme. Tussaud meets the Binding Theory. *Natural Language & Linguistic Theory* 10:1–31.

Jackendoff, R. 1996a. Semantics and cognition. In Lappin 1996: 539–560.

Jackendoff, R. 1996b. The architecture of the linguistic-spatial interface. In Bloom, Peterson, Nadel, and Garrett 1996: 1–30.

Jackendoff, R, 1997. *The architecture of the language faculty*. Cambridge, MA: MIT Press.

Jackson, S. 1981. Conversational implicature in children's comprehension of reference. *Communication Monographs* 48:237–249.

Jackson, S., and Jacobs, S. 1982. Ambiguity and implicature in children's discourse interpretation. *Journal of Child Language* 9:209–216.

Jakobson, R. 1939. Signe zéro. In *Mélanges de linguistique, offerts á Charles Bally* (pp. 143–152). Geneva: Georg.

Jakubowicz, C. 1984. On markedness and binding principles. *Proceedings of the North Eastern Linguistics Society* 14:154–182.

Jayaseelan, K. A., 1988. Emphatic reflexive X-self. *Working Papers in Linguistics* 5:1–20. Hyderabad, India: Central Institute of English and Foreign Languages.

Jespersen, O. 1917. *Negation in English and other languages*. Copenhagen: Høst.

Jespersen, O. 1927. *A Modern English grammar on historical principles, Part III.* Vol. 2, *Syntax*. Heidelberg: Carl Winters Universitätsbuchhandlung.

Johnson-Laird, P. 1983. *Mental models: Towards a cognitive science of language, inference, and consciousness*. Cambridge: Cambridge University Press.

Josephson, J., and Josephson, S. 1994. *Abductive inference*. Cambridge: Cambridge University Press.

Kadmon, N. 1984. Indefinite noun phrases with cardinality indication. Ms., University of Massachusetts, Amherst.

Kadmon, N. 1987. *On unique and non-unique reference and asymmatric quantification*. Ph.D. dissertation, University of Massachusetts, Amherst.

Kamp, H. 1981. A theory of truth and semantic representation. In J. Groenendijk, T. Janssen, and M. Stokhof (eds.), *Formal methods in the study of language*, Vol. 1 (pp. 277–321). Amsterdam: Mathematisch Centrum.

Kamp, H., and Reyle, U. 1993. *From discourse to logic*. Dordrecht: Kluwer.

Kant, E. 1933 [1781]. *Critique of pure reason*. (Trans. N. K. Smith). London: Macmillan. [Translation of 1781, *Kritik der reinen Vernunft*. Riga: Hartknoch.]

Karttunen, L. 1976. Discourse referents. In J. D. McCawley (ed.), *Notes from the linguistic underground* (pp. 363–386). New York: Academic Press.

Kasher, A. (ed.) 1998. *Pragmatics: Critical concepts*. Vol. 4, *Presupposition, implicature, and indirect speech acts*. London: Routledge.

Katz, J. J. 1987. Common sense in semantics. In Lepore 1987: 157–234.

Kaufman, D. 1994. Grammatical or pragmatic: Will the real Principle B please stand? In B. Lust, G. Hermon, and J. Kornfilt (eds.), *Syntactic theory and first language acquisition: Cross-linguistic perspectives*. Vol. 2, *Binding, dependencies, and learnability* (pp. 177–200). Hillsdale, NJ: Lawrence Erlbaum.

Kay, P. 1990. Even. *Linguistics and Philosophy* 15:59–112.

Kay, P. 1992. The inheritance of presuppositions. *Linguistics and Philosophy* 15:333–379.

Kay, P., and Zimmer, K. 1976. On the semantics of compounds and genitives in English. *Proceedings of the California Linguistic Association Conference* 6:29–35.

Keenan, E. O. 1998 [1976]. The universality of conversational postulates. In Kasher 1998: 215–229 [Reprinted from 1976, *Language in Society* 5:67–80.]

Kempson, R. 1975. *Presupposition and the delimitation of semantics*. Cambridge: Cambridge University Press.

Kempson, R. 1980. Ambiguity and word meaning. In S. Greenbaum, G. Leech, and J. Svartvik (eds.), *Studies in English linguistics* (pp. 7–16). London: Longman.

Kempson, R. 1986. Ambiguity and the semantics-pragmatics distinction. In C. Travis (ed.), *Meaning and interpretation* (pp. 77–104). Oxford: Blackwell.

Kempson, R. 1996. Semantics, pragmatics, and deduction. In Lappin 1996: 561–598.

Kempson, R., and Cormack, A. 1981. Ambiguity and quantification. *Linguistics and Philosophy* 4:259–309.

Kempson, R., and Cormack, A. 1982. Quantification and pragmatics. *Linguistics and Philosophy* 4:607–618.

Kenny, A. J. 1966. Practical inference. *Analysis* 26:65–75.

Kibrik, A. 1996. Anaphora in Russian narrative prose: A cognitive calculative account. In B. Fox (ed.), *Studies in anaphora* (pp. 255–304). Amsterdam: John Benjamins.

Kiparsky, P. 1982. Lexical morphology and phonology. In P. Kiparsky (ed.), *Linguistics in the morning calm* (pp. 3–91). Seoul: Hanshin.

Kiss, K. É. 1991. The primacy condition of anaphora and pronominal variable binding. In Koster and Reuland 1991: 245–262.

Klein, E. 1980. A semantics for positive and comparative adjectives. *Linguistics and Philosophy* 4:1–45.

König, E. 1991. *The meaning of focus particles: A comparative perspective.* London: Croom Helm.

König, E., and Traugott, E. 1988. Pragmatic strengthening and semantic change: The conventionalizing of conversational implicature. In W. Hüllen and R. Schultze (eds.), *Understanding the lexicon* (pp. 110–124). Tübingen: Niemeyer.

Koster, C. 1994. Problems with pronoun acquisition. In Lust, Hermon, and Kornfilt 1994: 201–226.

Koster, J. 1986. *Domains and dynasties: The radical autonomy of syntax.* Dordrecht: Foris.

Koster, J. 1994. Towards a new theory of anaphoric binding. In Lust, Hermon, and Kornfilt 1994: 41–70.

Koster, J., and May, R. 1982. On the constituency of infinitives. *Language* 58:116–143.

Koster, J., and Reuland, E. (eds.) 1991. *Long-distance anaphora.* Cambridge: Cambridge University Press.

Kripke, S. 1977. Identity and necessity. In S. P. Schwartz (ed.), *Naming, necessity, and natural kinds* (pp. 66–101). Ithaca, NY: Cornell University Press.

Kroch, A. 1989. Language learning and language change: Comment on D. Lightfoot, The child's trigger experience: Degree-0 learnability. *Behavioral and Brain Sciences* 12:348–349.

Kuno, S. 1973. *The structure of the Japanese language.* Cambridge, MA: MIT Press.

Kuno, S. 1987. *Functional syntax: Anaphora, discourse, and empathy.* Chicago: Chicago University Press.

Ladd, R. 1980. *The structure of intonational meaning.* Bloomington, IN: Indiana University Press.

Lafon, J.-C. 1968. Auditory basis of phonetics. In B. Malmberg (ed.), *Manual of phonetics* (pp. 76–104). Amsterdam: North-Holland.

Lakoff, G. 1971. Presupposition and relative well-formedness. In D. Steinberg and L. Jakobovits (eds.), *Semantics: An interdisciplinary reader in philosophy, linguistics, and psychology* (pp. 329–340). Cambridge: Cambridge University Press.

Lakoff, G. 1972. Hedges: A study in meaning criteria and the logic of fuzzy concepts. In *Proceedings of the Chicago Linguistic Society* 8:236–287.

Lakoff, G. 1973. Some thoughts on transderivational constraints. In B. B. Kachru et al. (eds.), *Issues in linguistics* (pp. 442–452). Urbana: University of Illinois Press.

Lakoff, G. 1974. Syntactic amalgams. In M. W. Galy, R. A. Fox, and A. Bruck (eds.), *Proceedings of the Chicago Linguistic Society* 10:321–344.

Lakoff, G. 1987. *Women, fire, and dangerous things*. Chicago: University of Chicago Press.

Landman, F. 1986. Conflicting presuppositions and modal subordination. In A. M. Farley, P. T. Farley, and K. E. McCullough (eds.), *Proceedings of the Chicago Linguistic Society: Parasession on pragmatics and grammatical theory* 22:195–207.

Lang, E. 1984. *The semantics of coordination*. Amsterdam: John Benjamins.

Langacker, R. 1977. Syntactic reanalyis. In C. Li (ed.), *Mechanisms of syntactic change* (pp. 57–140). Austin, TX: University of Texas Press.

Langacker, R. 1987. *Foundations of cognitive grammar*, Vol. 1. Stanford, CA: Stanford University Press.

Langacker, R., and Munro, P. 1975. Passives and their meaning. *Language* 51:789–830.

Lappin, S. (ed.) 1996. *Handbook of contemporary semantic theory*. Oxford: Blackwell.

Lascarides, A., and Asher, N. 1993. Temporal interpretation, discourse relations, and commonsense entailment. *Linguistics and Philosophy* 16:437–493.

Lasnik, H. 1991. On the necessity of Binding Conditions. In R. Freidin (ed.), *Principles and parameters in comparative grammar* (pp. 7–28). Cambridge, MA: MIT Press.

Laver, J. 1994. *Principles of phonetics*. Cambridge: Cambridge University Press.

Leech, G. 1983. *Principles of pragmatics*. London: Longman.

Lehmann, C. 1988. Towards a typology of clause linkage. In J. Haiman and S. Thompson (eds.), *Clause combining in grammar and discourse* (pp. 181–226). Amsterdam: John Benjamins.

Lepore, E. (ed.) 1987. *New directions in semantics*. New York: Academic Press.

Levelt, W. J. M. 1989. *Speaking: From intention to articulation*. Cambridge, MA: MIT Press.

Levesque, H. 1990. All I know: A study in autoepistemic logic. *Artificial Intelligence* 42:263–310.

Levin, N. 1987. A pragmatic concomitant of gapping. *ESCOL' 87*:176–186.

Levin, N., and Prince, E. 1986. Gapping and causal implicature. *Papers in Linguistics* 19:351–364.

Levine, J. E. 1990. Pragmatic implicatures and case: The Russian dative revisited. *Russian Language Journal* 44 (147–149):1–27.

Levinson, S. C. 1979. Pragmatics and social deixis. *Proceedings of the Annual Meeting of the Berkeley Linguistic Society* 5:206–223.

Levinson, S. C. 1983. *Pragmatics*. Cambridge: Cambridge University Press.

Levinson, S. C. 1987a. Minimization and conversational inference. In Verschueren and Bertuccelli-Papi 1987: 61–129. [Reprinted in A. Kasher (ed.) 1998, *Pragmatics: Critical concepts*, Vol. 4, pp. 545–612. London: Routledge.]

Levinson, S. C. 1987b. Pragmatics and the grammar of anaphora. *Journal of Linguistics* 23:379–434.

Levinson, S. C. 1987c. Explicature explicated. *Behavioral and Brain Sciences* 10:722–723.

Levinson, S. C. 1988a. Putting linguistics on a proper footing: Explorations in Goffman's concepts of participation. In P. Drew and A. Wootton (eds.), *Erving Goffman: Exploring the interaction order* (pp. 161–227). Cambridge: Cambridge University Press.

Levinson, S. C. 1988b. Generalized conversational implicature and the semantics/pragmatics interface. Mimeo, Linguistics Department, Stanford University, Stanford, CA.

Levinson, S. C. 1989. Relevance. *Journal of Linguistics* 21:455–472.

Levinson, S. C. 1991. Pragmatic reduction of the binding conditions revisited. *Journal of Linguistics* 27:107–161.

Levinson, S. C. 1995a. Three levels of meaning. In F. Palmer (ed.), *Grammar and meaning* (pp. 90–115). Cambridge: Cambridge University Press.

Levinson, S. C. 1995b. Interactional biases in human thinking. In E. Goody (ed.), *Social intelligence and interaction* (pp. 221–260). Cambridge: Cambridge University Press.

Levinson, S. C. 1996. Frames of reference and Molyneux's question: Cross-linguistic evidence. In Bloom, Peterson, Nadel, and Garrett 1996: 109–170.

Levinson, S. C. 1997. From outer to inner space: Linguistic categories and non-linguistic thinking. In E. Pederson and J. Nuyts (eds.), *With language in mind: The relationship between linguistic and conceptual representation* (pp. 13–45). Cambridge: Cambridge University Press.

Lewis, D. 1969. *Convention: A philosophical study*. Cambridge, MA: Harvard University Press.

Lewis, D. 1972. General semantics. In D. Davidson and G. Harman (eds.), *Semantics of natural language* (pp. 169–218). Dordrecht: Reidel.

Lewis, D. 1979. Score-keeping in a language game. In R. Bauerle, U. Egli, and A. von Stechow (eds.), *Semantics from different points of view* (pp. 172–187). Berlin: Springer-Verlag.

Li, C., and Thompson, S. 1981. *Mandarin Chinese: A functional reference grammar*. Berkeley and Los Angeles: University of California Press.

Lieberman, P., and Blumstein, S. 1988. *Speech physiology, speech perception, and acoustic phonetics*. Cambridge: Cambridge University Press.

Lightfoot, D. 1989. The child's trigger experience: Degree–0 learnability. *Behavioral and Brain Sciences* 12:321–375.

Linebarger, M. 1991. Negative polarity items and linguistic evidence. *Proceedings of the Chicago Linguistic Society: Parasession on Negation* 27:165–188.

Löbner, S. 1987. Quantification as a major module of natural language semantics. In J. Groenendijk, D. de Jongh, and M. Stokhof (eds.), *Studies in discourse rep-*

resentation theory and the theory of generalized quantifiers (pp. 53–85). Dordrecht: Reidel.

Lucy, J. 1993. Reflexive language and the human disciplines. In J. Lucy (ed.), *Reflexive language: Reported speech and metapragmatics* (pp. 1–32). Cambridge: Cambridge University Press.

Lust, B. (ed.) 1986. *Studies in the acquisition of anaphora*. Dordrecht: Reidel.

Lust, B., Hermon, G., and Kornfilt, J. (eds.) 1994. *Syntactic theory and first language acquisition: Cross-linguistic perspectives*. Vol. 2, *Binding, dependencies, and learnability*. Hillsdale, NJ: Lawrence Erlbaum.

Lyons, J. 1977. *Semantics*. Vols. 1 and 2. Cambridge: Cambridge University Press.

Lyons, J. 1981. *Language and linguistics: An introduction*. Cambridge: Cambridge University Press.

Lyons, J. 1995. *Linguistic smantics: An introduction*. Cambridge: Cambridge University Press.

Maling, J. 1984. Non-clause-bounded reflexives in Modern Icelandic. *Linguistics and Philosophy* 7:211–241.

Marslen-Wilson, W., and Tyler, L. 1980. Towards a psychological basis for a theory of anaphora. *Proceedings of the Chicago Linguistics Society: Parasession on Pronouns and Anaphora* 16:258–286.

Martin, R. M. 1987. *The meaning of language*. Cambridge, MA: MIT Press.

Matsumoto, Y. 1995. The conversational condition on Horn scales. *Linguistics and Philosophy* 18:21–60.

Matthews, P. H. 1981. *Syntax*. Cambridge: Cambridge University Press.

May, R. 1987. Logical form as a level of linguistic representation. In Lepore 1987: 305–336.

Mazuka, R., and Lust, B. 1994. When is an anaphor not an anaphor? In Lust, Hermon, and Kornfilt 1994: 145–176.

McCafferty, A. S. 1987. *Reasoning about implicature: A plan-based approach*. Ph.D. dissertation, University of Pittsburgh, Pittsburgh, PA.

McCarthy, J. 1980. Circumscription: A form of non-monotonic reasoning. *Artificial Intelligence* 13:27–39, 171–172. [Reprinted in Ginsberg 1987: 145–152.]

McCarthy, J. 1986. Applications of circumscription to formalizing common sense knowledge. *Artificial Intelligence* 28:89–116.

McCawley, J. 1978. Conversational implicature and the lexicon. In Cole 1978: 245–259.

Mehler, J., Sebastian, N., Altmann, G., Dupoux, E., Christophe, A., and Pallier, C. 1993. Understanding compressed sentences: The role of rhythm and meaning. In P. Tallal, A. M. Galaburda, R. Llinas, and C. von Euler (eds.), *Annals of the New York Academy of Sciences: Temporal information processing in the nervous system* 682:272–282.

Miller, G., and Johnson-Laird, P. N. 1976. *Language and perception*. Cambridge, MA: Harvard University Press.

Milsark, G. 1974. *Existential sentences in English*. Ph.D. dissertation, Massachusetts Institute of Technology, Cambridge, MA.

Mitchell, B. 1985. *Old English syntax*. Vol. 1, *Concord, the parts of speech, and the sentence*. Oxford: Clarendon Press.

Mitchell, J. E. 1986. *The formal semantics of point of view*. Ph.D. dissertation, University of Massachusetts, Amherst.

Moore, R. C. 1985. Semantical considerations on nonmonotonic logics. *Artificial Intelligence* 25:75–94. [Reprinted in Ginsberg 1987: 127–136.]

Moore, R. C. 1986. Problems in logical form. In B. Grosz, K. Jones, and B. Webber (eds.), *Readings in natural language processing* (pp. 285–292). Los Altos, CA: Morgan Kaufman. [Reprinted from 1981, *Proceedings of the ninth annual meeting of the Association for Computational Linguistics*. Urbana–Champaign, IN: ACL. pp. 117–124.]

Moravcsik, E. A. 1972. Some cross-linguistic generalizations about intensifier constructions. *Proceedings of the Regional Meeting of the Chicago Linguistic Society* 8:271–277.

Morgan, J. 1978. Two types of convention in indirect speech acts. In Cole 1978: 261–280.

Moxey, L., and Sanford, A. 1993. *Communicating quantities: A psychological perspective*. Hillsdale, NJ: Lawrence Erlbaum.

Moyne, J. A. 1971. Reflexive and emphatic. *Language* 47:41–63.

Naylor, P. B. 1986. On the semantics of reduplication. In P. Geraghty, L. Carrington, and S. Wurm (eds.), *FOCAL I: Papers from the Fourth International Conference on Austronesian Linguistics: Pacific Linguistics* C–93:175–185.

Neale, S. 1992. Paul Grice and the philosophy of language. *Linguistics and Philosophy* 15:509–559.

Newmeyer, F. J. 1980. *Linguistic theory in America*. New York: Academic Press. [2nd ed. 1986.]

Newstead, S. 1995. Gricean implicatures and syllogistic reasoning. *Journal of Memory and Language* 34:644–664.

Ni, W., Crain, S., and Shankweiler, D. 1996. Sidestepping garden paths: Assessing the contributions of syntax, semantics, and plausibility in resolving ambiguities. *Language and Cognitive Processes* 11:283–334.

Nichols, J. 1983. Switch-reference in the Northeast Caucasus. In Haiman and Munro 1983: 245–265.

Nunberg, G. 1978. *The pragmatics of reference*. Mimeo, Indiana University Linguistics Club, Bloomington, IN. [Reprint of Ph.D. dissertation, 1977, City University of New York.]

Nunberg, G. 1995. Transfers of meaning. *Journal of Semantics* 12:109–132.

O'Connor, K. 1987. Disjoint reference and pragmatic inference: Anaphora and switch reference in Northern Pomo. Paper presented to Wenner-Gren Conference on "The role of theory in language description". Jamaica, November 1987. [Published as O'Connor 1993.]

O'Connor, K. 1993. Disjoint reference and pragmatic inference: Anaphora and switch reference in Northern Pomo. In W. A. Foley (ed.), *The role of theory in language description* (pp. 215–242). Berlin: Mouton de Gruyter.

Parker, F., Riley, K., and Meyer, C. 1990. Untriggered reflexive pronouns in English. *American Speech* 65:50–69.

Partee, B. 1984. Nominal and temporal anaphora. *Linguistics and Philosophy* 7:243–286.

Peirce, C. S. 1932. *Collected papers of C. S. Peirce, Vol. 2.* Cambridge, MA: Harvard University Press.

Pica, P. 1984. On the distinction between argumental and non-argumental anaphors. In W. de Geest and Y. Putseys (eds.), *Sentential complementation* (pp. 185–194). Dordrecht: Foris.

Pica, P. 1987. On the nature of the reflexivization cycle. In J. McDonough and B. Plunkett (eds.), *Proceedings of the North Eastern Linguistic Society* 17:483–500.

Pica, P. 1991. On the interaction between antecedent-government and binding: The case of long reflexivization. In Koster and Reuland 1991: 119–136.

Platzack, C. 1987. The Scandinavian languages and the null-subject parameter. *Natural Language & Linguistic Theory* 5:377–401.

Pollard, C., and Sag, I. A. 1992. Anaphors in English and the scope of binding theory. *Linguistic Inquiry* 23:261–303.

Pollard, C., and Sag, I. A. 1994. *Head-driven phrase structure grammar.* Stanford, CA: CSLI and Chicago University Press.

Politzer, G., and Noveck, I. 1991. Are conjunction rule violations the results of conversational rule violations? *Journal of Psycholinguistic Research* 20:83–103.

Pople, H. E. 1973. On the mechanization of abductive logic. *International Joint Conference on Artificial Intelligence* 73:147–152.

Popper, K. 1959. *The logic of scientific discovery.* London: Hutchinson.

Poznanski, V. 1992. *A relevance-based utterance processing system.* Technical Report No. 246, University of Cambridge Computer Laboratory, Cambridge.

Postal, P. 1974. *On raising.* Cambridge, MA: MIT Press.

Prince, E. 1981. Toward a taxonomy of Given-New information. In Cole 1981: 223–255.

Pustejovsky, J. 1995. *The generative lexicon.* Cambridge, MA: MIT Press.

Putnam, H. 1958. Formalization of the concept "about." *Philosophy of Science* 25:125–130.

Putnam, H. 1975. *Mind, language, and reality: Philosophical papers.* Vol. 2. Cambridge: Cambridge University Press.

Quirk, R., Greenbaum, S., Leech, G., and Svartvik, J. 1972. *A grammar of contemporary English*. London: Longman.

Radford, A. 1981. *Transformational syntax*. Cambridge: Cambridge University Press.

Read, C., and Hare, V. C. 1979. Children's interpretation of reflexive pronouns in English. In F. R. Ekman and A. J. Hastings (eds.), *Studies in first and second language acquisition* (pp. 98–116). Rowley, MA: Newbury House.

Recanati, F. 1989. The pragmatics of what is said. *Mind and Language* 4:295–329.

Recanati, F. 1993. *Direct reference: From language to thought*. Oxford: Blackwell.

Reggia, J., and Nau, D. 1984. An abductive non-monotonic logic. In *Proceedings of the 1984 Non-monotonic Reasoning Workshop* (pp. 385–395). New Paltz, NY: American Association for Artificial Intelligence.

Reinhart, T. 1983. *Anaphora and semantic interpretation*. London: Croom Helm.

Reinhart, T. 1986. Center and periphery in the grammar of anaphora. In Lust 1986: 123–150.

Reinhart, T., and Reuland, E. 1991. Anaphors and logophors: An argument structure perspective. In Koster and Reuland 1991: 283–322.

Reinhart, T., and Reuland, E. 1993. Reflexivity. *Linguistic Inquiry* 24:657–720.

Reiter, R. 1978. On reasoning by default. In D. L. Waltz (ed.), *TINLAP 2: Theoretical issues in natural language processing 2* (pp. 210–218). New York: ACM.

Reiter, R. 1980. A logic for default reasoning. *Artificial Intelligence* 13:81–132. [Reprinted in Ginsberg 1987: 68–93.]

Reuland, E. 1994. Commentary: The non-homogeneity of Condition B and related issues. In Lust, Hermon, and Kornfilt 1994: 227–246.

Reuland, E., and Koster, J. 1991. Long-distance anaphora: An overview. In Koster and Reuland 1991: 1–26.

Rizzi, L. 1989. On the format for parameters: Comment on D. Lightfoot, The child's trigger experience: Degree–0 learnability. *Behavioral and Brain Sciences* 12:355–356.

Roberts, C. 1987. *Modal subordination, anaphora, and distributivity*. Ph.D. dissertation, University of Massachusetts, Amherst.

Rosch, E. 1977. Human categorization. In N. Warren (ed.), *Advances in cross-cultural psychology*, Vol. 1 (pp. 1–49). London: Academic Press.

Ross, J. F. 1981. *Portraying analogy*. Cambridge: Cambridge University Press.

Ross, J. R. 1970. On declarative sentences. In R. A. Jacobs and P. S. Rosenbaum (eds.), *Readings in English transformational grammar* (pp. 222–272.) Waltham, MA: Ginn.

Ruhl, C. 1989. *On monosemy: A study in linguistic semantics*. Albany, NY: SUNY Press.

Russell, B. 1905. On denoting. *Mind* 14:479–493. [Reprinted in R. Marsh (ed.), 1956, *B. Russell: Logic and knowledge*. London: George Allen and Unwin.]

Sacks, H., and Schegloff, E. 1979. Two preferences in the organization of reference to persons in conversation and their interaction. In G. Psathas (ed.), *Everyday language: Studies in ethnomethodology* (pp. 15–21). New York: Irvington.

Sadock, J. 1978. On testing for conversational implicature. In Cole 1978: 281–297.

Sadock, J. M. 1981. Almost. In Cole 1981: 257–272.

Sadock, J. M. 1983. The necessary overlapping of grammatical components. In *Proceedings of the Chicago Linguistic Society: Parasession on the interplay of phonology, morphology, and syntax* 19:198–221.

Sadock, J. M. 1984. Whither radical pragmatics? In D. Schiffrin (ed.), *Meaning, form, and use in context* (pp. 139–149). Washington, DC: Georgetown University Press.

Sadock, J. M. 1991. *Autolexical syntax: A theory of parallel grammatical representations*. Chicago: University of Chicago Press.

Sadock, J., and Zwicky, A. 1985. Speech act distinctions in syntax. In T. Shopen (ed.), *Language typology and syntactic description*. Vol. 1, *Clause structure* (pp. 155–196). Cambridge: Cambridge University Press.

Safir, K. 1992. Implied non-coreference and the pattern of anaphora. *Linguistics and Philosophy* 15:1–52.

Sag, I. 1981. Formal semantics and extralinguistic context. In Cole 1981: 273–294.

Saleemi, A. P. 1997. Review of Y. Huang, The syntax and pragmatics of anaphora. *Journal of Pragmatics* 28:103–128.

Sanford, A., and Garrod, S. 1981. *Understanding written language*. Chichester, UK: Wiley.

Sapir, E. 1921. *Language. An introduction to the study of speech*. New York: Harcourt, Brace.

Sapir, E. 1930. *Totality*. Language Monograph Number 6. Washington, DC: Linguistic Society of America.

Saussure, F. de 1916. *Cours de linguistique générale*. (Ed. C. Bally and A. Sechehaye). Paris: Payot. [Republished as *Course in general linguistics*, Trans. W. Baskin, 1966. New York: McGraw-Hill.]

Scharten, R. (1997). *Exhaustive interpretation: A discourse-semantic account*. Ph.D. dissertation, Catholic University Nijmegen.

Schegloff, E. A. 1972. Sequencing in conversational openings. In J. J. Gumperz and D. Hymes (eds.), *Directions in sociolinguistics* (pp. 346–380). New York: Holt, Rinehart, and Winston.

Schegloff, E. 1979. Identification and recognition in telephone conversation openings. In G. Pasthas (ed.), *Everyday language* (pp. 23–78). New York: Irvington.

Schegloff, E. 1996. Some practices for referring to persons in talk-in-interaction. In B. Fox (ed.), *Studies in anaphora* (pp. 437–486). Amsterdam: John Benjamins.

Schelling, T. 1960. *The strategy of conflict*. Cambridge, MA: MIT Press.

Schiffer, S. R. 1972. *Meaning*. Oxford: Blackwell.

Schmerling, S. 1975. Asymmetric conjunction and rules of conversation. In Cole and Morgan 1975: 211–231.

Searle, J. 1969. *Speech acts*. Cambridge: Cambridge University Press.

Searle 1975. Indirect speech acts. In Cole and Morgan 1975: 59–82.

Searle, J. 1979. *Expression and meaning*. Cambridge: Cambridge University Press.

Searle, J. 1986. Meaning, communication, and representation. In Grandy and Warner 1986: 209–228.

Sells, P. 1987. Aspects of logophoricity. *Linguistic Inquiry* 18:445–479.

Sells, P., Zaenen, A., and Zec, D. 1987. Reflexivization variation: Relations between syntax, semantics, and lexical structure. In M. Ida, S. Wechsler, and D. Zec (eds.), *Working papers in grammatical theory and discourse structure* (pp. 169–243). Stanford, CA: CSLI. Publications.

Senft, G. 1986. *Kilivila, the language of the Trobriand Islands*. Berlin: Mouton de Gruyter.

Seuren, P. (ed.) 1974. *Semantic syntax*. Oxford: Oxford University Press.

Seuren, P. 1998. *Western linguistics: An historical introduction*. Oxford: Blackwell.

Shibatani, M. 1972. Three reasons for not deriving "kill" from "cause to die". In J. P. Kimball (ed.), *Syntax and semantics* (pp. 125–138). New York: Seminar Press.

Sigurjónsdóttir, S., Hyams, N., and Chien, Y.-C. 1988. The acquisition of reflexives and pronouns by Icelandic children. In E. Clark and Y. Matsumoto (eds.), *Proceedings of the Annual Child Language Forum: Papers and reports on child language development* (pp. 97–106). Stanford, CA: Stanford University Press.

Singer, M. 1994. Discourse inference processes. In Gernsbacher 1994: 479–516.

Soames, S. 1982. How presuppositions are inherited: A solution to the projection problem. *Linguistic Inquiry* 13:483–545. [Reprinted in Kasher (ed.) 1998: 69–140.]

Soames, S. 1989. Presupposition. In D. Gabbay and F. Guenthner (eds.), *Handbook of philosophical logic IV* (pp. 553–616). Dordrecht: Reidel.

Soames, S. 1998. How presuppositions are inherited: A solution to the projection problem. In A. Kasher (ed.), *Presupposition, implicature, and direct speech acts* (pp. 69–148). London: Routledge.

Solan, L. 1987. Parameter setting and the development of pronouns and reflexives. In T. Roeper and E. Williams (eds.), *Parameter setting* (pp. 189–210). Dordrecht: Reidel.

Sperber, D., and Wilson, D. 1986. *Relevance*. Oxford: Blackwell.

Sperber, D., and Wilson, D. 1987. Précis of *Relevance*. *Behavioral and Brain Sciences*, 10:697–754.

Sperber, D., and Wilson, D. 1995. *Relevance*. 2nd ed. Oxford: Blackwell.

Stalnaker, R. 1972. Pragmatics. In D. Davidson and G. Harman (eds.), *Semantics of natural language* (pp. 380–397). Dordrecht: Reidel.

Steever, S. 1977. Raising, meaning, and conversational implicature. *Proceedings of the Chicago Linguistic Society* 13:590–602.

Stirling, L. 1993. *Switch-reference and discourse representation.* Cambridge: Cambridge University Press.

Strawson, P. 1950. On referring. *Mind* 59:320–344.

Strawson, P. 1986. 'If' and '⊃'. In Grandy and Warner 1986: 229–242.

Syromiatnikov, A. 1981. *The ancient Japanese language.* Moscow: Nanka.

Thagard, P. 1978. The best explanation: Criteria for theory choice. *Journal of Philosophy* 74:76–92.

Thomason, R. H. 1974. Introduction. In R. Thomason (ed.), *Formal philosophy: Selected papers of Richard Montague* (pp. 1–70). New Haven, CT: Yale University Press.

Thomason, R. H. 1987. Accommodation, meaning, and implicature: Interdisciplinary foundations for pragmatics. Ms., University of Pittsburgh. [Printed as Thomason 1990.]

Thomason, R. H. 1990. Accommodation, meaning, and implicature: Interdisciplinary foundations for pragmatics. In P. R. Cohen, J. Morgan, and M. E. Pollack (eds.), *Intentions in communication* (pp. 325–364). Cambridge, MA: MIT Press.

Toney, A. 1963. *150 masterpieces of drawing.* New York: Dover Publications.

Traugott, E. 1998. The role of pragmatics in semantic change. Paper presented to the Conference of the International Pragmatics Association, Rheims, July 1998.

Traugott, E., and Heine, B. (eds.) 1991. *Approaches to grammaticalization*, Vol. 2. Amsterdam: John Benjamins.

Traugott, E., and König, E. 1991. The semantics-pragmatics of grammaticalization revisited. In Traugott and Heine 1991: 189–218.

Tryon, D. T. 1970. *Conversational Tahitian.* Canberra, Australla: ANU Press.

Ureland, S. 1981. The development of Dutch and West Frisian reflexives between 1879 and 1979. In M. Gerritsen (ed.), *Taalverandering in Nederlandse dialekten* (pp. 250–263). Muiderberg, The Netherlands: Coutinho.

Vaccari, O., and Vaccari, E. 1948. *Japanese conversation-grammar.* Tokyo: Vaccari.

Van Deemter, K., and Peters, S. (eds.) 1996. *Semantic ambiguity and underspecification.* Stanford, CA: CSLI publications.

Van der Auwera, J. 1995. Conditional perfection. In A. Athanasiadou and R. Dirven (eds.), *On conditionals again* (pp. 169–190). Amsterdam: John Benjamins.

Van der Auwera, J. 1996. Modality: The three-layered Scalar Square. *Journal of Semantics* 13:181–195.

Van der Auwera, J. 1997. Pragmatics in the last quarter century: The case of conditional perfection. *Journal of Pragmatics* 27:261–274.

Van der Sandt, R. 1988. *Context and presupposition*. London: Croom Helm.

Van Kuppevelt, J. 1996. Inferring from topics: Scalar implicatures as topic-dependent inferences. *Linguistics and Philosophy* 19:393–443.

Van Riemsdijk, H., and Williams, E. 1986. *Introduction to the theory of grammar*. Cambridge, MA: MIT Press.

Van Valin, R. 1990. Functionalism, anaphora, and syntax. *Studies in Language* 14:169–219.

Verschueren, J., and Bertuccelli-Papi, M. (eds.) 1987. *The pragmatic perspective*. Amsterdam: John Benjamins.

Vincent, N. 1989a. Observing obsolescence: Comment on D. Lightfoot, The child's trigger experience: Degree–0 learnability. *Behavioral and Brain Sciences* 12:360–361.

Vincent, N. 1989b. Constituentization. Paper delivered at the Ninth International Conference on Historical Linguistics. Rutgers University, New Brunswick, NJ, August 1989.

Visser, F. T. 1963. *An historical syntax of the English language, Part 1*. Leiden: Brill.

Vonk, W., Hustinx, L., Simons, W. 1992. The use of referential expressions in structuring discourse. *Language and Discourse Processes* 11:301–334.

Von Wright, G. H. 1971. *Explanation and understanding*. London: Routledge and Kegan Paul.

Wainer, J. 1991. *Uses of nonmonotonic logic in natural language understanding: Generalized implicatures*. Ph.D. dissertation, Pennsylvania State University. [Published by UMI Ann Arbor].

Ward, G., and Hirschberg, J. 1985. Implicating uncertainty: The pragmatics of fall-rise intonation. *Language* 61:747–776.

Webber, B. 1979. *A formal approach to discourse anaphora*. New York: Garland.

Welker, K. 1994. *Plans in the common ground: Toward a generative account of conversational implicature*. Ph.D. dissertation, Ohio State University, Columbus.

Wexler, K., and Manzini, M. R. 1987. Parameters and learnability in Binding Theory. In T. Roeper and E. Williams (eds.), *Parameter setting* (pp. 41–76). Dordrecht: Reidel.

Wheeldon, L. R., and Levelt, W. J. M. 1995. Monitoring the time course of phonological encoding. *Journal of Memory and Language* 34:311–334.

Wilkins, D., and Hill, D. 1995. When 'GO' means 'COME': Questioning the basicness of basic motion verbs. *Cognitive Linguistics* 6:209–259.

Wilkins, W. 1988. Thematic structure and reflexivization. In W. Wilkins (ed.), *Syntax and semantics*. Vol. 21, *Thematic relations* (pp. 191–214). New York: Academic Press.

Williams, E. 1997. Blocking and anaphora. *Linguistic Inquiry* 28:577–628.

Wilson, D. 1975. *Presuppositional and non-truth-conditional semantics*. New York: Academic Press.

Wilson, D., and Sperber, D. 1986. Pragmatics and modularity. *Proceedings of the Chicago Linguistics Society: Parasession on pragmatics and grammatical theory* 22:67–84. [Reprinted as Wilson and Sperber 1991.]

Wilson, D., and Sperber, D. 1991. Pragmatics and modularity. In S. Davis (ed.), *Pragmatics* (pp. 583–595). Oxford: Oxford University Press.

Winograd, T. 1972. *Understanding natural language*. New York: Academic Press.

Yang, D.-W. 1983. The extended binding theory of anaphors. *Language Research* 19:169–192.

Ziff, P. 1975. On H. P. Grice's account of meaning. In D. Steinberg and L. Jakobovitz (eds.), *Semantics* (pp. 60–65). Cambridge: Cambridge University Press.

Zipf, G. K. 1949. *Human behavior and the principle of least effort: An introduction to human ecology*. New York: Hafner.

Zribi-Hertz, A. 1989. Anaphor binding and narrative point of view: English reflexive pronouns in sentence and discourse. *Language* 65:695–727.

Zribi-Hertz, A. 1995. Review of Y. Huang, The syntax and pragmatics of anaphora. *Lingua* 96:179–189.

Name Index

Adams, M., 423
Allen, S., 45, 52, 142
Ameka, F., xxi
Anderson, S., 177
Andronov, M., 351
Appelt, D., xvii
Ariel, M., xvii, 273, 409, 411
Aristotle, 30, 64, 74
Aronoff, M., 369
Arundale, R. B., xxi, 5, 379
Asher, N., 123, 161, 352, 423
Atlas, J., xv, xxi, 1, 4, 22, 41, 43, 45, 46, 64,
    74, 76, 77, 78, 79, 80, 82, 88, 89, 90, 91,
    109, 111, 114, 115, 116, 117, 156, 159,
    171, 177, 185, 189, 203, 207, 222, 241,
    256, 257, 258, 361, 375, 376, 380, 381,
    386, 387, 388, 390, 391, 392, 395, 397,
    401, 402, 403, 410
Austin, P., 23, 335, 336, 381, 402
Avramides, A., 13, 380, 398

Bach, K., xxi, 23, 24, 165, 169, 170, 188,
    194, 195, 196, 197, 198, 214, 217, 231,
    257, 258, 262, 375, 379, 380, 381, 383,
    384, 392, 396, 397, 398, 400, 402, 409
Bacon, F., 43
Baker, G. P., 192, 308, 415, 416, 420
Bar-Hillel, Y., 31, 34, 115, 163, 273, 278,
    299, 410
Barton, E., 183, 184
Barwise, J., xvii, 167, 177, 191, 208, 209,
    210, 226, 228, 229, 388, 397, 402
Bayer, S., 24, 134, 262, 264
Berlin, B., 152
Bickerton, D., 338, 340
Bierwisch, M., 372, 424
Blakemore, D., xvi
Blass, R., 148
Bloomfield, L., 125, 137

Blumstein, S., 381
Bohnemeyer, J., 96
Bolinger, D., 291, 296, 298, 307
Botha, R., 152
Bouchard, D., 308, 312, 323
Bourdieu, P., xiii, 386
Bréal, M., 137
Brown, P., xxi, 13, 24, 45, 46, 89, 264, 407,
    408, 423
Burrow, T., 352
Burton-Roberts, N., 80, 391
Burzio, L., 409, 416
Bybee, J., 263

Caldwell, R., 352
Calvert, D. R., 28, 382
Cann, R., 95
Cantrall, W. R., 319, 320, 333
Carberry, S., 380
Carden, G., 335, 338, 339, 340, 361, 419
Carnap, R., 31, 34, 115, 273, 278, 299, 391,
    410
Carston, R., xvii, 48, 89, 91, 114, 120, 121,
    123, 134, 194, 195, 196, 199, 238, 254,
    257, 258, 392, 393, 400, 403
Chafe, W., 237
Changeux, J. P., 2
Charniak, E., 45, 384
Cherry, C., 410
Chien, Y-C., 344, 361
Cho, Y. Y., 411
Chomsky, N., xiii, 5, 8, 29, 163, 166, 190,
    210, 248, 261, 265, 266, 280, 281, 282,
    283, 296, 308, 309, 310, 324, 343, 364,
    382, 397, 408, 413, 418, 423
Chung, S., 337, 418, 422
Clark, E., xxi, 237, 370, 376
Clark, H. H., xix, xx, 29, 30, 117, 126, 139,
    140, 237, 258, 376, 386, 395, 397

Claudi, U., 263
Cohen, L. J., 31, 44, 46, 198, 199, 206, 214, 380
Cole, P., xv, 256
Comrie, B., 95, 96, 239, 329, 335, 364, 408
Cooper, R., 388
Cormack, A., 211
Corne, C., 339
Crain, S., 424
Cruse, D. A., 90, 101, 103
Culy, C., 414

Davis, S., xv
De Morgan, A., 68
Dimitriadis, A., 411
Dixon, R. M. W., 90, 152, 335, 336
Donnellan, K. S., 217, 226, 227, 228, 229, 230, 404
Dowty, D., 290, 299, 319, 411, 412
Dulany, D., 424

Eades, D., 336
Eco, U., 386
Edmondson, J. A., 333, 351, 417, 418
Edwards, D., xx, 384
Emeneau, M., 352
Enç, M., 177, 192, 242, 243, 246, 397, 405, 411
Erasmus, D., 145
Evans, G., 278, 284, 335, 413
Everaert, M., 342, 417, 419

Faltz, L. M., 263, 325, 330, 331, 335, 341, 349, 350, 416, 417, 419, 420, 421
Farmer, A., xx, 328
Fauconnier, G., 104, 236, 237, 245, 333, 388
Fillmore, C., 99, 177, 397
Fodor, J., 187, 190, 257, 397, 405
Fogelin, R., 388
Foley, W., 276, 365
Ford, C. E., 403
Fox, B., 271, 273, 291, 409
Fox Tree, J., 395
Frederking, R., 111
Frege, G., 390
Fretheim, T., 90

Garnham, A., 269
Garrod, S., 269, 424
Gazdar, G., xv, xix, 1, 20, 35, 48, 49, 64, 75, 76, 77, 78, 79, 80, 81, 98, 108, 109, 110, 111, 125, 158, 161, 162, 163, 198, 201, 212, 214, 252, 255, 296, 297, 384, 385, 386, 387, 388, 390, 391, 395, 396, 402, 406, 423

Geach, P. T., 333
Geiss, M., 117
Geniusiene, E., 338, 351
Geurts, B., 407
Ginsberg, M., 43, 45, 46, 275, 383
Goodman, N., 208
Gordon, D., 395
Grandy, R., xv, 382
Green, G., 380, 382
Greenbaum, S., 147, 150
Greenberg, J., 126, 128, 137
Grice, H. P., xv, xix, 6, 11, 12, 13, 14, 15, 16, 17, 18, 19, 20, 21, 22, 29, 35, 37, 38, 41, 46, 48, 53, 55, 63, 72, 73, 74, 75, 78, 91, 92, 108, 111, 112, 113, 135, 136, 165, 166, 169, 170, 171, 172, 181, 186, 187, 189, 194, 195, 198, 199, 225, 236, 258, 260, 361, 371, 372, 373, 377, 379, 380, 381, 382, 386, 391, 396, 398, 399, 402, 403, 404
Grodzinsky, Y., 292, 293, 294, 344
Gundel, J., 94, 95, 411

Haas, W., 101
Hacker, P., 192
Hagège, C., 314, 315, 420
Haiman, J., xvi, 75, 112, 113, 123, 126, 135, 136, 142, 146, 148, 276, 317, 330, 342, 394, 414
Hale, K., 303
Hamblin, C. L., 49, 163
Hamilton, Sir W., 68
Harbert, W., 265, 282, 308, 310, 311, 312, 313, 328, 414, 415
Harbsmeier, C., 420
Harder, P., 96
Hare, V. C., 344
Harman, G., 54, 380, 383, 384
Harnish, R., xv, xx, 1, 13, 23, 95, 98, 100, 117, 159, 170, 184, 207, 262, 328, 381, 390, 398
Harris, R. A., 394
Haviland, J., 117, 126, 303, 334, 386, 389, 393, 420
Hawkins, J., xvi, 92, 93, 127, 155, 390, 397
Hedberg, N., 94, 95, 411
Heim, I., 60, 62, 63, 93, 167, 182, 193, 248, 249, 250, 252, 253, 255, 385, 397, 402, 406
Heinämäki, O., 97
Heine, B., 263
Hellan, L., 306, 310, 315, 326, 417
Herskovits, A., 118, 207, 223, 237
Higginbotham, J., 413
Hill, D., 94
Hilton, D., 424

Hinds, J., 421
Hintikka, J., 77, 333, 387
Hirschberg, J., xvi, xvii, 64, 78, 80, 82, 99, 101, 102, 104, 105, 107, 108, 120, 162, 212, 255, 380, 385, 387, 390, 391, 396, 403
Hirst, G., 174
Hobbs, J., xvii, xx, 12, 45, 46, 60, 61, 62, 63, 117, 125, 126, 165, 167, 237, 238, 276, 375, 397, 404, 423
Holdcroft, D., 17, 52
Holland, J. J., 44
Holyoke, K. J., 44
Hong, K. -S., 411
Hopper, P., 263
Horn, L. R., xv, xvi, xix, xx, xxi, 1, 4, 5, 6, 12, 15, 24, 38, 40, 41, 47, 52, 64, 68, 69, 74, 75, 76, 77, 78, 79, 80, 81, 82, 83, 84, 85, 86, 87, 88, 89, 90, 91, 98, 102, 103, 105, 107, 109, 110, 111, 115, 117, 120, 122, 124, 127, 128, 129, 130, 131, 132, 133, 134, 135, 136, 137, 139, 140, 141, 142, 143, 145, 146, 150, 155, 156, 157, 162, 169, 181, 185, 190, 194, 197, 210, 211, 212, 213, 222, 224, 237, 239, 240, 254, 255, 262, 264, 274, 277, 278, 286, 287, 290, 296, 297, 331, 333, 355, 356, 361, 364, 365, 369, 381, 385, 386, 387, 388, 389, 390, 391, 392, 393, 394, 396, 403, 407, 408, 411, 412, 413, 414, 415, 418
Hornstein, N., 265
Householder, F. 140
Huang, Y., xv, xvi, xx, xxi, 210, 301, 312, 313, 316, 326, 329, 330, 346, 351, 352, 353, 354, 355, 356, 357, 358, 364, 365, 381, 407, 408, 411, 414, 416, 417, 421, 422
Hünnemeyer, F., 263
Hustinx, L., 409
Hyams, N., 361

Jackendoff, R., 8, 192, 243, 245, 282, 298, 306, 307, 372, 397, 398, 424
Jackson, S., 370
Jacobs, S., 370
Jakobson, R., 115, 137
Jakubowicz, C., 340, 344
Jayaseelan, K. A., 333
Jespersen, O., 68, 84, 342
Johnson-Laird, P. N., 33, 42, 54
Josephson, J., 42

Kadmon, N., xx, 64, 88, 89, 90, 162, 179, 182, 193, 219, 248, 249, 250, 385, 389, 406

Kamp, H., 25, 62, 88, 122, 163, 167, 193, 205, 247, 248, 249, 250, 251, 252, 385, 406
Kant, E., 75, 386
Kaplan, D., 191, 243, 245, 246, 247
Karttunen, L., 180
Kasher, A., xv
Katz, J. J., 190, 240, 241, 404
Kaufman, D., 340, 344, 361
Kay, P., 77, 161, 207, 397, 403, 417
Keenan, E., 177, 397, 423
Kempson, R., xvii, xix, xx, 25, 88, 89, 90, 103, 182, 190, 210, 211, 212, 240, 254, 255, 256, 257, 376, 389
Kenny, A. J., 43, 45
Kibrik, A., 273
Kiparsky, P., 139
Kiss, K. É., 303, 306
Klein, E., 203
König, E., 263, 333, 351, 370, 416
Koster, C., 325, 344, 351, 422
Koster, J., 265, 282, 286, 311, 312, 313, 316, 332, 345, 412, 414, 419, 422
Kripke, S., 188, 226, 228, 229, 404
Kroch, A., 422
Kuno, S., 237, 297, 307, 315, 316, 319, 320, 322, 356, 411, 413, 414, 415, 421

Ladd, R., 102, 391
Lafon, J. -C., 381
Lakoff, G., xix, 192, 243, 395, 406, 408
Landman, F., 193, 253
Lang, E., 122, 125
Langacker, R., 243, 263, 332, 417, 420
Lascarides, A., 123, 161, 423
Lasnik, H., 299, 300, 301, 412
Laver, J., 382
Lee, Y. -S., 414
Leech, G., 14, 74, 134, 147, 15
Lehmann, C., 276
Lehrer, A., 101
Levelt, W. J. M., 28, 46
Levesque, H., 48
Levin, N., 393
Levine, J. E., 97
Levinson, S. C., xii, xiii, xvi, xvii, xx, 4, 7, 12, 14, 17, 23, 24, 30, 38, 40, 41, 43, 45, 46, 51, 54, 55, 57, 59, 64, 74, 75, 76, 79, 80, 89, 91, 96, 111, 112, 114, 115, 116, 117, 120, 121, 156, 157, 158, 159, 171, 177, 178, 181, 195, 197, 201, 207, 214, 217, 222, 224, 242, 252, 257, 258, 263, 264, 272, 277, 283, 284, 297, 303, 305, 307, 334, 347, 353, 359, 361, 364, 372, 380, 383, 383, 384, 385, 388, 391, 392, 392, 395, 401, 402, 403, 407, 408, 409, 411, 412, 413, 416, 418, 420, 423

Lewis, D., 12, 29, 60, 177, 233, 391, 399, 402
Li, C., 354, 421
Lieberman, P., 381
Lightfoot, D., 361, 362
Linebarger, M., 134, 262
Löbner, S., 86, 131
Lucy, J., 237
Lust, B., 312, 316, 325, 340, 345, 351, 418, 421
Lyons, J., xx, 5, 93, 101, 102, 127, 128, 237, 381

Maling, J., 310
Manzini, M. R., 313, 361
Marslen-Wilson, W., 382
Martin, P., xvii, 46, 218
Matsumoto, Y., 80, 102, 388
Matthews, P., xx, 8, 125, 376, 407
May, R., 240, 286
Mazuka, R., 312, 316, 325, 345, 351, 418, 421
McCafferty, A. S., xvii, 46, 52, 385
McCarthy, J., 48, 276, 384
McCawley, J., 137, 140, 141, 142
McDermott, D., 45, 384
McMahon, A., 422
Mehler, J., 28
Meyer, C., 415
Mill, J. S., 68
Miller, G., 33
Milsark, G., 297
Mitchell, B., 177, 341, 358, 419, 422
Mitchell, J. E., 237
Mohanan, K., xx
Moore, R. C., 48, 209, 386, 399, 402
Moravcsik, E. A., 332, 333
Morgan, J., 23, 24, 46, 134, 262, 380
Moxey, L., 424
Moyne, J. A, 333
Munro, P., 317, 332

Nau, D., 384
Naylor, P. B., 150, 151
Neale, S., 380
Newmeyer, F. J., 394
Newstead, S., 424
Ni, W., 424
Nichols, J., 237, 319
Nisbett, R., 44
Noveck, I., 424
Nunberg, G., 217, 236, 245, 376

Ochs, E., 423
O'Connor, K., 237, 315, 316, 317, 319, 346, 356

Pagliuca, W., 263
Parker, F., 415
Partee, B., 122, 151, 208, 399, 400
Pederson, E., xxi
Peirce, C. S., 44, 384
Perlmutter, D., xx, 418
Perkins R., 263
Perrault, R., xx
Perry, J., xvii, 167, 177, 191, 226, 228, 229
Peters, S., xx, 25, 240, 376, 397
Pica, P., 312, 414, 417
Plank, F., 333, 351, 417, 418
Platzack, C., 422
Politzer, G., 424
Pollack, M., 46, 380
Pollard, C., 282, 297, 306, 307, 310, 321, 323, 324, 325, 407, 416
Pople, H. E., 42, 384
Popper, K., 31, 115, 274
Poser, W., 382
Postal, P., 324
Poznanski, V., 385
Prince, E., 94, 393
Pullum, G., 386
Pustejovsky, J., 240, 376
Putnam, H., 115, 217, 388, 391

Quirk, R., 147, 150, 151

Radford, A., 281, 286
Read, C., 344
Recanati, F., 170, 192, 194, 195, 196, 197, 238, 258, 399, 400
Reggia, J., 384
Reinhart, T., 181, 182, 248, 265, 278, 280, 283, 290, 292, 293, 294, 295, 296, 297, 298, 299, 301, 302, 306, 307, 319, 329, 344, 359, 411, 412, 418, 422
Reiter, R., 47, 383
Reuland, E., 265, 280, 282, 306, 311, 313, 316, 329, 332, 351, 412, 414
Reyle, U., 122, 163, 247, 248
Riley, K., 415
Rizzi, L., 417
Roberts, C., xx, 193, 397, 406
Rosch, E., 101
Ross, J. R., 319, 376, 394
Ruhl, C., 165, 184, 240, 376
Russell, B., 180, 219, 231, 377, 403, 404

Sacks, H., 113, 149
Sadock, J. M., xix, 8, 15, 88, 184, 290, 392, 397, 406, 411
Safir, K., 412, 415

Sag, I., xx, 191, 233,236, 237, 242, 245, 246, 282, 297, 306, 307, 310, 321, 323, 324, 325, 402, 406, 407, 416
Saleemi, A. P., 407
Sanford, A., 269, 424, 424
Sapir, E., 84, 150
Saussure, F. de, 137
Scharten, R., xvii, 90, 389
Schegloff, E., 113, 114, 149, 179
Schelling, T., 6, 29, 30, 53, 258, 259
Schiffer, S. R., xix, 29, 380, 398
Schmerling, S., 123, 124, 392, 394
Searle, J., xix, 23, 134, 217, 381, 385, 397
Sells, P., 237, 314, 315, 316, 351, 356, 421
Senft, G, 337
Seuren, P., 203, 389, 394, 423
Shankweiler, D., 424
Shibatani, M., 141, 142
Sigurjonsdottir, S., 361
Simons, W., 409
Singer, M., 424
Soames, S., 77, 78, 161, 163, 385, 391, 396
Solan, L., 340, 344, 361
Sperber, D., xii, xvi, xix, xx, 4, 5, 12, 22, 24, 25, 30, 42, 52, 55, 56, 57, 59, 74, 118, 135, 164, 167, 174, 184, 186, 187, 190, 194, 195, 196, 207, 236, 238, 239, 240, 257, 258, 361, 371, 372, 375, 380, 384, 385, 392, 396, 397, 398, 399, 400, 405
Stalnaker, R., 49, 249, 399
Steever, S., 407
Stewart, W., 335, 338, 339, 340, 361
Stickel, M., xvii
Stirling, L., 314, 315, 316, 317, 318, 347, 356, 414, 415
Strawson, P., 20, 180, 217, 219, 231, 377, 403
Svartvik, J., 147, 150
Syromiatnikov, A., 421

Thagard, P., 44
Thomason, R. H., xvii, 12, 17, 46, 52, 60, 61, 63, 385, 399
Thompson, S., 354, 403, 421
Toney, A., xxi, 2
Traugott, E., 263, 370
Tryon, D. T., 337
Tyler, L., 382

Ureland, S., 342

Vaccari, E., 421
Vaccari, O., 421
Van der Auwera, J., 119, 388, 392
Van Deemter, K., 240, 376
van der Sandt, R., xx, 77, 381

Van Kuppevelt, J., xvii, 25, 90
Van Riemsdijk, H., 413
Van Valin, R. D., 276, 307, 365, 415
Vincent, N., xx, 362, 407, 419, 420
Visser, F. T., 340, 341, 342, 419
Vonk, W., 409

Von Wright, G. H., 30, 45
Wainer, J., xvii, 48, 423
Ward, G., 102, 402
Warner, R., xv, 382
Webber, B., 267
Welker, K., xvii
Wexler, K., 313, 344, 361
Wheeldon, L. R., 28
Wilkins, D., xxi, 94, 306
Williams, E., 369, 413
Wilson, D., xii, xvi, xix, xx, 4, 5, 12, 22, 24, 25, 30, 42, 52, 55, 56, 57, 59, 74, 118, 135, 164, 167, 174, 184, 186, 187, 190, 194, 195, 196, 199, 207, 209, 210, 214, 236, 238, 239, 240, 257, 258, 361, 371, 372, 375, 380, 384, 385, 392, 396, 397, 398, 399, 400, 405
Winograd, T., 31, 174, 271

Yang, D-W., 417

Zacharski, R., 94, 95, 411
Zaenen, A., 351
Zec, D., 351
Ziff, P., 29
Zimmer, K., 207
Zipf, G. K., 6, 26, 112, 115
Zribi-Hertz, A., 282, 297, 308, 320, 321, 322, 325, 329, 365, 414, 415, 416
Zwicky, A., 117, 392

Subject Index

'A-first account' of Binding patterns, 283, 285–327
  characterized, 283, 286–289
  diachronic relation to B-first, 347–348
  disjoint reference pragmatic, 318–319, 414 n.47
  first approximation, 285–291
  second approximation, 292–298
  problems for:
    c-command, 297–298, 303–305
    constructional oppositions, 296–297
    contrasts over reference vs. logophoricity, 316–317, 322–323, 327, 345–347
    order of antecedent/anaphor, 290–291
    language variation, 300–301, 310–311, 313–317
    overlap of pronouns and reflexives, 290, 308, 313–317, 319–324, 345–347
    pseudo-Anaphors, 324–326
  See also Binding Conditions
A-vertex of square of oppositions, 65, 82, 83–84
abnormal expressions. *See* markedness
abductive inference, 42–44, 384 n.33, n.35
  and implicature, 45, 46, 60
  of laws, 44
  in local pragmatics, 46
  nonmonotonicity of, 43
  from nonpropositions, 257–258
'aboutness'
  constraint on scales, 80, 121
  informativeness and, 275
accommodation, xvii, 12, 60–63, 233, 249, 251, 385 n.47, n.48, 399 n.17, 405 n.55
  defined, 60
  and failed reduction of GCIs, 60–63
  vs. gratuitous nature of GCIs, 61, 63
acquisition, of language, xii, 23, 140, 264, 340, 344, 361–362, 416 n.59, 422 n.93

and implicature, 264, 280, 344, 361–362, 370
  of reflexives (*see* Anaphors, Binding Conditions, reflexives)
addressee, vs. speaker. *See* speaker
adjectives, epistemic, 131–132
  gradable, semantic generality of, 184–185
  I-implicatures of, 127–129, 404 n.51
  scalar implicatures of, 86–87
adverbs, quantificational, 86
affirming the consequent, 44
affixal negation. *See* negation
African languages, Western, 314, 350, 414 n.46, 416 n.59
Afrikaans, 152–153, 342
agreement, pragmatic vs. syntactic, 262, 407 n.2
AI. *See* artificial intelligence
Aktionsart, 124
alethic modality, 84
all. *See* quantifiers
'all over' inference, 100. *See also* color terms
Algonquian, 415 n.51
alternates, marked vs. unmarked, 136–137
  constructional, 108–111
  lexical, saliency and, 32, 36, 80, 100
  scales and, 75–111
  referring expressions, 149
  See also contrast, Q-implicature
ambiguity
  of Anaphors with pronouns, 337–338, 418 n.65, 422 n.92
  avoidance of, 14, 135, 290
  and informational strength, 297
  lexical, 176–177
  of negation, 129–130
  of pronouns, 269–270, 337
  of referring expressions, 226–230, 233, 398 n.10

ambiguity (cont.)
  vs. semantic generality, 20–21, 88–89, 135,
    165, 184, 228–229, 376 (*see also*
    monosemy)
  of scope (*see* scope)
  structural, 174–176, 376
Amerindian languages, 416 n.59
Anaphors, Chomskyan, 267, 270, 281–283,
    286–290, 324–326
  acquisition of (*see* reflexives)
  ambiguous, 337–338, 418 n.65, 422 n.92
  anti-, 414 n.47
  covert, 337–338, 418 n.65
  'exempt', 324 (*see* pseudo-)
  and language change, 263–264, 338–342,
    344, 347–352, 355–358, 417 n.59, 419
    n.68–73, n.75
  languages without, 334–343, 418 n.62
  long-distance (LDA), 282, 283, 296, 310–
    317, 324–326, 414 n.42, n.43, n.44
    characteristics of, 312, 413 n.42, n.44
  non-clause-bound (NCBR), 311
  'one only' rule, 321, 415 n.50
  origin as emphatics, 332–334, 341–342,
    347–350, 358, 416 n.58, 420 n.81, n.83,
    421 n.84–85
  parameters and, 312–313, 360–363
  proto-, 358–359
  pseudo-, 282, 307, 313, 316, 323, 324–326
  raising of, 308, 312–313, 330, 363
  simplex vs. compound morphemes, 311–
    312, 332–333, 416 n.59
  weak vs. strong, 332, 413 n.38, 416 n.59
  See also anaphora, Binding Conditions,
    reciprocals, reflexives
anaphora
  'anaphoric potential', 269–270
  bound, 292–298
  and Binding (*see* Binding Conditions)
  in Chinese, 352–358
  clause-bound vs. long-distance, 311–317
  co-arguments, and, 304, 306–307, 325,
    328–332, 353–354
  complementary distribution of pronouns
    and reflexives, 283–284, 288, 290, 308
    breakdown of, 308–327, 414 n.44
    contrasts in more than reference, 316–
      317, 320–323
  configurational constraints on, 291, 292–
    303, 306 (*see also* Binding Conditions)
  coerces implicature, 179, 181, 250–251
  defined, 267
  and deixis, 179
  and determiners, 91–95
  in discourse, 271–273, 316
  and ellipsis, 183
  and epithets, 277, 399 n.14
  flexible interpretation of, 358
  and gaps, 270, 285, 305 (*see* zero-, *and*
    pronouns)
  'general anaphora pattern', 267–268, 272,
    285, 305
  in generative grammar, 265 (*see also*
    Binding)
  grammatical relations and, 306–307
  grammatical specification of, coreference
    only, 305
    domains only, 270
  implicature and, 272, 326
  I-Principle and, 272–276, 285, 299, 305,
    318, 325, 329–331
  M-Principle and, 272, 277, 285, 288, 290,
    301
  Q-Principle and, 277–280, 286–287, 290,
    294–297, 302, 305, 313–317, 319, 322–
    323
  restricted role of, 271–272
  linkage to antecedents, pragmatic, 270–
    271, 409 n.9
  and logophoricity, 314–317
  long-range, 282, 283, 296, 310–317, 325
  order of antecedent/anaphor, 290–292, 307
  pragmatic nature of, 272, 343
  and pragmatic resolution, 179, 181–183,
    217, 224–225, 249–250, 271, 324
  'precede and command' analysis of, 307
  and referential dependence, 268, 270, 353
  and semantic generality, 268–269
  and semantics, 248
  sentential, vs. discourse, 251, 267–273
  temporal, 122–124, 151
  thematic roles and, 306–307
  VP, 251, 267
  zero-, 146–149, 285, 305, 382 n.22
  See also Anaphors, Binding Conditions,
    coreference, pronouns, reference,
    reflexives
anaphoric expressions, 269–270
  scalar analysis of (*see* scales)
  semantic generality of, 269–270
  signals of switched reference, 95
anatomical adaptations for language, 28
and, 19, 80, 91, 122–127, 155, 199, 206,
    242. *See also* conjunction, connectives
anomaly, pragmatic, 199, 209–210
  semantic, 202–204, 209–210, 226 (*see also*
    contradiction)
antecedents, blocked, 290
  linkage is pragmatic, 270–273, 324–325
  no grammatical specification of, 270
  order with respect to anaphor, 290–291,
    307

uniqueness condition, 250
See also anaphora
antipassive, 304–305, 335, 419 n.77
antonymy, 127–129. *See also* sense
  relations
arbitrariness vs. motivation, in pragmatics,
  15. *See also* iconicity
argument from design, for GCIs, 27–35,
  382 n.21
Aristotelian categories, 386 n.2
articles, 17–18, 155, 156
  accommodation of, 60–63
  definite (*see* definite article)
  Grice's theory of, 17, 91
  indefinite, 17, 62–63, 89, 91–93
  phonetic subtypes of, 394 n.72
  scalar account of, 63, 91–93
  vs. zero-determiner, 146–147, 156
artificial intelligence, 25, 45, 167, 170, 275,
  423 n.1
aspect and implicature, 96, 124
attributive uses of referring expressions. *See*
  referential
Australian languages, 90, 125, 152, 269,
  270, 283, 303–305, 335–336
Austronesian languages, 335, 336–338
autoepistemic logic, 48
autohyponyms, 102–103, 394 n.66
autonomy of semantics from pragmatics.
  See semantics
auxiliary, 263
avoidance of expressions, 294. *See also*
  M-implicature, Q-implicature
Avoid Pronoun principle, 364, 407 n.4, 423
  n.95

bandwidth of human speech, 28, 35,
  169
'basic level' terms, 101, 102
because-clauses, 80, 210, 402 n.36
belief vs. knowledge, 78–79, 387 n.9
believe vs. *know*, 87, 129–133
best interpretation, inference to. *See*
  inference
'B-first account' of Binding Patterns, 284,
  327–344
  Australian languages and, 335–336
  Austronesian languages and, 336–338
  characterized, 328–332
  Chinese and, 353–358
  Creoles and, 338–340
  derivation of Condition A, 331
  derivation of Condition C, 331
  diachronically prior, 328
  disjoint reference presumption (DRP),
    328–331, 342, 347, 353

given by I-Principle, 329–331
over-ridden by M-Principle, 331–333,
  353
emphatics and reflexivity, 332–334, 337,
  347–348, 350, 420 n.81
M-implicated conjoint reference, 331–333,
  336–337
Old English and, 340–342
See also Binding Conditions
bias, in interpretation, 90, 389 n.28
biconditional, 37. *See also* conditional
  perfection
Binding Conditions, 265, 280–344
  acquisition of, 340, 344, 361, 416 n.59
    not in accord with nativist views, 344,
      361–363, 422 n.93
  c-command and, 281, 290, 292–298, 301–
    303, 306
  'compatibility requirement', 309
  counterexamples to, 282, 290, 301–303,
    310–317, 413 n.35, 413 n.40
  cross-linguistic variation in, 301, 303–
    305
  diachronic account of (*see* 'B then A'
    account)
  defined, 281–283
  domains (*see* domain)
  and language-change (*see* parameters)
  and LF, 265, 281, 308, 312
  nativism and, 338, 340, 343–344, 360,
    361–363
  nonconfigurational constraints on (*see*
    nonconfigurational, theme)
  parameters and (*see* parameters)
  pidgins and 'bioprogram', 338–340, 361
  pragmatic reduction of
    'A-first account', 285–327 (*see* 'A-first
      account')
    'B-first account', 327–344 (*see* 'B-first
      account')
    'B then A' account, 345–360 (*see* 'B then
      A')
  complimentarity of pronouns vs.
    reflexives in, 288, 290, 295, 313–317,
    319–327, 346
  Condition A reduced, 284, 327–344
  Condition B reduced, 283–284, 285–
    327
  Condition C reduced, 283, 286–289,
    298–301, 305, 412 n.31
  Y. Huang's account, 352–358, 421 n.87
  Lasnik's rejection of, 299–303
  logophoricity and, 314–317, 322–323
  Reinhart's account, 292–298
  style and dialect and, 301, 415 n.51, 416
    n.55

Binding Conditions (cont.)
  variant versions of, 265, 286, 290, 292–
    295, 303, 310, 312–313, 324–325, 326–
    327
  See also Anaphors, anaphora, pronouns
binding of variables. See variables
bioprogram hypothesis (Bickerton), 338,
    339–340, 361
blocking, in morphology, 139, 161, 369, 394
    n.69
  in default reasoning, 161
blocks world, 31
bottleneck, on speech encoding, 6–7, 28,
    381 n.16, 382 n.18, n.19
  asymmetry with comprehension, 28, 382
    n.20
boundedness of events, 96, 97–98
brevity, 14, 38, 114–115, 126
  equal, 108, 111
  and semantic generality, 115, 135, 181,
    267, 277
  See also I-Principle, Least Effort principle,
    minimal expressions, minimization
bridging inferences, 37–38, 61, 117, 126–
    127, 182, 232–233, 249
  with indefinites, 62–63, 127, 182
'B then A' account of Binding Patterns,
    284, 340, 345–360
  for Chinese, 352–358
  as diachronic pattern, 347–348, 360
  for English, 340–342, 347–349, 357–358
  Long-range reflexives and DRP, 346

calculability of implicatures. See
    conversational implicature
cancellation
  of implicatures, 15, 49–54, 56
  as ambiguity, 384 n.31
  at arbitrary distance, 51, 56–57, 163, 247,
    253, 384 n.31, 396 n.80, 406 n.56
  by common ground, 49–52, 162–163, 299
  by entailments, 50, 56–57, 155, 299–300
  by relevance, 88
  of presupposition, 252
  See also defeasibility, projection
cardinal numbers. See number words
case, grammatical, 97, 186
causal inferences, 122–123, 148, 182
  direct vs. indirect causation, 141–142, 224,
    297
causatives, 141–142, 208
causatives, lexical vs. periphrastic, 39, 141–
    142
c-command, 281, 290–298, 303, 411 n.24
  alternatives to, 306
  See also Binding Conditions

ceteris paribus assumptions, 45, 79, 208–
    209
Chamorro, 337–338
character vs. content (Kaplan), 245–247
child language. See acquisition
Chinese, 125, 285, 301, 311–312, 313, 316,
    334, 346, 352–358, 364, 420 n.83, 421
    n.88–89
clausal implicatures, 35–37, 50, 76, 82,
    108–111, 161, 296
  conditions for, 111
  constructional basis of, 108
  and epistemic uncertainty, 78, 108–109
  role in presupposition cancellation, 111
  vs. scalar, 161, 391 n.40
clausemate NPs, and anaphora, 306, 323–
    324
clauses, inferred connections between, 276.
    See also cohesion, I-implicature
closed-class morphemes, 90–98, 155
circumscription, 48, 275–276, 384 n.38
  See also nonmonotonic reasoning
coded meaning, vs. inference, 14, 15, 20, 21,
    31, 34, 54, 128, 130, 142, 162, 169,
    257, 273, 287, 334, 343, 374–376
  See also logical form, 'said', semantic
    representation, semantics
coercion, 246. See also intrusion
cognition, and pragmatics, 5, 21
  and semantics, 7, 241–242
  See also psychology, psycholinguistics
cognitive, effort, 57, 135
  linguistics, 21, 243, 372
cohesion, presumption of, 114, 116, 126,
    148, 276, 318, 409 n.13
coindexing, 282, 284, 292–293, 409 n.10.
  See also coreference, reference
collocational constraints, 261–262
color terms, 36, 100, 105, 140, 152, 184, 390
    n.33
come, and deictic verbs of motion, 94
commitment, of speaker. See speaker
common ground, augmentation of, 47, 48,
    49–54, 60, 193, 249, 384 n.36
communication, apparent certainty of, 53–
    54
  theory of, 11ff, 21–35, 187
  standard vs. three-leveled theory of, 22–
    27, 54–63
  See also meaning, meaning_nn
communicative content, of utterances
  communicative load, of entailments and
    implicatures, 70
communicative intention. See intention
comparatives, 87, 199–205
  degree adjectives as, 184–185, 242

intrusion of implicatures in, 199–205
semantic analysis of, 201–204, 401 n.31,
    n.32
See also intrusion
compatible alternates, 100, 102, 103
competence, vs. performance, 172, 397 n.5
    pragmatic, 22
complementary distribution
    of pronouns and reflexives, 283, 288, 290,
        308
    breakdown of, 283–284, 308–326, 414
        n.44
complementary interpretations, 34, 137, 150
completions and expansions. *See*
    impliciture
complex sentences, and implicature. *See*
    projection problem
componential analysis, of meaning. *See*
    lexical decomposition
components of linguistic theory, 166–167,
    171, 187, 243–244, 365, 368, 405 n.53.
    See also levels, modules
compositionality, bottom-up processing of,
    245–247
    vs. noncompositional fusion, 376
    pragmatic intrusion in, 189, 199, 205–206,
        213–214, 218, 233–234, 245–246
    See also intrusion
compound nominals, 61, 117, 147, 245
comprehension, 259
    asymmetry with production, 28, 382 n.20
conceptual structure. *See* cognition,
    language of thought
concessives, 82
conditional perfection, 37, 58, 117, 119–
    120, 159, 388 n.15, 392 n.49
conditionals
    Grice's analysis of, 19–20
    implicated, 125–126, 393 n.56
    implicatures of, 19, 20, 37, 50, 58, 108–
        109, 158, 296–297
    incremental processing of, 126, 163, 393
        n.57
    inferred vs. coded, 125–126
    intrusion of pragmatic inference in, 205–
        210, 251–253
    Kamp's analysis of, 163, 205
    and material conditional, 20
    order of antecedent vs. consequent, 126
    and presupposition projection, 252
    semantics of, 20, 205, 208–209
    suspension of inferences by, 81, 158, 252
    See also connectives, *if*, projection,
        suspension
conjunction
    asymmetric, 122–127, 154

asyndetic, 125–126
buttressing, 37–38, 117, 121, 122–127,
    138, 158, 199
Grice's analysis of, 19, 199
paratactic, 124–126, 147–148
reduction, 148–149, 394 n.70
See also connectives, *and, or, but*
connectedness, *see* cohesion
connectives, sentential, 18–20, 84, 91, 125,
    153–154, 386 n.53. *See also*
    conjunction, disjunction, conditionals
consistency, epistemic, 76–77
    of inferences, 77, 155–164
    and common ground, 49–52, 162–163,
        299
    not the only constraint on implicatures,
        52, 163
constituency, 303. *See also* c-command,
    nonconfigurational languages
Construction Grammar, 395 n.71
constructions. *See* intrusion
context
    and anaphoric resolution, 271
    bias in and default interpretations, 25–26
    change, and dialogue, 49–50
    and defeasibility (*see* defeasibility)
    dependence, and indexicality, 191–192,
        230, 242–243
    incremental model of, 50–54, 162–164, 193
    normal vs. special, 16
    types, 26
    See also common ground
contextuals, 191
contraction, 69–70
contradiction (self-contradictory utterances),
    57, 199–200, 202, 203–204, 208, 209,
    214–216, 233, 253, 404 n.49
contradictories, vs. contraries, 63–65, 83–
    86, 127–129, 130–132, 142–145, 222.
    See also negation
contrast, of expressions in salient
    oppositions, 32, 36, 76–111
    of forms, 135–142
    vs. gaps, 285 (*see also* anaphora, articles,
        pronouns)
    in morphological derivation, 139
    principle of, 140, 150
    in child language, 140
    of reference (*see* reference)
    in subjective meanings, 314–317, 319–321,
        327, 407 n.4, 415 n.54
    See also M-implicature, Q-implicature,
        scales
control, grammatical theory of, 363–364,
    408 n.4
flow of, in processing, 243–245

convention, and meaning, xix
Lewis's theory of, 29
of use, vs. convention of language, 23
See also standardization, short-circuited
inference
conventional implicature, 13–14, 166, 170,
213
conventionalization
of implicatures, 90, 134, 159, 237, 263–
265
of uses, 23
See also grammaticalization, short-
circuited inference
conversation, 14, 23, 113–114
analysis of, 113
conversational implicatures
actual vs. potential, 387 n.12, 395 n.73
calculability of, 15, 137, 141, 214
cancellability of, 15 (*see also* cancellation)
clausal (*see* clausal implicatures)
and communication, 21
conventionalization of (*see*
conventionalization)
vs. conventional implicature, 13–14
definition of, 15, 171, 194
and figures of speech (*see* figures of
speech)
generalized vs. particularized, 16–21 (*see
also those terms and* GCIs, PCIs)
language change (*see* language change,
grammaticalization)
and logical connectives (*see* connectives)
and logical form (*see* logical form)
and metaphor (*see* metaphor, figures of
speech)
nondetachability of, 15, 99
particularized (*see* particularized
conversational implicature, PCI)
and presupposition, 13, 111, 252
projection of (*see* projection)
typology of, 13–14, 16–17, 35–42, 373,
406 n.59
universality of, 15, 423 n.96
See also generalized conversational
implicature, I-implicature,
M-implicature, Q-implicature,
Relevance, etc.
cooperative principle, 112, 214
defined, 14
and nonverbal activity, 112
coordination problems, 29–30, 53–54, 258–
259, 371
coreference, 39, 115, 117, 149, 177, 181,
225, 250, 267–276, 288, 292–295
'accidental', 293
asserted vs. presupposed, 412 n.32

vs. bound variables, 267, 292–293, 301
and cohesion, 276, 318
and I-implicature, 181, 272, 273, 277,
287–288, 331
and I-Principle, 273–276
inferring, 273–276
and logophoricity, 312, 314–317, 346, 356
and M-implicature, 331–332, 347, 354
preference for, 273–276
See anaphora, Binding Conditions,
disjoint reference, variables
creoles, 338–340. *See also* pidgin and creole
languages
Chinook Jargon, 339
creolization process, 338–340
Guianese, 419 n.67
Haitian, 338–339
KiNubi, 339
Mauritian, 339
Palenquero, 339
cross-linguistic generalizations, 69, 118,
123, 134, 142, 146, 365, 370
cultural variation, xii

deductive inference, 42–43, 54
and implicatures, 42, 55–57, 257, 383 n.31
and sub-propositional representations, 257
See Relevance (Sperber-Wilson theory of)
deep or underlying structure, 129
default
inferences and grammar, 169
interpretation, xi, 11–12, 15, 21, 22ff
and metalinguistic reasoning, 6, 40–41,
104, 371
logics, 45, 46–49, 52, 53–54
modeling GCIs, 46–48
reasoning, 12, 42–54, 259
basis in communication, 53–54, 372, 383
n.26, 384 n.38, n.39
vs. default contexts, 25–26
vs. default logics, 54
derivative from implicature, 53–54
vs. flouts, 216
GCIs as prototype, 53–54, 372
rules, 47, 51
specific rules block general ones, 161
from sub-propositions, 259
types of, 42–49
defeasibility, 5, 42–54, 88, 123, 155–164, 192
and binding, 295–296, 299–303, 326
definition of, 42
differential, 78
and extralinguistic context, *see*
cancellation (by common ground)
as filtering by consistency, 163
and incremental context, 49–54, 162–164

as litmus test of grammar vs. pragmatics, 268, 278–279, 364–365, 408 n.6
models of, 45
nonmonotonicity and, 42
and semantics vs. pragmatics, 192
and syntax vs. pragmatics, 265, 268–280, 294, 295–296, 300–303, 318, 327, 363–365, 408 n.6
See also cancellability, context, projection
definite article, 60, 62–63, 92, 182–183, 217–235, 249–250
anaphoric use, 93
in bridging inference, 62–63, 127–127, 182
pragmatic resolution of, 180–183, 217–230
scalar implicature and, 220
uniqueness condition, 92, 219, 250, 385 n.49, 390 n.29, 399 n.13
See also articles, bridging
definite descriptions, 60–63, 182–183, 217–235
definite expressions, 61–63
as variables, 182
definiteness, 63, 248–250. *See also* articles, definite article
deictic determiners, 93–94, 390 n.29. *See also* deixis
deixis, 8, 93–94, 177–180
and anaphora, 179, 347
'exotic' parameters, 177
and definite descriptions, 217
and indices, 246
and noncancellability, 242, 247
and point of view, 347
pragmatic resolution of, 178–180
preemption over nondeictic expressions, 99, 180
and the 'said', 171
scalar implicatures of, 94
and truth-conditions
tests for deictic expressions, 242
and visibility-conditions, 177
See also indexicals
demonstratives. *See* deictic determiners
denial. *See* negation, metalinguistic
denotation, 137, 144, 245–246
shifted, 246
See also intension vs. extension, reference
deontic modality, 84
derivation. *See* morphology
design perspective on human communication, 27–35
detachability, 15, 99
determiners, 91–95. *See also* articles
diachrony, and pragmatics, 69–70, 103, 139, 185, 262–264, 268, 279–280, 338–342, 344, 347–352, 419 n.73. *See also*

grammaticalization, language change, semantic change
diagnostics, for kinds of GCI, 40–41
for scalar implicatures, 81–82, 84–86
disambiguation, 172, 232
implicatures and, 174–177
postponed, 189, 232
prosody and, 174
and 'what is said', 171
discourse, and anaphora, 267–273. *See also* conversation
discourse referent, 63, 179, 180, 248–249. *See also* anaphora
discourse representation theory (DRT), 26, 122, 163, 167, 172, 193, 218, 247, 248–256, 406 n.57
implicatures in, 248–256, 406 n.59
pragmatic vs. semantic conditions in, 253–256
disjoint reference, 224–225, 267, 277–280, 281–282, 295–303, 305, 310
characterized, 277, 281, 409 n.11
defeasibility and, 182, 277, 295–296, 299–303
disjoint reference presumption (DRP), 280, 328–331, 329–331, 342, 346–347, 353
defined, 328–330
I-Principle and, 330–331, 416 n.57
I-implicature and, 280, 328–331
M-implicature and, 277, 288–289, 301, 305, 331
pragmatic nature of, 319, 326, 343
Q-implicature and, 277–280, 302, 305, 317, 318–319
switch-reference and, 318–319
universally not grammatically stipulated, 319, 326, 365, 414 n.47, n.48
See also Binding Conditions, coreference, reference
disjoint reference presumption (DRP), 323, 329–331, 346–347, 353
disjunction, 19, 67, 81, 84, 108–109, 125, 154, 158, 209, 252
clausal implicatures of, 108–109, 154
exclusive vs. inclusive, 108, 154
Grice's analysis, 19
scalar implicatures of, 108–109, 154
and suspension of implicatures, 81, 159
distributional constraints, 261–262
division of pragmatic labor (Horn), 38, 137–155, 157, 277, 285, 333, 364, 365, 418 n.61
Dogrib, 415 n.47
domain
for anaphoric linkage, 271

domain (cont.)
  in discourse, 271, 321–322
  grammatical, 270–271
  binding domains, 281, 282, 286, 292–293,
    309, 312–313, 326, 354
  in acquisition, 361, 422 n.93
  and long-distance anaphors, 310–317, 345
  circumscription of, 48, 275–276
  of discourse, 274–275, 383 n.27, 385 n.50
  minimizing, 274–276, 410 n.16
  for point of view, 321–323, 354, 357, 414
    n.47
double negation, 38, 142–145. See also
  negation
double processing. See psycholinguistics
Dravidian, 352
DRS (discourse representation structure),
  122
DRT. See discourse representation theory
duals, logical, 67, 84
Dutch, 311, 342, 350, 416 n.59, 419 n.71–
  72
Dyari, 152
Dyirbal, 152

E-vertex of square of oppositions, 65, 82,
  83–84
economy, speaker's, 6, 112–113
  redundancy avoided in lexicon, 69–70,
    319, 326, 369–370
  See also least-effort principle, Zipf
ellipsis, 183–184, 189, 293, 376, 395 n.75
  and 'what is said', 172, 183–184
  implicatures of elided material, 184
elsewhere condition. See blocking
empathy, 312
emphatic markers, 304, 312, 331, 332–334,
  348, 350, 416 n.58, 420 n.81
  different types of emphasis, 333, 351
  intensification, 333, 350–351, 415 n.51,
    416 n.58
encyclopedic knowledge
  and cancellation of implicatures, 49–52,
    162–163, 299
  and disambiguation, 174, 176, 271
  and implicatures (see also common
    ground, context)
English
  binding patterns in, 285–298, 319–324
  dialects in, 415 n.51
  historical change in, 323, 340–342, 362
  Old, 335, 340–342, 349–350, 419 n.68–
    70
  Middle, 330, 341
  reflexives, long-distance, 319–324, 415
    n.53

subjective meaning of, 320, 413 n.40, 415
  n.54
enrichment rule, 114. See also I-Principle
entailment
  and cancellation of implicatures, 50, 56–
    57, 155, 299
  and definition of scales (see scales)
  and differential informativeness, 36, 76,
    79, 108–109, 273–274, 383 n.27
  and implicature, 196, 253
  nonentailing constructions, 108–109, 296–
    297
  and partial ordering, 105, 390 n.35
  scales (see Horn-scales, scales)
  and semantic representations, 191, 194,
    203, 241, 243
  and square of oppositions, 65, 385 n.50
  in theory of meaning, 168
  of what is said by what is implicated, 121,
    392 n.51
enthymematic argument, 56, 283 n.31
epistemic modality, 84, 131–132
epistemic modification
  of implicatures, 76–77, 387 n.6, n.7, n.10,
    n.11, 391 n.40
  and particularized strengthening, 78
  variable strength of, 77–78, 108–109, 387
    n.11, 396 n.77, 411 n.23
  See also knowledge, belief
ergative/absolutive, 304, 335–336
ethnography of speaking, 23
euphemism, 119, 128, 134, 138, 239, 264
even
events, 122–126, 148. See also conjunction
evidentials, 237, 315
evolution of language, 28, 381 n.16, 382
  n.17
Ewe, 420 n.79–80
exclusive vs. inclusive disjunction. See
  disjunction
existential
  import, 385 n.50
  quantification, 92, 200, 274–275
  statements, 93, 274
  See also some
explanation in linguistic theory. See levels,
  of linguistic theory
explicature, 24–25, 167, 190, 194–198, 211,
  238–239, 254, 392 n.46, 392 n.51, 400
  n.22
  definitions of, 194–197, 399 n.20
explicitness, pragmatic maxim of, 294,
  299
exploitation, of the maxims. See maxims,
  exploitation of
extension. See intension, reference

factives. *See* verbs
fallacy, of affirming the consequent, 44
  in human reasoning, 384 n.39
falsifiability, 274
felicity conditions, 23, 60–61, 166, 249–251,
  385 n.48
figures of speech, or tropes, 144–145, 163,
  210, 234–235, 238, 390 n.32. *See also*
  exploitation, flouting, irony, metaphor,
  metonymy
Fijian, 335, 336
file-change semantics, 167, 193, 248–249
filters. *See* projection
Finnish, 97
flouting, of the maxims of conversation. *See*
  figures of speech, maxims
focus, 94, 339, 341, 348, 351
force, illocutionary. *See* illocutionary force
form, linguistic
  marked vs. unmarked (*see* markedness)
  as trigger of inferences, 136
formalization, of pragmatic theory, 1, 49,
  52, 54, 78, 377, 423 n.96
formulae, ritual, 23
frequency, of expressions, 6
  and markedness, 136
  See also markedness
Frisian, 329
functionalism, 266, 363, 368
functional load, 132–133
function words, 90–98

game theory, 6, 29
gapping, 124, 126, 393 n.59. *See also*
  conjunction
'Gazdar's bucket', 49–50, 162
generality, semantic, 37
  narrowing of, 37, 184–186, 232
GCIs
  introduced, 11–21
  vs. PCI, 16–21
  See generalized conversational implicature
generalized conversational implicature
  (GCI), 11–21, 372–373
  borderline with PCIs, 102, 104–108, 396
    n.82
  calculation of, 141
  cancellation of, 49–54, 56–57
    by background assumptions, 50
    by entailments, 50, 56–57, 155, 299
    by inconsistent higher-ranked
      implicatures, 50–51, 77, 122, 155–164
    by relevance, 51–52, 88, 163–164
  as (supposed) category mistake, 55, 372–373
  close relation to linguistic structure, 17,
    22, 368–370

  as constraints on lexicalization, 64–71,
    143, 319, 369
  cross-linguistic generalizations and, 69,
    118, 123, 134, 142, 351, 365, 370 (*see
    also* cross-linguistic)
  defeasibility of (*see* defeasibility)
  default nature of, 16–17, 45–49, 162
  defined, 16, 162
  diachronic relation to PCIs, 263
  diagnostics for types, 40–42, 81–82, 83–84
  existence doubted, 380 n.5, n.6
  as explicatures, 196–197, 373, 385 n.41,
    392 n.46
  generation and filtering of, 162
  as gratuitous inferences, 59, 61
  and idiomatic uses of language, 22–24,
    134, 141, 367
  inconsistent, 39–40, 50–51, 77, 122 (*see
    also* projection)
  inside scope of logical operators, 172
  interactions between, 39–40, 153–164 (*see
    also* projection)
  intrusion into semantic content (*see*
    intrusion)
  joint effect of, 153–155
  and linguistic theory, 374–377
  mistaken for coded content, 18, 20, 68–69,
    374
  (attempted) reduction of, to nonce-
    inference, 54–71, 104–108, 123, 134,
    367, 386 n.54
  predictive power of, 59, 69–70, 289
  presumptive quality, 123, 127
  projection problem (*see* projection)
  psycholinguistic plausibility of, 162, 259,
    370
  regularity of, 68, 134
  relative priorities between, 39–40, 50–54
    (*see also* projection problem)
  rule-like, 47–48, 55
  scalar, 58 (*see also* Q-implicature, scales)
  from semantic representations, not truth-
    conditions, 380 n.2
  and semantics (*see* semantics/pragmatics
    interface)
  speaker's vs. addressee's perspective (*see*
    speaker)
  and square of opposition, 68–71
  stable patterns of, 64–71
  strength of, 411 n.23
  subliminal nature of, 17–18, 20, 69, 373
  tagging of, for cancellation, 163
  'traffic rules' between (*see* projection
    problem)
  and truth-conditions, 167
  typology of, 35–42, 170

generalized conversational implicature
(cont.)
See also conversational implicature,
GCI, I-implicature, M-implicature,
Q-inference
generative grammar, 265. *See also* Binding
Theory, Government and Binding,
grammar, Minimalist program, syntax
generative semantics, 237, 243, 333, 394 n.68
German, 342, 349–351, 364
Germanic languages, 311, 315, 330, 332,
335, 342, 416 n.59, 419 n.73, n.75
gesture, 179
givenness hierarchy, 94
goals, of interlocutors
and relevance, 17, 51–52, 163–164 (*see
also* plans)
Gothic, 311
governing domain, *see* domain
Government and Binding Theory (GB),
265, 270, 281–284, 304
grammar
and conventionalized implicature, 264, 266
overall models of, *see* linguistic theory
and pragmatics, 261–265, 362–365
as 'frozen pragmatics', 268
See also syntax
grammaticalization, 27, 69–70, 74, 124,
263–264, 268, 279, 339, 341–342, 347–
350, 362, 364
Greek, 285, 416 n.59
Grice's
circle, 172–198, 225, 236–243, 399 n.16
defined, 186
and two pragmatics, 187 (*see also*
semantics/pragmatic interface)
maxims (*see* maxims of conversation)
program, 12–21
theory of meaning, 12–13 (*see also*
intention, meaning_nm)
Gumbaynggir, 336
Guugu Yimithirr, 90, 125, 285, 303–305,
334, 364, 393 n.55, 412 n.34, 413 n.38,
419 n.770

Haitian creole, 338–339
Head-driven Phrase Structure Grammar
(HPSG), 306–307, 325–326
Hebrew, 335, 350
heuristics, 4–6, 31–35
and bottleneck on speech encoding, 28–35,
382 n.18
multiplication of message content, 31, 34
mutual assumption of, 34, 53–54, 73, 258–
259, 371
convert probabilities into certainties in
communication, 53–54, 258

role in recovering speaker's intentions, 30–
35, 53–54, 257–258, 371
'the marked message', 33
'the not said', 31
'the simply described', 32
See also I-Principle, M-Principle,
Q-Principle
Hindi, 125
Horn's scales. *See* scales
maxims, 40–41, 76, 136–137
honorifics, 264, 408 n.5
and agreement, 407 n.2
hyponyms, 101–103. *See also*
autohyponyms

I-vertex of Square of Oppositions, 65, 82,
83–86
pragmatic relation to O-vertex, 68–71
Icelandic, 311, 315, 316, 414 n.44, 416 n.59
iconicity, xvi, xix, 6, 75, 135–136, 142, 146,
150, 394 n.65
identity statements, 299–300, 412 n.32
idioms
generative theory of, 24
and three-leveled theory of meaning, 24–
27, 54, 134, 367
if, 19–20, 36–7, 91
and suspension of implicatures, 81, 252
(*see also* conditionals, connectives)
I-implicatures, 112–134
anaphora and, 115, 181–182, 217, 269–
272, 287–290
bridging (*see* bridging)
case, and, 186
of causatives, 141–142, 297
cohesion and, 276, 318 (*see also* bridging,
cohesion, conjunction, coreference)
compounds, 146–147, 186 (*see also*
compounds, nominal)
conditional perfection (*see* conditional
perfection)
conjunction buttressing (*see* conjunction)
from contradictories to contraries, 127–
134
contrast with Q-implicatures, 116, 119
coreference, 149, 177, 181 (*see also*
coreference)
and default logics, 48–49, 53
diagnostics for, 40–41, 119, 133–134
and ellipsis, 183–184, 395 n.72
and gaps (*see* zero-)
grammaticalization of (*see*
grammaticalization)
heterogeneity of, 118
intrusion of (*see* intrusion)
and language change, 347–348, 355–359,
370

and narrowing of meaning, 139, 185
negative strengthening (*see* negative
    strengthening, negation)
introduce semantic relations, 116
and M-implicatures, 137–155 (*see also*
    division of pragmatic labor)
and morphology, 143, 146–149
and Neg-Raising, 131–134 (*see also* Neg-
    Raising)
not independently glossable, 116, 120–
    121
and parataxis, 124–126, 147–148, 393 n.58
    (*see also* parataxis)
possessives, 118, 146, 186, 207, 223 (*see
    also* possessives)
and stereotypes, 114–115, 119, 138, 147,
    152, 223, 328–329, 333, 342, 370 (*see
    also* stereotypes)
tension with Q-implicatures, 116, 121,
    128–129, 133–134, 156
and zero-morphs or gaps, 146–149,
    285, 336–337, 364, 382 n.22, 411
    n.26
See also anaphora, articles, pronouns
illocutionary force, 23, 49, 381 n.11, 392
    n.50
vs. perlocutionary force, 23
implicature
vs. explicature and impliciture, 167, 194–
    198, 257–258, 392 n.46, 400 n.21, n.22,
    n.23, n.24
kinds of, 13–14, 40–41
    additive vs. subtractive, 406 n.59
phrasing of, 120–121, 196, 198
See also conventional implicature,
    conversational implicature, generalized
    implicature, particularized implicature
implicitness in communication. *See*
    I-Principle, impliciture
impliciture, 24–25, 167, 194–198, 392 n.46,
    400 n.21
defined, 194–195, 197, 400 n.22
incorporation of negation. *See* negation
indefinite article, 91–93
and nonuniqueness implicature, 92
See also definite article
indefiniteness. *See* definiteness
indeterminacy, of semantic content, 89,
    375–376. *See also* semantic
    representation, underspecification of
of syntax, 376
indexicals, 171–172, 242–243, 246
covert 'contextuals', 177, 185, 191–192,
    242
diagnostics for, 242
enlarged theory of, 191–192, 230, 242–
    243, 245–247

vs. implicatures, 191–192, 242–243, 405
    n.52
intrusion and, 192, 242
nondefeasible nature of, 242, 247
require pragmatic resolution, 177–180
and rigid designation, 242, 246, 405 n.52
and scope of negation, 405 n.52
and semantic interpretation, 177–180, 399
    n.12
standard view challenged, 177–180
See also deixis
indirect speech acts, 23, 141, 237, 408 n.5
indirection, 239. *See also* euphemism,
    politeness
Indo-European, proto, 417 n.59, 419 n.73,
    n.75
induction. *See* inductive inference
inductive inference, 42–43, 257, 384 n.32
nonmonotonicity of, 43
not basis of implicatures, 45–46
inference
abductive (*see* abduction)
ampliative, 258
and amplification of message content, 30–
    35
to best interpretation, 37, 44, 177, 257–
    259
and circumscription, 48, 275–276, 384
    n.36
and default logics, 42–49
defeasible, 42–54, 162–163
deductive (*see* deductive inference)
inconsistency between inferences, 39–40,
    48, 50–54, 56–57, 77, 122
inductive (*see* induction)
kinds of, 13–14, 42–54, 257–259
nonmonotonic (*see* nonmonotonic
    inference)
and processing effort, 55, 57–58
relative cheapness of, 29, 55, 382 n.22
and rhetoric, 382 n.22
and semantic representations, 241, 257–
    259
from sub-propositions, 257
information
asymmetry of
balance of, 112
increase by heuristics, 30–35
measures of, 31, 34
semantic, 31–35
theory of, 5–6, 383 n.24, n.26
informational strength, 76, 102
informativeness, 14, 273–276, 287, 409n.14
Bar-Hillel and Carnap's theory, 115, 273–
    275, 278, 299, 382 n.23, 410 n.15
defined, 115, 273–274
differential, 36, 76, 79, 100

informativeness (cont.)
  and entailment (*see* entailment)
  and existential quantification, 274
  information-theoretic, 383 n.24, n.26, 409
    n.14
  Popperian, 273–275, 278
  Principle of, 38, 114 (*see also* I-principle)
  semantic vs. information theoretic, 409–
    410 n.14
  types of, 273–275, 409 n.14, 410 n.16,
    n.18, n.19
  See also information, Q-implicature,
    Q-principle, scales
innate knowledge, of grammar. *See*
  nativism, universals
input/output relations of components. *See*
  theory of meaning, architecture of
intensification
  and M-implicature, 333, 348, 351. *See also*
    emphatic markers
  and reduplication, 150–153
intension vs. extension, 217–218, 225, 245–
  246, 391 n.45. *See also* character,
  reference
intensional vs. extensional contexts, 401
  n.30
intention, communicative, 4, 12–13
  recognition of, 13, 29–30, 52–53, 258–259,
    372
  logical problem of, 30, 379 n.3
  reflexivity of, 379 n.4
  regress of, 379 n.4, 380 n.1
  See also meaning-nn, m-intention
interaction, social, 21
interface, semantics/pragmatics. *See*
  semantic/pragmatic interface
  of syntax and semantics (*see* syntax)
  See also meaning, semantics
intolerant vs. tolerant quantifiers. *See*
  quantifiers
intonation, 212, 391 n.39. *See also* prosody
'introverted' predicates, 329–330, 342, 419
  n.74
intrusion, of pragmatics into semantic representations, 122, 164, 189–190, 192,
  198–234, 236–237, 238, 248–253, 373
  anaphora, and, 251, 272
  as coercions, 246–247
  constructions, intrusive, 198–217, 232,
    239, 251–256, 259
  defined, 198
  comparatives, 199–205
  conditionals, 205–210, 252–253
  negation, 210–213, 253–256
  referring expressions, 217–236, 238–239,
    249–251

default inference predicts, 259
defined, 168
figures of speech and, 210, 238–239
GCIs vs. PCIs and, 169, 236, 385 n.41
Grice's views on, 260
I-inferences and, 199, 201, 206–207, 210,
  221–223, 251
as indexicality, 192
kinds of, 239
M-inferences and, 201, 207–208, 223–224
Q-inferences and, 200–201, 205–206, 210–
  211, 213, 219–221, 249–251
and theory of meaning (*see* meaning)
See also discourse representation theory,
  pragmatics, situation semantics
intrusive constructions. *See* intrusion
Inuktitut, 142
I-Principle, 112–134
  and coreference, 115, 274–276 (*see also*
    coreference)
  and ellipsis, 183
  definition, 114–115
  and disjoint reference, 328–331 (*see also*
    disjoint reference)
  as heuristic, 32, 37, 48
  licenses inferences, 118
  speaker's maxim of minimization, 114, 126
  recipient's enrichment rule, 114
  and referential parsimony, 115
  relation to Grice's maxims, 37, 74–75, 112
irony, 163, 216, 234–235, 239–240
isomorphism
  of I-implicatures and semantic
    representations, 115, 116, 391 n.45
Italian, 420 n.78

Japanese, 102, 142, 312, 314, 315, 351, 419
  n.76, 421 n.84–85
Jiwarli, 336

Kilivila, 337
kinship terms, 102
know, 80, 133, 208
knowledge
  speaker's knowledge and implicatures, 76–
    77
  of use of language, 371
  See also encyclopedic, epistemic, mutual
    knowledge
Korean, 285, 315
Kwakiutl (Kwakwala), 177

language change, 139, 185, 262–264, 339–
  342, 362
  I-inferences as main engine of, 370, 394
    n.66

implicature and, 263–264, 370
See also grammaticalization, semantic
   change
language learning. *See* acquisition
language of thought, 7, 242, 372
Latin, 186, 350, 420 n.78
learnability, of pragmatics vs. universal
   grammar, 265, 279–280, 360, 361–363
   subset principle and, 361
least-effort principle (Zipf), 6, 112–113,
   135, 277, 319
   law of abbreviation, 115
   law of economic versatility, 115
levels, of linguistic theory, 8, 243–244, 367–
   368. *See also* components of linguistic
   theory
   and the burden of explanation, 374–377
   of meaning (*see* three-leveled theory of
      meaning)
lexical decomposition, 81, 140
lexical items
   constraints on (*see* lexicalization)
   contrast sets of (*see* contrast)
   doublets, 138–139
   meaning underspecified, 376
   vs. periphrasis, 140–142, 400 n.26
   and register, 138
   in semantic fields, 101–104
      taxonomies, 101–103
      compatibles, 102, 103
      incompatibles, 105
   See also monosemy
lexicalization
   constraints on scales (*see* scales)
   of negation (*see* negation)
   pragmatic constraints on, 12, 69–71, 91,
      143, 319, 369, 386 n.53, n.54
lexicon
   metalinguistic knowledge about, 6–7, 40–
      41, 119, 371
   pragmatic constraints on (*see*
      lexicalization)
   structure of, 79–108
      adjectives, 86–87, 100
      closed-class items, 90–98
      logical operators, 82–86
      marked/unmarked pairs, 138–140
      numerals (*see* number words)
      taxonomies, 101–103
      verbs, 87, 98 (*see also* verbs)
   See lexicalization, markedness, scales
linguistic theory. *See* components, levels,
   meaning
literal meaning
   vs. figurative use, 214–215, 402 n.38 (*see
      also* figures of speech)

vs. implicated content, 214–215, 240 (*see
   also* intrusion)
vs. indirect speech acts (*see* indirect speech
   acts)
vs. nonliteral uses, 23, 130, 132, 187, 197,
   204, 214–217, 226, 229, 232, 238, 240,
   402 n.38 (*see also* maxims, exploitation
   of; reference, speaker-)
litotes, 142–145. *See also* negation
'local pragmatics', 25, 167, 399 n.17
logic
   autoepistemic, 48
   deductive, *see* deductive inference
   inductive, 43, 44
   modal, 48
   See also inference, reasoning
logical form (LF), 8, 190–191, 195, 211,
   231, 238, 240–241, 249, 257, 292–293,
   295, 375–376
   Chomskyan LF, 190, 240, 265, 281, 405
      n.54
   and implicature, 171, 238
   underspecification and, 241, 249, 257–258,
      375–376, 399 n.17
   See also semantic representation
logical priority, of components in linguistic
   theory, 166, 172
logophoric pronoun. *See* pronoun
logophoricity, 284, 310–317, 356
   characteristics of, 314–315 (*see also*
      pronoun)
London school, 190, 256–257. *See also*
   Relevance (Sperber-Wilson theory of)

M-implicatures, 38–39, 89, 135–155
   and alternates, 136–137
   and anaphora, 181, 272, 277, 288–289,
      301–302, 305, 331–332, 333, 343–344
   and cases vs. postpositions, 97
   and compounds, 147
   and conjunction vs. parataxis, 126, 147–
      148, 393 n.55
   and disjoint reference (*see* disjoint
      reference)
   and double marking, 146, 357, 416 n.59,
      420 n.78, 422 n.91
   and double negation (*see* negation)
   and derivation, 139–140
   diagnostics for, 40–41
   form-basis of, 34, 38, 40, 126, 136
   intrusion into semantics (*see* intrusion)
   and lexical doublets, 138–140
   markedness and, 38, 136–155, 277, 288,
      326, 333–334, 337, 347, 369 (*see also*
      markedness)
   and negation, 142–145

M-implicatures (cont.)
  and periphrasis, 140–146
  and possessives, 146, 147
  and prepositions, 96, 147
  and reduplication, 150, 152–153
  and reflexives, 329, 331–334, 337, 341, 347
  and repetition, 149–153
  take priority over I-implicatures, 39–40, 137–138
  and zero-morphs, 146–149
  See also division of pragmatic labor, Manner, markedness
M-Principle, 38, 91, 135–155
  as heuristic, 33, 38, 136
  related to Grice's maxims, 38, 75
  relation to Relevance, 135–136
  See also Manner
Malagasy, 423 n.96
Manner, maxim of
  Grice's submaxims, 14, 19, 38, 135–136
  reduction of, 135–136
  Reinhart's, 294
  See also markedness, M-Principle
Manner implicatures, 135–136. See also M-implicatures
markedness
  concept of, 115, 137
  formal vs. semantic, 137
  heuristic based on, 33–34
  and Horn's division of pragmatic labor, 6, 26, 38, 136–139, 144, 277, 285, 364
  and iconicity, 136, 142
  and Manner, 91
  in morphology, 139–140, 152–153
  and negation, 70, 142–144
  and periphrasis, 39, 140–142
  and phonetics and prosody, 332–333, 395 n.72
  and prolixity, 6, 14, 38, 79–80, 114, 135–136
  and reference (see reference)
  as trigger of M-implicature, 136
  See also M-Principle, privative opposition
maxims of conversation
  clash between (see tension between below)
  exploitation (flouting) of, 112, 172, 214–216, 231–232, 234–235, 238–239
  Grice's, 14ff, 35, 37, 38, 386 n.2
  as heuristics, 31–39, 136
  number of, 55, 74–75, 164
  observation vs. flouting of, 15, 112
  reduction of, 55, 74–75
  tension between, 55, 116, 121, 133–134, 156–158 (see also projection)
  See also I-Principle, Manner and Relevance, M-Principle, Quality, Quantity, Q-principle

meaning
  composite nature of (see hybrid theory of below)
  conventional (coded), 170
  theory of, 7–9, 166, 374–377
    architecture of, 7–9, 166–168, 188, 243–244
      with double pragmatics, 187, 232–236
      with double semantics, 232–234, 236
      input/output structure, 166, 171–172, 187, 242, 243–244, 374–375
    received view of, 171–173
    two vs. three levels in, 22–27, 54–63, 73, 367
  hybrid theory of, 7ff, 13–14, 21, 166, 397 n.3
  literal (see literal meaning)
  nonnatural, 12 (see also meaning$_{nn}$)
  picture theory of, 4
  sketchy nature of encoded-, 2–8, 375–377
  speaker-, 22, 170 (see also speaker-meaning)
  timeless, 170
  See also Discourse Representation Theory, pragmatics, semantic representation, semantics, Situation semantics, utterance-meaning
meaning$_{nn}$, 12, 379 n.4, 398 n.7. See also M-intention
metalinguistic
  character of I- and M-implicatures, 40–41, 119
  reasoning and heuristics, 6–7, 371
  negation (see negation)
metaphor, and intrusion in semantics, 239
  and implicature, 163
metarules, 81
metonyms, 236–237, 238, 245–246
minimal expressions, 37, 62, 113–115, 124, 126, 268
  definition of, 115
  See also I-principle, maxim of minimization, semantic generality
minimal governing category. See domains, Binding Conditions
Minimalist program, 265, 281
minimization, maxim of, 113–115, 277. See also I-principle
m-intention, 13, 29, 114, 391 n.43. See also meaning$_{nn}$
mirror-image inference, 290, 295, 298, 326, 412 n.29. See complementary distribution
modality, 83–86, 140, 154, 391 n.38
modal logics, 48, 387 n.6, n.9, 388 n.13
model-theoretic semantics. See semantics

modularity
  Fodorean, 187, 190, 244, 372
    vs. linguistic component, 244, 372, 397
      n.4, 405 n.53
  in grammar, 21, 166, 261, 397 n.4
  in meaning, 21, 166, 171, 187, 192–193,
    192, 243–244
  and pragmatics, 371–372, 405 n.53
  representational, 424 n.4
monosemy, and implicature, 18, 20, 165,
  184
monotonicity
  and inferences, 42–55, 56–57, 192, 243.
    See also nonmonotonicity
mood, 315
Moore's paradox, 209, 386 n.1, 402 n.35
morphology, derivational, 139–140
  causative, 142
  negative, 142–143
  vs. periphrasis, 146
  reduplication, 152–153
mutual knowledge. See common ground,
  context, heuristics, salience

narrowing, of meaning
  Q-based vs. I-based, 185–186
nativism, 338, 344, 361, 363
necessity vs. possibility. See modality
negation
  affixal, 69, 134, 142–143
  and blocking of implicatures, 64, 80–82,
    162, 252–256
  contraction of, 69–70
  of contradictories, 144–145
  of contraries, 145
  contraries vs. contradictories, 64–65, 83–
    86, 127–129, 130–132, 142–145, 222
  and contrast sets, 103
  conventionalization of implicatures of, 134
  denials (see metalinguistic)
  double, 38–39, 127, 142–145
  I-implicatures of, 127–134, 142, 222
  and implicatures vs. presuppositions, 252–
    256
  implicit, 213
  incorporation of, 69–70, 82–83, 130–131,
    142–143, 212
  lexicalization and, 69–70
  litotes, 127, 142–145
  M-implicatures of, 127, 142–145
  metalinguistic, 210–213, 253–256
    as contradictions, 214
    definitions of, 211–212
    denials and retorts, 212, 253–256
    kinds of, 406 n.61
    as logical negation, 211–212, 253–254
    nonlogical type of, 212, 254

  properties of, 254
  scope over Q- and M-implicatures, 41,
    197, 210–213, 253–256
  psycholinguistic complexity of, 70, 81,
    145, 388 n.19, 392 n.49
  Q-implicatures and (see scales, square of
    oppositions)
  raising (see Neg-Raising)
  and scale reversal, 64, 388 n.17
  scope of, and lexicalization, 70
  strengthening by I-implicature, 127–134,
    143
  sub-contraries, 65, 83, 132
  See also square of oppositions
negative
  character of Q- and M-inferences, 40, 119
  expressions and M-implicatures, 142–145
  polarity items, 134, 212, 237, 262
  scales and Q-implicature, 36, 64–68, 80–
    82, 128–129, 254–255
  strengthening by I-implicature, 117, 127–
    134, 143, 222
  See also Q-implicatures, scales, square of
    oppositions
Neg-Raising (NR), 129–134, 159, 237, 262
neo-Gricean pragmatics, xv, 353, 381 n.9.
  See also radical pragmatics
neurocognition and language, 28
nonce interpretations, 12, 24, 25, 54–63,
  164
  inability to explain stable inference
    patterns, 71, 134, 386 n.54
  problem of inconsistent, 164
nonconfigurational
  constraints on binding, 303–307, 325
  languages, 297, 303–305
nondetachability, 99
  defined, 15
nonmonotonic reasoning, 42–54, 57, 192,
  275–276, 384 n.38, n.39
  types of, 42–49
nonnatural meaning, 12. See also meaning,
  meaning_nn, m-intention
normal expectations, 16, 32–33. See also
  stereotypes
Norwegian, 310, 311, 412 n.28, 416 n.59
noun phrases (NP)
  lexical (R-expressions), 270, 281, 285,
    286–287, 292–296, 298–303
  scale of reduction of, 270, 285, 288, 305,
    411 n.27
  types of, 277–286, 292, 300–301, 304, 326,
    409 n.12
  See also Binding Conditions, pronouns,
    R-expressions
NP. See noun phrases
NR. See Neg-Raising

number words, 25, 58, 87–90, 178, 249–
    250, 389 n.22
  ambiguity analysis of, 88–89
  'at least' interpretation of, 88, 250–251,
    406n.57, 389 n.26, 406 n.57
  vs. cardinal numbers, 88
  'exactly' interpretation of, 87–90, 175,
    204, 206, 219, 406 n.58
  PCI analysis of, 403 n.40
  semantic content of, 88, 250, 389 n.22,
    406n.57
  special properties of, 89–90
Nyawaygi, 335

oblique arguments, 282
Obstinate Theorist, 187, 215, 217, 225, 227,
    230–236, 240, 402 n.39
Occam's razor, 20
on, 33, 34
Ono, 148
oppositions. See contrast
or, 19, 81, 91, 153–154. See also disjunction
order, of reported events, 14, 19, 75, 122–
    127, 135, 199–201. See also conjunc-
    tion, buttressing
  of antecedents and anaphors, 290–291,
    307
  of antecedents vs. consequents, 126, 163
  of incrementation of context, 50, 162
  of lexemes in semantic fields, 102
  underlying scales, 105–108
O-vertex of square of oppositions, 65, 82,
    83–86, 143
  relation to I-vertex, 68–71
  O-to-E drift, 70, 143
  See also square of oppositions

Papago, 350
Papuan languages, 335
parameters
  pragmatic, 328
  syntactic, 300–301, 312–313, 360, 361–
    363
    vs. pragmatic explanations, 360–362
    and language change, 362, 422 n.94
parataxis, 124, 147–148
partial ordering, 105, 390 n.35
particularized conversational implicatures
    (PCIs), xvi–xvii, 13–21, 78, 103–108,
    163, 166, 169, 190, 236, 238, 263, 379
    n.3, 380 n.5–n.6, 385 n.41
  definition, 16
  vs. generalized, 16–21, 74, 89
  and inconsistencies with GCIs, 161
  (attempted) reduction of GCIs to, 104–
    108, 164

See also PCIs, conversational implicature,
    nonce interpretations, Relevance,
    speaker-meaning
performance. See competence vs.
    performance
periphrasis, 37, 140–146
perlocutionary acts/effects. See
    illocutionary acts
permissions, 49
person, first/second vs. third, in anaphora,
    387 n.7, 413 n.35, 413 n.40, 415 n.54
perspective, 312, 314, 320–321, 346–347,
    354
perspicuity, 14, 38, 135
phonetics and implicature. See markedness,
    prosody
phonology, 8
philosophy of language, 12–20, 23, 24, 64,
    68, 84, 87, 217, 226–231
pidgin and creole languages, 338–340
pirots, 29, 382 n.21
planning, in speech production, 46. See also
    goals, inference, plans, relevance
plans, 45, 46
  reconstruction of, 46, 380 n.4
  recognition of, 60
  and relevance, 17, 46, 51–52, 380 n.4
  See also goals, inference, relevance
plurality, 262
point of view, 237, 284, 320–322
  and logophoricity, 284, 314–316, 354, 356,
    414 n.47, 415 n.54
  See also perspective, reflexives
politeness, 14, 128, 145, 264, 423 n.96
polysemy, and implicature, 103
Pomo, Northern, 317
poset, 105. See also order
possessives
  interpretations of, 118, 146, 192, 207
  alienable vs. inalienable, 146
  and anaphora, 291, 305, 308, 309–310,
    412 n.28
possibility. See modality
PP-attachment, 174, 176
practical reasoning, 30, 43, 45, 52–53
  and intention, 45, 53
  and implicature, 45, 46, 52, 60
  nonmonotonic, 45
  and difficulties of reconstruction, 30,
    45
'pragmatics', 192–193, 243, 244
pragmatic intrusion, into semantic
    representations. See intrusion
pragmatic resolution of underspecification.
    See semantic representation
    (underspecification)

pragmatics
  as component of linguistic theory, 166,
    243, 365, 368, 371–372
  definitions of, 7–9, 168, 187, 243
  and explanation in linguistics, 266, 364–
    365, 374–377
  formal theory and, 377, 423 n.1
  local, 25, 167, 237
  generative grammar and, 237, 261–265,
    362–365
  heuristic potential of, 365
  innate bases, xii, 361
  interface, with semantics, *see* semantics/
    pragmatics interface
  nonmonotonic basis, 166, 192, 243
  predictive power of, 365, 367, 368–370
  as process rather than representation, 168,
    243
  and psychology, 28, 40, 78, 81, 90, 162,
    258–259, 405 n.53
  and psycholinguistics (*see* psycho-
    linguistic)s
  vs. semantics, 7–9, 23, 25, 192, 374–375,
    399 n.12
  and syntax, 261–365, 374, 407 n.4 (*see
    also* syntax)
    border between, 264–266, 268, 362–365
  universals of, xii–xiii, 15, 69, 266, 300–
    301, 361, 370, 423 n.96
  See also meaning, semantics
Prague school, 115, 137
preemption, 99–100
  and anaphora, 99–100
  of deictic words, 99
  and synonymy (*see* blocking)
preferred interpretation, xi–xiii, 1, 4, 9,
  11ff, 21, 22–27, 54, 59, 355, 367, 386
  n.55
  and explanation of stable inference
    patterns, 71, 386 n.54
  See also default interpretation, generalized
    conversational implicature,
    presumptive meanings
prepositions, 96, 222
presemantic pragmatics. *See* semantics/
  pragmatics interface
presumptive meanings, 1, 22ff, 127, 169,
  258–259, 367, 368. *See also* default
  interpretation, generalized
  conversational implicature
presupposition, 13, 23, 61, 166, 249, 252,
  397 n.2
  accommodation of, 61, 249, 251
  cancellation of, 111
  and conditionals, 256
  and conversational implicature, 111

  detachability of, 99, 111
  and factives, 61, 252
  and 'filters', 252, 256
  projection of, 111, 249, 252–253, 255–256
  triggers for, 60, 111
principles of language use. *See* I-, M-, and
  Q-Principles, maxims
Principles and Parameters. *See* Government
  and Binding
privative opposition, 202, 277, 286, 316,
  319, 356, 365. *See also* scales
PRO, 363–364
processing, and pragmatics. *See*
  psycholinguistics
production. *See* bottleneck, comprehension,
  psycholinguistics
projection
  of implicatures, 39–40, 80–82, 134, 155–
    164, 212, 252–253, 255–256, 289, 383
    n.28, 396 n.82
  consistency, with incremented context, 49,
    162
    with common ground, 49–52, 162–163,
      299, 330
  'filters' and 'holes', 252, 255–256
  M vs. I-implicatures, 137–155, 156–158,
    160, 277 (*see also* division of pragmatic
    labor)
  of presuppositions, 158, 163, 252–253, 255
  and negation, 162, 212–213, 254–255
  Q-clausal vs. Q-scalar, 161–162, 396 n.77
  Q vs. I-implicatures, 133–134, 155–159,
    395 n.74, n.76
  Q vs. M-implicatures, 157, 160–161
  and Relevance, 52, 163–164
  resolution schema, 157–158, 161–162, 289,
    330
    rationale for, 161, 411 n.23
  unified account for implicatures and
    presuppositions, 255–256, 396 n.78
  See also consistency, defeasibility,
    intrusion
prolixity, 38, 114, 267. *See* markedness
pronouns, 39, 181, 217, 277, 280
  agreement features of, 277, 312
  ambiguity vs. general purpose nature of,
    269–270, 409 n.7, 422 n.92
  c-commanding NPs, 290, 292–298, 302,
    413 n.35, n.36, n.37
  clausemate, as coreferential, 278–280
    as disjoint, 280, 288, 331
  complementary distribution of pronouns
    vs. reflexives, 283, 288, 308–326
    failure of, 307, 308–326, 412 n.29, 414
      n.44
  and control, 363–364

pronouns (cont.)
and determiners, 300, 304
emphatic, 263, 331, 333, 337, 348, 350
vs. gaps, 148–149, 285, 305, 336–337,
   364–365, 382 n.22, 411 n.26
logophoric, 314, 350, 414 n.45, 420 n.79–
   80
   contrast with ordinary pronouns, 317–
      318, 346–347, 356
   vs. LDA and Switch-Reference, 317, 414
      n.46
nonreflexive, 287–290
used reflexively, 336–343
obviative, 415 n.51
possessive, 291, 305, 308, 309–310, 412
   n.28
referential dependence, and, 268, 270, 284,
   287, 310, 312, 353–355
vs. referring expressions, 39, 62, 181, 267,
   269–270
vs. reflexives, 181, 237, 263, 267, 270, 271,
   277–280, 306–327, 410 n.19, n.20 (see
   also Anaphors, anaphora, Binding
   Conditions, reflexives)
semantic generality of, 181, 269–270, 409
   n.8
as variables, 267, 279, 292
vs. zeros (see gaps)
See also coreference, noun phrases,
   reference
proposition, 172, 186, 190, 194, 198, 236,
   239, 256–259, 273
inferred from nonpropositions, 257
informativeness of (see informativeness)
minimal expressed, 195–197, 258
nonlinguistic nature of, 190, 399 n.19
pragmatic resolution of, 256–259
sentences fail to express, 256
vs. subpropositional content (see
   propositional content)
and what is 'said', 194–198, 398 n.7
See also truth-conditions
propositional attitudes, 110
propositional content, 169, 193
determination by implicature, 174, 180,
   194
vs. sub-propositional, 194, 240–241, 257–
   258
See also semantic representation, truth-
   conditional content
prosody, 123, 174, 418 n.61. See also
   intonation, stress
proto-Indo-European, 417 n.59, 419 n.75
psycholinguistics
and asymmetry of production vs.
   comprehension, 28, 382 n.20, n.22

and negation (see negation)
and pragmatics, 5, 28, 162, 259, 370, 382
   n.22, 423 n.1, 424 n.3
and processing of implicatures, 5, 55, 162,
   245, 361, 370, 382 n.22, 424 n.3, 396
   n.80, 397 n.5, 409 n.12
double-processing in tropes, 216, 234–
   235, 239–240
psychology, and pragmatics. See
   pragmatics

Q-implicatures, 75–111
anaphora and, 181–182, 271–272, 286–
   289, 294–298, 301–302, 305, 317–318
cancellation of, 50–51, 81–82, 161
clausal (see clausal implicatures)
constraints on, 156–157 (see also scales)
and constructional opposition, 294–297,
   305 (see also clausal implicatures)
and contraries vs. sub-contraries (see
   negation)
and contrast sets, 32, 36, 64, 79–80
and contrast with I-implicatures, 119
diagnostics for, 40, 84–85
and differential informativeness, 36, 76,
   79, 100, 102, 287
inconsistency between, 50–51
and lexical alternates (see scales,
   alternates)
and lexicalization constraints, 69–70, 91,
   143, 369
and narrowing, 185–186
negative character of, 40–41
and numbers, see number words
and opposition between structures, 295–
   297
scalar (see scalar implicatures, scales)
and square of oppositions (see square of
   oppositions)
and switch-reference systems, 317–319
take priority over others, 39–40, 50–51
tension with I-implicatures, 116, 121–122,
   156–158
See also clausal implicature, contrast,
   scalar implicature, scales
Q-Principle, 75–111
definition of, 76
as heuristic, 31, 35
inferences due to (see Q-implicatures)
recipient's maxim, 76
relation to Grice's maxims, 35, 74–75
speaker's maxim, 76
See also Q-implicatures
Quality, maxim of, 14, 19, 20, 386 n.1. See
   also Moore's paradox, figures of
   speech

quantifiers
  domain of (*see* domain)
  English, 85, 389 n.22
  existential (*see* existential)
  implicatures of, 68–71, 76, 82–86
  monotone-increasing, 388 n.20
  negative, 83–86 (*see also* negation)
  and pragmatic resolution, 182–183
  scope of, 165, 237, 257
  and square of oppositions, 65
  tolerant vs. intolerant, 86, 131–133, 388
    n.21, 389 n.22
  universal (*see* universal)
Quantity implicatures. *See* clausal-, Q-,
    scalar-implicatures
Quantity, maxims of, 14, 19, 35, 37, 74–76,
    112
  first (*see* Q-Principle)
  second (*see* I-Principle)
  See also I-implicatures, I-Principle, Q-
    implicatures, Q-Principle

radical pragmatics, xv, 184, 185, 188, 242,
    256, 257, 381 n.8
raising
  of Anaphors (*see* Anaphors)
  of negation (*see* Neg-raising)
  of subjects, 363, 407 n.4
rather-construction, 213
rationality, 14, 48, 361, 371
Realism, 7–8, 167
reasoning, types of, 42–54
  with nonpropositions, 257
  vs. rule-based inference, 54, 383 n.30
  See also inference
receiver, of communication. *See* speaker
reciprocals, 267, 304, 309–310, 336–337.
    See also Anaphora, pronouns,
    reflexivity
recognition, of speakers, 113
reduction
  of linguistic expressions (*see* minimal
    expressions)
  of generalized implicature to nonce
    inference, 25, 54–63, 73, 386 n.54
  of grammar to pragmatics, 266 (*see also*
    syntax)
  of pragmatic inference to semantics, 25,
    73, 169 (*see also* semantics)
  redundancy constraints, on lexicalization,
    70, 80, 143, 319, 369, 370
reduplication, 150, 152–153, 208. *See also*
    M-implicature
reference
  attributive vs. referential (*see* referential)
  and anaphora, 94, 222, 225

and coreference (*see* coreference)
  disjoint (*see* disjoint reference)
  implicatural determination of, 180–183,
    189, 217–236
  overlapping, 412 n.29, 414 n.46
  parsimony in, 115 (*see also* I-Principle)
  to persons, 113–114, 149
  pragmatic approaches to, 217, 267–273
  and presupposition
  and referential dependence, 268, 270, 284,
    287, 305, 409 n.7
  necessary, 270, 310, 312
  resolution of the 'said', 171
  rigid designation and, 242, 246, 300
  speaker-, vs. semantic- (Kripke), 228–229,
    404 n.47, n.48
  Strawsonian vs. Russellian approaches,
    218–219, 226–227, 228, 231, 232
  -tracking, 273 (*see also* anaphora)
  See also anaphora, extension, pronouns,
    noun phrases
referential, vs. attributive uses of referring
    expressions (Donnellan), 226–230,
    300
  as implicaturally determined reference,
    226–227
referring expressions
  alternative, 149
  scale of, 92–94, 149
  See also reference
reflexives, 181, 237, 263, 267, 270, 271,
    277–280, 306–327
  acquisition of, 340, 344, 361–362, 416
    n.59, 422 n.93
  Anaphors vs. pseudo-Anaphors, 306–307,
    308, 323, 324–326
  antecedents of, 271, 345–346, 409 n.9
  binding domain of (*see* Anaphors, Binding
    Conditions, domain)
  clause-bound, 311, 323, 324
    vs. long-range (*see* long-range *below*)
  complementarity with pronouns, 283–284,
    288, 290, 308, 319–321, 345–347
  breakdown of, 308–327, 412 n.29, 414
    n.44
  in reference vs. logophoricity, 312, 314–
    317, 319–326, 345–347
  diachronic origins of, 347–352
  discourse-bound, 321–322
  disjoint interpretations of proto-reflexives,
    357
  emphatic-, 308, 320–321, 331–334, 341,
    348, 416 n.58
  origin from emphatics, 332–334, 341–
    342, 347–348, 416 n.58, 420 n.81, n.83,
    421 n.84–85

reflexives (cont.)
  languages without, 304–305, 323, 334–343
  and logophoricity, 284, 310–317, 320, 322, 345–348
  characteristics of, 314–315
  long-range, 282, 283, 296, 310–317, 319–327, 345, 357–358
  acquisition of, 361, 416 n.59
  contrast with pronouns, 319–327, 345–347
  more informative than pronouns, 278, 287, 316–317, 410 n.19, n.20
  nonuniversal, 334–343
  in oblique phrases, 290–291, 305, 308, 319–321
  and perspective or point of view, 314–316, 320–323, 346–347, 356
  'picture nouns' and, 308, 320, 324
  pragmatic resolution, of antecedents, 271, 409 n.9
  and referential dependence (see reference)
  semantic content of, 277–278, 312, 314–317, 319–324, 345
  and stereotypical actions, 329, 332–333, 342
  simplex vs. compound, 311–312, 352, 413 n.38
  singularity of, 321
  types of, 349–350, 359
  See also Anaphor, anaphora, Binding Conditions, reciprocals, reflexivity
reflexivity, 280, 304, 329–330, 334
  without Anaphors, 280, 304–305, 334–343
  grammatical relations and, 304
  implicated only, in some languages, 343, 334–343
  and introverted predicates (see introverted predicates)
  languages without coding of, 334–343
  marked nature of, 329, 331–334
  and 'middle' verbs, 338, 349–350
  and stereotypical transitive actions, 329–330, 332–333, 342
  verbal, 304–305, 325, 334, 349, 419 n.77
register, 138
reinforceability of implicatures, 15
relation, maxim of. See Relevance
relevance
  and ellipsis, 183
  generates only PCIs, 74
  goal- or plan-driven theory of, 17, 46, 51–52, 55, 163, 380 n.4
  Grice's maxim of, 14, 74
  interaction with GCIs, 51–52, 163–164
  and other maxims, 112, 135

Sperber-Wilson theory of, xvi, 12, 22, 52, 55–60, 135, 167, 197, 236, 238–240, 257, 371, 380 n.4, 382 n.22, 385 n.42, 390 n.28, 396 n.81, 399 n.18
  as balance of I- vs. M-principles, 55
  critique of, 55–59
repetition, 149–153
respect. See honorifics, politeness
retraction in conversation, 163
R-expression, 281, 301. See also noun phrase
rhetoric, 23, 145, 382 n.22
rigid designators, 242, 246. See also reference
Romance, 416 n.59, 419 n.73, 420 n.78
routinization, of inferences, 24. See also grammaticalization, short-circuited inference, standardization
R-principle (Horn), 40–41, 135–136, 396 n.82
Russian, 97, 349, 364

'said' vs. implicated, 13–14, 116, 194–198
  contradiction and, 215
  Grice's conception, 170–171, 398 n.7, n.8
  implicatural contributions to 'said', 172–186, 217–225 (see also intrusion)
  intuitions about, 197, 199–200, 205–206, 216 (see also truth-conditions)
  reference and, 171
  relation to logical form, 171
  relation to truth-conditions, 170–171
  indexicals, role of, 171
  variant views of, 194–198
salience
  of antecedents, 273
  and contrast, 32, 36, 80, 100, 107
  and games of pure coordination, 29ff, 258–259
  of readings, 90
satisfaction conditions, 171
scalar implicatures, 35–37, 50, 58, 76–108, 161, 383 n.29
  of adjectives, 86–87, 128–129
  blocking of by negation (see negation)
  cancellation of, 50–51
  by clausal implicatures, 81–82
  as default rules, 47
  definites vs. indefinites, 63, 91–95, 220
  diagnostics for, 81–82, 84–85
  entailment and (see scales)
  epistemic commitment and, 78–79, 387 n.8, n.8, n.11, 391 n.40
  in general vocabulary, 86–98
  intrusion into semantics, 200–201, 205–206, 210–213, 217–221, 234, 250–251

lower vs. upper bound, 88, 178
modals, 82–86, 154
negation and, 36, 64–68, 80–82, 128–129,
    211–213, 254–255
numerals (*see* number words)
quantifiers, 36, 47, 76, 82–86
positive vs. negative scales (*see* scales)
processing of, 245
and reflexives (*see* scales)
and semantic fields (Type I and II), 101–
    103
and switch reference, 317–319
See also Q-implicature, scales
scales
anaphoric expressions, 94, 181–182, 286–
    289, 310, 317–318, 348, 355
cases, 97
closed class morphemes and, 90–98, 155
constraints on, 79–80, 82, 98, 122, 156,
    391 n.38
  lexicalization constraint, 79–81, 120, 388
    n.15, 392 n.49, 412 n.28
  'aboutness' constraint, 80, 121, 388 n.16
  salience, 107–108
and contrast sets, 32, 36, 79–80
definition, 79
determiners, 91–95
entailment and, 79–82
  nonentailment scales, 98–103
function words and, 90–98
general vocabulary and, 86–104
Horn-, 36, 47, 52, 79–108, 274, 278, 286,
    296, 297
  conditions on (*see* constraints *above*)
Hirschberg-, 104–108, 120, 390 n.36, n.37
inversion, 88
and lexicalization patterns, 69–71, 80–81,
    143
metascales, 81, 182
mid-scalar items, 77, 83–86
negation and, 64, 80–82, 83–86, 128–129,
    162, 212–213, 255–256
nonentailment-, 36, 98–108
non-GCI scales, 82
nonce- (*see* Hirschberg-scales)
number words, 87–90, 178, 219
order relations underlying, 105
particularized, 103–108
placement on square, 84–86
positive vs. negative scales, 64, 254–255,
    388 n.17
pragmatic vs. semantic nature of, 88, 104–
    108
prepositions, 96
pseudo-scales, 79, 80, 99, 391 n.38, n.40
reflexives and, 278, 286, 353, 316–317

reversal of (*see* numbers, negation)
in semantic fields, 101–104
strong vs. weak items, 76, 81
summary of properties, 82
and square of oppositions, 65, 83–86, 388
    n.19
tenses, 95–96, 128–129
verbs, 87, 98–99, 110
See also Q-implicature, scalar-implicature
scientific reasoning, 44
scope, of logical operators
ambiguities of, 165, 375, 388 n.15
implicatures inside, 41, 172, 195, 196–197,
    253–256
raising and, 129–134, 165
and scope-free semantic representation,
    241, 257, 375
See also ambiguity, negation
self, 340–342
self-identification, 114
semantic change, 185, 262–264, 339, 341–
    342, 347–350, 362. *See also* diachrony,
    grammaticalization
semantic entailment. *See* entailment
semantic fields
structure of, and implicatures, 101–104
    (*see also* lexical items, scales)
semantic generality, 115, 135, 184–186,
    189, 274, 376
and anaphora, 225, 267–270, 287, 304
vs. indexicality, 191–192
resolution of, 184–186, 257–258, 376
and vacuity of representations, 184, 189
weak univocality vs. nonspecific (Atlas),
    185, 189, 242, 257, 381 n.8
semantic interpretation, 172
role of indexicals in, 177–180
semantic representation, 8, 168, 171, 240–
    242, 247, 256–259, 372, 375–377
vs. conceptual representations, 241–242,
    372
constraints on, from pragmatics, 377
decoded from syntactic structures, 193,
    194, 240, 248, 375
and entailment, 191, 194
enrichment by pragmatics, 194–198
and features (*see* 'markerese' *below*)
fragmentary, 168, 191, 238, 256–259, 399
    n.17
generality of, 135, 184–186, 240–242
and implicature, 171, 238, 377, 380 n.2
hybrid semantico-pragmatic nature of,
    168, 193, 247, 248–256, 259–260, 374–
    375, 405 n.55
pragmatic conditions 'in red ink' and
    erasable, 249, 253, 259, 384 n.37

semantic representation (cont.)
  interpretation, 7–8, 168, 191
  levels of, 168
  vs. logical form, 375–376, 380 n.2
  'markerese', 190, 240
  nature of, 375–377
  and scope, 165
    scope-free, 241, 257, 375–376
  semantic generality and (*see* semantic
    generality)
  sub-propositional nature, 194, 257
  and time, 122
  and underspecification, 8, 89, 168, 171,
    240–241, 256–259, 375–377
  and 'what is said', 171, 194–198
  See also logical form, intrusion
'semantic retreat', 190, 240–242
semantics
  author's assumptions, 7–9
  autonomy of, 166, 226, 232, 235, 244–245,
    397 n. (*see also* Grice's circle,
    presemantic pragmatics, semantics/
    pragmatics interface)
  controls pragmatic processes, 245
  definitional problems, 168
  division of labor with pragmatics, 165,
    168, 243–245, 398 n.6
  feature-theories of, 190
  interface with pragmatics (*see* semantics/
    pragmatics interface)
  and 'language of thought', 7, 242, 372
  model-theoretic, 6–7, 172, 193
  vs. pragmatics, 7–9, 170–172, 186–193,
    233–234
    as distinct processes over same
      representations, 168
    terminological difficulties, 194–195
  restricted theories of, 190
  scope of, 186, 190–191
  and sense relations, 191, 241
  truth-conditional, 7–8, 241, 248–253
  See also, DRT, meaning, Situation
    Semantics, truth-conditions
semantics/pragmatics interface, 165–260,
  374–375
  vs. abandoning the distinction, 192–193,
    243
  architecture of (*see* meaning)
  common representation with distinct
    contributions, 168, 193, 244, 374, 424
    n.3
  cyclical processing model of, 245
  and 'Grice's circle', 172–173, 186–187,
    236–243
  input/output models of, 166–167, 187,
    217, 236, 242, 243–244, 374–375, 397
    n.4

interleaving of processes, 168, 187, 236,
  242, 245, 374, 398 n.6, 405 n.55
intermediate phenomena (*see* intrusion,
  explicature, implicature)
modularity and, 187, 243–245, 371–372,
  397 n.4
presemantic pragmatics, 187–190, 215–
  217, 218, 226, 230, 231, 232–234, 238,
  239–240, 245, 247
recent trends, 167
and scope of operators, 165
terminology, 194–198
semiotics, 13, 26, 273
sense. *See* intension, monosemy
sense-relations, 168, 191, 194, 398 n.6
sentence vs. discourse, 267, 321–322, 415
  n.52
  vs. elliptical fragments (*see* ellipsis)
  -frame, 76, 108, 136
  vs. utterance (*see* utterance)
sentence-meanings. *See* utterance
sentence-types, minor, 392 n.50
Sheffer stroke, 386 n.53
short-circuited implicature, 24–25, 134,
  262–263, 408 n.5. *See also*
  conventionalization, standardization
simultaneity of events, 124
since, 36, 263
Sissala, 148
situation semantics, xvii, 26, 27, 167, 172,
  191, 208–210, 218, 229–230, 242–243,
  256
  described situation vs. utterance situation,
    191, 229–230
  indexicals in, 191–192, 230, 242–243
  utterance situation vs. resource situation,
    191
sloppy-identity, 293
some, 16–17, 36, 47, 65, 68, 77, 175, 200,
  297
space, deixis of, 94
  linguistic expressions for, 94, 96
  prepositions of, 96, 118, 207, 222, 237
Spanish, 350
speaker
  vs. addressee's perspective, 6, 28, 76, 114,
    136, 382 n.20, n.22, 373, 387 n.3
  commitment of, 76–79, 163, 384 n.36
  intentions of (*see* intention)
  knowledge of, 40
speaker-meaning, 4, 22–27, 54–63, 381 n.10
  distinctions in, 27
  vs. linguistic(sentence)-meaning, 228, 234
    (*see also* utterance)
  and reduction of GCIs to, 25, 54–63, 367
  See also nonce meaning, utterance-token-
    meaning

speaker-reference. *See* reference
specificity
  defined, 115
  vs. generality, 135, 185
  and I-principle, 114–116
speech, bottleneck in production of, 28, 382
    n.18, n.20
  neuroanatomical specializations for, 27–
    28, 381 n.16
  transmission rates in bps, 28, 382 n.19
speech acts, and satisfaction conditions, 171
  and utterance-types, 23
square of oppositions, 64–71, 82–86, 104,
    131–132, 388 n.15
  arithmetic, 82, 85–86, 131–132, 389 n.22
  and connectives, 66–67
  contraries vs. contradictories, 64–65
  and implicature (*see* scales)
  and logical operators, 66–67
  and modals, 66–67
  and quantifiers, 65
  sub-contraries as pragmatic, 65–71, 132
standardization of use, 23–24, 262, 381
    n.12
state descriptions, 115, 273–274. *See also*
    informativeness
statements vs. sentences, 256, 402 n.34. *See
    also* utterance
stereotypes, 6, 115, 391 n.40
  definition, 115
  and heuristics, 32–33, 37, 38
  and I-implicature, 114–115, 222–223,
    328–329
  inference in absence of, 127
  inference to, 117, 136–137, 142, 147, 148
  nonstereotypes and M-implicature, 136–
    137
strength
  differential, of GCIs, 41, 77–78, 411 n.23
  of scalar items (*see* scales)
  semantic (*see* informativeness)
stress, contrastive, 333, 334, 418 n.61. *See
    also* intonation, prosody
strong vs. weak
  constructions (*see* clausal implicatures)
  expressions (*see* scales, semantic
    generality)
structuralism, in semantics, 101
subcontraries, 65–71, 82–86. *See also*
    square of opposition
subjectivity, and anaphora, 312, 315, 320–
    321, 413 n.40, 415 n.54. *See also*
    logophoricity
'suspenders', 81, 84
suspension of implicatures, 81–82, 131, 252.
    See also cancellation
Swedish, 422 n.94

switch-reference, 317–319, 409 n.9, 414
    n.46
syllogisms, of difference kinds of inference,
    42–43
symbols and notations, ix–x, 387 n.5, n.6,
    388 n.13
synonymy
  avoidance of, 139
  denotational, and the M-Principle, 40–41,
    137
  and sense relations, 191, 241
  near synonymy and Neg-Raising
    predicates, 134
syntactic amalgams, 408 n.5
syntax
  and anaphora, 261–365
    restricted role in, 270–271
  binding (*see* binding)
  indefeasible patterns of, 265, 342, 364, 365
  interface with semantics, 8–9, 172, 190–
    191, 240–241, 243–244, 248, 281, 362–
    365, 374
  and interpretation, 262, 407 n.4
  and negation, 129
  and pragmatics, 261–365
    constraints on rules, 262, 407 n.4, 408 n.5
    constructions with pragmatic origins,
      264–265
    as rival explanations, 261–265, 362–365
    tests for pragmatic vs. syntactic
      character, 268, 278–279, 364–365, 408
      n.6
  universals of, 265, 297, 303, 319, 329

tacit coordination, 29, 258
Tahitian, 337
Tamil, 97, 153, 285, 332, 334, 351–352
tautology, 184
taxonomies, 101–104
temporal inference, 122–127, 158, 180, 199.
    See also order, tense, conjunction
    buttressing
tense
  and implicature, 95–96, 122–124, 180,
    263, 390 n.30, 400 n.25
  past, 95, 400 n.25
  perfect, 96
  and reference points, 122, 151, 199, 399
    n.15, 400 n.25
  semantic analysis of, 95
Thai, 300
the, 60–62, 147, 217–230. *See also* definite
    article
thematic roles, 282, 298, 303, 306
theme vs. rheme, 291, 298, 307. *See also*
    topic
theta criterion, 303, 413 n.38

theta roles. *See* thematic roles
three-leveled theory of meaning, 23–27, 54–63, 71, 367. *See also* meaning
together-implications, 37–38, 117, 207
tolerant vs. intolerant operators, 86, 131–133
topic vs. comment, 279
transderivational constraints, 392 n.48
transitivity, of implicatures, 390 n.31
transmission rates, of human speech, 28
'triggers' of inferences, 60, 111
tropes. *See* figures of speech, irony, maxims (exploitation of), metaphor, metonymy
truth-conditional content, of utterances, 166, 241, 248–249, 259. *See also* truth conditions
truth-conditional semantics. *See* semantics
truth-conditions
  intuitions about, 186, 189, 197, 199, 204, 205–206, 208, 209–210, 216, 219, 227, 229, 231, 232–233, 234–235
  and nonliteral uses of language, 402 n.39 (*see also* literal meaning, maxims, exploitation of)
  not the input to pragmatics, 380 n.2, 398 n.7
  pragmatic contributions to (*see* intrusion)
  properties of utterances not sentences, 256, 398 n.7, 402 n.34
  and semantic representations (*see* semantic representations)
  and nondeclaratives (*see* speech acts)
truth-functional connectives. *See* connectives
try, 98, 219, 390 n.31, 403 n.44
Turkish, 148, 285, 349
type/token distinction, 25
typology, markedness and, 329
  of anaphoric systems, 334, 344, 349, 359
  of implicatures (*see* conversational implicature)
  of inference types (*see* inference)
Tzeltal, 152
Tzotzil, 152

underspecification of semantic representations. *See* semantic representation
understatement, 145
universals
  Greenberg's, 126, 128
  of pragmatics, xii, 15, 69–70, 280, 300, 319, 329, 365, 370, 408 n.6, 423 n.96
  of semantics
  and universal grammar (UG), 265, 279–280, 297, 319, 329, 360, 408 n.6

universe of discourse. *See* domain
univocality of meaning. *See* monosemy
unmarked utterances. *See* markedness, I-principle
Uto-Aztecan, 420 n.78
utterance
  anaphoric reference to, 253–254
  definition of, 26–27, 163
  form, 26
  vs. sentence, as bearer of truth-conditions, 256, 402 n.34
  types vs. tokens, 25
  -type meaning (*see* utterance-type)
utterance-meaning, 22
  vs. sentence-meaning, 381 n.14
utterance-type vs. utterance-token, 1, 22ff, 25, 54–63, 71–72, 373, 381 n.10, 385 n.40
  See also meaning

variables, 182, 267, 279
  indexical, 191
  lexical NPs as, 301
  pronouns as, 279, 292–296
verb phrase (VP), 293, 303. *See also* nonconfigurational languages
verbs
  acquisition of, 140
  Aktionsarten of, 124
  causative, 141–142, 208, 297
  and clausal implicatures, 109–111
  denominal, 140
  factives, 61, 252
  introverted (inherently reflexive), 329, 332, 342
  modal, 140
  of motion (*see* come)
  Neg-Raising predicates (*see* Neg-Raising)
  of propositional attitude, 110, 129–131
  of saying, 110, 314
  and scalar implicatures, 87, 110
  subject-controlling vs. object-controlling, 364
Vietnamese, 125–126
visual interpretation, 2–4, 7
vocabulary. *See* lexicon, semantics field

Yucatec, 96

Zapotec, 335
zero anaphora. *See* anaphora
zero conjunction. *See* parataxis